Uncle John's OLD FAITHFUL BATHROOM READER

By the Bathroom Readers' Institute

Portable Press
San Diego, California

Portable Press/The Bathroom Readers' Institute
An imprint of Printers Row Publishing Group
10350 Barnes Canyon Road, Suite 100, San Diego, CA 92121
www.portablepress.com
e-mail: mail@portablepress.com

All correspondence concerning the content of this book should be addressed to Portable Press/The Bathroom Readers' Institute, Editorial Department, at the above address.

Publisher: Peter Norton
Associate Publisher: Ana Parker
Publishing / Editorial Team: Vicki Jaeger, Tanya Fijalkowski, Lauren Taniguchi
Editorial Team: JoAnn Padgett, Melinda Allman, J. Carroll, Dan Mansfield
Production Team: Jonathan Lopes, Rusty von Dyl

Created and produced by Javna Brothers LLC, Ashland, OR

Interior design by Lidija Tomas
Cover design by Michael Sherman
Cover illustrations by Sophie Hogarth

"*If someone says you're weird, say thank you.*" —*Ellen DeGeneres*

ISBN: 978-1-68412-086-4

Library of Congress Cataloging-in-Publication data available on request.

Printed in the United States of America

First printing: September 2017
21 20 19 18 17   1 2 3 4 5

OUR "REGULAR" READERS RAVE!

"I just really wanted to say thank you! I absolutely love your books. I have like 10 of them and I just bought your newest one. For a trivia buff like me, they are fantastic! Thank you again. I can't wait for the next installment."

—Ashley

"I can't remember the very first Bathroom Reader I read, but when I read it, I knew instantly that I was onto something good. Since that day, I've acquired all the annual editions. They are great! Keep it up!"

—Joe P.

"I absolutely love your books! They're always entertaining. Thanks to them, I'm always full of intriguing trivia (much to some of my colleagues' dismay...)."

—Christian B.

"I got my first Bathroom Reader for Father's Day from my kids and loved it. Now I have more than 25. I read them over and over again. My evening relaxation is to read one for an hour before bed."

—Carl S.

"For years I tried to find trivia books, and then when you started producing Uncle John's Bathroom Readers, I hit the trivia gold mine. Keep up the good work!"

—Don L.

"Thanks, Uncle John. Your books are the only way I can get my dad to read."

—Steven S.

"My first BR was the second Bathroom Reader...and I was hooked. I just recently moved, and one of the first boxes I opened (after the box with the bathroom necessities) was the one with the Bathroom Readers."

—Alex P.

THANK YOU!

The Bathroom Readers' Institute sincerely thanks the people whose advice and assistance made this book possible.

Gordon Javna

John Javna

John Dollison

Jay Newman

Brian Boone

Trina Janssen

Thom Little

Megan Todd

Kim Griswell

Brandon Hartley

Pablo Goldstein

Jahnna Beecham

Skye Hillgartner

Dan Mansfield

Tom Deja

Eleanor Pierce

Adam Bolivar

Lilian Nordland

Melinda Allman

Vicki Jaeger

Tanya Fijalkowski

Jonathan Lopes

Rusty von Dyl

Rod Parayno

Dave Blees

JoAnn Padgett

Peter Norton

Sydney Stanley

Sam and Alex

Gideon, Alex, and Baby Romeo

Glenn Cunningham

Egbert Sousè

J. Cheever Loophole

Alfred E. Newman

Quacky Duck

Porter the Wonder Dog

Thomas Crapper

"In theory, there is no difference between theory and practice; in practice, there is." —CHUCK REID

CONTENTS

Because the BRI understands your reading needs, we've divided the contents by length as well as subject.

Short—a quick read

Medium—2 to 3 pages

Long—for those extended visits, when something a little more involved is required

*Extended—for those leg-numbing experiences

*   *   *

THE OTHER WINSTON CHURCHILL

In the 1890s, future British prime minister Winston Churchill became aware of an American novelist who was also named Winston Churchill. The two began a correspondence, and in one letter the British Churchill suggested to the American, "Why don't you go into politics? I aim to be Prime Minister of England; it would be a great lark if you were president of the United States at the same time." The American Churchill did go into politics. He was elected to the New Hampshire legislature in 1903 and 1905, and ran for governor of the state in 1912, but lost.

When the British Churchill visited Boston in 1901, "Mr. Winston Churchill was the first to welcome me. He entertained me at a banquet…and we made each other complimentary speeches," the future prime minister recounted in 1930. "…Some confusion, however persisted; all my mails were sent to his address and the bill for the dinner came to me. I need not say that both these errors were speedily redressed."

INTRODUCTION

Well, that's 30 years of my life down the drain.

And what a long, strange drain it's been! When we first had this crazy idea to create a book just for the bathroom, we never dreamt that it would become a multi-million-selling book series. (I also never dreamt that it would last longer than my hair.) But here we are in 2017, still going as strong as ever.

That's why we decided to call our 30th annual edition *Old Faithful*—to remind you, our readers, that we're still the same core team that's been bringing you Bathroom Readers for three decades. Most of us have been here since the early days: Our four head writers—John D., Jay, Thom, and Brian—also used to have hair on their heads. And Trina, who organizes all of this madness onto the pages, has only been here for…has it already been five years?! My, how time flies when you're having fun.

Speaking of fun, that's the main ingredient that we try to put in every one of our books. Sure, we love to pass along interesting facts and odd stories—and a few of our articles tend to fall on the "serious" side—but in the end, our job is to entertain you. If you become smarter along the way, then…you're welcome!

And this edition, if I do say so myself, is right up there with our best ever. We've updated our "look" a bit *and* we've included all our favorite topics: dumb crooks, strange lawsuits, weird everything, bathroom news. And as usual, we have lots of new topics, like a bunch of interesting new uses for bamboo (bathroom tissue, bulletproof vests, and underwear), and once-common names— like Ebbo, Zawissius, and Waldswind—that haven't been in use for than a thousand years. What else is in here?

• **Pop culture:** Medical diagnoses of fictional characters, strange celebrity flings, rock star video games, and some really bad game shows.

• **Adventure:** Rescue on the high seas, a man who was stranded on a raft for more than a year, and a woman who got buried by a bear (and lived to tell the tale).

• **How-To:** We've got everything from how to make marshmallows and jelly beans to creative uses for old CDs and DVDs.

• **Mystery:** Ponder the identity of the "Isdal" woman, search homes for gruesome reminders of previous occupants, scratch your head over "murderabilia."

• **Origins:** The birth of the steering wheel, the story of Colonel Sanders, why a rabbit's foot is lucky (not for the rabbit), and how people got around before GPS.

• **For the wordsmiths:** Victorian puns, the secret language of computer hackers, bowling lingo, and why negative words (like "disgruntled") don't have a positive version (like "gruntled")

• **Quotes galore:** You'll find pearls of wisdom from the likes of Bill Nye, Michelle Obama, Rodney Dangerfield, a bunch of guys named Seth, and a bunch of guys who are not Brad Pitt.

• **Weird science:** The mystery of the mysterious hum in a Scottish town, the truth about whether getting revenge makes you feel better, and medical tests you can do at home

• **Random weirdness:** Nuclear false alarms, things hidden in corporate logos, beer in the news, and robot jokes.

Confession time: Picking out examples for the introduction is one of my favorite tasks to do before we go to press. Looking through the manuscript, it just amazes me how, year after year, my crackpot team continues to uncover new and surprising things to write about. And we really do go the extra mile to present it to you in fun and entertaining manner. I know it sounds cliché, but this truly is a labor of love.

So whether you're a new fan or an old faithful, we're proud to have been your rest stop along the Information Superhighway. (Of course, when we published the first edition, the Information Superhighway was just a dirt road.)

And who knows what Bathroom Readers will be like 30 years from now? Maybe you'll be able to download them straight into your brain. But then what would you do to pass the time in the bathroom? (We'll have to figure that one out.)

But in the meantime, we'll keep churning them out, and we hope you'll keep on reading them. As longtime fan Tom P. recently wrote on our Facebook page: "The only Bathroom Reader I don't like is the one that hasn't been published yet...and that's just because it hasn't been published yet! Keep 'em coming!"

No worries, Tom! We're already gearing up for the next one!

As always...Go with the Flow!

—Uncle John and the BRI staff

One last thing: Here's a heartfelt 21-flush salute to Sydney Stanley, the BRI's "fairy godmother." Since 2001 she's worked tirelessly behind the scenes to make sure our crackpot team could bring you these books each year. Bon voyage, Syd!

YOU'RE MY INSPIRATION

*It's always interesting to see where the architects of pop culture
get their ideas. Some of these may surprise you.*

The *Star Wars* Logo: When a 22-year-old graphic designer named Suzy Rice
met with director George Lucas in 1976 to create a title logo for his new space
movie, he told her he wanted something "intimidating." So Rice, who was
studying German typefaces at the time, took inspiration from Nazi propaganda
posters: "What I read was that (Joseph) Goebbels wanted a standardized font
without variations to be used for all signage throughout. So it struck me as
an indication of what I'd call 'fascist' design." Rice came up with a modified
Helvetica block font for the title. Lucas liked it…with one change: he wanted
her to join the "S" and the "T" in "STAR" and the "R" and "S" in "WARS."

Biff Tannen: For decades, it's been rumored that in 1989's *Back to the Future Part
II*, the "future" version of Biff—a megalomaniacal real estate mogul—was based
on real-life real estate mogul Donald Trump. In 2015, screenwriter Bob Gale
confirmed that Biff, his high-rise casino, and the fact that he makes everyone
call him "America's Greatest Folk Hero" were all modeled after Donald Trump.

Bullet Trains: Ever wonder why bullet trains have pointy noses? When the
trains travel at high speeds, air pressure builds up until it creates a small—but
loud—sonic boom. In the 1990s, Japanese engineer Eiji Nakatsu noticed that a
bird called a kingfisher could fly into the water at high speeds without disturbing
the surface. Nakatsu redesigned the bullet train's nose into a "50-foot-long steel
kingfisher beak" that not only decreases noise but increases speed.

Kate Moss: Moss is one of the few supermodels who's managed to stay famous
for three decades, and a big reason for that is her sense of style, which *Vogue*
described as "rock 'n' roll bohemianism." Inspirations: Mick Jagger and David
Bowie. "They're quite feminine but still with a tomboyish look, which I like."

The Sleeping Beauty Castle: While traveling through Europe in the early
1950s, Walt Disney visited Neuschwanstein Castle in the Bavarian Alps.
Nicknamed the "Fairy Tale Castle," it was built in the late 19th century (the
first castle we know of to have flushing toilets) by King Ludwig III. He wanted a
colorful castle in a beautiful setting to honor his musical hero, Richard Wagner.
Disney was so enamored by Neuschwanstein that he made it the basis for the
Sleeping Beauty Castle at his brand new-theme park, Disneyland.

TOURONS

Real questions asked by people on vacation.

...in Everglades National Park:

"Are the alligators real?"

"Are the baby alligators for sale?"

"What time does the two o'clock bus leave?"

...at the Grand Canyon:

"Was this man-made?"

"Do you light it up at night?"

"So is that Canada over there?"

...in Denali National Park:

"What time do you feed the bears?"

"What's so wonderful about Wonder Lake?"

"Can you show me where the Yeti lives?"

"How often do you mow the tundra?"

...in Mesa Verde National Park:

"Did people build this, or did Indians?"

"Why did the Indians decide to live in Colorado?"

...in Yellowstone National Park:

"Does Old Faithful erupt at night?"

"How do you turn it on?"

"When does the guy who turns it on get to sleep?"

...at Carlsbad Caverns:

"How much of the cave is underground?"

...in Yosemite National Park:

"Where are the cages for the animals?"

"What happened to the other half of Half Dome?"

"Can I get a picture taken with the carving of President Clinton?"

...in Glacier National Park:

"When do the deer become elk?"

"When do the glaciers go by?"

...in Sutter's Fort State Historic Park, Sacramento

"We cook over the fire here."
"Don't your pans melt?"

The "gin" in "cotton gin" has nothing to do with alcohol. It's slang for "engine."

CHEERS!

We propose a toast…to these facts about wine.

• The idea that wines improve with age isn't necessarily true. Experts say about 90 percent of wines should be consumed within a year of bottling, while others don't really get much better after 10 years have passed. The varieties that do get better with age: Bordeaux, Cabernet Sauvignon, and port.

• The custom of "toasting" with a glass of wine started in ancient Greece. A host would drink the first glass to show that the wine was safe to drink.

• One acre of grapevines yields about 13.5 barrels of wine. A barrel yields 24.6 cases; a case works out to 48 glasses. In all, the acre yields 15,940 glasses of wine.

• Wine is made almost entirely from grapes…but that doesn't mean it's vegetarian. Many big-batch commercial wines are filtered with a process that involves gelatin, which is an animal by-product. Result: tiny—even microscopic—bits of gelatin may be present in a glass of wine.

• Oldest bottle of wine: A bottle dating to AD 325 was found near Speyer, Germany, in 1867. (It's now on display in a museum.)

• Countries that drink the most wine per capita: Vatican City, France, Portugal, and Italy (which is also the world's biggest producer of wine).

• Medieval European measurement for wine: a "butt," which is about 126 gallons. (Also, a butt amounts to half of a "tun.")

• There's an enzyme in the human stomach that metabolizes ethanol, the type of alcohol found in wine. Men's stomachs naturally contain more than women's stomachs. Result: Women get drunk on wine a lot quicker than men do.

• Wine in space: In 1996 Buzz Aldrin brought a tiny vial of wine with him to the Moon so he could administer Communion to himself.

• In a 2017 lawsuit involving actor Johnny Depp and his business managers, it was revealed that Depp spends $30,000 a month on wine. (He also has a tattoo that reads "Wino Forever.")

THE SPEED OF STUFF

Life moves pretty fast sometimes. How fast? Check out these numbers.

Glass breaking. The cracks move at speeds of up to 3,000 mph.

Blood. It circulates at a rate of about three feet per second—a little more than 2 mph.

Signals from the brain. When you want to move your hand, your brain sends the signal to the muscles at a speed of about 250 miles per hour.

Rain. Regular, moderate precipitation falls from the sky at about 20 mph.

Snow. Most snow drifts down at 6 feet per second, or 4.1 mph.

Electricity. It travels across a copper wire at 96 percent of the speed of light. That's 643,791,964 miles per hour.

Urine. The average pee leaving the body amounts to about two cups over the course of 25 seconds. In terms of speed, that's 20 milliliters per second.

Typing. Typing at a rate of 60 words per minute is pretty fast, but in terms of land speed, it only works out to about 1 mph. (The average walking speed for a human is 3 mph.)

An ejected champagne cork. The contents are under pressure, so when that cork is finally released, it does so at a speed of 25 mph.

A fart. Gas leaving the body through the rear exit can do so as fast as 10 feet per second, or roughly 7 mph.

A bullet. The fastest ones shoot out of a gun somewhere near 1,800 miles per hour. (Which means Superman flies just a little bit faster than that.)

A sneeze. Not only does it propel about 100,000 germs into the air, but the air in a sneeze can move as fast as 100 mph. (Gesundheit!)

OOPS!

*It's always nice to hear about people screwing up even more than
you are. So go ahead and feel superior for a few moments.*

CRASH TEST DUMMY

There's a reason why engineers use mannequins to test car crashes: car crashes
really hurt! A 35-year-old Austrian engineer found that out the hard way in
2016 when he sat on top of a "machine used to test car crashes," reported
the *Daily Mail*, and then "asked his colleague to turn it on." For some reason,
the colleague obliged, and the engineer was instantly thrown face-first into a
concrete wall. He sustained serious injuries.

TIMBERRRRRRR!

Two neighbors in Pittston Township, Pennsylvania, got into a heated dispute.
A large tree in one of the neighbor's yards was dripping sap onto the car of the
other neighbor, Raymond Mazzarella (whose own house had been converted
into five apartments). The squabble came to a head one Saturday afternoon
in August 2016. Fed up with having to scrape the sap off his car, Mazzarella
grabbed a chain saw, and proceeded to cut down the tree. Bad idea: It fell onto
Mazzarella's house, causing significant damage. One of the tenants suffered minor
injuries, and the entire structure had to be condemned, rendering Mazzarella and
all five of his tenants homeless. "He decided it was the best thing to do, to get rid
of the tree," said police officer Terry Best. "Where he thought it was going to go,
I don't know."

FLY HIGH, BIRDSONG

In 2016, a 22-year-old University of Pittsburgh student named Grant Birdsong,
described as a "rising star" at the university, failed to live up to that high-flying
reputation when he fell off a building while trying to impress a girl. He'd just met
her that night, and at about 2:30 a.m. the two students climbed up a fire escape
to the roof of a three-story building that housed a restaurant. Right next to
it—well, about a foot and a half away from it—was another restaurant. Its roof is
about two feet higher. So that's a foot and a half away, and two feet up. Birdsong
thought he could make the jump…and immediately regretted his decision. He
missed the roof and slid down the narrow, debris-filled gap until he was wedged

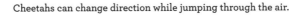

Cheetahs can change direction while jumping through the air.

("awkwardly," said news reports) between the two buildings about ten feet above the pavement. Suffering from lacerations and a badly broken ankle, Birdsong wasn't going anywhere for a while—for four hours, in fact. That's how long it took firefighters to cut through the wall of one of the restaurants and finally free Birdsong just after dawn. Meanwhile, the girl he'd tried to impress stayed there the entire time. He gave her a "thumbs-up" as he was being wheeled into an ambulance.

OFF THE RAILS

In 2014 France's national rail operator, RFF, paid 15 billion euros ($20 billion) for 2,000 high-speed trains as part of an overhaul of the country's aging rail system. But the project hit a huge snag when it was discovered that RFF gave the train company, SNFC, incorrect dimensions. According to BBC News: "They measured platforms built less than 30 years ago, overlooking the fact that many of France's regional platforms were built more than 50 years ago when trains were a little slimmer." After several hundred trains were built, RFF officials realized that—even though the trains would fit into most of France's 8,700 train stations—more than 1,300 train stations were too narrow. They all needed to have a few centimeters shaved off their platforms…which would cost a few more billion euros. "It's as if you'd bought a Ferrari and wanted to get it in your garage," explained RFF spokesman Christophe Piednoël, "only to discover the garage was not quite the right size because you'd never had a Ferrari before."

OOPS IN SPACE

In March 2017, NASA astronaut Peggy Whitson set a new record: at 57, she became the "oldest and most experienced woman on a spacewalk." So congrats all around. However, at the same moment that she was breaking the record, Whitson and her 49-year-old fellow spacewalker, ISS commander Shane Kimbrough, were making a rookie mistake. They were installing four 5-by-2-foot debris shields onto a vulnerable spot on the space station's hull where a docking port had been replaced. (Without the shielding, a piece of space junk can rip through the ISS's hull.) About midway into the seven-hour mission, Whitson and Kimbrough lost track of one of the heat shields. By the time they realized their goof, the shield was floating toward Earth and too far away to retrieve. Fortunately, they were able to complete the repair with the three remaining shields. Mission Control assured the frustrated spacewalkers that the lost shield would most likely disintegrate in the atmosphere, and that the chances of it coming back and hitting the station are unlikely.

Some research suggests that pickle juice can reduce muscle cramps.

OLD FAITHFUL FACTS

Old Faithful the book takes a vacation to *Old Faithful* the geyser.

Half of the earth's approximately 1,000 geysers are located in Yellowstone National Park. Old Faithful is not only the most famous geyser in the park but in the entire world.

Recipe for a geyser: groundwater flows through subterraneous fissures into a chamber that's being filled by superheated water. The superheated water boils the groundwater and converts it to steam, which has 1,600 times more volume than liquid water. There's only one place for all that boiling water and steam to go: up.

Eruptions top out at about 140 feet, but some exceed 180 feet—the height of a 15-story building.

In 2015 a young man named Zac Finley proposed to his girlfriend Laura Parkes in front of Old Faithful. He purposely chose a spot where his down-on-one-knee proposal would be caught on Yellowstone's live webcam. Parkes said yes, and the video of the proposal has since gone viral.

A five-minute eruption of Old Faithful spews out as much water as an average household uses in three weeks.

One reason Old Faithful is so reliable: unlike most geysers, it is not connected to—and therefore not affected by—any other thermal feature.

In 1903 President Theodore Roosevelt took a two-week trip to Yellowstone. He was reportedly awestruck by the big game and the scenery, but according to his guide, the geysers "bored" him.

The water that spews out of the geyser is 204°F; the steam can exceed 350°F.

Predicting Old Faithful's next eruption: If the previous one lasted more than 2½ minutes, the next eruption will come in 91 minutes. If the previous eruption lasted less than 2½ minutes, the next one will come in 65 minutes. (The timing has to do with how long it takes the underground chamber to fill up again.)

When the first white settlers discovered Old Faithful in 1870 (the Washburn Expedition), they used it to wash their dirty laundry. It reportedly tore wool garments to shreds, but worked just fine on linens and cottons.

America's oldest pet cemetery opened in 1896 in Hartsdale, NY. Over 70,000 pets are buried there.

VOTE FOR FATTMAN!

*Politics may be contentious, but there's still humor to be found
in it...like the names of these real people who ran for office.*

- **Janelle Lawless**, circuit court judge in Michigan

- **Mark Reckless**, member of British Parliament, representing Wales

- **Ryan Fattman**, state senator in Massachusetts

- **Dick Swett**, U.S. congressman from New Hampshire

- **Young Boozer**, state treasurer of Alabama

- **Timothy Shotwell**, candidate for sheriff in Clark County, Washington

- **Butch Otter**, governor of Idaho

- **Steve Strait** defeated **Becky Gay** in the 2002 Republican primary race for a seat in Alaska's state house (but didn't win the general election)

- **Moe Cotton**, candidate for state senator in Guam (His signs read "Pick Moe Cotton.")

- **Robin Rape**, constable in Brazoria County, Texas

- **Faye Ball** and **Don Cox** ran on the same ticket for seats on the Ewing Township, New Jersey, council

- **Dick Mountjoy**, California state assemblyman

- **Tiny Kox**, senator in the Netherlands ("Tiny" is a nickname; it's short for "Martinus.")

- **Harry Baals**, mayor of Fort Wayne, Indiana

- **Bill Boner**, mayor of Nashville, Tennessee

- **Frank Schmuck**, Arizona state senatorial candidate (he lost)

- **Diane Gooch**, Republican congressional primary candidate in New Jersey (she lost to a Tea Party candidate)

- **Ben Bushyhead**, county commissioner in North Carolina

- **Jay Walker**, write-in candidate for Pierce County, Georgia, tax assessor

- **Barb Queer**, county commissioner in Ashland, Ohio

- **Tripp Self**, judge on the Georgia Court of Appeals

- **Dave Obey**, U.S. congressman from Wisconsin

- **Krystal Ball**, Congressional candidate from Virginia in 2010 (who probably should've known she wouldn't win)

Some remote Christmas tree farms in Oregon are harvested by helicopter.

THE HARDEST-WORKING PERSON IN...

Who says you have to retire? Here are some folks who've proven that you don't.

...THE PAPERBOY BUSINESS

Honoree: Ted Ingram of Winterborne Monkton, England

Details: In 1942 Ingram, then 22, got a paper route to add to the income he made driving a tractor. He delivered the *Dorset Echo* for the next 72 years, more than 500,000 copies in all. And he delivered nearly all of them on a bicycle, taking to his car only after hip replacement surgery. Knee troubles forced him to give up the route for good in 2013, at age 93. In all those years the world's longest-serving paperboy took just two vacations, both in the 1960s, and one sick leave in 1950 after he broke his back.

...THE STOCK MARKET

Honoree: Irving Kahn of New York, New York

Details: Kahn began his Wall Street career as a 23-year-old "runner" (delivery boy) on the New York Stock Exchange in 1929. A few months later the stock market crashed, ushering in the Great Depression. Kahn survived (he made a handsome profit shorting stocks before the crash) and he rode out several more booms and busts over the years. A "value investor," his strategy was to buy stocks he thought were underpriced, then hold onto them until their value increased, and sell them for a profit. In 1978 the 73-year-old founded Kahn Brothers Group with his sons Alan and Thomas; by 2014 the firm was managing nearly $1 billion in assets and Kahn, 108, was still coming in to work three days a week. He died in 2015, a month after turning 109, still picking stocks to the very end.

...MEDICINE

Honoree: Dr. Leila Denmark of Athens, Georgia

Details: Denmark, a pediatrician, began a medical internship in Atlanta's Grady Hospital in 1928. In 1931 she opened her own practice and the following year she helped to develop a vaccine for whooping cough, which was often fatal to children. When her husband passed away in 1990, Denmark considered retiring after 62 years in practice, but decided against it. She continued on for another

11 years, retiring at 103…but only because her eyes became too weak for her to perform certain medical exams. By then she was treating the great-grandchildren of her earliest patients. Denmark lived another 11 years. At the time of her death at age 114 in 2012, she was the fourth-oldest person in the world.

…THE FEDERAL JUDICIARY

Honoree: Judge Wesley Brown of the Federal District Court for Kansas

Details: Brown graduated from law school in 1933 and practiced law for three decades before President John F. Kennedy nominated him to the federal bench in 1962. The U.S. Constitution allows federal judges to remain on the bench for life, and Judge Brown did just that. He was still hearing cases when he died in 2012 at the age of 104.

…THE AIR

Honoree: Ron Akana of Boulder, Colorado

Details: Akana was a 21-year-old student at the University of Hawaii in 1949 when he saw an ad in the paper for flight steward jobs on United Airlines. A job that offered access to the mainland was a big deal in those days, so Akana (and 400 others) applied for the eight openings…and he got one of them. He worked for United for the next 63 years, and saw a lot of changes in that time. Flights became nonsmoking; prop planes gave way to jets, which cut travel time to the mainland in half; stewards and stewardesses became "flight attendants." If you've ever flown United from Denver to Kauai or Maui, you may have been served by Akana. When he retired in 2012 at age 83, it was estimated that he'd flown more than 20 million miles—the equivalent of 40 trips to the moon and back.

…AN ICE-CREAM TRUCK

Honoree: Allan Ganz of Boston, Massachusetts

Details: Ganz started working on his father's ice-cream truck in the late 1940s when he was 10. He kept at it until he was 19, spent two years in the military, and then went back to working with his dad. He didn't buy his own truck until 1977, when he was 40. But he's had it ever since. As of 2016, the 79-year-old had logged 67 years driving up and down the Massachusetts North Shore selling ice cream out of his or his father's trucks, the longest career as an ice-cream man ever. He may have a few years left in him, too: his father didn't give up his truck until he was 86.

The Greenland shark can live for 200 years.

WHATEVER HAPPENED TO...

One day, they were making headlines. The next...they were gone. Here's where they went.

Who: Baby Jessica

Then: In October 1987, 18-month-old Jessica McClure was playing in her aunt's backyard in Midland, Texas, when she fell into an abandoned well. Over the next three days, millions of Americans were glued to their TV screens to watch emergency workers try to free "Baby Jessica." It ultimately took 58 hours for workers to drill through thick rock to dig a parallel shaft and a tunnel over to where Jessica was trapped. Baby Jessica's inspirational story was irresistible. A made-for-television movie about the ordeal was produced, and the McClure family got to visit the White House and meet Vice President George Bush.

Now: Baby Jessica didn't escape the well unharmed. Her toe got stuck and the lack of circulation led to gangrene, and amputation. But apart from that (and a broken arm and a scar on her forehead), she was fine. She graduated from high school in 2004, and two years later got married and had two kids. At age 25, she inherited a trust fund of $1.2 million made up of donations that had been sent to her during the well ordeal. She bought a home two miles away from her aunt's house. (It doesn't have any wells on the property.)

Who: Christopher Cross

Then: Soft rock was all the rage in the early 1980s, and the king of the genre was Christopher Cross. A high-voiced singer from Texas, he went to #1 in 1980 with his laid-back single "Sailing." At the 1981 Grammys, Cross beat some of the biggest acts in music—Bette Midler, Frank Sinatra, Kenny Rogers, Billy Joel, and Pink Floyd—to sweep the top four awards, the first time in Grammy history anybody won Record of the Year, Song of the Year, Album of the Year, and Best New Artist. (It's since happened only one more time, when Norah Jones did it in 2003.) Cross went on to score a string of super-smooth megahits like "Think of Laura," "All Right," "Ride Like the Wind," and "The Best That You Can Do," the theme song to the movie *Arthur*. For that one, Cross won an Academy Award for Best Original Song. It looked as if he would dominate the '80s.

Now: Cross's reign as the king of pop was short-lived, thanks to MTV and New Wave. Cross, a shy, heavyset guy in his mid-30s, was quite the contrast to young video-driven acts like Duran Duran and Michael Jackson. Cross was suddenly a square and his fame fell fast. His last hit, "Loving Strangers," reached #94 on the pop chart in 1986. Warner Bros. Records dropped him in 1988, but he continued to make music, and tour county fairs and casinos. He's released nine albums in the past 30 years on tiny labels like CMC, Ear…and Christopher Cross Records.

Who: Fernando Valenzuela

Then: In 1979 a Los Angeles Dodgers scout went to Mexico to check out a shortstop named Ali Uscanga. But when a 19-year-old pitcher named Fernando Valenzuela retired Uscanga with three straight strikes, the scout knew he had the next big star. Valenzuela amassed 162 strikeouts and a 3.10 ERA in the Dodgers' minor league system, enough to get a call to the big leagues for the Dodgers' drive to secure a division title in 1980. He pitched 18 innings without allowing any runs, and was selected to pitch for the Dodgers on opening day in 1981. Valenzuela was explosive, going 8-0 in his first eight starts, including five shutouts and an ERA of 0.50. "Fernandomania" soon hit, and that year the 21-year-old Valenzuela won the Cy Young Award and the Rookie of the Year Award, a National League first. He led the Dodgers to a World Series championship as well. Nobody could sustain those numbers, and Valenzuela settled into a decent career as part of the Dodgers rotation. He had another big year in 1986, amassing a 21-11 record and coming in second for the Cy Young Award. Once more, his numbers declined, but in his last full season in the majors in 1990, he threw a no-hitter.

Now: Valenzuela played for Mexican and American teams for a few years, and retired in 1997…until 2004 when, at age 43, he took the mound for Los Aguilas de Mexicali of the Mexican Pacific Coast League, and pitched for another three years. Today, he owns the Tigres de Quintana Roo of the Mexican League and provides commentary on Spanish-language TV broadcasts of Dodgers games.

Who: Larry Fortensky

Then: It wasn't especially surprising when Hollywood legend Elizabeth Taylor announced that she was getting married in 1991—this would be her eighth marriage. But *who* she was marrying made headlines: Larry Fortensky wasn't an actor or politician like Taylor's previous spouses, but a Los Angeles–area construction worker. The two had met at the Betty Ford Center in 1988, where Fortensky, who was 20 years younger than Taylor, had checked himself in after a DWI conviction. (He told *People* that "Elizabeth was in there for pills, I was in there for beer.") After being together for three years, the couple wed in a $2 million ceremony at Michael Jackson's Neverland Ranch; Fortensky's best man was Jose Eber, Taylor's hairdresser. Then Fortensky and Taylor's relationship faded from the tabloids…until 1996, when the couple announced they were getting divorced. Fortensky reportedly didn't like being treated as "Mr. Elizabeth Taylor." According to the terms of a prenuptial agreement, Fortensky got a flat sum of $1 million because they'd stayed married for five years.

The technical name for a unibrow is synophrys. (If you have one, you have the PAX3 gene.)

Now: Fortensky's life took a few bad turns. Shortly after splitting with Taylor, police found him intoxicated in an illegally parked motor home with no license plates, and he was arrested for drug possession. In 1999 he fell down a flight of stairs while drunk and was in a coma for six weeks, which left him with permanent memory loss. He and Taylor remained friends, reportedly talking on the phone a few times a month, and in 2009 Taylor gave him $50,000 to save the home he'd bought with his divorce settlement from foreclosure. When Taylor died in 2011, she left him $800,000. When Fortensky died in 2016, he was living with his sister, unable to work due to injuries sustained in his fall.

Who: Imelda Marcos

Then: In 1965 Ferdinand Marcos was elected president of the Philippines, and his wife, Imelda, a former beauty queen, became first lady. Seven years later, Marcos declared martial law and became a de facto dictator. He used his new power to crush all political opposition—the Marcos administration has also been accused of mass torture and executing its opponents. When opposition leader Benigno Aquino was assassinated in 1983, the People Power Revolution fought back. Violent revolts ultimately forced Marcos out of office in 1986. Through it all, Imelda Marcos lived a life of immeasurable luxury. She famously owned more than 3,000 pairs of shoes, most of them expensive, designer-brand. Those, along with clothes, artworks, and other personal effects, were paid for with billions stolen from the federal treasury.

Now: Forced to flee the Philippines in 1986, Imelda Marcos had to leave most of her treasure in the presidential palace. She abandoned more than 1,200 pairs of shoes, which new president Corazon Aquino (widow of Benigno) ordered to be put on public display as a reminder of the Marcos regime. When Aquino left the presidency in 1992, the display was dismantled and put into storage at the National Museum. The staff only became aware that they had shoes when they were inspecting the museum after a tropical storm in 2012 flooded the basement. By then the shoes had already been destroyed by termites, humidity, and mold. As for Ferdinand Marcos, he died in exile in Hawaii in 1989. Imelda Marcos went on trial in the United States, accused of using $200 million of Filipino federal funds to buy real estate in New York. She was acquitted, and in 1991 returned to the Philippines...and was arrested on corruption charges. But she posted bail and, while awaiting trial, ran for president. She lost. Back in court, she was convicted of corruption, and was sentenced to prison and a $4.3 million fine. The conviction was overturned in 1998. Marcos decided to stick with politics, and in 2010, she won election to the Philippines' House of Representatives.

Flower tip: If you want your rose bouquet to last longer, keep it at a temperature of 33-35°F.

INTELLIGENCE QUOTIENT

Words of wisdom…about lacking wisdom.

"We are all born ignorant, but one must work hard to remain stupid."
—Benjamin Franklin

"Intelligence is totally subjective; it's like sexiness."
—David Fincher

"Stupid people are ruining America."
—Herman Cain

"People who boast about their I.Q. are losers."
—Stephen Hawking

"Evil is relatively rare; ignorance is epidemic."
—Jon Stewart

"A brainiac notices everything, an ignoramus comments about everything."
—Heinrich Heine

"TALK SENSE TO A FOOL AND HE CALLS YOU FOOLISH."
—Euripides

"We're all idiots when we're young. We don't think we are, but we are."
—Helen Mirren

"One of the painful things about our time is that those who feel certainty are stupid, and those with any imagination and understanding are filled with doubt and indecision."

—Bertrand Russell

World record for longest-held breath: 24 minutes, 3.45 seconds.

ROBOTS IN THE NEWS

Get aware of what's going on in the world of robots…before they rise up and enslave us all.

LYING BOT

Thousands of websites use a program called Captcha to ensure that when you sign into your account, you're not robotic data-mining software, and are in fact a real person. Or a robot programmed to beat Captcha. A robotics enthusiast named Matt Unsworth programmed a robotic arm outfitted with a stylus to fool Captcha. When Unsworth's robot encounters a Captcha window that asks the user to check a box that says "I'm not a robot," it checks the box.

HUSBAND BOT

A French woman identified in press reports only as "Lilly" downloaded plans for a robot named Immovator and built it with a 3-D printer. Lilly identifies herself as a "proud robosexual," who always enjoyed the sound of robotic voices and then, as a young adult, realized she was physically attracted to them. Result: Lilly says she hopes to marry Immovator someday. She has to wait, though—because human-robot marriage is not yet legal in France.

BALL-IN-CUP BOT

The whole point of having robots is so that they can do jobs that are too hard for humans, right? Well, here's another difficult human task that can be outsourced to robots: playing that "get the ball on the string into the cup" game. A Japanese robot named Pepper, which learns to do things better the more it does them, was taught to play the game. After just 100 tries, Pepper had mastered the game—and now it never misses. Ever.

EDIBLE BOT

Engineers at MIT's Computer Science and Artificial Intelligence Laboratory have developed what they hope will be an alternative to some invasive surgical procedures. Drawing its inspiration from origami, it's a robot made of flat pieces that can self-fold and unfold as needed. The bot is slipped into a piece of sausage casing and the patient swallows it. Stomach acid then breaks the bot out of its casing, allowing it to unfold. Using a tiny magnet embedded in the robot, doctors guide it through the anatomy to where it needs to go. Possible uses:

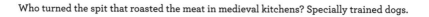

Who turned the spit that roasted the meat in medieval kitchens? Specially trained dogs.

retrieving swallowed objects, delivering medication, performing microsurgery, or serving as an organic "bandage" to help punctured or torn organs heal.

BURGER BOT

Robots are also great at doing monotonous tasks, and they do it without complaint…and without being paid. It makes sense, then, that someone would create a burger-flipping robot for fast-food restaurants. Enter Flippy, a "robotic kitchen assistant" designed to take over what its developer, Miso Electronics CEO David Zito, calls "the dull, dirty, and dangerous work around the grill." Flippy is a wheeled cart with a robotic arm and a sensor bar. It's small enough to fit in any kitchen in place of a human, and it gets plugged into the restaurant's computer system to receive orders and then cook them.

PING PONG BOT

In February 2017, *Guinness World Records* declared a robot named FORPHEUS the "first robot table tennis tutor." Developed by the Omron Corporation of Japan, FORPHEUS can teach any human the fundamental skills of table tennis…and also crush them at the game. It's powered by sensors—one sensor to track its human opponent's movements, and two vision centers that keep an eye on the ball and can move as quickly as 80 times a second. Tako Oya, lead developer of the FORPHEUS project, said that his company's goal is to create "a future where humans and machines harmonize together. So to achieve this we produced a robot that can play table tennis."

AIRPORT BOT

A trip to the airport—with all the security checks, metal detectors, and people running to catch connecting flights—can be a little dehumanizing. Oakland International Airport in California is trying to make the airport experience "a little more human" by installing a Pepper, a humanoid robot that serves as an information booth. According to its manufacturer, Pepper is "tall enough that you can't miss it, but not too big that it scares small children." With the aid of its onboard flat-screen monitor, Pepper can answer questions about the locations of the bathrooms, gates, and baggage claim. It also can point travelers into the direction of restaurants, such as the Pyramid Tap House, which is right behind Pepper's station, and which is paying SoftBank for Pepper's services. (Pepper displays the Tap House menu, but will suggest other restaurants if that one doesn't appeal to travelers.)

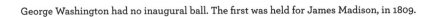

George Washington had no inaugural ball. The first was held for James Madison, in 1809.

DROP THAT PHRASE!

Drop everything—we've got the origin stories of some drop-based phrases.

AT THE DROP OF A HAT

Meaning: At the slightest provocation; immediately.

Origin: In the American Old West, the start of a sporting event, such as a boxing match or a race, was commonly marked by the dropping of a hat. That led to the idea of starting anything "at the drop of a hat." The phrase was first used in the late 1830s.

WAITING FOR THE OTHER SHOE TO DROP

Meaning: Anticipating a follow-up to something that has already occurred, usually with ominous underpinnings.

Origin: Etymologists say this phrase originated in the crowded tenement buildings that were prevalent in New York City in the 19th and early 20th centuries. Residents in the buildings' tiny apartments could hear every sound in neighboring apartments, including, as this story goes, a neighbor taking off his or her shoes before going to bed at night. After hearing the first shoe hit the floor, the listener would wait...for the other shoe...to...drop!

A DROP IN THE BUCKET

Meaning: A very small or inconsequential amount.

Origin: This phrase is pretty simple to understand. A drop of water is very tiny in a bucket full of water. But it's a lot older than you might guess: It actually appears in the Bible, in the book of Isaiah (which is believed to have been written in around the eighth century BC). *"Behold, the nations are as a drop of a bucket, and are counted as the small dust of the balance: behold, he taketh up the isles as a very little thing."*

GET THE DROP ON SOMEONE

Meaning: To gain an advantage over someone.

Origin: Another phrase with origins in the American West, this one in reference to firearms. If someone was holding you at gunpoint, they could be said to have "gotten the drop on" you. Unfortunately, nobody knows for sure exactly

African giant pouched rats are being trained to sniff out land mines. (They're too light to set them off.)

what that meant. According to *The Columbia Guide to Standard American English* (1983), by Kenneth George Wilson, it might have had to do with dueling pistols competitions: "The expression probably stems from the duelists' practice of awaiting the drop of a handkerchief by a third party as the signal to aim and fire. To get the drop was to be the first to respond to the signal." The earliest known use of the phrase was in 1869 by Philadelphia journalist Alexander K. McClure, who wrote of a particular gunslinger: "So expert is he with his faithful pistol, that the most scientific of rogues have repeatedly attempted in vain to get 'the drop' on him." The phrase gained its more general meaning sometime around the beginning of the 20th century.

DROP THE BALL

Meaning: Make a mistake or miss an opportunity, especially by failing to act in a timely manner.

Origin: It's believed to be a simple sports-based idiom, probably taken from football or baseball, where dropping the ball is of course a bad thing. It got its generalized meaning of failing by the early 1940s. (One of the earliest uses of the phrase was in Marcus Goodrich's best-selling 1941 novel, *Delilah*.)

> **THE NUMBER OF PAY PHONES IN THE UNITED STATES** *peaked around 1995, with 2.6 million in operation. Today more than 90 percent of Americans own cell phones, reducing the need for pay phones. There are only about 500,000 left.*

DROP A DIME

Meaning: Inform police about someone's illicit activities; betray; snitch.

Origin: This phrase comes from the days when coin-operated pay telephones were common. The cost of a local call on those phones in most parts of the United States from the 1950s until the 1980s: 10 cents—a dime. And because pay phones were public and could be used anonymously, they were commonly used to inform on criminals. In the 1960s, this led to the idea that anyone who had informed on someone had "dropped a dime" on that person, meaning they had dropped a dime in a pay phone and called the police on them. (This phrase led to another phrase—dime-dropper—for an informant or snitch.)

Douglas Adams (author of *The Hitchhiker's Guide to the Galaxy*) wrote for Monty Python in the 1970s.

BIRD ATTACKS

Real-life stories of real-life bird attacks.

AIR RAID

In February 2007, Nicky Moss, 38, one of the UK's top paragliders, was competing in an event in Australia when—at about 8,200 feet in the air—she was attacked by a pair of eagles. "I heard screeching behind me," Moss told Reuters, "and an eagle flew down and attacked me." The angry birds were wedge-tailed eagles, Australia's largest bird of prey—and they're huge. Their wingspans can exceed seven feet. (Bald eagles, by comparison, rarely exceed seven feet.) The giant eagles repeatedly attacked both Moss and the parachute-like sail of her paraglider, tearing gashes in it. What's worse, one of the eagles got caught in the support lines, which collapsed the sail and sent Moss into a rapid descent. "It swooped in and hit me on the back of the head," she explained, "then got tangled in the glider. So I had a very, very large bird wrapped up screeching beside me as I screamed back." The encounter didn't come to an end until the bird was finally able to free itself, after which it flew off. Moss—now only about 300 feet off the ground—was somehow able to land the damaged glider. "I see the eagles quite often and they are incredibly beautiful," Moss said, "but I must say I have never been so relieved to reach the ground."

ANOTHER AIR RAID

In 2011 a Russian paraglider named Vladimir Tsar'kov, 25, was about 850 feet above Bir-Billing Valley, in the Himalayans of northern India, when two huge birds suddenly appeared out of nowhere and attacked his sail. One of the birds immediately became entangled in the glider's lines, and the sail instantly collapsed. Tsar'kov had an emergency parachute, but it was too small to stop the fall. Result: he, his fluttering sail, and the still-entangled bird all plummeted uncontrollably toward the earth—a terrifying descent that ended with a crash into a large shrub, after which Tsar'kov and his load fell through the shrub's branches, finally landing on the ground. Amazingly, he suffered only scrapes and bruises. The bird was okay, too: after Tsar'kov got his wits about him, he carefully untangled the lines from its wings and talons, after which it flapped, hopped, and finally flew away to freedom.

Bonus: Tsar'kov was wearing a helmet-camera, so you can watch the whole thing—with lots of bleeps to hide all the Russian swear words—on YouTube.

The youngest person ever to bowl a perfect game: Hannah Diem of Seminole, Florida. She was 9.

THE BIRDS!

Around 3:00 a.m. on the morning of August 18, 1961, thousands of sooty shearwaters—large, gull-sized seabirds—staged what seemed to be an attack on the small towns along the coast of California's Monterey Bay, flying into homes, businesses, cars, and even any residents who ventured outside with flashlights to find out what was going on. A few hours later, people awoke to a macabre sight: the bodies of *thousands* of dead or stunned shearwaters littering yards, rooftops, and streets. To make matters worse, most of the birds had regurgitated the sardines they'd been gorging on in the bay—so they also *smelled* terrible. Bird experts concluded that the birds must have become confused in the fog, and headed for the lights of houses and cars—and flashlights—simply out of survival instinct. But that was proven incorrect…50 years later. In 2012 marine biologists studied the gut contents of zooplankton—tiny floating marine animals—that had been collected in Monterey Bay in the summer of 1961, and found that there had been a bloom of algae that is especially toxic to birds: it causes disorientation, seizures, and death in birds that eat it. The shearwaters, the scientists said, had undoubtedly consumed the toxic algae while gorging on fish, after which the sickened birds had staged the bizarre "attack." "It looks like attacking," lead scientist Sibel Bargu said, "but it's actually crashing into walls, because they are very disoriented."

Bonus: Alfred Hitchcock's 1963 classic horror film *The Birds* was loosely based on a short story by Daphne du Maurier. But the Monterey Bay incident played a part, too. Hitchcock lived not far from the bay at the time of the "attack," and is known to have called a local newspaper, asking for details.

KILLER GULLS

In July 2015, a young boy was in the backyard of his home in the seaside town of Newquay, in southwestern England, when a pair of large seagulls swooped down and attacked the boy's dog, an eight-year-old Yorkshire terrier named Roo. The terrified boy screamed for his mother, while the gulls—European herring gulls, one of the largest gulls in the world—viciously pecked at the tiny dog's head. The dog managed to run into the house, but once inside it collapsed. "I ran into the kitchen and saw Roo lying on his side and there was blood everywhere," the boy's mother, Emily Vincent, told the *Telegraph* newspaper. "Blood was coming out of his head. It was like a murder scene." She rushed the dog to the vet, but sadly, he didn't make it. It was later determined that the seagulls were protecting a nest they'd built on the roof of the family's home—but the family wasn't allowed to do anything about it. European herring gulls are a protected species—and it's illegal to kill them or disturb their nests. "I haven't stopped crying and I've now reached the angry stage," Vincent said. "It could have been my child that was hurt and there is nothing I can do about it."

Extra: A week later, European herring gulls attacked and killed a 20-year-old pet tortoise in a backyard pen in the nearby town of Liskeard. The tortoise's owner, Jan Byrne, said she found the gulls pecking at the overturned tortoise, eating it "like a crab."

BIRD ATTACK QUIZ

Who gets attacked by an ostrich? One internationally famous singer did. This story, which appeared in his autobiography, tells of a face-to-beak encounter he had while walking in the woods near his home one day. Fortunately, he was carrying a large stick that he'd picked up off the ground a few minutes earlier. See if you can guess who our famous ostrich-attack victim is. (Answer below.)

> When he started moving toward me I went on the offensive, taking a good hard swipe at him…I missed. He wasn't there. He was in the air, and a split second later he was on his way down again, with that big toe of his, larger than my size-thirteen shoe, extended toward my stomach. He made contact—I'm sure there was never any question he wouldn't—and frankly, I got off lightly. All he did was break my two lower ribs and rip my stomach open down to my belt. If the belt hadn't been good and strong, with a solid belt buckle, he'd have spilled my guts exactly the way he meant to. As it was, he knocked me over onto my back and I broke three more ribs on a rock—but I had sense enough to keep swinging the stick, so he didn't get to finish me. I scored a good hit on one of his legs, and he ran off.

Answer: The ostrich-attack victim was country music superstar Johnny Cash. He wrote about it in his 1997 memoir, *Cash: The Autobiography*. The attack occurred in the winter of 1981 when the singer was walking through the woods near his House of Cash compound in north-central Tennessee. The ostrich belonged to Cash—he had an exotic animal park on the property—and, according to Cash, it was usually friendly. So why had the usually friendly bird attacked him? Cash explained that the ostrich's mate had recently died, and that the loss had made the bird "cranky." (Sounds like a country song.)

LOST IN TRANSLATION

Movie titles often don't translate well. Foreign marketers have to get creative to get a film's point across, often with unintentionally hilarious results.

The Dark Knight: Knight of the Night (Spain)

Guardians of the Galaxy: Interplanetary Unusual Attacking Team (Taiwan)

The Help: Black and White World (Czech Republic)

Drive Angry: Super Speeding Cleaning Evil Accounts (Thailand)

American Pie: American Virgin Man (Hong Kong)

No Strings Attached: Sex Friends (France)

Dodgeball: Full of the Nuts (Germany)

Superbad: Horny All the Time (Israel)

The Professional: This Hit Man Is Not as Cold as He Thought (China)

The Terminator: Electronic Murderer (Poland)

Psycho: The Man Who Killed His Mother (Portugal)

Field of Dreams: Imaginary Dead Baseball Players Live in My Cornfield (China)

The Producers: Please Do Not Touch the Old Women (Italy)

Due Date: Odd Couple, Wacky Trip, Go Together in Time for Birth (Thailand)

Eternal Sunshine of the Spotless Mind: If You Leave Me, I Delete You (Italy)

Silver Linings Playbook: My Boyfriend Is a Psycho (Russia)

Little Fockers: Zany Son-in-Law, Zippy Grandkids, Sour Father-in-Law (Thailand)

Lost in Translation: Meetings and Failures in Meetings (Portugal)

The Gopher Hole Museum in Calgary, Alberta, exhibits taxidermied gophers dressed like people.

WHAT DO YOU EAT BEFORE THE GAME?

These professional athletes are the world's best, so who are we to question the fact that they are very methodical, superstitious even, about what they eat? (Well...we might question a few of them.)

• **Justin Verlander.** The Cy Young Award–winning pitcher eats Taco Bell before taking the mound. Specifically, he gets three Taco Supremes (no tomato), a Cheesy Gordita Crunch, and a Mexican Pizza (no tomato).

• **Wade Boggs.** The Baseball Hall of Famer ate chicken before every game. The preparation varied—fried, baked, or roasted—but it was usually a whole bird with a squirt of lemon juice.

• **Wayne Gretzky.** It started as just another meal early in the Great One's storied hockey career, but then he made it a pregame ritual. The meal: four hot dogs with mustard and onions.

• **Brian Urlacher.** The 258-pound NFL linebacker ate exactly two Famous Amos chocolate chip cookies on game day.

• **Caron Butler.** The NBA star chugged a two-liter bottle of Mountain Dew just before a game, hopping himself up on both sugar and caffeine. (His team, the Washington Wizards, made him stop because they said it was too unhealthy.)

• **Marshawn Lynch.** During the 2011 NFL season, the Seattle Seahawks running back was caught by TV cameras on the sidelines stuffing a handful of Skittles in his mouth. He apparently does this between plays, several times a game. He says it helps keep his energy up.

• **Derek Jeter.** The Yankees legend's pregame meal was an omelette and a stack of pancakes.

• **Charles Barkley.** In his playing days, the NBA legend known as "the Round Mound of Rebound" would start game day at McDonald's. His order: two Filet-o-Fish sandwiches, an order of large fries, and a Diet Coke.

- **Usain Bolt.** "The fastest man on earth" is also a devotee of McDonald's. He fuels himself with 20 Chicken McNuggets on race day.

- **Sam Bradford.** The Minnesota Vikings' quarterback doesn't eat one particular food before every game, but he does eat one particular amount. No matter what he eats, it has to be in quantities of three.

- **Claude Giroux.** The NHL all-star eats a grilled cheese sandwich (or two) before he takes to the ice.

- **Paul Pierce.** In sports, timing is everything. That could explain it: Not only did this NBA player eat a peanut butter and jelly sandwich before a game, he had to eat it exactly 55 minutes before the game started.

> **SUPER-SIZED:** *In 1986, Houston Rockets star center Hakeem Olajuwon appeared in a McDonald's commercial promoting Chicken McNuggets. He was supposed to "slam dunk" a McNugget in his mouth. The shoot took five hours and 100 takes to get right. And although he didn't have to, on every take, Olajuwon ate the McNugget. Result: he ended up eating the equivalent of one and a half chickens and three pounds of bread, marinade, salt, and other ingredients.*

- **Bryce Harper.** The Washington Nationals' outfielder eats Eggo frozen waffles (and only Eggos will do) slathered in peanut butter and honey just before a game.

- **Peyton Manning.** The retired NFL quarterback fueled up with a bowl of spaghetti and marinara sauce, a plain baked potato, a side of broccoli, two pieces of chicken, and some Gatorade before every game.

- **Laffit Pincay Jr.** This jockey has the second-most wins of all time in professional horse racing, with 9,530. His pregame "meal": a single peanut.

- **Lyoto Machida.** This Brazilian mixed martial arts light-heavyweight champion claims to derive medical and health benefits from his morning routine of drinking his own urine.

THE PHANTOMS OF PARIS

*Do you believe in ghosts? Paris is loaded with them. Here are a
few famous spots in the City of Light where believers claim
you're likely to encounter some spirited residents.*

THE LOUVRE

Every year, millions of people visit this museum to see the *Mona Lisa*, the *Venus
de Milo*, and other masterpieces. The building dates to the 12th century, when
it served as a fortress for Philip II. Since then, the grounds have borne witness
to wars, plagues, and other calamities, which is one reason why the Louvre is
considered by ghost hunters to be the most haunted place in France. Since it
was converted into a museum in 1793, visitors and staff have reported spectral
orbs, mysterious shadows, and human-looking figures lingering among the
artworks. French legend also tells of a gnomelike ghoul dressed in red that often
appears near the Louvre as a harbinger of national tragedy. Often referred to as
"the Little Red Man," the spirit is supposedly capable of offsetting impending
doom…for the right price. If the tales are true, he's bargained with French rulers
including Henry IV, Marie Antoinette, and Napoleon, who failed to heed the
Little Red Man's advice and suffered the consequences at the Battle of Waterloo.
The museum's other ghosts are said to include the spirits of French soldiers and
prisoners who were once held captive in its dungeon.

NOTRE DAME

According to local legend, a depressed woman known only by the initials "MJ"
visited the iconic cathedral in 1882. She wanted to climb up one of the towers
but was turned away by guards because women weren't permitted to enter that
area without a chaperone. So, MJ found one—an elderly woman who was
touring the main floor of the cathedral. As the two women reached the parapets,
MJ did what she came there to do: she flung herself over the side and landed
on one of the spiked railings below. Her ghost has been spotted near the tower's
gargoyles. Another legend claims that a locksmith commissioned to craft all
the locks for Notre Dame back in the 12th century was so overwhelmed by the
task that he asked the devil to help in his workshop. The devil agreed, and the
locksmith died a few days after finishing the project. His soulless spirit, it is said,
still wanders the grounds.

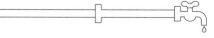

Short fact: Napoleon was 5'6", just one inch less than the average Frenchman of today.

PÈRE-LACHAISE

The grandiose tombs and elaborate statues featured in this cemetery attract countless tourists annually. It is the final resting place of Doors frontman Jim Morrison, whose spirit reportedly still hangs around his grave. Rock historian Brett Meisner had his photo taken next to Morrison's headstone in 1997 and was shocked by what he found when the film was developed. Standing behind Meisner was a pale figure with his arms outstretched, an iconic pose often struck by the Lizard King. The cemetery is also said to be home to the restless spirit of French novelist Marcel Proust, as well as two lovers who rise from their graves on opposite sides of the cemetery nightly and forlornly wander the grounds in search of one another.

THE PARIS CATACOMBS

Deep beneath the streets of Paris are the bones of no less than six million people. For most of the 18th century, the city's cemeteries couldn't keep up with all the victims of war, disease, and other fatalities. With nowhere else to turn, city officials began piling their bones in the catacombs—the maze of old limestone mines—that lay beneath Paris. Needless to say, the catacombs are thought to be haunted by countless spirits who are upset about the fact that their remains were so unceremoniously discarded. Many visitors have returned from the catacombs with videos of weird glowing lights and photos of spectral orbs. Others have reported being touched by invisible hands, being followed by illusory figures, and even the sensation of being strangled.

THE EIFFEL TOWER

Hundreds of visitors have committed suicide by jumping off the "Iron Lady," but the Paris landmark's ghost isn't among them. According to legend, a young woman asked her lover to meet her at the top of the tower, where she planned to tell him she was ending the affair. The woman hoped that the beauty of the city below would soften the blow of the difficult message she was about to deliver. But when they reached the top—before the woman was able to tell him the reason for the meeting—the man proposed marriage. Shocked, she began laughing nervously. The man was so humiliated by her disdain that, in a fit of rage, he pushed her over the edge and she fell to her death. Are the stories true? Head to the tower's top observatory platform late at night and you may hear the sound of her laughter...followed by bloodcurdling screams.

It took 17 years and $4.5 billion to renovate the Pentagon (1994–2011).

A PAGE OF CAGE

Words of wisdom—or something—from Oscar-winning actor Nicolas Cage.

"I was always shocked when I went to the doctor's office and they did my X-ray and didn't find that I had eight more ribs than I should have or that my blood was the color green."

"Every great story seems to begin with a snake."

"Sometimes people think I'm wearing a wig when I'm not wearing a wig, and then sometimes they think I'm not wearing a wig when I am wearing a wig."

"I would like to find a way to embrace what Led Zeppelin did, but in filmmaking."

"Dracula is one of my favorite characters in literature. Much of my lifestyle is modeled after him. I don't drink blood, but otherwise, I admire the sensibility."

"I think I jump around more when I'm alone."

"Superman is an American myth. Like the English have Shakespeare."

"I am not a demon. I am a lizard, a shark, a heat-seeking panther. I want to be Bob Denver on acid playing the accordion."

"I always add a year to myself, so I'm prepared for my next birthday. So when I was 39, I was already 40."

"I was being stalked by a mime—silent but maybe deadly. Somehow, this mime would appear on the set and start doing strange things. I have no idea how it got past security. Finally, the producers took some action and I haven't seen the mime since. But it was definitely unsettling."

"See my eyes. Respect them as you'd respect me."

"I actually choose the way I eat according to the way animals have sex. I think fish are very dignified with sex. So are birds. But pigs, not so much. So I don't eat pig meat."

"Nobody ever thinks clearly at the airport."

In Belgium, casinos have caged birds; patrons can bet on which one will sing the loudest and longest.

FLOWERS FOR MRS. KUROKI

It's certainly not unheard of for a man to show his wife that he loves her by giving her flowers. (The floral industry kind of depends on it.) But this many flowers? Say hello to Toshiyuki and Yasuko Kuroki.

TIME FOR A VACATION

Toshiyuki and Yasuko Kuroki got married in 1956 and started their family on a dairy farm near the town of Shintomi, on the southern Japanese island of Kyushu. With their two children, they spent the next 30 years caring for their herd of dairy cows, which grew to 60 in number. By the mid-1980s the couple was looking forward to the day, not too far off, when they could retire and take a nice long trip to see the rest of Japan.

But it was not to be: one day in 1986 Mrs. Kuroki, a diabetic, began having problems with her eyes. Her vision deteriorated rapidly and within a week she was almost completely blind. The shock of losing her sight so quickly sent her into a deep depression; not only did she not want to travel around Japan, she didn't want to leave the house. Formerly cheerful and outgoing, Mrs. Kuroki became a virtual recluse and rarely saw anyone outside the family.

SEED OF AN IDEA

Mr. Kuroki was at a loss for what to do…until one day he noticed some people admiring the fuschia-pink *shibazakura* flowers in his and his wife's small garden. Also known as moss phlox, the flowers bloom prodigiously and they have a strong, sweet fragrance. That gave Mr. Kuroki an idea: if he planted more shibazakura around the farm, their pleasing scent might encourage his wife to venture out of the house more often to smell them. And if the flowers attracted an admirer or two, chatting with them might lift Mrs. Kuroki's spirits.

The Kurokis farm is several acres, and Mr. Kuroki decided to plant as much of it as possible in shibazakura. He retired from the dairy business, sold his cows, and devoted the next two years to clearing trees, planting shibazakura, and tending to the young plants as they grew. He created footpaths through the fields, so that if anyone ever did stop by to admire the flowers, they would be able to walk out into the middle of the flowers and enjoy them all the more.

Physics fact: A warm basketball is bouncier than a cold one.

IN THE PINK

After two years of planting, the fields were ready; that March the shibazakura came into bloom. The rolling fields of pink that surrounded the Kurokis' home were a vivid contrast to the green pastures of the neighboring farms, and just as Mr. Kuroki hoped, they began to attract attention. Only a few visitors came by at first, mostly locals from Shintomi and surrounding towns. But as the years passed the numbers grew, and the story of Mr. Kuroki's gift to his wife spread. Soon people came from other parts of Kyushu to see the flowers, then from other southern islands, and then from all over Japan. The crowds grew so large that Mr. Kuroki converted a cow shed into a visitors' center filled with photographs and other displays. During March and April when the flowers are in full bloom, a hundred people or more drop by the farm each day to see the flowers and visit with Mr. and Mrs. Kuroki, who are usually in the visitors' center or out walking along the footpaths that run through the fields.

FLOWER POWER

It's a good thing that the Kurokis enjoy all the attention, because in early 2016 their story was profiled on the English language website Rocket24, and from there it spread all over the Internet. It's a safe bet that in coming years when foreign tourists travel to Japan each April for *Sakura Matsuri*, the annual Cherry Blossom Festival, more than a few of them will be adding another destination to their itinerary: a visit to the Kurokis' farm outside of Shintomi on the island of Kyushu. If they do drop by, they are likely to see Mr. and Mrs. Kuroki socializing happily with their visitors. Mrs. Kuroki still struggles with her blindness, but her depression has lifted and by all appearances she is as cheerful and outgoing as she was before she lost her sight. That she has made such a strong recovery from the depths of her despair is, for Mr. Kuroki, the greatest gift of all.

*   *   *

SIGN OF THE TIMES

A McDonald's billboard on the outskirts of Yass, New South Wales, Australia, suffered from some poorly thought-out design. The "M"-shaped Golden Arches were positioned right in front of the town name, so motorists were greeted with this as they drove into town:

ΛΛYASS
Open 6 a.m.

In 1520, King Henry VIII challenged French King Francis I to a wrestling match. (Henry lost.)

START ME UP

These real Kickstarter campaigns are good examples of 21st-century capitalism gone weird.

Grilled Cheesus: Toast the face of Jesus onto your cheese sandwich and turn lunch into a religious experience. Launched in 2012, this cheesy campaign was successfully funded by 286 backers to the tune of $25,604.

Mokase: It's a combination cell phone case/coffee dispenser. Just pop the coffee pod "wafer" into the side of the case, open the app, and press the empty cup on the screen. As the "cup" fills, the Mokase's battery heats water in the reservoir and, in seconds, the coffee is ready to pour. Mokase raised only €4,500 ($4,642) of the €75,000 ($82,331) goal, so Kickstarter suspended the campaign.

Poop: The Game: Feels Right Design launched their campaign in 2014 with a goal of $4,500. Patterned after the card game Uno, the goal is to run out of cards. Players take turns "pooping" (laying down a variety of Poop cards), but if they clog the toilet, they might get left with a handful of crap cards. Players say "Poop!" as they lay down cards. They raised $11,696.

Sprimo Personal Air-Quality Monitor: This portable monitor plugs into your iPhone to give you real-time readings of the air quality in your personal space. The device senses a variety of volatile organic compounds, from paint to perfume, bleach to body odor. It rates air quality on a scale from 0 (good) to 500 (hazardous). More than 1,300 backers pledged $72,053 so you, too, could soon walk around holding out your iPhone to check the air quality wherever you go.

Fidget Cube: An inconspicuous dice-shaped toy for fidgeters. The little cube has a toggle switch on one side, and a mini joystick, an indentation, three gears and a tiny metallic trackball, five buttons (three click; two are silent), and a spinning dial on each of the other five sides. Two fidgety brothers came up with the idea in 2012 and—with 154,926 backers pledging $6 million—rolled it out in 2016.

IllumiBowl: Started in 2014 as the world's first toilet bowl night-light, the latest version of IllumiBowl blasts toilet germs using non-UVC wavelengths of light that are "lethal to bacteria, but harmless to humans." The medical-grade anti-germ diode clips to the lip of the bowl like a deodorizer and is motion-activated. Light-wave energy zaps the bowl in regular intervals for 15 seconds and, once a day, for 8 minutes straight. Backers have pledged $90,000—ten times the goal.

Cin cin! The standard daily ration for Italian soldiers includes an 80-proof alcohol "breakfast shot."

A BRIEF HISTORY OF MARSHMALLOWS

Half of all marshmallows eaten in the summer are toasted over a fire.
Here are s'more marshmallow facts.

PILLOW TALK

Marshmallows have something in common with early soft drinks like 7 Up and Coca-Cola. They all started as medicines, and only later became popular as "junk" food. Coca-Cola contained cocaine and was originally marketed as a "brain tonic," used to treat everything from headaches to morphine addiction. 7 Up contained lithium citrate, a drug still used to treat bipolar disorder. Likewise, the ancient Egyptians extracted sap from the root of *Althaea officinalis*, a species of mallow plant that grows in marshes, and mixed it with honey to treat sore throats.

It wasn't until centuries later that the French added whipped egg whites and rose water to make *pâté de guimauve*, the first marsh mallow concoction similar to a modern marshmallow. The French are also credited with taking the marsh mallow (and the egg whites) out of marshmallows: extracting sap from marsh mallow roots is a tedious process, and in the early 1800s confectioners there began substituting gelatin and cornstarch in its place. That formula is still used today: even if you love marshmallows, you've probably never tasted marsh mallow, at least not in a marshmallow. (It can still be found in halva, a popular snack in the Middle East.)

GETTING IN SHAPE

The familiar shape of the marshmallow dates only to 1954, when a Los Angeles confectioner named Alex Doumakes patented a machine that extruded long cylindrical "ropes" of marshmallow onto a conveyor belt, then cut them into individual pieces. His machine is credited with turning marshmallows from a rare and costly delicacy, made by hand, into an affordable treat that people bought by the bagful.

Want to make your own marshmallows? See the recipe on page 367.

ACCORDING TO THE NATIONAL CONFECTIONERS ASSOCIATION, *Americans buy 90 million pounds of marshmallows per year—the same weight as 6,000 African elephants. How much does 6,000 elephants' worth of marshmallows cost? $125 million.*

The first Ferris wheel had 36 cars. Each car held 60 people.

THE DANGERFIELD FILES

Rodney Dangerfield (1921–2004) was one of the late 20th century's most revered stand-up comedians, but most people only knew his public "I get no respect" persona. Here are some odd facts about this fascinating man.

- Birth name: Jacob Cohen. He began his stand-up career as Jack Roy but failed to make an impact, so he quit show business and became an aluminum siding salesman in New Jersey. He didn't get back into comedy until his mid-40s. One reason for the abrupt career change may have been that the company Dangerfield worked for was under investigation by the FBI for fraudulent sales practices.

- Back then, successful comedians needed a good hook, and Dangerfield's "No one likes me" tag line wasn't really working. Then, one night at a comedy club, he overheard some mobsters complaining about their jobs, and one said, "I don't get no respect." Dangerfield liked the line so much that he used it in his next act. It got the biggest laugh he ever got, so he kept it for the rest of his life.

- Because he knew firsthand how difficult it was to succeed as a stand-up, Dangerfield was very helpful to other comedians. Among those whose careers he helped launch: Roseanne Barr, Rita Rudner, Bob Saget, Sam Kinison, Tim Allen, Jeff Foxworthy, Jim Carrey, and Jerry Seinfeld.

- Dangerfield's successful movie career didn't begin until he was 60 years old when he appeared in 1980's *Caddyshack*. He was paid $35,000 for the role, but later said that if he'd spent that time performing in Las Vegas, he would have made more than $150,000.

- In 1995 Dangerfield became the first comedian to own a website. He also claimed to have told the world's first Viagra joke (which we can't print here).

- The comedian's uniform: a suit with a white shirt and red necktie that he would frequently loosen. The suit and tie are on permanent display in the Smithsonian.

- When Dangerfield was at home, however, he preferred to wear a loose robe…and nothing else. (This put off more than a few interviewers who came to his house.)

- The two primary types of jokes in his act: his wife's infidelity and his unhappy childhood. The jokes about his wife were all made up, but the unhappy childhood stuff had a ring of truth. His father, a vaudeville comedian, abandoned the family when Dangerfield was very young, and he described his mother as "uncaring." His way of dealing with it: write jokes. He started at age 15 and never stopped.

If you hear "Mr. Mob" paged on a cruise ship, it's code for "man overboard."

- Who was the original Rodney Dangerfield? Jack Benny. It was the name of a cowboy character on Benny's radio show in 1941. Ricky Nelson later used the name as a pseudonym on his TV show *The Adventures of Ozzie and Harriet*. A nightclub owner suggested it to Jack Roy, who was looking for a new name, and Roy became Rodney Dangerfield.

- Later in his life, Dangerfield wanted to clone himself. His wife, Joan Child, still has a vial of Rodney's blood should human cloning ever become a reality.

- Joan also has a vial of Rodney's sweat in her refrigerator. The couple collected a bunch of it in the early 2000s so it could be sold at the MGM Grand in Las Vegas, but the casino refused due to "insurance issues."

- In private, Dangerfield was nothing like his public persona. He was soft-spoken and highly respected. But until the 1990s, he harbored a dark secret: he'd suffered from depression for most of his life. His coping mechanism was marijuana; he smoked it every day for nearly 60 years.

- In the 2000 movie *Little Nicky*, Dangerfield played Lucifer. In the 2005 movie *Angels with Angles*, he played God.

- In 1983 Dangerfield earned a spot on the Billboard Hot 100 singles list with his song "Rappin' Rodney." (It reached #89.) Sample lyrics:

> Steak and sex, my favorite pair
>
> (No respect, no respect)
>
> I have 'em both the same way, very rare
>
> (No respect, no respect)

- Dangerfield made more than 70 appearances on *The Tonight Show*.

- It's well known that Willie Nelson once smoked marijuana at the White House. What's less known is that so did Dangerfield. He snuck a joint while visiting Ronald Reagan in 1983. He also lit one up in a hospital's intensive care unit after having a mild heart attack (for which he was severely reprimanded).

- If he hadn't become a comedian, Dangerfield could have been a mathematician. According to his wife, he could perform complex math equations in his head.

- After playing goofy roles in several slapstick comedies, the comedian was lauded by critics for his dark dramatic turn in the 1994 Oliver Stone film *Natural Born Killers*. Dangerfield applied for membership to the Academy of Motion Picture Arts and Science in the hopes of winning an Oscar, but the academy rejected his application.

Black-eyed peas were once called *mogettes*, French for "nuns," because the eye looks like a nun's habit.

According to member Roddy McDowell: "He had failed to execute enough of the kinds of roles that allow a performer to demonstrate the mastery of his craft." Dangerfield's response: "Comedians don't get no respect."

• Rodney Dangerfield died in October 2004, at the age of 82. He's buried in Westwood Park Cemetery in Los Angeles. The inscription on his headstone: "There goes the neighborhood."

• Dangerfield's comedy is better watched than read, so do yourself a favor and check out his act online. In the meantime, here are some of Dangerfield's best.

"I tell ya, I get no respect. No respect. When I get in an elevator, the operator takes one look and says, 'Basement?'"

"What a childhood I had. My parents sent me to a child psychiatrist. That kid didn't help me at all."

"I was an ugly kid. When I was born, after the doctor cut the cord, he hung himself."

"The other night, outside my house, I saw a guy jogging naked. I asked him how come. He said, 'Because you came home early!'"

"Last night some guy knocked on the front door. My wife told me to hide in the closet."

"I feel sorry for short people, you know. When it rains, they're the last to know."

"What a kid I've got. I told him about the birds and the bees, and he told me about the butcher and my wife."

"With my wife, I got no sex life. She cut me down to once a month. Hey, I'm lucky—two guys I know she cut out completely."

"My uncle's dying wish was to have me sitting on his lap. He was in the electric chair."

"With my doctor, I don't get no respect. I told him I want a vasectomy. He said with a face like mine, I don't need one."

"If things go right, I'll be there about a week, and if things don't go right, I'll be there about an hour and a half." (In 2004, before entering a Los Angeles hospital for heart valve replacement surgery.)

My wife was afraid of the dark. She saw me naked, now she's afraid of the light!

Nearly 80% of the world's wedding dresses come from Suzhou, China.

THE DIFFICULT DECISIONS OF ROBERT E. LEE

If you look back on your life, you can probably point to a time or two where you were faced with a really tough decision. Had you chosen differently, your world would look very different right now. So it was for Confederate general Robert E. Lee (1807–70)—one of the most divisive figures in American history. To his fans, Lee was the hero of the Civil War—which explains why there are so many roads and schools named after him in the South. But to his critics, Lee was a traitor who fought to keep slavery legal. It turns out that Lee was just as conflicted as his legacy. Let's look at Lee's life through the scope of some of those choices to look at the impact they did have…and are still having today.

DECISION 1: MATHEMATICS OR MILITARY?

Robert Edward Lee was born in 1807 to one of Virginia's most wealthy and respected families. When he was 18 years old, he applied to West Point Military Academy in New York, which was expected of a young man of his social status. But late in life he confided to a friend that attending a military college was among his greatest regrets. It may seem like an odd comment for a man who was venerated as a war hero, but as a boy it was mathematics, not soldiering, that interested him. Robert was an intelligent child and could have studied to become a teacher, architect, or an engineer. But there was another factor in play: the once-proud family name had been tarnished.

Two centuries earlier (a few years before the Pilgrims landed at Plymouth Rock), Richard Lee I emigrated from England to begin a new life in what is now Virginia. That was Robert E. Lee's great-grandfather. Lee's grandfather was Colonel Henry Lee II, a prominent Virginia politician. And Lee's father, Henry "Light Horse Harry" Lee III, fought alongside George Washington in the Revolutionary War. In fact, at Washington's funeral in 1799, it was Harry Lee who famously described the late general and president as "first in war, first in peace, and first in the hearts of his countrymen." Harry Lee would go on to become Virginia's governor and then a U.S. congressman.

But things turned sour for the family when Harry's poor financial habits and risky business ventures led to bankruptcy and a one-year stint in debtor's prison. A few years later, during the War of 1812, Harry was nearly beaten to death after defending a friend who opposed the war. He fled to the West Indies to "heal," but it was more likely to escape his debts. He died before he could make it home.

HONOR THY FATHER

With his father gone, and his older brother away at Harvard, it was left to Robert to care for his invalid mother and help raise his younger siblings. His mother instilled in him a sense of honor, never letting him forget that he was born into a family that had produced a governor, a U.S. congressman, a U.S. senator, a U.S. attorney general, and four signers of the Declaration of Independence. Even so, the name "Lee" didn't have the clout it once did.

So one reason for Lee's application to West Point was to restore honor to his family. (Another reason: it was much cheaper than Harvard.) He nearly didn't get in because of his father's reputation, as by that point he had become known primarily as "the man who once wrote George Washington a bad check." But Lee was accepted, and that's where his rise began. An exemplary student, Lee earned zero demerits in his four years there, which is almost unheard of at the strict military academy. In 1829, after graduating second in his class, his high marks earned him the rank of second lieutenant in the prestigious Army Corps of Engineers. He then married Mary Custis, the great-granddaughter of Martha Washington. That alone went a long way to restoring the Lee name.

During the 1830s and early '40s, when the United States was at peace, Lee had the opportunity to put his math skills to work by fortifying the nation's borders. As a U.S. Army engineer, he helped map the line between Ohio and Michigan, and was part of the team that rerouted the Mississippi River back toward St. Louis.

MEANWHILE, IN TEXAS

A few years later, the United States went to war against Mexico over the annexation of Texas. Lee, now a captain, was dispatched there in 1847 to map routes over rough terrain that American soldiers could use to gain an advantage over the Mexicans. His tactical prowess led directly to winning several crucial victories…and eventually the war. And it put Lee on the map as a rising star in the U.S. Army. His commander, General Winfield Scott, called him "the very finest soldier I ever saw in the field."

When Lee was giving a speech to the troops during the Mexican-American War, one of the soldiers in attendance was Ulysses S. Grant, who admired Lee. When the war ended, the two men went their separate ways, on either side of the Mason-Dixon Line (which ran between Virginia and Maryland, and divided the nation between North and South). Little did they know their lives and their legacies would be forever linked.

Lick a frog, cure the flu? The South Indian frog has antiviral properties in the slime on its skin.

DECISION 2: CAPTURE BROWN, OR WAIT IT OUT?

In 1859, Lieutenant Colonel Robert E. Lee and a squad of marines were sent to Harpers Ferry, Virginia, to prevent a slave revolt. A group of 21 abolitionists led by a 58-year-old white Northerner named John Brown had taken over a military arsenal. Their mission: free every slave and kill their captors if they had to (which they had already done on a few occasions). At Harpers Ferry, Brown and his men captured several townspeople, including George Washington's great-grandnephew, and held them as hostages. When Lee arrived, his main objective was to capture Brown, but he was also there to ensure the safety of any townspeople, black or white, who refused to side with Brown. After a tense standoff, Lee sent one of his commanders to approach the arsenal with a white flag. Brown was told that if he surrendered, none of his men's lives would be lost.

> No," replied Brown, "I prefer to die here.

That brought Lee to his next big decision: Should he send his men in to capture by force and perhaps even kill Brown—whom he described as a "madman"—but doing so, possibly turn Brown into a martyr in the North, which would further divide the already divided nation? Or should Lee cut off Brown's provisions and wait him out, in the hope that the revolt would fizzle? Lee chose to send in the troops. They captured Brown after a bloody firefight in which several people were killed—including two of Brown's sons—but no hostages.

John Brown was convicted of murder, conspiracy to incite a slave uprising, and treason against the Commonwealth of Virginia. He was hanged for his crimes. Just as Lee had feared, Brown's death became a rallying cry for the North, though he was vilified as a murderer and a terrorist in the South. When Abraham Lincoln was elected president a year later on an antislavery platform (without winning a single state below the Mason-Dixon Line), many in the South saw that as the last straw. Slavery had been outlawed in the northern states for several decades, and most Southerners could see no other choice than to fight the "northern aggression" or lose their way of life. War was looming.

To read about Lee's next hard choice, turn to page 192.

*   *   *

Random Fact: The Confederate flag-adorned, "Dixie" playing Dodge Charger on *The Dukes of Hazzard* was named the General Lee. The car was modeled after one driven by a notorious Southern bootlegger named Jerry Rushing, who named his car Traveler—after Robert E. Lee's horse, Traveller.

Skunks have rotating scent squirters. They can hit a target from 20 feet away.

WHITE HATS; BLACK HATS

Hackers used to be an obscure subculture of tech genius nerds. Now they're at the forefront of our digital world. Here are some common hacker terms.

White hat. A "good" hacker—one that breaks into a company's computer system to find potential security flaws, often hired by the company to do so

Black hat. A "bad" hacker—one who takes down computer systems to steal information, or just for fun

Hacktivist. Someone like Edward Snowden—a hacker who breaks into systems to expose information for a political cause

State actor. A government-sponsored hacker

Fuzzing. When hackers input a ton of random data to overload or "fuzz" a computer system into crashing.

Brute force. An unsophisticated form of hacking into a server or an account: by guessing a password via trial and error

Jailbreak. Removing the security of a consumer electronics device, such as a smartphone. Purpose: to run unauthorized software or steal intellectual property.

Evil maid attack. Rather than breaking in remotely, the hacker accesses the target computer in person (like a person posing as a maid to break into an office)

DoS. Short for "denial of service," it occurs when a hacker completely shuts down a website

Sniffing. Browsing a network undetected using special software that allows a hacker to find commonly recurring sequences of data—or passwords.

RAT. Short for "Remote Access Tool," it's a nasty program a hacker installs remotely and gets full access to the targeted computer

Ransomware. A piece of hacking software that denies the computer's owner access their files…unless they heed a pop-up message that tells them to send money to the stated address

Doxing. Exposing the identity of someone on the Internet by gathering private information about them and then publishing those documents or "dox"

Script kiddies. What experienced hackers call novice hackers, or a derisive term for a not very skilled hacker.

Infosec. "Information security," also known as "cybersecurity," the sector of the information technology community that tries to prevent hackers from hacking.

Five dubious reasons given for commitment to a West Virginia mental asylum in the 1800s:…

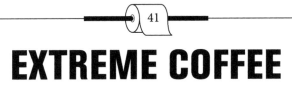

EXTREME COFFEE

How do you begin your day? Many of us get a little kick-start from the caffeine in a cup of coffee. Some people need more than a cup. As in enough to kill an elephant.

STRONG AND DEADLY

In 2016 a South African businessman named Sean Kristafor quit his corporate job to follow his passion: to make the strongest, most highly caffeinated coffee in the world. And through his company, Black Insomnia, he did it. The company's coffee is a sweet, nutty blend made from *robusta* coffee beans that have been specially roasted to maximize caffeine content. It's been chemically tested and measured to contain 58 milligrams of caffeine. That's 58 milligrams *per ounce*, or more than double the caffeine load of Starbucks' dark roast and about six times as much as an ounce of home-brewed coffee. This means one eight-ounce serving of Black Insomnia coffee packs about 700 milligrams of caffeine, which is almost twice the 400 milligrams that the FDA says should be anybody's limit. Black Insomnia has been challenged for caffeine supremacy by another coffee maker, called Death Wish. Before Black Insomnia came on the scene, Death Wish had a caffeine level of 54.2 milligrams per ounce…but it says that those figures are old, and that the coffee now contains 59.17 milligrams per ounce, which is more than Black Insomnia. (And both are more than anybody needs.)

AND TAKING NAMES

Viscous Coffee is a café in Adelaide, Australia, known for an espresso so strong that those who drink it may experience heart trouble and not be able to sleep for days. Concocted by Viscous owner Steve Benington, an iced coffee drink on the menu aptly named the A**kicker delivers five grams of caffeine—not milligrams, but grams. That's half of what is considered a lethal dose of caffeine, and roughly 60 times as much caffeine as is found in a regular cup of joe. A**kicker's ingredients: four shots of a thick, syrupy espresso, four ounces of drip coffee brewed for 10 days to extract the most caffeine possible, and eight ice cubes made from cold-drip coffee brewed over 48 hours so that each has the strength of two normal shots of espresso. Anybody who orders it must submit to a round of questioning from staff, to make sure they can handle it, and that they know what they're getting into—along with the recommendation to drink it over a period of three to four hours to lessen the shock to the system. Viscous says anyone who drinks an A**kicker can expect to stay wired for 12 to 18

…"Bad company," "parents were cousins," "bad whiskey," "political excitement," and "kicked by horse."

hours, although the person Benington created it for, an ER nurse who had to work an unexpected overnight shift, stayed awake for three days.

HOT STUFF

A recent fad in coffee shops in Indonesia is a style of preparation called Kopi Joss. This is the drink for people who like their coffee to be as hot as possible—so hot it's not safe for human consumption. Kopi Joss is prepared the way most coffee is made—water is forced through coffee grounds, and then poured into a cup. Then the daring barista goes over to a grill and, using metal tongs, removes a chunk of red-hot burning charcoal and carefully places it into the coffee. The charcoal melts a little and stays in the cup, creating a gray, goopy, puddinglike mixture even after the charcoal is removed. But Kopi Joss reportedly tastes pretty good—the charcoal eliminates the acidity of the coffee, which improves the taste and also limits the post-coffee upset stomachs many people experience.

IT'S NOT BANANAS

Despite its complex flavors, coffee blends pleasantly with whatever is added in, such as milk or flavored syrup. Or monkey saliva. One of the most annoying pests facing coffee farmers in Taiwan are Formosan Rock Monkeys. They love to pick coffee cherries as they're growing, getting a major caffeine buzz. Then they spit out the coffee beans that are inside the cherries and move along to get their next fix. It's not clear exactly how, but one of those frustrated Taiwanese coffee growers discovered that the beans that had been spit out by monkeys—and had monkey saliva all over them—made for a brewed coffee with a pronounced vanilla flavor. Farmers have started collecting the beans, but there's a relatively small amount of monkey-sucked coffee out there. Some years, the harvest is as low as eight pounds, and in other years it's been as high as 600 pounds. Cost to consumers: about $56 per pound.

CRYSTAL COFFEE

There are a lot of caffeine options in the world today: colas, energy drinks, and energy shots to name a few. But for some people, nothing beats coffee. One major negative of java is that frequent consumption can leave teeth stained. Brothers David and Adam Nagy hated that, so they figured out a way to keep all the caffeine in coffee while also making the beverage itself clear. Clear Coffee, say the Nagys, smells and tastes like coffee, but looks like water. (Others say it tastes more like a coffee-flavored drink, or water that has a few drops of coffee essence in it.)

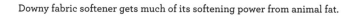

Downy fabric softener gets much of its softening power from animal fat.

FELLINI

Here are some tips on how to live la dolce vita *from Federico Fellini, the legendary Italian film director who directed…La Dolce Vita.*

"Life is a combination of magic and pasta."

"There is abundant testimony that if we choose love rather than self, we gain immeasurably."

"Regrets are a waste of time. They're the past crippling you in the present."

"Nothing is more honest than a dream."

"If there were a little more silence, maybe we could understand something."

"I think that one can have luck if one tries to create an atmosphere of spontaneity."

"If you see with innocent eyes, everything is divine."

"Happiness is simply a temporary condition that precedes unhappiness. Fortunately for us, it works the other way around as well. But it's all a part of the carnival, isn't it?"

"Experience is what you get while looking for something else."

"The visionary is the only realist."

"Money is everywhere, but so is poetry. What we lack are the poets."

"All art is autobiographical. The pearl is the oyster's autobiography."

"We can all pretend to be cynical and scheming, but when we're faced with purity and innocence, the cynical mask drops off."

"Everyone knows that time is Death, that Death hides in clocks."

"If you do what you were born to do, you will never grow old."

"There is no end. There is no beginning. There is only the infinite passion of life."

"Remember, this is a comedy."

LATE NIGHT NO-SHOWS

*Every night, late night talk show hosts come into our homes to tell a few jokes,
interview a celebrity, introduce the band, and say good night. It's a job that
many entertainers want—but not all do. Here are some who said no.*

THE DAILY SHOW with AMY SCHUMER

When Jon Stewart announced that he planned to leave *The Daily Show* in 2015
because, he said, doing the show wasn't as "satisfying" as it had once been,
Comedy Central went after a number of high-profile comedians to replace him
as host. Chris Rock was asked, and he accepted—but he only wanted to do the
show through the end of the 2016 presidential election season. Comedy Central
wanted someone permanent, so Rock was out. The network also looked inside
the network, approaching *Inside Amy Schumer* star Amy Schumer. She turned it
down because, as she told *The Daily Beast*, it was too safe. "Picturing being in a
building and knowing what I was going to do for five years—I love *not* knowing.
And I've never done anything safe or to make money for that reason." *Parks
and Recreation* star Amy Poehler passed on the gig, as did *Louie* star Louis C.K.
Ultimately, Comedy Central selected low-profile Trevor Noah, a South African
stand-up comic who had joined *The Daily Show* as a contributor just a few
months before Stewart's exit.

THE LATE, LATE SHOW with NORM MACDONALD

In 1998 Don Ohlmeyer, NBC vice president in charge of late night, personally
fired *Saturday Night Live* cast member Norm Macdonald. Reason: As host of
the comic news segment "Weekend Update," Macdonald had frequently—and
brutally—made fun of O. J. Simpson. Ohlmeyer was friends with Simpson, and
he'd had enough of Macdonald's teasing. But while he had one high-powered
enemy, Macdonald also had a high-powered ally: David Letterman. A week
after he was fired, Macdonald got a call from a producer at Letterman's CBS
talk show, who asked if he'd like to film some man-on-the-street segments for
that program. A few days later the producer called back to say that somebody
else had gotten the job. But what the producer didn't tell Macdonald was that
he was in contention for another job—to host a talk show in the time slot
after Letterman's show, which Letterman's company, Worldwide Pants, was
developing. Without Macdonald even knowing he was up for the job, CBS
executives overruled Letterman and hired *Daily Show* host Craig Kilborn to host
The Late, Late Show.

Did you buy any? 7-Eleven sells 45 million gallons' worth of Big Gulps each year.

THE TONIGHT SHOW with BOB NEWHART

When Jack Paar left *The Tonight Show* in 1962, he was the second entertainer—following Steve Allen—to host the late-night franchise. NBC considered several major comedians to replace him, including Groucho Marx and Jackie Gleason. But it ultimately came down to two guys: Johnny Carson, the host of a game show called *Who Do You Trust?* and Bob Newhart, at the time one of the hottest comedians in the country. His album *The Button-Down Mind of Bob Newhart* had hit #1 and won Newhart the Grammy for Best New Artist. Newhart was too busy touring and recording more albums to take on a daily gig, and so NBC went with Carson…who hosted *The Tonight Show* for nearly 30 years.

THE CONAN O'BRIEN SHOW

In 2001 Conan O'Brien's contract as host of NBC's *Late Night* was about to expire, which meant he could entertain offers from other networks. And other networks were eager to poach the popular host. Fox, which hadn't put a late night show on the air since *The Chevy Chase Show* was canceled after just six weeks in 1993, made O'Brien a very nice offer. Not only would he get an earlier time slot—weeknights at 11:00 p.m., instead of 12:30 a.m.—but they'd pay him $21 million a year…seven times what he was earning at NBC. But O'Brien turned it down, mostly because he was hoping to succeed Jay Leno as host of *The Tonight Show*. In 2009 O'Brien got his wish, and inherited *The Tonight Show*…only to have NBC pull him off the show after 10 months in order to reinstall Leno.

LATE NIGHT with DANA CARVEY

When NBC passed on *Late Night* host David Letterman to succeed the retiring Johnny Carson as host of *The Tonight Show* in 1992 (in favor of Jay Leno), Letterman jumped to CBS to host *The Late Show*, which aired in direct competition with Leno's *Tonight*. That left an opening at *Late Night*. NBC asked *Saturday Night Live* creator Lorne Michaels to produce the show and find its new host. Michaels already had a guy in mind: *SNL*'s biggest star at the time, Dana Carvey, the comedian behind such characters as the Church Lady and Garth on "Wayne's World." NBC pursued Carvey hard, giving him $1 million just to consider hosting *Late Night*, along with gifts, such as a Beatles album signed by all four Beatles. The news that Carvey might be taking the job was leaked, and *TV Guide* put him on the cover with the headline "Letterman's Heir Apparent." But in spite of all that, Carvey turned down NBC. Lorne Michaels's second pick: Carvey's friend and former *SNL* writer Conan O'Brien, who'd already been hired as a writer and producer for *Late Night with Dana Carvey*.

Authorities can get a DNA sample from a licked envelope.

OOEY GOOEY PLAYSCHOOL

What's in a name? Ask the owners of these real day-care centers.

Mad Tots Learning Center

Martini Kids Club

Small Minds of Tomorrow

Graves

Your Child Is Mine Preschool

Hugz 'N' Hissy Fits

Ann's Teenie Weenie

Hannibal Children's Center

Showers of Learning

Tiny Minds Family Child Care

The Little Willie Center

Best Little Schoolhouse N Texas

Dik-in-aa-gan Child Care Center

The Swamp

Babble-On Day Care

Little Monsters

Elm Street Childcare

Drop a Tot

Pooh County Day Nursery School

Sunshine Childcare
(has no windows)

Beyond Care, Inc.

Happy Hours Preschool

Little Gulls & Buoys

Ripley Do-Da's Learning Center

Vermonsters Day Care Center

Ooey Gooey Playschool

Wahaha Childcare Center

Allie Gator Playskool

Olive Juice Child Development
Center

Tiny Hiney Daycare

Board of Child Care

Blackbutt Childcare

Kickin' Kids After School Care

Threats Child Care Center

Ankle Biters Home Day Care

Eenie Meenie Einstein's

Tatertots
(located in Idaho)

Li'l Squirts

The Village Children

Little Stinkers Daycare

Poet e. e. cummings dedicated his book *No Thanks* to the 14 publishers who turned it down.

BETWEEN THE PAGES

In case you don't happen to have a bookmark on hand, here are a few things your fellow readers have used as handy placeholders.

A librarian from Georgia found a taco pressed like a flower in the middle of a library book. It was squeezed so flat, she had no idea it was there until she opened the book.

Inside an old copy of A *Wrinkle in Time*, a Goodreads patron from Utah found a photo of his dad and his sixth-grade teacher, together at the prom.

The Hallelujah songbook was published in 1854. The book is subtitled A *Book for the Service of Song in the House of the Lord*. Inside? A rare-books dealer in New York found a hand-drawn bull's-eye, used for target practice and dated 1902. Eight bullet holes were a testament to how well the owner could handle a Marlin repeating rifle. Conclusion: Not very well. Only two shots made it into the inner circle.

While working in the children's department, a Salt Lake City librarian found a baby carrot flattened inside a copy of a children's book written by Marc Brown. The book's title: *D.W. the Picky Eater*.

A Michigan man found a $500 savings bond inside a ratty old book about soccer and tracked down its owner through the names inscribed inside. Turns out the recipient had been given the bond as a birthday present before using it as a bookmark. The family had torn the house apart looking for the bond but never found it. Somewhere along the line, the book was donated to charity. Eleven years later, the man who bought the book returned the bond to the girl—now a college student—who used it to pay some of her expenses.

A California college student found everything he needed to roll a joint inside an old medical textbook: marijuana leaves (neatly dried and pressed) along with a pack of No. 7 rolling papers.

An Oregon woman found a tuition receipt from Southern Oregon College (now Southern Oregon University) made out to her mother in a book she inherited. Cost of one semester's tuition for the 1965–66 school year: $124.

The "tusk" of the narwhal is actually a tooth. It can grow up to 9 feet long.

Inside a tattered first edition of *Exodus* by Leon Uris, a gleeful used-book buyer found a yellowed 1961 program from a meeting of the Atlanta Jewish Welfare Fund. Listed on the program as giving the address: Leon Uris. The program had been signed by Uris himself before being stuck inside the book and promptly—or so it seems—forgotten.

A Utah public librarian found a ten-page letter (single-spaced), addressed jointly to President Obama and the Vatican, stuffed inside a copy of Gabriel Garcia Márquez's *Love in the Time of Cholera*. The letter's topic: the need for more religious books in libraries. Ironically, the book is about a man who has 622 illicit love affairs.

A New York bookseller found a tiny bright orange life vest in a kids' book titled *Bats in the Dark* (1972). The vest once belonged to an Action Jackson action figure—a toy that was made by Mego Toys in the early 1970s to compete with Hasbro's more popular G.I. Joe. (It flopped.)

A Brooklyn woman found a copy of *Rock This!* by Chris Rock in an abandoned shopping cart. It seemed like a good subway read, so she took the book aboard with her. Inside the pages? $200 cash.

A Macon, Georgia, library worker was hefting the *Chilton Car Repair Guide* onto a shelf when a wrench fell out and landed on her (Ouch!) foot.

A researcher in Norfolk, England, opened a 17th-century scientific pamphlet on Halley's comet. Out fell a fried egg so old that it shed blue spores all over his shoes before it bounced across the floor.

An out-of-towner bought a treasure of a cookbook from the Cat's Meow, a used bookstore in New Mexico. What made it special? The forty $1,000 bills hidden among the recipes. The book had been part of a large collection from a wealthy woman's estate. Since the $1,000 note hasn't been printed since 1934, each bill would have been worth up to seven times its face value.

Inside a copy of *The Thundering Herd* by Zane Grey (1925), a rare-books dealer from Oneonta, New York, found a pass for someone named C. Robert Rau to visit the House of Representatives. It was dated July 12, 1955, and signed by Massachusetts representative John W. Heselton. Too bad it wasn't signed by one of two other Massachusetts representatives to the 84th Congress—John F. Kennedy or Tip O'Neill.

Gore-Tex, the waterproof jacket coating, is made out of stretched-out Teflon.

GPS FINDS ITS WAY

If you don't already have GPS on your smartphone or in your car, you probably will soon. And as soon as you start using it, you start becoming more and more dependent on it. So how did this system get off the ground?

DOPPLER EFFECT–IVE

Here's a topic you might not have thought about much since you studied physics in school: the difference between how a car horn sounds when you're riding in the car and how it sounds when you're standing on the side of the road as the car passes by. Inside the moving car, the sound of the horn is steady and unchanging. But when you're standing on the side of the road, the sound you hear is higher in pitch as the car approaches you, and lower in pitch as the car drives away. This phenomenon is called the *Doppler effect*, and it's what makes the Global Positioning System possible.

The origin of the GPS system dates back to the dawn of the Space Age. Just a day or two after the Soviet Union launched *Sputnik*, the world's first artificial satellite, on October 4, 1957, two physicists at Johns Hopkins University realized that if they listened for *Sputnik's* beep-beep-beeping radio signal and measured how its frequency was altered by the Doppler effect, they could calculate the satellite's location. Then they realized that if the satellite's location was known, but an observer's location on Earth was not, they could use the Doppler effect to calculate the observer's position, too. Launch enough satellites into orbit so that at least four are always passing overhead no matter where in the world an observer is, and it becomes possible to determine the position of *any* observer, *any* time, *anywhere* on Earth.

THE DOLLAR EFFECT

The physics of such a system is straightforward enough, but the cost of launching dozens of satellites into orbit (and dozens more in perpetuity as the old ones wear out) was prohibitive. It wasn't until the Cold War, when the U.S. military needed a way for submarines to quickly and accurately determine their position before launching nuclear missiles, that anyone was willing to spend the billions of dollars needed to put such an expensive system into operation.

The first prototype GPS satellite was launched in early 1978, and by 1983 several more were in orbit. In those days the system was intended solely for military use, and it might have stayed that way had tragedy not struck on

In the 16th and 17th centuries, married people wore their wedding rings on their thumbs.

September 1, 1983. On that day a navigational error caused Korean Airlines flight 007 to stray more than 400 miles off course into restricted Soviet airspace, where it was mistaken for a U.S. Air Force reconnaissance plane…and shot down by the Soviets. All 269 people aboard, including a U.S. congressman from Georgia named Larry McDonald, were killed.

At the time, the GPS system was still in development, with many more satellites remaining to be launched before the system came online. But President Ronald Reagan ordered that when it did become available, it should be made available for civilian use to prevent similar tragedies from occurring.

THAT'S CLOSE ENOUGH

The GPS system became fully operational in April 1995. At first the signal was deliberately degraded for civilian users, a feature called "selective availability." The military did this specifically to deny enemies of the United States the ability to use civilian GPS equipment as precision guidance devices for drones and other weapons. Selective availability made the signals accurate only to within 300 feet, instead of 3 feet or less. A special code, which was changed every 24 hours, was needed to restore the degraded signal to full strength, and only the military had the code.

Over time, though, selective availability became increasingly obsolete. Reason: civilian manufacturers found ways to defeat it and make their GPS receivers more accurate even without knowing the daily code. That's why, in 1996, President Bill Clinton ordered that the feature be turned off no later than 2006. But the U.S. military was already at work developing secret new technologies to deny GPS to its adversaries in crisis zones without affecting other users around the world, and by May 2000 those systems were in place. Selective availability was turned off for good, six years ahead of schedule, and ever since then, all users, military and civilian, receive the full-strength signal from the 32-satellite system…or do they?

For that part of the story, turn to page 255.

*   *   *

RANDOM FACT

In some European hospitals, premature babies are given crocheted octopuses. The infants seem to respond better to the stuffed octopuses than to other toys. One theory as to why: Octopuses bring back memories of the umbilical cord.

Banana trees are technically herb plants.

FIRST IN FLIGHT

There are certain things people expect on a flight. And we're not talking about a lack of legroom or a delay. Here are the origins of some of the standard amenities.

First flight attendant. There were flight attendants before there were commercial airlines. In 1912 a German man named Heinrich Kubis served passengers on the *Schwaben*, a zeppelin. (Kubis was working the *Hindenburg* when it caught fire and crashed. He jumped out of a window and survived.)

First female flight attendant. Until 1930, airlines in the United States and Europe hired only men (like Kubis) to attend to passengers' needs during flights. Then United Airlines hired a registered nurse named Ellen Church as an attendant, in case there were any mid-flight medical emergencies. Because medical emergencies are a rare occurrence, United and other airlines expanded the job and renamed them "stewardesses" and "air hostesses"…and put them to work serving meals and drinks.

First in-flight magazine. Nearly every airline has an in-house magazine, which they give away for free. They're extremely general interest, and all are a derivative of the very first one, *Clipper Travel*, first published by Pan American World Airways in 1952. There are now more than 150 different in-flight magazines. The longest-running: *Holland Herald*. It has been available on Dutch carrier KLM's flights since it was first published in 1966.

First airsickness bag. Also known as barf bags, these folded paper sacks are available on planes in the event that a passenger—for whatever reason—has to puke. In 1949 an inventor named Gilmore Schjeldahl devised the first plastic-lined, paper airsickness bag for Northwest Orient Airlines. Before that, barf bags were made from wax paper or cardstock. Schjeldahl's plastic one was revolutionary in that it didn't leak. (Bonus fact: the Guinness World Record for the largest collection of barf bags belongs to a Dutch investment consultant named Nick Vermeulen. He has more than 6,000 bags from 1,100 airlines.)

First SkyMall catalog. For years, the backseat pocket on airline seats came stocked with an in-flight magazine, an airsickness bag, and a SkyMall catalog. The catalog offered hot dog cookers, foot massagers, plastic garden rocks that hid spare keys, and dozens more must-have gadgets. The company was created in 1990 by entrepreneur Bob Worsley, whose initial concept was to allow

Why do Barnum's Animal Crackers boxes come with strings attached? To hang on a Christmas tree.

passengers to order things when their flight touched down, and have them ready for pickup in the terminal 20 minutes later. When that proved to be a logistical nightmare, SkyMall became a conventional catalog, with goods shipped to the buyer's home. SkyMall has since been grounded—it filed for bankruptcy in 2015.

First in-flight meals. American airline companies used to serve complimentary hot meals—it was a standard part of any flight that was at least a few hours long. Now, coach passengers pay extra for meals. The first airliner to feed passengers was a British carrier—Handley Page Transport in 1919. And much like today, the menu was a sandwich, a piece of fruit, and a piece of chocolate. Cost: three shillings. Hot, knife-and-fork meals debuted in 1936, when United Airlines installed warming trays in its planes, and served meals cooked in airport kitchens.

First in-flight movie. In 1921 Aeromarine Airways operated tourist flights on amphibious airplanes in Chicago—partially in the air, and partially on Lake Michigan. On the short trip, it showed a film about the Windy City called *Howdy Chicago*. The first feature film shown on an airline was another silent movie—*The Lost World*, on a London–Paris flight in 1925 (the film was 75 minutes long; the flight was 30 minutes.) The first sound film on a plane: *By Love Possessed*, starring Lana Turner and Efrem Zimbalist Jr., on a TWA flight from New York to Los Angeles in 1961.

WHY DO AIRLINES SERVE PEANUTS AND PRETZELS? *A British study found that dry air and loud background noise (like an airplane engine) tends to lessen the ability to perceive sweet and salty tastes. Because of that, airlines offer salty foods to counteract the blandness.*

First airline to serve peanuts. Peanuts have been served on airline flights since the 1940s. But Southwest Airlines, which started service in 1971, was one of the first no-frills "budget" carriers and the first one to offer only peanuts. It was part of an advertising campaign in which they marketed themselves as the airline where passengers could "fly for peanuts." (Widespread peanut allergies—along with rising prices of nuts—have led most airlines to discontinue the practice in favor of safer and cheaper crackers or pretzels.)

Jerry Lewis was nominated for the Nobel Peace Prize in 1977 (for his Labor Day MS telethons).

DOME DODGERS

Nobody likes to move—it's a hassle to pack up all your stuff and head for someplace new and unfamiliar. But sports teams do it all the time, and perhaps no other team move was as shocking as when the Brooklyn Dodgers left for Los Angeles in 1957. Here's why the team skipped town after decades in Brooklyn.

HEY, EBBETS!

When the Brooklyn Dodgers first started playing at Ebbets Field in 1913, baseball wasn't yet the popular sport it became a decade or two later. The stadium, located in the Brooklyn neighborhood called Flatbush, sat 18,000 fans when it opened, but was slowly expanded to a maximum of 32,000 seats by the mid-1950s—which, as far as Dodgers owner Walter O'Malley was concerned, was still too small to host a team of such stature; the Dodgers had appeared in nine World Series by that point.

So, much like professional sports team owners do today, O'Malley started considering the possibilities of a new stadium—and he wanted the City of New York to pay for it. The commissioner of the New York City Parks Department, Robert Moses, was happy to oblige…provided that he and the municipal government got to decide where the stadium would be built. Moses wanted to put the new ballpark in Flushing Meadows in Queens. The city would pay for it, and the city would own it. What a deal!

NO DEAL

Not for O'Malley. Before owning the Dodgers, he'd made his fortune as a real-estate developer. He knew that part of the financial benefits of owning a sports franchise was owning the stadium, so he rejected Moses's offer. His counteroffer: He wanted Moses to condemn a large parcel of land along Brooklyn's Atlantic Railroad Yards under a federal law called Title I, which allowed the city to condemn unused land for public works projects. Then, O'Malley figured, he could buy the land from the city at a bargain rate. Moses wasn't having any of it, in part because he thought (correctly) that O'Malley was just trying to get a good deal on the land, but also because he didn't believe a baseball stadium fell under the category of "public-works." Moses had a stricter interpretation—he defined public works to mean projects like playgrounds, bridges, and subsidized housing.

The phrase "o'clock" comes from a contraction of "stroke of the clock."

But O'Malley simply didn't want to move the Brooklyn Dodgers to Flushing Meadows. He told Moses, "If my team is forced to play in the borough of Queens, they will no longer be the Brooklyn Dodgers." Apparently that didn't matter to Moses, and he basically gave O'Malley an ultimatum: the *only* way the city would pay for a new ballpark was if it was the one in Flushing Meadows. Moses didn't want a gigantic new stadium anywhere in Brooklyn, citing concerns over traffic and a need to redo subway and streetcar schedules and routes. Also factoring into Moses's rejection of O'Malley's plan was that on those four city blocks of abandoned land in downtown Brooklyn, O'Malley wanted to build a domed stadium—the *first* domed stadium.

A DOME IDEA

Domed stadiums became the rage in professional sports after the Houston Astrodome opened in 1965. It was a way to host outdoor sporting events for tens of thousands of spectators in regions where rain, snow, or heat were a factor. Some of the most famous domes in sports history: the Kingdome in rainy Seattle, the Metrodome in snowy Minneapolis, and the Astrodome in scorching Houston. In the 1950s, the idea of building a domed ballpark was scoffed at. It would be an architectural novelty—maybe even an impossibility.

In May 1955, after architect Norman Bel Geddes politely rejected O'Malley's request to devise an Ebbets Field renovation plan that included building a roof over it, O'Malley wrote to quirky architect and inventor Buckminster Fuller. Fuller was known for creating domed structures, and at one point proposed building a dome over midtown Manhattan. But when given the chance to build one over a stadium, Fuller jumped at the idea and turned the task over to students in the graduate-level architecture class he taught at Princeton University. Led by a budding architect named T. William Kleinsasser, the students designed a plan for a domed stadium in Brooklyn.

Among the proposed features of the dome, which would have opened on O'Malley's favored site in 1960:

- It would seat 52,000 people.

- It would use a real grass playing surface.

- It would be 300 feet tall and 750 feet in diameter.

- It would be covered in a transparent domed top.

- The roof would be retractable.

- It would be air-conditioned.

Probably not what you thought: Zebras are actually black with white stripes.

- Bordering the stadium: a village with new shops and restaurants.

- Under the stadium: a 5,000-car parking garage with four entrances.

- The cost: $6 million, but privately funded.

OUT OF TOWN

Moses was right to have reservations about squeezing all of that into four city blocks in the heart of Brooklyn. The city wouldn't permit it, and O'Malley had no choice but to move the team, especially after he'd already made a deal to sell Ebbets Field to a real-estate developer, in part to force action on the new stadium.

Moses and the City of New York essentially called O'Malley's bluff. The city council of Los Angeles, following the news of the new stadium developments, reached out to the Dodgers owner in 1955 and again in 1956, suggesting he make the Dodgers the first Major League Baseball team to play in Los Angeles. After the dome deal fell through, O'Malley accepted the offer and the Dodgers played their last game in Brooklyn on September 24, 1957. In the 1958 season, the Brooklyn Dodgers became the Los Angeles Dodgers.

What New Yorkers didn't count on was that at the same time the Dodgers left New York, the New York Giants were moving to San Francisco. (The owner, Horace Stoneham, was planning to move to Minneapolis, but O'Malley and others convinced him to move to the West Coast instead.) Suddenly, the biggest city in the United States, which had once fielded three Major League Baseball teams, had only one, the New York Yankees.

Major League Baseball quickly scrambled to fill that void, and in 1962 awarded the city an expansion team, the New York Mets. Initially, the Mets played in the Giants' old stadium, the Polo Grounds, but two years later they were playing in Shea Stadium—a stadium built by the city and owned by the city. It was built on the exact parcel of land in Flushing Meadows that Moses had offered O'Malley as a new stadium for the Dodgers.

Oddly enough, right across the street from where the Brooklyn dome would've sat is the Barclays Center. The arena is home to the Brooklyn Nets of the NBA.

IN ADDITION TO THE NEW YORK GIANTS' MOVE *to San Francisco, lots of other sports teams headed west in the early '60s. The Washington Senators relocated to become the Minnesota Twins in 1961, and in the NBA, the Minneapolis Lakers moved to Los Angeles, and the Philadelphia Warriors moved to San Francisco.*

One of the hardest products to recycle: A Pringles can. (It's made of metal, plastic, cardboard, and foil.)

UNCLE JOHN'S STALL OF FAME

*Uncle John is amazed—and pleased—by the unusual ways
people get involved with bathrooms, toilets, and so on.
That's why he created the "Stall of Fame."*

Honorees: Six inmates of the Cocke County Jail in downtown Newport, TN

Notable Achievement: Using the can to break out of the can

True Story: On Christmas Day 2016, one of the inmates noticed that the bolts on a leaky jailhouse toilet were rusted out. The water had also damaged the concrete behind the toilet, making it possible for the inmates to rip it off the wall and shimmy through the hole where the toilet had been. After they made it outside, they pulled the toilet back in place to make it appear as if nothing was amiss, then they climbed over the fence and made their escape.

Four inmates were captured by the end of the day, a fifth turned himself in, and the sixth was captured three days after the escape. At last report, the hole had been sealed up with steel plating until more extensive repairs could be made. "We've had a lot of issues with the jail and there is a need for a better facility," Cocke County sheriff Armando Fontes told reporters. "We've made repairs when we find things, but you don't always know what the problems are."

Honoree: Roy Riegel, a lifelong New York Mets fan who died in 2008

Notable Achievement: Being memorialized in a way that honors his love of baseball and his profession—plumbing—at the same time

True Story: When Riegel died at the age of 48, his close friend Tom "Porky" McDonald obtained some of his ashes from his mother so that he could pay tribute to his pal by scattering them in ballparks around the country. McDonald planned to sprinkle the ashes on the *field* at each park, but when he went to a Pirates game in Pittsburgh, it was too windy. His next stop was the Metrodome, home to the Minneapolis Twins, but somehow, McDonald thought, scattering the ashes at an *indoor* stadium didn't seem right. A few hours later, he and a friend were drinking beer at a pub near the Metrodome, trying to figure out what to do with Riegel's ashes when McDonald got up to use the restroom. That's when the idea came to him. When he returned to his seat he told his friend, "I just took care of Roy."

McDonald now follows the same ritual every at every park he goes to: he waits until the game is underway, then when nature calls, he uses the facilities himself, then flushes, sprinkles a small portion of his friend's ashes into the bowl, and flushes again. (He bypassed the toilets at Wrigley Field, because the Chicago Cubs were the Mets' rivals.)

By 2017 McDonald had flushed Riegel's ashes down the toilets of 16 different ballparks, and had enough ashes left for one more flush. Those he was saving for an upcoming visit to the minor-league ballpark in North Carolina where the 1988 movie *Bull Durham* was filmed.

" *I know people might think it's weird, and if it were anyone else's ashes, I'd agree,"* McDonald told the New York Times. *"But for Roy, this is the perfect tribute to a plumber and a baseball fan and just a brilliant, wild guy.* "

Honoree: Wendell Boyd, 10, a clever kid who lives with his family in Mars Hill, Maine.

Notable Achievement: Cooking up a friendly purple potty "protection racket" to raise money for the American Cancer Society

True Story: When Wendell was six years old, he was diagnosed with a brain tumor. Two surgeries and a slow recovery later, he was cancer-free, back to his old self and eager to find a way to raise money to help fight cancer. After looking around online for ideas, in 2014 Wendell came up with one of his own. He got ahold of an old toilet, painted it purple, and started leaving it on people's lawns around Mars Hill.

Each time the toilet is left on a lawn, the bowl of the toilet is filled with beautiful flowers, and taped to the tank is a sign that reads "Flushing Out Cancer." The sign offers homeowners three options: for a $10 donation to the Maine chapter of the American Cancer Society, Wendell and his folks will take the toilet away. For $20, the homeowner can "give" the toilet to a friend and have it moved to their lawn. For a $30 donation, the homeowner can purchase "toilet insurance" that ensures the toilet will never be left on their lawn again.

In two years, Wendell and his painted purple potty were flush with success: they raised more than $5,500 in donations for the American Cancer Society, making him one of the most prolific fund-raisers for the Maine chapter. By the summer of 2016, he'd expanded to *two* fund-raising toilets. The original still decorates lawns around Mars Hill, and the number two toilet (Get it? *Number two!*) is extorting contributions in nearby Easton. To date, "No one has said, 'Come get this, I don't want it,'" he says. "Some people have asked to keep it even longer—to show it off."

A violent whirlpool is called a maelstrom.

ATLAS OF THE WORLD

"HEY SHRIMP!" If you're a 97-pound weakling (like Uncle John), you'll want to read the amazing story of strongman and mail-order fitness guru Charles Atlas.

IN LIKE A LION

Charles Atlas's rise from scrawny kid to wealthy hunk is a classic American story. He was born Angelo Siciliano, and he emigrated to the United States from Calabria, Italy, through Ellis Island in 1903, at the age of 10. As a teenager in Brooklyn, Siciliano was weak, slight, and small for his age, and the other kids picked on him. He later said he was inspired to build up his muscles by two of his favorite sights in Brooklyn: a statue of Hercules at the Brooklyn Museum, and a lion at the Prospect Park Zoo.

Siciliano was watching the lion stretch his bulging muscles one day. He noted to himself that the lion had gotten his muscles without using barbells, and suddenly realized that the lion was "pitting his muscles against one another." In other words, Siciliano accidentally "discovered" isometric and isotonic exercises—weight-training measures in which muscles are held still or tight while tense. Examples: holding a push-up in the "up" position for as long as possible, or standing in place and pressing out against the sides of a doorframe. The exercises were born of necessity. Siciliano didn't have any money, so like that lion, he didn't have access to weight sets. But it turned out he didn't need them. Using his techniques, within a few years he had developed a 47-inch chest, a 32-inch waist, and lots and lots of muscles.

PERFECTLY DEVELOPED

Siciliano left high school in 1908 and took a job as a leatherworker in a pocketbook factory. He worked there until 1916, when he started earning his living as a model for sculptors and artists. Meanwhile, he spent all his free time bodybuilding. In 1921 he decided to go pro, competing in an open bodybuilding competition at Madison Square Garden. He won the competition and the title "World's Most Beautiful Man." The next year, he won again, beating more than 700 competitors, and received a new title: "World's Most Perfectly Developed Man." In fact, promoters decided to cancel the event for future years because there was no way anybody could beat Siciliano.

And it was at those contests that Siciliano started going by his stage name: Charles Atlas. Why that name? Because a friend told him he looked like a statue

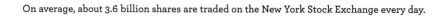

On average, about 3.6 billion shares are traded on the New York Stock Exchange every day.

of Atlas that perched atop a hotel on Coney Island. It was an apt comparison: Atlas was a Titan in Greek mythology who held the heavens on his back.

THE TENSION BUILDS

Atlas's prize for being named the World's Most Perfectly Developed Man was his choice of either a screen test for a new Tarzan movie, or $1,000 cash (about $15,000 today). Atlas took the cash and used it to start a business to sell his muscle-building techniques in the form of a mail-order pamphlet. While he came up with the techniques, the course itself was written primarily by seasoned fitness writer Frederick Tilney, who also wrote training programs for another physical culture guru, industry pioneer Bernarr Macfadden. Atlas and Tilney became business partners.

But the business wasn't successful and was on the verge of shutting down until Atlas met an advertising industry veteran named Charles Roman in 1928. Tilney sold Roman his share of the company, and he and Atlas became equal partners in Charles Atlas Ltd. Roman knew exactly how to market the World's Most Perfectly Developed Man. First, he came up with the name "Dynamic-Tension" for Atlas's regimen. Then he arranged public appearances and photo shoots to help turn Atlas into a celebrity. Atlas provided a needed distraction, and even an inspiration, to Depression-era America, as crowds gathered to watch him tow a train or bend metal bars. Roman even arranged to have Atlas's measurements sealed in a time capsule at Oglethorpe University in Atlanta as a message to future humans on "the ideal proportions of the 20th century man."

CHARLES ATLAS *took inspiration from statues...and he also worked as a sculptor's model. A bronze statue of the first U.S. Secretary of the Treasury, Alexander Hamilton, stands on the south side of the Treasury Building in Washington, D.C. It was sculpted by James Earle Fraser, who used Charles Atlas as his model.*

97-POUND WEAKLINGS REJOICE

The most notable of Roman's ideas was placing ads for Charles Atlas's "Dynamic-Tension" mail-order course in comic books, directly appealing to the teenage boys they were hoping to reach. If you've ever read a comic book, you've probably seen an ad for Charles Atlas's muscle-building system. They started with a comic strip featuring a scrawny kid on a beach date with his girlfriend, only to get picked on by a bully who calls him "skinny," or "shrimp," and kicks sand in his face. The kid then transforms himself into a big strong guy, goes back to the beach, and socks the bully right in the nose. Next to the strip was Atlas's sales pitch for his training program, including Atlas's confession that, like the boy in the comic, he too was once a "97-pound weakling." But not anymore, as shown by the photo of a muscle-bound Atlas wearing nothing but leopard-print briefs.

Atlas's personal appearances and comic-book ads continued regularly for decades. By the 1950s, more than a million people had sent away for the "Dynamic-Tension" 12-lesson muscle-building course. It also included nutrition tips, suggestions on proper sleep habits ("GET UP! If you linger and hesitate you are weakening your will power!"), and even confidence builders ("Go steadily on from one success to another").

MUSCLING ON

And Atlas continued to serve as the public image of his own company all the way until 1965—he started to retreat from the business after the death of his wife sent him into a depression. Shortly before his death at age 79 in 1972, Atlas sold his share of the company to Charles Roman. Despite the loss of the program's public face, Roman kept the company going, continuing to pitch it almost entirely through those comic-book ads. Shortly before *his* death in 1999, Roman sold the whole thing to a New Jersey businessman named Jeffrey Hogue, who hasn't changed much about Charles Atlas Ltd. Images of Atlas are still front and center, and those campy, retro ads are still used, both in comic books and on the company website.

Also unchanged is Atlas's "Dynamic-Tension" course. It's still 12 lessons that come in a three-ring binder with "no weights or gym required." The only major addition to the program since Atlas and Roman devised it in the 1920s is that it's now available in Spanish as well as English.

*   *   *

RANDOM ORIGIN: THE MIC DROP

The "mic drop"—in which someone ends a speech or a song on a particularly strong note...and then drops the microphone before walking off stage—was popularized by President Barack Obama when he did it on a 2012 episode of *The Tonight Show*. But it actually dates back to 1983 when comedian Eddie Murphy used it to end his concert film *Delirious*.

The Great Blizzard of 1888 dumped 40 in. of snow on New York City. Drifts were 30–40 feet high.

POLITICS: EUROPEAN STYLE

We travel "across the pond" for govern-mental blunders both befuddling and bemusing!

ENTRAPMENT

Imagine walking to your car—parked in front of your house—and discovering that someone had painted a dotted line around it, and then painted the word "DISABLED" next to it…and that there was ticket on your windshield for parking in a disabled space. That actually happened to a Londoner named Matt Armstrong. "I thought it was an April Fool's Day joke," he told the *Telegraph* after discovering his suddenly illegally parked car with a parking ticket for £110 ($136) on April 1, 2016. But it was no joke: the local town council had issued the work order to create the disabled parking space, so road workers painted the space (even though there was a car parked there). And a traffic officer came by later and wrote the ticket. After Armstrong complained to town leaders and received no response, he did a little digging and discovered what had happened: two years earlier, his elderly neighbor had made a request to the town council for that parking space to be changed to disabled for her ailing husband. But by the time the council finally got around to it, her husband had been dead for two months. And Armstrong's car was now parked in the spot. Once the mix-up was brought to light, Armstrong's fine was dismissed…but now he has to find somewhere else to park.

SMEAR TACTICS

In February 2015, Scott Harris—a Conservative council member from Portsmouth, Hampshire, England—decided to strike back at what he believed was unfair treatment by his critics. Angry that local feminist groups were protesting a proposed £180,000 cut to domestic violence services, Harris wrote an email to his closest confidants: "The tricks by the Lib Dems, the lies and the smear are disgusting. Quite frankly it might be a good idea to play dirty this time." Then he listed several people and groups he could "compile some stuff on," including a constituent named Sameen Farouk, a Liberal Democrat whom Harris described as having a "clear political vendetta." Then Harris hit the send button. Oops: the email inadvertently got sent to a much larger group than he'd intended…even to some of the people he was targeting. One of those was Farouk, who wrote back and said, "I want to tell you that I feel personally disappointed. You don't need to snoop around behind my back or collect information on me surreptitiously." When the gaffe was made public, Harris issued an apology and said he learned his lesson: "Local politics is about representing people and their opinions, and the number one consideration for me as a newly elected councillor is to listen to people and represent them in an open and honest way."

NO CLASS

Llanfynydd Primary School in Wales had everything a primary school should have—clean classrooms, teachers, administrators. But it was missing one very important component: students. Because of demographic changes, the school's numbers kept dwindling until late 2014, when the final 11 students were transferred to other schools. Yet because of "bureaucratic red tape," the school was required to remain open. According to the *Guardian*, "The 'statutory process' by the Labour-led Welsh government dictates that the school cannot officially close until a consultation has been carried and a formal decision is made." For some reason, the consultation had to wait until the end of the following semester. Result: the school remained open for seven months—at a taxpayer cost of £50,000 ($62,000)—even though there were no students.

> **WALES,** *which is part of the United Kingdom, has two official languages: Welsh and English. Virtually the entire population knows English, but less than 20 percent is fluent in Welsh.*

YOU GO YOUR WAY

A conservative mayor and a socialist mayor in adjacent Paris suburbs got into a bitter feud in 2009 over a heavily traveled road—the D909—that went through both their towns and into the French capital. To ease congestion in Levallois-Perret, Conservative mayor Patrick Balkany changed the D909 to a one-way street…out of his town and into Clichy-la-Garenne, which Socialist mayor Gilles Catoire saw as an attempt to cause traffic problems in his town. So he retaliated by making the D909 a one-way street in the opposite direction. You can guess what happened next: "Commuter chaos, road rage, and gridlock," reported the *Telegraph*. Traffic was so chaotic that French national police had to come in to untangle the mess. After the signs were fixed, the case went to court. The winner? The Conservative. Before he changed his sign, Mayor Balkany had conducted a traffic study that concluded there would be no major traffic issues, whereas Mayor Catoire did not.

Candy fact: Circus Peanuts are made of banana-flavored marshmallows dyed orange.

UNSOLVED MYSTERY: THE LARGS HUM

Most people who live in Largs, a popular seaside resort town in southwest Scotland, cannot hear the "Largs hum." But for those who can hear it, it's enough to drive them nuts.

DID YOU HEAR THAT?

In the summer of 1999, a Scottish woman named Georgie Hyslop became a widow when her husband Roy died after heart surgery. The couple had recently moved to Wales, but Georgie was lonely without Roy. So she returned home to Scotland and bought a house in Largs, a seaside town 33 miles west of Glasgow.

On the first night in the unfamiliar new home, an annoying humming sound kept her awake all night. It sounded like a diesel truck idling outside, but when Hyslop stepped out onto the street, there was no truck. Oddly, even though the hum seemed to come from outside, it was louder inside the house. The building appeared to amplify the noise, the way the sound box of a guitar amplifies the sound of the strings when they're strummed. Or maybe the house just blocked out other outdoor sounds, making the hum easier to hear.

As the days passed, the noise got worse. Hyslop began to suffer from sinus pain, earaches, nosebleeds, and chest pains, and was often sick to her stomach. She started leaving the radio on to drown out the hum, and took long drives with her dog, Isla, to get a break from it. At night she slept fitfully; when the hum was really loud, she camped out in a tent in the backyard. "You're lucky if you can get an hour's sleep at night," Hyslop told the *Sunday Telegraph* in 2001. "It gives you headaches, your ears pop when you come in, you feel your nose bursting, and your chest crushing in."

HEAR SAY

Hyslop is not alone: reports of the "Largs hum" date back to the 1980s. But only about one in 50 people in the town hear it. Women are more likely than men to hear it, and middle-aged people are more likely than young or old people. And no one knows why. Similar hums have been reported in other places, including Bristol, England; Taos, New Mexico; and Ankara, Turkey, to name just a few. In 2012 a high school teacher named Glen MacPherson began to hear a hum in

In 2014 the U.S. Army changed its tattoo regulations, prohibiting new ones on exposed arms and legs.

Sechelt, British Columbia. That prompted him to launch a website called the World Hum Map that lets hum sufferers enter their information into a database. As of 2017, the site lists 5,000 reported hum locations around the world.

HEAD GAMES

At first, few people other than the suffering "hummers" believed that the noises existed. One study conducted in the 1990s concluded that hummers were actually suffering from *tinnitus*, or ringing in the ears, which gives the sensation of hearing a sound that isn't really there. "Everybody who has tinnitus complains at first of environmental noise," Jonathan Hazell, head of research at the Royal National Institute for the Deaf, told the *Independent* newspaper in 1994. "'Hummers' are a group of people who cannot accept that they have tinnitus."

Since then, however, other scientists have been able to detect the Largs hum, including in Hyslop's home, where they used special equipment to detect a low noise at the frequency of 50–60 hertz (cycles per second), which is within the rage of human hearing. A second hum in the range of 700–862 megahertz (million cycles per second) has also been detected, leading to the theory that the hum is caused when these two hums (and perhaps others) combine to create a "beat frequency" that only a handful of especially sensitive people can hear.

CAUSE AND EFFECT

So what is it that causes the Largs hum and others like it? Theories include cell towers, wind turbines, buried natural gas pipelines, electromagnetic radiation from power plants, secret military projects, UFOs, and "mass delusion"—the theory that people begin to "hear" the hum only after being told that it exists.

There is another theory, however, that gains plausibility from the fact that Largs and many other places where hums are heard are located on or near the ocean. According to this theory, when storms disturb the ocean surface, they create powerful waves. Some of this wave energy is transmitted to the ocean floor, where it causes oscillations in the earth's crust. It is this oscillation that people who are sensitive to low frequencies perceive as the hum. And because the hum is transmitted through the earth's crust, it is heard more easily indoors, where other sounds from the outside world are muffled. That's the theory, but more research will be needed before it can be confirmed. Georgie Hyslop will likely be spending a lot more nights in her tent before anyone knows for sure.

Some hums are mysterious, others can be traced to their source. That part of the story is on page 337.

GOING POSTER

*What's the difference between a photo and a poster? A poster is a photo that's been cropped,
edited, blown up, edited, mass-produced on cheap paper…and purchased by millions. Here's
a look behind some of the most famous and best-selling posters of all time.*

CHE

In March 1960, leftist revolutionary Che Guevara, clad in a black beret, briefly
joined Fidel Castro onstage at a memorial for those who lost their lives in the
explosion of the munitions ship *La Coubre* when it was docked in Havana's
harbor. While Castro delivered a eulogy, Guevara stood off to the side, which is
when photographer Alberto Korda took his picture. It was later published under
the title *Guerrillero Heroico*, or "Heroic Guerrilla." The simple, black-and-white
photo became a poster eight years later when Irish artist Jim Fitzpatrick applied a
two-tone treatment to make a striking, contrasting image of Guevara's face, and
he placed it against a red background. Fitzpatrick initially allowed his work to
be distributed without a copyright to encourage its spread and the "power to the
people" message of Guevara…but it was also widely reproduced by capitalists on
T-shirts, postcards, coffee mugs…and posters. In 2011 Fiztpatrick told reporters
that he wanted to copyright the image. Reason: he wants to give Guevara's
family control of its usage and reproduction.

PINK FLOYD'S BACK CATALOG

In 1996 graphic designer Storm Thorgerson and his design firm, Hipgnosis, were
hired to make a TV commercial to advertise the re-release of the back catalog
of British rock band Pink Floyd, including *Atom Heart Mother*, *Dark Side of the
Moon*, *Wish You Were Here*, *Animals*, and *The Wall*. When Thorgerson suggested
to the band's label, EMI, that he wanted to take the suggestion literally—and
film a bunch of young women with their bare backs painted with the cover art
of a different Pink Floyd album—the executives loved it. But they thought it
would be better as a promotional poster for record stores than as TV commercial.
A body painter named Phyllis Cohen actually painted the images on the

> **PINK FLOYD'S** The Dark Side of the Moon *stayed on the
> Billboard charts longer than any other album—741 weeks, or
> 14 years and 3 months.*

models—and the women had to stay perfectly still for five or six hours while she worked. The finished product by photographer Tony May was so striking that EMI decided to not distribute the poster for free to record stores, but to sell it directly to fans.

FARRAH FAWCETT

Before she became the star of *Charlie's Angels*, Fawcett was doing mostly TV commercials and modeling work. Her management team thought she might get the attention of more casting agents if her résumé included a picture of the blonde bombshell in a bikini, so in 1975 they hired photographer Bruce McBroom to take one. McBroom went to Fawcett's house (where she lived with her husband, Lee Majors, star of *The Six-Million Dollar Man*), and had her pose by the pool in front of an old Southwestern-style blanket that McBroom had been using to cover the back seat of his car. Fawcett tried a number of swimsuits before deciding on a red one-piece because it covered a scar on her stomach. A year later, Fawcett landed the role on *Charlie's Angels*, and the humble picture of Fawcett in a swimsuit was licensed out to poster publishers. It went on to sell 12 million copies—still a record for the best-selling poster of all time.

> *The reason that the all-American boy prefers beauty to brains is that he can see better than he can think.*
>
> —**Farrah Fawcett**

EINSTEIN WITH HIS TONGUE OUT

The influential physicist Albert Einstein was being honored at an event at Princeton University in 1951 to mark his 72nd birthday. United Press International photographer Arthur Sasse tried but couldn't get Einstein to smile for a photograph—the scientist said he'd been smiling for photographers all day and he was tired of it. But Sasse (and other photographers) kept insisting Einstein give them a grin. Annoyed, he stuck out his tongue instead, and Sasse caught the image of Einstein, along with scientist Dr. Frank Aydelotte and his wife. Ironically, the grouchy Einstein later found Sasse's picture to be his favorite photo of himself. He contacted UPI and ordered reproductions of it, with the Aydelottes and everything that wasn't his face and tongue cut out. Then he sent them as greeting cards to his friends. Knowing they had a good thing going, UPI then licensed the photo for use as a poster.

The board game Scrabble was originally called Lexico.

NATIONAL BOOZES

Okay—they're not official national drinks, but these unusual spirits are difficult to find outside their native lands. Proost! (That's Dutch for "cheers!")

THE NETHERLANDS

Drink: Genever

Story: Food historians consider this the predecessor of gin because, like gin, it's made from juniper berries. A 17th-century Dutch chemist named Franciscus Sylvius is usually credited as its inventor, but other sources say it may have been distilled as early as the 13th century. Genever is available in two varieties: *jonge* (which tastes like vodka) and *oude* (similar to whiskey). According to tradition, both versions are served in tulip-shaped glasses filled to the brim. The first sip must be taken without lifting the glass, so as not to spill even a single drop. Currently, only a few distilleries scattered across Europe are legally allowed to use the name "Genever," which is one of the reasons it's tough to find in America. It's most popular in the Netherlands and Belgium.

PERU

Drink: Chicha

Story: This "corn beer" was created over 2,000 years ago by the Incas of South America, who drank it during rituals and religious festivals. It's still prepared the traditional way in some parts of Peru. A group of women work together on the first few steps of the simple process: they chew up corn kernels and spit them into clay jars filled with water. The kernels ferment and, a few weeks later, the chicha inside is ready to drink. In accordance with centuries-old tradition, it's typically served in hollowed-out gourds. It's also made without bodily fluids and with other grains or even with fruit juice. Different varieties are found throughout South and Central America, especially in Peru, Colombia, Bolivia, Ecuador, and Costa Rica.

RUSSIA

Drink: Kvass

Story: This mildly alcoholic beverage is popular in the summertime in Russia and the Ukraine, and dates back to the Middle Ages. Made from fermented black or rye bread, kvass is sold by sidewalk vendors who dispense it from

Oilbirds, or *guácharos* (S. America), navigate with echolocation, like bats. They're the only birds that do.

wheeled yellow tanks during the warmest months of the year. Customers can add other flavors to their glasses—raisins, mint, and berries being the most popular. You'd have to drink a lot of it to get drunk, though. The alcoholic content of kvass is typically 1–1.5 percent.

JAPAN
Drink: Yogurito

Story: Fermented in the Netherlands and bottled in France, Yogurito is sold only in Japan by Suntory, a company that produces a wide variety of international alcoholic beverages, including Gilbey's Gin, Cruzan Rum, Hornitos Tequila, Jim Beam Bourbon…and this liqueur made from yogurt (in case you couldn't tell from the name). At 16 percent alcohol, it's usually drunk straight, although some fans prefer to mix it with orange or pineapple juice, or soda water. End result: a drink with the consistency of a smoothie but with the boozy punch of a spirit.

FRANCE
Drink: Génépi

Story: This herbal liqueur looks like olive oil and is made from a type of wormwood that grows only in certain areas in the French Alps and the Pyrenees. Like absinthe (which also contains wormwood), its strong flavor is an acquired taste, and it is served as a digestif after large meals. Most bottles contain a few twigs from the wormwood plant.

*   *   *

REAL TEAM NAMES

- The Coachella Valley High School Arabs (California)
- The Laurel Hill School Hobos (Florida)
- The Orofino Maniacs (Idaho)
- The Freeburg Midgets (Illinois)
- Wahpeton Wops (North Dakota)
- The Butte Pirates (Montana)
- The Hoopeston Cornjerkers (Illinois)

COMIC THOUGHTS

Who has a better perspective on comedy than comedians?

"A wonderful thing about true laughter is that it just destroys any kind of system of dividing people."

—John Cleese

" I never defend my material. Comedy is subjective. "

—Sarah Silverman

"Faith in the face of disappointment is only enhanced by laughter in the face of pain."

—Marc Maron

"Most comedy comes out of misery."

—Seth Rogen

"There are certain things I don't joke about. If it's about somebody else, it's fine. If it's about me, I think it's totally insensitive!"

—Gilbert Gottfried

"Laughter is the best medicine... you know, besides medicine."

—Bo Burnham

"He taught me that the world is open for play, that everything and everybody is mockable in a wonderful way."

—Robin Williams, on his mentor, Jonathan Winters

"The only honest art form is laughter, comedy. You can't fake it...try to fake three laughs in an hour–ha ha ha ha ha–they'll take you away, man."

—Lenny Bruce

"You found it offensive? I found it funny. That's why I'm happier than you."

—Ricky Gervais

The first tomato ketchup was marketed as diarrhea medicine.

PHRASE ORIGINS: BORN AT SEA

Mrs. Uncle John told Uncle John he was getting a little broad in the beam. Uncle John put down his doughnut and told us to look up that phrase. We did... and voilà!—an article chockablock with nautically born phrases.

ALL AT SEA

Meaning: Confused or uncertain about what to do

Origin: Before technological advances enabled sailors to determine their location at any time, seafarers were essentially lost once they were out of sight of land and without landmarks by which they could navigate. From that came the phrase "all at sea" to describe someone in a confused or bewildered state.

GIVE A WIDE BERTH

Meaning: To keep a safe distance from; to avoid

Origin: The most common definition of the word "berth" in relation to shipping is "a designated location where a ship can be moored," such as at a spot alongside a wharf, or simply a designated anchorage inside a harbor. But "berth" also refers to having enough distance to maneuver a ship safely. By the 17th century, the meaning had evolved to simply mean "working room." The broader, nonshipping use of the phrase came about in the mid-1800s.

BY AND LARGE

Meaning: In general; on the whole; all things considered

Origin: According to our records, we've used this phrase eleven times in the history of the *Bathroom Reader*—and we never knew it had a nautical origin. Here's the story: a ship sailing *against* the wind is said to be sailing "by the wind," while a ship sailing *with* the wind (with the wind coming from behind it) is said to be sailing "large." By the late 1600s, a ship that sailed well regardless of wind direction was said to be able to sail both "by and large." Over the centuries, the phrase moved into the landlubber world and morphed into "in general"—the meaning it still has today.

How does Russia's Hermitage museum keep mice away? With a "staff" of more than 70 cats.

ANCHORS AWEIGH

Meaning: Time to depart; get ready to go

Origin: This phrase dates to the late 1600s, and it is very commonly written "anchors *away*" (and now you get to correct anyone who spells it that-a-way). In the old days, to "weigh" something simply meant to hoist or lift it. "To weigh anchor" meant to lift the anchor from the seafloor, so that the ship could sail. The prefix "a" meant "at"; an anchor being lifted was said to be "at weigh." (The prefix "a" can have other meanings, including "in" or "on," and is found in many nautical terms, such as *aboard, adrift, afloat, aground, ashore,* and *astern*.)

BROAD IN THE BEAM

Meaning: Having wide hips or a big butt

Origin: The "beam" is a ship's width at its widest point, measured at the waterline. A sleek, high-speed sailing vessel, for example, will have a relatively narrow beam, while a ship focused more on stability than speed, such as an ocean freighter, will have a much wider beam. The phrase "broad in the beam" first appeared as a reference to stout, broad ships in the 1600s; in the early 1900s, that meaning was transfered to (wide) humans.

CHOCKABLOCK

Meaning: Very full; crammed

Origin: This phrase is more popular in the UK and Australia than in North America. It came from the shipping world's use of the block-and-tackle multi-pulley system for loading heavy cargo. Simply: *blocks* are pulleys; *tackle* is the name for an assembly of blocks and a rope. As a ship was near to being fully loaded, additional loading became difficult because the blocks in the block-and-tackle system got too close together to function properly. Etymologists say "chockablock" came from such situations, probably just as rhyming slang. It may also be related to the "chock" in *chock-full*, a term more familiar to Americans, which is of unknown origin, but has basically the same meaning as "chockablock."

HIGH AND DRY

Meaning: Helpless; stranded; abandoned

Origin: By the first half of the 1700s, when an unlucky ship became grounded and, when the tide went out, was left stuck fully on land, it was said to be "high and dry"—for fairly obvious reasons.

New Zealand's Whanganui River, central to the Maori culture, has the official legal status of a person.

IN THE OFFING

Meaning: Likely to happen soon; impending

Origin: "Offing" is a term from the 1600s, meaning "the distant part of the sea as seen from the shore." If you were standing on a dock waiting for a ship to arrive and saw it coming over the horizon, the ship was said to be "in the offing." Such a ship would soon arrive at dock in short order, so over the centuries, the phrase was borrowed from the nautical world and used to apply to *anything* that was expected to happen soon.

TAKEN ABACK

Meaning: Surprised and put out by something unexpected

Origin: Did you sail too close to the wind and have your sails drop and be blown back against the mast, leaving you stalled in the water? Then you were *taken aback*, according to the original meaning of this early 1600s phrase. It got its more well-known meaning in the mid-1800s.

THE CUT OF YOUR JIB

Meaning: One's appearance, style, or overall manner of being

Origin: A *jib* is simply a type of sail: a triangular, forward-positioned sail usually used as a booster sail to a ship's mainsail. Different countries had differently shaped jibs, which allowed sailors to identify the nationality of distant ships by the "cut"—or shape—of those sails. The "cut of a jib" migrated from the sea to its idiomatic usage on land by the early 1800s.

> **ASK THE EXPERTS**
> *QUESTION: Why is the left side of a ship called the "port" side?*
> *ANSWER: The left side was originally the "larboard" side. It was probably changed because it sounded too much like the term for the right side of the ship—the "starboard" side. "Starboard" comes from* steor *and* bord, *from Old English terms for a boat's "steering board," which was on the right side. "Larboard" may derive from the Swedish* ladda, *meaning "loading," because ships were loaded on their left side. "Port" could have the same meaning—the side put to the dock when the ship was in port.*

A volcanic "bomb" is lava that's ejected into the air and solidifies into rock before...

REALITY BITES

Every decade has a TV fad that leads to big hits…and big flops. The most popular format today: reality shows. Some, like Top Chef *and* Survivor, *are winners…and then there are these.*

THE WILL (2005)

Unlike the usual reality show concept of strangers competing to win a big cash prize, the contestants on *The Will* were all family and friends of one person—a multimillionaire named Bill Long. The contest: to be named the beneficiary of Long's will. CBS canceled the show after just one episode. (Long's wife was the eventual winner.)

WHO'S YOUR DADDY? (2005)

Like *The Bachelorette*, except instead of a lonely woman who had to choose a partner from a group of men, the contestant was an adoptee who had to identify her biological father.

THE BRIEFCASE (2015)

Each episode featured two families, both of whom were in dire financial straits. Each family was given a briefcase that contained $101,000, and then had to decide whether to keep all the money, or share it with the other family. One TV critic called it "cynical and repulsive," but in all in six episodes, every single family opted to share the money with the other family.

I WANNA MARRY "HARRY" (2014)

This *Bachelor* clone allowed single women to compete for a date with Prince Harry. Well, not really the English royal, but another young redheaded man who kind of looked like Prince Harry. (Hence the quotation marks around "Harry.") Despite Prince Harry being a well-known and frequently photographed person, the contestants seemed to really think "Harry" was the real deal.

THE MONASTERY (2006)

Like MTV's *Real World*, seven strangers are picked to live together, but not in a house—in a Benedictine monastery in the New Mexico desert. For 40 days.

…it lands. Exception: a "cow pie bomb," which splats when it lands.

MR. PERSONALITY (2003)

Unlike other dating shows, the bachelorette on this show had to choose a mate based on his personality, not his looks. But because TV is a visual medium, audiences had to see the guys. Result: All the male suitors wore silver gladiator masks that obscured their appearance. Bonus: The host of *Mr. Personality* was former White House intern Monica Lewinsky.

DATING IN THE DARK (2009)

Sort of like *Mr. Personality*, in that it downplayed looks. Except that on this show, nobody could see anybody. The three male and three female contestants hung out in a dark room (giving new meaning to the term "blind date") while a night-vision camera showed the audience what was happening.

PLAYING IT STRAIGHT (2004)

Yet another bizarre variation on *The Bachelorette*. Of the small army of guys the female contestant could choose from, half were heterosexual and half were homosexual (in other words, not interested in her). Each episode, the woman had to eliminate contestants she thought might be gay. If, at the end of the series, the last man standing was straight, the woman and the guy split the money, but if he was gay and had "fooled" her into thinking he was straight, he got all the money. (It aired for only one season; they split the money.)

ARE YOU HOT? (2003)

Do good looks really matter? They did on this show. In fact, that's all that mattered. Male and female contestants, generally clad in swimsuits, would come out onto the stage, and actor Lorenzo Lamas and model Rachel Hunter would discuss their physical attributes while highlighting flaws with a laser pointer. Lamas and Hunter would then judge whether the contestant was "hot" (or not).

HE'S A LADY (2004)

The eleven macho man contestants were told they were going to be on a show called *All American Man*, which would crown the toughest of tough guys as its winner. But it was bait-and-switch by the producers—they were actually on a cross-dressing competition show. Challenges in each episode involved how to put on makeup, how to participate in a beauty pageant, and how to plan a wedding.

Hawaiian blueberries, or *Ohelo ʻAi*, are red.

WHAT'S THE POINT?

Stretching in a line from New York all the way to California, hundreds of concrete arrows, some more than 70 feet long, have been set into the landscape. Why are they there? The answer is in the mail.

DAY TRIPPERS

When the U.S. Post Office introduced airmail service in 1920, the mail could only be flown during daylight hours, when pilots could see where they were going. In an age before sophisticated navigation systems, flying after dark was just too dangerous. The pilots who transported the mail navigated by following roads, rivers, railroad tracks, and prominent landmarks as they made their way across the country. When these landmarks weren't visible, they didn't fly.

At dusk, airborne planes landed at designated airfields near railroad lines. The mail they were carrying was then loaded onto trains, which hauled it through the night until daybreak. Then the mail was loaded onto a new airplane and flown again until dark. At that rate, it took about three and a half days to get mail from New York City to San Francisco, only a day less than sending it entirely by rail, and at much greater risk and expense. If airmail service was going to survive, it was going to have to get much faster, and that meant flying at night. But how?

A SHOT IN THE DARK

On February 21, 1921, the post office launched a night-flying experiment when it sent two planes east from San Francisco, and two more west from New York. The planes were flying the first stretch in what was, in effect, a cross-country relay, much in the way that the Pony Express had operated 60 years earlier. When the pilots landed, their mail sacks were transferred to another airplane with a fresh pilot, who flew the mail to the next stop. As the planes made their way across the country, small towns along the route lit the way by keeping large bonfires burning through the night.

That was how the experimental flights were *supposed* to go, but that's not exactly what happened. The westbound flights were grounded in Chicago when a snowstorm hit. And one of the eastbound flights ended when the pilot, William Lewis, crashed his plane and was killed. But the other eastbound plane made it all the way to Hazelhurst Field in New York, delivering the mail just

Rapper Lil Jon owns a diamond and gold "Crunk Ain't Dead" chain that weighs 5 lb. Value: $500,000.

33 hours and 20 minutes after it left San Francisco. That's about 65 hours faster than sending the mail by train. The very next day, Congress voted to give the Air Mail Service $1.25 million to develop the system further.

TRANSCONTINENTAL AIRWAY

Two years later, Congress appropriated additional funds to create a lighted airway across the entire United States. From San Francisco through Nevada, Utah, Wyoming, Nebraska, Iowa, Ohio, Pennsylvania, and New York, planners devised a system of beacons and emergency runways spaced from 10 to 30 miles apart, depending on the terrain. At each location, a 50-foot-tall steel tower was erected with a rotating spotlight installed at the top.

The beacons were spaced close enough together so that when a pilot was passing over one of them, the next one would be visible in the distance. That worked in clear weather, but on a day when it was overcast and visibility was poor, the pilot might need help finding the next beacon. For that reason, the foundations for the beacon towers were poured in the shape of giant, 70-foot arrows, which pointed the direction to the next beacon. The concrete arrows were painted bright yellow to make them more visible from the sky.

LIGHTS OUT

By the late 1920s, 284 beacons had been built in a line along the 2,665-mile route from New York to San Francisco. The Transcontinental Airway System, as it was called, was a technological marvel. It worked so well that other countries imitated it. There was even talk of using light ships or anchored buoys to create routes across the Atlantic and Pacific Oceans.

But as effective as the system was, it was soon eclipsed by other advances in aviation technology. Newer planes were more reliable and flew higher, faster, and farther, eliminating the need for so many emergency runways. Radio navigation systems made it possible for pilots to follow a radio signal for hundreds of miles, even in poor visibility. That made the light beacons obsolete, and the system was dismantled in the 1940s. The towers ended up as scrap metal, which was used to build tanks and ships during World War II. In coastal areas, many of the giant concrete arrows were destroyed to prevent enemies from using them as navigation aids. But many still survive to this day, the only physical reminders of the days when pilots could fly all the way across the country by sight without getting lost in the dark.

The ASPCA was founded to combat cruelty to horses.

NEITHER JELLY NOR FISH

These creatures are not of this earth.

• A jellyfish doesn't have a front or a back, only a top and a bottom.

• Jellyfish lack eyes (or a brain, for that matter). They have tiny receptors that can sense light and dark. They use gravity to navigate.

• Something else jellyfish lack: teeth. Instead, they have *nematocysts*: tiny barbs filled with painful venom that they use to ensnare and immobilize their prey.

• In 1991 NASA sent thousands of jellyfish into space and bred them to see how their offspring would fare back on Earth. Result: Not good. Their gravity sensors developed abnormalities, and they couldn't swim well. (This doesn't bode well for future humans born in space.)

• What's longer than a blue whale? A lion's mane jellyfish, which can exceed 120 feet in length. (But blue whales weigh 130 times more.)

• Jellyfish breathe through their skin. And they eat and go to the bathroom through the same orifice.

• Only about 5% of a jellyfish is solid matter. The rest is water. So little mass means they can tolerate greater pressure, which allows some species of jellyfish to dive to more than five miles below the ocean's surface.

• What do a snowflake, a pizza, and a jellyfish have in common? They are all *radially symmetrical*, which means that they can be divided in half along multiple planes. (Most animals, like us, are *bilaterally symmetrical*, which means we can only be cut in half on one plane straight down the middle.)

• Stay away from dead jellyfish, because they can sting you too. Even *part* of a dead jellyfish can sting you.

• Because jellyfish aren't fish, aficionados refer to them as "jellies."

• Myth-conception: Peeing on a jellyfish sting can ease the pain. It might take your mind off the pain for a moment, but the three most effective remedies are seawater, vinegar, and time.

• Different names for groups of jellyfish: *bloom, swarm,* and *smack.*

• Some fish in the *Caranx* genus are impervious to jellyfish stings. This allows them to evade predators by hiding inside jellyfish swarms.

"Her Majesty" on the Beatles' *Abbey Road* is considered the first hidden track on a record album.

• Jellyfish live half their lives upside down: Young jellies, called *polyps*, attach themselves to the seafloor, and their mouths and stomachs face upward. When jellyfish reach their adult, umbrella-shaped stage—called the *medusa* stage—they let go and as soon as they're free-floating, they invert themselves so their mouths face downward.

• *Turritopsis dohrnii*, a small jelly that lives in the Mediterranean, is the only animal that scientists consider "immortal" because of its ability to transform itself from a medusa back to a polyp, theoretically over and over again…if it doesn't get eaten. Work is underway to figure out just how they do that.

• Some jellyfish use bioluminescence to scare and confuse predators. One species, *Atolla wyvillei*, flashes a blue "burglar alarm" when danger is near. Others can emit a glowing slime that sticks to predators and then makes *them* visible.

• Very few species of jellyfish are endangered. Reason: overfishing. Because their natural predators (sea turtles and certain fish species) are declining, massive jellyfish swarms are showing up more and more around the globe. In 2015 a mile-wide swarm was spotted off the British coast.

• Often mistaken for a jellyfish, a Portuguese man o' war is actually a *siphonophore*—related to jellyfish, but different in that it isn't a single organism; it's a colony of specialized individuals called *zooids*, each performing different functions but working together as one.

• The U.S. Navy is trying to develop an underwater robot that swims like a jellyfish.

• The box jellyfish is one of the most venomous creatures on Earth. They kill more than 100 people a year.

• Spoiler alert: In Sir Arthur Conan Doyle's 1926 story "The Adventure of the Lion's Mane," about a science professor who was killed on a beach, Sherlock Holmes deduces that the murderer is…a lion's mane jellyfish. (Then Holmes kills it with a rock.)

> A jellyfish is little more than a pulsating bell, a tassel of trailing tentacles and a single digestive opening through which it both eats and excretes— as regrettable an example of economy of design as ever was.
>
> **—Jeffrey Kluger, *Time* magazine science writer**

Saturn has such a low density that it would float on water. (It's a gas giant.)

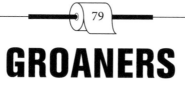

GROANERS

Brought to you by Puncle John.

- I tried to tell the doctor that I didn't want a brain transplant, but he changed my mind.

- What does an annoying pepper do? It gets jalapeño face.

- How do Stop, Yield, and Merge talk to each other? They use sign language.

- Telling puns in an elevator is just wrong on so many levels.

- That colander movie wasn't very good. The plot had too many holes. I was straining to understand it.

- Uncle John's bakery burned down. Now his business is toast.

- It took me forever to eat that clock. Very time-consuming.

- I just ate a bunch of Scrabble tiles. My next trip to the bathroom might spell disaster.

- That jerk just threw milk and butter at me! How dairy!

- A stork is strong enough to carry a little baby. Bigger babies require a crane.

- The most groundbreaking invention ever: the shovel.

- What does Jesus drive? A Chrysler.

- Hey, buddy, wanna put two of every animal on a boat? I Noah guy.

- The ambassador didn't get sick because she has diplomatic immunity.

- Little Brian refused to take his nap, so he was sent to jail for resisting a rest.

- That clown just paid my bill for me! What a nice jester!

- "Who's that woman standing between the goal posts?" "Annette."

- Peter Pan just won't stop flying around ever since he went to Neverland.

- I've been to the dentist a lot recently, so I know the drill.

- Two antennas met on a roof, fell in love, and got married. The wedding ceremony wasn't much, but the reception was excellent.

No joke: Gelomancy is the "art" of predicting the future by listening to someone's laughter.

SNEAKY LOGOS

These well-known logos have hidden visual messages. Can't picture it? Look 'em up.

FedEx. The shipping giant's well-known logo is a blocky, purple and orange "FedEx." But check out the space between the "E" and the "X." Did you ever notice the white arrow?

Baskin Robbins. Everyone knows the slogan of the world's largest ice cream maker—"31 flavors"—but not everyone sees the "31" in its familiar pink and blue "BR" logo. The humps in the "B" make up the "3," and the vertical line on the left side of the "R" makes the "1," both of them rendered in pink, setting them off from the rest of the logo.

Vaio. This computer brand's logo is a wavy line making up a "V" and an "A," followed by an "IO." The wavy line is a sine wave, representing an old-school analog signal, and the "IO" represents the binary digits 1 and 0, which is how digital information is transmitted. Together, it represents the analog-to-digital history of information technology.

Bronx Zoo. The logo of America's largest city zoo shows the words "Bronx Zoo" beneath the silhouettes of an two zebras—with outlines of the city's famous skyline hidden in the negative space between the zebras' legs.

Toblerone. The symbol representing this chocolate company, maker of distinctive prism-shaped bars of chocolate, has the word "Toblerone" under an image of a mountain peak. Look closely at the mountain: there's a bear hidden in it. (It's standing up, and appears to be dancing.) A bear is the traditional symbol of the city where this company was founded—Bern, Switzerland.

London Symphony Orchestra. A simple, stylized "LSO" in one flowing red line makes up the logo of this famous orchestra. Look again: it's the head and arms of a person—seeming to be conducting an orchestra.

Amazon. This famous logo features the word "amazon" (all lowercase letters), with an orange arrow underneath it. Look closer: the arrow goes from the first "A" to the "Z" in Amazon—because you can get anything from A to Z from Amazon. (The arrow also looks a like a smile, suggesting that the company makes its customers happy.)

The original Chewbacca costume was made of goat hair, yak hair, and rabbit hair.

THE LOOOONG EXPERIMENT

You've heard the expression "as slow as molasses moving uphill in winter"? Here's the story of something even slower.

CRUDE EFFORT

In January 1961 a man named John Mainstone began a new job as a physics lecturer at the University of Queensland in Brisbane, Australia. On his first day, one of his colleagues showed him around the department, and in one room he pulled an experiment out of a cupboard. Still underway, it had been set up in the 1920s by Thomas Parnell, a physics professor long retired and now dead.

The experiment looked simple enough: it was a glass funnel filled with ordinary asphalt or "pitch," a derivative of crude oil used to pave roads. The funnel sat on a stand, and beneath the stand was a glass beaker to catch any pitch that dripped from the funnel. A glass cover, called a bell jar, protected the apparatus from dust.

The "pitch drop experiment," as it was called, had been sitting in the cupboard since the 1930s. In all that time, only three drops of the stuff had dripped from the funnel—the first in 1938, the second in 1947, and the third in 1954. A fourth was now hanging like a teardrop from the bottom of the funnel. It must have looked to Mainstone as if it could fall into the beaker at any moment, but as his colleague explained, years might pass before it finally did.

DRIP...

Professor Parnell had created the experiment back in 1927 by pouring heated, softened pitch into a sealed funnel and letting it settle there for three years. In 1930 he unsealed the bottom of the funnel and the pitch began to flow. The purpose of the experiment was to demonstrate to his students that some substances, like pitch, may appear solid at room temperature but are actually very slow-moving liquids. If you hit a slab of pitch with a hammer, for example, it will smash into pieces, just like a rock. But if you put it in a funnel as Parnell did, it will slowly flow out, like water dripping from a faucet, because it's actually a liquid, albeit one with extremely high viscosity, or resistance to flow. The pitch that Parnell placed in the funnel was so viscous that it took, on average, eight years for a single drop to form and drip from the funnel.

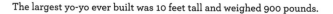

The largest yo-yo ever built was 10 feet tall and weighed 900 pounds.

PITCHING IN

Mainstone was fascinated by the experiment and agreed to become its custodian. His job: check the display once or twice a day to see how the fourth drop was progressing. He suggested that the experiment be taken out of the cupboard and placed on public display, so that other people could enjoy it as well.

The head of the physics department rejected the idea, insisting that "nobody would be the slightest bit interested." There were even people who wanted to toss the display in the trash, but Mainstone managed to save it. It was still there in the cupboard in May 1962, when the fourth drop fell into the beaker…and no one was there to see it. It was still there eight years later in August 1970, when the fifth drop fell. Once again, nobody saw it. (In fact, no one had *ever* seen a drop of the pitch fall, because experiments like this one were rare, and it only takes about a tenth of a second for a drop of pitch to fall into a beaker. Managing to be there at just the right tenth of a second in that eight-year span takes persistence, dedication, and more than a little luck.)

THE END IS NEAR

A new head of the physics department took over in 1972, and he liked Mainstone's suggestion of putting the pitch drop experiment on public display. So it was moved to the entrance hall of the physics building and set up in its own glass case. That's where it was in April of 1979, when the sixth drop seemed close to falling.

Mainstone was determined to be there when it did fall. He wanted to understand the precise mechanical process that causes a drop to break free and fall into the beaker. He knew that in the final stages the drop hangs by three or four slender strands of pitch, and he theorized that the drop finally falls when one of those slender strands breaks, and the remaining strands are too weak to hold the drop any longer. But he couldn't be sure until someone actually saw one fall.

One Saturday afternoon, the end appeared to be just days away. Mainstone had to decide whether to spend the rest of that day at work, in the off chance that it might drop, or go home, as he promised his wife, to help her around the house. After studying the drop carefully, he saw no signs of an imminent fall, and went home. He did not return Sunday, and by the time he arrived for work on Monday morning, the drop had fallen, again with no one to witness it.

Mainstone's next chance came in the summer of 1988, when the seventh drop was getting near. This time he kept a close watch on the experiment. But as he recounted to an interviewer in 2013, at some point "I decided that I needed a cup of tea or something like that, walked away, came back, and lo and behold

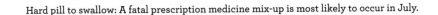

Hard pill to swallow: A fatal prescription medicine mix-up is most likely to occur in July.

it had dropped. One becomes a bit philosophical about this, and I just said, 'Oh well, let's be patient.' "

PITCH IMPERFECT

The wait for the eighth drop to fall took even longer, because the university installed air conditioning in the physics building, and cooler temperatures made the pitch flow more slowly. This time Mainstone had to wait 12 years, until November 2000, for the drop to fall. By then he was semiretired and traveling in the UK when he received an e-mail from a colleague warning that the fall might happen at any moment. Mainstone was disappointed that he wouldn't be there to see it in person, but he took comfort in knowing that the physics department had set up a camera to record the event…that is, until two more e-mails arrived. The first reported that the drop had fallen; the second reported that the camera had malfunctioned and failed to film the fall. Four times since 1962, drops had fallen into the beaker. Mainstone missed them all.

TO THE LAST DROP

By the summer of 2013, Mainstone was in his late 70s. He was still the custodian of the pitch drop experiment, and he hoped to be there to see the ninth drop fall, perhaps in 2014. This time, not one but three cameras were set up to film the drop, so that one camera would film the action even if two others failed. But Mainstone didn't make it. He died in August 2013, before the drop fell.

Mainstone did have one consolation before he died: Trinity College in Dublin had their own pitch drop experiment, dating to 1944. It had been long ignored, but the growing interest in Mainstone's experiment convinced the faculty at Trinity to pull theirs off the shelf, where it sat beneath decades of accumulated dust. A number of drops had already fallen, but no one knew when, because no one had paid any attention. This time would be different: When someone noticed in April 2013 that a drop looked like it was about to fall, a camera was set up to record it. At about 5:00 p.m. on July 11, it filmed the pitch as it fell into the beaker. Mainstone saw the footage; it was "tantalizing," he told his colleagues. He died six weeks later.

Even if Mainstone had lived, he wouldn't have seen the ninth drop fall. The beaker was so full of pitch from the first eight drops, that in April 2014 Mainstone's successor decided to replace it with an empty one. But when he lifted the bell jar, the base wobbled and the ninth drop just snapped off. Don't despair, though: the tenth drop should fall sometime in 2028, and there's enough pitch in the funnel to last another 100 years.

Not just a scientist: Sir Isaac Newton also ran England's Royal Mint for 30 years.

DON'T CALL ME GENGHIS

Be it because of translation errors, honorifics bestowed, or assumed names, many historical figures are known by names that are not really their names.

Genghis Khan. The name by which we know the leader of the Mongols who conquered most of Asia in the 13th century is an honorific—it means "ruler of all." Genghis Khan's birth name was Temujin, which means "blacksmith."

Jesus Christ. The New Testament was written in Greek, which used the Greek form of the name, Iesous. That was Latinized into Iesus, and when the letter J developed, it entered into languages such as Spanish and English as Jesus. Jesus's original Hebrew name was Yahushua, or, in some other accounts, Yeshua. As for Christ, that means "messiah" or "anointed one" in Greek, so that's not his last name. At the time and place he lived, Yahushua would have been known as "son of Joseph," or "Yosef." Therefore, in his own time, Jesus Christ's name was something more like Yahushua ben Yosef. ("Ben" means "son of.")

Nelson Mandela. Born in 1918, the future freedom fighter was part of the ethnic isiXhosa group native to eastern South Africa. His father named him Rolihlahla, a isiXhosa word that means "pulling the branch of the tree," but colloquially it's closer to "troublemaker." When Mandela started attending school, which was run by the British colonial government, it was common practice for the teachers to give the African students Western names that were more pronounceable. Hence, he acquired the name Nelson.

Muhammad. In sixth-century Arabia, it was customary to include several generations' worth of ancestors in one's name, so the full birth name of the prophet of Islam is: Muhammad Ibn Abdullah, Ibn Abdul Mutalib, Ibn Hashem, Ibn Abd Zanat, Ibn Abd Kusay, Ibn Kilab, Ibn Murra, Ibn Kaab, Ibn Louay, Ibn Ghaleb, Ibn Fihr. ("Ibn" means "son of.")

Christopher Columbus. The explorer who "sailed the ocean blue / in the year 1492" was born in Genoa, a part of what is now Italy, with the name Cristoforo Colombo. But his great voyage was funded by, and in the name of, the Spanish crown. So his name was translated into the history books first as the Spanish-sounding Cristóbal Colón. When English historians wrote about him, they adapted his name once more, anglicizing it to Christopher Columbus.

Largest dog litter on record: Tia, a Neapolitan mastiff, gave birth to 24 puppies (2005).

Nicolaus Copernicus. The 16th-century astronomer who boldly theorized that planetary bodies revolved around the Sun, not Earth, was born in 1473 in Poland. When his theories became known in western Europe, his name was anglicized. Real name: Mikolaj Kopernik.

Confucius. Similarly, when the Chinese philosopher's works spread to Europe in the 17th century, his name was westernized from its original form: Kong Qiu.

Voltaire. The 18th-century French philosopher and author used a pen name. His real name was François-Marie Arouet, but he reportedly resented his father so much (his father wanted him to become a lawyer, not a writer) that he abandoned the family name. Why he chose "Voltaire" is unclear. Historians think it might be an anagram of a Latinized spelling of Arouet, his real surname.

Peter. An early apostle of Jesus as well as the first pope, Peter's real first name was Simeon, or Simōn. When the Bible was written, he was given the name Peter, or in the Greek of the New Testament, Petros, which means "rock." When it was translated into Latin, it became Petrus and made its way into English as Peter.

Vladimir Lenin. His real first name is Vladimir, but his real family name was Ulyanov. When he began his political career, which culminated with the Communist takeover of Russia, he started using the alias Lenin. He did that to remind both himself and others of how the government he helped overthrow had once imprisoned him in Siberia near the Lena River.

Plato. History remembers one of the greatest and most important philosophers of all time with what could be essentially a fat joke. According to a third-century biography, he was really named Aristocles, son of Ariston. A teacher nicknamed him Plato, which comes from the Greek word *plauteta*, which means "broad and wide." In other words, a teacher called his student chubby, and the name stuck... forever.

Che Guevara. The Cuban revolutionary wasn't Cuban and he wasn't named Che. Ernesto Guevara Lynch (his great-great-great-great grandfather was Irish) was born in Argentina, and emigrated to Cuba in the early 1950s to join Fidel Castro's band of Cuban revolutionaries. Guevara got his nickname during the revolution because while talking he said "che" a lot. Unknown to the Cubans, "che" is a filler word in Argentine Spanish, similar to "uh" or "um" or "you know?" in American English. They called him Che and it stuck.

Truth in advertising: Hidden Valley Ranch Dressing was invented at Alaska's Hidden Valley Ranch.

KNOW YOUR BANDITS

Add this to the many ways that crime does not pay: if law enforcement agencies or the media pick your nickname, you may not get one as snappy as Butch Cassidy and the Sundance Kid. At last report, all of these bandits were still at large.

THE MOLE BANDIT

Description: Asian male approximately 30 years old, 5'6" tall, weighing 140 lb., wanted for robbing or attempting to rob six banks in the San Diego area in 2014. In each heist, he wore dark aviator sunglasses, a baseball cap, and a hoodie with the hood pulled up over the baseball cap.

Details: If you were thinking this baddie got his nickname by tunneling into bank vaults or performing some other really cool molelike behavior, think again. "The robber has a mole over his lip on the left side," says the FBI. That's it. And he's not very good at robbing banks. Three of the Mole Bandit's attempted six heists failed. The FBI won't say how much he got away with in his three successful jobs, but the reward for information leading to his identification, arrest, and conviction is just $1,000, or $167 per (attempted) heist.

THE BAD BREATH BANDIT

Description: Caucasian male, 6'0" tall, weighing 210–250 lb., wanted for six bank robberies in 2014 and a seventh in 2016, all of them in the Sierra Nevada foothills of Northern California.

Details: It's not clear whether the Bad Breath Bandit really has bad breath. The nickname is an FBI joke, because he wears a disposable surgical mask when he pulls his bank jobs. That, and his wraparound sunglasses and a San Francisco Giants baseball cap do such a good job of concealing his facial features that witnesses have a hard time estimating his age; he could be anywhere from his mid-20s to his late 40s. His getaway vehicle may be a red Dodge Durango.

THE BAD HAIR BANDIT

Description: African American male in his late 40s or early 50s, 5'10" tall, weighing about 200 lb., wanted for robbing five banks in the Dallas, Texas, area in the first half of 2016. He makes his getaways in a white four-door sedan believed to be a late model Nissan Altima.

Details: This robber conceals his appearance by wearing an ugly gray wig in some bank heists, and an ugly black wig in others. He may be the same person

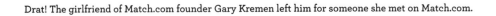

who robbed a bank in Mesquite, Texas, in March 2015 while wearing an ugly wig (held on with a headband) and a fake beard. Either that or Texas has two Bad Hair Bandits at large at the same time. Dallas Crimestoppers is offering a $5,000 reward for information leading to the arrest of their Bad Hair Bandit.

Note: Authorities caught a third Bad Hair Bandit—48-year-old Cynthia Van Holland. She is now serving 10 years for robbing 21 banks in Washington, Idaho, Montana, and California while wearing a variety of ugly wigs.

THE JUST CHECKING BANDIT

Description: Caucasian male in his mid 30s, brown hair, about 5'7" tall, with a small build, weight unknown.

Details: This bandit's nickname immortalizes the moment he lost his nerve in the middle of his first bank job. In May 2015, he handed a note to the teller at a branch of the California Bank and Trust in San Diego, demanding cash. When the teller tried to clarify what the man wanted, he grabbed the note back and fled. As he was leaving, he said to the teller, "I just wanted to see what would happen." The man may have learned his lesson: since then, no one matching his description has tried to rob a bank in the San Diego area. (The FBI is not offering a reward for information leading to his arrest.)

THE GEEZER BANDIT

Description: Caucasian male in his late 60s, 5'10" tall, average build, and weighing 190–200 lb. He is wanted for 16 California bank robberies from 2009 to 2011. "Typically, the man enters the bank, approaches the teller, and presents a demand note for cash. He carries a small-caliber pistol that he threatens to use if the teller does not comply with his demands," says his FBI wanted poster.

Details: The nickname "geezer" refers to the man's advanced age. He looks and acts like he's ready for a nursing home. But he may not be as old as he appears: in his sixteenth bank heist, a hidden die pack exploded as the man was making his getaway, and security camera footage from outside the bank shows the ink-stained fogey sprinting away at an "abnormally fast" speed for someone his age. That and eyewitness accounts describing his wrinkle-free hands and unnatural skin tone has led to speculation that he may have been wearing a mask or makeup to hide his—or her—true features. If so, he may be one of the few people who's ever been called a "geezer" and takes it as a compliment. (Then again, his failure to rob any more banks since 2011 may mean he really was an old man…and he died.)

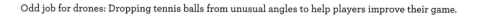

Odd job for drones: Dropping tennis balls from unusual angles to help players improve their game.

WE NAMED HER FARBERTA

Looking to name your little one something besides Aidan, Graydon, Braden, or Jaden?
Try one of these names…which were popular in medieval times.

- **Hoger** (Old German for "mind, heart" and Saxon for "spear")

- **Falatrude** (Old German for "falcon")

- **Abone** (Old English for "obscure")

- **Ulfkell** (Icelandic, it translates to "wolf kettle")

- **Tallboys** (Old French for "woodcutter")

- **Zawissius** (Czech for "spite")

- **Wigbert** (Old High German for "battle brightly")

- **Waldswind** (Saxon for "authority")

- **Ebbo** (Old German for "boar")

- **Ashwy** (Old English, meaning "spear made from an ash tree")

- **Witugis** (Old German for "wood")

- **Odart** (Saxon for "wealth")

- **Wendelswith** (Early German for "strong")

- **Godo** (Old Dutch for "God")

- **Dado** (Saxon for "deed")

- **Dodo** (Old German for "sponsor")

- **Dudo** (Latin for "people")

- **Loup** (Middle French for "wolf")

- **Brunger** (From an Old English word that means "brown")

- **Radegund** (A Saxon word that translates to "battle advisor")

- **Eupraxia** (Greek for "well")

- **Rogue** (Old Icelandic for "crow")

- **Knightwine** (Put together, the two Old English words mean "knight" and "friend")

- **Sixt** (Greek for "polished")

- **Pagan** (Latin for "rustic")

- **Alanteus** (Early German for "whole")

- **Farberta** (feminine version of Farbert—Old German for "journey")

- **Amblard** (Early German for "vigor" or "bravery")

- **Drudmund** (Frankish for "foreigner" or "slave")

- **Notger** (Early German for "necessity")

- **Sisbert** (Old High German for "song of lament")

- **Evergrim** (Two Old German words that together mean "fierce boar")

The 1899 "Horsey Horseless" was a car with a wooden horse's head attached. The inventor…

POT-ERGEISTS

These bathroom poltergeists remind us of Moaning Myrtle, the ghost who haunts the girls' bathroom at Hogwarts in the Harry Potter book series. Are bathroom ghosts for real? Who knows—but they make for some great bathroom reading.

Haunted Bathroom: The women's restroom in the White Lion pub, in the town of Yateley, in southern England.

Haunted By: A ghostly female figure wearing a white hood.

Boo! When the pub's burglar alarm went off mysteriously in October 2015, the pub keeper, Andy Froker, reviewed the security camera footage to see if he could identify what had set off the alarm. At one point in the video, a wispy apparition materializes at the entrance to the ladies' room at the top of the stairs. It loiters there briefly before dropping out of the image. Regulars at the pub say the mysterious image is the hooded figure of a woman who has been seen—and felt—around the White Lion "quite often."

> *I live in the building and so I can feel it when I pass the ghost,*

the pub's manager, Kate Staniszewska, told the London *Daily Mail* in 2015. "I've lived here six months and it's happened a few times, but this is the only place I've seen it." (Care to make that a double? The White Lion has a second spirit— that of former owner James Rogers, now deceased. Rogers's favorite tankard still sits in a special place in the bar, and regulars say he has been known to set off the burglar alarm if anyone moves the tankard from its proper spot.)

Haunted Bathroom: The one on the tour bus that Scott Weiland, lead singer of the Stone Temple Pilots, was riding in when he died from a drug overdose in 2015.

Haunted By: The ghost of Scott Weiland.

Boo! Former Creed lead vocalist Scott Stapp has battled his own demons over the years. They seemed to have caught up with him when he rented the same tour bus that Weiland died on, and had what he describes as a "crazy, mystical experience"—Scott Weiland speaking to him from beyond the grave.

"I remember being in the bathroom, looking in the mirror, on the bus, and really feeling like I could hear him saying, 'Dude, this could have been you. And this could be you if you continue that path. Don't do what I did. Don't go down that road,' " Stapp recounted to GQ magazine in 2017. At the time, he was fighting a losing battle to stay sober, but the experience in the bus bathroom caused Stapp to "further my commitment to my recovery," he says. "It was definitely one of those God moments. I get goose bumps right now just talking about it. It was a God moment."

MOANING MYRTLE *(full name: Myrtle Elizabeth Warren) was the ghost of a 14-year-old girl…and yet in the* Harry Potter *movies, she was played by British actress Shirley Henderson. Her age while filming Myrtle's first appearance in* Harry Potter and the Chamber of Secrets: *37*

Haunted Bathroom: The women's restroom on the 86th floor of the Empire State Building in New York City.

Haunted By: A female ghost, said to be that of a woman who committed suicide by jumping off the building after World War II.

Boo! According to one version of the story, in the mid-1980s a tourist visiting the 86th-floor observation deck saw a distraught woman dressed in 1940s clothing. When she tried to comfort the woman, the woman explained that her husband had died in the war and she couldn't live without him. Then she removed her coat and passed through the suicide barrier as if it wasn't there, and jumped off the building.

Shocked by what she'd just seen, the tourist ran into the women's restroom and splashed some water on her face. Then when she looked up, she saw the suicidal woman standing at the next sink touching up her makeup as she looked into the mirror. After she finished, the woman went out onto the observation deck and jumped off again. More than one person has reporting seeing a jumping female ghost that repeats the act over and over after materializing in the ladies' room, but the ghost doesn't always tell the story about her husband dying in the war. This has led some believers to suspect that the ghost is actually that of Evelyn McHale, a single 23-year-old woman who leapt to her death in 1947. (Her fiancé, a college student named Barry Rhodes, survived her.) Or maybe observation deck regulars have made up the ghost-in-the-bathroom story to keep the lines in the ladies' room from getting too long.

Haunted Bathrooms: The ones in Dumfries House, East Ayrshire, Scotland. Technically, the bathrooms aren't any more haunted than the rest of the house, but the place is said to be haunted by a ghost who smells like he didn't get to the bathroom in time.

What's the "Zion Curtain"? A Utah law requiring that alcoholic drinks be made out of customers' view.

Haunted By: One of the Earls of Dumfries (which one is unclear).

Boo! The 18th-century mansion was a private home until 2007, when it was purchased by a charitable trust headed by Prince Charles. That's when the trouble started: During private tours of the residence, a stink described by head curator Charlotte Rostek as "the smell of incontinence" would suddenly appear out of nowhere, "usually in very inconvenient situations. Suddenly people would get a bit shifty and look around them, and there was this very, very unpleasant smell," she told Glasgow's *Herald* newspaper.

More than $3 million was spent renovating the house to open it to the public in 2008, and Rostek hoped the repairs would solve the problem. No such luck: "I did smell it the other day. I just got a whiff of it," she told the paper in 2016. Visitors to the house have also reported seeing the stinky earl entering one of the bedrooms where two members of the Dumfries family are known to have died.

Haunted Bathroom: A first-floor restroom in the Galvez, a century-old historic beachfront hotel on Galveston Island in Texas.

Haunted By: A ghost wearing heavy boots.

Boo! The many ghosts that are said to haunt the Galvez are one of the hotel's selling points. Guests book rooms in the hopes of seeing the "Ghost Bride" who hanged herself in one of the turrets on the roof; the little girl bouncing a ball in the lobby; and Sister Katherine, a nun who is said to have drowned in the 1900 hurricane and who may have been buried on the land where the hotel was later built. The ghost that haunts the restroom on the first floor near the music hall is one of the hotel's creepier spirits, and he apparently likes to have the bathroom to himself. Once, when a guest popped into the restroom late at night after using the hot tubs, the lights suddenly went out and the woman could hear boot steps approaching her. Then the sound of loud breathing, and a man's voice that ordered, "Get out!"

*   *   *

PLAYING CHICKEN

Birds collide with U.S. military jets more than 3,000 times a year, costing the government as much as $80 million in repairs. Engineers call the collisions "bird strikes." To help design bird-proof jets, they test new aircraft with "chicken guns"—compressed-air cannons that fire four-pound chickens (at 400 miles per hour) at the windshields and engines of standing jets manned with dummy crew members.

English muffins were invented in the United States. They weren't popular in England until the 1980s.

PANTY HOSE SOLUTIONS

Panty hose—wardrobe staple of grandmas everywhere. Uncomfortable and impractical, they seem to be fading out of fashion…but don't throw yours away yet! They have surprisingly practical applications that go far beyond the world of hosiery.

PROBLEM: Broken fan belt

SOLUTION: If you drive an older model car (one with a V-belt), the waistband from a pair of panty hose makes a decent emergency replacement. Cut off the legs (and excess material), and install the leftover loop until you can make it to a mechanic.

PROBLEM: Bug bites and blisters

SOLUTION: If you're camping, hiking, or gardening in an area with ticks or chiggers, wearing panty hose will protect your legs while still letting your skin breathe. It will also decrease friction in your shoes, so you'll get fewer blisters.

PROBLEM: Small object lost on the floor

SOLUTION: Slip the leg of a pair of panty hose over the nozzle on your vacuum's hose and secure it with a rubber band. Carefully move the nozzle along the area where you lost the item, and you will eventually find your lost earring, screw, contact lens, or other hard-to-see item attached to the makeshift filter.

PROBLEM: Hairbrush buildup

SOLUTION: Cut the foot off a pair of panty hose and slip it over your hairbrush. Secure with a rubber band around the neck of the brush, and push the fabric down so that the bristles poke all the way through. Use your brush normally, and when hair builds up around the bristles, slip off the cover to remove the hair.

PROBLEM: Bugs in the garden are eating the melons

SOLUTION: Insert a small melon (or squash) into a panty hose leg, and tie the top of the leg to a garden stake so that it's suspended above the ground. The mesh will protect it from bugs (and rodents) on the ground, and still allow it to grow.

PROBLEM: You need to change the water in your fish tank

SOLUTION: Pull the foot of a pair of panty hose over the nozzle of a wet-dry shop vacuum, and secure it with a rubber band. Now you can remove the water from the tank without having to mess up your tank's gravel and decorations. (But don't forget to remove the fish from the tank first.)

First mention of sausages in print: In 4,000-year-old Sumerian texts found in Mesopotamia.

THE "RED SCARE"

Here's a Stall of Fame member who earned his claim to bathroom fame by being written up in a medical journal. (Warning: If you're reading this at breakfast, you might want to wait until you've finished eating.)

SEEING RED

In 1971 a 12-year-old polio survivor (unnamed in all subsequent press reports) made medical history—of sorts—when he contracted a scary medical condition that he first noticed following a trip to the bathroom. Besides having contracted polio years earlier, the boy suffered from a seizure disorder. He also had a history of mild constipation and a tendency to eat odd things, such as coffee grounds. So it's understandable that when he went to the bathroom that day in 1971 and saw that his "number two" was bright reddish-pink, his mother rushed him to the hospital. The boy was kept under observation for four days while doctors tried to find the source of what they assumed was internal bleeding.

"The stool had no abnormal odor, but looked like strawberry ice cream," Dr. John V. Payne wrote. It was "unassociated with abdominal pain or other symptoms," and "physical examination upon admission revealed no acute distress and normal vital signs."

Chemical analysis showed no trace of blood in the boy's stool. That was good news, but it brought the doctors no closer to finding out what was wrong with him. Test after test failed to shed any light on what was causing his condition.

MYSTERY SOLVED?

The boy pooped pink for the next two days, and then his "business" mysteriously returned to normal. That prompted doctors to quiz the boy's mother more thoroughly about what her son had eaten before falling prey to the malady. The mother described how, in the two days leading up to his hospitalization, the boy had eaten big bowls of a new breakfast cereal called Franken Berry, which had been introduced by General Mills only a few weeks earlier. If you've ever eaten Franken Berry, you'll know that it's strawberry-flavored and bright pink in color. In the early 1970s, much of that color was provided by Red No. 2, an artificial and indigestible food coloring. So…if you eat a bunch of red dye and your body can't digest it, where does it go? You guessed right: it leaves your body the same way as everything else you eat. And because it hasn't been broken down by the digestive process, it exits your body every bit as reddish-pink as when it entered.

By now the doctors were pretty sure they'd figured out what had caused the boy's condition. Just to be sure, though, before they released him from the hospital they let him eat four big bowls of Franken Berry cereal. When his pink poop returned, they sent the boy home with instructions to go a little bit easier on the Franken Berry.

BY ANY OTHER NAME

To alert any physicians who might soon have similar encounters with pink-pooping kids in the emergency room, Dr. John Payne wrote a case study titled "Benign Red Pigmentation of Stool Resulting from Food Coloring in a New Breakfast Cereal (The Franken Berry Stool)," which was published in the February 1972 issue of the medical journal *Pediatrics*.

It doesn't take a marketing genius to realize that selling a breakfast cereal to parents becomes more difficult when it has this effect on their kids. The problem is not helped when a doctor names the condition "Franken Berry Stool." Nearly half a century later, the folks at General Mills are still reluctant to discuss the Franken Berry Stool incident, so it's difficult to pin down the precise date when they switched to *digestible* food coloring. But it's a safe bet that it didn't take them long. (They would have had to do it eventually, because the U.S. Food and Drug Administration banned the use of Red No. 2 as a food additive in 1976.)

COLOR CODES

Three more foods with a reputation for "off-color" behavior:

Nerds Cereal (1988). Red No. 2 wasn't the last indigestible food coloring, as the parents of a five-year-old boy discovered when he was admitted to a Virginia hospital with what appeared to be blood in his stool, this time orange-red in color, not reddish-pink. The condition was diagnosed as "Nerds Turds," caused when the boy ate an entire box of orange and red Nerds cereal, a spin-off of the popular candy. His case was written up in *Pediatrics*, too.

Peeps Oreos (2017). Eat too many of these seasonal Oreos with pink centers flavored like the famous Easter marshmallow treats and you yourself will be "in the pink" a few hours later.

Halloween Whopper (2015). Burger King customers who tried this seasonal item—a burger served on a black bun—were in for a spooky surprise. The bun got its dark color from a mixture of A1 steak sauce and the dyes Blue #1 and Red #40. The result: green poop.

Blueberries. 'Nuff said.

90% of phones in Japan are waterproof. Reason: People use them in the shower.

ROADKILL REPORT

ROADKILL? SOUNDS FISHY.

In December 2015, a man named Arthur Boyt found a dead dolphin on a beach near his hometown of Davidstow, in the far southeast of England. He took the carcass home...and ate it for Christmas dinner. Boyt, 76, insists he's been collecting, cooking, and eating roadkill since he was a teenager. The animals he's eaten include badgers, weasels, hedgehogs, squirrels, otters, foxes, rabbits, sparrows, deer, pigeons—and a bat. The 2015 Christmas feast was special, though: it was the first time he'd ever found a dolphin. How would he rate the meal? "I've got to admit, it's nothing to write home about," he told the *Guardian*. "It's not very fishy or oily. I fried it up and it was quite tough." When news got out about Boyt's dolphin dinner, he was informed that it is actually illegal to eat dolphin—because all dolphins in the UK are "royal fish" that belong to the British crown. Boyt's reply: "I don't suppose the Queen will be interested in getting back a dolphin that has been dead for a month or more."

ROADKILL COUTURE

In 2013 Pamela Paquin, an unemployed single mom in Jaffrey, New Hampshire, came up with a unique way to earn a living: she got a "fur buyer's license" so that she could sell animal furs. Then she went to a local taxidermist to learn how to skin and prepare animal skin...and started collecting and skinning roadkill she found near her home. And then she worked with a seamstress to turn the furs into clothing—muffs, scarves, hats, wraps, leg warmers, and more. She took samples of her roadkill-fur clothes to New York City—and they were an instant hit. Today her company, Petite Mort Fur ("little death"), is based in Boston and sells roadkill clothing to clients all over the world. The animals collected and skinned for the furs include foxes, rabbits, otters, raccoons, beavers, deer, mink—and even bears. Paquin says using the pelts of roadkill animals is an ethical way to produce fur, unlike the farming of fur animals, a practice she opposes. "All this fur is being thrown away," Paquin says. "If we can pick that up, we never have to kill another fur-bearing animal again." Prices for her items range from $45 for coyote fur pom-pom earrings, to $2,500 for a fawn scarf and belt. (Bonus: every Petit Mort product comes with a note telling where and when the animal was found.)

SLUTS, VILLIANS & BOORS

Over the centuries, these words' meanings have changed to almost their exact opposite.

PECULIAR (1400s)
Then: Belonging exclusively to, as in customs peculiar to a certain country
Now: Odd or different. Often suspicious, as in "his peculiar behavior"

CUNNING (1300s)
Then: Knowing or knowledgeable
Now: Tricky and slightly sinister

BOOR (1500s)
Then: A simple farmer or peasant
Now: A rude, insensitive lout

BLACKGUARD (1700s)
Then: A castle servant who, among other things, cleaned sooty pots
Now: A bad guy or scoundrel

RETALIATE (1600s)
Then: To return in kind—good or evil
Now: To get revenge or fight back

CRAFTY (1700s)
Then: Skilled in the manual arts, such as making soap or tooling leather
Now: A wily person who is probably up to no good

SLY (1200s)
Then: Skillful
Now: Sneaky or deceitful

COUNTERFEIT (1300s)
Then: To imitate, or model on a lofty ideal
Now: Fake, as in counterfeit money

SLUT (1400s)
Then: A fond term for an untidy woman or girl, as in "Our little daughter Susan is a delightful slut"
Now: A promiscuous woman

SMIRK (1100s)
Then: An open, sincere smile
Now: A smug, taunting smile of satisfaction, possibly at someone else's misfortune

SUE (1300s)
Then: To follow, as in "ensue"
Now: To take action in a court of law.

VILLAIN (1300s)
Then: A farmhand
Now: A character, usually in a book or movie, who does bad things

Ahead of their thyme: In 1856 a vegetarian commune was founded in the Kansas Territory.

MOVIE INSPIRATIONS

*It's always interesting to see where the architects of pop culture
get their ideas. Some of these may surprise you.*

The Ring (2002). This American remake of the 1998 Japanese horror film
Ringu—based on a 1991 novel by Kôji Suzuki—tells the story of a girl who
was thrown into a well and then later climbs out as a terrifying ghost. The
inspiration for Suzuki's book: a 14th-century folk tale about a servant girl named
Okiku. According to the tale, she was thrown into a well at Himeji Castle in
western Japan after rejecting the advances of a lovelorn samurai. Every night
thereafter, Okiku's ghost would climb out—with wet black hair and a long, white
dress—to torment her killer.

Bates Motel (1987). It's one of the most famous shots in movie history—the
Gothic architecture of the rustic hotel framed against a moody sky. That scene
from *Psycho* (1960) looks eerily similar to a 1925 painting by Edward Hopper
called *House by the Railroad* (which is based on a house in Haverstraw, New
York). When Alfred Hitchcock was directing *Psycho*, he not only "borrowed" the
look of the house; the mood and framing of the entire film were directly inspired
by that painting. (Hopper was said to be "honored" when the movie came out.)

Blade Runner (1982). You're probably familiar with the iconic Edward
Hopper painting *Nighthawks*, which depicts four people inside a corner diner,
viewed from outside at night. Director Ridley Scott knows that painting well…
and so did all of the production designers on his sci-fi film *Blade Runner*: "I
was constantly waving a reproduction of this painting under the noses of the
production team to illustrate the look and mood I was after."

Creed (2015). Directed and cowritten by Ryan Coogler, this drama told the
story of retired boxer Rocky Balboa (Sylvester Stallone), who agrees to train
his late nemesis's son, Adonis Creed (Michael B. Johnson), while battling
non-Hodgkin's lymphoma. Coogler wasn't really a *Rocky* fan, but his father
was. Coogler's father was also gravely ill…and that gave him an idea. "What if
this happened to my father's hero?" he told *The Wrap*. "And what if there was a
young guy in his life, and we were following their relationship?" Coogler decided
to give Rocky his father's illness, and to make that "young guy" the illegitimate
son of Apollo Creed. Result: *Creed* was a critical and commercial success.

SQUATTER'S RIGHTS
...AND WRONGS

You've probably heard the phrase "squatter's rights." It's a term for taking over unoccupied or abandoned land or buildings without ownership or permission. Every state has different laws about how property may be acquired by squatting or "adverse possession," but here's the thing: despite the name, it's not a right. That doesn't stop some folks from moving in, though.

OREGONIAN VACATION

In October 2015, a family in Medford, Oregon, went on a vacation, and hired someone to check in on their home while they were gone. A couple of weeks later, when the house-sitter went over to make sure everything was okay, they found a 63-year-old man living there. Police say that Raymond Calvert broke in and literally made himself at home. Calvert's defense: "squatter's rights." His defense was immediately dismissed, because a home left by people who went away on vacation does not, legally speaking, fall under the definition of "abandoned property."

THE NIGHT THE LIGHTS GOT CHANGED IN GEORGIA

Beverly Mitchell went on a two-week vacation to Greece in 2004, locking up her Douglasville, Georgia, home before she left. She returned to find a stranger living in her house. Not only that, but the squatter, Beverly Valentine, had completely redecorated the place. She even ripped out the carpet in favor of hardwood floors, and took down the pictures off the wall and replaced them with her own. Valentine had also moved in her own washer and dryer, brought along a dog, and called the electric company so the utilities would be in her name. (Police arrested the woman, who unsuccessfully claimed "squatter's rights.")

YOUR FRIEND SAID IT WAS COOL

In 2012, U.S. Army specialist Michael Sharkey was deployed to Afghanistan, and then was stationed in Hawaii, where he moved with his wife. He asked a friend to occasionally check in on his New Port Richey, Florida, home to make sure nobody broke in. The friend didn't do a very good job, because while he was gone, a family broke into the house, changed the locks, and lived there. When

Sharkey returned in 2014 and tried to evict the squatters, they claimed that they had gotten verbal permission from Sharkey's friend to live there, in exchange for making repairs to the house. Both Sharkey and the friend denied that agreement ever took place. Local police refused to evict the squatters, claiming it was a "civil matter." Eventually, the bad feelings they created in the rest of the neighborhood forced the squatters out—especially when one of them was charged with larceny for stealing electricity from another home, and another was found to be in violation of her probation.

AIRBNBEHEREFOREVER

In the summer of 2014, Cory Tschogl placed her Palm Springs, California, condo on Airbnb, a service that allows people to rent homes for short periods, as if they were hotel rooms. Two men booked the condo for 44 days, but at the time of their arrival they'd only paid for 30 days. On day 31, Airbnb informed Tschogl that the renters were not paid up, so Tschogl went to them directly. Under California law, because the men had technically been living in the home for 30 days, they *could* claim squatter's rights. So Tschogl hired a lawyer to try to evict them. The men lawyered up, too, suing Tschogl for reimbursement of medical bills after one of them got sick from drinking unfiltered tap water in the condo. And then, two months after the ordeal began…the two men abruptly moved out and dropped all the lawsuits. More good news: Airbnb paid for all of Tschogl's legal bills.

*   *   *

JOHN LENNON, THE MEAN BEATLE?

"The songs George and Ringo sang were songs that used to be part of my repertoire—the easier ones to sing."

"90 percent of the people on this planet were born out of a bottle of whiskey on a Saturday night."

"I like 'Honky Tonk Women,' but I think Mick [Jagger] is a joke, with all that f*g dancing."

"I think Paul died creatively."

"If there's such a thing as genius—I am one. And if there isn't, I don't care."

"You have to be a b****** to make it, and that's a fact."

"Love means having to say you're sorry every 15 minutes."

La Pinta was only a nickname for Columbus's ship. Nobody knows what the real name was.

ACCORDING TO THE LATEST ANIMAL STUDY

*Can chickens count? Do dogs dig Motown? If a rat wears pants,
does it make him a better lover? Here are the results from some
of the more unusual animal studies we've come across lately.*

Study: "The Effect of Different Genres of Music on the Stress Levels of Kenneled Dogs," *Physiology & Behavior*, March 2017

Purpose: To see if dogs find some types of music more relaxing than others.

Methodology: In a 2015 study, researchers at the University of Glasgow (Scotland) played classical music to dogs in a rescue shelter and found that it helped to reduce their stress levels. But the effect wore off over time, either because the dogs became used to classical music or grew bored by it. In this follow-up study, the researchers alternated classical music with four other genres: soft rock, reggae, pop, and Motown. A different genre was played each day for five days. The dogs' heart rate and cortisol levels were measured, and behaviors that indicate stress, such as barking and standing (in preference to lying down), were monitored.

Findings: "Dogs were found to spend significantly more time lying and less time standing when music was played, regardless of genre," the researchers noted. "Heart Rate Variability was significantly higher, indicative of decreased stress, when dogs were played Soft Rock and Reggae, with a lesser effect observed when Motown, Pop and Classical genres were played." There was also evidence that each dog had its own individual music preference, much like humans.

The positive behavioral effects remained constant over the five days of the study, instead of declining like they did when only classical music was played. This suggests that "the effect of habituation may be reduced by increasing the variety of auditory enrichment provided."

Study: "Evolutionary Trade-Off Between Vocal Tract and Testes Dimensions in Howler Monkeys," *Current Biology*, November 2015

Purpose: To determine if there's a relationship between the power of a male howler monkey's mating calls and the size of his testes.

Methodology: Primatologist Leslie Knapp, who chairs the University of Utah's Department of Anthropology, and a team of researchers calculated the volumes of 255 howler monkey hyoid bones, which are U-shaped bones that support the tongue and larynx. (The larger the hyoid bone, the deeper and louder the howler monkey's call.) The research team also collected data on 66 howler monkeys from other published studies, and measured 21 howler monkeys living in zoos. In addition, males who lived in "multi-male" groups with females were compared with males who lived in "single-male" groups and had exclusive access to the females in the group.

Findings: The howler monkeys with the largest hyoid bones, and thus the loudest mating calls, were found to have the smallest testes. Howler monkeys with smaller hyoid bones and weaker mating calls had the largest testes. Furthermore, "as the number of males per group increases, testes volume also increases" and hyoid bone size decreases.

The researchers theorize that the monkeys who howl the loudest are better able to keep other males away and can mate exclusively with the females in the group. Thus they don't need to "invest" as much in sperm production, since they are not competing against other males to produce offspring with the females. Males whose calls are not strong enough to keep other males away from the females in the group must compensate by investing more in sperm production, to increase the chances that they are the male who produces offspring with the females. "These results," writes Knapp, "provide the first evidence of an evolutionary trade-off between investment in precopulatory vocal characteristics and postcopulatory sperm production."

Study: "Thinking Chickens: A Review of Cognition, Emotion, and Behavior in the Domestic Chicken," *Animal Cognition*, January 2017.

Purpose: To find out if chickens are really the "dumb clucks" that they're commonly thought to be.

Methodology: The paper's author, Lori Marino, undertook a broad survey of the existing peer-reviewed research "on the leading edge of cognition, emotions, personality, and sociality in chickens" to see how their intelligence compares to other bird species and to mammals.

Findings: Chickens are intelligent in ways that were surprising even to Marino: chicks as young as five days old "are able to perform arithmetic operation to a total of five objects. When they were presented with two sets of objects of different quantities disappearing behind two screens, they were able to successfully track which screen hid the larger number by apparently performing simple addition and subtraction."

Chickens have also demonstrated the ability to reason, to perceive time intervals, and there's even evidence to suggest that they can anticipate future events. They're also capable of "Machiavellian intelligence," which means they can

> *Of course, females develop counter-strategies and eventually stop responding to males who call too often in the absence of food.*

perceive things from another chicken's point of view and use this information to manipulate and deceive the other chicken. Males will make "food calls" even when there is no food available, for example, in order to lure females closer, and will cluck more quietly during courting rituals if male rivals are within earshot. "Of course, females develop counter-strategies and eventually stop responding to males who call too often in the absence of food," Marino writes, offering another indication of intelligence. "My overall conclusion is that chickens are just as cognitively, emotionally and socially complex as most other birds and mammals in many areas."

Study: "Effect of Different Types of Textiles on Sexual Activity," *European Urology*, 1993

Purpose: To determine what effect, if any, the wearing of different types of pants has on the sex lives of rats.

Methodology: Seventy-five male rats were divided into five groups of 15 rats each. The first group was dressed in 100 percent polyester pants; the second in 50/50 percent polyester/cotton mix pants; the third in 100 percent cotton pants; the fourth in 100 percent wool pants. The fifth group was the control group: they wore no pants at all. "Sexual behavior was assessed before and after 6 and 12 months of wearing the pants, and 6 months after their removal."

Findings: The groups that wore all-cotton pants or all-wool pants showed "insignificant changes" in sexual activity, but the rats who wore polyester and polyester/cotton mix pants were another story. They showed marked declines in sexual activity. "The reduction was more manifest in the polyester than in the polyester-cotton mix group, and at the 12 month than at the 6 month of examination," the author, Dr. Ahmed Shafik, noted in the paper. "Six months after the removal of the pants, [sexual activity] returned to the pre-test levels."

Bonus: On the basis of these findings and others in similar studies he conducted, Dr. Shafik wondered if wearing polyester underwear might be a viable form of birth control in human subjects. So he recruited 14 married men who were hoping to conceive children and had them wear a 100 percent polyester "suspensory sling" (use your imagination) in place of ordinary underwear for a year. His findings: "All men became azoospermic [infertile] after four months… pregnancies did not occur during this period," he wrote. After the year was up and the volunteers returned to wearing whatever underpants—if any—they had worn before the study, fertility returned to normal after five months. "Five couples achieved the planned-for pregnancy," Dr. Shafik wrote.

Velcro sales struggled for 20 years before they finally began to take off in the late 1970s.

BOWLING LINGO

You probably know what a strike and a gutter ball are—but what about a baby split? Or a sombrero? Not likely, we're guessing. So put on your funny-looking shoes and let's learn some terminology from the great game of ten-pin bowling.

‖NTRODUCTION

Because several of these bowling terms require you to know the numbers assigned to bowling pins as they're standing in their familiar triangle-shaped pattern at the end of a lane, here's a handy diagram to use as a reference.

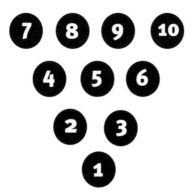

For instance, what's a "7-10 split"? It's when just the 7 and 10 pins are left standing after the first shot in a bowling frame. Look at the diagram above—and you can see why it's considered one of the hardest shots in the game. (If some of the splits in this glossary are hard to picture—the "picket fence," for example—use this diagram to get a picture of the split in your head, as understanding all the different possible split combinations is an essentially important part of bowling.) Now—on to the terms.

Anchor. The last player to "roll" (bowl) in team format bowling. In five-player team play, for example, each player bowls two frames, and the player who bowls last—usually the player with the highest average—is called the team's "anchor." According to bowling historians, the term originated in 1913, when a bowler named Hans Arfsparger, playing in the fifth position for the Anchor Brewing team in Milwaukee, Wisconsin, "struck out" (meaning he bowled three strikes in the final frame of a game) in 94 games straight.

The word "dude" is said in *The Big Lebowski* 160 times (and the Dude drinks 9 White Russians).

Approach. The wooden surface, usually maple on lanes made from wood, behind the foul line, from which the bowler rolls the ball. Also: the start of a bowler's motion, leading up to the delivery of the ball.

Arrows. Also known as "darts," these are the seven dark, pointed marks on the surface of a bowling lane, in a "V" configuration, between 12 and 16 feet past the foul line. Experienced bowlers typically aim their ball at the arrows, rather than at the pins. They're commonly made from inlaid walnut, but cheaper bowling alleys simply paint them on.

Baby split. A "split" is when you leave at least two pins standing after your first shot, and those pins are relatively far apart—making for a difficult second shot. More precisely, it's any combination of pins left after the first shot that 1) doesn't include the head pin (the #1 pin); and 2) includes two pins that weren't next to each other when all ten pins were standing. A "baby split" is when just the 2 and 7 pins, or just the 3 and 10 pins, are left after the first shot. Why "baby" split? Because these are easy splits to convert into a spare, meaning these combinations of pins are relatively easy to knock down with the second shot.

Baby split with company. A baby split with one extra pin left standing—the 2, 7, and 8 pins or the 3, 9, and 10 pins.

Big four: The 4-6-7-10 split. Also called *big ears*, *double pinochle*, and *golden gate*. The first American professional to convert this split on TV during a pro bowling match was Walter Ray Williams Jr., during an ESPN telecast in June 2005. It hasn't been done since.

Bridge. The distance separating the finger holes in a bowling ball.

Brooklyn strike. For a right-hander, it's a strike from a ball that crosses the lane from right to left and strikes the pins to the left of the headpin, between the 1 and 2 pins, rather than between the preferred 1 and 3 pins. For left-handers, it's the opposite—a ball that strikes between the 1 and 3 pins. (In some parts of the country, it's called a *Jersey*.)

Dots. Rows of small, dark marks on 1) the approach, which bowlers can use as guides to set their feet; and 2) on the lane itself, which players can use as guides for their rolls. Like the arrows, they can be either inlaid or painted on.

For more lingo to make you sound like a pro the next time you're at the lanes, roll on over to page 385.

Enjoy your meal!
A McDonald's in Marino, Italy, has a transparent floor so customers can see the Roman road...

UNCLE JOHN'S PAGE OF LISTS

Random bits of information from the BRI's bottomless files.

11 Most Expensive Cities to Move to in 2016

1. Hong Kong, China
2. Luanda, Angola
3. Zürich, Switzerland
4. Singapore, Singapore
5. Tokyo, Japan
6. Kinshasa, Dem. Rep. of the Congo
7. Shanghai, China
8. Geneva, Switzerland
9. N'Djamena, Chad
10. Beijing, China
11. New York City

The 8 Planets in Our Solar System and Their Predominant Hues

1. Mercury: Gray
2. Venus: Pale yellow
3. Earth: Blue
4. Mars: Red
5. Jupiter: Orange
6. Saturn: Gold
7. Uranus: Aquamarine
8. Neptune: Blue

7 Non-Food Companies that Tried to Sell Food

1. Lamborghini: Vodka
2. *Chicken Soup for the Soul* books: Dog food
3. *Cosmopolitan* magazine: Yogurt
4. *For Dummies* books: Wine for Dummies
5. Donald Trump: Steaks
6. Colgate: TV dinners
7. Televangelist Jim Bakker: Survivalist food buckets

7 U.S. Army Units

1. Squad: 8–12 soldiers
2. Platoon: 15–30
3. Company: 80–150
4. Battalion: 300–800
5. Regiment/brigade: 2,000–4,000
6. Division/legion: 10,000–15,000
7. Corps: 20,000–40,000

12 Teetotalers

1. Donald Trump
2. 50 Cent
3. Tyra Banks
4. Jim Carrey
5. Tom Cruise
6. Henry David Thoreau
7. David Bowie
8. Samuel L. Jackson
9. Jay Leno
10. Jennifer Lopez
11. Penn &...
12. Teller

5 Strange Things for Sale on eBay

1. Guinea pig armor ($1,150)
2. Ghost in a jar ($50,922)
3. Zagami, the Martian meteorite ($450,000)
4. Four golf balls that were eaten by a python ($1,400)
5. Toronto mayor Rob Ford's "crack tie" (worn when he confessed to smoking crack) ($1,445)

...and ancient skeletons that were discovered when the restaurant was being constructed.

WEIRD NEW GADGETS

Not long ago, the idea of a tiny computer in your pocket that made phone calls would have seemed impossible. Perhaps some of these devices will be commonplace in the future, too.

SHOCK TO THE SYSTEM

Fitbit and smart watch users can make their devices send alerts when it's time to do certain things, such as move around if they've been sitting for too long. But those are just warnings. They can be easily ignored, and they lack consequences. Not so with a smart watch produced by a company called Pavlok. Users can program the watchlike "behavior training device" to "administer an electric stimulus" whenever they engage in a habit they're trying to break. In other words, it delivers a small (but harmless) electric shock. The company says that its customers have used Pavlok to quit smoking, to stop biting their nails, to prevent oversleeping, and to get up and exercise more.

THE SHOCK *administered from a Pavlok behavior training device can be set anywhere from 17 to 340 volts. The voltage of an electric chair is about 2,000 volts.*

A MAJOR TURNOFF

Most hearing aids work by amplifying sound into a device worn inside one or both ears. A company called Knops has invented what it calls a "volume button" for your ears—basically a reverse hearing aid. Rather than turning up the volume of the outside environment, these turn it down. The user puts these devices, which resemble wireless earbuds, in their ears, and turns a knob on the side of the Knops to determine how much environmental noise they want to hear, from all to some to none. Knops are not electronic—they are completely mechanical. They can completely shut out all noise, and are ideal for people who require silence to concentrate in noisy places, like a coffee shop or an office.

HAIR IT IS

Several divisions of hair-care giant the L'Oreal Group partnered with the high-tech French firm Withings (now part of Nokia) to create the Hair Coach—the

A bolt of lightning is about five times hotter than the Sun.

world's first "smart hairbrush." It looks like a regular hairbrush, but with a little black circle right in the middle. That's actually a highly sensitive, sophisticated microphone. As the user brushes their hair, the microphone can pick up sounds of hair cracking and breaking. It gathers this information and other data relating to the user's brushing habits and sends it all to an app on the user's smartphone, providing a "hair health score" of 1 to 100. It also suggests changes into how to improve hair health and address problems the Hair Coach noticed, such as frizziness and split ends.

SNORE NO MORE

One part of the Nora looks like an oblong white egg that fits in the palm of a hand—like a sleek computer mouse. But it's actually a gadget that promises to help the user stop snoring. The Nora is placed on a bedside table, and as the user sleeps, it can pick up on the faintest, earliest signs that some snoring is about to start. That's when the other part of the Nora—a pillow insert—springs into action. The Nora sends a signal to a tiny pump in the insert, telling it to inflate or deflate. The insert will gently rise or fall, which changes the position of the snoring sleeper's head and neck, opening air passageways to prevent snoring before it can even begin.

A FRIDGE TOO FAR

We've all been at the store, debating whether or not to buy something because we can't remember if we've still got enough on hand back in the fridge at home. The FridgeCam from Smarter makes that minor worry a thing of the past. It's a camera that's placed inside the fridge, and whenever the door is opened, the camera uses that moment of light to take a picture of the refrigerator's contents. It then uploads the images to the Internet, allowing users to see for themselves exactly what's in the fridge without even needing to be there. Cost: $128.83.

PURRFECT

A Portland-based company called PDX Pet Design has solved a problem that cat owners may not even have known they had: They're missing out on the social bonding between cats that they get by licking each other. That's why the company created LICKI brush. It's a brush/tongue extender. The human owner simply fits the LICKI brush over his or her tongue, and then uses it to groom their feline pet, "making it feel like a kitten again by getting an intimate tongue bath from its mother."

Odds that a Russian man born in 1923 died in World War II: 80 percent.

THE CLASS OF 2016

A huge number of famous people died in 2016. Not only were they widely respected, but as these two pages confirm, they were highly quotable.

"I think there should be laughs in everything. Sometimes it's a slammed door, a pie in the face, or just a recognition of our frailties."
—Alan Rickman (1946-2016), actor

"It's always helpful to learn from your mistakes because then your mistakes seem worthwhile."
—Garry Marshall (1934-2016), writer/director

"It isn't the mountains ahead to climb that wear you out; it's the pebble in your shoe."
—Muhammad Ali (1942-2016), boxer

"A long time ago, I realized that I loved to sing, dance, and make people laugh. The trick is finding something that you like and sticking with it."
—Debbie Reynolds (1932-2016) actor

"YOUTH AND BEAUTY ARE NOT ACCOMPLISHMENTS."
—Carrie Fisher (1956-2016), actor and author

"Concentration comes out of a combination of confidence and hunger."
—Arnold Palmer (1929-2016), golfer

"I'll tell you what the public likes more than anything, it's the most rare commodity in the world: honesty."
—Merle Haggard (1937-2016), singer/songwriter

"You learn something out of everything, and you come to realize more than ever that we're all here for a certain space of time, and then it's going to be over, and you better make this count."
—Nancy Reagan (1921-2016), former First Lady

"Just remember, strength and courage. If you stand on principle, you'll never lose."
—Janet Reno (1938-2016), former U.S. Attorney General

"Life is just a party, and parties weren't meant to last."
—Prince (1958-2016), musician

"It's not the hair on your head that matters; it's the kind of hair you have inside."
—Garry Shandling (1949-2016), actor

"There is a crack in everything, that's how the light gets in."
—Leonard Cohen (1934-2016), musician

"You never really understand a person until you consider things from his point of view."
—Harper Lee (1926-2016), author

"We are humans. There is a finite end to this life and we're all going to face it, and a little silliness can help."
—Alan Thicke (1947-2016), actor

"Except for a few guitar chords, everything I've learned in my life that is of any value I've learned from women."
—Glenn Frey (1948-2016), musician

"MACHO DOES NOT PROVE MUCHO."
—Zsa Zsa Gabor (1917-2016), actor

In Italy, children play Lupo Mangia Frutta ("Fruit Eating Wolf"), a game similar to Duck, Duck, Goose.

LOST AT SEA, PART I

Two complete strangers set out on a two-day fishing trip.
Only one came back…fourteen months later.

BACKGROUND

José Salvador Alvarenga was all alone in a foreign country. After running into trouble in his native El Salvador (which involved a bar fight and some stab wounds), he fled north to Mexico, leaving his young daughter and his parents behind. There he started a new life as a commercial fisherman in the village of Costa Azul, at the southern tip of Baja California. By November 2012, Alvarenga was 37 years old and hadn't spoken to his family for nearly a decade. He always said he wanted to become successful before returning home, and that may have been on his mind as he readied his 25-foot fiberglass boat for his next job—a 30-hour trip in the Pacific to catch shark, tuna, and mahi-mahi. But shortly before launching, Alvarenga's usual partner dropped out. So he made a few calls and found a replacement, 22-year-old Ezequiel Córdoba, a local soccer player who went by the nickname "Piñata." Although the experienced boatsman and the rookie deckhand had never met each other before, they were anxious to get out on the water and make some money. If the trip went as planned, Alvarenga would earn about $200, of which $50 was promised to Córdoba.

The trip did not go as planned.

THE IMPERFECT STORM

They set out before dawn on November 17, 2012, and the first leg of the voyage went well; Alvarenga and Córdoba were hauling in fish, quickly filling up the large icebox. However, a huge windstorm from the north—known as a *norteño*—was brewing on the mainland and rolling out to sea. A more cautious fisherman probably wouldn't have risked the trip, especially with an inexperienced shipmate, but Alvarenga was hoping he could get bring in a sizable catch and get back to shore before the weather turned too sour.

Before they could make it back to Costa Azul, 10-foot waves started tossing the tiny boat around so fiercely that it started filling up with water. The two men worked through the night to keep afloat. At one point Córdoba was swept overboard, and Alvarenga had to pull him back in by his hair. Making matters worse, the full icebox was making the small boat top-heavy. One big wave could flip them over. So the men reluctantly dumped their catch and then cut the fishing lines.

But the storm wouldn't let up.

By the next morning, Alvarenga had managed to get them back to within about 15 miles from shore. Then the boat's motor sputtered out, and they couldn't get it started again. Alvarenga radioed for help, but he couldn't give his exact location because their GPS unit hadn't survived the night, and high winds and heavy rain made searching for them nearly impossible. In addition, the small boat had no mast or cabin, so it was too low in the water to be seen from far away. Not long after, the radio died…and the powerless vessel was getting blown farther and farther out to sea.

ADRIFT IN THE PACIFIC

Five days later, the *norteño* finally subsided, but before a search could get underway the boat had drifted far beyond the point where the pilots would look for it. So when no trace was found, the authorities assumed that the two fishermen had perished. They hadn't—Alvarenga and Córdoba were able to ride out the rough seas by tying several lines of buoys to the hull, which helped to keep the boat from capsizing in the high waves. During the storm, they drank rainwater, but that quickly ran out. And most of their food and supplies had either been thrown overboard or got swept away. The most useful tool they had left: a small knife. They probably would have starved, but Alvarenga figured out how to catch fish with his hands—but only from the boat. The shark-infested waters made swimming for fish too dangerous.

Several more days passed, and no more rain came. So on top of having to eat the fish raw, the two men were forced to drink their own urine to stay alive, and that was making them severely dehydrated because of the high salt content. And their only escape from the burning midday sun was to hide inside the icebox. Before long, the realization set in that they were floating toward the middle of the largest expanse of ocean on Earth, and rescue seemed less and less likely. They could feel themselves slowly dying.

BY THE SKIN OF THEIR TEETH

It would be nearly two more weeks before the first rainfall finally came. Overjoyed, Alvarenga and Córdoba let the big drops fall right into their mouths. Then, with their thirst quenched, they collected water in every bottle or bucket they had left.

And with each new day, Alvarenga was coming up with new ways to keep them both alive. He caught small fish by hand and then used them to lure seabirds and sea turtles…while always keeping watch for sharks. He was even

Soccer players in the World Cup run an average of 7 miles per game. (The refs run even more.)

able to scoop up jellyfish and swallow them whole (getting stung in the throat was a small price to pay). At one point they found a bag of garbage floating by and ate the contents—spoiled food—like it was a gourmet meal. When there was no freshwater available, Alvarenga drank turtle blood by sucking it out with a tube from the boat's broken motor. Córdoba, however, wasn't adapting to the survival tactics as well. He couldn't bring himself to drink the turtle blood, and he could barely stomach the raw meat. He was getting weaker.

ADIOS, AMIGO

As the days turned into weeks, and weeks into months, the two strangers bonded. They passed the time by telling each other about their families, and vowed that if only one of them made it back, then he would visit the other man's mother.

Then, about four months into their ordeal, Córdoba ate a raw bird that they later discovered had eaten a sea snake, which is one of the most venomous snakes in the world. The young man survived, but he was never the same after that. He became too afraid to eat anything at all. Alvarenga couldn't even get him to drink any water. He tried bargaining and even forcing water down his shipmate's throat, but Córdoba was either unable or unwilling to keep himself alive. There was nothing Alvarenga could do except watch as the only companion he had in the world starved to death.

Suddenly, Alvarenga was all alone…but his epic journey was just getting started.

To find out how he made it home, turn to page 347.

To find out how he made it home, turn to page 347.

*   *   *

ITS EMPTY EYES ARE WATCHING YOU

Do you believe in haunted dolls? According to a report by Vice UK, there's a thriving haunted doll market on eBay. One recent ad read: "WARNING: Extremely negative doll possessed by sexually sadistic demon!" In the product description, the seller wrote that the little girl doll (which looks innocent enough in the picture) was removed from a Pennsylvania asylum after it closed. "This doll gives off very nasty vibes…she is abusive to all the other dolls I have. Please think it over carefully before bidding. I will not take her back!" A bidding war ensued, and the doll eventually sold for $1,500, which seems to be about the going price for a haunted doll these days.

Although they're defunct in the U.S., Kenny Rogers Roasters restaurants are going strong in Asia.

HOW MUCH FOR THE SWATCH WATCH?

For our 30th anniversary edition, we decided to look back at what some distinctively 1987 items cost back in 1987…and how much those "vintage" items can fetch today.

TEDDY RUXPIN

Then: The hot toy of the time, an animatronic teddy bear that reads stories to kids, cost $60.

Now: An in-the-box, never-used, mint-condition Teddy sold in 2016 for $1,000.

CELL PHONE

Then: A brand-new wireless, battery-operated Radio Shack cell phone sold for $1,495.

Now: You can find a used version on eBay for about $30.

MIKE TYSON'S *PUNCH-OUT*

Then: A copy of the video game for the Nintendo Entertainment System cost $49.99.

Now: An unopened copy can fetch about $1,525 from a collector.

FORD TAURUS

Then: A brand-new Taurus (on the market since 1986) sold for $11,161.

Now: National Appraisal Guides values the '87 Taurus at about $1,400.

THREE MEN AND A BABY ON VHS

Then: A brand-new VHS copy of the top-grossing movie of the year was $79.95.

Now: A used copy can be had for about $3. A brand-new one: about $4.

SONY DISCMAN

Then: The portable, battery-operated CD player sold for $249.99.

Now: A factory-sealed Discman can fetch about $200 on eBay. A used one: about $20.

The "UFO Trail" in Chile averages one new UFO sighting per week.

CAMCORDER

Then: A VHS camcorder that fit comfortably on your shoulder cost $699.99.

Now: Make new home movies the old-fashioned way…for just around $70.

A G.I. JOE ACTION FIGURE

Then: A G.I. Joe action figure sold at toy stores for $4.99.

Now: If you kept it "mint on card" (in its original plastic package), it's worth $50.

PICTIONARY

Then: A copy of the hot new board game cost $30.

Now: A pre-owned "first edition" of the board game can be had for about $30.

TICKETS TO A BROADWAY MUSICAL

Then: Tickets to see *Cats* or *The Phantom of the Opera* were $60 each.

Now: Revivals of both shows are currently running on Broadway, where the average ticket price is around $115.

BON JOVI'S *SLIPPERY WHEN WET*

Then: An LP of the best-selling album of the year went for $9.98.

Now: An unopened, cellophane-wrapped copy of the LP is worth about $50.

SWATCH WATCH

Then: A Swatch with a cool rubber watch band was $29.95.

Now: Collectors pay upwards of $90 for the same watch.

2-LITER OF NEW COKE OR PEPSI FREE

Then: A 2-liter of either soft drink cost 89¢.

Now: If you really want to buy a bottle of old soda, it may cost you as much as $200 on eBay.

JORDACHE JEANS

Then: A pair of acid-wash Jordache jeans ran about $26.

Now: "Vintage" is in! And you can find '80s-era jeans like this for…about $26.

Heil Honey, I'm Home was a 1990 Hitler-themed British sitcom. It was canceled after one episode.

YOU DO...WHAT?

You may not have heard of any of these jobs, but most of them affect your life daily.

THE JOB: Information security consultant

DESCRIPTION: Businesses, hospitals, and government agencies make sure their valuables are secure by hiring an information security consultant to break into their buildings and steal things. ISCs don't just analyze data, they also physically attempt to get past a system with any tools they can muster.

THE JOB: Face feeler

DESCRIPTION: Cosmetic companies hire face feelers, or sensory scientists, in order to determine a beauty product's performance. They are specially trained to analyze the effects of lotions, razors, and other skin-care products through touch. Whether or not a product makes it to the store depends on the data they collect.

THE JOB: Professional snuggler

DESCRIPTION: A snuggler provides "cuddling" to people in need of physical touch. That sounds suspicious, but the snuggling is strictly nonsexual. Snugglers say their services are helpful for those dealing with loneliness after a breakup or the loss of a loved one, and there's scientific evidence that it actually works.

THE JOB: Avalanche controller

DESCRIPTION: Sometimes the best way to prevent avalanches is to start them, and that's what avalanche controllers are hired to do. They monitor geographic areas that create avalanches, and if the situation becomes hazardous, they set off smaller avalanches by throwing mild dynamite charges at the target from a helicopter, and larger ones with a remote-controlled fuel-air explosive.

THE JOB: Nautical cowboy

DESCRIPTION: The job is exactly what it sounds like. Most of the meat you eat is imported from outside the country, and nautical cowboys, or livestock transportation specialists, ensure the cattle make it through the voyage safely. The job is more dangerous than handling livestock on land, but it comes with the added bonus of international travel, a higher paycheck, and a strong bond with the livestock—which turns many nautical cowboys into vegetarians.

Michael Eisner's severance pay when he left Disney in 2005 was reportedly $1 billion.

THE JOB: Chief listening officer

DESCRIPTION: Professional eavesdropping? Yes—that's how big companies find out about their brands' popularity and what products or services the market wants. Chief listening officers (they usually have degrees in marketing) spend their time looking for casual mentions of their brands on social media platforms and analyzing public opinion.

THE JOB: Pet food taster

DESCRIPTION: Just like human food, pet food needs to be tested before it hits the market. Pet food tasters try each new formula to make sure that it tastes as advertised, and contains the proper amount of nutrients for your pet. They also test the packaging to make sure that the product is owner and pet friendly. They are just tasters, not eaters, and they spit out the food after they test it.

THE JOB: Snake milker

DESCRIPTION: Snake milkers extract the venom from poisonous snakes so it can be used to create antivenin and new medicines. A snake milker handles the venomous snakes directly, and provokes the snakes into biting the top of a container so that the venom released can be collected. The job can be lucrative, but a deadly bite is always a possibility.

THE JOB: Professional bridesmaid

DESCRIPTION: Bridesmaids are traditionally tasked with the planning and running of pre-wedding events, as well as helping out on the big day. But bridesmaids have their own lives, so professional bridesmaids can be hired to perform all traditional behind-the-scenes bridesmaid duties, providing personal assistance, planning, and emotional support through all stages of wedding planning and during the wedding itself. They don't usually serve as actual bridesmaids during the ceremony, but will for an extra fee.

THE JOB: Professional pusher

DESCRIPTION: This job is specific to Japan, where public transit is the main form of transportation. It can be hard to fit everyone who needs to be on the train onto the train, so a professional pusher is hired by the station to shove everyone inside the train car so that the doors can close safely. They either use their hands while wearing white gloves, or use a clear plastic rectangle to apply pressure to avoid inappropriate contact with the commuters.

And it's your fault! Workplace stress is estimated to cost U.S. businesses up to $300 million a year.

LOST AND FOUND: GRUESOME EDITION

WARNING: These stories are fascinating…but pretty creepy, so if you're even a little bit squeamish, skip this article

HORROR HOUSE #1

Carpenter Bob Kinghorn was renovating a house in a Toronto, Ontario, neighborhood in July 2007 when he found something wrapped in newspaper beneath the floorboards of the home's attic. He opened it…and found a mummified infant. "It was all crunched up in a fetal position," Kinghorn later said to reporters. "It was pretty horrific." The deceased child, a boy, had lain hidden there for more than 80 years. (The newspaper it was wrapped in was dated September 15, 1925.) Medical examiners said the boy appeared to have died shortly after birth, but there was no way to determine a cause of death. A CBC investigation found that the owners of the house in 1925 were Wesley and Della Russell, and that Mrs. Russell was admitted to a Toronto psychiatric hospital in 1934. Four days after arriving at the hospital, staff records indicate that she spent the afternoon repeating, "I'm a murderer but I can't get away. I'm a murderer but I can't get away." She died in a sanatorium 19 years later.

The CBC also located Russell's 92-year-old niece, who was living in the house at the time of the baby's death. She couldn't add any details to the story, but thought the baby must have been the child of Della Russell's younger sister. She didn't believe her Aunt Della could have been involved in the boy's death. The mummified remains were there through a succession of homeowners, all of them unaware of its presence. The baby was buried at a Toronto cemetery in October 2007, in a ceremony attended by more than 100 people. Bob Kinghorn was the sole pallbearer.

HORROR HOUSE #2

In August 2010, Gloria Gomez, manager of the Glen-Donald Apartments near MacArthur Park in Los Angeles, found three abandoned steamer trunks in the building's basement. The Glen-Donald was built in the 1920s, and had been the home of some of the city's most elite residents over the decades, including some Hollywood stars. Gomez opened the old trunks using a screwdriver, excitedly hoping to find antique treasures. Inside the first two trunks she found…nothing.

Désalpes is the Swiss tradition of adorning cows with flowers as they come down from summer pastures.

The third did contain some things, though—stocks, a fur stole, some photographs and postcards…and two leather doctor's satchels. And inside the satchels? The bodies of two small infants, a boy and a girl, wrapped in newspapers dating to the 1930s. Medical examiners said one of the infants appeared to have died shortly after birth, and that the other may have been stillborn. Police were able to determine that the trunks belonged to a woman named Janet Barrie, who'd been the live-in nurse of George and Mary Knapp from the 1930s to the 1960s. Police located one of Barrie's relatives, who agreed to provide DNA evidence…and Barrie turned out to be the children's mother. Why the remains were hidden away in a steamer trunk remains a mystery.

The identity of the children's father couldn't be determined, but there's some suspicion that it was George Knapp. He and Barrie were married after Mary Knapp died in 1964. The couple continued to live in the Glen-Donald apartment until George Knapp died in 1968. Barrie then moved away, leaving the steamer trunks behind. She died in Canada in 1992.

HORROR HOUSE #3

In October 2003, Stephen and Deena Roberts of Brownwood, Texas, decided to remodel the unused second-story attic of the large A-frame home they'd been living in for three years. Reason: their two children were growing up, and they needed their own bedrooms. As they inspected the attic, Deena noticed something she'd never seen before: a small door in the back of a built-in closet. She opened it, peered into a musty crawl space, and saw a plastic garbage bag. Inside that was a paper bag…and inside that were the mummified remains of a newborn baby. The couple immediately called the police, who sent the garbage bag to medical examiners in Austin, where they identified the remains of two more newborns inside the bag. After years of investigation, the following facts were determined: the house was built in 1987 by James and Doris Bowling; the couple lived there until they died—James in 1999 and Doris in 2000—after which their three adult children sold the family home. Two of those children were located by investigators. They agreed to give DNA samples to police, and the infants were proven to have been their siblings. (The shocked Bowling children said they knew nothing about the newborns). Even more macabre, medical examiners determined that all three newborns were born and died around 1960—roughly 40 years before they were discovered—meaning that James and Doris Bowling brought the deceased infants with them when they moved into the house in 1992. How the infants died and why the Bowlings never reported the deaths remains unknown.

We don't want to speculate, but Kami, the HIV-positive Muppet, hasn't been seen since 2009.

THE SHOW MUST GO ON...AND ON

Here are some folks who didn't let a little thing like age or time served knock them off the stage, the silver screen, the radio, or the TV.

Herbert "The Cool Gent" Kent

Claim to Fame: Longest DJ career in radio history

Details: In 1944 the 16-year-old Kent got a job hosting a classical music show at WBEZ radio in Chicago. Over the years he worked at 11 different stations in and around Chicago, and he is credited with helping launch the careers of numerous Motown greats like the Temptations, Martha and the Vandellas, and Smokey Robinson. In October 2016, he celebrated his 88th birthday and his 72nd year on the air. A few weeks after that, he delivered what turned out to be his final radio broadcast, and then died at home a few hours later.

Betty White

Claim to Fame: The longest TV career of any actor

Details: White's career is as old as broadcast television itself: she was just three months out of high school in 1939 when she and a friend sang songs on a broadcast of an experimental television station in Los Angeles. That was the same year that NBC began airing the first regular television broadcasts. TV was suspended during World War II (1941–45), but when it returned after the war so did White, and she's been on TV ever since. In 2017 she turned 95 and marked her 73rd year on the tube.

I'm a health nut. My favorite food is hot dogs with French fries. And my exercise: I have a two-story house and a very bad memory, so I'm up and down those stairs.

—Betty White

Dercy Gonçalves

Claim to Fame: The longest acting career, period

Details: Gonçalves, who was born in Brazil in 1907, ran away from home when she was 15 and joined a traveling theater troupe. She performed regularly on stage, film, and TV for the rest of her life. Her final role was in the 2008 film *Nossa Vida Nao Cabe Num Opala* (*Our Life Does Not Fit Into an Opal*) at the age of 101, bringing her 86-year acting career to an end. She died later that year.

Dave Ward
Claim to Fame: Longest career as a TV news broadcaster

Details: In 1966 Ward was hired as a news reporter for KTRK in Houston, Texas. Two years later he was promoted to anchor of the 6:00 p.m. news, a job he held until the end of 2016, when he retired at the age of 77 after more than 50 years at the station. At last report he was still making occasional TV appearances, but he no longer anchors the news.

Hanna Meron
Claim to Fame: Longest theater career

Details: Meron, who was born in Berlin, Germany, in 1923, made her first stage appearance in a children's theater at the age of four. When the Nazis came to power, she emigrated with her family to France, and then to the British mandate of Palestine, which became the state of Israel in 1948. She continued acting even after losing her left leg in a 1970 terrorist attack. She appeared in several films over the years and at least one TV sitcom, but she never left the theater. She broke the record for longest theater career in 2011 when she was 87, and continued acting until shortly before her death in 2014 at the age of 90.

Dick Goddard
Claim to Fame: Longest career as a TV weather forecaster

Details: Goddard got his introduction to meteorology in the U.S. Air Force in the late 1950s. After he left the service he studied broadcasting at Kent State University in Ohio, then in 1961 he landed his first TV weather forecasting job at KYW Channel 3 in Cleveland. In 1980 he moved to WJW Channel 8 and delivered weather forecasts there for the next 38 years until he retired in 2016 at the age of 85, after 55 years on the air.

*　　*　　*

"If world peace was as important to people as getting tweeted back by their favorite celebrity, we'd live in a blissful Utopia."

—Adam Levine

Al Roker and Lenny Kravitz are cousins.

SHAW'S ALPHABET

Here's the story of how a major English writer tried to make the world abandon the Latin alphabet in favor of something very, very different.

THE SHAWGA BEGINS

Irish playwright George Bernard Shaw is widely regarded as one of the best English-language writers of all time. Among his major works, many of which are still produced today, are *Saint Joan*, *Caesar and Cleopatra*, *Major Barbara*, and *Pygmalion*, which was adapted into the musical *My Fair Lady*.

Shaw was also a prolific and outspoken essayist. In the late 19th and early 20th centuries, he wrote dozens of articles espousing the benefits of revolutionary ideas such as socialism, feminism, and vegetarianism. But the cause he felt most strongly about was his desire to preserve and beatify the English language. While the plot of *Pygmalion* (and *My Fair Lady*) focuses on the romance between a Cockney flower girl and the professor who teaches her to speak properly, Shaw wrote the play specifically to emphasize the need for people to be more eloquent. In the preface to the play, Shaw wrote: "The English have no respect for their language, and will not teach their children to speak it. The reformer England needs today is an energetic phonetic enthusiast; that is why I have made such a one the hero of a popular play."

One way Shaw thought that English could be improved was to abolish the standard, 26-letter English alphabet. He believed the system of different, elaborately shaped letters was arbitrary, and a waste of time, energy, and ink. Nor did it make sense for words with the same letters and letter combinations to have completely different pronunciation. So when he died in 1950, he stipulated in his will that a contest be held to develop a new English writing system. The person who created the best Shaw, or Shavian, alphabet, as it was to be called, would receive a cash prize of £500 and the rights to publish Shaw's play *Androcles and the Lion* with the new system. The rules: The alphabet had to contain at least 40 letters and eliminate the need for letter groupings to create common phonetic sounds, as well as diacritical marks.

AS EASY AS ꩜ ꞁ ꞇ

The winners: a team of four scholars led by 71-year-old academic and linguist Ronald Kingsley Read. (Yes, the guy who invented a new letter system was named *Read*.) Read's system consisted of 48 letters, exceeding the requirement of Shaw's will. As for capital letters, there are none in the Shaw alphabet. Read devised a "namer dot" placed by the letter to efficiently indicate—and with as little effort as possible—that the word is a proper name. Also, certain sounds in the English language that require two letters, such as "th" in a word like "that," got their own dedicated character.

TAKE A LETTER

Here is Read's Shaw alphabet, along with the sounds each short little line or loop was supposed to represent.

ꞁ	"pih" as in "pip"
ꞁ	"bih" as in "bit"
ꞁ	"tuh" as in "task"
ꞁ	"duh" as in "dead"
ꞁ	"kuh" as in "kick"
ꞁ	"guh" as in "gang"
J	"f" as in "fail"
ꞁ	"vuh" as in "vow"
ꝺ	"th" as in "thigh"
ꝺ	"th" as in "they"
ꞁ	"sss" as in "so"
ꞁ	"z" as in "zoo"
ꞁ	"sh" as in "sure" or "shore"
ꞁ	"zh" as in "treasure"
ꞁ	"chuh" as in "church"
ꞁ	"juh" as in "judge"
\	"yuh" as in "yes"
/	"wuh" as in "went"
ꞁ	"huh" as in "hungry"
ꞁ	"ha" as in "ha-ha"
c	"law" as in "lollipop"
ꞁ	"rah" as in "roar"
ꞁ	"muh" as in "mine"
\	"nuh" as in "nothing"
ꞁ	"ih" as in "if"

The son of a seamstress, U.S. president Andrew Johnson sewed his own clothes.

ㅓ "ea" as in "beat"

ㄴ "eh" as in "egg"

ㄷ "aye" as in "age"

ㅗ "ah" as in "mash"

ㄱ "eye" as in "iced"

ㄱ "ah" as in "ado"

ㄱ "uh" as in "up"

ㄱ "awe" as in "on"

ㅇ "oh" as in "moat"

ᴠ "uh" as in "book"

ᴧ "oo" as in "snooze"

ㄑ "ow" as in "out"

ㄱ "oy" as in "oil"

ㄹ "aw" as in "ah-ha"

ㄹ "awe" as in "awesome"

ㅁ "are"

ㄴ "or"

ᴖ "air"

ᴗ "urr" as in "urge"

ᴖ "arr" as in "array"

ᴖ "ea" as in "ear"

ᴦ "ian" as in "Egyptian"

ᴎ "yew" as in "you"

ALPHABET SOUP

The Shavian alphabet failed to catch on. For while it did require less effort to use than the traditional Latin-based English alphabet, it also required a lot of effort to learn it—and people weren't interested in relearning a language they already knew. (Especially one with an alphabet that was nearly twice as long as the old one.) Read did publish his "simplified" version of *Androcles and the Lion*, and for years ran a general-interest magazine in the Shaw alphabet. He also developed two simpler versions—one called Quikscript and another called Soundspell—and all three are available as computer fonts. But there's not much use for them (except in articles like this) because the alphabet was never widely adopted.

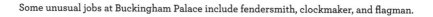

Some unusual jobs at Buckingham Palace include fendersmith, clockmaker, and flagman.

WEIRD BEER NEWS

There's nothing all that weird about beer itself. A magical combination of water, yeast, barley, and hops, sure, but not weird. But these stories about it sure are.

CHIP, CHIP, HOORAY!

At about 3:00 a.m. one night in July 2016, two semi trucks collided on Interstate 95 in Brevard County, Florida. One of the vehicles was carrying a load of Doritos, and the other was on its way to deliver cases of canned Busch Beer. Chips and beer were spilled all over the highway, shutting down two southbound lanes for hours. "Neither driver was hurt," said a spokesperson for the Florida Highway Patrol, "but you had Doritos and Busch beer all over I-95. That's like a Super Bowl commercial right there."

LOCATION, LOCATION, LOCATION

BrewDog is a Scottish brewery that specializes in making really weird beers. (For example, in 2010 it unveiled the End of History—one of the strongest beers ever made, with an alcohol content of 55 percent. It came in a bottle shoved inside a taxidermied squirrel.) BrewDog opened a taproom in Columbus, Ohio. Sample brews: Dead Pony Club, Jet Black Heart, Elvis Juice, and Cocoa Psycho. Now they want to put another business next door: the world's first beer-themed hotel. BrewDog is trying to raise $6 million to build the DogHouse, which will have a beer fridge in every room's shower. Other amenities will include malted barley massages, beer for breakfast, and beer-filled hot tubs.

TOTALLY PUNK

Graeme Wallace works as the packing manager for BrewDog. One day in early 2016, he was preparing to ship out a batch of 200,000 cans of Punk IPA (the company's signature beer) all over the United Kingdom. Personally, he didn't think there was anything particularly "punk" about the beer, so he took upon himself to stamp "MOTHER F***** DAY" along with the product code on the bottom of all 200,000 cans. BrewDog higher-ups didn't find out for a few weeks, when BrewDog drinkers noticed the code and started posting pictures of the naughty word on social media. BrewDog issued a recall for the 200,000 offensive cans. As for Graeme, he wasn't fired—bosses thought it was so funny that they named him employee of the month.

NAMASTE

Yoga is an ancient form of exercise and spiritual practice that guides participants to a better overall state of well-being. Beer is also ancient, but it's not *quite* as healthy as yoga. Nevertheless, a German yoga studio called BierYoga has successfully combined the two concepts. "We take the philosophies of yoga and pair it with the pleasure of beer-drinking to reach your highest level of consciousness," says yogi Jhula, the inventor of BierYoga. After starting out as an activity class at festivals in Berlin, BierYoga is now being taught in the United States, Canada, and Australia. And it's not just doing yoga while drinking a beer. A bottle of suds is used as a prop in all of the exercises—adherents use the bottles in their practice. For example, they might balance a beer on their heads during a "tree pose," or hoist the beer upward in a "sun salutation." (Then they get to drink it.)

BEER WITH A WU-TANGY FLAVOR

Pretty much anything can be used to give beer a special or distinctive flavor, from fruits to chili peppers to coffee. Apparently, music can make a beer stand out, too. In 2016 Dock Street Beer of Philadelphia created a pineapple-and-orange-flavored golden saison beer that was aged by the Wu-Tang Clan. This is to say, the brewers strapped an iPod and a speaker to the side of the barrel where the beer is stored, and played a constant, repeating playlist of songs by the '90s rap group. "I listen to music every day in the brewery and I've wanted to do a series of beers based on the music I like," says Dock Street brewmaster Vince Desrosiers. "It started as a joke, and then we wondered if the bass would cause enough vibration to move the yeast around and create some different flavors."

WASTE NOT, WANT NOT

Remember how we said coffee can be used to change a beer's flavor? Japanese brewery Sankt Gallen tried that. Except it procured coffee beans harvested from a huge pile of elephant poop. The brewery got the beans from the Golden Triangle Elephant Foundation, an elephant preserve in Thailand. The elephants there were fed a style of coffee bean called "Black Ivory." The beans then passed undigested through the elephants…and came out the other end. Next, the beans were collected and used to flavor a beer called Un, Kono Kuro. And while it's maybe not the grossest part of this story, it is pretty gross that Sankt Gallen calls the beer a "chocolate stout" even though the beer doesn't contain any chocolate.

COLD WAR SECRET: PROJECT FURTHERANCE

For decades the public position of the U.S. government has been that only the president can order a nuclear strike. The reality, it turns out, is quite a bit more complicated.

THE BIG ONE

From the beginning of the atomic age, American presidents have had to wrestle with the question of who should control the country's nuclear weapons—the military or the civilian government. After the bombing of the Japanese cities of Hiroshima and Nagasaki in the closing days of World War II, many in the armed forces argued that since the bombs were tools of war, the military, not the president, should decide when, where, and how they should be used. But President Harry Truman (1945–53) saw it differently. He thought the president and the president alone should have the power to order a nuclear attack.

❝ *You have got to understand that this isn't a military weapon,* ❞

Truman said in 1948. "It is used to wipe out women and children and unarmed people, and not for military uses. So we have got to treat this differently from rifles and cannon and ordinary things like that." Truman feared that if the military was given unfettered control over atomic bombs, "some dashing lieutenant colonel" might decide on his own "when would be the proper time to drop one."

BEHIND THE SCENES

As far as anyone outside the highest levels of government knew, that was where the matter stood for the next 40 years: only the president could order a nuclear attack. But behind the scenes, the thinking inside of government began to change as soon as the Soviet Union tested their first atomic bomb in the summer of 1949, then followed it up with a much more powerful hydrogen, or *thermonuclear*, bomb in 1955. (The United States detonated its first hydrogen bomb in 1952.)

Once the Soviets started stockpiling their own nuclear weapons and developing long-range bombers to deliver them to the United States, the possibility of a surprise first strike loomed large in the minds of American military planners, who

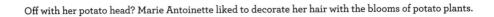

Off with her potato head? Marie Antoinette liked to decorate her hair with the blooms of potato plants.

well remembered the bombing of Pearl Harbor less than a decade before. What if the Soviets dropped an atomic bomb on Washington, D.C., and the president was either killed in the attack or couldn't be located? Even if he was still in charge, he might not be able to contact the military if communications were knocked out in the attack. So who would order the nuclear counterstrike? If no one else was able to do it, American bombers loaded with nuclear weapons might be destroyed on the runway waiting for orders to retaliate that would never come.

IKE'S SECRET ORDERS

Truman's successor, Dwight D. Eisenhower (1953–61), was just as reluctant to delegate his war powers. Like Truman, Eisenhower worried that doing so might make it possible for someone to "do something foolish down the chain of command" as he put it, by starting a nuclear war on his own. But Eisenhower eventually decided that the risks associated with doing nothing were even greater, and in the late 1950s he issued a series of orders, collectively code-named Furtherance, that gave senior military commanders "pre-authorization" to order nuclear attacks—but only under certain emergency conditions.

GO CODES

The Furtherance orders envisioned two sets of circumstances in which the president would be unable to order the use of nuclear weapons:

• **The first:** If time was of the essence. If, for example, the Soviets suddenly attacked U.S. and NATO forces in Western Europe and "the urgency of time and circumstances clearly does not permit a specific decision by the president," then the commander of those forces could use nuclear weapons against the attacking forces without consulting the president. In such a case, the size of the response would be "limited to such size and numbers of weapons and to such targets as are necessary," and the authorization to use nuclear weapons remained in effect "only until it is possible…to communicate with the president."

• **The second:** If the United States itself was attacked and the president was killed or went missing as a result. In this case the orders were to activate the Single Integrated Operational Plan (SIOP), the military's plan for a full-scale nuclear war against the Soviet Union, China, and the Soviet bloc countries in Eastern Europe.

The SIOP was to be activated even if the attack on the United States was made with conventional forces, not nuclear weapons. And both the Soviet Union and China would be targeted in the counterstrike, even if it wasn't clear who was responsible for the attack. Indeed, both would be targeted even if it wasn't clear that *either* of them had anything to do with it. And even if the

Political protest: Maryland's 1775 $4 bill depicts King George III trampling the Magna Carta.

initial attack appeared to be some kind of an *accident*, the stakes were so high that the Furtherance orders required a full nuclear retaliatory strike anyway.

So what would a full-scale nuclear war look like? Over a period of 28 hours, wave after wave of B-52 bombers and Jupiter, Atlas, and Trident nuclear missiles would strike 3,729 targets in the Soviet Union, China, North Korea, and Eastern Europe. The SIOP called for the most valuable targets to be hit by as many as six nuclear weapons each, to be sure they really were destroyed. Military planners estimated that more than 220 million people, including more than half the Soviet population, would be killed immediately, and tens or perhaps hundreds of millions more would die later from burns, radiation sickness, exposure, and other causes. Why strike so hard? The Atomic Energy Commission estimated that 39 million Americans would die in the first hours of a full-scale nuclear war with the Soviet Union, which was why so much emphasis was placed on hitting the Soviets as hard as possible. American military planners wanted to make the ensuing war as one-sided in favor of the United States.

SHHH!

The idea of delegating a president's war powers under any circumstances was so controversial that Eisenhower admitted he was "very fearful of writing papers on the matter." Even after the Furtherance orders were put on paper, they were shown only to a handful of senior military officials—the ones who would order the nuclear strikes if the president was unable to. These officers were given strict orders not to share the information with anyone, and as far as anyone knows, they didn't. The orders remained one of the best-kept secrets of the Cold War, and were revealed to the public only in the 1980s.

TIME FOR A CHANGE

The Furtherance orders remained in effect for the rest of Eisenhower's presidency, and for that of his successor, John F. Kennedy. But by the mid-1960s, the idea of launching a full-scale nuclear war in response to a conventional or even an accidental attack came to be seen as overkill. During Lyndon B. Johnson's presidency, the orders were revised to give the military more flexibility. If the Soviets attacked with only conventional weapons, the United States would respond in kind, inaugurating a policy of no first use of nuclear weapons. And instead of a full-scale attack against both the Soviet Union and China, military commanders could launch a limited response against whichever country they believed was responsible for the first attack. The changes went into effect in 1968, moving America a step or two back from the brink of nuclear war.

Besides Rosie the Riveter, there was Wendy the Welder, Bertha the Burner, and Jenny on the Job.

HOW MUCH DO THEY MAKE?

Everyone wants to know how much the other guy is getting. It's human nature. Only problem: After you read this, you might wonder if it's too late for a career change.

NFL referees. In 2013 the average salary for an NFL referee was $173,000. And according to the stipulations in their latest contract, that will rise to $201,000 by 2019. Sound like a lot? Maybe, but keep in mind that aside from officiating games, referees can spend up to 30 hours a week viewing game footage, keeping up on the NFL's complex rules, and doing administrative work. On the other hand, the job only requires about six months of work a year—unless the refs are picked to officiate playoff games and the Super Bowl, in which case they are paid big bonuses—and for most, being a referee is actually a side job.

Baggage handlers. The people who do the physical work of loading and unloading baggage from commercial airliners at airports around the country make about $24,000 a year. Supervisors average about $49,000.

Veterinarians. According to the latest figures from the Bureau of Labor Statistics, American veterinarians make an average of about $88,000 a year. The highest-paid make more than $150,000.

Coal miners. The average annual pay of the roughly 83,000 coal miners in the United States: about $82,000.

MLB umpires. Starting salary for Major League Baseball umpires: about $120,000. Annual salary for senior umpires: $350,000 or more. MLB umpires have between four and six months off every year, and, like NFL referees and officials in many other professional sports, many have other jobs during the off season.

Professional commercial extras. If they are members of the Screen Actors Guild-American Federation of Television and Radio Artists, the union that represents screen entertainers, a person who appears as a nonspeaking extra in a TV commercial earns a base pay of $366—a day. And that's for an eight-hour workday. If they work longer than that, the first two hours of overtime are paid at about $550 an hour. After that, it's about $730 an hour. Some commercial extras do the work as a career—and can earn as much as $80,000 a year. Base pay for nonunion commercial extras: as little as $60 a day. The work of a commercial extra, union or nonunion, often entails waiting to be called to appear in a scene, and many days they do no actual work at all. But they still get paid.

Crane operators. The average annual salary of American crane operators is about $55,000.

Surgeons. Surgeons, according to the Bureau of Labor Statistics, are physicians "who treat diseases, injuries, and deformities by invasive, minimally invasive, or noninvasive surgical methods, such as using instruments, appliances, or by manual manipulation." Those who have their own practices earn an average annual salary of about $256,000; those in hospitals make about $213,000. (Neurosurgeons, who specialize in surgery of the brain and spinal column, earn a lot more: an average of about $540,000 annually.)

Dental assistants. Dental assistants average about $37,000 a year.

Janitors. Public school janitors earn an average yearly salary of about $29,000. (Note: that's the *national* average. Janitors in New York City public schools are paid around $109,000 a year.)

Butchers. Butchers in grocery stores and specialty meat shops in the United States earn an average of $29,000 a year.

Phlebotomists. Phlebotomists—the people who draw blood in hospitals, clinics, blood donor centers, etc.—earn $31,000 a year on average.

Plumbers. Plumbers are included in a category of workers with pipelayers, pipefitters, and steamfitters, and are described as workers "who install and repair pipes that carry liquids or gases to, from, and within businesses, homes, and factories." They make an average of just over $50,000 a year.

NBA referees. National Basketball Association referees make the most of any refs in American professional sports. Entry level salary: $150,000. Salary of senior NBA refs: $550,000 or more a year. (Referees in the Women's National Basketball Association make about $500 per game, or up to $19,000 a year.)

School bus driver. The average American school bus driver gets an annual salary of about $31,000 a year.

The first U.S. airmail was sent by balloon from Lafayette, Indiana, in 1859. The intended destination...

THE DREAM BEAM

The story of a health-care breakthrough that sounded too good to be true…because it was.

THE BEAM IS STILL ALIVE

More than 29 million Americans have diabetes. To manage the disease, they monitor their blood glucose levels by pricking their finger and putting a drop of blood on a little strip that goes into a machine and gives an accurate reading in less than a minute. Miraculous as that is, it still involves painful needles and expensive glucose test strips, which make up a $2.5 billion market. With all that money, and millions of diabetics clamoring for advanced medical technology to replace painful finger sticks, a few companies set out to find a better way. In 1991, the Maryland medical technology company Futrex announced that it had developed a way to measure blood glucose without drawing blood—by shining a laser through the skin.

The company's president, Robert Rosenthal, demonstrated the product in public, and investors were hooked: Within three years, Futrex had raised $1.85 million in venture capital. Plans to start selling shares in the company were underway for 1995, along with bringing to market the product they were calling the Dream Beam.

But after distributing its prospectus to 20,000 potential investors, Futrex abruptly, and without reason, canceled its initial public offering. However, once a company starts talking about an IPO and has the potential for millions of dollars changing hands, that gets the attention of the Securities and Exchange Commission (SEC). That agency's mission: "protect investors, maintain fair, orderly, and efficient markets, and facilitate capital formation." In other words, to root out stock scams. Which is precisely what was going on at Futrex. The Dream Beam, it turns out, didn't work at all.

> **UNCONTROLLED** *diabetes can lead to sugar "spilling" into the urine. Centuries ago, that's how diabetes was diagnosed. In the late 1600s, renowned English physician Thomas Willis diagnosed it using a technique called uroscopy…or tasting urine.*

A DREAM DEFERRED

The data that the company always cited, both to its investors and to the U.S. Food and Drug Administration (which was still working its way through the

…was New York City, but the balloon only made it as far as Crawfordsville, 30 miles away.

approval process for the device) was a 1991 study conducted at New York's Mt. Sinai Medical Center. Blood sugar readings were taken from infrared scans of patients' fingers, and compared to tests done in the traditional finger stick/glucose strip method. Futrex said that the laser readings provided the same results as the blood draw method. In reality, the readings were wildly different, indicating that the laser did not work.

Futrex conducted more studies in 1992, with more infrared readings compared to more blood readings. Again, no correlation was found…so Futrex simply dismissed the study out of hand. But Futrex kept working toward bringing the Dream Beam to market, hoping that they'd somehow have the technology worked out by the time it was ready for consumers. And with every test and every study, they obtained the exact same results: the Dream Beam didn't work.

Meanwhile, Futrex CEO Bob Rosenthal kept attending investor meetings and doing product presentations with prototypes of the Dream Beam, in which he would demonstrate it on himself. Amazingly, he'd tell attendees that the reading "seemed correct," because he was a diabetic and knew what different levels "felt" like. It turns out that before each presentation, a Futrex employee had rigged the device to display a preprogrammed number when Rosenthal turned it on and pretended to test his blood sugar. The machine wasn't testing his blood at all.

THE DREAM IS DEAD

In 1996, the SEC formally charged Futrex and Rosenthal with fraud. Without admitting or denying the allegations, the defendants consented to the SEC findings, and Rosenthal was ordered to pay a $50,000 fine. According to the SEC, "neither the Dream Beam nor any other infrared blood glucose analyzer tested by Futrex has ever been capable of predicting blood glucose levels accurately." Further, "not one of Futrex's top scientific and technical employees has ever reviewed or analyzed any data that would support claims made by Rosenthal and Futrex that the blood glucose analyzer, as configured by Futrex, actually works."

It's been more than 20 years since the Dream Beam catastrophe, but the idea of through-the-skin lasers testing blood sugar has not been abandoned. And the technology is at about the same place where it was 20 years ago. A study in 2012 reviewed ten different technologies that are being studied in an effort to find a way to test blood glucose without needles and pain, but the study's authors concluded that we still have a long way to go. "At this stage" the authors said, "we are still far away from achieving the goal of noninvasive blood glucose monitoring, with many technical issues yet to be resolved."

Millions of diabetics are patiently waiting.

The "figgy pudding" in "We Wish You a Merry Christmas" refers to plum pudding…which contains no plums.

WEIRD WORLD MUSEUMS

When traveling, you could see the usual sites listed in every guidebook…
or you could check out one of these quirky museums.

Museum: Instant Ramen Museum
Location: Osaka, Japan
Details: In 1958, a Japanese inventor named Momofuku Ando perfected instant ramen noodles. Just add boiling water, and it made a meal! Since then, Ando's invention has been enjoyed by millions around the world (especially college students…because it's so cheap), and has been produced by many different companies, including the one Ando founded: Cup Noodles. This museum, located in Ando's hometown, is devoted to the history of the instant noodle, and includes exhibits where guests can roll their own noodles, and design their own noodle bowl.
Be sure to see: The walk-through tunnel decorated with the labels from more than 800 different packages of ramen.

Museum: Meguro Parasitological Museum
Location: Tokyo, Japan
Details: Countless museums feature exhibits on animals and even insects, but what about the common parasite—creatures that live inside of (and off of) other living creatures? This one-of-a-kind museum in central Tokyo gives them their proper due with exhibits on parasite diversity, the life cycle of the parasite, and more than 300 parasite specimens on display. (Credentialed scientists can visit the museum's research library, which contains 60,000 more parasite specimens.)
Be sure to see: A preserved tapeworm that was removed from a real human's small intestine. (It's 8.8 meters—about 29 feet—long.)

Museum: Funeral Carriage Museum
Location: Barcelona, Spain
Details: Housed in a building that's adjacent to the Montjuic Cemetery, the museum focuses on a very specific element of the grieving process—the hearses that carried the deceased to their final resting place. The Funeral Carriage Museum is the final resting place of more than a dozen old-fashioned—and extremely ornate—horse-drawn funeral carriages dating back as far as the 18th century. (The museum also has three early motorized hearses.)

Snap! On average, the U.S. Patent Office receives applications for 20 new mousetrap patents each year.

Be sure to see: The museum's library on death customs from around the world. The collection comprises 3,600 books and periodicals on what people do with their dead, from the prehistoric era to the present.

Museum: Vampire Museum

Location: Paris, France

Details: The museum is an exhaustive, *undying* look at the history of the fictional bloodsucker through centuries of literature and film. Visitors (by appointment only) can explore exhibits on vampire rituals in Parisian cemeteries, check out a genuine medieval vampire-killing kit (the kit is real, not the vampires), and a painting of a vampire made by a convicted French murderer.

Be sure to see: The collection of autographs of every actor who's ever played Dracula on screen.

Museum: Cancún Underwater Museum

Location: Cancún, Mexico

Details: The 500 life-size statues that sit on the ocean floor off the coast of this Mexican resort town are covered in sea vegetation, suggesting that they're ancient artifacts from a lost civilization. But they're not. The clay sculptures were built specifically to foster marine life, a collaboration between marine biologists and sculptor Jason deCaires Taylor. The entire museum is underwater, so visitors can only experience the art by snorkeling, scuba diving, or taking a glass-bottom boat ride.

Be sure to see: *Inertia*, a sculpture of an overweight man sitting on a couch watching television.

Museum: Museum of Broken Relationships

Location: Zagreb, Croatia

Details: After they ended their relationship in 2003, Croatian artists Olinka Vistica and Drazen Grubisic decided to create a traveling exhibition devoted to relics of other people's romances gone sour. The museum became a permanent fixture in 2010, providing visitors with "a chance to overcome the emotional collapse" of a breakup. The museum also takes donations—things former lovers have left behind, such as letters, fuzzy handcuffs, wedding rings, stuffed animals, cookies, and unused wedding dresses. (There's a new satellite of the Museum of Broken Relationships located in Los Angeles, California.)

Be sure to see: The "Exe Axe," used by a German woman to chop up all of her ex's furniture. You'll find it in the "Rage and Fury" room.

Cold shoulder: In ice-skating, judges can deduct points for "inappropriate costume."

I HEARD IT ON THE GOOGLE

Was President Obama planning a coup d'état as his presidency was winding down?
According to the world's largest search engine, the answer seems to be yes.

THAT'S A FACT(?)

You may have noticed that sometimes when you do a Google search, Google will select what it believes is the best answer and highlight it in a special box, rather than giving you a list of websites to visit for more information. If you Google "how many feet in a mile," for example, Google will respond with a box that reads "1 mile = 5,280 feet." It replies to the query "20th president of the United States" with a box that reads "President of the United States (20): James A. Garfield," along with Garfield's portrait.

These special boxes, which were introduced in 2014, are called "featured snippets in search," and Google only serves them up when it believes that the answer it is providing to your query is factually correct and beyond dispute. But featured snippets are selected by computers, not humans. Google processes more than 5 billion queries each day, and every once in a while it selects an unreliable website and serves up a ridiculous answer such as "According to the *Daily Star*, Theresa May is our new prime minister but already online users have exploded with rumours that she is actually a lizard in disguise."

DOUBLE TROUBLE

The situation was made worse when Google introduced a "smart speaker" called Google Home in 2016. Google Home is like a stereo speaker connected to the Internet: When you ask it a question, like Siri on an iPhone or Google Now on an Android phone, it searches the Internet for the answer. When it finds what it believes is the best answer, it recites the information aloud through the speaker.

And that's where the trouble starts. When you read a web page that's full of nonsense, there are often visual cues to warn you that the source is unreliable: silly headlines, unprofessional graphics, or ads for ridiculous products that suggest the site may not be as reliable as *Scientific American* magazine or the BBC. But when the same nonsense is read *to you* through the speaker of Google Home, all of those visual cues are stripped away. You are left with Google telling you that Theresa May is a lizard in disguise, with the same authoritative voice that tells you there are 16 ounces in a pound and 50 states in the United States of America.

Squid go through water tail first, not head first.

OOPS!

Google admits that it isn't perfect. "Featured snippets in search provide an automatic and algorithmic match to a given search query, and the content comes from third-party sites. Unfortunately, there are instances when we feature a site with inappropriate or misleading content," a company spokesperson told reporters in March 2017. "When we are alerted to a featured snippet that violates our policies, we work quickly to remove it. We apologize for any offence this may have caused."

The biggest boo-boos are often posted on Facebook and other social media sites, where they quickly go viral and find their 15 minutes of Internet fame. Here are some of the more bizarre examples we've found:

Query: "Is Obama planning a coup?"
Featured Snippet: "According to details exposed in Western Centre for Journalism's exclusive video, not only could **Obama** be in bed with the communist Chinese, but **Obama** may in fact be **planning** a communist **coup** d'état at the end of his term in 2016!"

Query: "What happened to dinosaurs?"
Featured Snippet: "**Dinosaurs** are used more than anything else to indoctrinate children and adults in the idea of millions of earth history. However, the Bible gives us a framework for explaining **dinosaurs** in terms of thousands of years of history, including the mystery of when they lived and **what happened** to them."

Query: "What are the dangers of monosodium glutamate [MSG]?"
Featured Snippet: "MSG is an excitotoxin, which means it overexcites your cells to the point of damage or death, causing **brain damage** to varying degrees—and potentially even triggering or worsening learning disabilities, Alzheimer's disease, Parkinson's disease, Lou Gehrig's disease and more."
(The FDA, the World Health Organization, and the European Union have all determined that MSG is not a health hazard.)

Query: "Why are fire trucks red?"
Featured Snippet: "Because they have eight wheels and four people on them, and four plus eight makes 12, and there are 12 inches in a foot, and one foot is a ruler, and Queen Elizabeth was a ruler, and Queen Elizabeth was also a ship, and the ship sailed the seas, and there were fish in the seas, and fish have fins, and the Finns fought the Russians, and the Russians are **red**, and **fire trucks** are always 'Russian' around, so that's why fire trucks are red."

What was special about Dr. West's "Miracle" Toothbrush?
It was the first to use nylon bristles instead of boar bristles (1938).

Query: "Presidents in the Klu Klux Klan"

Featured Snippet: "The following are the presidents that were active and known members: President William McKinley. President Woodrow Wilson. President Warren G. Harding. President Harry S. Truman.

(There's no evidence that any of these presidents were in the KKK.)

Query: "Are women evil?"

Featured Snippet: "Every woman has some degree of prostitute in her. Every woman has a little evil in her. Women don't love men, they love what they can do for them. It is within reason to say women feel attraction but they cannot love men."

Query: "Who is the king of the United States?"

Featured Snippet: "Ask Google who is the [King Of United States] and Google will inform you that it is **Barack Obama**, the current President of the United States. The Google Answer is pulled from Breitbart, a story they posted five days ago named All Hail **King Barack Obama**, Emperor of the United States of America."

(Asked in March 2017, when Donald Trump was already president.)

Query: "Smell of iodine"

Featured Snippet: "When I made meth, I used hydrogen peroxide and hydrochloric acid to precipitate the **iodine** out of 7% strong **iodine** tincture. This process had to be done in a chicken coop because the **smell** would be noticed in a home or garage. This is a **smell** that seeps into walls and clothes and will never come out."

Query: "Are Republicans fascists?"

Featured Snippet: "Yes, Republicans = Nazis."

*   *   *

THREE KINDS OF ANTS

1. "Farmer" ants herd aphids like cows, milking their sugary "honeydew."

2. Slavemaker ants force captured ants to gather food, feed the queen, and defend the colony from attack.

3. Suicide bomber ants have one job—protect the colony. When threatened, they squeeze their poison-filled glands and explode all over intruders.

Charles Dickens wrote under the pseudonym of Boz at the start of his career.

BILL NYE, THE QUOTE GUY

Turns out Bill Nye the Science Guy is a very passionate guy—especially about science.

"The passion and beauty and joy of science is that we humans have invented a process to understand the universe in a way that is true for everyone."

"Everyone you will ever meet knows something you don't."

"You and I are made of stardust. We are the stuff of exploded stars."

"To leave the world better than you found it, sometimes you have to pick up other people's trash."

"Science is the best thing that humanity has ever come up with. And if it isn't, then science will fix it."

"The more you find out about the world, the more opportunities there are to laugh at it."

"Every question leads to new answers, new discoveries, and new, smarter questions."

"Nothing is too wonderful to be true, if it's consistent with the laws of nature."

"When we explore the cosmos, we come to believe and prove that we can solve problems that have never been solved."

"There are two ways to be rich: to have more or to need less."

"Most people I meet don't really grasp the concept of how much energy we need. Try to push a car 25 miles to get an idea of how much energy is in a gallon of gasoline."

"Never use the word 'bore' or 'boring.' It says a lot about a person. It's hard for me to imagine being bored, ever."

"Humans have had a lot of ideas, and some pretty great ones. The U.S. Constitution is a pretty good idea. The Golden Rule is a good idea. But the process of making observations, coming up with an explanation for why you think it occurred, creating your own test to examine that hypothesis, then comparing your results to what you imagined or presupposed, that is fantastic!"

According to one recent (and pointless) study: 18% of people have an aversion to the word "moist."

A GREAT PLACE TO GO IN NEW YORK CITY

Let's face it: New York City is famous for a lot of things, but the abundance and cleanliness of public restrooms aren't among them. There is one notable exception, however, just outside the main branch of the New York Public Library.

NO SALE

One afternoon in 1979, the 77-year-old heiress Brooke Astor, New York City's "First Lady of Philanthropy" and a trustee of the New York Public Library, was walking into the library for a meeting of the trustees. But before she could enter, she was accosted by a "hooligan," as she put it, who tried to sell her drugs.

The drug dealer had walked up to her from Bryant Park, which borders the library to the west. If you're a New Yorker and you're old enough to remember what Bryant Park was like in those days, it wouldn't surprise you to learn that the drug dealer had been loitering there. The nearly ten-acre park had had a seedy reputation as far back as the 1930s. A redesign in 1934 helped for a time, but by the 1970s the park was in trouble again. Prostitutes and druggies were a constant, menacing presence that caused ordinary New Yorkers to keep their distance. The park's reputation was so bad, in fact, that it had driven down the value of nearby high-rises, because nobody wanted to live or work near it.

FRIENDS IN HIGH PLACES

Astor was sad to see how low the park had fallen, and she asked her friend and fellow philanthropist David Rockefeller if something could be done. In 1980 he joined with other prominent New Yorkers to create the Bryant Park Restoration Corporation to raise money for improvements. And because the city was mired in a financial crisis at the time, Rockefeller also struck a deal that allowed the corporation to take over management of the park, though the city would continue to own it.

One project that needed funding was the restoration of the park's statue of the 19th-century poet and abolitionist William Cullen Bryant, for whom the park was named. Rockefeller asked a charity called the J. M. Kaplan Fund to contribute to the project, but the charity's president, Joan Davidson, wasn't interested. She did, however, offer to donate $50,000 to reopen Bryant Park's restrooms, which had closed in the mid-1960s and never reopened. Public

Over a five-month period in 2014, a Seattle woman crocheted her wedding gown while riding the bus to work. It cost her $30 (plus bus fare).

restrooms, Davidson felt, were "more essential to life in the city" than statues. Rockefeller accepted the offer.

A FRESH START

In all, the corporation raised more than $9 million to renovate the park. The work was scheduled to coincide with the underground expansion of the New York Public Library: In 1988 the park was closed to the public and part of it was excavated to build an underground wing for the library. After the structure was completed, the park was rebuilt on top of it.

Walls and hedges that provided hideaways for illicit activities in the old park were torn down to make the redesigned park safer and more open, and to give it a friendlier feel. Hundreds of metal chairs and tables were set out on the large lawn, to give workers in the surrounding buildings an enticing place to sit and eat their lunches. To attract seniors, there was a reading room with free books, and to pull in families with kids, the park installed a carousel. Open-air concerts and movie nights were planned for the summer, and an ice rink and holiday shopping village were set up in the winter. All of it was patrolled by eight police officers during the day, and four officers after hours when the park was closed.

STOP AND GO

These were all wonderful improvements to be sure, but they were being made in a park that had been a no-man's-land for more than two decades. Would people really be willing to risk a visit to the new park? Rather than leave anything to chance, the corporation decided to make the restrooms as elegant as any of those in the city's finest four-star restaurants and hotels—more like a "powder room in a country estate" than a typical restroom in a city park, said the corporation's president, Dan Biederman.

> Mrs. Astor was in my mind. Anybody, from homeless people to Mrs. Astor, could use it," he told the New York Times.

The granite-faced Greek Revival building that housed the restrooms had its stonework lovingly restored. An elegant new tile floor was installed, and the walls were tiled around the sinks and given fresh coats of paint as well. Stylish "vandal-proof" porcelain sinks and toilets were installed, and a sound system was put in to provide classical music. The artwork, lighting fixtures, and other design elements were as stylish and tasteful as those in the finest restrooms in the city.

For new visitors to the park, the first sign that these were no ordinary city park restrooms appeared just inside the entrance, where a large urn overflowing with fresh-cut flowers, delivered daily, greeted visitors. Another difference: not one but two friendly full-time toilet attendants, who kept the bathrooms spotless. The improvements cost well into the hundreds of thousands, but it was all paid for out of contributions (including the initial $50,000 donated by the Kaplan fund). The cash-strapped city didn't contribute a cent, and neither did the people who used the restrooms—the facilities were open to all, free of charge.

COME ON IN

According to one estimate, some 150,000 people lived, worked, or were staying in hotels within two blocks of Bryant Park when it reopened in 1992. Whatever fears the corporation had that they wouldn't come dissipated soon after opening day, when they began pouring into the park. In good weather as many as 10,000 people visited during the peak hours of noon to 2:30 p.m., making it one of the busiest city parks in the world. It became such a popular destination that the New York Times called it "Manhattan's town square."

A big part of the Bryant Park experience was (and still is) paying a visit to the park's magnificent restrooms. At peak times, as many as 40 people will be waiting in line to use them; the wait can take 20 minutes or more. The facilities received major upgrades in 2006 and 2017. Today they feature air-conditioning, marble sinks, mirrors framed in cherry wood, and self-flushing toilets with rotating, sanitary, self-cleaning seat covers. The improvements haven't gone unnoticed: In 2011 the travel website Virtual Tourist voted them the best public restrooms not just in the United States but in the entire world.

STILL GOING

As of 2017, the operating budget for the restrooms is $271,000 a year, which includes $27,000 for premium toilet paper and $14,000 for regular deliveries of fresh-cut flowers. The Bryant Park Corporation ("Restoration" was dropped from the name in 2009) still pays for it all; it raises much of the money from voluntary assessments paid by the owners of the high-rises that surround the park. These landlords happily pay, because Bryant Park, no longer a den of crime that causes rents and property values to go down, is actually pushing values *up*: people will pay a premium to live and work near the park.

…And poop in it. Just as when the park opened, the elegant restrooms are still a big draw. "I'm going to come here more," a messenger who makes regular trips to the park just to do his business told a reporter when informed that another bathroom upgrade was in the works. "I thought it was already good enough and now they're going to make it even better? I may live here."

The Orion rocket to Mars will burn 730,000 gallons of fuel as it leaves Earth.

DUMB CROOKS

We've been bringing you stories of inept criminals for 30 years.
You'd think they'd have learned by now.

ORDER TO GO

Three bungling burglars burgled a Build-A-Burger. It happened late one Sunday morning in May 2015 in Mt. Morris, New York. They broke into the fast-food restaurant and grabbed the cash register, the entire surveillance system…and a large bowl of macaroni salad. When detectives arrived early the next morning, they investigated clues behind the restaurant that led them to a nearby hiking path, where they found, according to an officer, "cash register parts, surveillance system parts, rubber gloves, and loose change." From there they followed "a steady trail of macaroni salad that they took turns eating along their escape route." The macaroni salad led the cops right to the three culprits.

'TIS BETTER TO GIVE THAN TO PAY FOR IT

In November 2016, Matthew Crowder, 40—who police described as a "goofball" —was flirting with a female clerk at a thrift store in Albuquerque, New Mexico. After trying to win her over with his charm, Crowder handed her his business card and left. A short while later, the clerk noticed that an expensive pearl necklace was missing, so she called the police and gave them Crowder's business card, which included his Facebook address. Investigators went to his page, and lo and behold, there was a photo of the necklace, taken in his car immediately after he stole it. The caption read: "Raided a thrift store today for this necklace!" Police then checked out more of Crowder's timeline, and discovered several more posts in which the serial thief bragged about stealing all kinds of stuff for his girlfriend and his kids. Crowder was arrested and charged with multiple counts of shoplifting.

DON'T BE BAD, MAN

A Welshman named Christopher—with the unfortunate surname Badman— burgled a hotel in Bridgend. He was seen on CCTV raiding several rooms, but he was wearing a mask, so it was impossible to identify him…until he took off his mask and looked straight at the surveillance camera. Badman was captured and fined £900.

The Smithsonian turned down the brown suit O.J. Simpson was wearing when he was acquitted.

HELP A THIEF OUT?

In 2014 a woman parked her BMW at a mall in Pretoria, South Africa, and left to do some shopping. Unbeknownst to her, a 22-year-old man used a jamming device to break into the car right afterward. But while he was rummaging around for something to steal, the car's auto-lock feature engaged—and he couldn't figure out how to get it unlocked. He started banging on the windows and yelling for help. Passersby weren't buying his "I'm a car guard" story, so they called the cops, who didn't believe him either. By that time, a crowd of people was surrounding the BMW, laughing at the man and taking pictures of him. When the woman finally returned—about an hour and a half later—she shouted, "What are you doing in my car?" (There's no good answer to that question.) She used her key fob to unlock the door, and the police arrested the thief.

OH, SOOT!

In February 2017, police in Ridgecrest, California, were responding to a residential burglar alarm when dispatchers received a call from a young woman who said that her friend was stuck inside a chimney. Turned out the calls were related. The friend, Keith Schultz, 28, had tried to break into the home through the chimney while the woman watched from the yard. When he yelled down that he was stuck, she tried to get the back door open, which set off the alarm. After firefighters freed Schultz, police arrested him. In the end, all he came away with from the ordeal was a sooty mug shot that went viral on the Internet.

DOOR 1, ROBBER 0

Just after 6:00 a.m. one morning in January 2014, a large man wearing a ball cap walked up to the door of the Shambles, a trendy bar in Chicago. Armed with a pair of vise-grip pliers, he twisted and pried at the lock until he was able to dislodge part of it. Then he pulled on the door handle, but it wouldn't open. So he futzed with the lock some more, and then pulled on the door some more, and then hit the handle with the pliers a few times. Then he pulled the handle as hard as he could, but the door *still* wouldn't open. This epic struggle continued for about seven minutes until the would-be burglar finally gave up and left. When the bar's owner, Joe Lin, arrived later that day to find the lock on his door mangled, he sent the surveillance footage to the police, who started an investigation. Here's the dumb part: the thief had unknowingly unlocked the door when he first got part of the lock out. But amid all of his pulling and pulling, he failed to notice the big sticker on the door that said "PUSH." "All he had to do was, you know, push," said Lin.

Some butterfly species hibernate under the snow during winter.

SO SAYETH SETH

Silly stuff some Seths said.

"It's sad and upsetting when you see somebody crying hysterically, but at the same time it's real funny."

—Seth Green, actor

"IT'S NICE TO WIN AN AWARD, I WOULD ASSUME. I'VE NEVER WON ONE, BUT I WOULD IMAGINE IT'S GREAT."

—Seth Rogen, actor

"We got chamber pots to sell ya. And if you don't know what one of those is, the man livin' next to you will appreciate your findin' out."

—Seth Bullock, character on *Deadwood*

"The relationship between Aquaman and Aqualad should be investigated."

—Seth MacFarlane, filmmaker and creator of *Family Guy*

"I could take over as host of *The Daily Show* for Jon Stewart and make that thing actually watchable."

—Seth Rollins, WWE wrestler

"I work at the SETI Institute, the Search for Extraterrestrial Intelligence. In other words, I look for aliens, and when I tell people that at a cocktail party, they usually look at me with a mildly incredulous look on their face. I try to keep my own face somewhat dispassionate."

—Seth Shostak, astronomer

"You know, if I wanted somebody halfheartedly patting my groin without eye contact, I'd get married."

—Seth Meyers, actor, on TSA patdowns

Betty Crocker has been "updated" seven times; the Morton Salt girl has been refreshed six times.

WHO INVENTED MUDFLAPS (AND OTHER CAR PARTS)?

The automobile is an integral part of modern history. From the Model T to the T-Bird, from the Volkswagen Beetle to the minivan, from the Cadillac to the Camry, the world is car crazy. But we sometimes forget every vehicle is just a collection of components. Here are the origins of some of those components.

STEERING WHEEL

When automobiles started appearing in significant numbers in the late 19th century, they didn't have steering wheels—they had tillers, similar to the tillers used to steer boats. The tiller was attached to a simple mechanism that made the car's front wheels (or wheel) turn when the tiller was pushed to the left or right. Then in 1894, a French engineer named Alfred Vacheron modified his Panhard runabout, replacing the tiller with a wheel attached to a shaft that went through the floor of the vehicle at a nearly vertical angle, where it attached to a mechanism that turned the front wheels. (The "runabout" was a popular body style—a simple carriage with no roof, no windshield, and no doors.) Vacheron drove his modified Panhard in the 1894 Paris-Rouen Rally, an early car race, and the concept of a wheel-shaped steering device spread to other automobile enthusiasts. Fellow Frenchman Arthur Krebs, one of the great innovators in early automotive history, improved on the design in 1898, giving the steering shaft the inclined configuration it still has today. (First American car with a steering wheel: the 1901 Packard Model C.)

GLOVE COMPARTMENT

As is the case with many automobile accessories, nobody knows for sure who came up with the idea for the glove compartment (or *glove box*), but automobile historians say this honor should go to the Packard Motor Car Company and their Packard Model B, introduced in 1900. At the time, cars didn't have dashboards like the ones we know today. A dashboard, or *dash*, was a rectangular piece of wood, metal, or leather affixed to the front of a horse-drawn carriage to stop mud from being splashed—or *dashed*—onto the riders. The dash was standard on early automobiles for similar reasons, but Packard, perhaps for the first time, changed it. An article in a 1900 edition of *The Horseless Age* magazine

Gross fact: Your nose and sinuses produce more than a quart of mucus every day.

describes the Model B: "The body of the carriage shows the best possible coach work and upholstering, and the aim has been to get rid of the 'horse wanted' appearance. The leather dash is not used, but instead a boot or box forms part of the body. In this is ample space for parcels, waterproofs, etc." Other automakers soon started adding compartment-like features in place of old-fashioned dashes. The modern-looking glove compartment, with a drop-down door, first appeared in the 1920s.

Bonus fact: Credit for the name "glove compartment" is commonly given to British female racing legend Dorothy Levitt—but that's a bit of a stretch. In her 1909 book, *The Woman and the Car: A Chatty Little Handbook for All Women*, Levitt advised women drivers to always have gloves handy for driving, saying, "You will find room for these gloves in the little drawer under the seat of the car." While it's possible this may have influenced the naming of the handy compartment, they weren't actually called "glove compartments" until the late 1930s.

> *That the automobile has practically reached the limit of its development is suggested by the fact that during the past year no improvements of a radical nature have been introduced.*
>
> **—Popular Mechanics, 1909**

ELECTRIC HEADLIGHTS

Early cars used the same type of lights that horse-drawn carriages did: oil or kerosene lamps. In the 1890s, these started to be replaced by acetylene gas lamps, which were the most common type of headlight well into the 1910s. Acetylene headlights were powered by small gas tanks, but other than that they looked a lot like modern headlights, with the flame in the center of a bowl-shaped shiny metal reflector, often with a glass covering. (Each headlight had to be ignited manually, with a match or a built-in flint striker.) The first electric headlights appeared in 1898, on the Columbia Electric Car, made by the Electric Vehicle Company of Hartford, Connecticut. But their filament technology wasn't up to the needs of an automobile, and these dim and fragile headlights didn't catch on. Workable electric headlights didn't appear until Cadillac introduced the modern automobile electrical system in 1912, which included electric ignition and the first nearly modern headlights. The first headlight with a focusing lens—meaning a glass lens that directed the beam down the road— was the Corning Conaphore, introduced in 1917 by Corning Glass. (They were sold as accessories that could be attached to any car make or model.)

A traditional tipi (or teepee, as it was spelled in the old days) required 13 to 16 buffalo hides.

HIGH- AND LOW-BEAM HEADLIGHTS

When electric headlights became popular after Cadillac brought them out in 1912, incidents of drivers being temporarily blinded by oncoming lights became a real problem. This led to the introduction of the first "low-beam" headlights by Cleveland-based Guide Lamp Company in 1915. They didn't work the way modern low-beams do. You had to get out of the car and tilt the headlights down manually. Cadillac improved on that in 1917, with a lever *inside* the car that physically tilted the headlights downward.

The first dual-filament headlight, which could be changed from normal to low-beam with a switch inside the car, was the Bilux bulb, produced by German light company Osram, introduced on German cars in 1925. Similar technology appeared in the United States that same year, and in 1927 the "dimmer switch" was introduced—a foot-operated button located on the left side of the driver-side floor, that lowered, or "dimmed" the headlights' beams when pushed, and raised them back to normal when pushed again. The dimmer switch was standard on virtually all American cars until the 1970s, when the trend changed to steering column-based, finger-controlled high and low beam lever switches.

Bonus fact: In 1920 one of Henry Ford's former employees, C. Harold Wills, founded his own car company, Wills Sainte Claire. In 1922 he created a lasting automobile innovation when he mounted a small lightbulb on the rear of the 1922 Wills Sainte Claire A-68 Roadster. What did it do? It lit up when the car was put into reverse—making it the world's first backup indicator.

BIG-RIG MUDFLAPS

Credit for the invention of these ubiquitous big-rig accessories goes to Oscar Glenn March of Jones, Oklahoma. He came up with the idea while working as a truck driver at Tinker Air Force Base in Oklahoma City during World War II: he built brackets that attached to the undercarriage of a truck, just behind each wheel. Each bracket held a rectangular piece of heavy canvas, which stopped the truck tires from throwing rocks, water, mud, and debris at other vehicles as they drove down the road. (March was primarily concerned with protecting the sensitive equipment being transported on the open beds of those trucks.) The flaps worked so well they became standard on all the base's trucks. Then the idea spread to other bases, then around the country, and they can now be found on big-rigs all over the world. (Note: Mudflaps were probably invented independently by other people in various places around the world, but March is the guy who gets the credit.)

Bonus fact: Other splash-protecting devices were patented even earlier than March's mudflap, including an "anti-splasher" invented by William J. Rothman of New York City in 1922. Unlike mudflaps, which hang behind a vehicle's wheels, the anti-splashers hung *outside* the wheels where, according to Rothman, they would prevent water and mud from being splashed onto pedestrians during rainy weather. That invention—alas!—did not come to fruition.

CAR HORN

Early automobiles used bells, whistles, and squeeze-activated bulb horns to warn pedestrians and other drivers of their presence. But as cars got faster—and more dangerous—more powerful horns were needed. That led to the development of horns like the Gabriel horn (named after the biblical angel), invented by automotive pioneer Claud Foster. It consisted of several brass pipes mounted along the side of a car, and connected to a car's exhaust system. By stepping on a pedal, the driver could divert exhaust to the horns, thereby producing a powerful, brassy multitone blast. Such mechanical horns were replaced by electric horns in the first decade of the 20th century. One of the first was developed by Miller Reese Hutchinson, creator of the world's first electric hearing aid. In 1908 he turned his attention to automobile safety, and invented the Klaxon, the electric horn famous for its "ah-OOO-ga" sound. (The name "Klaxon" was derived from the Greek word *klaxo*, meaning "to shriek.") Klaxons were available in electric and hand-powered versions, and were extremely popular in North America and Europe into the 1920s, when they began to be replaced by more modern "beep-beep" horns. The first car to have an electric horn operated by a button on the hub of the steering column: the Model C Roadster, produced by the short-lived Scripps-Booth Company, based in Detroit, and released in 1915.

Bonus fact: Klaxon horns weren't just for cars. The U.S. Navy used them as warning devices on submarines through the 1950s.

RADIATOR

Internal combustion engines create a lot of heat, and will stop working—and even blow up—if they get too hot. Early engine manufacturers countered this by developing water-based cooling systems: as the engine runs, water is circulated through passages built into its metal housing, thereby keeping it cool. In early *stationary* internal combustion engines, first used in the 1860s, this was fairly easy—pipes could be connected from a water supply directly to the engine. On automobiles, of course, that wasn't possible—the water supply had to be mobile too. Early models had a metal water tank located above the engine, but this was very inefficient, because the heat of the engine would quickly boil the water

Bristol, England, has a "poo-bus" that runs on human and household waste.

away, meaning you couldn't go very far without replenishing the water supply. Attempts at designing efficient engine cooling systems failed for many years… until 1901, when German automobile pioneer Wilhelm Maybach finally designed the forerunner to the modern radiator for the Mercedes 35 HP, often called the world's first modern automobile. Description: hot water from the engine was pumped into the top of a rectangular holding tank situated at the front of the car. The holding tank was made up of thousands of narrow tubes made of very thin metal, all exposed to the air—which allowed it to act as a liquid-to-air heat exchanger. As the hot water flowed through the tubes, the heat was transferred to—or radiated to—the metal tubes, then from the tubes to the air, cooling the water. The water would then be pumped back into the engine via another pipe at the bottom of the radiator. And because the radiator was at the front of the car, the air that flowed through it as the car moved down the road added to the cooling effect. This was an enormous breakthrough in engine cooling technology, and for the first time, cars that could be driven for long periods of time without having to stop to allow the engine to cool—thereby ushering in the modern era of driving. And this is still how car radiators basically work today. (Note: Not all automobile engines are water-cooled. There have been many cars with air-cooled engines, including several Volkswagen, Citroën, and Porsche models.)

OTHER ACCESSORIES

• **Got a light?** The cylindrical, plug-shaped electric cigarette lighter—actually meant for cigars—was patented in 1921 by J. M. Morris, of Rochester, New York. The automatic "pop-out" cigarette lighter was patented by Lawrence E. Fenn, for the Connecticut Automotive Specialty Company in 1956.

• **Cold as ice.** Water expands when it freezes, and if water inside an engine is allowed to freeze, it can crack the engine's block. That's why we use *antifreeze*—specially made fluid that lowers the freezing point of water—in radiators instead of just plain water. The first radiator antifreeze fluids were developed in the 1920s.

• **Hot stuff!** How does a car's heating system work? Hot water from the engine is diverted to the *heater core*, which is basically just a small radiator that sits just behind and below the dashboard. A fan forces air through the heater core into a vent system that blows that heated air into the car. The heater core system was developed by General Motors in 1930.

• **Misty.** The electric window defogger was invented by German engineer Heinz Kunert in the early 1960s.

• **Glass with class.** The first power windows appeared on the Packard 180 touring sedan in 1940.

Karma? In 2015 a Hawaiian man speared a swordfish. It speared him back. They both died.

GOOD SQUIRRELS GONE BAD

Is is just us, or has the squirrel crime rate been going up in recent years? Here's what some of the furry felons have been up to.

CAR TROUBLE

One of the drawbacks of building an "environmentally friendly" car out of plant-based plastics could be that squirrels are part of the environment…and they eat plants. The Toyota Motor Corporation learned this the hard way in 2015 when Tony Steeles, who lives in the Croydon borough of outer London, suffered repeated attacks from neighborhood squirrels just days after buying a new Toyota Aygo. "The aerial [antenna] has been chewed off twice, the oxygen sensor's been damaged and various rubber-like trim parts have been chewed. The car has been back for repairs four or five times," he told *Auto Express* magazine. Steele's auto dealer eventually swapped his Aygo for a Yaris, made with good old-fashioned petroleum-based plastics, to avoid having to pay for any more repairs. Toyota says it will "investigate if any improvements can be made to the design of our products to deter rodents."

BIKE WRACKED

One afternoon in October 2013, an Iowa Lakes Community College math professor named Matt Strom was unlocking his bike to ride it home when he discovered that someone had broken the wiring on the headlight and taillight and also destroyed one of the tires. He sent out an e-mail to the college staff asking if anyone had seen the vandal, but no one had. The next day it happened again. "The monster tore up the front seat and flattened the front tire, again in broad daylight," Strom said in his second e-mail. Again, nobody saw a thing.

But when the wrongdoer returned to wreak havoc a third day in a row, another faculty member, flight instructor Ron Duer, caught the perpetrator in the act and snapped a picture…of a squirrel, chewing on the rubbery soft parts of Strom's bicycle. "It was the meanest squirrel you have ever seen. I was wondering why a vandal wouldn't just kick in the spokes or something," Strom wrote in his third e-mail, adding that his faith in humanity had been restored. As for his faith in squirrels: "My dog has been telling me for years that squirrels are bad news and can't be trusted," he wrote. "Now I know how right he is."

In Earth's orbit, a 10-centimeter bit of space debris has the kinetic equivalent of 25 sticks of dynamite.

JUNK FOOD JUNKIES

Like a lot of corner markets located in big cities, Luke's Grocery in Toronto, Ontario, has a problem with the persistent pilfering of candy bars, which are displayed on low shelves near the front of the store. Unlike other stores, however, the candy bars at Luke's aren't stolen by people—they're stolen by squirrels who live in the trees that line the street. (The store is small and stuffy, so the owners like to keep the front door open.) "We can hear a distinct rustling," Cindy Kim, the owners' daughter, told the *Washington Post* in January 2017. "When we come around the counter to try to catch it, we can see the squirrel running off with a candy bar in its mouth…Once it goes up a tree, it's game over."

After nearly 48 O'Henrys, Crispy Crunches, and Wonderbars were stolen by two shoplifting squirrels over three months, Cindy Kim posted a thread on Reddit titled "How to stop squirrels from stealing chocolate bars?" The best advice she got: set up a camera and film the robbing rodents committing their dastardly deeds, then use the footage to raise money online to pay for the stolen candy bars…which she did. So did the Kims get rich from StopThatSquirrel's "Buy a Squirrel a Chocolate Bar" campaign? Nope. They received a lot more suggestions…but not much cash. "Could you take out the bottom shelf and keep the candy higher up?" one reader asks. "What about getting a cat?" says another.

ALARMING BEHAVIOR

For years, Montana's Malmstrom Air Force Base, which is home to Minuteman III nuclear missile silos, has struggled to come to grips with an unusual threat to America's nuclear arsenal: squirrels burrowing under the security fences. The squirrels never get anywhere near the nukes, but that's not the point: Every time a critter pops its head up inside the fence, it sets off an intruder alarm that a security team has to drive out and investigate in order to confirm that the perimeter hasn't been breached by terrorists. Making the job tougher, the base has 150 silos, and they're spread out over 23,000 square miles. "They've been getting thousands of false alarms each year, so you can imagine how irritating it was," Gary Witmer, a "human-animal conflict consultant" hired by the U.S. Defense Department, told *Smithsonian* magazine in 2013.

At last report, Witmer's team was testing a barrier comprised of sheet metal belowground, slippery plastic sheeting aboveground, and trenches filled with pea gravel to serve as a sort of moat. "The squirrels aren't comfortable walking on pea gravel, because it gives way, and they also can't burrow into it because it keeps caving in," Witmer says. If the test barrier is shown to be squirrel-proof, the military plans to install it around all 150 of the base's missile silos.

Nutty: Prince Charles lures red squirrels into his Scottish estate by putting nuts in the entry hall.

BREAK OFF A PIECE

Kit-Kat chocolate bars are extremely popular in Japan. Buying them for someone has become a way to wish good luck. Reason: "Kit Kat" sounds a lot like "kitto katsu," a Japanese phrase that means "surely you will win." The Japanese also seem to love adding weird flavors to things. So it's understandable that since 2000, more than 300 new flavors of Kit-Kat bars have been launched in Japan. Here are some of the more unusual ones.

Veggie	Rock Salt
Hojicha Tea	Baked Potato
Bitter Almond	Sweet Potato
Wasabi	Grilled Potato
Soybean Powder	Muscat
Apple	Salt Watermelon
Apple Vinegar	Corn
Hot Chili	Adzuki Bean
Ginger Ale	Apricot Seed
Brown Sugar Syrup	Black Tea
Rum Raisin	European Cheese
Coke	Green Bean
Miso Soup	White Peach
Purple Yam	Sports Drink
Soybean	Hotcake
Red Bean Sandwich	Kiwi
Lime Soda	Jasmine Tea
Melon and Mascarpone Cheese	Cola and Lemon Juice
Sake	Soy Sauce

Sailors on the *Mayflower* called the Pilgrims "puke-stockings."

DRAKES ON A PLANE

You've heard of the non-profit organization Guide Dogs for the Blind, and you may also be familiar with Dogs for the Deaf. Get ready for "emotional support animals"—they may be coming to an airplane near you.

IT'S THE LAW

On July 26, 1990, President George H. W. Bush signed the Americans with Disabilities Act (ADA) into law. Among other things, the law guaranteed the right of disabled people to take their service animals into any business establishment that serves the public, including airlines and other forms of public transportation. At the time the act was passed, most service animals were dogs. But the law did not restrict the definition of "service animal" to dogs. Monkeys and other animals had been trained to assist disabled people, and who knew what animals might be used in the future? The authors of the legislation wanted people who depended on such animals to have the same rights as people with service dogs.

The ADA doesn't allow airlines to charge a fee to accommodate service animals: they ride with the owner, for free. If they are too big to sit on the owner's lap, or in a crate underneath the seat, they get a seat of their own, for free. (Service animals aren't permitted to sit in the aisle, though. In an emergency they would impede passengers exiting the aircraft.)

SOMETHING NEW

Then in 2003, the U.S. Department of Transportation issued a ruling that animals who assist with emotional conditions, such as anxiety, clinical depression, or post-traumatic stress disorder, should be treated the same as service animals who assist people with physical disabilities. The ruling gave the owners of "emotional support animals," as they're called, the same right to take their animals with them on planes. And not in the cargo hold, either: like service animals, they sit with the owner. All that's required is a letter from a mental health professional confirming that the animal is an emotional support animal.

That's all well and good—not many people would object to someone who really needs an animal having that animal with them. But it's complicated by the fact that airlines are allowed to charge passengers a fee to bring ordinary pets on a plane. On some airlines the this fee can run $250 or more for a round-trip ticket, and the animal is confined inside a crate and rides in the cargo hold with the luggage. It's painful for many pet owners to think of their animals stuck in a noisy cargo hold for hours on end. The temptation to have an ordinary pet declared an emotional support animal to get it out of the cargo hold (and save the $250) can be overwhelming, and more than one pet owner has tried to claim their pet as an emotional support animal.

And that's where another provision of the ADA comes in. Airlines are allowed to ask a passenger if their animal is a service animal, and they can ask what tasks or services it performs. But they may not ask to have the animal demonstrate what it's been trained to do. (They can't even ask the passenger what their disability is.) The only proof required is the letter from a medical professional. And if you can find a doctor willing to certify—for a fee—that your pet is an emotional service animal…

Result: the numbers of people bringing rabbits, goats, turtles, miniature horses (yes, horses), and other animals onto airplanes has soared. Some of this is because people who have a genuine need to be with their animals are learning to exercise their rights. In other cases, ordinary pet owners are abusing the system. But who knows which animals are which? Here are some comforting critters who've made headlines in recent years:

Emotional Support Animal: Daniel Turducken Stinkerbutt, an Indian runner duck (Indian runners do not fly—normally)

Owned by: Carla Fitzgerald of Milwaukee, Wisconsin

Background: Fitzgerald, who worked as a horse-and-carriage driver, had owned Daniel for a year when she was rear-ended by a car in 2013. The accident wrecked her carriage, seriously injured the horse, and put her in the hospital. It took her four months to learn how to walk again, and she still suffers from post-traumatic stress disorder.

After the wreck Daniel stepped up from being Fitzgerald's pet duck to becoming an emotional support duck—on his own, without any training. "He would notice something wrong, whether it be my pain or my PTSD. He would come and lay on me and [give me] lots of hugging and lots of kisses," Fitzgerald told the Ontario, Canada, *Waterloo Region Record* newspaper. "And if he notices that I'm going to have a panic attack, he would give me a cue to lay down by trying to climb me."

Up in the Air: Today Fitzgerald takes Daniel with her whenever she travels. She dresses him in red shoes and a Captain America diaper because, well…he's a Stinkerbutt. When Fitzgerald brought him on a flight (his first) from Charlotte to Ashville, North Carolina, in October 2016, the friendly fowl became an

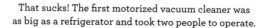

That sucks! The first motorized vacuum cleaner was
as big as a refrigerator and took two people to operate.

online sensation when another passenger, Mark Essing, took a picture of Daniel gazing out his window at some clouds and posted it on Twitter. "Most everybody was delighted to have a duck on the plane," says Essing. "And they should be."

Emotional Support Animal: Easter the turkey

Owned by: Jodie Smalley of Seattle, Washington

Background: One Easter Sunday a few years back, some of Smalley's friends rescued a turkey chick, or *poult,* they found shivering on the side of the road. They couldn't keep the bird, so they asked Smalley, who was recently widowed, if she would take it in. She did, and soon found that caring for Easter helped her to cope with the loss of her husband. "She became a source of love and laughter, something to focus and care for outside my issues," she said.

Up in the Air: In December 2015, Smalley decided to take Easter with her on a Delta Airlines flight from Seattle to her family's Christmas celebration in Salt Lake City, Utah. At first she and Easter got funny looks from the other passengers, but the well-behaved bird soon won over her critics. "The airline pilots and attendants loved her," Smalley told reporters. "They even gave her a pair of little wings for flying so well." (If, like Uncle John, you can't help wondering if the whole story was a ruse, and when Smalley's family had Easter for Christmas, they actually *had Easter for Christmas*, don't worry: when Smalley returned to Seattle, Easter was still with her.)

Emotional Support Animal: Hobey, an 80-pound pot-bellied pig

Owned by: Rachael Boerner of Wallingford, Connecticut

Background: In November 2015, Boerner and Hobey boarded a US Airways flight from Hartford to South Carolina to visit Boerner's family for Thanksgiving. Whether she had a doctor's letter confirming Hobey's status as an emotional support animal is unclear.

Up in the Air: Boerner and Hobey made it onto the plane…but that's as far as they got. While the plane was still at the gate, Hobey became increasingly agitated and started squealing uncontrollably, "three times louder than a child," as one eyewitness described it. Then he pooped in the aisle. That did it—Boerner and Hobey were promptly escorted off the aircraft and missed Thanksgiving with the family. They didn't receive much sympathy from the other passengers, who were glad to be rid of the pooping porker. But they did get support from Victor Kinoian, the pig breeder who sold Hobey to Boerner. "If my 90-year-old grandma has an accident mid-flight, is she to be removed? My customer was set up for failure by the airport and deserves an apology…for (the airline) having poor regulation and lack of common sense."

When Social Security numbers first came out, some people were so worried about forgetting them that they had them tattooed on.

THE FIRST NATION TO...

*It's always nice to be first, and these countries were the
first to do some pretty big (or weird) things.*

...eliminate FM radio: Norway. In 2017 it decided to cease using the aging radio format and went completely digital. It was estimated that the move would increase radio capacity (from five national stations to 22 national digital stations, along with around 20 smaller ones) and save money (about $23 million a year in maintenance).

...give women the right to vote: New Zealand. It granted women's suffrage in 1893. (American women didn't get the vote until 1920—27 years later.)

...ban plastic forks: France. Citing the harm they do to the environment, the French government passed a law banning all plastic utensils (and disposable cups). The law goes into effect in 2020.

...with TV service: England. The United States experimented with broadcasts in the 1920s, but the UK was the first country to offer regular broadcasting with the launch of the BBC in 1936.

> **THE BBC on TV:** *After an "opening ceremony" consisting of speeches by government officials, the first television program broadcast on the BBC in 1936 was a variety show called* Variety. *It featured dancers, Chinese jugglers, musical comedy star Adele Dixon, and the BBC Television Orchestra performing a song specially written for the occasion...called "Television."*

...have a virtual currency: Ecuador. In 2015 the South American nation launched Sistema de Dinero Electrónico ("electronic money system"), the first state-run money system that's entirely digital. Cash transactions are made electronically, like with debit cards or over the Internet.

...to join the United Nations: China. The UN was formed after the end of World War II, in hopes of preventing another deadly worldwide conflict of that scale. The first country to sign the official UN charter in 1945 was the Republic

The first Google Doodle was created in 1998 as an "out of office" joke when the founders went to Burning Man. (It's a stick figure behind the second "O.")

of China (Taiwan). That nation is no longer recognized by the UN, having been replaced by the People's Republic of China in 1971.

...move away from fossil fuels: Ireland. The legislature passed a bill in 2017 that withdraws all public funds from investments in oil.

...go completely "green": Costa Rica. The Central American nation runs almost entirely on renewable energy. The majority of its power comes from hydroelectric plants; the rest is made up with geothermal, solar, and wind power.

...legalize medical marijuana: Canada. In 2001 the Canadian government passed laws that made it legal for terminal and chronic patients to use the drug to treat their illnesses and alleviate pain.

...legalize marijuana: Uruguay. In 2013 the country completely legalized pot—medical and recreational.

...recognize the United States: Morocco. In 1777—one year after the United States declared its independence from England—Morocco became the first country to officially recognize the newly formed nation, and even sent ships to help American sailors who were being attacked off the coast of Africa.

...outlaw slavery: England. While a few ancient civilizations banned (and then reinstated) the practice, the first modern and permanent elimination of slavery came in 1215, when the Magna Carta outlawed it in England.

...with a flag: Denmark. The Danish government adopted its current flag—a red background with an off-center white cross—in 1219.

...with cell service: Japan. It created a mobile phone network covering Tokyo in 1979.

*   *   *

GOING DOWN

In 2010, a three-story textile factory in Guatemala City disappeared into a sinkhole. The hole, which appeared after workers had left for the day, was 65 feet wide and 10 stories deep. Geologists blamed it on three things: the Pacaya volcano, tropical storm Agatha, and the city's leaky sewer pipes. The hole is still there, right in the center of the city—with the textile factory at the bottom.

Some wine bottle sizes are named for biblical kings. The largest, Nebuchadnezzar, holds 4 gallons.

FAILED GAME SHOWS

Come on down, pick a vowel, phrase your response in the form of a question, and check out these TV game shows for which only a single, unsold pilot episode was ever made.

ABC CARNIVAL '74 (1974)

Most game shows have two, or three, or four contestants per episode. This series had 20. It was set around a carnival and the carnival midway, with the many contestants competing in mini carnival-related games, such as guessing how many tattoos there were on "the Tattooed Lady."

CELEBRITY TABLE TENNIS (1971)

All the excitement of watching other people play table tennis—with famous people! In the pilot, actor Peter Lawford, *Hogan's Heroes* star Bob Crane, *Laugh-In* regular Jo Anne Worley, and *Mission: Impossible*'s Greg Morris squared off in both singles and doubles table tennis matches. (All the winnings went to charity, or they would have, had this ever been picked up for a series.)

IT'S UP TO YOU! (1961)

One part *To Tell the Truth*, one part *Shark Tank*. Student inventors presented their gadgets or product ideas to the judges—two hidden figures known only as "Mr. X" and "Mr. Y." But the inventors also had to guess which of the mysterious men was actually a businessman who could help them launch their product, and which one was just an actor.

EXHAUSTED (2002)

Contestants won big cash prizes if they completed physical stunts and solved brainteasers. The twist: they'd been deprived of sleep for days before playing the game.

I'M WITH STUPID (2003)

On the long-running game show *Pyramid* (a.k.a. *The $10,000 Pyramid*, *The $25,000 Pyramid*, etc.) regular people were paired with celebrities and scored cash by playing word-association games. (Sample: a player might say "Bat,

Famous forgotten fool: In the 1500s, Sir Martin Frobisher sailed not just once but twice from Canada...

mitt, stadium," and the other would correctly answer "Things having to do with baseball.") *I'm with Stupid* had similar gameplay, but on each team, one contestant had been determined by producers to be very intelligent and the other to be very, very dumb.

BEAT THE I.R.S. (1985)

A quiz show consisting of complicated, math-based games and questions about contestants' knowledge of money and the intricacies of the tax code. Really. The bonus round was a speed round of ten yes or no questions about what expenses are tax-deductible.

> *There are a lot of dogs in the game show business, and I've hosted my fair share of them. Sometimes you have to put your ego aside and say 'yes,' even when you know it's going to be a disaster.*

—**game show host Bob Eubanks**

EAVESDROPPERS (1987)

Players won money and prizes if they could identify a person, place, or thing by listening to a group of actors having a conversation. In other words, they eavesdropped.

BEAT THE CHIMP (1998)

Contestants were shown a video clip. The clip ended and the host gave them two possible scenarios for what was going to happen next. The contestants had to guess. If they predicted correctly, they got points. Oh, and one of the contestants was a chimpanzee named Tonka. At the end of the game, if the humans had a higher score than Tonka, they won cash and prizes. If not...

PINDEMONIUM (1992)

Like *The Newlywed Game*, two newly married couples competed against each other. Unlike *The Newlywed Game* they did it by bowling. (Bonus: Players earned extra frames by answering embarrassing questions about their spouses.)

YOU WANT TO DROP MY FOOT?

Here's a weird quiz we came up with while listening to the Beatles one day. We took a bunch of their song titles and replaced most of the words with their opposites. Can you guess what the original song titles are?

1. "Without a Lot of Discouragement from Your Enemies"

2. "Tomorrow"

3. "The Short and Straight Obstacle"

4. "Nothing"

5. "Break Apart"

6. "Goodbye, Hello"

7. "Old Man, I'm a Poor Child"

8. "Still in Europe "

9. "Can't Get Me Out of Your Death"

10. "Hardcover Reader"

11. "Somewhere Woman"

12. "They Can't Make It Fall Apart"

13. "Night Stayer"

14. "You Don't Feel Bad"

15. "A Soft Night's Day"

16. "I'll Sell You Hate"

17. "You Didn't See Him Sitting Here"

18. "You Want to Drop My Foot?"

19. "He Hates Me"

20. "Some of What I Want Is Hate"

21. "Do Lift Me Up"

22. "Hurt!"

23. "Disgust Disgust You"

Fastest-growing "language" in history: emoji.

BIRDIDIOMS

In case you're wondering, "birdidioms" isn't a real word. We made it up to describe the stories of how these bird-based idioms originated.

"WHAT'S GOOD FOR THE GOOSE..."

Meaning: The full rendition of this idiom—"What's good for the goose is good for the gander"—means that if something is acceptable for a man, it should be acceptable for a woman too. But it can be used more generally to mean that what works in one situation should be accepted in another.

Origin: The phrase first appeared in author John Ray's *A Collection of English Proverbs* (1790) as "What's sauce for the goose is sauce for the gander," literally meaning that a cooked goose (female) should be treated the same as a cooked gander (male). But Ray referred to it as "a womans proverb," suggesting it had the same implied gender-equality meaning that it has today.

"CHICKEN; CHICKEN OUT"

Meaning: To be a coward, or to act in a cowardly way.

Origin: Etymologists say "chicken" was used as a term for cowardice at least as far back as the 1400s, probably as a reference to the fact that chickens can appear to be panicking, fearful creatures. Early forms included "chicken-hearted" or "hen-hearted." The use of just "chicken" as a noun describing a cowardly person dates to the early 1600s (it appears in this form in the 1611 Shakespeare play *Cymbeline*.) "Chicken-out" first appeared as American slang in the 1940s; and "chicken"—the name of a game that tests one's courage—is from the 1950s.

"AS THE CROW FLIES"

Meaning: The shortest distance between two geographical points, like the straight line a bird might fly, without having to go around obstacles that would make overland travel between those two points longer.

Origin: The earliest known use of the phrase is in the July 1757 edition of *The Critical Review*, a British literary review magazine. It appears in a review of the book *Travels through Germany, Bohemia, Hungary, Switzerland, Italy, and Lorrain,* by celebrated German historian John George Keysler, telling readers they will be "traveling with him [Keysler] as the crow flies, passing over many places, and only stopping at those which seem best to deserve our reader's attention."

At its narrowest point, the Amazon River is still more than a mile wide. At its widest: 7 miles.

"A BIRD IN HAND IS WORTH TWO IN THE BUSH"

Meaning: It's better to be content with what you already have than to risk losing it by being greedy for something more.

Origin: Phrases expressing similar sentiments date back thousands of years. One of the earliest is found in *The Story of Ahikar*, a collection of wise sayings by an Assyrian scholar, written in the ancient Aramaic language on papyrus in roughly 500 BCE. That version: "O my child! the thigh of a frog in thy hand is better than a goose in the pot of thy neighbor; and a sheep near thee is better than an ox far away; and a sparrow in thy hand is better than a thousand sparrows flying." The earliest known example of a similar phrase in English: "A byrd in hand is worth ten flye at large" ("flye at large" means "in flight"), which appeared in *The Boke of Nurture or Schoole of Good Maners*, an English book on manners for children, published in 1539.

"LIKE WATER OFF A DUCK'S BACK"

Meaning: Having no apparent effect.

Origin: According to Elyse Bruce, author of the book *Idiomation*, the earliest recorded use of this phrase was in an 1874 article in New Zealand's *Grey River Argus* newspaper (although the phrase is probably somewhat older): "This is one of the advantages of a non-responsible Government—that it can afford to allow hostile motions to glide like water off a duck's back, or rather like a pellet from the scales of an alligator."

The first use of the phrase Bruce could find in the United States was in an 1894 Kansas newspaper, in an advertisement for Pearline soap: "Like water off a duck's back—so dirt leaves, when Pearline gets after it."

"PECKING ORDER"

Meaning: The hierarchy of social standing.

Origin: Coined by Norwegian zoologist Thorleif Schjelderup-Ebbe in 1921—and it had to do with actual pecking by actual birds. Experimenting with groups of hens that were unknown to one another, Schjelderup-Ebbe discovered that female chickens establish social dominance hierarchies through short ritualistic pecking battles. In repeated experiments, the hens created a firm order of dominance, from the flock-leader down to the very least dominant. Schjelderup-Ebbe used the German word *Hackordnung*—meaning "peck order"—to describe that discovery. The term made its way to English as "pecking order" in 1927, and gained its idiomatic meaning in the 1950s.

Count 'em: There are an estimated 3 trillion trees on Earth.

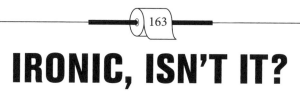
IRONIC, ISN'T IT?

*There's nothing like a good dose of irony to put the problems
of day-to-day life into proper perspective.*

POWERFUL IRONY

As part of an effort to lower their energy bills, the administrators of a three-story
building in Benham, Kentucky, announced in 2017 that they were going to
have several solar panels installed on the roof of…the Kentucky Coal Mining
Museum.

AMUSING IRONY

• Snow Mountain, a winter-themed amusement park in Atlanta, Georgia,
churns out 360 tons of man-made snow every day. In January 2017, hazardous
road conditions in the area and forced Snow Mountain to close. What was the
cause? A couple of inches of snow.

• "The feeling of flying like a bird!" That's the motto for "Crystal Wing," a roller
coaster at the Happy Valley amusement park in Beijing. In March 2016, the coaster
got stuck mid-ride for almost 20 minutes after an emergency auto-lock engaged.
What happened? A bird landed on a safety sensor.

MCIRONY

When music star Pharrell Williams was a teenager in Virginia in the 1990s,
he got fired from not one, not two, but *three* McDonald's. "I was lazy," he
later recalled. "I was only good at eating the McNuggets." Good thing
Williams wasn't lazy when it came to songwriting: in 2003, he co-wrote
McDonald's iconic "I'm Lovin' It" jingle.

IRONY IN THE NAME OF SCIENCE

In 2016, after a dead orca washed up in British Columbia, the National
Oceanic and Atmospheric Association (NOAA) launched an investigation and
determined that the animal most likely died of a fungal infection. Cause of the
infection: a tagging dart that was shot into the whale…by the NOAA. Standard
protocol is to use sterile darts, but when this particular orca—known as L95—
was originally tagged, the first dart missed. In their haste, the researchers pulled
it back and then shot the dart again without resterilizing it, and it infected the

whale. The worst part: orcas are on the Endangered Species List, and the tag was part of an NOAA study to figure out ways to protect them.

THY NAME IS IRONY

Two financial firms—one from France and one from San Francisco—got into a legal dispute over which firm can use the name "Andersen"…as in Arthur Andersen—the name of the disgraced financial firm that went belly-up as a result of the 2001 Enron scandal. After the French firm announced it was changing its name to Arthur Andersen International in 2015, Andersen Tax in San Francisco threatened to sue them for trademark infringement. (No word of anyone fighting over rights to the name "Enron," though.)

SO IRONIC IT HURTS

• A Frenchman named Patrick Edlinger was known as the "god of free climbing." The *Independent* wrote that he was among the best in the world at "overcoming sheer vertical rock faces and horizontal overhangs, often without safety ropes." Edlinger died in 2012 at the age of 52 after falling down a flight of stairs.

• Bill Hillman, a 35-year-old author and thrill seeker from Chicago, loves to run with the bulls in Pamplona, Spain. "I become one with the fiercest, most majestic animal on Earth," he says. He really became one with a rampaging Pamplona bull in 2014 when he tripped and fell and "the bull pierced his horn through my right thigh and lifted me into the air." Perhaps Hillman could have avoided injury if he'd only read the book *Fiesta: How to Survive the Bulls of Pamplona*…by Bill Hillman.

CRACKS IN THE IRONY

An iconic New York City building located at 280 Broadway, known for its old *New York Sun* clock, is in disarray. The old facade is crumbling so badly that an enclosure was built over the sidewalk to keep people from getting hit by falling concrete. There's been scaffolding on some parts of the building since 2011. And in 2016, the subceiling in the basement collapsed, causing a parking garage to be closed indefinitely. City council members have been complaining for years that the building is in violation of several codes, and nearby residents are concerned for their safety (one street vendor described it as "horrible and dangerous"). It just so happens that this building is the headquarters of the Department of Buildings, the agency in charge of making sure all of the city's buildings are safe and up to code. "Yes," said a DOB spokesperson, "we are aware of the irony."

Graven images? New trend in the funeral business: Tombstones that display videos of the deceased.

HIGH-TECH WORKOUT UNDERWEAR

Better workouts through underwear technology.

CHROMAT AEROS SPORTS BRA

What It Does: Integrates computer technology into a sports bra to keep the wearer cool.

Details: Incorporated in the design of the bra is a button-sized Intel microcontroller that monitors the wearer's breathing rate, body temperature, and perspiration levels. When the bra detects an increase in physical activity, the microcontroller opens carbon-fiber vents built into the bra, allowing air to circulate through it. The vents remain open until sensors detect that the wearer has cooled down, at which point the microcontroller closes them up again. According to Chromat, the bra "enables the wearer to break through barriers such as overheating to achieve peak performance."

OMBRA SPORTS BRA

What It Does: Analyzes the wearer's workouts and provides tips on how to improve them.

Details: A small black box attached to the lower band of the OMbra tracks the wearer's breathing rate, heart rate, and calories burned during the workout. The information is transmitted to an app on the wearer's smartphone for analysis. The app's "Digital Coach" then offers tips on how to get more out of each workout.

2UNDR GEARSHIFT PERFORMANCE BOXER BRIEFS

What It Does: Provides "in-your-pants air-conditioning."

Details: The founders of 2UNDR say they drew inspiration from kangaroos to add what they call a "Joey Pouch" to their entire line of underwear. The front panel of each undergarment has a hole that opens to the Joey Pouch. When putting on the skivvies, the wearer puts his "junk" into the pouch. The pouch prevents chafing by minimizing skin-on-skin contact and provides extra support (like a bra cup) while also improving airflow around the male anatomy.

Popular activity in China: having your ears cleaned by roadside earwax removers.

The Joey Pouches on 2UNDR's Gearshift briefs contain an additional cooling feature: a lining of ColdSkin thermal reduction fabric that 2UNDR says can lower the temperature of an overheating crotch by as much as 6°F. "ColdSkin can absorb a certain amount of heat in key areas and dissipate it to the outer atmosphere," the company says. "The combination of fast-drying microfiber filaments and the 100% all-natural mineral embedded within the filaments helps the body's own natural air-conditioning system regulate these key heat sensitive zones."

GUNZE SMART WORKOUT UNDERSHIRT

What It Does: Takes smart underwear technology like the OMbra's one step further by uploading fitness information to the cloud for third-party "workout professionals" to evaluate.

Details: Why settle for a digital coach? This undershirt, developed as a joint project by Japanese underwear maker Gunze and electronics giant NEC, is made of "conductive metallic textiles" that continuously monitor the wearer's heart rate, caloric intake, and posture. The data is uploaded to NEC's cloud (via the wearer's phone), where fitness companies and other businesses can access the information and provide personalized advice to the wearer of the undershirt.

BUBBLES DOUBLE-O PANTIES

What It Does: Acts like push-up bras for your butt cheeks.

Details: Now that these other garments have gotten you back in shape, why not show it off? The Double-O line of "booty bra" undergarments contain a pair of holes on the backside, one for each of your cheeks—hence the name "Double-O." Your cheeks poke through the holes and are hoisted aloft by the sturdy fabric at the bottom of each hole, giving your rear a more protruding and gravity-defying appearance. Or as the folks at Bubbles put it, "a noticeable butt lift effect."

*   *   *

FLUBBED HEADLINE

"Amphibious Pitcher Makes Debut"

—*East Oregonian*, June 8, 2015, describing Pat Venditte, the Oakland A's ambidextrous pitcher

New York was named for the Duke of York, not the English town of York.

TERRRIBLE TYPOS

Everyone makes misteaks.

• An Irish politician named Mary Lou McDonald sent out campaign mailers in 2016 in which she quoted legendary IRA member Bobby Sands. However, the quote lacked the impact she'd hoped for because of what came right before it: "As Booby Sands once said…"

• A sign outside a KFC advertised, for only $2.99, a "Loaded Bowel."

• These two typos made news in May 2016: The graduation program at Texas Christian University said it was Texas Christian "Univeristy." And on a California high school's faux-leather diploma covers, printed in fancy gothic lettering, were the words "Ontario High Shcool."

• This sad newspaper death announcement took an odd turn: "Remembering a wonderful daughter and sister. Your special smile and genital face, something time can never erase."

• In 2016, hackers from Bangladesh used forged documents to fool New York's Federal Reserve Bank into transferring huge sums of money into their account. The heist was up when a bank official noticed that the thieves misspelled "foundation" as "fandation." Up to that point, the hackers had received $81 million of the money they'd requested. Although they got away, the typo ended up costing them nearly $800 million more.

• An unfortunate new home listing in Round Lake, Illinois, began with "Attention Incestors!"

• When *Time* magazine ran a full-page ad in the *Wall Street Journal* in 2016, they put an unnecessary apostrophe in the most embarrassing spot it could go: "Don't miss the newest venture by the editor's of *Time*."

• This just in from Channel 18 News in Lexington, Kentucky: "5 Arrested in Math Lab Bust."

• In Reston, Virginia, in 2016, the Air Line Pilots Association wanted to send a clear message that it was against allowing Norwegian Airlines (NAI) to operate in the United States. But the message was confusing to everyone who saw it because it said "Deny NIA." And a lot of people saw the message because it was done in skywriting.

Thomas Jefferson wanted new states to have "classical" names like Metropotamia and Pelisipia.

ANTI-JOKES

They're not the typical HA-HA kind of funny…but they're still pretty funny.

What's red and smells like blue paint?
Red paint.

Why was six afraid of seven?
It wasn't. Numbers are not sentient and do not feel fear.

Knock-knock.
Who's there?
Your old friend, David.
David! What a lovely surprise, please come in!

What did the lawyer say to the other lawyer?
"We are both lawyers."

How do you confuse a blonde?
Paint yourself green and throw forks at her.

A horse walked into a bar. Many of the other patrons immediately left, having identified the potential danger in the situation.

What's brown and sticky?
A stick.

Your mother is so fat that she should lose weight so as to avoid any long-term health risks.

What do you call a woman on the Moon?
An astronaut.

What was the last thing the old man said before he kicked the bucket?
"Hey, how far do you think I can kick this bucket?"

What's red and bad for your teeth?
A brick.

What's worse than finding a worm in your apple?
War.

What did the farmer say when he lost his tractor?
"Where's my tractor?"

What's a vampire's favorite dessert?
Vampires aren't real.

What do a banana and a helicopter have in common?
Neither of them is a mailman.

Why isn't Helen Keller a good driver?
Because she died decades ago.

CELEBRITY COUPLINGS

We heard a rumor that Penny Marshall and Cindy Williams (Laverne & Shirley) once double dated with Simon and Garfunkel. We could only verify half of that rumor. But here are some fascinating stories of celebrity flings that we could verify.

PENNY MARSHALL & ART GARFUNKEL

Meetup: Marshall was depressed after a bitter divorce from her husband, Rob Reiner, in 1981, but it got even worse when her TV show, *Laverne & Shirley*, started slumping in the ratings. Then Marshall met singer Art Garfunkel (Carrie Fisher introduced them), who was also depressed following the suicide of his girlfriend. After Garfunkel guest-starred as a beatnik on a *Laverne & Shirley* episode, the two stars became friends…and then more than friends. Before Marshall knew it, she was traveling around the world with Art Garfunkel… along with Paul Simon and his wife, Carrie Fisher. "One of the most thrilling nights in my life," recalled Marshall, "was when Simon and Garfunkel sang in my apartment." The couple credit each other with lifting each other out of the doldrums, and they were pretty happy together for five years.

Split Up: Then Marshall and Garfunkel realized they could be just as happy as friends, which they've remained since (unlike Simon and Garfunkel).

TOM CRUISE & SOFIA VERGARA

Meetup: In 2005, four years before Vergara's breakout role as Gloria Pritchett on *Modern Family*, the Colombian-born immigrant was trying to make it as an actress in Miami. That's when Will Smith met her and invited her to a pre-Oscars party in Los Angeles. Vergara had no idea that she was being set up. According to journalist Lawrence Wright's award-winning book, *Going Clear: Scientology, Hollywood and the Prison of Belief*, Smith was recruiting potential wives for his friend, renowned Scientologist Tom Cruise, following Cruise's divorce from Nicole Kidman and his recent breakup with Penelope Cruz. After their first meeting, which Wright alleges was recorded with hidden cameras, Vergara was "smitten" with Cruise's smile and his charm…and the two dated briefly.

Split Up: Cruise tried to convince Vergara, a Catholic, to join him as a Scientologist. She said no on the spot and broke off all contact. When asked about the affair in 2011, all that Vergara said was, "I don't want to talk about that." (Two other women that Cruise allegedly "interviewed": Jennifer Garner and Scarlett Johansson.)

In Brazil, a group of dolphins herd fish toward fishermen and signal when they should cast their nets.

CONAN O'BRIEN & LISA KUDROW

Meetup: Before they became household names, O'Brien and Kudrow were in the same improv class together. "He was really smart, really funny," recalled Kudrow, "and he thought I was funny." So they started dating.

Split Up: Beyond the ability to make each other laugh, there wasn't much of a romantic spark, and the relationship never got too serious. But the fling did end up having a dramatic effect on both of their lives. Kudrow was embarrassed that she wasn't very good at improvisation, and told O'Brien that she was seriously considering quitting show business. He was able to convince her that she was still very funny and talented and should focus her talents on acting. So Kudrow kept at it, and a few years later, she landed her breakout role as Phoebe on *Friends*.

O'Brien was also at a crossroads. Even though he was a successful writer for *Saturday Night Live*, he wanted to do something in front of the cameras (hence the improv class). While they were dating, Kudrow gave him an idea: "I remember saying," she recalled years later, "'If (David) Letterman's leaving his late-night show, he's irreplaceable. So better it be someone we don't know at all.'" O'Brien didn't think he was famous enough to even audition for such a high-profile job, but Kudrow pressed him to "look into it." He did, and a year later took over as David Letterman's *Late Show* replacement. (O'Brien and Kudrow are still good friends.)

MERYL STREEP & JACK NICHOLSON

Meetup: This (alleged) love affair took place (allegedly) during the filming of the 1987 movie *Ironweed* when Streep was 37 and Nicholson was 50, and it sent Hollywood gossip writers into a frenzy. After the two stars had played warring spouses in the 1985 drama *Heartburn*, many news outlets reported that Streep "couldn't stand Nicholson" and vowed never to work with him again. Apparently not. According to Marc Eliot's biography, *Nicholson*, "Often during shooting, his Winnebago seemed to be balanced on four overworked Slinkys. One unnamed source told Mitchell Fink, of the *Los Angeles Herald Examiner*, that...

> Whatever is going on inside that Winnebago, it's starting to get out of hand, to the point where it's embarrassing a lot of people on the set.

Split Up: What did go on in that Winnebago? The two stars maintain they were just "practicing their lines." Streep was (and still is) married, and Nicholson was in a relationship with Angelica Houston (and secretly seeing

Veronica Cartwright on the side). Regardless of what occurred in or out of the Winnebago, Streep and Nicholson have remained close. When Streep was awarded the AFI Life Achievement Award in 2004, Nicholson gave a touching speech: "You transcend talent," he said to her from the podium. "To me, you are perfect and I love you very much. God bless you, and God bless America."

RYAN REYNOLDS & ALANIS MORISSETTE

Meetup: The Canadian-born singer met the Canadian-born actor at Drew Barrymore's 27th birthday party in 2002, and Morissette was smitten with Reynolds. They started dating, and then things got really serious: in 2004, Reynolds asked Morissette to marry him. "He's just such a supportive creature," she said at the time. "I feel so loved by him, in a trampoline kind of way." But what bounces up, must bounce down.

Split Up: The couple never set a wedding date, and in 2007 they announced their breakup through their respective publicists, who insisted the split was amicable (gossip sites say otherwise). What went wrong? It's uncertain, but a few months later, Ryan announced his engagement to Hollywood beauty Scarlett Johansson. (Those two did get married…and then divorced two years later.) And though Morissette has never given a reason publicly for the split, her 2008 album *Flavors of Entanglement* is still regarded as one of the saddest "breakup albums" ever. From the song "Torch": "These are the days of raw despondence. I miss your warmth and the thought of us bringing up our kids." Reynolds hasn't said much publicly about the relationship over the years, but in 2016, when he was on *The Today Show*, Matt Lauer asked him to sing a lyric from any famous 1990s song, and Reynolds half-heartedly sang the chorus of his ex-fiancée's biggest hit, "Isn't It Ironic?"

CARRIE FISHER & CHRISTOPHER DODD

Meetup: In 1985 the former Princess Leia and the future U.S. senator were set up on a blind date at a Washington, D.C., restaurant. And the man who set them up: Senator Ted Kennedy. According to Fisher's book *Shockaholic*, the odd double-date got even odder when Senator Kennedy turned to her and asked, "So, do you think you'll be having sex with Chris at the end of your date?" Fisher, who wasn't drinking that night (she'd recently gotten out of rehab), answered, "That probably won't happen." It didn't happen that night, but Fisher said they went out a few more times, when things…did happen.

Split Up: The romance didn't blossom, and the actress and the politician went their separate ways. In 2007, when Dodd was asked about the tryst, he had no comment, only saying, "It happened a long time ago in a galaxy far, far away."

WEAVE ME ALONE

What's in a fabric? It's how the threads are woven that gives them their special look.

Damask. A class of fabrics characterized by raised, elaborately designed patterns—usually of flowers, fruit, and animals—that have a different sheen from the fabric's background. The weaving style dates to the early Middle Ages, and is named after the ancient Silk Road city of Damascus (in modern-day Syria), one of the major centers of damask fabric trade. Traditional damasks were made from silk, but today they're made from many other materials, including wool, linen, cotton, and synthetics. Damask is most commonly used for upholstery, wall coverings, and curtains, but it can be found in clothing, too.

Houndstooth. Also known as dogstooth, this is the name of a fabric pattern that originated in wool garments worn by 19th-century shepherds in the Scottish Lowlands (the south of Scotland). The pattern is made with alternating bands of light and dark thread, and is characterized by rows of irregularly shaped, pointed squares, which were thought to resemble dogs' teeth—hence the name. It is most famously associated with the fictional detective Sherlock Holmes, who was depicted wearing a houndstooth deerstalker cap. You won't see many deerstalkers being worn today, but you can see houndstooth in wool jackets and many other types of clothing, as well as upholstery. (A version of houndstooth with small, pointy squares is called "puppytooth.")

Felt. It's the world's oldest textile, but it isn't woven—it's created by compressing fibers using heat and water. It was produced in ancient times throughout the Middle East, Rome, Greece, and Asia. Samples from 6500 BC have been found in Turkey. There are various legends about felt's origins, including one that, after 40 days on Noah's ark, the combination of urine and constant trampling on the fleece that the animals shed created a carpetlike layer of felt on the ship.

Seersucker. This lightweight fabric is intentionally woven to have a wrinkled or puckered texture, usually in a striped or checkered pattern. First produced in India during the British colonial era, it got its name from the Hindi *sirsakar*, which was borrowed from the Persian words *sheer* and *shakar*, meaning literally "milk" and "sugar," probably a reference to the fabric's smooth (milk) and lumpy (sugar) texture. Seersucker became fashionable in the early 20th century in the American South, where clothes—especially men's suits—made from the light, airy fabric were a good way of dealing with the region's muggy summers.

Cooking tip: if you're low on iron, cook with a cast-iron skillet. The food will absorb some of the iron.

SAME-SIDE SQUABBLES

Sports history includes thousands of bench-clearing brawls, but not nearly as many that pitted teammate against teammate.

BILL ROMANOWSKI vs. MARCUS WILLIAMS

Bill Romanowski is considered as one the best linebackers to ever play in the NFL…but is also regarded as one of the dirtiest. Romanowski was fined tens of thousands of dollars during his career for late hits, punches, kicks, spitting, and even throwing the football into an opponent's crotch. He'd do those kinds of things to any opposing player—even his own teammates. During a 2003 Oakland Raiders intrasquad practice game, tight end Marcus Williams blocked Romanowski. Romanowski responded by knocking Williams's helmet off of his head, and then punching him in the face. Williams's left eye socket was shattered, and it ended not only his season but his career. Williams sued Romanowski for millions, but was awarded $340,000 in lost wages and medical expenses. Amazingly, though, Romanowski kept his spot on the Raiders' roster.

DARRYL STRAWBERRY vs. KEITH HERNANDEZ

By the start of spring training in 1989, New York Mets star Darryl Strawberry still hadn't negotiated a new contract with the team. His teammate Keith Hernandez had reportedly sided with management during the dispute, which rubbed Strawberry the wrong way. As a photographer was arranging players for the official team photo after a practice, Strawberry refused to sit beside Hernandez, saying, "I only want to sit next to my *real* friends." Hernandez made a remark about Strawberry's agent, and Straw threw a punch. (He missed.) Both men then had to be restrained.

GENO SMITH vs. IK ENEMKPALI

Before the 2015 NFL season began, New York Jets quarterback Geno Smith agreed to appear at teammate IK Enemkpali's football camp, asking for little more than the $600 cost of a plane ticket to get him there. But Smith never showed. When the team reconvened that fall, Enemkpali confronted Smith about his absence and demanded that Smith pay back the $600 he'd spent on the unused plane ticket. Smith's response: he stuck a finger in Enemkpali's face and told him to shut up. That didn't sit well with the 261-pound linebacker. He punched Smith in the jaw; the injury cost Smith half a season. Enemkpali was suspended for four games by the NFL and was cut by the Jets.

Zippo lighters got their name because the inventor liked the sound of the word "zipper."

GILBERT ARENAS vs. JAVARIS CRITTENTON

In late 2009, Washington Wizards teammates Javaris Crittenton and JaVale McGee got into an argument over McGee's gambling debts. When star player Gilbert Arenas tried to break it up, Crittenton threatened to shoot him. Arenas called his bluff. The next day, Arenas put four handguns in Crittenton's locker with a note asking him to "choose one." According to teammate Caron Butler's book *Tuff Juice*, the next time Crittenton saw Arenas, he pulled his own gun (it was loaded) and aimed it at Arenas. The league hadn't yet decided how to punish Arenas and Crittenton, but when Arenas mimed shooting his teammates during a pregame player introduction, commissioner David Stern decided to suspend both men for the rest of the 2009–10 season.

JONATHAN PAPELBON vs. BRYCE HARPER

In the home stretch of the 2015 MLB season, the Washington Nationals were trying to eke out a spot in the playoffs. Every win counted, and tensions among players were high. During a game against the Phillies, Washington relief pitcher Jonathan Papelbon got upset at star teammate Bryce Harper, who he thought should've at least tried to reach first base after hitting a routine pop-up fly. As Harper went back into the dugout, Papelbon yelled, "You gotta run that ball out!" Harper muttered something under his breath, to which Papelbon responded by wrapping both of his hands around Harper's neck and squeezing. Teammates quickly broke up the fight, and Papelbon was suspended for four games. (The incident occurred just a few days after Papelbon had been suspended for intentionally throwing a pitch at a batter's head.)

LATRELL SPREWELL vs. P. J. CARLESIMO

The 1997–98 season did not get off to a good start for Golden State Warriors player Latrell Sprewell and coach P. J. Carlesimo. Sprewell was upset when the coach pulled him out late in a close game against the Los Angeles Lakers. A few weeks later at a practice session, Carlesimo criticized Sprewell's passing skills, telling him his throws needed to be "crisper." Sprewell responded by telling the coach that he wasn't in the mood…and then threatened to kill him. Carlesimo replied, "I'm right here." That's when Sprewell ran to the sidelines and choked Carlesimo, dragging him to the ground until teammates pulled him off and security escorted him out of the building. Fifteen minutes later, Sprewell snuck back into practice and went after Carlesimo again, trying to deliver a couple of punches before he was restrained again. Sprewell was suspended for the rest of the NBA season and was traded.

The grasshopper swarm that hit the Great Plains
in 1875 was estimated to be 1,800 miles long and 110 miles wide.

THE BEST PEOPLE

In 2002 the BBC aired a TV series called The 100 Greatest Britons, *a countdown show that presented a list of the nation's most important historical figures, compiled from a viewer poll. It was a ratings hit, which inspired TV producers in dozens of other countries to do the same. Here's who viewers in several nations think are their all-time best and brightest.*

UNITED STATES

The Greatest American (Discovery Channel, 2005)

1. Ronald Reagan. America's 40th president

2. Abraham Lincoln. America's 16th president

3. Dr. Martin Luther King Jr. Civil rights leader

4. George Washington. Revolutionary War hero and America's first president

5. Benjamin Franklin. Writer, scientist, and one of America's Founding Fathers

UNITED KINGDOM

The Greatest Britons (BBC, 2002)

1. Sir Winston Churchill. Prime minister from 1940 to 1945, and from 1951 to 1955. He led Britain and the Allies to victory over Hitler and the Axis powers in World War II. (He also won a Nobel Prize for Literature.)

2. Isambard Kingdom Brunel. Renowned architect and civil engineer during the Industrial Revolution of the 19th century. He designed, among other things, the Great Western Railway, the Clifton Suspension Bridge, and numerous transatlantic steamships, bridges, and tunnels.

3. Princess Diana

4. Charles Darwin. The scientist who popularized the theory of evolution.

5. William Shakespeare. He wrote plays.

CANADA

The Greatest Canadian (CBC, 2004)

1. Tommy Douglas. Premier of Saskatchewan from 1944 to 1961 who introduced universal, government-sponsored health care in his province, which became the basis for Canada's national health care system.

Ben Franklin published "The Drinkers Dictionary," with 228 slang phrases for being intoxicated.

2. Terry Fox. After having a leg amputated due to cancer, the 22-year-old ran across Canada in 1980 on one natural leg and one prosthetic one. He died in 1981, but the annual series of Terry Fox Runs across the country continues to raise millions for cancer research.

3. Pierre Trudeau. Prime minister from 1968 to 1979 and 1980 to 1984. The young, charismatic politician (earning comparisons to John F. Kennedy) helped cement Canadian identity during his terms in office, which included making the country officially bilingual, passing numerous progressive reforms, and fighting hard against Quebec becoming independent.

4. Frederick Banting. Doctor and scientist. In 1923 Banting and Scottish scientist John Macleod won the Nobel Prize for Medicine after discovering the hormone insulin and, thereby, the cause and treatment options for diabetes.

5. David Suzuki. A pioneering and outspoken environmentalist. He was also the host of the popular TV series *The Nature of Things*.

FRANCE

Le Plus Grand Français de tous les temps, or "The Greatest Frenchman of All Time" (France 2, 2005)

1. Charles de Gaulle. The most prominent and influential French politician of the 20th century. De Gaulle headed the exiled French government during the World War II Nazi occupation, and then led the postwar provisional government before being elected president.

2. Louis Pasteur. "The father of microbiology." His work led to the universal acceptance of germ theory, which led to vaccines against rabies and anthrax, and the development of pasteurization, the process by which milk was treated to kill bacteria and limit the spread of food-borne illnesses.

3. Abbé Pierre. Catholic friar. The charity he founded in 1949—Emmaus—now serves millions of poor and homeless people in more than three dozen countries.

4. Marie Curie. Scientist. Born in Poland but a naturalized French citizen, Curie's pioneering research on radioactivity won her two Nobel Prizes.

5. Coluche. Actor and comedian. He starred in movies, had his own TV show, ran a joke campaign for the presidency, and started a charity called Restaurants du Coeur ("Restaurants of the Heart"), which feeds more than 50,000 hungry people every day.

A real person named Willy Wonka lived in Blue Hill, NE, and corresponded with Roald Dahl.

ARGENTINA

El Gen Argentino, or "The Argentine Gene" (Telefe, 2007)

1. José de San Martín. The 18th-century general who successfully led Argentine armies against Spain and won the nation's independence.

2. René Favaloro. Cardiac and thoracic surgeon. In the late 1960s, he developed the now-standard medical procedure of bypass surgery.

3. Juan Manuel Fangio. Formula One driver. He was one of the sport's earliest and most successful stars, winning the world championship five times in the 1950s.

4. Alberto Olmedo. Popular actor and comedian. He starred in a string of ribald, sex-themed comedies in the 1970s and 1980s, and in his own semi-improvised sketch comedy show in the 1980s called *No Toca Botón!*

5. Che Guevara. Marxist revolutionary and advocate of the working class and poor. He's most famous for helping install Fidel Castro as dictator of Cuba.

GERMANY

Unsere Besten, or "Our Best" (ZDF, 2003)

1. Konrad Adenauer. The first chancellor of West Germany after World War II. He worked aggressively to create a new, peaceful Germany by encouraging economic growth and close ties with the United States, the UK, and France.

2. Martin Luther. Theologian. In the 16th century, Luther protested against corruption in the Roman Catholic Church by nailing his list of grievances ("Ninety-Five Theses") to the door of a chapel in Wittenberg, leading to the Protestant Reformation, and causing multiple new Christian sects to split from the Catholic Church.

3. Karl Marx. Political scientist and author of *The Communist Manifesto* and *Das Kapital*, which became the blueprints for communism.

4. Sophie and Hans Scholl. Brother and sister who led the White Rose, a student resistance group in Nazi Germany during World War II. They were convicted and executed for high treason in 1943 after they were caught handing out antiwar leaflets at the University of Munich.

5. Willy Brandt. Chancellor of West Germany from 1969 to 1974. Brandt won the Nobel Peace Prize in 1971 for his work in trying to improve relations between Western Europe and Communist-controlled Eastern Europe.

The lava flows from the 2017 eruption of Mt. Etna could be seen from space.

FILM NAME ORIGINS

You know the names—now find out where they came from!

***O Brother, Where Art Thou?* (2000).** In the classic 1941 film *Sullivan's Travels*, a Depression-era director wants to make a serious movie about the nation's poor, titled *O Brother, Where Art Thou?* But after traveling the country disguised as a hobo to gather research for the film, he decides the world needs comedies more than serious films. Joel and Ethan Coen took the fictional film title for their film—about three Depression-era hobo-ish characters on a journey of their own.

***Gattaca* (2007).** This science-fiction film, starring Ethan Hawke, Uma Thurman, and Jude Law, is about a futuristic society where "perfect" children are created via genetic manipulation. The film's title (and the name of a corporation that features prominently in the film) is a reference to the DNA-based storyline: "Gattaca" is derived from G, A, T, and C, the first letters of the four nucleobases that make up DNA—guanine, adenine, thymine, and cytosine.

***The Lost Boys* (2007).** This cult classic horror film, which featured a young Kiefer Sutherland, Corey Haim, and Corey Feldman, revolves around a gang of teenage vampires in the fictional town of Santa Carla, California. The name was taken from J. M. Barrie's "Lost Boys"—the boys led by Peter Pan who, like vampires, never grow up.

***The Breakfast Club* (1985).** John Hughes's coming-of-age classic is about five high school kids who spend an all-day detention session together. One of the five (in the film's final scene) gives the group the nickname "the Breakfast Club." Hughes got the name from a friend, whose son went to New Trier High School in Winnetka, Illinois. At New Trier, the school's daily detention session—which took place in the morning—was nicknamed "the Breakfast Club."

Indiana Jones. The title character of George Lucas and Stephen Spielberg's 1981 movie *Raiders of the Lost Ark* was originally named Indiana Smith. "Indiana" was the name of an Alaskan Malamute that George Lucas had in the 1970s. But Spielberg didn't like "Smith" as a surname, so Lucas suggested "Jones." Bonus fact: "Indiana" isn't Jones's real first name—it's "Henry." The story of Lucas's Malamute is referenced in 1989's *Indiana Jones and the Last Crusade*, when Jones father, Henry Jones Sr. (Sean Connery), insists on calling Indiana "Junior," saying, "We named the *dog* 'Indiana.'"

The U.S. state with the highest median household income is Maryland; the lowest is Mississippi.

WISE GUYS

Wise words from thoughtful thinkers.

"Do one thing every day that scares you."
—Eleanor Roosevelt

" *If you are always trying to be normal, you will never find out how amazing you can be.* "
—Maya Angelou

"It is better to be thought of as a fool than to open your mouth and remove all doubt."
—Abraham Lincoln

"If you let your head get too big, it'll break your neck."
—Elvis Presley

"FOLLOW YOUR DREAMS, EXCEPT FOR THE ONE WHERE YOU'RE NAKED IN CHURCH."
—Rev. David Ault

"When you battle with your conscience and lose, you win."
—Henny Youngman

"The sun, with all those planets revolving around it and dependent upon it, can still ripen a bunch of grapes as if it had nothing else in the universe to do."
—Galileo Galilei

"Money won't make you happy...but everybody wants to find out for themselves."
—Zig Ziglar

Dutch word for their traditional wooden shoes: *klompen.*

CRASH!

Statistics say you're more likely to die in a car crash on the way to the airport than in an airplane. But those statistics relate to commercial airliners. Google "small plane crash" and the numbers soar. Here's proof that the skies aren't so friendly.

THE LONG AND SHORT OF IT

Pilot Tico McNutt might have thought the most dangerous animal he would encounter in a 2004 trip to Botswana would be the wild African dogs he came to study. Not so. The Cessna C172 he was piloting had a close encounter at Santawani airstrip in Botswana's Okavango Delta with…a giraffe. McNutt emerged shaken…but not injured. As for the giraffe? When the wing of McNutt's plane slammed into the long-necked animal, it took out the plane…and giraffe.

BIN THERE DONE THAT

Personal aircraft are one of the perks some wealthy families enjoy, but they can also be a curse. Take the bin Laden family. Rumored to be worth at least $7 billion, they've had more than their share of small plane fatalities.

• Mohammed bin Awad bin Laden, father of Osama bin Laden, died in 1967 when his Beechcraft 18 crashed while landing in Saudi Arabia. The 73-year-old was on his way a to wedding—his. He was scheduled to marry wife number 23.

• In 1988 Osama's half-brother died after his small plane hit power lines in San Antonio, Texas.

• Then, on July 31, 2015, Osama's stepmother and his sister were killed when the business jet they were flying in overshot a runway in southern England. The Phenom 300 business jet hit an embankment, flipped over, and smashed into an adjacent car lot. Cause of the crash: The jet, say investigators, was coming in way too fast—40 percent more than the recommended rate of speed. Another reason: the speeding pilot would have been inundated with warnings, instructions, and messages, and his "mental capacity could have become saturated."

ESCAPE FROM RIKERS ISLAND

On February 1, 1957, Charles Naylor had just scored the gig of a lifetime: playing piano with the popular music act Fred Waring's Pennsylvanians. To celebrate, he and his wife Phyllis decided to flee the blizzard howling in New

York City and hop onto a Douglas DC-6A for Miami. Bad decision. Less than a minute after takeoff from La Guardia, the plane's wing sheared off—possibly after clipping a pole—and the aircraft dove…straight into the prison yard on Rikers Island. Charles and Phyllis stumbled from the burning wreckage into the snow. As screams filled the night, Rikers Island assistant deputy warden James Harrison made a crazy decision: he ushered 57 inmates into the flame-filled yard, not knowing whether they would help, as he hoped, or try to escape in the confusion. There were horrors all around. Twenty people, including an infant, lay dead or dying. A stewardess who was helping passengers had her nose and ears burned off. Despite the danger—and the possibility of escape—when the warden checked the cells at the end of the harrowing night, all were present and accounted for. The parole board released 30 inmates for their heroism and reduced the sentences of another 16. The assistant deputy warden's crazy decision earned him the Correction Department's highest award: the Medal of Honor. And the Naylors? They survived, but Charles's career as a pianist was over. His badly burned fingers couldn't stretch the way they once had, so he turned to composing. And Phyllis never set foot on a plane again.

> **THE "RIKERS"** *in Rikers Island is an anglicized version of Rycken. Abraham Rycken was among the first wave of Dutch settlers in New York in the 1630s. The land that now houses the Rikers Island prison belonged to Rycken's family until 1884, when they sold it to the City of New York for $180,000.*

WHAT A CROC!

It's not unusual for a passenger to carry a duffel bag onto a small plane. What is unusual is for the passenger to be carrying a crocodile in the bag. That's what the sole survivor claimed caused the crash of a LET 410 turboprop plane flying from Kinshasa to Bandundu airport in the Democratic Republic of the Congo. The route was the air equivalent of a taxi ride, and it wasn't unusual for passengers to bring along chickens and other animals. But apparently a crocodile was too much, even for the Congolese. When the three-foot-long croc escaped from its bag, the flight attendant freaked. She ran toward the cockpit and a panicked planeful of passengers followed. The sudden shift in weight sent the plane into a nosedive and it "fell out of the sky like a leaf," as one witness reported. Twenty people died. (Note: The croc survived the crash, but not by much—a bystander killed it with a machete.)

Billiard balls used to be made of ivory from the tusks of Asian elephants. One tusk yielded up to five balls.

AM/FM

While you're turning on the news or putting on some music, dozens of radio station employees are buzzing around the studio trying to make sure that there's no "dead air" (silence), barking terms like these to save time and create the magic of radio.

Birdie: A small amount of feedback that sounds like a tweeting bird

Howlround: Lots of feedback

Bleeble: A brief bit of music used for transition

Cans: Headphones

Doughnut: A nationally run commercial that has a spot for a local affiliate to add in their own specific ad; it's called a doughnut because there's a hole in the middle

Ramp: Lyrics-free music that the DJ can talk over, either as background for an ad or the introduction to a song—it's "ramping up"

Hitting the post: When a DJ's banter is timed perfectly so they talk right up to the "post"—the point when a song's lyrics begin

Clear-channel: Not to be confused with media conglomerate Clear Channel, it's a technical term for a major radio station that's been given FCC clearance to be the only station with that frequency (101.9 or 97.1, for example) in an area of up to 750 miles wide

Antenna farm: That place on the edge of town where all of the TV and radio transmitting towers sit

Across mike: Speaking sideways into a microphone to cut down on excessive, extra popping and hissing sounds

Cough button: A mute button on a microphone (or control board), so that the DJ can cough and not have it go out over the air

Drive time: TV's "prime time" is in the evenings; in radio, most people are listening in their cars while commuting to work: 6–10 a.m. and 4–7 p.m.

Woodshedding: When a DJ marks up a script to place in pauses and inflections; one slash indicates a pause, two indicates a long pause, and an underline is for emphasis; the little marks look like axe marks

Stop set: A long commercial break, so named because the DJ gets to "stop" working for a while

Clock: A chart for radio personalities that shows a day's complete schedule, worked down to the minute, including station breaks, ads, and who is working when

Twig: A radio antenna

To get through Prohibition, Anheuser-Busch sold a near-beer soft drink called Bevo.

MAKE YOUR OWN BUBBLE GUM

Everyone remembers the thrill of learning to blow bubbles with bubble gum. Here's another memory waiting to be made: blowing bubbles with gum you've made yourself. But first, a tasty refresher on the history of bubble gum.

POP CULTURE

If you're a lover of chewing gum, you have these four people to thank for it:

1. General Antonio López de Santa Anna (1794–1876). Military leader and eleven-term president of Mexico. By 1869 he'd also been overthrown eleven times and was living in exile on Staten Island, New York, where he was trying to raise money for a revolution that would put him in power for the twelfth time. He planned to raise the money by finding an industrial use for *chicle*, the latex rubber sap of the sapodilla tree, which was native to Mexico's Yucatán peninsula.

2. Thomas Adams (1818–1905). Santa Anna gave some chicle to Adams, his secretary, who set out to find a way to *vulcanize*, or stabilize, chicle the same way that Charles Goodyear had invented a process for vulcanizing India rubber in 1844. Adams did not succeed. He did, however, observe Santa Anna chewing chicle, just as the people of the Yucatán had for centuries. Finally accepting the fact that the stuff could not be used to make toys, rain boots, or tires, Adams tried boiling some chicle (no sugar, no flavoring)…and created the world's first chicle-based chewing gum. It sold for a penny a piece and was far superior to the tree sap and paraffin wax, a byproduct of petroleum, that people chewed in those days. (Santa Anna never did return to power and died broke in 1876.)

3. William Wrigley Jr. (1861–1932). In 1891 Wrigley used every dollar he had—$32—to launch a business selling "Wrigley's Scouring Soap." He gave free samples of baking powder to anyone who would buy his soap, until he realized that people wanted the baking powder more than the soap. So he went into the baking powder business, giving away free samples of chewing gum as a premium with every sale. Then he realized that people wanted the gum more than the baking powder…and he went into the chewing gum business. More than any other person, Wrigley is responsible for turning America into a nation of gum chewers by advertising his Spearmint and Juicy Fruit gums in every corner of the United States. In 1915 he mailed free sticks of gum to every address in every

---

Japan's SkyCycle is a bicycle-powered "roller coaster." Its tracks are four stories off the ground.

phone book in America—more than 1.5 million homes in all. (He figured that if people could afford a telephone, they could afford gum.) He did it again in 1919, to the 7 million U.S. households who now owned telephones.

4. Walter Diemer (1904–1998). In 1928 Diemer, 23, was a newly-hired accountant with Fleer, a Philadelphia gum and candy maker. He liked to experiment with recipes in his spare time, which is how, purely by accident, he stumbled across a formula that was stretchier, less sticky, and produced better bubbles than the company's earlier attempts to bring a bubble gum to market. Diemer added pink food coloring (he was out of every other color), and took five pounds of the stuff—soon to be called Dubble Bubble—to a grocery store. It sold out by the end of the day. Americans have been chewing bubble gum ever since.

A RECIPE FOR HOMEMADE BUBBLE GUM

Ingredients:

- ⅓ cup "gum base" pellets, the modern equivalent of chicle, which gives chewing gum its chewiness and texture. It's sold in specialty supermarkets and baking stores, and can also be ordered online.

- 3 tablespoons corn syrup
- 1 teaspoon glycerin
- ½ teaspoon citric acid
- ¾ cup confectioners' sugar
- ½ to 2 teaspoons flavoring extract or flavored gelatin
- Food coloring

Directions:

Combine gum base, corn syrup, glycerin, citric acid, and flavoring in a microwave-safe bowl. Microwave on high for 60 seconds, then remove and stir with a spoon. Microwave for another 30 seconds and stir until the ingredients are thoroughly combined. Stir a few drops of food coloring into the mixture.

Pour about half the confectioners' sugar into a pile on a clean, solid work surface. Make a "well" by creating an indentation in the center of the pile.

Pour the gum base mixture into the well. Be careful! The mixture will still be hot. Let it cool for 3–5 minutes.

When the mixture has cooled enough to allow you to work with it, knead it (like bread dough) for 10–15 minutes.

When the mixture gets sticky, knead in some of the remaining sugar.

When the gum has been thoroughly kneaded, press or roll it out flat on your work surface, and then cut into individual pieces.

Lose weight—send e-mails instead: The adhesive glue on an envelope has 1.7 calories per gram.

LOONY LOTTERY WINNERS

What would you do if you won the lottery? Pay off some bills? Buy a new car? Probably.
Or would you spend your windfall on something a bit more off-kilter?

WEATHER IT MAKES SENSE OR NOT

In 2008 Alan Rowley of Selston, England, won £1.9 million (about $2.4 million) on a Lucky Dip lottery ticket. Among his immediate purchases were a few of the usual big ticket items that lottery winners go for, including a brand-new house and a brand-new car. But then he spent £20,000 (about $25,000) on a professional-grade, state-of-the-art, electronic weather forecasting system. Rowley says he only has a passing interest in meteorology "like most people have," but he wanted to be able to know exactly what the weather would be like before he decided whether to go to professional cricket matches, because he hates to get stuck in the rain.

HAVING A BALL

In 1996 John McGuinness won £10 million in Scotland's National Lottery. Two years later, after having given away £3 million to friends and having spent millions on cars and houses, he decided to invest in a professional soccer team. But in doing so, he unwittingly guaranteed the team's debt. Due to that debt— and a bank loan scheme set in action by the team's other owners—McGuinness wound up losing his entire £4 million investment. By 2007 he was bankrupt.

SCHOOLED

In 2013, 84-year-old Gloria Mackenzie of Florida won what as at the time the largest Powerball jackpot in history: $590 million. That kind of money means that she could buy or fund almost anything she wanted, and it was just a drop in the bucket. So she did what anyone would do—she bought a new house and then gave away millions to friends and family. But then she heard that the high school in East Millinocket, Maine, that she had attended (and later worked at as a teacher) was so run-down that it was about to get shut down. The $1.8 million needed to repair it (particularly its roof) just wasn't there. So Mackenzie did what very few people could do: she wrote a check to Schneck High School for $2 million, which was enough to renovate the building (with a little something extra left over).

Neil Young, Bob Seger, and Pete Townshend all refuse to license any of their music for streaming.

MOVIE ON THIS

Cynthia Stafford and her father took the $67 million lump sum option when they won a $112 Mega Millions jackpot in 2007. Cynthia then used most of her share to fulfill her lifelong dream of producing movies. Lacking any business experience, she first donated $1 million to the Geffen Playhouse in Los Angeles, which enabled her to talk to industry mogul David Geffen, and get his financial advice. Then, after taking a two-day seminar on filmmaking, Stafford started Queen Nefertari productions. The company has released four small-budget movies to date, including the romantic comedy *The Brass Teapot* and the horror parody *Holla II*, which reportedly performed well on home video.

GRAPPLING WITH SUCCESS

A guy named Jonathan Vega won $35 million in a 2008 Powerball jackpot, and he spent almost all of it to fulfill a lifelong dream: to get involved with professional wrestling. He started his own company called Wreslicious—a women-only wrestling league in which the participants all wore skimpy outfits. Vega himself even took to the ring on a few occasions as league CEO "J. V. Rich." The company got some spotty TV coverage in 2010, but it went bankrupt by the end of the year, taking Vega's wealth with it.

GOING GAGA

Adrian Bayford of Suffolk, England, won £148 million in a 2012 Europe-wide lottery—the equivalent of about $190 million. That made Bayford the second-richest British lottery winner in history and gave him enough money to fulfill a dream: to amass the world's most valuable collection of Lady Gaga memorabilia. Bayford bought Gaga costumes, shoes, rare records, and lots more. After all, he had to have something to fill up the £6 million mansion he bought that will serve as a Lady Gaga museum and memorabilia store. (He also bought a bunch of Beatles, Madonna, and *Star Wars* stuff—but that was just to sell in the store.)

LIKE A BATTLEFIELD

Ray and Barbara Wragg of Sheffield, England, won the equivalent of $15 million in 2000. They've spent very little of it on themselves, preferring to give it away. The main recipients: the two local hospitals, Weston Park Hospital and Sheffield Children's Hospital. In addition to that, in 2004 they footed the bill for 50 English veterans of World War II to revisit Italy for the 60th anniversary of the Battle of Monte Cassino.

The word "unfriend" has been around since the 1200s.

DOGS YOU DON'T KNOW

Everyone's familiar with at least some species in the Canidae *family of mammals—the domestic dog, wolf, coyote, and even the red fox (insert* Sanford and Son *joke here). Here are some of their wild canine cousins that may be a little less familiar.*

RACCOON DOG

Native to: Forested regions of eastern Asia (including eastern Siberia, China, Vietnam, the Koreas, and Japan).

Description: Raccoon dogs actually do look like raccoons: they have short, squat bodies with short legs; thick, grizzled, gray, brown, black, and reddish fur; and a short, bushy tail. They also have small heads and raccoonlike faces with wide cheeks, short pointy noses, and even black "mask" markings around the eyes. They're small—just 15 to 20 inches tall, 20 to 28 inches in length, and their weight varies from about 8 pounds in early summer to 20 pounds in late fall.

Notable Characteristics: The reason raccoon dogs go through such a dramatic weight change is because they semi-hibernate during the winter, and they're the only canine species that does. (They don't go into full hibernation; they go into a dormant period during winter, during which they spend most of their time in burrows, usually in pairs, surviving primarily off the fat they built up during the summer.) They're also one of only two canine species that can climb trees (the other is the North American gray fox).

Bonus Fact: From the 1920s to the 1950s, the government of the Soviet Union introduced raccoon dogs into several parts of western Russia, hoping to boost the fur industries in those regions. The transplanted populations spread over the following decades, which is why wild raccoon dogs can now be found in Poland, Sweden, Norway, Germany, Austria, and even France.

BUSH DOG

Native to: Forests and wet savanna lands throughout Brazil and surrounding countries, and north into Central America.

Description: Except for their color, bush dogs look a lot like otters. They have long, stout bodies; very short legs (they stand just 12 inches tall at the shoulder); short reddish fur; short dark tails; and otterlike heads with small, rounded ears.

Notable Characteristics: Bush dogs live in family units of up to 12 members. They hunt alone or in packs, and their prey consists primarily of large South American rodents, especially paca, agouti, and capybara—the world's largest rodent species (it looks like a giant guinea pig). Preying on animals like the semiaquatic capybara is natural for bush dogs because they've become semiaquatic too: they always live near bodies of water, they have partially webbed feet, and they're great swimmers—even underwater. (Which means that bush dogs not only resemble otters—they act like them, too.)

Bonus Fact: In South America bush dogs have several different names, including *perro de agua*, meaning "water dog," and *perro vinagre*, meaning "vinegar dog." Why "vinegar dog"? Because their urine smells like vinegar.

DHOLE

Native to: Forests, rain forests, and jungles in southern Asia (including India and China) and Southeast Asia (including Thailand, Vietnam, Sumatra, and Indonesia).

Description: Dholes look like long, lanky foxes. They have red fur on their heads and backs; white throats and underbellies; long, slender legs; long, bushy black tails; pointy snouts; and big, upright, rounded ears. They can stand 22 inches tall at the shoulder, reach 3 feet in length, and weigh more than 44 pounds.

Notable Characteristics: Also known as Asiatic wild dogs, Indian wild dogs, and red dogs, dholes live in clans of between five and twelve members, led by one dominant monogamous pair. They hunt alone or in packs, feeding on berries, insects, frogs, lizards, rodents, deer, wild boar—and sometimes even monkeys. Unfortunately, their numbers are diminishing, due primarily to loss of habitat and to disease from domestic dogs and cats. It's estimated that there are just 2,500 adult dholes left in the wild today.

Bonus Fact: Dholes are known for their wide range of vocalizations, including a high-pitched whistle, a two-tone yap-squeak, a chickenlike cluck, and what is sometimes described as a "scream."

ETHIOPIAN WOLF

Native to: Alpine meadows in the Ethiopian Highlands, a rugged mountain chain in central and northern Ethiopia—and *only* at altitudes above 9,600 feet.

Description: Slender and long-legged, somewhat like coyotes in size and shape, with short, tawny-red coats, white throats, and patches on their bellies.

Notable Characteristics: Evolutionary biologists say Ethiopian wolves are the most highly specialized of all the canine species. They are believed to have descended from wolves that ventured from Europe and Asia into Africa during the last ice age, roughly 100,000 years ago. Over the ensuing millennia, they evolved into the unique species they are today. Most wolf species around the world prey primarily on large ungulates, such as moose and deer, and have stout, powerful jaws with large teeth suited to capturing that prey. Ethiopian wolves, on the other hand, have narrow, pointy jaws, with much smaller teeth—perfectly suited to capturing the burrowing rodents that are abundant in the region, such as the big-headed mole rat. Today, these wolves are almost totally dependent on those rodents for their survival, and that has come at a cost: the habitat in which these rodents live is increasingly being lost, primarily to agriculture, and the wolf's range has subsequently shrunk to just six small and specific regions in the Ethiopian Highlands. There are believed to be fewer than 600 Ethiopian wolves left in the wild today.

Bonus Fact: In 2016 the South Korean company Sooam Biotech—which specializes in cloning animals—announced that it would be attempting to clone Ethiopian wolves in the hopes of saving the species from extinction.

BAT-EARED FOX

Native to: Savannas and grassland terrains in two separate and distinct locations in eastern and southern Africa.

Description: Bat-eared foxes have sandy gray bodies, with darker fur on their muzzles, eye rings, ears, feet, and tail. And they are probably the most recognizable canid species, mostly because of their enormous upright ears. The ears can be up to five inches long—huge considering the fact that these tiny canids stand just 12–16 inches tall at the shoulder. (And their small, pointy-nosed heads do make them look like bats.) Those ears are useful not just for hearing: they're full of blood vessels, which allows the bat-eared fox to shed heat during those regions' intense hot seasons.

Notable Characteristics: Bat-eared foxes can live in small groups of adults and pups, or as just one mating pair and pups. They're very good diggers, and they dig several deep dens throughout their territories, each with several chambers and entrances and exits. They use the dens to escape predators (lions, jackals, hyenas, and eagles) and extreme temperatures, and to raise their pups. And unlike most canine species, the males participate in pup-raising as much as the females do…and often more.

Bonus Fact: The most unique feature of the bat-eared fox is that their primary food is termites. They also eat other kinds of insects, including ants, crickets, spiders, and scorpions, which makes the bat-eared fox the only primarily insectivorous dog species in the world. They have even developed teeth that are suited for that bizarre diet: they have up to eight extra molars, which allows them to grind the hard exoskeletons of insects, and they have between 46 and 50 teeth—the most of any canine species. (They also occasionally eat small rodents, lizards, bird eggs, and plants—including desert truffles.)

A FEW MORE WILD DOG SPECIES

Darwin's Fox. There are only around 250 of these small, foxlike dogs left in the wild. Most of them are on the island of Chiloe, off the Pacific coast of Chile; the remainder are in a small area of the nearby mainland. They're named for famed British naturalist Charles Darwin, who encountered one of these foxes while exploring the region in 1834. (Darwin wrote that he snuck up behind it—and killed it with a hammer. The dead fox was stuffed, taken back to England, and put on display in London's Zoological Society museum.)

Crab-Eating Fox. Another South American canid, these small gray dogs survive on a diet of bird and turtle eggs, insects, lizards, amphibians, and fruit, but during the wet season they dig through mud to find their favorite food—crabs. (Like Darwin's fox, the crab-eating fox is called a fox because of its foxlike appearance, but neither are related to the true foxes; a genus that includes the red fox, Arctic fox, and ten other species found around the world.)

Tibetan Sand Fox. One of the true foxes, these small, stout-bodied, short-legged, thick-coated dogs—known for their strange, squarish faces and squinty eyes—live in the barren steppes and sandy near-deserts of the Himalayan Plateau in Tibet, Nepal, India, and Bhutan—at altitudes of 11,000 to 17,000 feet.

Maned Wolf. The tallest wild dogs in the world, standing 35 inches high at the shoulder. They're long-legged, lean, and graceful-looking, with a long reddish coat, black lower legs, and a distinctive black mane. More than 50 percent of their diet is plant matter, including bananas, guavas, sugarcane, and a wild tomatolike fruit known as the wolf apple. (Bonus: The maned wolf marks its territory with urine, which has a very strong odor—it's said to smell like marijuana—which is why it has the nickname "skunk wolf.")

Epicyon haydeni. These wild dogs can be found across the Lower 48 of the continental United States, from Florida to Oregon. They have huge, powerfully muscled bodies weighing up to 370 pounds. They have massive skulls, with squashed, somewhat lionlike muzzles, and extremely powerful jaws that can crush bones. (But don't be afraid! You can only find fossils of *Epicyon haydeni* across the United States…because they went extinct 12 to 6 million years ago. They are the largest canid species ever recorded.)

TAUTOLOGY!

Tautologic phrases are expressions in which something is said twice using different words. (From tautologos—Greek for "repeating what has been said.") Each word works on its own, but together it sounds more emphatic. Here are some "typical examples." (Hey, that's one!)

Short summary

Close proximity

The evening sunset

Hot water heater

First priority

Overexaggeration

New innovation

Future predictions

Necessary requirement

Please RSVP

Free gift

Added bonus

I made it with my own hands

Return again

I heard it with my own ears

First and foremost

Great big

Say it out loud

Take turns, one after the other

Sad misfortune

All well and good

Prepay in advance

Royal Crown

Tuna fish

Bread rolls

Young children

Manly man

Devoted disciples

Completely devoid

Repeat that again

I am my father's son

New addition

Daylight

Speed Racer

Cassette tape

Electric power

The Amazon molly fish is asexual. It reproduces by creating female clones of itself.

THE DIFFICULT DECISIONS OF ROBERT E. LEE, PT. II

How we make the tough decisions shapes our lives. It can also define "greatness." Would you do what Robert E. Lee did? (Part I of the story starts on page 37.)

DECISION 3: WHICH SIDE SHOULD I FIGHT FOR?

Next came the most difficult decision of Lee's life. He was both a proud American and a proud Virginian. Today, it's accepted that the federal government is responsible for setting the national agenda with regard to laws, taxation, education, and more. In the 19th century, Washington, D.C., had a lot less direct oversight over people's lives. The states made their own laws— including laws relating to slavery. Like most Americans of his generation, Lee's loyalty was to his state first, and his country second.

That didn't mean he wasn't alarmed when several Southern states— South Carolina, Alabama, Georgia, Texas, and Louisiana—seceded from the Union after Lincoln was elected. Lee feared that Virginia's leaders would follow suit, and he thought it was a major overreaction to the problem, stating, "I do not believe in secession as a constitutional right, nor that there is sufficient cause for revolution."

But after Virginia's lawmakers voted by a narrow margin to secede in April 1861 and join the newly formed Confederate States of America, Lee suddenly found himself as a man without a country. He didn't want to fight for either side. He sought the counsel of General Scott, director of the Confederacy's War Department. Scott's advice: "You cannot sit out the war." The situation became even more complicated after President Lincoln, an admirer of Lee, offered him the chance to lead the Union army in the war. Lee had to think about it for a few days. "I look upon secession as anarchy," he confided. "If I owned the four millions of slaves in the South I would sacrifice them all to the Union, but how can I draw my sword upon Virginia, my native state?"

SACRIFICE

So when it came down to choosing between the North and the South, Lee chose neither. He chose Virginia. Turning down Lincoln's offer, he resigned his commission with the U.S. Army after serving with distinction for 32 years. A few weeks later, Lee accepted Confederate president Jefferson Davis's offer to

History's first all-woman duel was fought in Liechtenstein in 1892, after Princess Pauline Metternich...

serve in the Army of Northern Virginia, the first line of defense against invading Union soldiers. Within a year Lee would be in charge of the entire Confederate military.

History buffs can only speculate about what would have transpired had Lee accepted Lincoln's offer, but it's hard to imagine a worse fate than a war that killed more than 620,000 people. In his 2014 book, *A Disease in the Public Mind*, historian Thomas Fleming theorizes that the outcome would have been much better: "General Lee would have remained in command of the Union army, ready to extinguish any and all flickers of revolt. By expertly mingling his troops so that Southern and Northern regiments served in the same brigades, he would have forged a new sense of brotherhood in and around the word 'Union.' At the end of President Lincoln's second term, it seems more than likely that the American people would have elected Robert E. Lee as his successor."

DECISION 4: FOLLOW ORDERS, OR FOLLOW MY HEART?

But that didn't happen, and four years later, the Confederacy had all but lost the Civil War. And Lee knew it. After some early successes in driving off invading Union troops—which earned him a lot of respect on both sides—Lee lost both of his major incursions into the North at the battles of Antietam and Gettysburg, two of the bloodiest of the war. Lee, now in his mid-50s, was suffering from heart problems that kept him sidelined for weeks at a time. After Gettysburg, he even tried to resign his commission, but President Davis talked him out of it. Yet despite the losses, the Confederate soldiers still looked up to him. Why? Unlike many commanders who traveled with servants and slept on soft beds, Lee chose to be with his troops, both on and off the battlefield. Lee biographer Peter S. Carmichael wrote that the soldiers had

> "extraordinary confidence in their leader, extraordinary high morale, a belief they couldn't be conquered. But at the same time it was an army that was being worn down. Lee was pushing these men beyond the logistical capacity of that army."

As the South ran low on supplies, and the desertion rate among Confederate soldiers increased, Lee proposed a radical plan: train the slaves to fight. That idea did not go down well. "The proposition to make soldiers of our slaves is the most pernicious idea that has been suggested since the war began," complained Georgia governor Howell Cobb. "The day you make a soldier of them is the

...and Countess Kielmannsegg started arguing over a flower arrangement. (Nobody knows who won.)

beginning of the end of the Revolution. And if slaves seem good soldiers, then our whole theory of slavery is wrong." President Davis agreed with Cobb, and Lee's request was denied. Lee told Davis there was only one option left: surrender to the North so no more lives would be lost for a losing cause.

Davis wasn't ready to give up, though. He ordered Lee to keep the war going by using guerrilla tactics—sending small squads into Northern strongholds to fight, hand-to-hand if necessary. Knowing that a guerrilla war could go on for years, Lee found himself in yet another difficult position: should he follow the orders of his commander-in-chief, or do what he thought was right? On April 9, 1865, with his troops heavily outnumbered in the town of Appomattox Courthouse, Virginia, Lee knew it was time. "I suppose there is nothing for me to do but go and see General Grant," he said. "And I would rather die a thousand deaths." The two generals held an official ceremony in which Lee surrendered, and the Civil War was over.

> *Robert E. Lee is the greatest military genius in America, myself not excepted.*
> —**Union army general Winfield Scott, 1870**

DECISION 5: RETIRE IN PEACE, OR WORK FOR PEACE?

When Lee chose to align himself with Davis, not Lincoln, he was effectively renouncing his U.S. citizenship. So when the war ended, he was a man without a country. He couldn't vote, much of his land had been seized in the war (including his home, the Custis-Lee Mansion, which is now Arlington National Cemetery), and he was nearly broke. According to South Carolina writer Mary Chestnut in *Civil War Diaries*, right after the war she overheard Lee telling a friend that he "only wanted a Virginia farm—no end of cream and fresh butter, and fried chicken." But as much as he yearned for a quiet life, Lee's sense of duty brought him to the White House to publicly advocate for Reconstruction. That made him, according to Civil War scholar Emory Thomas, "an icon of reconciliation between the North and South."

See page 452 for the rest of the story.

Arlington National Cemetery is the only place where servicemen from every U.S. war are buried.

BOARD WITH TV

Most classic board games are the same—players race around a track and collect something. There's not much strategy involved. So how can game designers keep consumers interested? By licensing a popular TV show and basing the game play on its characters. Result: some very silly games. Here are a few based on sitcoms and cop shows of the past.

Show: *Dark Shadows*

Game: *Barnabas Collins Dark Shadows Game* (1969)

Details: The creepy soap opera ran for ten months before Jonathan Frid joined the cast as the charismatic vampire Barnabas Collins. Then, running in an after-school time slot on weekdays, the series became a big hit with kids…so a board game centered on the vampire was released. Object of the game: move around a board and collect little plastic bones that are stored in a little plastic coffin. The first player to assemble a complete skeleton wins. That doesn't have much to do with vampires, but the game did include a free pair of glow-in-the-dark vampire teeth.

Show: *ALF*

Game: *The ALF Game* (1987)

Details: ALF was an alien (or Alien Life Form), and among his many extra terrestrial quirks was that he loved to eat cats. He was always trying to snag Lucky, the cat that lived next door with Mrs. Ochmonek. In *The ALF Game*, players rolled one die to advance on Lucky, and another die to control Mrs. Ochmonek. The player won if ALF got to feast on the cat before Mrs. Ochmonek caught up with him.

Show: *Green Acres*

Game: *The Green Acres Game* (1965)

Details: It was similar to *Monopoly*…except that instead of amassing real estate, players had to buy farm equipment—as much as you need to start running your farm.

Show: *Leave It to Beaver*

Game: *Leave It to Beaver: Rocket to the Moon* (1959)

Details: Remember the episode of this 1950s sitcom when Wally and the Beaver built a rocket and flew to the moon? That's because that episode doesn't exist. Nevertheless, the show was so popular that several *Beaver* board games that had

---

By 1950 chestnut blight had killed virtually all 4 billion mature American chestnut trees in the U.S.

nothing to do with the show—except for the face of Jerry "the Beaver" Mathers on the box—hit toy stores. In this one, players traveled through space.

Show: *Laverne & Shirley*
Game: *Laverne & Shirley* (1977)
Details: On the late 1970s sitcom set in the early 1960s, Laverne and Shirley were always trying to get boyfriends. In this board game aimed at little girls, players competed as either Laverne or Shirley, and the winner was whoever amassed the most hours going out on dates, as determined by the game cards.

Show: *Gomer Pyle, U.S.M.C.*
Game: *Gomer Pyle* (1964)
Details: Goooooolly! Each player is given a small troop of army guys. Object of the game: place the men in the correct formation on the board to form a salute to Sergeant Carter.

Show: *12 O'Clock High*
Game: *12 O'Clock High* (1965)
Details: This card game allowed fans of the World War II fighter pilot show to play "Go Fish" with special cards that had pictures of different World War II planes on them. The winner had to gather all four cards of as many "squadrons" as they could in order to be proclaimed "Wing Commander."

Show: *Barney Miller*
Game: *Barney Miller* (1977)
Details: The characters on *Barney Miller* never seemed to do much police work. They just sat around the precinct and chatted most of the time. Nevertheless, the *Barney Miller* board game was a thorough exercise in crime-solving. It had players assuming the role of one of the show's weary detectives and, with a stack of evidence cards and warrants, book all four of the suspects that appear on their "Most Wanted" poster.

Show: *The Dick Van Dyke Show*
Game: *The Dick Van Dyke Board Game* (1964)
Details: On each turn, if they were lucky, players landed on a spot on the game board that awarded them a puzzle piece. The pieces were then placed together at the center of the board. The winner was the first player who completed a full-color cast photo of *The Dick Van Dyke Show* (which was broadcast in black and white).

Q: Name the geologic time period we're living in. A: The Anthropocene, which means "human epoch."

ACCORDING TO THE LATEST RESEARCH

Do the fortunes of defendants in juvenile courts rise and fall with football? Would you be happier if you spent more time nude in public? Read on and all will be revealed.

Study: "Emotional Judges and Unlucky Juveniles," *National Bureau of Economic Research*, September 2016

Purpose: To determine if there's any correlation between the length of sentence imposed on defendants in juvenile court, and "unexpected outcomes of football games played by a prominent college team in the state." The point of the study, the authors note, was to look at judges, "the conduct of whom should, by law, be free of personal biases and emotions."

Methodology: Two Louisiana State University researchers examined juvenile court records from 1996 to 2012 and compared the length of sentences handed down with the performance of LSU's football team the previous Saturday. They focused particular attention on upset losses: games that LSU was expected to win, but lost.

Findings: "Upset losses increased length [of sentences] imposed by the judges by 6.4 percent and the effect of an upset loss on judicial decisions seems to persist throughout the week following a Saturday game. Close losses and upset wins, on the other hand, have no impact...Importantly, the results are driven by judges who have received their bachelor's degrees from the university with which the football team is affiliated...The effects of these emotional shocks are asymmetrically borne by black defendants."

Study: "Factors Associated with the Disposition of Severely Injured Patients Initially Seen at Non-Trauma Center Emergency Departments: Disparities by Insurance Status," *JAMA* (*Journal of the American Medical Association*) *Surgery*, May 2014

Purpose: To see if a critically injured patient's "insurance status"—whether they have medical insurance or not—influences whether they are transferred from an ordinary emergency room to a hospital equipped with trauma center, where they are less likely to die. (Hospitals are much more likely to be paid when they treat an insured patient than when they treat an uninsured patient.)

What do Warren Buffett, Tom Brokaw, and Tom Cruise have in common? They all had paper routes as kids.

Methodology: Stanford University School of Medicine researchers studied 4,513 cases from 2009 in which patients suffering from major trauma were admitted to 636 "non-trauma centers"—ordinary emergency rooms—around the country. They looked at which of these patients were kept at the non-trauma center, and which ones were transferred to hospitals that had trauma centers, where they would receive better care. (A critically injured patient is 25 percent less likely to die if they are treated at a trauma center.)

Findings: "We found that insured, critically injured trauma patients are much less likely to be transferred out of non-trauma center emergency departments than uninsured trauma patients after adjusting for patient, injury, and hospital characteristics," the study's authors note. "Given that transfer to a trauma center has been shown to reduce mortality, these insured patients may be receiving suboptimal care."

"It's the opposite of the overly aggressive transfer of a poor patient," Dr. Arthur Kellermann, dean of the U.S. Military Medical School, told *PBS NewsHour* in 2014. "This is actually suggesting that patients who have coverage may not be getting transferred as quickly as they should be."

Study: "Naked and Unashamed: Investigations and Applications of the Effects of Naturist Activities on Body Image, Self-Esteem and Life Satisfaction," *Journal of Happiness Studies*, January 2017

Purpose: To find out if participating in "naturist" (nudist) activities improves the participants' body image.

Methodology: Dr. Keon West of the University of London conducted an online survey of 850 British subjects of all ages, ethnicities, and religions. He also conducted assessments of naturists at two public events: "Bare All for Polar Bears" at Yorkshire Wildlife Park, and at Waterworld, a gathering hosted by British Naturism in Stoke on Trent in west central England. He assessed the participants right before they removed their clothes, and just before they put them back on.

Findings: "Participants experienced immediate and significant improvements in body-image, self-esteem, and life satisfaction," something West speculates may be due to "exposure to 'non-idealized' bodies," which helps participants to become more accepting of their own perceived imperfections. "Initial analyses of the data suggests that seeing other people naked is more important than being seen naked yourself," he writes. "The data also seemed to find that the benefits hit a ceiling after about 20 naturist events a year—further naturist activity beyond this did not appear to make a difference."

U.S. president Warren G. Harding had a "Poker Cabinet" that played twice a week.

BANKSY REVEALED!

It's one of the biggest mysteries in pop culture: Who is the real "Banksy," the internationally renowned street artist known for satirical anticapitalist and antigovernment graffiti? Some people have made it their business to unmask the elusive artist.

ALL THE WAY TO THE BANKSY

The British street artist known as Banksy is one of the most famous artists in the world today…except that nobody knows who he (or she) really is. The anonymity is partly out of necessity, because a lot of Banksy's art is technically illegal. It's graffiti—richly rendered, highly realistic, and charged with social commentary. For example, prior to London's hosting of the 2012 Olympics, Banksy painted a mural of a child laborer sewing a Union Jack flag. Another time, he created a large image of Dorothy from *The Wizard of Oz* being detained and searched by police. But who is Banksy? Here are some leading theories.

Theory: Banksy is a famous musician named Robert Del Naja.

Proof: In the 2010 Oscar-nominated documentary about Banksy, *Exit Through the Gift Shop*, Del Naja made a brief appearance, referring to Banksy as a "close friend." He also provided the soundtrack for the film. (Del Naja is a founding member of the electronic music group Massive Attack.) Banksy and Del Naja, who sometimes uses the stage name "3D," may be more than close friends. Someone noticed that in 2010, Banksy's murals and street art appeared in major cities right around the same time that Massive Attack played shows there. For example, a Banksy mural showed up in San Francisco on May 1, 2010—three days after a Massive Attack concert there. A Banksy piece appeared in Toronto on May 9, the same day as a Massive Attack gig in the Canadian city. Similar coincidences occurred in Boston and Los Angeles. Del Naja, who also happens to be an accomplished artist, has publicly addressed the theory that he is Banksy, calling the idea "greatly exaggerated." (Which isn't a denial.)

Theory: Banksy is a French artist named Thierry Guetta.

Proof: That Banksy documentary, *Exit Through the Gift Shop*, spends a lot of its screen time focusing on the story of Thierry Guetta, a French man who tracks the movements of Banksy and other street artists. He ultimately becomes a street artist himself, opening a studio in Los Angeles under the name "Mr. Brainwash." His work is similar to Banksy's, suggesting that they could be one and the same.

Ouch! Ancient tattooing technique: pulling soot-covered thread through your skin with a bone needle.

On the other hand, art critics contend that there's no way Guetta is really Banksy, citing the fact that Guetta's art is not nearly as good as Banksy's.

Theory: Banksy isn't one person—it's a collective of like-minded artists who have learned similar artistic techniques to make their works look uniform.

Proof: This theory was posited by Canadian artist Chris Healey in the HBO documentary *Banksy Does New York*. Healey first made the claim in 2010, with little evidence to back up the story, that Banksy is actually a team of seven people, and their leader is a woman. Adding to the intrigue, in 2013 a Twitter user spotted five guys in Brooklyn setting up what would soon be unveiled as a Banksy exhibit called *Siren of the Lambs* (dozens of puppet animals sticking their heads out of a truck labeled "Farm Fresh Meats" and squealing as they drive around New York City's Meatpacking District). Having multiple Banksys *would* explain how the artist is able to debut new work all over the world within a very short timeframe.

Theory: Banksy is a guy from Bristol named Robin Gunningham.

Proof: In 2016 a team of researchers at Queen Mary University in London conducted a test in geographic profiling, which is usually used to track serial criminals across locations and cross-reference their findings with other data to narrow in on a suspect. The QMU researchers cross-referenced a list of 10 possible Banksy identities against 192 instances of buildings that Banksy had "tagged" with his graffiti in the English cities of London and Bristol. The most frequently hit buildings were a pub and a park in the edgy Bristol neighborhood of Easton, both a close distance away from a home where one of the Banksy possibilities lived. His name: Robin Gunningham. He avoided interview requests by the media, but some of his old school friends didn't. They said he was a standout art student when he was a teenager. Gunningham also had a nickname: "Robin Banks"…which isn't a far leap to "Banksy."

Theory: British artist Nick Walker, whose work resembles Banksy's, is Banksy.

Proof: In 2008 a reader of the website Gawker claimed to have seen a man painting street art on the outside wall of a Greenwich Village bar. The stenciled image of a little boy with a sledgehammer raised up above a fire hydrant certainly looked like a Banksy piece, and the tipster claims they boldly asked the guy painting it if he was Banksy…and he said yes. Several commenters on Gawker disputed the claim, saying that the painter was more likely Walker, another British street artist. Bucky Turco, a writer for the website Animal New York, decided to investigate. He asked a waitress at the bar if she knew who the artist was, and she reported that it was Banksy…and that it was also Nick Walker.

Land mines were used in the American Civil War. Unexploded ones are still being unearthed.

ACHOO! (PLEASE PASS THE BAMBOO)

Stronger than steel when stretched and sturdier than concrete when compressed, bamboo is fast becoming the new "it" plant. It grows like grass…because it is grass. It can be harvested by mowing and quickly regrows, just like the grass on your front lawn. Here are a few of the products now being made from bamboo.

TISSUE. Bamboo tissue is perfect for cold and flu season. Reason: it's naturally antibacterial and antifungal. It's also soft and easy on the skin (especially important after a few days of constant nose-blowing). It's also hypoallergenic, and it's healthier for skin than regular or even recycled tissue. Why? Because no pesticides or fertilizers are used to grow it, and no chemicals are needed to process its fibers. Bamboo tissues are biodegradable. And no trees have to be cut down to keep your shnoz clean.

BULLETPROOF VEST. India—second only to China in bamboo production—has a National Bamboo Mission that is working to create and test new products. One of the latest: bamboo bulletproof vests. The jackets are half the weight of conventional vests and much cheaper. Scientists believe that the tensile strength of bamboo jackets will absorb the impact of shots fired from AK-47s. (No word on whether test subjects will be volunteers…or conscripts.)

BEER. In 2011, a young Mexican entrepreneur named Mauricio Mora Tello won a scholarship from China's Ministry of Commerce. His winning idea: to enter the craft beer market with a brew made from bamboo. Tello spent two months in China testing various types of bamboo and figuring out which part of the plant could provide a viable extract. In the end, he used bamboo leaves and created a spicy brown ale—Bambusa artisanal beer—that he launched at the Puebla Beer Fest in 2012. Wondering why bamboo beer makes sense in Mexico? So were we. Turns out small bamboo plantations are sprouting up across the northeastern mountains in the state of Puebla, and with an average consumption of 62 liters of beer per capita annually, Bambusa could find a home in Mexico.

SUNGLASSES. Vincent Po started Panda Sunglasses with a three-pronged plan: create a product that incorporated his Chinese heritage, give back to those less fortunate, and quit his day job. In late 2011, Po and two college friends launched a Kickstarter campaign to fund their idea—a company that makes sunglasses with bamboo frames. They raised $20,000 with a business model Po calls "conscious capitalism." The conscious part: first, for every pair of sunglasses sold, Panda donates one eye exam and a pair of eyeglasses. Second, bamboo! The eco-friendly woody grass releases 30 percent more oxygen into the air and absorbs more CO_2 than trees do. Coolest of all, bamboo sunglasses won't sink to the bottom of the pool if they fall off. They float.

UNDERWEAR. The advertising claims about undies made from 100 percent organic bamboo are extraordinary. They say it's more absorbent than cotton and it's breathable, which means no itching or sticking. One marketer promises bamboo briefs "won't smash your willy" or "wedgie your buns," and are guaranteed to keep your "hoo-hoo" happy.

BRIDGES. Chinese researchers are on their way to building bridges out of bamboo that a truck can drive across. Bamboo beams are made by cutting strips from large stalks of bamboo, then layering the strips and bonding them together with glue. A team of just eight workers built a 32-foot-long bridge in a village in southern China in a single week, and they did it without heavy equipment. Sound too lightweight for traffic? Nope. The bridge can support trucks weighing up to 16 tons. Another plus: bamboo is far more economical than steel or concrete.

SKATEBOARDS. The North American maple tree might soon be going the way of the dodo. Why? Skateboards. With more than six million produced annually, skateboards are the current #1 contributor to maple tree deforestation, edging out maple flooring. It takes 40 to 60 years for a maple tree to grow big enough to be harvested. Bamboo, on the other hand, takes only 3 to 5 years to mature. But bamboo is lighter than maple. Can it stand up to the kind of thrashing skateboards routinely take? Apparently, yes. In test after test, bamboo boards flexed but didn't break. Most skaters find their bamboo boards last three times as long as their maple boards. Bamboo boards haven't replaced maple yet, but the strength and flexibility, combined with affordability, make them a good bet for the future.

CHARCOAL. Activated bamboo charcoal has been used in Asia for centuries, and is now finding its way into American homes as well. Because it absorbs water, a bowl of bamboo charcoal can regulate humidity in your house. How? It "drinks down" the excess moisture in the air and then releases it when the air is dry. Because it emits negative ions (or so we're told), bamboo charcoal can balance out the positive ions emitted from your TV, computer, and other electronics. Placed under your pillow, it will absorb night sweats or other smelly nocturnal emissions. In fact, activated bamboo charcoal can absorb foul odors anywhere they may be found…including in the bathroom.

It's estimated that in the U.S., wild or "feral" hogs do $1.5 billion worth of property damage each year.

EXTRAS! EXTRAS!

When you see a poster for the classic 1959 film Ben-Hur *that reads "Starring Charlton Heston and a Cast of Thousands," you might wonder who those thousands are. They're the 10,000 anonymous toga-wearing slaves, chariot drivers, and soldiers in the movie. Hollywood has a term for these background actors—extras. Their specialty: blending in, avoiding the limelight, and being just another face in the crowd. They're the hardest-working people in show business…but nobody knows their names.*

RIGHT OUT OF CENTRAL CASTING

"Central Casting" isn't just a generic term for the movie department that provides stereotypical actors—it's a real thing. Central Casting was established in Burbank, California, in 1925 for the purpose of providing extras, body doubles, and stand-ins for the movies. By 1929, the company had more than 17,000 extras on its books. Extras were generally expected to bring their own wardrobe, spend all day on the set of a film, and do whatever was asked of them in the background, even if it was dangerous. Standard payment: two dollars a day and a box lunch. By 1941, these nameless players had concerns about what they were being asked to do for so little pay and long hours, so they formed a union— the Screen Extras Guild (SEG).

The SEG not only guaranteed that the extras were paid well, they also gave a cash value to each task that extras were asked to perform. A cowboy extra would get one fee. If he was asked to walk a horse, holding its reins, he'd get another. If he was then asked to get on the horse and ride, that would be yet another fee. Each new request was officially called "special business," but to the extras, it was called a "whammy," because of the bump in pay. With five or six whammys and overtime pay, an extra's $18-a-day pay rate could jump to almost $100.

BIT BY BIT

In Cecil B. DeMille's epic 1956 film *The Ten Commandments*, extras were given a whammy for wearing body paint, another whammy for gluing on sideburns, and two whammys for slogging through the mud. And if one of those extras was asked to hand Charlton Heston (as Moses) a scroll, this was called a "special bit" and was worth $50. If Moses gave that extra an order, and the extra was told to reply, "I shall!" that extra was now a "day player," which upped his salary to $150 a day, and meant that he was being paid a wage rate set by the talking-role actors' union, the Screen Actors Guild.

Atmospheric rivers can carry as much as 20 times the amount of water as the Mississippi River.

FILMMAKING FOR DUMMIES

As extras' pay increased, film studios needed to find a cheaper way to create crowd scenes. Enter stuffed dummies. Stanley Kubrick, director of the 1960 film *Spartacus*, was the first to use these nonhuman extras, supplementing the live battle scenes with 150 costumed and wigged dummies at $45 apiece. The cost-saving device was quickly adopted by other directors and studios.

But even at $45 each, dummies weren't practical for use in larger crowd scenes. So in 2003, a special-effects man named Joe Biggins started the Inflatable Crowd Company to create the 7,000 blow-up torsos with painted faces and clothes that became the audience at the Pimlico Racetrack in the movie *Seabiscuit*. Since then, that company's inflatable extras have been seen but not noticed in more than 80 feature films, including *Million Dollar Baby*, *Iron Man 2*, and *The King's Speech*. The obvious benefits of hiring nonhumans, says Crowd in a Box, another inflatable extra company: "No water, no food, no bathroom breaks and no 'I have to leave early.' Hundreds at the cost of 20 real people."

MASSIVE CROWDS

Nowadays extras have more to fear than dummies or inflatables taking their jobs. Most filmmakers use CGI (computer generated images) to simulate crowds of people. For the film *The Lord of the Rings* (2001), director Peter Jackson asked designer Stephen Regelous to develop software that could generate hundreds of thousands of soldiers for the battle sequences. Regelous created Massive (Multiple Agent Simulation System In Virtual Environment), which is now available for the home market, meaning any budding filmmaker can create casts of thousands.

Don't worry, though. Extras will always have work. Reason: there's still no computer substitute for the smiling waitress who pours the lead character's coffee, or the doorman who opens the star's cab door, or the regular office workers who stand in the crowded elevator behind the romantic couple in a love scene. Not yet, anyway.

Movies that use "inflatable extras" in the crowd scenes.

Contagion	*American Gangster*	*Rocky Balboa*
Angels and Demons	*Blades of Glory*	*Flags of Our Fathers*
Frost/Nixon	*We Are Marshall*	*Akeelah and the Bee*
The Great Debaters	*Forever Strong*	*Memoirs of a Geisha*
Oceans 13	*Spider-Man 3*	*Dodgeball*

The Dolby Theater, where the Oscars are held, is actually part of a shopping mall.

SADDAM SPEAKS

Iraqi dictator Saddam Hussein was big news from the 1980s through the 2000s. But it wasn't until years after his death that the world got to hear his story in his own words.

DEBRIEFING THE DICTATOR

Saddam Hussein (1937–2006) became the president and dictator of Iraq in 1979—a position he held for 24 years. In that time, he invaded Iran in 1980, waged a genocidal campaign against the Kurdish people of northern Iraq in 1988, and invaded Kuwait in 1990.

The United States went to war with him twice. After he invaded Kuwait in August 1990, President George H. W. Bush organized a military coalition of 39 states that drove Hussein out of Kuwait in 1991. That was the first time—the Gulf War.

Part of the cease-fire agreement that ended the Gulf War was that Hussein had to destroy all of his weapons of mass destruction, or WMDs. But by early 2003, President George W. Bush (son of George H. W.) had become convinced that Hussein was stockpiling the banned weapons, and in March 2003 the United States invaded Iraq a second time to seize them. The Iraqi government fell in April 2003 and Saddam went into hiding, but was captured and arrested eight months later. The WMDs that were used to justify the invasion of Iraq were never found, because they did not exist. The United States' intelligence agencies got it wrong: Hussein had not been stockpiling the weapons after all.

The capture of Saddam Hussein by American forces offered FBI interrogators a rare opportunity to peer into the mind of a dictator and better understand his motives for invading Iran and Kuwait, and for expelling UN weapons inspectors from Iraq in 1998. Had the inspectors been allowed to continue their work, they might have helped to prevent the war, by providing proof that Saddam *wasn't* stockpiling WMDs. So why did Saddam kick them out? He gave answers to these and other questions while under interrogation in what was called "Operation Desert Spider." The following are excerpts from FBI agent George Piro's interrogation transcripts, which were declassified in 2009.

ON THE IRAN-IRAQ WAR

• "According to Hussein, Iran would have occupied all of the Arab world if it had not been for Iraq. As such, Iraq expected the Arab world to support them during and after the war. However, Iraq saw the opposite, especially from Kuwait.

At the end of the war as Iraq began the rebuilding process, the price of oil was approximately $7 per barrel. In Hussein's opinion, Iraq could not possibly rebuild its infrastructure and economy with oil prices at this level. Kuwait was especially at fault regarding these low oil prices."

FATHER OF THE MOTHER: *After Iraq invaded Kuwait in 1990 and the U.S.-led Operation Desert Storm was mobilized to drive him out, Saddam said in a speech that "the great showdown has begun. The mother of all battles is underway!" The expression "mother of all" to describe the biggest ever was a common phrase in the Middle East and Mediterranean for hundreds of years. But it's Saddam's speech that marked its introduction into English.*

ON THE INVASION OF KUWAIT

• "Hussein stated that he devised the plan for the invasion of Kuwait…The invasion was accomplished within two and a half hours, equivalent to that previously estimated. Hussein stated it should have taken no more than one hour. He believes it should have occurred more quickly than originally estimated due to support for the invasion from the Kuwaiti people. Hussein reiterated a previous statement to the interviewers that Iraq was asked by the Kuwaiti people to invade their country in order to remove the Kuwaiti leadership. When asked to clarify how Kuwaiti citizens communicated their desires to the Iraqi government prior to the invasion, Hussein stated some, not all, Kuwaitis felt this way. He added, 'we felt they were asking.' "

• "During Iraq's occupation of Kuwait, Hussein denied knowledge of the commission of atrocities by the Iraqi military. These atrocities include the punishment [and] executions of Kuwaiti individuals who prayed on their roofs, who failed to hang pictures of Hussein, who displayed pictures of the previous Kuwaiti royal family, or who wrote anti-Iraqi graffiti. Hussein stated, 'This is the first time I have ever heard this.' He added, of the mentioned punishable offenses, he particularly does not believe two of them were designated as crimes. First, the Iraqi government did not force Iraqis to display pictures of Hussein, therefore, the government would not have forced Kuwaitis to do this. In Iraq, citizens voluntarily chose to display Hussein's picture in their homes. Second, neither Iraqis, nor Kuwaitis are prohibited from praying anywhere, including their roofs."

ON THE PERSIAN GULF WAR

• "When questioned regarding Iraq's usage of Kuwaitis, Japanese, and Westerners as human shields during the first Gulf War including the positioning of them at key sites such as communications centers and military positions, Hussein denied that such individuals were taken to Iraqi military positions. He added that the Iraqi government did not, however, prevent individuals from volunteering as human shields to protect facilities such as communications centers. When questioned whether such volunteers existed in 1991, Hussein replied, 'I do not remember.' "

• "Regarding the igniting of [150] oil wells in Kuwait by withdrawing Iraqi forces and the subsequent environmental disaster deemed one of the worst in history, Hussein asked, 'More than Chernobyl?' He requested to know the number of people who died in Kuwait because of the smoke created by the fires. Hussein denied that Iraqi forces ignited the oil wells. He acknowledged that Iraqi forces burned "oil in trenches" as they were retreating…Hussein stated his belief that it would not be a crime for the Iraqi military to burn oil in order to prevent planes from attacking them. If such an event took place, this would have been an act of a desperate person who had no weapons remaining with which to defend himself."

ON THE 9/11 ATTACKS

• "Hussein stated Osama Bin Laden's ideology was no different than the many zealots who came before him. The two did not have the same belief or vision. Hussein claimed he had never personally seen or met Bin Laden…Hussein stated the Iraqi government did not cooperate with Bin Laden. Agent Piro asked Hussein 'why not' since Iraq and Bin Laden had the same enemies, the United States and Saudi Arabia. Agent Piro then cited the quote 'my enemy's enemy is my brother.' Hussein replied that the United States was not Iraq's enemy, but that Hussein opposed its politics. If he wanted to cooperate with the enemies of the United States, Hussein would have with North Korea, which he claimed to have a relationship with, or China."

• "Hussein stated that the United States used the 9/11 attacks as a justification to attack Iraq. The United States had lost sight of the cause of 9/11."

For more of what Saddam Hussein told the FBI, turn to
Part II of Saddam Speaks on page 437.

…"traps, fake hallways, escape routes, hidden doors, and places to hide swords."

MUSICIAN VIDEO GAMES

Video games are weird to begin with—the most popular ones involve a yellow circle eating ghosts, or a plumber saving a princess. But they get epically weird when famous rock stars get involved.

JOURNEY (1983)

Bally Midway had developed some pretty cutting-edge technology for 1983: It had mounted a camera onto a video game cabinet that took high-scoring players' photos (in grainy black and white) and posted them alongside their scores. But after a disastrous test marketing period—many female players "flashed" the camera—Bally utilized it for a video game starring the rock band Journey. Atop tiny pixelated bodies were tiny, pixelated black-and-white photos of the band members as the game unfolded. As a variety of their hits blared, players directed Journey to travel to different planets to locate their instruments, stolen by an interplanetary warlord. Journey then must return to Earth and play a concert… fighting off crazed fans who are also trying to steal their instruments.

PSYCHO CIRCUS: NIGHTMARE CHILD (2000)

Made to promote Kiss's 2000 would-be comeback album *The Nightmare Child*, this is a Kiss-based video game that doesn't technically feature Kiss. Instead, it's about a Kiss cover band, whose members are granted superpowers by a mystical force. Then they use those superpowers to hunt down and shoot bad guys.

THE THOMPSON TWINS ADVENTURE (1984)

The October 1984 issue of *Computer and Video Games* magazine came with a free bonus: a vinyl record that contained a video game. Readers were instructed to copy the record onto a cassette tape, and then play the game on computers with a cartridge drive, such as the ZX Spectrum or Commodore 64. The game itself: *The Thompson Twins Adventure*, in which the three members of the New Wave band ("Hold Me Now," "Doctor! Doctor!") must search a beach, a cave, and a forest for ingredients "the Doctor" needs to make a potion. (What the potion actually did was the subject of a write-in contest, with the winner getting to meet the Thompson Twins.)

Pinball was illegal in the U.S. from the 1940s to the 1970s. (It was considered a form of gambling.)

THE BLUES BROTHERS (1992)

The pretend blues musicians portrayed by Dan Aykroyd and John Belushi on *Saturday Night Live* and in the 1980 movie of the same name are in a pickle: They're trying to get to their own concert on time but, as is usually the case with the Blues Brothers, the police are trying to catch them and lock them up. The player can choose to be either Jake or Elwood Blues as they traverse a prison, river, and a city, collecting blues LPs to rack up points and throwing warehouse crates at the cops.

50 CENT: BLOOD ON THE SAND (2009)

Tough-guy rapper 50 Cent ("In Da Club," "Magic Stick") has been hired by a promoter to play a concert in a war-torn Middle Eastern country (which is never named in the game). Although the promoter promises to pay the rapper $10 million, he says after the concert that he doesn't have the money. But as collateral, he gives 50 Cent a diamond-and pearl-studded skull. But then a terrorist steals the skull, so 50 Cent and his group, G-Unit, have to hunt down the terrorist to get the skull back so 50 Cent can get paid. The journey involves shooting bad guys in the city streets, shooting bad guys with a Humvee-mounted machine gun, and shooting bad guys in helicopters from another helicopter.

SURF CITY (1994)

This nostalgic CD-ROM game features three classic surf music acts: Jan & Dean, the Ventures, and the Beach Boys. While songs from all three bands play (particularly Jan & Dean's "Surf City"), the player explores an idyllic California beachside town called (naturally) Surf City, where it's perpetually the innocent early 1960s. Among the activities: bowling at the Beach Bowl, decorating a surfboard, hitting the drive-in burger place, learning surf lingo, playing "Spin the Bottle," and checking out the "Video Jukebox," which plays videos by…Jan & Dean, the Ventures, and the Beach Boys.

REVOLUTION X (1994)

This game offers a look at the dark, far-off future year of…1996. By then, a coalition of corporations and military leaders called the New Order Nation has taken over the world. In the process, they ban TV, music, and video games. The resistance is led by members of the band Aerosmith, who are kidnapped by New Order Nation goons after playing a secret gig. It's up to the player to kill a bunch of New Order Nation bad guys to rescue Aerosmith.

OCTOPUSSY AND FRIENDS

How did Ian Fleming come up with all those memorable (and sometimes naughty) titles for his James Bond novels? We went on a secret mission and found out...

GOLDFINGER (1959). The title of this early Bond book came from the title character, Auric Goldfinger, who, like many of the characters in Ian Fleming's books, is named after a real person—British architect Ernö Goldfinger. And although Fleming is believed to have based the character on American gold mining magnate Charles Engelhard Jr., when Ernö Goldfinger found out the fictional villain was named after him, he sued Fleming...and won an undisclosed amount of money in an out-of-court settlement. (Bonus fact: *Auric* is a Latin-based word meaning "pertaining to gold.")

FROM A VIEW TO A KILL (1960). Fleming took the title for this short story from "D'ye Ken John Peel?" (*ken* meaning "to know"), a song written in 1820 by English composer John Woodcock Graves, about the famed huntsman John Peel. The lines from which the title was derived:

> From the drag to the chase / from the chase to the view / From a view to the death in the morning.

A popular alternate version of the song had the last line as "From a view to a kill in the morning," and Fleming got his title from that version. (The 1985 film—which is nothing like Fleming's short story—shortened the name to *A View to a Kill*.)

THE SPY WHO LOVED ME (1962). This is the only Bond novel told in the first person, and it's not told by Bond—it's told by its Canadian heroine, Vivienne Michel. The spy who loved her is Bond. (Like *From a View to a Kill*, the 1977 film "adaptation" of this novel is completely original, and the title refers to the affection between Bond and the film's "Bond girl," Soviet spy Anya Amasova—Agent Triple X—played by Barbara Bach.)

YOU ONLY LIVE TWICE (1964). This title is sometimes attributed to 17th-century Japanese haiku master Basho—but that's incorrect. It actually comes from a haiku written by Bond himself in the novel. Here's what happens: Bond is sent to Japan, where he becomes friends with the head of the Japanese intelligence service, Tiger Tanaka. Tanaka asks Bond if he's familiar with Basho. Bond says no, and Tanaka tries to teach him about haiku, and has Bond try to

Signs in Hawaii Volcanoes National Park warn visitors not to roast marshmallows over the hot lava.

write one himself. Bond writes: *You only live twice / Once when you're born / And once when you look death in the face.* The title was taken from that poem. The 1967 film adaptation of *You Only Live Twice* was written by British author Roald Dahl (*Charlie and the Chocolate Factory*). It is only loosely based on the novel, and doesn't feature the haiku scene that gave the story its title. Instead, they have the bad guy, Ernst Stavro Blofeld, say the words "You only live twice, Mr. Bond" after he captures Bond, as a reference to the fact that Bond had faked his own death earlier in the film.

***OCTOPUSSY* (1966).** One of two short stories in a book titled *Octopussy and the Living Daylights.* (The other story was *The Living Daylights.*) They were the last Bond stories Fleming wrote. In the book, which, like all Bond novels, was written on Fleming's estate in Jamaica, "Octopussy" is the name of an actual octopus. It's the pet of the story's villain, World War II hero-turned-criminal—and amateur octopus expert—Major Dexter Smythe. According to his biographers, Fleming got the name "Octopussy" from the name of a wooden coracle—a small, roundish, oar-driven boat—that was given to him by his neighbor (and lover) in Jamaica, Blanche Blackwell. In the film, "Octopussy" is the nickname of the Bond girl, who says she got it from her father—Major Dexter Smythe.

***THE LIVING DAYLIGHTS* (1966).** At a critical moment in this story, Bond shoots the rifle out of the hands of a female Russian assassin just as she's about to kill someone. He later remarks that it must have "scared the living daylights out of her"—and that became the title of this book.

EXTRAS

• The 1995 film *GoldenEye* was the first Bond film that was not based on a Fleming novel or short story. It was named after GoldenEye—Fleming's estate in Jamaica. (Fleming is believed to have taken the name from his time as a British Naval Intelligence commander, during which he ran an operation to spy on the Spanish government, code-named "Operation Goldeneye.")

• In the 1997 film *Tomorrow Never Dies*, another film with no connection to Fleming's books, the villain is a media mogul named Elliot Carver, who runs a newspaper called *Tomorrow.* Screenwriter Bruce Ferlstein originally titled the film *Tomorrow Never Lies*—referencing that newspaper. He got the idea while trying to come up with a title for the story and listening to the Beatles song "Tomorrow Never Knows." Some producers argued that *Tomorrow Never _Dies_* would be better— but *Tomorrow Never _Lies_* actually won out. The only reason the film ended up being called *Tomorrow Never Dies*: an assistant accidentally typed "Tomorrow Never Dies" when the title was sent to MGM.

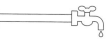

World's largest tree: India's Thimmamma Marrimanu, a banyan tree that has a 5-acre canopy.

UNCLE JOHN'S "CREATIVE TEACHING AWARDS"

If schools handed out degrees for dumb, these teachers would have earned a Ph.D.

Subject: Gun safety

Winner: Peter William McKenzie, a Japanese language teacher at St. Norbert College in Queens Park, a suburb of Perth, Australia

Approach: One night in 2013, McKenzie was on a trip with some of his students at the Forest Edge Recreation Camp in Waroona, Western Australia, when he happened to find a Gamo 0.177 air rifle in a camp work shed. The air rifle looked a lot like a hunting rifle, so McKenzie, ever the life of the party, took the gun and snuck up on some kids sitting around an unlit campfire. Then he leapt out of the dark and screamed "Time for bed!" while pointing the air rifle at the kids.

What Happened: Someone reported the incident to the authorities and McKenzie was dragged before a disciplinary board, found guilty of "unsafe handling of a firearm and an intention to scare students," and suspended from teaching for a year. "The teacher acknowledges his actions were reckless, irresponsible, and constituted a moment of 'utter stupidity,'" the disciplinary board found. (McKenzie says he made sure the air rifle was unloaded before pulling the prank.)

Subject: Arts and crafts

Winner: Lindsay Blanc, 29, a kindergarten teacher in Tampa, Florida

Approach: In April 2015, one of the kindergarteners in Blanc's class was talking during a music lesson, so she sent him to sit at a table in the classroom's "time out" area. Then she showed a video to the other kids. Because the disruptive five-year-old had been naughty, she didn't want him to watch the video and told him to sit facing away from the screen. When he kept turning around to watch the video, she taped his eyes shut with duct tape.

What Happened: When other kids reported to their parents what had happened, they contacted the school and Blanc was removed from the classroom and reassigned to work in the district offices while her case was reviewed. She denied covering the boy's eyes with duct tape, but the school board didn't buy her story and in July 2015 they voted to suspend her from teaching without pay, the first step in firing her from the district altogether.

Subject: Chemistry

Winner: Gu Ming, who teaches Traditional Chinese Medicine manufacturing at a vocational school in Guizhou Province, China

Approach: Why stop at traditional medicines? Gu also evaluated his students on their ability to drink strong liquor, which he himself administered in shot glasses during the final exam.

> Those who [finish] a full glass of liquor get a full 100 mark for their exam, half glass gets 90 marks, and a sip gets 60. Those who do not drink at all will fail,

one of his students posted on the social media site Weibo, China's answer to Facebook and Twitter.

What Happened: When some of Gu's students complained to the college administration, he was suspended. But he had a lot of defenders on Weibo, who argued that Gu was merely preparing his charges for the business world. "Many of the students may go to sales meetings, and how much one can drink may decide how many deals he can seal," one of Gu's supporters posted online. "There is a culture of gaining other people's trust and recognition through drinking, which is sad but true." Gu admitted that he told his students that they were being graded on how well they downed the shots he served them, but he says he was only joking; serving them strong liquor was his way of bidding them farewell. (The associate dean, Fu Guisheng, says that Gu behaved the way he did because he was drunk at the time.)

Subject: History

Winner: Richard Wright Jr., who taught music to intellectually disabled students at the Alden Road Education Center in Jacksonville, Florida, in 2016

Approach: For Black History Month in February 2016, Wright (who is white) decided to teach his students a song about the Underground Railroad using a role-playing game. He told the kids to pretend to be slaves, and instructed his two teaching assistants, both of whom were African American, to hold up stuffed animals—representing vicious dogs owned by slaveholders—and chase the children around the room. One assistant refused to participate; the other told Wright that he was trivializing a painful chapter in African American history, and doing so with children whose cognitive abilities were so low that they weren't going to understand the lesson anyway.

What Happened: When the school district learned of Wright's "lesson," it suspended him for 30 days without pay. "A reasonable person would know the historical significance of this reality and be conscious of the level of discomfort and pain this could likely represent to individuals of African-American descent when asked to pose as dogs chasing slaves through forests," the district concluded in a report on the incident.

Subject: Communications

Winner: Dean Liptak, a former pro wrestler–turned–science teacher at Fivay High School in Florida

Approach: In March 2015, Liptak got so frustrated by students using their smartphones in class that he bought a "cellphone jammer" online and brought it to school without informing his superiors. He says he checked with local police first and they advised him that there was no state law prohibiting the use of such devices.

What Happened: Liptak should have checked with the feds, because it's the Federal Communications Commission, not state governments, that regulates such devices. And federal law prohibits "the operation, marketing, or sale of any type of jamming equipment." Reason: criminals and terrorists can use them to interfere with emergency calls, preventing people from dialing 911 when they need help. Liptak's device jammed a nearby cell tower, prompting Verizon to send investigators to the school to look for the interference; that's how he got caught with the device. The district suspended him for five days without pay.

The incident wasn't Liptak's first run-in with the authorities. In 2013 he ran afoul of his superiors after giving his kids a science quiz that contained violent themes such as "A northbound car with a velocity of 100 meters per second ran over a baby with a momentum of 800 kilogram meters per second, what is the mass of the car?" "He's kind of extreme," student Braxton Mora told the UK's *Daily Mail* newspaper. "He's a little out there."

*   *   *

NO JOKE

The king of Tonga liked Bank of America's financial advisor Jesse Bogdonoff so much that, in 1999, he gave him a title—"Court Jester." A more appropriate title might have been "court magician" because within three years, Bogdonoff, a California businessman, made $26 million of the country's assets completely disappear. He moved the Tongan portfolio into an obscure fund called the Millenial Asset Management Company, which wiped out the Tonga Trust Fund. King Taufa'ahau Tupou IV was not amused and sued Bogdonoff. The Jester settled the suit, agreeing to pay Tonga $100,000, plus part of his income for ten years and half the royalties from any book or movie deal. (There wasn't one.)

TREPANNING WITH JOHN & YOKO

You need to read this story like you need another hole in your head.
(Only the first part of that sentence is true.)

THIS IS NOT A DRILL

In March 1969, John Lennon and Yoko Ono spent their honeymoon at a posh hotel in Amsterdam, where they staged their infamous "Bed-in for Peace." Among the reporters and well-wishers that Lennon invited was a 34-year-old Dutchman named Bart Huges. He was summoned there because the Beatle had a strange request: "I want a third eye." Lennon wasn't talking about a metaphorical, spiritual third eye, but an actual *hole* drilled in his forehead. This controversial procedure is called *trepanation*, and we've written about it before in past editions of Uncle John's Bathroom Reader. But when we found out that one-quarter of the Fab Four nearly got holes drilled in his head, we knew we had to drill down a little deeper into this strange subject.

Trepanning (from the Greek *trypanon*, "a borer") has been practiced since prehistoric times to treat everything from headaches to demons. But in the late 1960s, trepanation became something of a fad for the burgeoning New Age movement. The best known among them was Huges, a Dutch librarian who had been expelled from medical school a few years earlier for his rampant drug use. In 1964 he published a "scientific" paper—in scroll form—called "Homo Sapiens Correctus," in which he claimed that ever since humans learned to walk upright, gravity has prevented enough blood from flowing up to the brain, and that drilling a hole in the forehead would relieve pressure and thus increase "brainbloodvolume." Or something like that. The benefits: increased energy and creativity, and even better: a "permanent high." Marijuana and LSD are temporary, Huges preached; trepanation is forever.

BEATLE-MANIAC

John Lennon, who was well known for trying to find new ways to expand his consciousness, really wanted Huges to drill a "third eye" in his head. As much of a kook as Huges may have been (and according to pretty much every medical professional, he was a kook), he warned Lennon against the procedure, telling him, "I am certain you already have it. Third eye people are your kind of people." Metaphorically, Huges was speaking about the Beatles' and Lennon's massive influence on popular culture. But the "it" to which he was *specifically* referring is an actual hole in about 10 percent of adults' craniums known medically as a *fontanel*. A better-known term is "soft spot," which all babies have. A fetus's skull is connected in sections, and the fontanel helps relieve the pressure of the rapidly growing brain (it also helps the head fit through the narrow birth canal). Most people's skull plates have fused together by adulthood, which is why Huges recommended trepanation. However, he insisted that Lennon still had his…hole. "But John kept wanting it," Huges recalled many years later, "and I kept telling him, 'Don't drill it. It's a deception. You will notice no difference!'" It wasn't until Yoko Ono took Huges's side that Lennon let the matter go. For a while.

"WE KNOW A GUY"

Later, back in England, John and Yoko invited Paul and Linda McCartney over for dinner one night, and Lennon brought up the subject again. "You fancy getting the trepanning thing done?" Lennon asked.

McCartney had no idea what he was talking about, so Lennon explained, "Well, you kind of have a hole bored into your skull and it relieves the pressure."

McCartney thought he was kidding.

"No, this isn't a joke," Lennon assured him. "Let's go next week, we know a guy who can do it, and maybe we can all do it together!"

McCartney politely refused: "Look, you go and have it done, and if it works, great. Tell us about it and we'll all have it."

So did John Lennon ever go through with the procedure? All reports point to no.

FOR THE RECORD: *John Lennon's final album was* Double Fantasy, *a collaboration with Yoko Ono, released in 1980. It was his first album after having dropped out of the public eye for five years to raise his son, Sean. Every major record label made a bid for the rights to release Lennon's comeback album, and Geffen Records won out. Reason: David Geffen was the only person who took Yoko seriously as a musician.*

The oversized claw of the Pink Floyd pistol shrimp makes a loud "BANG!" when it snaps shut.

MUG SHOT T-SHIRTS

Did your mother ever warn you to always wear clean underwear, just in case you end up in the emergency room? Here's an updated warning for the Internet age: Be careful what your T-shirt says, in case it ends up on your mug shot.

"America's Most WANTED"

"It's okay—I'm a ninja."

"Will You Harness Your Potential?"

"POOP"

"I'm a virgin but this is an old t-shirt"

"Internet was down so I thought I'd come outside today."

"WORK HARD PLAY HARD"

"I quit the band—now I just play with myself"

"Wish You Were Here"

"WARNING: You have the RIGHT to remain silent"

"Do I look like I care?"

"I've turned to the Dark Side"

"Tried to be GOOD But I got BORED"

"I ♥ midget porn"

"Y_U AR_ AN ID_OT"

"I'm out of my mind—please leave a message"

"I ♥ Crystal Meth"

"I may not be Mr. Right"

"I saw your mom on the Internet"

"Drunk as $*&%!"

"Cleverly disguised as a responsible adult"

"Out on Bail"

"I can get away with anything."

"GUILTY"

"I AM the law!"

"I'm Rick James BITCH"

"D.A.R.E. Role Model"

"STOP LOOKING AT MY SHIRT"

Three old-fashioned swear words: *Sard! Gadsbudlikins!* and *Potzblitz!*

ONE FALSE MOVE AND I'LL FOAM YOU!

In combat, "friendly fire" usually means being shot at accidentally by someone on your side of the conflict. Here it describes high-tech weapons that "fill the gap between shouting and shooting" by disabling an adversary without physically harming them.

HOT STUFF

Weapon: Active Denial System

How it works: Nicknamed the "heat ray," the ADS is a vehicle-mounted "directed energy" weapon designed for crowd-control applications, such as breaking up prison fights, or providing security around embassies and other sensitive buildings. Kind of like a microwave oven that can be fired at people, it shoots a beam of high-frequency energy that penetrates less than 0.02 inch into human skin. (One difference: microwave ovens use lower-frequency energy that penetrates more than half an inch into the food that is being cooked).

The energy from the ADS excites water molecules in the outermost layer of skin, causing a burning sensation that has been described as similar to touching a hot lightbulb. While painful, the ADS system has a lower risk of injury than tear gas, rubber bullets, water cannons, and other non-lethal weapons that have been used for crowd control in the past. It was deployed in Afghanistan in 2010 but never used, although why it wasn't used is unclear.

THIS IS A STICK UP

Weapon: Sticky Foam

How it works: It's basically military-grade "silly string"—that stuff that kids shoot out of spray cans at birthday parties. The military version is so sticky that it incapacitates human targets by causing them to stick to the foam, themselves, and their surroundings, much like flies on flypaper or rats in a glue trap.

Sticky Foam was deployed in Somalia in 1995, but problems quickly arose: the goo clogged the guns from which it was fired, for one thing. It's also hard to free and then transport someone entrapped in the foam, and the risk of suffocating someone sprayed in the face is high. At last report, the military was looking into developing a "foam-based vehicle arresting system" to disable

Encyclopedia Britannica's 1768 edition divided Homo sapiens into five groups:...

approaching suicide bombers by encasing their cars in "several cubic meters of high-strength foam." There are also reports that the foam is being deployed at nuclear weapons storage facilities as an extra layer of defense: if the heavy steel doors protecting a stockpile of nukes come under attack, the defenders inside can spray the entrance with a large volume of foam, creating a barrier that will trap or at least slow the attackers, buying time for reinforcements to arrive.

ON THE WATER

Weapon: The Slimeball

How it works: It's a proposed two-part weapon system designed to immobilize ships and boats by gumming up surrounding waters and making them as thick as road tar. Proposed in 2009 by Lieutenant Commander Daniel Whitehurst, a U.S. Navy researcher, the system consists of a thick layer of sticky foam (see above) that floats on the water's surface, and a "submerged gel barrier that will impede movement through a ship channel." The foam and gel could be contained in bombs, missiles or other munitions and used against sheltered harbors, port facilities, and similar targets.

Though the weapon is still on the drawing board, Whitehurst argues that "the individual components of Slimeball already exist or can be manufactured to designers' specifications…Additionally, the existing U.S. inventory of munitions appears adequate for delivering the Slimeball to a variety of potential targets." So the system could potentially be developed and deployed quickly if the Pentagon ever decided to do it.

SLIP-SLIDING AWAY

Weapon: Mobility Denial System

How it works: Who says everything has to be sticky? The Mobility Denial System uses a "highly slippery, viscous gel" to make concrete, asphalt, wood, and even grass so slippery that people or vehicles that come in contact with the stuff will be immobilized on the spot. "The substance severely reduces surface friction and results in a loss of traction or control," wrote Captain Andrew B. Warren, a Marine Corps officer assigned to the project. "Riots, protests, noncombatant evacuations, and sanction enforcement are just a few of the situations where this kind of tactical barrier would be most useful." The stuff can even be sprayed on walls to prevent people from climbing them, even with a ladder. (It could probably be sprayed on the ladder, too.) Bonus: when a person's shoe or a vehicle tire comes in contact with the gel, the material "is transferred to uncoated surfaces, making them slippery as well."

...the American, the European, the Asiatic, the African, and the "monstrous."

"I'M NO BRAD PITT"

You're not the only one, brother.

"In this business, you're either Brad Pitt right away, or you're already going down the ladder."
—Skeet Ulrich

"For me, personally, I'm a 5'5" leading man. I'm no Brad Pitt or anything."
—Jeremy Luke

"If I could be anyone, it would be Brad Pitt."
—David Fincher

"I'm certainly not Tom Cruise or Brad Pitt."
—Jason Statham

"I'm clearly not Brad Pitt, and I'm never going to be Brad Pitt."
—Paul Giamatti

"The real challenge is if you don't look super sexy, like a Brad Pitt, you're going to have to try harder."
—Jack Black

"Unless you look like Brad Pitt, it's really hard to have full control of your character."
—Vincent D'Onofrio

"Heartthrobs are a dime a dozen."
—Brad Pitt

"No matter what heights you achieve, even if you're Brad Pitt, the slide is coming, sure as death and taxes."
—James Caan

Old-time cures for flatulence: drinking chamomile tea and blowing tobacco smoke into the rectum.

ACCEPTED (NOT)

It's a huge moment for a young student when the acceptance letter from their dream college arrives. But it's horrible for the student when it turns out that the college made a mistake.

UNIVERSITY OF CALIFORNIA, DAVIS. In March 2002, UC Davis sent letters to 105 high school students letting them know that they'd been admitted to the institution. Except that those students hadn't actually been accepted, and the letters were sent in error. All of this was detailed in the correction email that Davis officials sent to the affected students…on April Fool's Day.

JOHNS HOPKINS UNIVERSITY. The prestigious Maryland school had already informed around 300 applicants that they *hadn't* made it into JHU in 2014. It must have been confusing, then, when the school followed up that mass email a few weeks later with another email telling the rejected students that they *had* been accepted. It gets worse. A few hours later, the school had to send out yet another email letting those same 300 students know that the email they'd received earlier that day was the one that had been a mistake…and they actually *hadn't* been admitted to Johns Hopkins.

COLUMBIA UNIVERSITY. Even Ivy League schools make mistakes. In February 2017, applicants to Columbia's Mailman School of Public Health postgraduate program began to receive acceptance letters, saying the school was "delighted to welcome them" come fall. Then, a little over an hour later, 277 of them received a second email: Their acceptance letters had been sent in error.

UNIVERSITY OF BUFFALO. The largest number of people ever told they'd been accepted into a college…and then told that they hadn't: around 5,100. It happened in April 2016 at the University of Buffalo. The accepted-then-rejected students accounted for one-fifth of everybody who applied to UB that year. According to the school, someone in the admissions office had intended to send out an email reminding students to get their financial-aid paperwork in order, but instead mistakenly sent the prewritten "You're in!" letters.

CARNEGIE MELLON. In 2015 the Pittsburgh university accidentally told 800 applicants via email that they'd been accepted to study at the school. The problem was that many of them hadn't actually been formally accepted yet, and the letters had been sent out early due to a computer error. Ironically, the 800 students had applied to CMU's graduate program in computer science.

The game Life started out in 1860 as The Checkered Game of Life, which had moral messages.

NUCLEAR FALSE ALARMS

Remember the Cold War? From 1947 until 1990, international politics were dominated by the tense arms race between the Soviet Union and the United States. Both nations had nuclear arsenals…and both kept their fingers on the trigger. Given that, it's easy to understand how there might be a few false alarms.

OCTOBER 24, 1962

Incoming! Sometime on or before the 24th, the Soviet Union launched a Mars probe and "parked" it in Earth orbit before sending it on to the red planet. That's far as it ever got: the probe malfunctioned in orbit and exploded. And the blast was detected by the early warning radar system of the North American Air Defense Command (NORAD), which mistook it for a nuclear missile attack against the United States.

…Never mind: The mishap occurred during the Cuban Missile Crisis, when Cold War tensions were at their highest. Both the United States and the Soviet Union were on hair-trigger alert, watching for any sign that the other was about to start a nuclear war. That may be why, more than 50 years later, very little information has been released about how NORAD responded to the incident. "The event is shrouded in mystery," Scott Sagan writes in *The Limits of Safety: Organizations, Accidents, and Nuclear Weapons*, "and, unfortunately, the NORAD Command Post logs covering possible dates for the launch remain classified."

OCTOBER 28, 1962

Incoming! Five days later, just as the Cuban Missile Crisis seemed to be winding down, NORAD received a report from a radar installation in Moorestown, New Jersey, that a nuclear missile had been launched from Cuba and would strike Tampa, Florida, in two minutes. NORAD went on full alert, but on such short notice there was little they could do before the missile reached its target.

…Never mind: Two minutes passed and Tampa wasn't destroyed. A few minutes later NORAD received a call from New Jersey explaining what had happened: "Moorestown now informs [us] that a test tape [simulating a nuclear attack from Cuba] had been inserted in the equipment," reads the log. While the test tape was running, an orbiting satellite—or, possibly, debris from the destroyed Mars probe—had appeared over the horizon unexpectedly, confusing the operators into believing that the simulation was real. Normally there was another office that alerted controllers when orbiting satellites or other tracked objects were about to appear on the horizon, but that office had been reassigned to other duties because of the Cuban Missile Crisis.

MAY 23, 1967

Incoming! During daylight hours on that Tuesday, the three radar installations in Alaska, Greenland, and the United Kingdom that were part of NORAD's Ballistic Missile Early Warning System were disrupted by intense, unexplained interference that had never been seen before. The fact that all three stations were hit at the same time suggested to NORAD controllers that the interference was man-made: the Soviet Union had to be jamming the radar installations deliberately. The jamming was itself an act of war, and because it prevented NORAD from detecting incoming nuclear missiles, there was the possibility that it was being done to conceal an attack on the United States that was imminent or already underway.

In those Cold War days, a number of U.S. Air Force bombers carrying nuclear weapons were always in the air, but the jamming incident prompted the Strategic Air Command (SAC) to put additional bombers on "ready to launch" status, parked next to runways and ready to be deployed on short notice.

...Never mind: Catastrophe was averted—but only due to the fact that the Air Force Weather Service had recently begun monitoring the sun for solar flares, which release bursts of radiation that can cause electromagnetic disruptions on Earth. The "jamming" on May 23 was caused by one of the most powerful solar storms of the 20th century, one that caused electromagnetic interference for a week and made the *aurora borealis,* or northern lights, visible as far south as New Mexico. When it was informed of the solar storm, SAC took its bombers off ready-to-launch status; the solar storm eventually died out and so did the interference. "An important and long-lasting outcome of this storm," wrote Dr. Delores Knipp in her 2016 article in the journal *Space Weather,* "was more formal Department of Defense support for current-day space weather forecasting."

NOVEMBER 9, 1979

Incoming! Early on the morning of the 9th, National Security Advisor Zbigniew Brzezinski was awakened by a call from a military aide reporting that NORAD's early warning radar system had detected the launch of 250 Soviet nuclear missiles against targets in the United States. Moments later, the aide called back: now more than 2,200 missiles were on their way. Ten U.S. Air Force fighters were in the air already and many more soon would be; President Jimmy

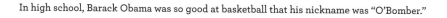

In high school, Barack Obama was so good at basketball that his nickname was "O'Bomber."

Carter had less than ten minutes to decide whether to launch a counterstrike.

Brzezinski paused a moment to digest this information. Then just as he was about to call President Carter and wake him with the news, the military aide called a third time to report that NORAD's other early warning systems hadn't detected any further signs that missiles had been launched. When it became clear a few minutes later that none of the targets had been destroyed, the alert was canceled. Brzezinski let Carter sleep. (He let Mrs. Brzezinski sleep, too: even when the attack appeared to be real, he saw no point in waking her up just to tell her she was going to die.)

...Never mind: So what caused the NORAD computers to think that an attack was underway? Someone loaded a training tape simulating a full-scale nuclear attack into computers that were—supposedly—offline, in order to test their software. Sound familiar? Somehow the test bled over to the online computers, and they interpreted it as a real attack. NORAD's computer programmers later tried to reproduce the error in order to prevent it from happening again...but as NORAD itself admitted, "the precise mode of failure could not be replicated." Whether NORAD ever did figure out how to fix the problem is unknown.

SEPTEMBER 26, 1983

Incoming! Not long after midnight Russian time, an alert sounded at the Serpukhov-15 bunker near Moscow. The underground facility was the command center for Oko, the USSR's system of early warning satellites, which had just detected the launch of a single nuclear missile against the USSR from a silo in the United States.

The officer on duty, Lieutenant Colonel Stanislav Petrov, thought it odd that the United States would start a nuclear war against his country by firing a single missile, so he dismissed the alert as a false alarm. A few minutes later another alert sounded, then a third, a fourth, and a fifth. Each alert reported the launch of another lone missile toward the USSR. Five missiles still seemed like too small a number to start World War III, so acting purely on "a funny feeling in my gut," as Petrov later put it, he reported the alerts to his superiors as false alarms. He figured the odds were 50-50 that his hunch was correct; had he reported the alerts as genuine, there's a good chance that the Soviet leadership would have ordered a retaliatory nuclear strike against the United States.

...Never mind: When Soviet ground radar failed to detect any sign of incoming missiles, the alarms were confirmed as false. An investigation later revealed that what the early warning satellites had mistaken for incoming missiles was actually...sunlight, reflected off of clouds.

The main shopping area of Rodeo Drive in Beverly Hills is only three blocks long.

THIS IS A TEST

Ever wonder how home medical tests you get at the pharmacy actually work? Here's how.

BLOOD SUGAR. Part of how diabetics stay healthy is with constant monitoring of their blood sugar levels—if it's too high or too low too often, it can lead to complications like blindness or gangrene. So people with diabetes test their *blood glucose* levels each day. It's done by pricking the finger with a *lancet* to extract a drop of blood, which is then placed on a glucose test strip and inserted into a device called a *glucometer*. The strip is embedded with a chemical called *glucose oxidase*—an enzyme that reacts to the glucose present in the blood. That reaction generates a tiny electrical signal. The glucometer measures the strength of that jolt, and it translates the level of the charge into a number reflecting the amount of glucose in the blood. The higher the charge, the higher the number on the meter's display screen, which indicates the amount of sugar in the blood.

PREGNANCY. There are a lot of hormone shifts in a woman's body when she becomes pregnant. For example, shortly after an egg is fertilized, a placenta is created (it spreads nutrients from mother to baby). The placenta, which secretes a hormone called hCG, short for *human chorionic gonadotropin*, starts growing about six days after conception, so pregnancy tests are most effective *after* those six days. An at-home pregnancy test works by binding the hCG molecule, which is present in urine, to an antibody in the pregnancy test. (It's in the spot where urine is supposed to be placed.) The antibody in the test *only* binds with hCG, and a positive result on the test is technically a positive result for hCG. If there's no hCG for the test to find, it's because the hormone is only present in pregnant women, and a negative result is triggered.

OVULATION. Ovulation tests are similar to pregnancy tests—a little urine can inform a woman about whether she's at the most fertile place in her menstrual cycle. Technically speaking, ovulation tests don't predict fertility in real time. They're actually ovulation *predictor* kits—they indicate that the ideal period of fertility is as much as 24–36 hours away. A hormone called *luteinizing* is always present in urine (and blood). One to two days before ovulation occurs, there's a surge in the body's production of this chemical—about two to five times the normal rate. An antibody on a test strip reacts with a high level of luteinizing. If it's present, the test kit will display a positive sign, such as a smiley face or "+" symbol.

The guillotine is named for Joseph Guillotin. (He did not invent it, and opposed the death penalty.)

"FINGER-LICKIN' GOOD"

*Colonel Harland Sanders (1890–1980) has been gone for so long now that
even many KFC fans may not realize that he was a real person, and not
just a fictional corporate icon like Betty Crocker or Mr. Clean.*

LET'S MAKE A DEAL

In 1930 the Shell Oil Company made a tantalizing offer to a struggling 39-year-
old gas station owner named Harland Sanders. The country had just entered
the Great Depression and Sanders, who'd run a Standard Oil gas station in
Nicholasville, Kentucky, had just gone out of business. Before times got hard,
Sanders had sold more gasoline at his station than any other had for miles
around. He was a natural-born salesman.

The Shell executive explained to Sanders that the company was planning to
build a new service station in Corbin, Kentucky, at the junction of U.S. Route
25, which runs from north to south, and Routes 25 East and 25 West. They
wanted him to run it, and they offered to let him have the station for no money
down, in exchange for a percentage of his gasoline sales. Bonus: Shell would
add two bedrooms, a bathroom, and a small kitchen to the gas station so that
Sanders, his wife, and their three children could live there rent-free.

Sanders took the deal and moved his family into the Shell station. "It was
there," he later wrote, "that I started my restaurant business and put my plain
and simple knowledge of food and cooking to work."

A LATE DINNER

Sanders's start in the food business was modest, to say the least: He moved his
dining-room table into the front of the Shell station. Every night when he
cooked dinner, he set it out on the table where his customers, many of them
truck drivers sick of eating in greasy spoons, could see it. "We'd stall on eating
for a while, figuring we'd sell some of our food," Sanders remembered.

> *Sometimes we'd sell one meal, sometimes we'd sell them
> all. If we did, I'd start cooking all over again.*

Word soon spread that "Sanders' Servistation and Cafe" in Corbin was one of
the few places on the road where a person could get a decent home-cooked meal.

According to one study, playing Tetris can reduce cravings for food and block the effects of PTSD.

The business grew, and about a year later Sanders opened a larger restaurant across the street, with three tables and a lunch counter. That's when he added a new item to the menu that he had avoided serving earlier: pan-fried chicken. The dish had long presented problems for restaurant owners, because it took a half an hour to prepare. Diners—especially truckers on a schedule—weren't willing to wait that long for their food, so the chicken had to be fried in advance. If a restaurant owner made too much, the unsold pieces went to waste. If they didn't make enough, their customers might drive off to look for another café. So Sanders didn't serve it. It wasn't until business was really booming that he decided to add it to the menu.

PRESSURE TACTICS

Then in 1939, Sanders was invited to see a demonstration of a pressure cooker at the local hardware store. A pressure cooker is basically a pot with locking lid that allows steam from boiling water to build up pressure inside the pot. The heat and steam pressure cooks foods in a fraction of the time it would take if they were steamed or boiled in an ordinary pot.

The hardware store owner thought a pressure cooker might enable Sanders to prepare vegetables he served in his restaurant more quickly, so he told Sanders to bring some to the store. Sanders showed up with green beans and loaded them into the pressure cooker as instructed. They cooked in just 3½ minutes, and they looked and tasted better than green beans cooked in an ordinary pot. Sanders was so impressed that he bought eight pressure cookers on the spot.

Before long, he began to wonder if it would be possible to put *cooking oil* in a pressure cooker instead of water and use it to fry chicken. He gave it a shot and soon he found a way to make crispy, flavorful chicken that was not too greasy on the outside, tender and juicy on the inside, and that cooked to a finish in just eight minutes. He added it to the menu and it sold spectacularly well.

ROAD KILL

Business at the restaurant was so good that Sanders tore down the gas station and built a 142-seat restaurant and motel on the site. He renamed the enterprise the Sanders Court and Cafe. For a time he owned a second restaurant and motel in Asheville, North Carolina. He likely would have finished out his career as a successful hotel and restaurant owner, little known outside of Kentucky and North Carolina. But in the mid-1950s, disaster struck. Twice.

First, the highway was resurveyed and the junction between Route 25 and Routes 25 East and West, which had been right in front of Sanders's business, was moved farther away. That cut his business in half. A few years later,

Interstate 75 was built parallel to Route 25, but seven miles to the west. That caused his trade to dry up entirely. Sanders sold the business at public auction, and by the time he paid off his debts, he was broke. Now 66 years old, his main source of income was his Social Security check, which paid just $105 a month.

BUCKET LIST

About the only thing that Sanders salvaged from the ruins of his business was his method for making fried chicken in pressure cookers, and his "secret blend of eleven herbs and spices." The chicken had already attracted the interest of other restaurant owners, and Sanders had licensed it to a handful of franchisees. He collected a four-cent royalty on every chicken they cooked.

His first franchisee was a Salt Lake City restaurateur named Pete Harman, who added a few marketing touches of his own. To call attention to the product's exotic origin—and to differentiate it from traditional Southern fried chicken, which was dry and crusty by comparison—Harman accepted his sign painter's suggestion that he call it "Kentucky Fried Chicken." Harman also came up with the slogan "It's finger lickin' good." Within a year or two, he began packaging 14 pieces of chicken, five rolls, and a pint of gravy in a cardboard takeout "Bucket O' Chicken" for families who wanted a break from cooking, but still wanted a meal they could eat at home.

MEET THE COLONEL

After Harman added Kentucky Fried Chicken to the menu, his business more than tripled, with most of the increase coming from fried chicken sales. His success (and that of other early franchisees) convinced Sanders that if he could sell enough franchises, he might make enough to live on. So he loaded a pressure cooker into his car along with a cooler filled with raw chicken, a sack of flour, and his mixture of eleven herbs and spices, and began driving around the country paying sales calls to one restaurant after another.

He also updated his image: Back in 1931, Sanders had supported a candidate named Ruby Luffoon for governor, and after Luffoon won the election, he made Sanders an honorary Kentucky colonel (see page 283). Sanders hadn't done much with the title before, but now he began using the name Colonel Sanders in business, and he changed his appearance to look the way he thought a Kentucky colonel should look: he grew a mustache and goatee, and had them bleached to match his white hair. He also wore a black string tie and a long black frock coat, which soon gave way to a white, double-breasted suit.

His new gentlemanly appearance opened a lot of doors, but he still had to sell his chicken. He did this by offering to cook up a batch in the restaurant's

kitchen at a time of day when business was slow. Then he served it to the staff. If they liked it, Sanders would stick around for another day or two to prepare chicken for the restaurant's customers, with the understanding that if *they* liked the chicken, the restaurateur would sign up for a franchise.

CLOSE TO HOME

The work was difficult and slow-going: Sanders had to drive a lot of miles and cook a lot of chicken for every restaurant he signed up as a franchisee. He slept in his car and accepted every complimentary meal he was offered to save on expenses. But his hard work paid off: The restaurants that signed up soon found they had a hit on their hands…and word of their success spread. Within a couple of years, Sanders didn't have to travel anymore—he could sit in his office at home, now in Shelbyville, Kentucky, and field the offers that came pouring in.

By 1960 more than 200 restaurants in the United States were selling Kentucky Fried Chicken; three years later the number had tripled to more than 600. The business was still a mom-and-pop operation: Sanders handled the sales and the paperwork and his wife, Claudia, mixed the secret spice blend and mailed it to the franchisees. (To this day the franchisees still do not know the formula.) But as Sanders himself admitted, by 1963 "my business was beginning to get too big for me, no matter how much energy and time I put into it." In 1964 he sold the business for $2 million. He agreed to stay on as a spokesperson for the company and collect a salary of $40,000 a year, soon raised to $75,000 ($562,000 today), for life.

THE BIG TIME

As rapid as Kentucky Fried Chicken's growth was from 1956 to 1964, after Sanders sold the business it grew even more rapidly, thanks in large part to the chain's first national advertising campaign and its promotion of Colonel Sanders as a living image of the brand. By 1970 the number of Kentucky Fried Chicken outlets had grown to more than 2,700, Sanders had become one of the most famous men in America, and Kentucky Fried Chicken's share price soared: a $5,000 investment made in 1964 was worth more than $3.5 million in 1970.

In his lifetime, Colonel Sanders saw his idea grow beyond his wildest dreams and reward him with more wealth and fame than he knew what to do with. And though he finally had financial security, he never did retire; he continued to travel more than 250,000 miles a year on behalf of Kentucky Fried Chicken until shortly before his death in 1980 at the age of 90. "I just say the moral of my life is don't quit at age 65, maybe your boat hasn't come in yet," he told an interviewer in the late 1970s. "Mine hadn't."

In 2017 the CTF Pink, a 59.6-carat pink diamond, sold for $71.2 million.

COLONEL SANDERS SPEAKS

Words of wisdom from a brave man who made a success with chickens.

"I've only had two rules: Do all you can and do it the best you can. It's the only way you ever get that feeling of accomplishing something."

"There's no reason to be the richest man in the cemetery. You can't do any business from there."

"Anyone who's reached 65 years of age has had a world of experience behind him. He's had his ups and downs and all the trials and tribulations of life. He certainly ought to be able to gather something out of that so he can get a new start."

"If you've got time to lean, you've got time to clean."

"I think the Lord has kept me here on Earth for a purpose, either to do good for somebody else or to punish me for something I've done."

"Wealth, like happiness, is never attained when sought after directly. It comes as a byproduct of providing a useful service."

"The easy way is speedy, the hard way arduous and long. But, as the clock ticks, the easy way becomes harder and the hard way becomes easier."

"Hard work beats all the tonics and vitamins in the world."

"This title of Colonel before my name is like the honorable Sir in front of yours, my dear Sir Lawyer. It means absolutely nothing."

"One has to remember that every failure can be a stepping-stone to something better."

"A lot of people have said to me, 'Why don't you retire?' I tell them, 'A man will rust out quicker than he'll wear out.' So, I keep right on going."

"If my story is different, it's because my life really began at age 65 when most folks have already called it a day."

"I've got no idea when I am going to retire. Whenever they pick me up and take me to the funeral home, I guess."

The Saltstraumen Strait in Norway gets the world's strongest whirlpools—33 feet wide and 16 feet deep.

THE TERMINATOR, STARRING CARRIE FISHER

Some roles are so closely associated with a specific actor that it's hard to imagine that he or she wasn't the first choice, but it happens all the time. For example, could you picture…

Eddie Murphy as Jules Winnfield (*Pulp Fiction*, 1994). According to a hand-typed want list that was leaked on Reddit in 2015, director Quentin Tarantino had four people in mind to play the Scripture-reciting gangster: Eddie Murphy, Laurence Fishburne, Clarence Dutton, and Samuel L. Jackson. Jackson got the part and became a household name because of it. Other almost-casting surprises: the role of Vincent Vega was written for Michael Madsen, not John Travolta. Uma Thurman wasn't even on Tarantino's original list for Mia Wallace. Who was? Robin Wright, Virginia Madsen, Debra Winger, Phoebe Cates, and Marissa Tomei. And Bruce Willis ended up playing Butch the boxer, but Tarantino also considered Matt Dillon, Sean Penn, Nicolas Cage, and Johnny Depp.

Matt Damon as Lee Chandler (*Manchester by the Sea*, 2016). Matt Damon produced writer-director Kenneth Lonergan's story about a grieving janitor who must raise his dead brother's son, and John Krasinski was originally going to star, but the project took too long to get going, so Krasinki dropped out. Damon was going to take over the lead role, but he'd already signed on to star in *The Martian*. Lonergran asked Damon to recommend a new lead. "I wasn't interested in producing it for another actor, unless it was someone I grew up with and loved dearly," said Damon. So he offered it to his friend Casey Affleck, who was in a career slump at the time. "I knew he would be able to do it in a way where I wouldn't regret giving it to him." Damon was right: Affleck won the Golden Globe and the Academy Award for Best Actor.

Carrie Fisher as Sarah Connor (*The Terminator*, 1984). *Star Wars* fans never got a chance to see Princess Leia take on Ahh-nold, but if director James Cameron had his way, it would have been Fisher instead of Linda Hamilton. One problem: Fisher never wanted to be a "movie star"—only a writer and an occasional actor. She also turned down lead roles in *The Princess Bride*, *The Accused*, and *The Blue Lagoon* and said that if she'd known *Star Wars* was going to be such a megahit, she would have turned that part down as well.

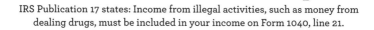

IRS Publication 17 states: Income from illegal activities, such as money from dealing drugs, must be included in your income on Form 1040, line 21.

Jake Gyllenhaal as Frodo Baggins (*The Fellowship of the Ring*, 2001).
When Gyllenhaal's agent got him the audition, he neglected to tell him one important thing: the character has an English accent. Not knowing that, Gyllenhaal read for Frodo in an American accent, and director Peter Jackson was not impressed, telling him: "You are the worst actor that I have ever seen." The part went to another American: Elijah Wood. (Had Gyllenhaal known about the accent and landed the role, he wouldn't have been available to make two other movies that came out in 2001: *Donnie Darko* and *Bubble Boy*.)

John Lennon as Stephen Falken (*WarGames*, 1983). This Matthew Broderick movie about a high school computer geek who nearly starts World War III went through a lot of changes in the years it took to get it to the screen. One big one: the scientist who designed the computer defense system was going to be "an astrophysicist in a wheelchair," inspired by Stephen Hawking. According to *WarGames* co-writer Walter Parkes: "We always pictured John Lennon, because he was kind of a spiritual cousin to Stephen Hawking." Lennon (who had acted in a few movies) was reportedly interested, but he was assassinated while the movie was still in preproduction. The role went to another Brit: John Wood.

Mel Gibson as Max Rockatansky (*Mad Max: Fury Road*, 2015). The three original *Mad Max* movies (1979–85) made Mel Gibson a superstar, and director George Miller wanted Gibson to reprise the role for a reboot in the late 1990s, but then reality reared its head: shortly after the movie started production in Australia, the September 11, 2001, terror attacks occurred, causing 20th Century Fox to postpone the movie because, according to Miller, "the American dollar collapsed against the Australian dollar, and our budget ballooned." The film was going to resume production in the Outback in 2003, but massive rainfalls ruined the shooting location, so they moved the project to Namibia, Africa…and then the Iraq War started. Tensions in the region forced the movie to be postponed yet again. Miller moved on to direct *Happy Feet* (2006), and by the time he was ready to get back on *Fury Road*, Mel Gibson had not only gotten considerably older, he was embroiled in controversy over his drunken, racist rants. So Miller decided to recast Max with a younger actor. Jeremy Renner campaigned for the role, unsuccessfully. Other names that were rumored: Channing Tatum, Sam Worthington, and Heath Ledger (who many feel would have gotten the part if he hadn't died). In the end, Miller cast English actor Tom Hardy. The wait was worth it: *Fury Road* has since been hailed as one of the best action movies of all time, and even got an Oscar nomination for Best Picture.

In Vietnam, everyone celebrates their birthday on the New Year.

FOUNDING FATHERS

You know the names. Here's a look at the people behind them.

WILBER HARDEE

After a stint in the U.S. Navy during World War II, Wilber Hardee settled down in Greenville, North Carolina. Over the next ten years, Hardee opened a string of diners, and had some success, but he had his eye on another restaurant concept—the McDonald's that opened in Greensboro in late 1959. He decided to try to copy it. So in September 1960, at age 42, Hardee started his first drive-in hamburger stand, which he named Hardee's. Thanks to its location—a popular "cruising" spot near the East Carolina University campus—and its simple, inexpensive menu: fresh charcoal-grilled hamburgers for 15¢, cheeseburgers for 20¢, shakes for 20¢, and fries for a dime, it did extremely well. It did so well, in fact, that two local businessmen, Jim Gardner and Leonard Rawls, paid Hardee $1,500 to franchise the concept with a second location. More franchisees bought into the Hardee's model, but Hardee himself was soon out of the company. In 1962 he was playing poker with Gardner and Rawls, wagered his controlling stake in the company…and lost. Disheartened, Hardee sold the rest of his share of the business to the duo and walked away. Hardee opened many other restaurants, but never achieved the success of Hardee's.

WALTER SCHLAGE

Born in Germany in 1882, Schlage had a knack for gadgets and mechanics, so his father sent him to study (and work) at the prestigious Carl Zeiss Optical Works, where he learned drafting and mechanical engineering. After that, Schlage drifted, working as the engineer of a Brazilian sailing ship, as an instrument maker in England, and as an electrician at Western Electric in San Francisco. Around 1909, he stopped drifting and started inventing. In 1909 he received his first patent, for a doorknob that completed an electrical circuit (when the door opened, the room's lights came on). He spent the better part of the 1910s developing the product for which he is best known: the first bored cylindrical lock, which used fewer parts and was much more easily installed than the standard mortise locks of the day. In 1920 he started the Schlage Lock Company with three friends, each of whom contributed $10, to produce Schlage's cylindrical lock, which was named the "A series" lock. By 1925 the company was producing 20,000 locks a month. Walter Schlage died in 1946, but the company is still around, making security products and keyless entry systems…and still making the "A series" lock.

What is malism? The doctrine that the world is evil.

DANIEL SWAROVSKI

Born into a family of glassworkers in North Bohemia—where glass was and remains a major industry—20-year-old Daniel Swartz was in Paris in 1882, and attended an exhibition promoting that newfangled concept of electricity. It was there that he saw an electric machine that could cut and grind glass. Such a device could open up possibilities—and opportunities—for his family's business. But those early machines were really just novelties, so Swartz spent the next 10 years developing what turned out to be the first practical electric glass grinder. In 1895 he founded a company in Wattens, Austria, which had the cheap hydroelectric power he needed to run the machines, and started making lead crystal glass "gems." (He also changed his name from Swartz to Swarovski to avoid the increasing anti-Semitism in Europe.) Swarovski's crystals looked like diamonds but weren't nearly as expensive. The value, he said, was in the craftsmanship that turned glass into ultra-bright, light-refracting gems. Jewelry made with Swarovski crystals quickly became popular with Europe's elite and came to be associated with luxury. The company is still around today and still operates out of Wattens with more than 30,000 employees, manufacturing sculptures, chandeliers, optical instruments, and, of course, crystal gems.

GEORGE AND ALFRED RAWLINGS

In 1887 the Rawlings brothers opened a sporting-goods store and catalog business in St. Louis. Their main products: fishing tackle, guns, and golf supplies, along with a few gloves for the emerging sport of baseball. A few months later, the store burned down, and the Rawlings brothers decided to focus on the catalog business and make the sporting goods themselves to cut out the middleman. Among the initial products sold by the Rawlings Manufacturing Co.: the first-ever set of football shoulder pads, called "Armor Clothing," and the first all-weather football. In 1906 the brothers secured a deal with the St. Louis Cardinals to provide their uniforms. That led to the company manufacturing baseballs for the minor leagues. All the while, the company made simple leather baseball mitts, which were essentially just padded gloves. Cardinals pitcher Bill Doak didn't like his glove, so in 1919 he sewed a few pieces of rawhide in between the thumb and forefinger slots, separating them and giving him better control. He took the idea to Rawlings, which adopted the design. It became their best-selling glove for more than 25 years. The company continues to make gloves, along with other sporting goods. In 1977 Rawlings became the official ball supplier for Major League Baseball.

A new microscope, the Mesolens, can create 3-D images of the structures inside cells.

THE MARS SQUIRREL

Did NASA send one or more squirrels to Mars? Some people believe they did…and say they have the photographic evidence to prove it.

OUT OF THIS WORLD

Not long after NASA landed its one-ton, car-sized Curiosity rover on Mars in 2012, the rover began exploring and sending pictures back to Earth, as part of its mission to study the climate and geology of the Red Planet. The images weren't all that exciting, at least not for the layperson: Mars is a barren wasteland, after all. (At least that's what NASA *wants* us to think.) But that hasn't stopped conspiracy theorists and others from pouring over the thousands of photos taken by Curiosity and scanning them rock by rock by rock, looking for any sign that NASA knows more than it admits to the public.

SEEING IS BELIEVING

In 2012, someone struck gold when they zoomed in on one of the rocks in a wide-angle photo of the Martian landscape. This particular rock looked uncannily like a squirrel crouching between two other rocks. Could it be…

"It's a cute rodent on Mars!" Scott Waring, editor of the UFO Sightings Daily website, posted on December 4. "[It] looks similar to a squirrel camouflaged in the stones and sand by its colors." How did it get to Mars? Waring believes it arrived with the Curiosity. "A lot of people are emailing me saying that this squirrel was part of a NASA experiment to test how long it would live on the surface of Mars and I believe this does sound like something they might do," he writes. "Why would they not tell us about it? Because the squirrel would be expected to die eventually and that would get PETA [People for the Ethical Treatment of Animals] to fight against them in a court of law."

ROCK ON

NASA says the squirrel is just a rock. It owes its squirrel-like shape to "wind erosion and mechanical abrasion and breakdown chemical weathering," Joy Crisp, a scientist on the Curiosity mission, told Space.com in 2013. Rather than move the rover in for a closer look, NASA sent it on a one-year, five-mile trek to a nearby mountain. (Since then, Waring has found "evidence" of a groundhog and a monkey living on Mars as well. NASA has no comment.)

VICTORIAN JOKES

We tend to think of England's Victorian era (1837–1901) as straitlaced, moralistic, and humorless. But maybe the Victorians did like a good laugh. Some British historians have made a project of gathering jokes and puns from magazines and newspapers of the day, and although they probably won't have you rolling on the floor, these examples may give you some insight into how humor has changed.

Who is the greatest chicken-killer in Shakespeare?
Macbeth, because he did murder most foul!

If all the seas were dried up, what would Neptune say?
I really haven't got a notion.

What is the difference between a tube and a foolish Dutchman?
One is a hollow cylinder and the other a silly Hollander.

"See here, waiter. I've found a button in my salad."
"That's all right, sir, it's part of the dressing."

If William Penn's aunts had a pastry shop, what would be the prices of their pies? The pie-rates of Penn's aunts.

> *Speak properly, and in as few words as you can, but always plainly, for the end of speech is not ostentation, but to be understood.*
> —**William Penn**

Why is the devil riding a mouse like one and the same thing?
Because it is synonymous.

What do you call men who hate long sentences?
Criminals.

Irate father: I never gave my father impudence when I was a boy!
Son: Maybe he didn't need it!

Before settling on "America," mapmakers considered *Amerige*, which means "Land of Americus."

What's the difference between Joan of Arc and a canoe?

One is Maid of Orleans and the other is made of wood.

Why is a badly conducted hotel like a fiddle?

Because it is a vile inn.

What is the difference between stabbing a man and killing a hog?

One is assaulting with intent to kill; the other is killing with intent to salt.

Why is a dog like a tree?

They both lose their bark once they're dead.

Husband: "I am a millionaire. Haven't I money enough for both of us?'"

Wife: "Yes, if you are moderate in your tastes."

How do you keep a dog from going mad in August?

Shoot it in July.

A novelist is a queer creature. His tale comes out of his head!

Why should the number 288 never be mentioned in company?

Because it is two gross.

Doesn't it make you dizzy to waltz?

Yes, but one must get used to it, you know. It's the way of the whirled.

There's only one melancholy fact about calendars. There's no time when its days are not numbered.

About the only thing that prevents some men from telling bare-faced lies is a moustache.

*　　*　　*

I'VE BEEN CLOWNED

When Queen Elizabeth I was 29, smallpox left her with a scarred complexion that she covered with a deadly paste of white lead and vinegar. When her skin got worse, the queen ordered all mirrors taken away. With no mirrors, mischievous servants would often paint a red dot on the oblivious queen's nose.

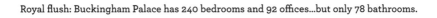

Royal flush: Buckingham Palace has 240 bedrooms and 92 offices...but only 78 bathrooms.

HOME ALONE?

When you hear the floorboards creak, or notice some food missing, do you wonder if there's someone else in the house? These folks did…and they were right.

BOY'S IN THE ATTIC

One night in September 2012, a 41-year-old woman in Rock Hill, South Carolina, identified in news reports as "Tracy," heard strange noises in her attic. The single mother of five sent her two oldest sons up to check it out… but they found nothing. "The kids were saying, 'You're hearing things. You're getting old,'" Tracy told reporters. But later that night, at around 2:30 a.m., she heard the noises again—and then saw nails popping out of the ceiling. She immediately called a nephew, who came over to the house…and found a man sleeping in the attic. The man fled before police arrived, but Tracy recognized him: it was her ex-boyfriend—who she'd broken up with 12 years earlier. For years he'd been sending her love letters, begging her to go out with him again. But she had steadfastly refused. Police said the man, who must have been living in the cramped space for a number of days, had rigged an air vent in the attic floor…so that he could peek down at Tracy while she was in her bedroom.

CLOSET CASE

In 2008, a 57-year-old man in the town of Kasuya, on Japan's southern Kyushu Island, started noticing food mysteriously disappearing from his refrigerator and cupboards. The man lived alone, so he figured someone must have been breaking into his home. In order to catch the intruder, he installed a security system with cameras that he could monitor on his cell phone while he was out of the house. Sure enough, not long after setting up the cameras, the man watched as a middle-aged woman walked around his home. The shocked homeowner called the police, who found no signs of a break-in. The police made a search of the home and property—and found nothing. Finally, one of the officers slid open a small door at the top of a built-in closet in a room the man rarely used—and saw a woman curled up on a small futon in the tiny space. The woman, 58-year-old Tatsuko Horikawa, told police she was homeless, and had been living in the man's closet for about a year. She had been sneaking out when the man went to work, she said, to find things to eat. Police told news reporters that Horikawa appeared "unusually clean," and must have made regular use of the man's shower. (She was charged with trespassing.)

Good news? Perique Tobacco Liqueur really is made with tobacco.

THE FLINTSTONES ROCKS

Perhaps the most notable thing about the classic 1960s animated TV show The Flintstones *(aside from it being a blatant knockoff of* The Honeymooners*) was its Stone Age puns. Everything with a name had some kind of reference to rocks or stones. Here are a few yabba-dabba-doozies from various* Flintstones *TV shows and movies.*

LOCATIONS

- **Rock Vegas** (Las Vegas)
- **Sand-and-Stony-o** (San Antonio)
- **Hollyrock** (Hollywood)
- **Mexirock** (Mexico)
- **Rockapulco** (Acapulco)
- **Texarock** (Texas)
- **New Rock City** (New York City)
- **Rockarabia** (Saudi Arabia)

CELEBRITIES

- **Jackie Kennerock** (Jackie Kennedy)
- **Conrad Hailstone** (Conrad Hilton)
- **Gina Lodabricks** (Gina Lollobrigida)
- **Gary Granite** (Cary Grant)
- **Rock Pile Hudstone** (They had to change Rock Hudson?)
- **Mick Jadestone and the Rolling Boulders** (Mick Jagger and the Rolling Stones)
- **Eppy Brianstone** (Beatles manager Brian Epstein)
- **Stony Curtis** (Tony Curtis)
- **Ed Sullystone** (Ed Sullivan)
- **Ann-Margrock** (Ann-Margret)
- **Alvin Brickrock** (Alfred Hitchcock)
- **Greta Gravel** (Greta Garbo)
- **Clark Gravel** (Clark Gable)
- **The Beau Brummelstones** (1960s band the Beau Brummels)

ATHLETES

- **Red Granite** (Red Grange)
- **Bronto Crushrock** (Bronko Nagurski)
- **Arnold Palmrock** (Arnold Palmer)
- **Floyd Patterstone** (Floyd Patterson)
- **Sonny Listone** (Sonny Liston)
- **Sandy Stoneaxe** (Sandy Koufax)
- **Lindy McShale** (Lindy McDaniel)

In China, you can buy cans of fresh air from the Rocky Mountains.

> **SOMETHING TO CHEW ON:** *Flintstones Chewable Vitamins are still the top-selling children's vitamin, even though the TV show was canceled more than 50 years ago. They were a revamp of a failed kids' vitamin called Chocks, made by Miles Laboratories.*

- **Roger Marble** (Roger Maris)
- **Mickey Marble** (Mickey Mantle)
- **Jack Nickrock** (Jack Nicklaus)
- **The Indianrockolis 500** (The Indianapolis 500)

ENTERTAINMENT

- **Cinderellastone** (Cinderella)
- **Perry Masonite** (Perry Mason)
- **Perry Gunite** (Peter Gunn)
- **Count Rockula** (Count Dracula)
- **Rockzilla** (Godzilla)
- **Frankenstone** (Frankenstein)
- **Tar Wars** (Star Wars)
- **Adobe Dick** (Moby Dick)

- **Superstone** (Superman)
- **Hercurock** (Hercules)
- **James Bondrock** (James Bond)

OTHER

- **Arthur Quarry Dance Studio** (Arthur Murray Dance Studio)
- **The Cavern on the Green restaurant** (The Tavern on the Green)
- **Prinstone University** (Princeton)
- **Chevrock** (Chevron gas station)
- **Cave Scouts** (Cub Scouts)
- **Hatrocks** (a hillbilly family, a play on the Hatfields)
- **Rolls-Rock** (Rolls-Royce)
- **First Rock War** (World War I)

*   *   *

A TIGER TALE

In 2013, a wild Bengal tiger actually broke *into* Nandankanan Zoological Park in India. This was after he spent several days lurking in the forest not far from the tigress enclosure. Rather than attempt a capture, zookeepers left a door open next to the tigress enclosure and then locked it after the male sauntered in. For the next few weeks, zoo staff and townspeople debated whether to keep the male in captivity…until he took matters into his own paws. One night he climbed an 18-foot "tiger-proof" wall and vanished back into the forest.

The first pencil with an attached eraser had the eraser inside the pencil…

JUST PLANE WEIRD

If you happen to be reading this in midair, you mightwant to turn to another page and save this one for when you're back safely on the ground.

AN OFFER HE COULDN'T REFUSE

In 2015 Italy's civil aviation authority suspended the license of a helicopter pilot (unnamed in press reports) for flying too low over the city of Rome and dropping rose petals on the funeral procession of crime boss Vittorio Casamonica, while a band played the theme from *The Godfather*. Single-engine helicopters are prohibited from flying over the Eternal City, and even aircraft that are permitted must remain above 1,000 feet. The pilot broke both of those rules, as well as the one that prohibits throwing unauthorized objects out of aircraft. Rosy Bindi, the head of the Italian parliament's anti-mafia committee, condemned the gaudy funeral as "yet another wound for Rome" that "humiliated all Italians."

EVERYONE ELSE WAS AWAKE

Pakistan International Airways suspended one of its most senior pilots, Captain Amir Akhtar Hashmi, in April 2017 after passengers photographed him snoozing in the business-class cabin for more than two hours. Hashmi was supposed to be instructing a trainee pilot during the flight from London to Islamabad. Instead, soon after takeoff he handed the controls over to the trainee and went to take his nap. (First Officer Ali Hassan Yazdani remained with the trainee in the cockpit, but he was sitting in the observer's seat and would have been of little assistance in an emergency.) Hashmi denies any wrongdoing: "It is a wrong allegation that I took a two-and-a-half hour sleep during the flight," he told reporters. "I did not sleep during the said flight." (In 2009 an Air France flight crashed in the Atlantic Ocean en route from Brazil, killing 228 people, when the captain turned control of the flight over to two junior pilots and left the cockpit to take a nap.)

BARE-PLANE

In October 2016, British Airways suspended pilot Colin Glover, 51, after the *Sun* newspaper published a series of lurid photos it said showed Glover piloting a commercial flight while wearing nothing but a pair of womens' stockings. In some photos the nearly naked person (his face isn't shown) is resting his feet on the control yoke while the plane is in autopilot mode; in others a pornographic

...Sharpening one end revealed the eraser; sharpening the other revealed the lead.

magazine is propped up on the center console covering some gauges. (How can aviation experts be certain that the photos were taken in an actual aircraft, and not a flight simulator? Because a few of the naughty photos were taken in an airplane bathroom…and flight simulators don't have bathrooms.)

Glover denies he's the man in the photos. But even if it is proven to be him, he could be in just as much trouble for not wearing his seat belt as for stripping out of his uniform. "It's very serious," an unnamed 777 pilot told the *Sun*. "A pilot could possibly deal with turbulence while naked, but if he was hurt and couldn't open the door to get help, it could endanger the aircraft. He's more likely to be injured when he is not strapped in."

NO PARKING

Two pilots for IndiGo, India's largest airline, were suspended following an incident in February 2016 when they mistook an ordinary road in the city of Jaipur for a runway and tried to land on it. They most likely would have, too, had their aircraft's Enhanced Ground Proximity Warning System not shrieked an alarm when they got too close to the ground. When the alarm sounded, they aborted the landing, found the runway, and landed safely on it.

PHOTO FINISH

In early 2017, the British Royal Air Force fired pilot Lieutenant Andrew Townshend, 49, after he sent a military passenger jet into a nosedive while fiddling with a camera in the cockpit. According to investigators, Townshend was "bored" and had been snapping photos through the windshield when he set his Nikon camera down in front of his seat's armrest. But then he slid his seat forward, and the camera inadvertently pushed the aircraft's "side stick" control, disengaging the autopilot and sending the plane into a steep dive. It dropped 4,400 feet in just 29 seconds.

Copilot Lieutenant Nathan Jones was in the galley getting tea when the plane went into its dive. He was thrown up into the ceiling by the force and had to crawl along the ceiling to get back into the cockpit. Once there (still stuck to the ceiling), he managed to reach down and pull back on the control stick gently enough to ease the plane out of its nosedive without "snapping the wings off." He is credited with saving the 187 people on board, many of whom, like him, were "pinned to the ceiling and thought they were going to die," according to news reports. Townshend pled guilty to negligently operating the aircraft and was given a four-month suspended prison sentence; at last report, Jones was still recovering from his injuries.

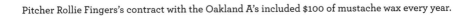

Pitcher Rollie Fingers's contract with the Oakland A's included $100 of mustache wax every year.

NICKNAME ORIGINS

If you've ever wondered how "Dick" is a shortened form of Richard, Uncle Jack's Bathroom Reader has got you covered.

Name: James
Nickname: Jim

Story: James has been a popular name in Scotland for hundreds of years, but it didn't really catch on in English until the Scottish king James I became king of England in 1603. (He's also the "King James" of the King James Bible.) In a Scottish brogue, "James" sounds more like "Jems." Spoken with an English accent (without a brogue), it transformed into Jem, and then Jim.

Name: Richard
Nickname: Dick

Story: The name Richard originates in an early form of German as Rikharthu. Over the centuries, Rikharthu evolved into Ricohard, and entered Old English as Richeard. In the 12th and 13th centuries, English scribes, who had to write everything by hand, adopted a series of abbreviations to save themselves time and labor. Among the shortened versions: Richard was written as Rich or Ric. In medieval times, rhyming was a popular way to create nicknames, so Ric became Dick.

Name: Margaret
Nickname: Peggy

Story: Margaret has been a common English name since the 11th century, and even further back in other European languages. Dozens of names are some variant of Margaret (which comes from *margarite*, an Old French word that means "gemstone"), including Rita, Megan, Greta, Gretchen, Madge, Margo, and many more. Maggie became a pretty obvious nickname from Margaret, and then that got shortened to Meg. Add in the English rhyming tradition, and Meg turned into Peg, and then turned into its diminutive form, Peggy.

Name: Charles
Nickname: Chuck

Story: In Middle English (which dates to the 11th and 12th centuries), the word *chukken* meant "cluck" (like a chicken). Because both "Charles" and "chukken" started with the same two letters and sound, the latter caught on as a nickname for the former. The concept then fell out of favor for a few centuries, until the name "Chuck" was revived in William Shakespeare's popular play *Macbeth*, when Lady Macbeth affectionately calls her husband Chuck.

Name: Henry

Nickname: Hank

Story: The original form of Henry is the Dutch name Hendrick, and the Dutch nickname for Hendrick is Henk. When Hendrick entered English as Henry, the nickname version followed along, with only a minor Anglicization—a change of the letter "e" to an "a."

Name: Edward

Nickname: Ted

Story: Ted is short for Theodore, but it's also a nickname for Edward. In the Middle Ages of England, unlike today, there weren't all that many names to choose from. So many people in a village might have the same name... such as Edward. Rather than inventing new names, English speakers simply started creating variations on the name by swapping out or adding letters to the beginning of the name. Result: rhyming nicknames, such as Tedward. More variations on that were then formed by shortening, and Tedward was easily shortened to Ted.

Name: Sarah

Nickname: Sally

Story: Another example of how a new name was spun off from another when the original name became overused. Sarah was a very common name for women 400 to 500 years ago. (It's from the Bible—Abraham's wife was named Sarah, and it's Hebrew for "noblewoman.") Rather than coming up with a word that rhymed with Sarah to derive a nickname, the R sound was replaced with an L sound to create "Sallah," which evolved into Sally.

Bonus fact: Replacing an R sound with an L sound led to another common name for women. The "r" in Mary was replaced with an "l," and it became Molly.

*　　*　　*

A REAL SIGN (SEEN IN INDIA)

DO NOT: Bend, Borrow, Break, Cut, Cleave, Clip, Crush, Divide, Endanger, Harm, Mutilate, Pare, Pinch, Pick, Pluck, Pull, Sever, Snip, Snap Off, Steal, Take, Touch, Twist Off, or Remove the Flowers

If the U.S. ever gets a 51st state, the flag will need three rows of nine stars and three rows of eight.

HANAKO OF THE TOILET

*If you ever have occasion to visit a children's school in Japan, use
the third stall in the third-floor bathroom at your own risk.
Better yet, just wait until you get back to your hotel.*

KID STUFF

When you were growing up, did your parents ever scare you with stories about
the boogeyman? Tales of a shadowy creature that punishes children for bad
behavior is common to many cultures—Spain has El Coco, Slavic countries
have Baba Yaga, India has Bihar, Mediterranean countries have Babau, and so
on. Moms and dads in Japan have a similar tradition. But where the American
boogeyman is usually described in vague and amorphous terms, the stories
that Japanese parents tell about scary imaginary beings are more defined—and
they're frequently centered in the bathroom. Traditionally considered unclean
even when kept perpetually immaculate by the most fastidious of housekeepers,
bathrooms were often hidden away in a dark corner of the house. Ghosts were
said to live in the toilet, and parents liked to tease children about a hairy hand
rising up out of the water and pulling kids down into the sewage pipes.

SCHOOL SPIRIT

It stands to reason that with such a spooky start, some kids might come up with
their own scary legends around the bathroom. And sure enough, they have.

One of the most popular has to do with *Toire no Hanako-san*, or "Hanako of
the toilet." The legend is believed to date back to the 1950s, when Hanako was
a popular girls' name. Toire no Hanako-san is said to haunt the third toilet stall
of third-floor girls' bathrooms in elementary schools (assuming their school has
a third floor.) And she is said to have died a horrible death, the details of which
vary from school to school: in some she died in a World War II bombing raid; in
others she was killed by one or both parents, or by a stranger; in still others she
committed suicide after she was bullied by schoolmates.

Whatever the case, for a few generations now, word has spread from one
schoolchild to another that if they stand outside the third stall in the third-floor
girls' restroom, knock three times, and ask, "Are you there, Hanako-san?" a voice
will answer, "I'm here." When they enter the stall, they will be greeted by the
ghost of a girl in a red skirt. That's it—Toire no Hanako-san is creepy and scary
and sometimes slams bathroom doors, but she's not dangerous.

In India, people are buying cow dung patties off the Internet to burn—the smell is nostalgic to them.

Like a game of telephone, the tale has grown with each telling. In some schools, instead of a little girl appearing, kids believe a bloody human hand will emerge from the toilet stall. In other schools the hand is not bloody, and in still others the voice that replies "I'm here" is that of a three-headed lizard *pretending* to be Hanako-san, and it will eat any child foolish enough to enter the stall.

MORE SPOOKS

In some schools, the bathrooms are haunted by a legless female ghost named Kashima Reiko, who died after she was run over by a train. That's also how she lost her legs. She asks, "Where are my legs?" of anyone who enters the bathroom, and if they don't give the correct answer ("*kamen shinin ma*," or "mask death demon," which may also be the phonetic root of her name), she will rip their legs off, leaving them as disfigured as she is.

Another scary schoolhouse bathroom spirit is Aka Manto (Red Cape), known in some places as Aoi Manto (Blue Cape), a male ghost who haunts the last stall in the girls' bathroom. Sometimes the ghost is said to be that of a man so beautiful in life that he had to wear a white mask to stop every woman he met from falling in love with him. He's still so charming that most schoolgirls who hear his voice are powerless to resist him.

According to one version of the tale, when a child in the last stall is seated on the toilet doing their business, the disembodied voice of Aka Manto will ask, "Which do you prefer, the red paper or the blue paper?" If the child chooses red, Aka Manto will slash their throat or chop off their head, causing their blood to flow down their back until it looks like a red cape. If the child chooses blue, Aka Manto will kill them by choking them until they turn blue.

CAPE FEAR

Another version of the story says that the ghost will ask the child if they want a red or blue *cape*. The child who chooses red will have their blouse torn off and a cape-shaped patch of skin ripped from their back; the child who chooses blue will have the blood drained from their body until they turn blue.

Choosing yellow for the toilet paper or the cape—even though Aka Manto hasn't offered yellow as an option—results in the ghost shoving the child's head into the bowl of the toilet they've just used (so it's a good idea to flush before answering the question). Answering with any color other than red, blue, or yellow causes a pair of hands to rise up out of the toilet and drag the child down to hell. The only way to emerge unscathed from the toilet paper/cape conundrum: don't answer at all…and wait for the demonic spirit to leave.

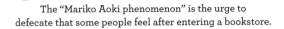

The "Mariko Aoki phenomenon" is the urge to defecate that some people feel after entering a bookstore.

WATCH THIS!

Smart watches and fitness trackers are mini computers that monitor the wearer's exercise, heart rate, sleep patterns, and other health information. Sometimes they do a little bit more.

UNDER ATTACK

In the summer of 2015, 62-year-old Dennis Anselmo, a contractor from Morinville, Alberta, was building a fence in Edmonton when he suddenly didn't feel well. He decided to rest for a while, thinking that he must be coming down with the flu. But then he started messing around with his brand-new Apple Watch. One of the device's features is that it constantly measures the user's heart rate; Anselmo's was running at 210 beats per minute, more than twice what it should have been. Anselmo suspected the fatigue and dizziness he was experiencing might not be flu symptoms, but signs of a heart attack. He called an ambulance and was rushed into heart surgery and lived to tell the tale.

HAVE A HEART

A 42-year-old man (unnamed in news reports) was admitted to the emergency room at New Jersey's Our Lady of Lourdes Medical Center in 2016. He'd just suffered a seizure, and reported a heartbeat that was both irregular and rapid. Doctors had a hard time determining whether the seizure triggered the irregular heartbeat, or if his heart problems were an undiagnosed, chronic condition. Then they tapped into the data collected by the man's Fitbit Charge HR. After looking at his vitals from the exact moment he'd had the seizure, they were able to discern that the seizure caused the strange heart problems. They were then free to perform a lifesaving procedure called an electrical cardioversion.

SURGE PROTECTOR

An 18-year-old British woman named Sarah-Jayne McIntosh got a Fitbit Surge for Christmas in 2015. Two weeks later, it saved her life. She was studying quietly when the device alerted her that her heart rate had jumped from 88 beats per minute to 210—and she was just sitting there reading, not doing anything physically strenuous. McIntosh immediately called an ambulance and was taken to a hospital, where doctors discovered an undiagnosed heart ailment—a misfiring chamber in the heart. If she had been left untreated any longer, doctors say, McIntosh would probably have died.

When the Vienna zoo got its first giraffe in 1828, the novelty of it inspired a pastry, a perfume, and a hairstyle.

LUCKY FINDS

Have you ever found something valuable? It's one of the best feelings in the world. Here's the latest installment of a regular Bathroom Reader feature—a look at some folks who found really odd and valuable stuff.

CARGO BYE-BYE

The Find: A stolen sports car

Where It Was Found: On a cargo ship

The Story: In 1967 a young New York lawyer named Ivan Schneider bought himself a present. He'd just won his first big court case, so he rewarded himself with a shiny new car—a Jaguar XK-E convertible. But he didn't get to enjoy it for long. A few months later it was parked in front of his Manhattan apartment. "I went downstairs," he told CNN years later, "and it was gone. I was devastated." The police couldn't find the thieves *or* the car, and that was the last that Schneider heard about it for 45 years. Then, when Schneider was 82, he got a call from U.S. Customs informing him that his Jaguar had been discovered in Los Angeles during a routine inspection of a cargo ship bound for the Netherlands. (Four other stolen cars, including a 1969 Corvette, were also recovered.) Schneider had the Jag—which he bought for $5,000—shipped to Miami Beach, where he planned to have it restored to its original glory at a cost of about $50,000…but then it would be worth around $100,000. "Who would think a car would show up 45 years later?" he mused. "When I found out they weren't kidding, I was thrilled."

A REALLY GOOD LUCK CHARM

The Find: The largest pearl ever found

Where It Was Found: Off Palawan Island in the Philippines

The Story: In 2006, a fisherman (who has chosen to remain anonymous) was heading back to shore when his boat's anchor became snagged on something big. He dove into the water to investigate and discovered that the something big was a giant clam. And inside of it was a pearl the size of a bed pillow. The fisherman freed the anchor and then lugged the 75-pound pearl up to his boat. Not realizing the magnitude of his find, he took it home and put it under his bed, only touching it before fishing trips for "good luck." And there it stayed for ten years. Then, when he had to move, he gave it to his aunt, local tourism officer Aileen Cynthia Maggay-Amurao, for safekeeping. She knew instantly that it was valuable, even more so after she did some research and discovered that the largest pearl ever reported weighed "only" 14 pounds. At last report, experts had yet to confirm the find, but if it is what it appears to be, this massive pearl will be worth around $100 million. For now, it's on display at the New Green City Hall in Puerto Princesa.

THE LUCKY SEVEN

The Find: Seven rare baseball cards

Where They Were Found: In a paper bag

The Story: By 2016, Joe Orlando had been working as a professional sports authenticator for 17 years, and in that time he'd verified some of the most valuable baseball cards in existence. So when a collector contacted Orlando about a potentially huge find, he took it with a grain of salt. "After you see so many beautiful Mickey Mantle cards and authentic Babe Ruth autographs, it takes something very special to really grab your attention." Result: when the collector told him that he'd discovered seven Ty Cobb cards printed between 1909 and 1911, Orlando assumed they were fakes, which is most often the case. But that was not the case. "The cards," he explained,

> "were unearthed in a rural town after a Southern family was combing through the possessions of their great-grandparents. They were found inside a torn paper bag on the floor. Initially, the family thought the bag was merely filled with trash and planned to discard it. One of the family members decided to sift through the contents, which included a number of postcards and other paper products. Beneath this small pile of items were the Cobb cards lying facedown at the bottom of the bag."

The family took the cards to a local dealer, who then called Orlando. It wasn't until he actually saw the cards that Orlando started to suspect that they might be the real thing. And sure enough, after some vigorous testing, the cards—now being referred to as the "Lucky Seven Find"—turned out to be authentic. Even though they're faded, they're in otherwise good condition. Estimated worth: more than $1 million. Orlando had one word to describe this lucky find: "miraculous."

> *One of the advantages of being disorganized is that one is always having surprising discoveries.*
>
> **—A. A. Milne**

Does it bug him? A newly discovered moth with yellow "hair" has been named *Neopalpa donaldtrumpi.*

STENCH ON THE BEACH

The Find: A lump of whale vomit

Where It Was Found: On a beach in Somerset, England

The Story: In August 2016, Alan Derrick, 67, and his son Tom, 39, were taking a walk on Sand Point when Tom picked up a waxy, gray lump that weighed about two and a half pounds and smelled like "walking into a very old, damp building." Tom asked his dad if he knew what the thing was. "If that's what I think it is," replied Alan, "then guard it with your life." It was. Whale vomit—technically called *ambergris*—is prized by perfume makers, who will pay very high prices for it. The Derricks listed their lucky find on eBay; so far there's no word as to whether it sold, but the asking price: £65,000 ($85,000).

IT'S FOR PAUL

The Find: A lost Beatles record

Where It Was Found: Hidden in plain sight

The Story: In 1964 Paul McCartney and John Lennon wrote a song called "It's for You" for an up-and-coming singer (and fellow Liverpudlian) named Cilla Black. It reached #7 in the British charts. A few years later, Black gave the acetate demo of the song to her brother, who was an avid music collector. He labeled the record sleeve "It's for You" and the artist as "Demo," assuming that it was Cilla's demo version. Then the record stayed in that sleeve for more than 50 years. After Black died in 2015, her nephew Simon White—who inherited the collection from his father—had the record (and several others) appraised by Stephen Baily at the Beatles Shop in Liverpool. They got to the Cilla Black demo last, and expected to hear her demo version of "It's for You." But then, "as soon as I heard it," recalled Baily, "I thought, 'Oh God, that's not Cilla Black, it's Paul McCartney.'" Everyone assumed that McCartney's demo had long been taped over—even McCartney himself. "I can't think of finding anything better," boasted Bailey, "unless I discover there is a sixth Beatle." Only one copy of the demo was made, and it was given to McCartney. The record was later sold at auction to a private collector for £21,060 ($32,000). It's unknown if the public will ever get to hear Paul's long-lost version of the song.

*   *   *

"The world is a book and those who do not travel read only a page."

—St. Augustine

Some early hot-air balloons were equipped with silk-covered oars, for rowing through the air.

HOW TO MAKE JELLY BEANS

These jelly beans won't be quite as shiny as the ones you buy in the store, but they'll taste better—not just because they're homemade, but also because you can choose any flavors and colors you want.

WHAT YOU'LL NEED

- 2 cups superfine sugar
- 1 cup water
- ¼ ounce unflavored gelatin
- ½ cup of your favorite juice, with the pulp (if any) removed. If you're an adult and prefer jelly beans with a little "spirit," mix one of your favorite cocktails and use ½ cup in place of the juice.
- ¼ teaspoon salt
- 2 tablespoons cornstarch
- Nonstick cooking spray
- A candy thermometer

- Jelly bean molds, enough to make 150 jelly beans. They're available in craft stores and online. (If you're feeling creative, you can use molds shaped like coffee beans, gummy bears, or any other shape that strikes your fancy.)
- A large bowl filled with ice cubes, or a kitchen sink filled with ice water
- Parchment paper
- Food coloring
- A large jar with a tight-fitting cover, such as a mayonnaise jar with a lid

NOW GET COOKING

Jelly Bean Innards

Spray the jelly bean molds with the nonstick cooking spray. Set aside.

In a large saucepan, combine ¾ cup of water with 1¼ cups of superfine sugar and the gelatin. Bring to a boil over medium heat, stirring regularly to ensure that the gelatin and sugar dissolve completely.

Using the candy thermometer, keep an eye on the temperature of the boiling mixture, and as soon as it reaches 230°F (about 25 minutes), remove it from the

A sting from Australia's "suicide plant" feels like "being burnt with acid and electrocuted at the same time."

stove and set the saucepan in the bowl of ice cubes or the sink filled with ice water to stop the mixture from cooking any further.

Quickly stir the salt, the juice (or cocktail), and a few drops of food coloring into the mixture.

Immediately pour the mixture into the jelly bean molds.

Allow the molds to cool at room temperature for four to six hours, then place in the freezer for ten minutes to really firm up the jelly beans before removing them from the molds.

Remove the beans from the molds and set on the parchment paper. Lightly dust with cornstarch.

The Hard Outer Shell

Combine ¼ cup water with ¾ cup superfine sugar and a few drops of the food coloring.

Pour this mixture into the large jar. Add the jelly beans and seal tightly. Tilt the jar at a 45-degree angle, then hold the jar by the lid and begin rotating it so that the jelly beans tumble through the water/sugar/food coloring mixture. If you happen to have a (clean) hobbyist's rock tumbler handy, you can also tumble the jelly beans in that.

Continue rotating the jar for 10–15 minutes, until the beans are thoroughly coated.

Remove the beans from the jar and return to the parchment paper. Allow them to dry overnight, then turn the beans over and allow the other side to dry for several more hours.

> **ALL YOU CAN EAT:** *Today, Jelly Belly Jelly Beans sells 50 "official flavors," including Chocolate Pudding, Chili Mango, Crushed Pineapple, Cotton Candy, Kiwi, and Caramel Corn. When it launched in 1976, it produced just eight: Very Cherry, Tangerine, Lemon, Green Apple, Grape, Licorice, Root Beer, and Cream Soda.*

*   *   *

"If you can't make it good, at least make it look good."

—Bill Gates

First star to put handprints in the cement outside
Grauman's Chinese Theatre: 1920s actress Norma Talmadge.

POPE-POURRI

English poet Alexander Pope (1688–1744) popularized the epigram: a short quote that contains wit and wisdom, and often rhymes—basically the Tweets of the 18th century.

"Our proper bliss depends on what we blame."

"It is with narrow-souled people as with narrow-necked bottles: the less they have in them, the more noise they make in pouring it out."

"Never elated, while one man's oppress'd; Never dejected, while another's bless'd."

"Lo, what huge heaps of littleness around!"

"He who tells a lie, is not sensible of how great a task he undertakes; for he must be forced to invent twenty more to maintain that one."

"If a man's character is to be abused, there's nobody like a relative to do the business."

"Hope springs eternal in the human breast. Man never is, but always to be blest."

"If you want to know what God thinks about money, just look at the people He gives it to."

"A little knowledge is a dangerous thing. So is a lot."

"A work of art that contains theories is like an object on which the price tag has been left."

"Some old men, by continually praising the time of their youth, would almost persuade us that there were no fools in those days; but unluckily they are left themselves for examples."

"What Reason weaves, by Passion is undone."

"A person who is too nice an observer of the business of the crowd, like one who is too curious in observing the labor of the bees, will often be stung for his curiosity."

"What some call health, if purchased by perpetual anxiety about diet, isn't much better than tedious disease."

"Wit is the lowest form of humor."

Are they bananas? Russia is planning to send a spacecraft crewed by monkeys to Mars by 2020.

SATURN IS A GIANT UFO!

…and other headlines from Uncle John's favorite newspaper, the Weekly World News.

OBAMA ADDS HIMSELF TO
MOUNT RUSHMORE

GOOGLE STREET VIEW OF HEAVEN

TWINKIES: THE NEW
SUPERFOOD

COOKIE MONSTER MUGS KIDS
IN TIMES SQUARE

ALIENS FOUND IN HEDGE
FUND LEADER'S BRAIN

JAY-Z NAMED SECRETARY OF STATE

ASTEROID TO BOUNCE
OFF EARTH TODAY

JERSEY DEVIL SPOTTED
IN OKLAHOMA

WILD HOGS TAKE ATLANTA!

MEN ON "ENDANGERED
SPECIES" LIST

*DALAI LAMA RETIRES—MOVES
INTO PLAYBOY MANSION*

RAM AND DEER TO MARRY
ON VALENTINE'S DAY

"TOY STORY 4" WILL BE RATED R

GOD PARTICLE FOUND
IN NEW JERSEY

GIANT'S ARM FALLS ON CAR

CROCODILE DUNDEE
FOUND ALIVE!

CHAOS CLOUD TAKES VIRGINIA

NFL TO BECOME FLAG
FOOTBALL LEAGUE

GHOST KICKED OUT OF
CEMETERY

*ALIEN ICE FALLS
ON BROOKLYN*

CHICAGO TO BE RENAMED
"OBAMA CITY"

*WOMAN FINDS
GIANT KFC BUCKET!*

POPE JOINS HELL'S ANGELS

IRS TO HOLD DANCE MARATHON

*FLYING WITCHES
ARRESTED IN KANSAS*

ABE LINCOLN WAS A WOMAN!

At the time of the American Revolution (1765–83), about 20% of New York City residents were slaves.

GPS TKO? DIY

More and more people are using GPS to help get them where they need to go. But the system is controlled by the U.S. military and they can turn it off anytime they want. If you were a foreign government, wouldn't you want to do something about that? Some already have.

OUT OF ORDER

In February 1999 a group of Pakistani soldiers and Kashmiri militants crossed the "Line of Control" that divides the state of Kashmir into Indian- and Pakistani-controlled areas, and moved into strategically important positions on the Indian side. The rugged, mountainous area is sparsely populated during the harsh winter months, and it wasn't until early May that the Indian military discovered the incursion and attacked. After three months of heavy fighting, they managed to drive the Pakistanis out of most of the territory they had occupied; international diplomatic pressure forced Pakistan to withdraw from the rest.

The Indians had hoped to use GPS technology during the conflict. Whether they did is unclear: As we told you on page 49, the U.S. military has the ability to disable GPS in conflict zones without affecting users elsewhere in the world. It's possible that the military, at the behest of the Clinton administration, disabled the system in Kashmir during the conflict, perhaps to prevent it from escalating into a nuclear war. If they did so, they're not telling.

Many in India do believe the United States denied them access to GPS, and frustration from the incident convinced the government that it needed its own satellite navigation system. And India isn't the only country to feel this need. Here are some alternatives that have already been built or are on the way:

THE INDIAN REGIONAL NAVIGATION SYSTEM

Description: Also known as NAVIC ("boatman" or "navigator" in Hindi, and short for "NAVigation with Indian Constellation"), the Indian system consists of seven satellites in geosynchronous orbit, which keeps them in the sky over India 24 hours a day.

Details: Unlike GPS, which is global, NAVIC is regional. It covers India and extends nearly 1,000 miles beyond its borders to encompass China, the Middle East, the Indian Ocean, and parts of Africa and Australia. The first satellite was launched in 2013, and the seventh and final one went into orbit on April 28, 2016. The system became fully operational for military and civilian users in the fall of 2016.

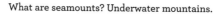

GLOBAL NAVIGATION SATELLITE SYSTEM (GLONASS)

Description: GLONASS is the Soviet Union's response to GPS—a satellite-based navigation system that would allow Soviet ballistic missiles to strike their targets with an accuracy of about 65 feet.

Details: The first of 24 satellites was launched in October 1982; the system was complete by 1995. But keeping all 24 satellites in orbit was another problem. Economic difficulties made it impossible to replace the old satellites as fast as they wore out, and by 2001 only six satellites were still in orbit.

When the economy recovered in the 2000s, Russian president Vladimir Putin made launching new GLONASS satellites a top priority. In 2011 the system became fully operational for the first time since 1996. Samsung Galaxies, iPhones, and other smartphones have been capable of receiving both GPS and GLONASS signals since 2015; using both systems at once makes the phones' navigation software more accurate than when they use only GPS signals.

BEIDOU

Description: BeiDou ("Big Dipper" or "Northern Dipper") is the name of two different Chinese satellite navigation systems.

Details: BeiDou-1, which became operational in 2000, is an experimental, three-satellite regional system that covers China, India, Southeast Asia, the Philippines, and parts of Japan. BeiDou-2 is a global system that has been under construction since 2007. As of 2017, it provided coverage of the Asia-Pacific region and is scheduled to go worldwide by 2020, when all 35 satellites in the system have been put into orbit.

GALILEO

Description: It's the European Union's satellite system. Unlike the others, it is intended primarily for civilian use. But like the others, it was created to provide an independent service that could not be shut off by outsiders in a crisis.

Details: The first Galileo satellite was launched in 2011, and as of December 2016, 18 of 30 planned satellites were in orbit. That's enough to provide what Galileo calls early operational capability. Full operational capability won't be available until 2019.

Perhaps because it is designed for civilians, Galileo offers a unique two-way global search-and-rescue function: When a lost or stranded person activates an emergency beacon, the rescue center that receives the call will be able to reply to the beacon, letting the stranded party know that help is on the way.

The world's largest coin, 220 lb. of pure gold, was stolen from a Berlin museum. Police think the thieves hauled it off in a wheelbarrow.

30 FOR 30

This is the 30th Uncle John's Bathroom Reader! It puts us into the special club of "things of which there are more than 30." Here are some other members of the club.

30th in line to the British crown. When Queen Elizabeth II dies (or abdicates), her son Prince Charles is first in line to become the UK's new monarch. After Her Majesty's various other sons, grandchildren, cousins, nieces, and nephews, the 30th in line for succession (out of 56 officially listed royals) is Tane Mahuta Lewis, the son of Lady Davina Lewis (daughter of Prince Richard, Duke of Gloucester). Tane was born in 2012.

30th president. After President Warren G. Harding died in San Francisco while on a tour of the West in 1923, his vice president, Calvin Coolidge, took the oath of office and became the 30th president of the United States.

30th *30 for 30*. In 2009 ESPN began a documentary series called *30 for 30*. The title referred to their plan to make 30 documentaries about sports and athletes in honor of the network's 30th anniversary. The network has since aired nearly 100 episodes about everything from the XFL to Mike Tyson to Tonya Harding. The 30th *30 for 30* was the 2010 film *Pony Excess*, about the demise of the Southern Methodist University football program—the first and only time a collegiate athletic team was shut down by the NCAA for secretly paying its players.

30th person in space. Cosmonaut Yuri Gagarin was the first human in space, orbiting Earth in *Vostok 1* in 1961. American astronaut Alan Shepard was number two, aboard the *Freedom 7* in May 1961. After many more Russian and American missions, *Gemini 11* left Earth in September 1966. Onboard were veteran astronaut Pete Conrad and rookie Richard Gordon, the 30th person to ever leave Earth. Along with Conrad, Gordon docked with an Agena Target Vehicle, the first-ever rendezvous between two orbiting spacecrafts.

30th Perry Mason TV movie. Based on a series of novels by Erle Stanley Gardner (he wrote 82), the popular TV courtroom drama *Perry Mason*, starring Raymond Burr as Mason, aired on CBS from 1957 to 1966. In 1985 NBC revived the series in the form of made-for-TV movies, with Burr reprising his role. Over the next decade, Burr appeared in 26 *Perry Mason* movies, until his death in 1993. But that didn't end the series. NBC made four more Perry Mason movies with other actors playing Mason-like superlawyers. The 30th and final one was *A Perry Mason Mystery: The Case of the Jealous Jokester*, which aired in 1995 and starred Hal Holbrook as lawyer "Wild Bill" McKenzie.

30th pope. The 30th official leader of the Roman Catholic Church was Pope John II of Alexandria. Prior to being named pope in the year 505, he was a priest who lived a monastic life alone in northern Egypt's Nitrian Desert.

30th state. The first Europeans to explore America's upper Midwest were French explorers and fur traders in the 1600s. The British took over the region in 1763, after the French and Indian War. But the area that came to be known as the Wisconsin Territory (it means "grassy place" in the Chippewa language) didn't come under American control until after the War of 1812. Attracted by farming, logging, and mining, thousands of European immigrants moved there. By the end of the 1840s, Wisconsin's population had grown to 300,000, which facilitated its admission to the Union as the 30th state in May 1848.

30th Hardy Boys mystery. Teen sleuths Frank and Joe Hardy were at it again in *The Wailing Siren Mystery* (1951), the 30th published Hardy Boys mystery novel. (The plot involves a mysterious yacht, a missing wallet containing $2,000, a stolen truck full of rifles, and a siren that will not stop wailing.)

30th Nancy Drew mystery. Nancy Drew could do what it took *two* Hardy Boys to do: solve mysteries. In the 30th edition of this long-running children's mystery series, *The Clue of the Velvet Mask* (1953), Nancy thwarts a gang of thieves who rob the homes of socialites while they're out attending musicals and lectures.

30th Best Picture winner. At the 30th annual Academy Awards in March 1958, the Oscar for Best Picture went to *The Bridge on the River Kwai*, a drama set in Burma during World War II. The film also won the Oscar for Writing Based on Material from Another Medium (now known as Best Adapted Screenplay). It went to French writer Pierre Boulle, who wrote the 1952 source novel *Le Pont de la rivière Kwaï*. But Boulle, who didn't know English, did not write the screenplay—Carl Foreman and Michael Wilson did. They'd been "blacklisted" for their Communist sympathies, and received no credit for their work on *Kwai*.

30th wedding anniversary gift. The perfect traditional anniversary gift for a couple celebrating one year of marriage is something made of paper, on year three it's leather, and on year 13 it's lace. The traditional gift for a couple celebrating 30 years of marriage: pearls. (In other words, it's a great time for a husband to give his wife pearl earrings.)

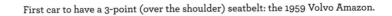

First car to have a 3-point (over the shoulder) seatbelt: the 1959 Volvo Amazon.

TV WISDUMB

In real life, these clueless sitcom characters would be pitied.
But they're on TV, so we get to laugh at them.

"I thought Ultimate Robot Fighting was real, like pro wrestling; but it turns out it's fixed, like boxing."
—**Fry,** *Futurama*

"Well, there is no way *Star Wars* is better than *The Planet of the Apes*. I mean, those apes were really good actors!"
—**Kelso,** *That '70s Show*

Frasier: "Everybody, I'd like you to meet my date, Dr. Lilith Sternin, M.D., Ph.D., Ed.D., A.P.A."
Woody: "Boy, it sure isn't spelled like it sounds."
—*Cheers*

"It's better to have a gun and need it, than to not have a gun and not need it."
—**Ricky,** *Trailer Park Boys*

"The whole reason we have elected officials is so we don't have to think all the time. Just like that rain forest scare a few years back: our officials saw there was a problem and they fixed it, didn't they?"
—**Homer,** *The Simpsons*

"Now, like a great Eastern religion says, it's all about striking a balance between the ping and the pong."
—**Kelly,** *Married with Children*

"Success is 1 percent inspiration, 99 percent perspiration, and 2 percent attention to detail."
—**Phil,** *Modern Family*

"You know what they say — you can lead a herring to water, but you have to walk really fast or he'll die."
—**Rose,** *The Golden Girls*

The "Cotard delusion" is a psychological condition in which a person thinks that they are already dead. ("Dead" is when a person is dead.)

THE ACCIDENTAL FARMER

*Bob Fletcher was an agricultural inspector working in California's
Central Valley in the early 1940s. He might have stayed one, too,
had the outbreak of World War II not changed everything.*

INFAMY

Shortly before 8:00 a.m. on the morning of December 7, 1941, Japanese
military forces attacked the U.S. naval base at Pearl Harbor, on the Hawaiian
Island of Oahu. More than 2,400 soldiers were killed in the attack, 18 warships
were sunk or damaged, and 188 aircraft were destroyed. The surprise attack was
just the opening shot in a military campaign that stretched across Southeast
Asia and the Pacific. In the days and weeks that followed, the U.S. territories of
Guam, Wake Island, and the Philippines fell to the Japanese. So did the British
possessions of Hong Kong, Malaya (part of modern-day Malaysia), Burma, and
Singapore, as well as the Netherlands Indies (part of modern-day Indonesia) and
the nation of Thailand.

As one territory after another was captured by Japan, for a time it seemed
like their advance might never be stopped. Would Australia be next? The West
Coast of the United States? With much of the Pacific Fleet destroyed or knocked
out of commission at Pearl Harbor, an invasion of the western United States was
a very real—and terrifying—possibility.

GUILT BY ASSOCIATION

One group that fell victim to the hysteria that followed was the Japanese
American community of families who lived on the West Coast. Many were
descended from immigrants who settled in the United States as far back as the
1860s; ties to their ancestral homeland were tenuous at best. No matter: In
February 1942, President Franklin D. Roosevelt signed Executive Order 9066,
which authorized the military to designate the entire state of California, as well
as parts of Arizona, Oregon, and Washington, as "military areas" from which
"any or all persons may be excluded." As a consequence of the order, more than
110,000 Japanese immigrants and Japanese American citizens were forced from
their homes and transported to internment camps far from home. There they
were kept under armed guard for the rest of the war. It was the largest forced
relocation in American history.

At 58, Teddy Roosevelt tried to get Congress to approve
volunteer divisions so that he could fight in WWI. (He failed.)

"OUSTER OF ALL JAPS IN CALIFORNIA NEAR!" screamed one *San Francisco Examiner* headline in February 1942. The forced internments were popular with the American public, but one man who was appalled by them was Bob Fletcher, a 33-year-old state agricultural inspector who had gotten to know many Japanese American farmers in the Central Valley, the agricultural heart of California. Some of these families had been on the land for three generations. With no way to pay their bills while they were locked away in the camps for years on end, they risked losing everything they had.

One Japanese American who Fletcher knew fairly well was a farmer named Al Tsukamoto. Around the time that notices appeared on telephone poles in the town of Florin, near Sacramento, ordering Japanese Americans to report to the train station in nearby Elk Grove to be taken away to internment camps, Tsukamoto came to Fletcher with a request. Two of his neighbors, the Okamotos and the Nittas, were looking for someone to manage their farms while they were interned. If Fletcher was willing to run their farms, keep the books, and pay the bills while the families were away, whatever money was left over was his to keep as payment for his labor.

BACK TO THE LAND

Fletcher had been raised on a walnut farm, and during the Great Depression he managed a peach orchard. But he had no experience growing Flame Tokay table grapes, which was the two farms' main crop. Nevertheless, he was bothered by the fact that decent people like the Okamotos and the Nittas could lose their farms, so he agreed to do it. Then when Tsukamoto decided he needed someone to take over his farm as well, Fletcher agreed to look after all *three* farms. He quit his job as an agricultural inspector and moved into an unoccupied bunkhouse on Tsukamoto's farm. Tsukamoto had invited Fletcher to move into his own home, but Fletcher was uncomfortable with the idea of living there when Tsukamoto could not, so he stayed in the bunkhouse.

There must have been times when Fletcher wondered what he'd gotten himself into, because he was soon putting in 18-hour days tending Flame Tokay grapes, strawberries, blackberries, boysenberries, and olive trees—more than 100 acres of produce in all. In addition to the hard work, he also had to put up with the disapproval of his neighbors, many of whom supported the forced internments and considered Fletcher a "Jap lover" who was aiding and abetting the enemy. Once he was nearly shot when someone fired a gun into Tsukamoto's barn while he was inside. But he toughed it out, and in defiance of his neighbors he kept the farms going until the war ended, the internment camps closed, and the families were able to return home.

The first saxophones were made of wood.

Those families that still *had* homes, that is: of the 2,000 Japanese and Japanese Americans who had lived in and around Florin before the war, only about 20 percent, or some 400 people, returned to live there after the war. Where would the rest have stayed? Their homes and farms were gone—foreclosed upon or otherwise stolen from them when they were imprisoned in the camps.

WELCOME MAT

When the Nittas, the Okamotos, and the Tsukamotos began making their way back to Florin, they too must have wondered what awaited them. What they found was what they'd hoped they'd find: their homes and farms still intact, and Bob Fletcher tending to their crops. He was newly married to his wife Teresa, who was helping him with the farm chores. (Even after marrying, the Fletchers did not move into the Tsukamotos' house, which would have been more comfortable for the newlyweds than the spartan bunkhouse. But doing so felt wrong, so they didn't—"It's *their* house," Teresa Fletcher explained.)

The families did find one surprise when they got home: money in the bank. The agreement the Nittas, the Okamotos, and the Tsukamotos made with Fletcher was that if their farms managed to eke out a profit, he could keep the money in payment for his labor. But Fletcher decided to split it with them, and their half was in the bank, earning interest—a sizable nest egg that they could use to restart their lives.

A LASTING FRIENDSHIP

Fletcher must have enjoyed farmwork because after the war he bought a ranch of his own, and raised hay and cattle. He also volunteered for the Florin Fire Department and served 12 years as fire chief. He retired in 1974 and lived to the age of 101. On his 100th birthday in July 2011, his family threw a huge birthday bash. Teresa, his wife of 66 years, was by his side, as were his son, three granddaughters, and five great-grandchildren. So were quite a handful of Nittas, Okamotos, and Tsukamotos. And though Fletcher never sought recognition for the helping hand he gave his neighbors during the war, they were eager to share his story. "We had forty acres of Flame Tokay grapes and we would have lost it if Bob didn't take care of it," Doris Taketa told the *Sacramento Bee*. She was 12 when her family was sent with to an internment camp in Arkansas. "My mother called him God," she said, "because only God would do something like that."

When asked by reporters at the birthday party why he did what he did, Fletcher's answer was simple. "They were the same as everybody else," he said. "It was obvious they had nothing to do with Pearl Harbor."

Hang Son Đoòng, Vietnam's mammoth cave system, is so big that it has forests growing in it...

YOU CALL THAT ART?

Is it art just because someone says it is? You decide…

Artist: Phil Hansen, an American painter

Artwork: *Value of Blood*

Description: It's a portrait roughly one foot wide and nine feet high. The painting surface is unusual—it's 6,000 bandages, with the absorbent pad side out. The "paint" on the bandages is even more unusual: it's Hansen's blood. Hansen made the painting over the course of five months in 2007, using 500 milliliters (about two cups) of his blood, which was extracted (by a friend) in his studio. Subject of the portrait: former North Korean leader Kim Jong-Il.

Artist: Noritoshi Hirakawa, an internationally acclaimed Japanese conceptual artist and filmmaker

Artwork: *The Home-Coming of Navel Strings*

Description: For the 2004 Frieze Art Fair, an annual art exposition that takes place in London's Regent's Park, Hirakawa created an exhibit consisting of a woman seated in a chair, reading books, all day long, for five days straight. That's not all. Every morning the woman pooped on the floor near the chair, and the poop remained there for the rest of the day while the woman read her books. That's still not all. Hanging on the wall behind the woman was a photographic print depicting a human sphincter.

> *Great art is great because it inspired you greatly. If it didn't, no matter what the critics, the museums, and the galleries say, it's not great art for you.*
> **—Yoko Ono**

Artist: Gianni Motti, an Italian sculptor based in Geneva, Switzerland

Artwork: *Clean Hands*

Description: Motti's artwork, displayed at the 2005 Art Basel fair in Basel, Switzerland, consisted of a bar of soap sitting on a square of black velvet inside a small glass box. But according to Motti, it wasn't just any bar of soap—it was made from fat sucked out of the body of former Italian prime minister

…It has stalagmites over 200 feet tall and an opening large enough to fit a skyscraper.

Silvio Berlusconi. Motti claims he bought the fat from the Swiss clinic where Berlusconi had a liposuction procedure in 2004. "I came up with the idea because soap is made of pig fat," Motti said, "and I thought how much more appropriate it would be if people washed their hands using a piece of Berlusconi." He added that Berlusconi's fat "stunk horribly, like rancid butter or stale cooking oil."

Note: The clinic denied having sold Berlusconi's fat to Motti, but that didn't stop the bar of soap from being sold—for $18,000—to a private collector. It has been displayed several times around the world since.

Artist: Chris Trueman, an art professor at Fullerton College and Santa Ana College in Southern California

Artwork: *Self-Portrait with Gun*

Description: This portrait of a young boy dressed as a cowboy and holding a rifle was made from 200,000 dead ants. Where do you get 200,000 ants? Online. Trueman bought the ants from a company that sells them as food for pet lizards. (Cost: about $2,500.) And they were alive, so Trueman had to kill all the ants himself—using cotton balls soaked in nail polish remover, a trick he says he learned in the Boy Scouts. Then, using tweezers, he stuck the ants, one at a time, to a sheet of Plexiglas smeared with sticky resin, carefully arranging them to create the image. Trueman said the portrait took several years to make, "because at one point I started to feel bad about killing all of the ants and I stopped the project for over a year." He completed it in 2010, and when it was displayed in a San Diego art gallery, news of the work went viral, resulting in its sale to the Ripley's Believe It or Not museum in Los Angeles. Price: $35,000.

Artist: Miru Kim, a Korean-American artist, photographer, illustrator…and pig fan

Artwork: *I Like Pigs and Pigs Like Me* (104 hours)

Description: Kim had a shedlike structure built in front of a Miami art gallery, as part of the 2011 Art Basel Miami fair. The floor of the shed was covered with several inches of dirt, topped with a layer of straw. Also in the shed: two live pigs. And Kim. Naked. For four days. (Actually for 104 hours.) Kim spent the four days eating and sleeping with the pigs, as people watched through a large window in one side of the shed. "My work, I hope," Kim said afterward, "brought some consciousness to the audience about how close in essence human beings are to animals like pigs."

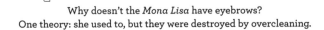

Why doesn't the *Mona Lisa* have eyebrows?
One theory: she used to, but they were destroyed by overcleaning.

THE CHRISTMAS BIRD COUNT

Here's a holiday tradition that you may not have heard of
if you're not a bird-watcher. It's more than
a century old and still going strong.

BIRD MAN

Frank Chapman was an ornithologist, publisher of *Bird-Lore* magazine, and curator of birds at New York City's American Museum of Natural History at the turn of the 20th century. He enjoyed Christmas as much as anyone, but there was one yuletide tradition he abhorred: "side hunts," in which groups of people divided into teams and spent the day roaming the countryside shooting every animal they came across. The hunted included rabbits, foxes, squirrels, and plenty of birds. Not for food—hardly any animals were eaten—but for sport. At the end of the day each team counted their kills, and the team that had the most animals was the winner.

Chapman wanted to come up with a replacement for the side hunts that wouldn't involve the pointless slaughter of so many animals, especially birds. Why not count the birds *without* killing them, in a "Christmas Bird Count"? He published his idea in *Bird-Lore* magazine and on Christmas Day 1900, 27 people (many of them Chapman's friends and colleagues) in 25 locations around the United States and Canada went out and counted all the birds they could find.

CIRCULAR LOGIC

The method used to count the birds was simple enough: the participants drew a circle on a map, then spent the day roaming around the territory inside the circle and making note of all the birds they saw. To avoid counting the same birds twice, whenever the participants doubled back along their route they only counted birds of species they hadn't seen before. At the end of the day, tallies were made of both the number of individual birds seen, and the number of species. The totals were sent to Chapman at *Bird-Lore* magazine. He did his count in Englewood, New Jersey, and saw 18 different bird species. In Pacific Grove, California, a bird-watcher counted 36 species, the most of any location.

The counts continued each year afterward. Publicity in *Bird-Lore* magazine, soon to become *Audubon* magazine, helped the number of participants and counting sites to grow over time. As the years passed, the counts became more standardized: Volunteers organized themselves into groups of at least ten people, and retraced the same routes in the same circles every Christmas, so that the results could be compared from year to year.

YEAR BY YEAR

Bird counts are not precise—how does anyone accurately count a flock of birds in flight? And how can anyone be certain that as they hike around the countryside, some of the birds aren't moving with them and being counted more than once? There's no way to be sure, but the results are still meaningful. Cold winters mean frozen ponds and lakes—and declining numbers of waterfowl in northern bird counts. As the climate changes, where these birds migrate to—and whether they need to migrate at all—has also changed. It all gets picked up in the annual Christmas Bird Counts.

After a few house finches escaped or were released from cages on Long Island, New York, in 1940, the counts marked the progress of the birds' descendants year to year as they multiplied and spread along the Atlantic coastline from Maine to North Carolina. The finches eventually numbered in the tens of thousands and occupied a range of more than 170,000 square miles.

COUNTER REVOLUTION

Today the Christmas Bird Count is organized by the Audubon Society; participants count more than 50 million birds representing 2,400 different species in a typical year. People who aren't up for a daylong outing in winter weather can do their part by counting the birds that visit designated feeders. It all adds up. In the more than 115 years that the Christmas Bird Count has been around, hundreds of thousands of volunteers have assembled the largest, longest, and most comprehensive collection of data on the changing North American bird population in existence. The data is made available to researchers free of charge, and has been analyzed in hundreds of scientific studies over the years. Agencies like the U.S. Fish and Wildlife Service use the information to plan how best to protect wild birds and their habitats, both today in the future.

If you're interested in participating in a bird count, it's a safe bet there's a group active near you, no matter where you live: Today more than 71,000 volunteers count birds in 2,400 different locations, including all 50 states, every Canadian province and territory, plus more than 100 locations in Latin America and on islands in the Caribbean and the Pacific.

If you hear "Zulu, Zulu, Zulu" on a cruise ship PA system, there's a fight somewhere on board.

SEYMOUR BUTTS

Years ago, punny imaginary book titles and their authors were a hallmark of joke books. For example: Under the Grandstands *by Seymour Butts, or* Robots *by Anne Droid. Get it? Here's a bunch of new ones.*

How to Choose a Steak
by Porter House

Stringed Musical Instruments
by Amanda Lynne

Mountain Climbing Techniques
by Andover Hand

The First Nuclear Weapons
by Adam Baum

Blowout!
by Vlad Tire

Off to Market
by Tobias A. Pigg

Battle Axes
by Tommy Hawk

Don't Come Near Me!
by Vera Way

The Long Island Chain
by Archie Pelago

Red Vegetables
by Bea Troot

Housing Construction
by Bill Jerome Holmes

Deep-Fried Foods
by Chris Coe

Six Feet Under
by Doug Graves

Not Optional
by Mandy Torry

Why I Hate the Sun
by Gladys Knight

The Paper Route
by Avery Daye

Stop Arguing!
by Xavier Breath

Championship Tennis Matches
by Davis Skupp

Playing with Firecrackers
by Huell B. Sari

Installing Carpets
by Walter Wahl

Fun Outdoor Activities
by Alf Resco

Proper Lawn Care
by Ray King

The Odds of Coin Tossing
by Taylor Hedds

Ghosts in the Closet!
by Emma Fraid

The Best Books Ever Written
by Paige Turner

In college, Richard Nixon was called "Iron Butt" for his long hours of studying.

SUPER BLOOPERS

A movie based on a comic book requires us to turn off our brains and accept that grown men and women can fly around wearing tacky costumes. Three keys to making it believable: create a realistic world, try—if at all possible—to base the heroes' powers on real science, and don't commit obvious continuity errors. Here are some examples where filmmakers lost their superpowers.

X-MEN: FIRST CLASS (2011)

Scene: Magneto (Michael Fassbender) telepathically lifts Shaw's (Kevin Bacon) submarine out of the sea. The vessel floats through the air at a 45-degree angle and then crashes on the beach, rolling over several times before finally coming to rest on its belly. The sub is in tatters, and everything inside of it should be, too.

Blooper: When Magneto walks through the wreckage and enters Shaw's living quarters, it's in perfect condition. The books and potted plants are still on the bookshelves; not even a couch cushion is out of place.

CAPTAIN AMERICA: CIVIL WAR (2016)

Scene: A ticking hand grenade is thrown into an armored truck.

Blooper: Hand grenades don't tick.

DEADPOOL (2016)

Scene: Ajax (Ed Skrein) stabs Deadpool (Ryan Reynolds) in the side of his head. Thanks to Deadpool's super healing abilities, he's able to pull the knife out and keep on fighting.

Blooper: Apparently Deadpool's head mask has healing abilities as well, because in the next shot there is no knife hole in the fabric. (Later in the scene, however, there *is* a hole in the fabric.)

THE DARK KNIGHT (2008)

Scene: Having just robbed a bank, the Joker (Heath Ledger) puts a hand grenade in the bank manager's (William Fichtner) mouth. The grenade's pin is attached to a string, which is attached to a getaway bus. The Joker walks to the bus, gets in, and when it pulls away it pulls the pin, leaving the grenade in the manager's mouth. A few seconds later, the grenade (which is ticking) detonates.

Blooper: There's no logical reason for the bank manager to have left the grenade in his mouth after the Joker left. His hands weren't tied, so he could have easily taken it out or even spit it out. But for some reason, he kept it in his mouth the whole time with a worried look on his face (which is odd, because a few moments earlier, he'd bravely taken a shot at the Joker). Luckily for the manager it was a *joke* grenade. It emitted a harmless gas…but he had no way of knowing that.

BATMAN (1989)

Scene: The Joker (Jack Nicholson) has tainted all of Gotham City's beauty products; whenever someone puts on makeup, they will laugh maniacally and die a few minutes later. Gotham officials place a citywide ban on wearing makeup. In a humorous scene, two newscasters, whose every blemish is showing because they're not wearing makeup, announce the ban.

Blooper: The ban was in place for everyone…except Batman's love interest, Vicki Vale (Kim Basinger), who wears makeup throughout the entire movie, even in the scene directly following the newscast. And she doesn't laugh hysterically and die.

THE AMAZING SPIDER-MAN (2012)

Scene: A SWAT team is trying to capture Spider-Man (Andrew Garfield).

Blooper: One of the cops is looking through the scope on his automatic rifle, but you can clearly see that the scope cover is closed.

ANT-MAN (2015)

Scene: Ant-Man (Paul Rudd) gets sucked into a vacuum cleaner.

Blooper: According to the movie's "science," Hank Pym (Michael Douglas) learned how to shrink himself by compressing the space within and between atoms. If that were really possible, then Ant-Man would still have all of the same atoms—and the same mass—so he would weigh the same as when he was normal sized and therefore be way too heavy to get sucked into a vacuum cleaner. He also wouldn't be able to run along the barrel of a gun without the gunman dropping it. Nor would he be able to float. (The original comics explained this conundrum by saying that Ant-Man's mass was "displaced into an unknown dimension," but the movie makes no mention of it.)

SUPERMAN (1978)

Scene: Jor-El (Marlon Brando) puts his infant son in a spaceship and launches it toward Earth just before his planet explodes. During the trip through space, the child is taught everything about Earth's history, right through the late 20th

---

…but sugar-sweetened Coke is ok. It's sold with special yellow caps.

century. A hologram of Jor-El later tells Superman (Christopher Reeve) that he has been dead for thousands of years, which is how long the infant's journey to Earth took.

Blooper: If Krypton had been destroyed thousands of years ago, there's no way Jor-El could have taught his son modern Earth history. By then, he would have been dead for millennia.

SUICIDE SQUAD (2016)

Scene: While in Tehran, Iran, the Chairman (Aidan Devine) opens up a binder and begins reading left to right.

Blooper: The binder is printed in Farsi (Persian), so he should be reading right to left.

> **ONE OF THE MOST FAMOUS GOOFS** to ever make it into the final cut of a movie occurs in Alfred Hitchcock's 1959 classic North by Northwest. During the scene in the Mount Rushmore cafeteria, Eve (Eva Marie Saint) and Roger (Cary Grant) argue, and then Roger gets shot, startling everyone. Almost everyone—a child extra in the scene has his ears covered to protect himself from the loud noise five seconds before the "surprise" gunshot.

MAN OF STEEL (2013)

Scene: Lois Lane (Amy Adams) falls out of a plane while a singularity is sucking everything else up toward it, even the plane.

Blooper: Why isn't Lois herself affected by the singularity? After Superman (Henry Cavill) flies in and saves her, even with his super strength he has to struggle to escape it. But Lois just fell.

WATCHMEN (2009)

Scene: Dr. Manhattan (Billy Crudup) is narrating his origin story when he says that "a circulatory system is seen by the perimeter fence" describing a glowing, blue skeletal figure.

Blooper: Despite his godlike powers and intelligence, Dr. Manhattan apparently doesn't understand basic anatomy. The circulatory system is comprised of the heart and blood vessels, but the being that he's describing features the brain and spinal cord. Dr. Manhattan should have said "nervous system."

When a person is struck by lightning, their skin breaks out in Lichtenberg figures, which is a rash pattern shaped like a lightning bolt.

DUNBAR'S DOG BITE SCALE

Who knew there was an actual scale used to measure the severity of a dog bite? It's actually a useful tool in determining whether a biting dog can be "reformed."

BARKGROUND

According to the Centers for Disease Control, there are about 4.5 million dog bite incidents in the United States every year. But those numbers can be confusing, because there is disagreement on the proper definition of a "dog bite." Is a bite an incident that draws blood? Does a "nip" count as a "bite"? What about a "grab and shake" that causes bruising (and terror!) but doesn't draw blood? And these aren't just trivial musings: the definition of what constitutes an actual bite is argued in court cases across the country on a regular basis. Doctors, veterinarians, and statisticians need some kind of agreed-upon criteria in order to properly study and treat wounds, to assess dogs' behavior, and to keep meaningful tallies of dog bite incidents.

With that in mind, Dr. Ian Dunbar, an internationally acclaimed veterinarian and animal behaviorist, developed the "Dunbar Dog Bite Scale," which categorizes dog bite incidents into six different levels, from least to most serious. The scale is used by doctors, veterinarians, and legal organizations all over the world today. Here is the scale, along with Dr. Dunbar's comments on each level in the scale, for *Bathroom Reader* readers only. (Note: Other, similar scales exist, but Dr. Dunbar's is the most commonly used one today.)

Dr. Ian Dunbar's Dog Bite Scale (Official Authorized Version)
An assessment of the severity of biting problems based on an objective evaluation of wound pathology.

LEVEL 1 INCIDENT. Fearful, aggressive, or obnoxious behavior but no skin contact by teeth.

LEVEL 2 INCIDENT. Skin contact by teeth but no skin puncture. However, there may be skin nicks (less than one-tenth of an inch deep) and slight bleeding caused by forward, backward, or lateral movement of teeth against skin, but no vertical punctures.

Analysis and recommendation: Levels 1 and 2 comprise over 99 percent of dog incidents. The dog is certainly not dangerous and more likely to be fearful, rambunctious, or out of control. Wonderful prognosis for rehabilitation. Quickly

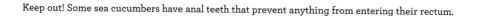

Keep out! Some sea cucumbers have anal teeth that prevent anything from entering their rectum.

resolve the problem with basic training, plus numerous bite-inhibition exercises and games.

LEVEL 3 INCIDENT. One to four punctures from a single bite with no puncture deeper than half the length of the dog's canine teeth. May be lacerations in a single direction, caused by victim pulling hand away, owner pulling dog away, or gravity (dog jumps, bites, and drops to floor).

Analysis and recommendation: Prognosis for rehabilitation is fair to good, provided you have owner compliance. However, treatment is time-consuming and not without danger. Rigorous bite-inhibition exercises are essential.

LEVEL 4 INCIDENT. One to four punctures from a single bite with at least one puncture deeper than half the length of the dog's canine teeth. May also have deep bruising around the wound (dog held on for a number of seconds and bore down), or lacerations in both directions (dog held on and shook its head from side to side).

Analysis and recommendation: Dog has insufficient bite inhibition and is very dangerous. Prognosis for rehabilitation is poor because of the difficulty and danger of trying to teach bite inhibition to an adult hard-biting dog and because absolute owner compliance is rare. Only work with the dog in exceptional circumstances, e.g., the owner is a dog professional and has sworn 100 percent compliance. Make sure the owner signs a form stating that they understand that: 1. The dog is a Level 4 biter and is likely to cause an equivalent amount of damage *when* it bites again (which it most probably will), and should therefore be confined to the home at all times and only allowed contact with adult owners; 2. Whenever children or guests visit the house, the dog must be confined to a locked room or roofed, chain-link run with the only keys kept by the adult owner (to prevent children or guests entering the dog's confinement area); 3. The dog is muzzled before leaving the house and only leaves the house for visits to a veterinary clinic; 4. All incidents must be reported to the relevant authorities—animal control or police. Give the owners one copy of the form, keep one copy for your files, and give a third copy to the dog's veterinarian.

LEVEL 5 INCIDENT. Multiple-bite incident with at least two Level 4 bites, or multiple-attack incident with at least one Level 4 bite in each.

LEVEL 6 INCIDENT. Victim dead.

Analysis and recommendation: The dog is extremely dangerous and mutilates. The dog is simply not safe around people. I recommend euthanasia because the quality of life is so poor for dogs that have to live out their lives in solitary confinement.

Do not disturb: Maya Angelou did her writing only in cheap hotel rooms.

TV'S LAST LINES

Great books' first lines are memorable. So are movie catchphrases. Can you match these last bits of dialogue with the classic TV shows they concluded? (Answers are on page 501.)

1) "I'm sorry, we're closed."

2) "The sky's the limit."

3) "I went ahead and ordered some for the table."

4) "Hey, you've been great! See you in the cafeteria!"

5) "There's a lot of beauty in ordinary things."

6) "Should we get some coffee?" "Sure. Where?"

7) "You can't take a picture of this. It's already gone."

8) "We've been waiting for you."

9) "We're going forward into the future, not back into the past." "If only we had the choice."

10) "Winning!"

11) "I'm ready."

12) "Tomorrow."

13) "New day, new ideas, new you."

14) "You'll always be my sisters. Always."

15) "I'll see you back in the States, I promise. Just in case, I left you a note."

a. M*A*S*H*

b. Seinfeld

c. Downton Abbey

d. The West Wing

e. Cheers

f. Lost

g. Six Feet Under

h. Friends

i. The Golden Girls

j. Mad Men

k. Star Trek: The Next Generation

l. Two and a Half Men

m. Parks & Recreation

n. The Office

o. The Sopranos

In Victorian England, entire families would go to prison for debt, including newborn babies.

"SPACE POOP CHALLENGE"

One of the harsh realities of life in space is that in an emergency, astronauts may have to live in their space suits for days on end. If that ever does happen, how will they go to the bathroom? That's the question NASA hopes to answer.

WHEN YOU GOTTA GO...

There are three situations during a typical mission to the International Space Station in which the astronauts may not have access to a bathroom when they need one: 1) on their way to the space station at the start of the mission; 2) on their way back to Earth at the end of the mission; and 3) during spacewalks, when they are outside the station and can't get back inside easily or quickly. None of these circumstances require the astronauts to go more than ten hours without access to a toilet, so the solution, while awkward, is simple: they wear diapers inside their space suits. And if they have to go, they go.

Even in an emergency, such as if a module of the ISS were to be struck by a piece of space debris and losing pressure, if the astronauts had to evacuate the station they'd be back on Earth in less than a day, so once again, diapers would suffice.

But what about on a mission to Mars, when Earth will be many months away instead of only hours? If a spacecraft on its way to the Red Planet were to be hit by a micrometeoroid and lose pressure, the astronauts might be stuck inside their space suits for several days until they repaired the damage and were able to repressurize the spacecraft. In such a situation a single diaper, worn for days, would not be good enough.

OUT-HOUSE

Ordinarily NASA tackles such challenges with in-house engineers or assigns them to a contractor, but in October 2016 it took a more novel approach. Working with a crowdsourcing website called HeroX, it launched a contest called the "Space Poop Challenge" and invited all comers to take a stab at coming up with an in-suit "fecal, urine and menstrual management system" that would enable an astronaut to remain in their space suit for 144 hours straight. Why 144 hours? The most likely explanation is because 144 hours adds up to six days. (It's also possible that someone at NASA has a sense of humor: 144 hours is also 12 dozen hours. What's another word for 12 dozen? *Gross!*) Any solution entered in the contest would have to be simple enough for an astronaut to operate in

Les Machines de l'île in France is an amusement park of mechanical animals.

microgravity while wearing bulky spacesuit gloves. It would also have to either store the liquid and solid waste somewhere inside the suit, or remove it entirely.

Entrants were given from October 11 until December 20, 2016, to come up with ideas and submit them to NASA. The first prize was $15,000; second prize was $10,000; and third prize was $5,000.

READY, SET, GO!

When NASA gave contestants just over two months to invent something, it wasn't sure how many people would enter. It was pleasantly surprised to receive more than 5,000 proposals from nearly 20,000 people all over the world, including many who worked in teams. After studying the entries for two months, in February 2017 NASA announced the winners. And they are…

Third Place: SWIMsuit Zero Gravity Underwear

Inventor: Hugo Shelley, a product designer in the UK

Details: The underwear looks a lot like a pair of spandex biking shorts with front and rear catheters attached—the external type of catheter, so they're worn over the anatomical areas in question, not inserted into them, which would be way too uncomfortable if worn for six days straight. An electronic mechanism disinfects liquid and solid waste and pumps it into a sealable, compressible pouch on the leg of the garment.

Second Place: Air-PUSH Urinary Girdle

Inventors: Space Poop Unification of Doctors (SPUDs), a team consisting of dentist Katherine Kin, environmental engineer Stacey Louie, and physician Tony Gonzalez, all from Houston, Texas

Details: The device resembles the cup of an athletic supporter, one with two small air hoses attached at the top, and a larger hose at the bottom. Air flows through the upper hoses into the cup, blowing any urine or menstrual fluids into the larger hose at the bottom, and from there to a storage pouch inside the suit. Bonus: the airflow is generated by the astronauts themselves as they move around while wearing the space suit, so there are fewer mechanical parts to break.

Note: The Air-PUSH girdle does not address the issue of astronaut poop—an odd choice for an entrant in a contest called the Space Poop Challenge, but NASA judges were nonetheless impressed enough to award the team the $10,000 second prize. (They're number two!)

The punishment for smuggling silkworms out of China in the 5th century BC: death.

First Place: MACES Perineal Access & Toileting System (M-PATS)

Inventor: Colonel Thatcher Cardon, a U.S. Air Force flight surgeon stationed at Laughlin Air Force Base in Texas

Details: The system consists of an airlock, called a "perineal access port," installed on the crotch of the astronaut's space suit, and a series of toileting "tools" that can be passed through the airlock without the space suit losing air pressure. Cardon drew inspiration from "keyhole" surgeries, in which complicated operations are performed by inserting narrow surgical tools through tiny incisions. "They can even replace heart valves now through catheters in an artery. So [a tiny opening] should be able to handle a little bit of poop," he says.

Cardon was disgusted by the idea of storing six days' worth of human waste inside a space suit. So unlike the other two winners, his system removes the waste from the suit for storage or disposal elsewhere.

Tools of the Trade:

• One of Cardon's tools is an inflatable bedpan that can be inserted through the airlock while deflated, then maneuvered into position and inflated with a squeeze bulb. A vacuum hose drains the bedpan and sucks the waste out of the spacesuit. Afterward, the bedpan is deflated and removed through the airlock.

• If the astronaut only has to urinate, a vacuum hose with a male- or female-specific external catheter can be inserted through the airlock.

• After an astronaut has completed their business, a bidet tool can be used to wash affected areas, and after that, a tool called a "hygiene wand" that substitutes for toilet paper can also be used. It consists of a vacuum hose covered with a bunched-up tube of terry cloth at the tip that's used to wipe the affected area. Then when the job is finished, the soiled fabric is pulled "through the middle of the wand so that fresh fabric slides forward…in a motion similar to a sock being turned inside out," Cardon says. The result is a wand that's clean and ready for the next use.

• Cardon has even devised special mens' and womens' underwear that can be inserted and removed through the airlock, so that astronauts can change into fresh undies without having to remove their space suits.

HERE WE GO AGAIN

If you missed the Space Poop Challenge, fear not! The agency was so impressed by the entries that it's considering doing more contests. "We enjoyed seeing the innovative approaches, given such a demanding scenario," says engineer Kirstyn Johnson. "Others at NASA are now thinking about ways we can leverage a crowdsourcing approach to solve more of our spaceflight challenges."

NASCAR was formed to keep racing honest—
and to stop promoters from running off with the prize money.

LADY KILLERS

If you're a fan of Dateline *or one of the other crime newsmagazines on TV, you might like these stories of gruesome murders committed by women. (And maybe you can lessen the horrifying impact by imagining Keith Morrison as the narrator.)*

THE COUNTESS OF BÁTHORY (1560–1614)

In the early years of the 17th century, girls from peasant villages in the medieval kingdom of Hungary (now western Slovakia) started disappearing. They had been hired to work as maids in Cachtice Castle—the home of Countess Elizabeth Báthory. Born to a noble family in 1560, Báthory was married to a baron at the age of 14, but her social standing was higher than his, so she kept her family name. When the daughters of nobles, who'd been sent to the castle for tutoring, started to disappear, the issue could no longer be ignored, and in 1610 Hungarian authorities finally launched an investigation. Their findings: with the aid of her servants, the countess had tortured and murdered the girls, possibly as part of "virgin blood rituals" meant to preserve the countess's youth, and buried them in the castle or on its grounds. The exact number of her victims is unknown—but historians put it somewhere between 100 and 650. *Guinness World Records* calls Elizabeth Báthory the most prolific female killer in history. Three of her servants were executed for their parts in the murders. Báthory was sentenced to solitary confinement in her castle, where she died four years later.

AMELIA DYER (1837–1896)

On March 30, 1896, a package was found in the river Thames, near the town of Reading in southern England. Inside the package: the strangled body of a baby, just a few months old. Police were able to decipher a faded name and address on the package, which led them to 57-year-old Amelia Dyer in the nearby town of Caversham. Police quickly determined that Dyer was a "baby farmer," a woman who took in children in exchange for a fee. This was an accepted practice in Victorian England, especially for children born out of wedlock. Dyer placed ads in newspapers offering her services, for which she charged £10—about two months' wages for a lower-class worker—and a box of clothing.

In the days that followed, police dredged the local river and turned up the bodies of six more young children. As the investigation continued, the reality of the situation became clear: Dyer had been taking in babies for more than 30 years, and had pocketed the money meant for their care and then killed

Kaktovik, Alaska, has so many polar bears they have a Polar Bear Patrol to run them out of town.

them. At first the children were killed by neglect, or by giving them overdoses of sedatives. Later, Dyer had strangled them, sometimes just hours after taking them in. She did this in a succession of towns in southern England over three decades, moving when local authorities became suspicious, and using aliases to keep them off her trail. (Amazingly, she had actually been caught once. In 1879 she was convicted of neglect when several children under her care died in the span of a few years. But she was sentenced to just six months in prison, and returned to her grisly work as soon as she was released.) Although Dyer was convicted of the murder of just the one child (there wasn't enough evidence to charge her with any others), she is believed to have killed as many as 400. She was hanged in London's Newgate Prison on June 10, 1896.

LEONARDA CIANCIULLI (1894–1970)

One day in 1939, Cianciulli, a 45-year-old shopkeeper in the northern Italian town of Correggio, welcomed a local woman, Faustina Setti, into her home. Cianciulli was a fortune-teller of sorts, and she'd been counseling Setti, a 73-year-old spinster, on how to get a husband. But she actually had other business in mind: during the course of the visit, Cianciulli drugged Setti, and killed her with an axe. She then chopped Setti's body into pieces (saving the blood in a basin), dissolved them in a large pot containing a mixture of water and caustic soda, and dumped the resulting sludge into a septic tank.

> *She kept the blood until it dried, then crushed it into powder, mixed it with flour, and used it to make "crunchy tea cakes," which she served to visitors.*

Over the following several months, Cianciulli did this two more times, both times with older, local women she was "helping" in one way or another. The third victim was her last, because someone had witnessed her going into Cianciulli's home. Upon being confronted by police, Cianciulli confessed her crimes, providing all the details of the three murders. She had performed the ritualistic murders, she explained, as black magic, to protect the life of her eldest son, who was preparing to serve in World War II. (Cianciulli had given birth to 14 children. Ten had died young, and she was very protective of the surviving four.) Cianciulli spent several years in prison, and died in an insane asylum in 1970 at the age of 76.

DOROTHEA PUENTE (1929–2011)

In November 1988, police were called to a boardinghouse in a run-down section of Sacramento, California, to look for a man who'd been reported missing by

his social worker. The boardinghouse, which was home mostly to indigent elderly people, was managed by 59-year-old Dorothea Puente. She'd served time in jail for crimes that included forging checks, prostitution, and, in the early 1980s, drugging and robbing three elderly men. Yet somehow, despite her history, Puente was able to take over management of the boardinghouse in 1985. When police noticed freshly turned soil in the yard, they launched an investigation that uncovered the remains of seven people, all former residents of the boardinghouse. Puente had killed them with overdoses of sleeping pills, then stored the bodies in an upstairs room in the house until it was safe to bury them in secret. Why had she killed them? So she could cash their Social Security checks, which continued to arrive after their deaths. Police linked Puente to two more killings: an unsolved murder of one of her boyfriends in 1985, and the overdose death of a business partner in 1982, which had been ruled a suicide at the time. In 1993 Puente was convicted of three murders (the jury was deadlocked on the other six). She was sentenced to life in prison without the possibility of parole, where she died in 2011 at the age of 82.

GRISELDA BLANCO (1943–2012)

Blanco grew up in the slums of Colombia's notorious cocaine capital, Medellín, and started a life of crime when she was still a preteen. She moved to New York in the 1970s, and became one of the early pioneers of the cocaine trade. In 1975 she was indicted on smuggling charges but escaped to Colombia, only to return to the United States in 1979, this time to Miami, Florida. There she lived a life of luxury and flamboyance, always on the run from the FBI and the DEA, and at the same time overseeing a smuggling operation that brought millions of dollars' worth of cocaine—every month—from Colombia to cities all across the United States. (Net worth during this time: around $2 billion.) She also earned a reputation for ruthlessness. Blanco was a central figure in the "Miami Drug Wars," the deadly battles between rival drug gangs that saw hundreds killed on Miami streets in the late 1970s and 1980s. She is believed to have ordered the murders of at least 40 people—possibly as many as 250—and was personally responsible for many more. Blanco was arrested in Los Angeles in 1985 and was eventually convicted of three murders, one of them a two-year-old boy who'd been shot in a botched hit of a former Blanco enforcer. She served 19 years in prison before being deported back to Colombia in 2004. In 2012 she was gunned down by assassins on a motorcycle while leaving a butcher shop in Medellín.

Bonus fact: Blanco took her nickname—*La Madrina*, "the Godmother"— seriously. How seriously? She named one of her sons Michael Corleone Blanco, after the lead character in the *Godfather* films.

...Ravenclaw, and Hufflepuff—on a plane and wrote them down on the back of an airsickness bag.

WHILE YOU'RE WAITING...

*Airport terminals offer a lot more than just prepackaged sandwiches and Starbucks nowadays.
Here are some unique time-killers to make your next layover a bit more entertaining.*

MOVIE THEATER

Portland, Oregon, has a thriving arts community, and that fact is proclaimed
to travelers almost immediately upon their arrival at Portland International
Airport. The Hollywood Theatre, one of the city's many independent houses,
operates a branch at the airport. It seats 17 travelers (and has standing room
for as many as 49) and runs a 20-minute loop of short movies made by local
filmmakers.

FRESH PRODUCE

Portland also has a reputation as a food city, where many chefs make magic out
of locally grown produce. Some of that local produce can be purchased at the
airport and taken back to where travelers call home. Capers Café, a restaurant
with an airport location, runs a miniature farmers market two days a week on the
concourse, offering a few tables of fresh berries and melons for sale.

BUTTERFLIES

Singapore is the natural home of dozens of different species of butterflies, and
40 of them are on display at a network of massive, enclosed tropical gardens
at the country's Changi Airport. It's highly likely that one of the more than
1,000 butterflies that lives in the oasis will land on a nearby fern as you walk
through...or even on your shoulder.

GRUNGE ROCKERS

Seattle was the site of the 1990s "grunge rock" revolution that made
international stars out of bands like Pearl Jam, Nirvana, and Soundgarden.
Many of those grunge bands got their start on Seattle record label Sub Pop. The
company's heyday is behind them, but now it operates a Sub Pop gift shop at
Seattle-Tacoma International Airport. Fans can buy CDs, T-shirts, and posters—
and if they're lucky, they'll hand their money to Mark Pickerel, who is the store's
assistant manager and one-time drummer for Screaming Trees.

Great! Something else to worry about: Operating room fires affect about 600 U.S. patients every year.

ICE SKATING

In addition to a rotating slate of "Plaza Parties" in an area outside its main terminal, Denver International Airport operates an ice-skating rink in the winter. It's open all day, travelers can skate as long as they want, and they can borrow skates, all free of charge. On the other side of the world, Incheon International Airport in Seoul, South Korea, offers a skating rink too, but this one has big, lit-up icy trees in the middle to create an "ice forest" effect.

VIDEO GAMES

If parents need to occupy kids during a long international journey—or they need to blow off some steam themselves—they're lucky if they've got a layover at Charles de Gaulle Airport in Paris. It hosts several Sony PlayStation kiosks—and they're free to play.

ART

Many airports have fine art installations; a few, such as Paris's Charles de Gaulle and Amsterdam's Airport Schiphol, even have art galleries. One of the best is the SFO Museum in San Francisco International Airport, which features exhibits on a variety of subjects, including Hindu religious sculptures, a history of flight attendant uniforms, shoes of the world, and 19th-century gambling machines.

THE SYMPHONY

Brisbane Airport in Australia has an artist-in-residence program. Different fine artists have been invited to hang out at the airport and interact with travelers as they make things. Past artists-in-residence include Robert Brownhall, who made paintings of different areas of the airport while he was there, and the Queensland Symphony Orchestra, which presented six unannounced classical concerts throughout the airport's domestic and international terminals.

DENTISTRY

Some people consider air travel to be a painful ordeal, on par with going to the dentist. Well, maybe some of those people can kill two birds with one stone if they've got a layover in São Paulo. Travelers at the Brazilian city's São Paulo-Guarulhos International Airport can visit the on-site dental practice. The team of licensed dentists provides checkups, teeth cleaning, whitening, and X-rays.

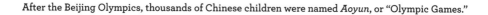

After the Beijing Olympics, thousands of Chinese children were named *Aoyun,* or "Olympic Games."

TWO _____S GO INTO A BAR

Bar jokes have only been around since the 1950s, but they're some of our favorites.

Two peanuts walk into a bar. One was a salted.

An E-flat walks into a bar. The bartender says, "Sorry, we don't serve minors."

An amnesiac walks into a bar. He sidles up to the prettiest woman at the bar and says, "So, do I come here often?"

A fish walks into a bar. Bartender says, "Shouldn't you be in school?"

A measle virus walks into a bar. Bartender says, "Shots for everybody!"

A zombie walks into a bar and says to the bartender, "Give me a stiff drink."

A guy walks into a bar and orders a beer. He hears someone say, "Hey, mister! Nice pants! Nice shirt! Nice tie! Nice shoes!" But when he looks around there are no other customers in the bar. The bartender points at a bowl sitting on the bar. "It's the pretzels," he says. "They're complimentary."

The past, present, and future walk into a bar. (It was tense.)

Charles Dickens walks into a bar and orders a martini. The bartender asks, "Olive or twist?"

A Roman walks into a bar, holds up two fingers, and says to the bartender, "Gimme five beers."

A panda goes into a bar and asks the bartender, "Have you seen my brother?" "I don't know," the bartender says. "What does he look like?"

An amoeba walks into a bar. Bartender says, "Pay the tab before you split."

Two fonts walk into a bar. "Get out!" shouts the bartender. "We don't serve your type here."

A grizzly bear goes into a bar and says "I'll have a.........beer." "Sure," the bartender says, "but why the big pause?"

A Frenchman goes into a bar. A parrot wearing a baseball cap is sitting on his shoulder. "That's pretty neat," the bartender says, "where did you get him?" "France," the parrot says. "They've got millions of them over there."

"Fortified" wine has extra alcohol added to it to make it stronger. Examples: sherry, port, and madeira.

KENTUCKY FRIED COLONELS

You've heard of Colonel Harland Sanders, founder of the Kentucky Fried Chicken empire. (His story is on page 226.) Sanders did serve in the U.S. Army, but he never earned the rank of colonel. So how'd he get it? Here's the story of a Kentucky tradition more than 200 years old.

MAN OF WAR

Isaac Shelby (1750–1826) was a Revolutionary War hero and Kentucky's first governor. He served his first term from 1792 to 1796, and a second term from 1812 to 1816. He made it clear that he would have preferred not to serve the second term, but the War of 1812 was looming, and he agreed to come out of retirement and see the state through the national crisis.

In July 1813, General William Henry Harrison asked Governor Shelby to raise a force of Kentucky soldiers and lead them into battle against the British. Shelby agreed, and on October 15, 1813, his force of 3,500 volunteers helped win the Battle of the Thames, in what is now the province of Ontario, Canada.

After the war, Shelby appointed one of his former officers, Charles Todd, to serve as an aide-de-camp on his staff with the rank of colonel—the first official "Kentucky colonel." As Todd's rank implied, he served the governor as a military aide. The time when Kentucky governors needed military aides on their staff would soon pass, but the tradition of awarding prominent citizens with the title was just getting started. More than 200 years later, awarding someone a commission of Kentucky colonel remains the highest honor a governor of Kentucky can bestow. More than 140,000 people have received the title since 1813, an average of nearly 700 per year.

FIGUREHEADS

In the 1820s, Kentucky colonels served as uniformed bodyguards, assigned to protect the governors as they went about their official duties. But as the years passed, the job became entirely ceremonial, with no bodyguarding required. Kentucky Fried Chicken founder Colonel Harland Sanders, the most famous Kentucky colonel of them all, owes his colonelcy not to his secret recipe for fried chicken but to the fact that he was a political supporter of Ruby Laffoon, who was the state's governor from 1931 to 1935. Laffoon commissioned more than 5,000 colonels during his four years in office, or about five times the number awarded by all of his predecessors combined. Laffoon's successor, Governor

Happy Chandler, was not impressed; he reverted to tradition by appointing only about a dozen new colonels each year, and always on the first Saturday in May, during the running of the Kentucky Derby. (Tickets to the derby and to a special derby eve colonels' banquet are two of the perks of being appointed a Kentucky colonel; a third is the right to be addressed as "Honorable." Most colonels decline the "Honorable" honor and humbly prefer to be addressed simply as "Colonel.")

Since then, governors have alternated between issuing scads of commissions, like Ruby Laffoon, or only a handful, and only to the most deserving nominees "in recognition of noteworthy accomplishments and outstanding service to a community, state or the nation." How many to award is left entirely to the discretion of the sitting governor, who then forwards the names to the secretary of state's office, which is responsible for printing the commission certificates. Governor Steve Beshear (2007–2015) awarded so many colonels' commissions—about 16,000 each year—that the state reduced the size of the paper on which the commission certificate was printed, in order to save money.

SOME FAMOUS KENTUCKY COLONELS

- Colonel Elvis Presley
- Colonel Shirley Temple
- Colonel Pope John Paul II
- Colonel Bill Clinton
- Colonel Whoopi Goldberg
- Colonel Wayne Newton
- Colonel Tiger Woods
- Colonel Betty White
- Colonel Johnny Depp
- Colonel Hunter S. Thompson
- Colonel John Glenn
- Colonel General Norman Schwarzkopf

One famous colonel who's not a Kentucky colonel is Colonel Tom Parker, Colonel Elvis Presley's longtime manager. Reason: He's a Louisiana colonel. In 1948 Parker was awarded a colonel's commission in the Louisiana State Militia by Governor Jimmie Davis, a former country singer who won his gubernatorial election with Parker's help in 1944.

NICE TRY

"There's something mystical about the Kentucky colonel that other states have tried to create, and it has not been successful," says Colonel Glen Bastin.

For a look at some states that have tried to emulate the "Kentucky colonel" concept—with varying degrees of success—turn to page 403.

In 1953 an annoyed viewer invented Blab-Off, a switch to turn off the sound of TV commercials.

UNCLE JOHN'S PAGE OF LISTS

Random bits of information from the BRI's bottomless files.

7 Candies that Debuted in the 1920s

1. Oh, Henry!
2. Reese's Peanut Butter Cups
3. Baby Ruth
4. Mounds
5. Milky Way
6. Mr. Goodbar
7. Milk Duds

9 Music Acts Who Licensed Alcoholic Beverages

1. KISS: Destroyer Beer
2. Justin Timberlake: Sauza 901 Tequila
3. Marilyn Manson: Mansinthe
4. Sammy Hagar: Beach Bar Rum
5. Whitesnake: Zinfadel
6. Pharrell: Qream Liqueur
7. Ludacris: Conjure Cognac
8. Hanson: Mmmhop Beer
9. Kenny Chesney: Blue Chair Rum

8 Onomatopoeic Pig Noises from Around the Globe

1. "Oink oink" (English, German)
2. "Boo boo" (Japanese)
3. "Knor knor" (Dutch)
4. "Nöff-nöff" (Swedish)
5. "Hrgu hrgu" (Russian)
6. "Chrum chrum" (Polish)
7. "Hunk hunk" (Albanian)
8. "Groin groin" (French)

8 Methods of Asexual Reproduction

1. Fission
2. Binary fission
3. Budding
4. Vegetative propagation
5. Sporogenesis
6. Fragmentation
7. Parthenogenesis
8. Apomixis

5 Songs About Buses

1. "Magic Bus" The Who
2. "Bus Stop" The Hollies
3. "Double Dutch Bus" Frankie Smith
4. "Get on the Bus" Destiny's Child
5. "Thank God and Greyhound" Roy Clark

14 Former *Daily Show* Correspondents

1. Stephen Colbert
2. Steve Carell
3. Kristen Schaal
4. Ed Helms
5. John Oliver
6. Samantha Bee
7. Jason Jones
8. Jessica Williams
9. Olivia Munn
10. Rob Corddry
11. Mo Rocca
12. Larry Wilmore
13. Michael Che
14. Josh Gad

Coincidence? The numbers on a roulette wheel add up to 666.

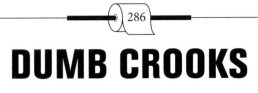

DUMB CROOKS

We've been bringing you stories of inept criminals for 30 years.
You'd think they'd have learned by now.

ALL BRAWN, NO BRAINS

Loud screeching, banging, and swearing noises woke several tenants at a
Kingsport, Tennessee, apartment complex in the middle of the night in February
2015. When the tenants looked out their windows, they saw three men trying to
drag and roll a large safe across the parking lot. The ruckus got even louder when
the safe landed on one of the men's feet. A few minutes later the cops arrived,
followed the drag marks to a nearby apartment, and knocked on the door.
Willard Harmon, 41, opened the door and invited the officers in. Inside were
two other men (one of them was Harmon's 27-year-old son) and a 200-pound,
unopened safe sitting on the kitchen floor. Harmon insisted that they found it in
an alley, but a little detective work proved otherwise. That same safe had been
stolen from a warehouse earlier that evening. How'd they know? There were
scrapes on the warehouse floor that led police to broken glass; the glass matched
the glass from their car's hatchback, which hit the safe and shattered when they
tried to close it. All three men were arrested. Adding insult to injury: the safe
was empty.

PLUMB STUPID

Fun fact: In the UK, slot machines are called "fruit machines." (This tidbit
will come in handy later.) On a crime spree across England in 2016, Benjamin
Robinson, 29, and Daniel Hutchinson, 24, used a screwdriver to break into
dozens of fruit machines and steal thousands of pounds worth of cash and coins.
They were careful enough to wear ski masks when they committed the crimes,
but their vanity got the best of them afterward: they removed their masks and
snapped several "celebratory selfies" with their loot. (In one of the images,
Hutchinson is displaying a cheeky smile while placing his finger over his mouth
in a "shoosh" pose.) When the duo was later stopped at a police checkpoint,
they might have had a chance at explaining away the cash and the coinage, and
maybe even the masks and the screwdriver, but not the incriminating selfies.
That's what put the fruit machine bandits in jail. Detective Chief Inspector Matt
Walker (who's watched a few too many cop shows) told reporters, "We knew we
hit the jackpot when we investigated these lemons."

What's *sphenopalatine ganglioneuralgia*? The scientific name for "brain freeze."

THE HANGOVER, PART IV

Don't you hate it when you wake up after a night of partying and there's a penguin in your apartment? Rhys Owen Jones, 21, and Keri Mules, 20, couldn't exactly recall how the bird got there, but the two Welsh tourists suspected it might have something to do with their drunken visit to Sea World on Australia's Gold Coast the night before. Not knowing what to do with the bird—a seven-year-old fairy penguin named Dirk—they decided to let it go in a nearby canal. Concerned witnesses called the police, who just happened to be looking for a missing penguin. Dirk was returned to Sea World, and the witnesses led police to Jones and Mules. When they were apprehended, they were informed that, in addition to stealing Dirk, they had also swam with the dolphins and set off a fire extinguisher in the shark enclosure. The pair was fined $1,000 each and told to write a letter of apology to Sea World and to the people of Australia.

> And the judge told them, "Perhaps next time you are at a party you will consider drinking a little less vodka.

MIXED MESSAGES

In March 2017, a Scotsman named Gregor Ford wanted to get rid of his Odyssey putter, so he posted it for sale on Facebook. After an exchange with a potential buyer, Ford tweeted a screenshot of the conversation on his Twitter account. As of this writing, the tweet had amassed more than 90,000 likes. Here's why:

Golf Putter For Sale: £25

Dumb Crook: Hi is this still for sale?

Seller: Hi, yes I still have it. Are you interested?

Dumb Crook: Yes mate where can you meet me. I'm in East Kilbride.

Seller: If you come and pick it up you can have it for £20.

Dumb Crook: Awryt mate am goiny meet some geezer for a new putter, wanty come with me and we'll just do him and take it off him lol

Dumb Crook: Sh*t that was meant for ma pal

Dumb Crook: But its not about you

Dumb Crook: Where do u live

*   *   *

"Civilization is a race between education and catastrophe."

—H. G. Wells

From 1932 to 1967, there was a casino in the Nevada State Prison.

THE STRONGEST MEN IN THE WORLD

Before the mid-20th century, people didn't have as many entertainment options as they do today. Mostly, they'd go to see live shows: vaudeville, music hall performances, circuses, and touring exhibitions. And one of the most popular attractions were the strongmen—burly, often scantily clad men who would exhibit amazing feats of strength and might. In their day, they were among the most famous athletes—and celebrities—in Europe and the United States. Here's a look back at some of the world's strongest strongmen.

ZISHE BREITBART

Siegmund Breitbart, nicknamed "Zishe" or "sweet" by his Yiddish-speaking parents, was born in Lodz, Poland, in 1883. At the age of three, he already exhibited some amazing capabilities. The story goes that while playing in his father's blacksmith shop one day, a heavy iron bar fell on him…and he lifted it off himself with little effort. As a child, he was expelled from several schools for fighting—because other kids always challenged him, and Breitbart always won. In the early 20th century, Poland was under Russian control, and Breitbart was drafted to fight in World War I. He was taken as a prisoner of war by Germany, but after the war he opted to stay in Germany. The 6'1", 225-pound Breitbart joined a traveling circus, performing as an acrobat and strongman. When the circus stopped in Bremen, Germany, in 1919, the director of another, more popular circus, the Circus Busch, poached Breitbart and made him that show's opening act…and soon, the star.

Breitbart was nicknamed "the Iron King," and for good reason—his act consisted almost entirely of manipulating that mighty metal. He'd bend iron rods into horseshoes, twist iron bars into flowers, bite through iron chains, pull a coach full of people with an iron handle placed in his mouth, and pound iron nails into a board using only his fists. Then he'd lay on the stage and let two guys on motorcycles chase each other round…running over his chest. Or he'd climb a ladder while holding a train wheel in his teeth…with three men holding onto it.

Breitbart's feats were impressive, but his act also had a political message. Anti-Semitism was rising in Europe between the world wars, and Breitbart became a hero and a role model for European Jews. While he did his act, he was flanked by the Zionist flag (which would later become the flag of Israel). In addition to being "the Iron King," the Circus Busch billed him as "Shimshn-hagibr," or "Samson the

Flyin' flop: Lockheed Martin created the *Sea Shadow*, the boat equivalent of a stealth plane…

Mighty," comparing him to the biblical figure. His presence on stage dispelled the stereotypical, racist notion that Jewish men were weak. He starred in two German films, endorsed products, marketed a bodybuilding course, wrote a memoir, and inspired folk songs and popular sayings such as "If a thousand Breitbarts were to arise among the Jews, the Jewish people would cease being persecuted."

Trying to perform one of his signature stunts is what ultimately killed him. In 1925, Breitbart was hammering a nail into a board with his hand, as he'd done hundreds of times before. Only this time the nail slipped and was driven into his leg. The nail was rusty, and Breitbart contracted sepsis (blood poisoning). Eight weeks of hospitalization and ten surgeries, including the amputation of both legs, couldn't save the great Breitbart, and he died at the age of 42.

LOUIS UNI

French strongman Louis Uni had many nicknames. Among them were "King of Athletes," "Demigod of Strength," and "Apollon" (the French name for the Greek god Apollo). Standing 6'2" and weighing 260 pounds, and sporting an impressive handlebar mustache, Uni was a showman first and an athlete second—which is to say that unlike the other major strongmen of the era, he didn't train, or learn specialized lifting techniques to achieve his feats. He used pure force and will.

After running away to join the circus at age 14, Uni was returned home to his parents by the police, who then made him wait a couple of years before allowing him to leave home to work as a performer at the Folies-Bergère theater in Paris. There he was discovered by a promoter who took Uni on tour as "the strongest man in the world." Uni's signature routine: He'd appear onstage dressed as a prisoner and locked in a cage. Then he'd bend the iron bars, break out, and run away from actors dressed as policemen. His other specialty: lifting a train axle—with two iron wheels attached—over his head.

He ultimately took over a major Paris music hall called the Café Fontaine and renamed it the Café Apollon, where he staged theatrical acts and performed himself in between. Uni scaled back his frequency of performances following a horrific injury incurred in a 1913 performance. The stunt called for him to push back against two cars—one on either side. He kept the vehicles at bay...until he fell to the ground, having torn most of the muscles in both of his arms.

Uni continued to appear occasionally onstage and even in silent films almost up until his death at age 66 in 1928. Amazingly, he didn't die in a performance—he was taken down by an abscess in his throat that burst while he was sleeping, and he unknowingly swallowed the fluid inside.

> 🦆 **TALL TALE:** One of Louis Cyr's greatest performances was his wrestling match against a famous sideshow performer named Edouard Beaupré in March 1901. Standing nearly eight feet tall, Beaupré was one of the tallest men on earth. And he weighed 365 pounds—the exact same weight as Cyr, who was only 5'10" tall. Nevertheless, in the battle between the incredibly tall man and the incredibly strong man...Cyr won.

LOUIS CYR

Born in Quebec in 1863, he was so strong by the age of 12 that he was able to find work as a lumberjack in one of French Canada's many timber camps. He could lift entire logs, but what he really wanted to be able to do was lift an entire cow off the ground: Cyr loved stories about the ancient Greek warrior Milo of Croton, who was so strong that he was said to have once carried a bull on his shoulders. Cyr trained himself to do it by lifting a sack of grain that he made a little heavier each day...and then carrying it for a couple of miles. It worked—by age 15, he could lift more than 200 pounds. At age 18, the 5'10", 310-pounder, nicknamed "Canadian Samson" (because, besides his strength, he had long hair like the biblical Samson), entered a strongman contest in Boston and won the whole thing when he lifted a horse clean off the ground.

Cyr toured Quebec in the 1880s as "the Strongest Man in Canada," performing feats of strength such as lifting 3,000 pounds on his back, and lifting a 200-pound dumbbell with just one hand. Even that was too easy for Cyr. He once pushed a 500-pound train car up an incline with one finger. One of Cyr's greatest stunts involved both of his arms being tethered to horses. Then the horses were ordered to pull. Rather than letting them pull his limbs out of their sockets, Cyr stood his ground—neither horse could ever budge him. He topped that in 1895 by lifting, on his back, a platform upon which 18 men were seated. It weighed two tons.

Within ten years, Cyr's weight had increased to 400 pounds, and his health was failing. When he died of kidney disease in 1912 at the age of 59, he was still one of the most famous men in Canada. He died in Montreal, where a bronze statue of Louis Cyr still stands.

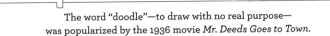

The word "doodle"—to draw with no real purpose—
was popularized by the 1936 movie *Mr. Deeds Goes to Town.*

NOT-SO-GREATEST HITS

Greatest hits albums are a marketing tool—a way to repackage old songs and call it a new product. And consumers must fall for it, because record labels keep doing it…even if the artist didn't have any real hits or much commercial success.

CHUCK MANGIONE
GREATEST HITS

In 1978 Mangione delivered one of the most memorable soft rock hits ever: "Feels So Good"—an instrumental song powered by Mangione's flugelhorn. It's the only flugelhorn song to ever top the charts…and it was also Mangione's only hit. But that hasn't stopped Mangione's record company from releasing 10 separate "Best of" compilations.

GIN BLOSSOMS
OUTSIDE LOOKING IN: THE BEST OF THE GIN BLOSSOMS

This '90s alternative rock band had a few hits, including "Hey Jealousy," "Found Out About You," and "Allison Road." But the group broke up after making just two albums. Nevertheless, the Gin Blossoms' label released this compilation—without the band's knowledge.

NELSON
20TH CENTURY MASTERS: THE MILLENNIUM COLLECTION

Nelson was a pop-rock band fronted by Matthew and Gunnar Nelson, the twin sons of rock 'n' roll teen idol Rick Nelson. They had one #1 hit, "(Can't Live Without Your) Love and Affection," which spent one week at the top of the charts in 1990, and three other minor hits by the end of 1991. And that was it.

CAPPADONNA
CAPPADONNA HITS

The Wu-Tang Clan is one of the most successful and critically acclaimed hip-hop groups of all time. Many of its members have enjoyed hit solo albums, particularly Method Man, RZA, and Ol' Dirty Bastard. Cappadonna, also a member of the group, has quietly released eight albums. None have produced any hits; *Cappadonna Hits* contains songs from Cappadonna's first two albums.

Disney's research library has 11 vaults of animation cels, concept art, and storyboards preserved from every movie the studio has ever made.

TONE LŌC
"WILD THING" AND OTHER HITS

The gravelly voiced rapper had two huge hits in 1989: "Wild Thing" and "Funky Cold Medina." And those were the only two hits he ever had, so the title of his greatest hits album is a bit misleading.

SHAQUILLE O'NEAL
THE BEST OF SHAQUILLE O'NEAL

Who knew O'Neal even had a recording career? In the early '90s, he released two rap albums, *Shaq Diesel* and *Shaq Fu: Da Return*. Highlights of both were compiled onto this 1996 album, rounded out with "Biological Didn't Bother," a rap song O'Neal wrote in praise of his stepfather.

YOUNG MC
THE BEST OF YOUNG MC

The rapper released six albums, but his only two hits ("Bust a Move," "Principal's Office") came off his first one, *Stone Cold Rhymin'*. So what's *The Best of Young MC*? It's *Stone Cold Rhymin'* with the songs' order rearranged.

ENUFF Z'NUFF
COVERED IN GOLD

This second-tier hair metal band had two hits in 1989: "New Thing" and "Fly High Michelle." Its last album came out in 2009…in Japan and England, but not in the United States. Nevertheless, there are three Enuff Z'nuff greatest hits collections, including this one. (Number of gold records awarded to Enuff Z'nuff: zero.)

MILLI VANILLI
BEST OF THE BEST

Fab and Rob were off to a great start, with three #1 singles—until the revelation in 1990 that the duo didn't sing on their records and lip-synced in concerts destroyed their career. Despite the scandal, their hits were extremely popular—but they were also unavailable until this 2006 collection because all the band's albums were pulled from stores after the lip-syncing debacle.

Star Wars has been adapted for shadow puppets, a one-man play, a photoessay with action figures, and a ballet.

WEIRD CANADA

O, Canada: where the mountains are capped with snow, the maple trees and beavers are abundant, and the news stories are really, really strange.

IT RHYMES WITH DUCK

Taking the court for Alberta's Medicine Hat College Rattlesnakes in 2015: 6'6" forward Guy Carbagiale…and we can't print his last name. The player, an international student from Brazil who is of German descent, has a last name that is spelled exactly like the most famous of all English curse words—the f-bomb— although he insists that it's pronounced "foo-kee." "It doesn't mean what people think it means," he told a reporter. "In German, it means *fox*." (No, that word is *fuchs*.) But he turned out to be a pretty good player, averaging 18 points a game and being named to the All-Canada college basketball team.

ROLLING ALONG

In October 2016, a 25-year-old man from Scugog Township, Ontario, was run over by an out-of-control car. It happened to be *his* car. He was backing out of his driveway, but had left the door open. As the car moved, he fell out, but the automobile kept rolling, and ran right over his leg. That obstacle still wasn't enough to stop it, and the car kept going, eventually coming to a stop after hitting two mailbox posts. He was treated for a broken leg at a local hospital and then released…into the custody of police, who charged him with impaired driving—not surprisingly, he'd been drinking at the time of the accident.

DUTY CALLS

Until 2013, Eric Manu lived a humble life, working as a gardener and living with his wife and baby in Vancouver. But then he got a call about a new job: he was the heir to the throne of a 6,000-person tribe in the African nation of Ghana. The previous king was Manu's uncle, and he had died without fathering any children. So Manu moved to Ghana in 2015—part-time—to rule the tribe.

EGGS AND SAUSAGE

One evening in October 2016, a Vancouver man heard a strange noise coming from his kitchen. He investigated and found something that was indeed strange: a man he didn't know, at his stove, cooking some eggs he'd gotten out of the homeowner's refrigerator. Oh, and also, the stranger was completely naked. Upon being discovered, the invader fled the house…but left his clothes. Police easily found him, though—he was the guy wandering around a Vancouver neighborhood naked. Amazingly, in 2013 police responded to another call about a man who'd broken into a house to cook eggs in the nude—but it was a *different* guy.

> " *There are few, if any, Canadian men that have never spelled their name in a snow bank.* "
>
> —Douglas Coupland, author

IT'S TOUGH BEING TOUGH ON CRIME

The town of Williams Lake, British Columbia, has such a high crime rate that the city council was fed up. In February 2016, they passed a motion (unanimously) to inject GPS tracking devices into "high-risk" criminals and repeat offenders. That way, the local government can keep tabs on them before they commit another crime. While the law was challenged by legal experts for violating privacy laws, it doesn't really matter because injectable GPS tracking devices haven't been invented yet.

CANADIANS ARE TOO NICE

No good deed goes unpunished. Dane Rusk of Regina, Saskatchewan, was issued a $175 traffic ticket in June 2016. His crime: not wearing a seat belt. Rusk had actually pulled over to hand $3.00 to a homeless man asking for money on the side of the street. But he wasn't really a homeless man: he was a Saskatoon police officer in disguise, dressed up to look like a homeless man as part of a sting operation to nab drivers who weren't wearing their seat belts. When Rusk unbuckled his seat belt to lean across the passenger seat and hand off the money through the window, he was busted by the bogus beggar.

LIGHTS OUT

A driver was caught speeding on a stretch of highway outside of Guelph, Ontario, one night in July 2016. Not only was he was traveling at 108 kph (67 mph) in a 70 kph (45 mph) zone, but he doing so without his headlights in an area that had no streetlights. The man argued (unsuccessfully) that he had the lights thing under control, because he'd strapped a flashlight to his head.

In a 2017 experiment, vending machines charged a "time tax." Healthy snacks popped out…

POSITIVE-NEGATIVE WORDS

Do negative words like "disheveled" or "reckless" have a "positive" version? Some do.

Disgruntled. The prefix "dis" usually means "not," as in *dissatisfied*. But it can also be used to indicate an extreme state. Example: to be *disgruntled* means to be *very* gruntled. *Gruntled* is an arcane word meaning "slightly unhappy."

Disheveled. *Chevel* is an Old French word for hair. *Deschevelé* meant "uncovered hair," and evolved to also mean "messy hair." There's no such word as *sheveled* in English. (But if there was, it would mean "hairy.")

Inert. It means "without the ability or strength to move," which isn't far from the meaning of its Latin root, *iners*—lacking skill. Inert derives from *iners*; there's no such word as "ert" to indicate *having* the ability or strength to move.

Ineffable. This word describes an emotion or sensibility that's difficult to express in words. It's derived from French, and survives in English. What didn't survive: *effable*, an obscure academic word that describes pronounceable sounds.

Disgust. It comes from the French word *gustare*, which means "to taste." *Disgust* literally means "distasteful," but English didn't absorb "gust," which would just mean "tasteful."

Reckless. The root of "reckless" is the German *reck*, which means "care." *Reckless* is care*less*. The opposite form, *reckful*, never caught on in German or in English.

Disembowel. Definition: to eviscerate or remove the bowels of something. It replaced the word *embowel*, which meant the exact same thing. Although confusingly, "embowel" was also used to mean "enclose"—which is the opposite of its other meaning, and probably how the word *disembowel* came about.

Postpone. It means "to delay or reschedule an event," but is there a word that means to move something up to before its prescheduled time? Yes—*prepone*. It's used only among English speakers in India.

Innocent. It comes from the Middle English word *nocens*, which meant "to harm." Adding "in" created a word that meant "harmless" or "pure." *Innocent* stayed in the language, but *nocent* didn't—it was replaced by "guilty."

DOOMSDAY!

*On page 222 we told you about five incidents involving nuclear false alarms.
Here's a different kind of tale that's just as scary: a NORAD alert
warning that World War III was already underway.*

Incoming! On October 5, 1960, a group of defense contractors were in
Colorado Springs, Colorado, touring the Cheyenne Mountain bunker that
served as the headquarters for the North American Air Defense Command
(NORAD). They were there because a new NORAD early warning radar
installation in Thule, Greenland, had just become operational.

On the tour, the contractors were shown a numerical threat level indicator
that was mounted on a wall above a giant map of the world. The indicator was
flashing a bright red number 1, the lowest threat level. Suddenly it changed to
2, then 3, then 4, and then 5, the highest threat level there was. Was this part
of the tour, or some kind of drill? Neither: The radar installation at Thule was
reporting that the USSR had just launched a massive nuclear missile strike
against the United States.

...Never mind: The visitors were hustled out of the room as both NORAD
and the Strategic Air Command (SAC) went on full alert. But doubts began
to arise when the warning system was unable to calculate any of the incoming
missiles' impact points. In addition, Soviet premier Nikita Khrushchev was visiting
New York. It seemed unlikely that the USSR would attack the United States
when their own leader was there. The alert was soon dismissed as a false alarm.

An investigation found that what the early warning system had detected
was actually...the moon, rising over Greenland. "It was indeed radar echoes
from the moon that had caused the false alarm," a Defense Department report
concluded. "Improved 'gating' procedures...were later instituted in order to
prevent another false moon alarm."

Déjà Vu: Just over a year later on November 24, 1961, SAC went on alert
again when the line to Thule went dead. When a controller tried to report the
problem to NORAD, that line was dead too. Had both sites been taken out in
a nuclear strike? Hundreds of nuclear bomber crews were placed on high alert,
ready to take off and attack targets in the Soviet Union...when a lone bomber
circling over Thule made contact with the base and was able to confirm that
it hadn't been nuked. The alert was canceled; the problem was later traced to
a faulty AT&T switch that had gone bad and cut off all communication links
between SAC and NORAD.

The stairs of medieval castles were always built in clockwise circles
(from the bottom up), to give their owners the advantage in a swordfight.

COMING TO A RESTROOM NEAR YOU?

It wasn't that long ago that hand dryers, touchless faucets, and self-flushing toilets were marvels of restroom technology. Here's a look at some more recent innovations that may soon be just as common.

LOOKY-LOOS

Product: Restroom Visitlizer System

What it does: The system, which is designed to be installed in several restrooms at once, uses sensors located in the doorway to count how many people enter each of the restrooms over a given period of time. A second set of sensors "sniffs" the air at each location to detect the presence of ammonia, hydrogen sulfide, and other "naturally occurring" chemicals. When the system determines that enough people have used a particular restroom (or that the air is too smelly), it sends a text message to the custodian alerting them that the restroom needs cleaning. The system makes it possible for custodians to make more efficient use of their time, says Dennis Quek, a spokesperson for Convergent Smart Technologies, the Singaporean company that invented the system. "One cleaner can take care of more toilets—some which aren't so heavily used—and he doesn't have to walk around to physically check the toilets."

THE FACE IS FAMILIAR

Product: Facial recognition toilet paper dispensers

What it does: The dispensers, which were installed in China's popular Temple of Heaven cultural site in 2017, are mounted on a wall just inside the entrance to the restrooms. Users who need toilet paper must stare into a camera for three seconds: the dispenser memorizes their facial features, then discharges about a two-foot length of paper. That's all they get—the dispenser will not give any more toilet paper to the same face until nine minutes have elapsed. The machines were installed to combat a rash of "toilet paper kleptomania," as the *South China Morning Post* put it, often by local senior citizens who have fixed incomes and can't afford to buy their own. So...what happens if a person is in distress and needs more paper? "If we encounter guests who have diarrhea or any other situation in which they urgently require toilet paper, then our staff

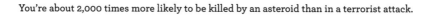

You're about 2,000 times more likely to be killed by an asteroid than in a terrorist attack.

on the ground will provide the toilet paper directly," says a Temple of Heaven spokesperson.

HELP IS ON THE WAY

Product: The SmartSafe Restroom Scream Detector

What it does: Not everything that happens in restrooms is good or even acceptable. The SmartSafe system, developed by a South Korean company and installed inside women's restrooms at Seoul National University, has palm-sized sensors that detect heat and smoke just like ordinary smoke detectors. But they can also detect the sound of a person screaming. When a scream is detected, the sensor activates security lights and sirens, and automatically alerts the police that someone in the restroom is in distress. The system was developed in 2016, after a woman was murdered in a public restroom near the campus. The hope is that the sensors will deter crime by discouraging attacks in restrooms that have them, and if that fails, thwart attacks in progress by scaring the attacker away. "The device alone can't save all women under threat in restrooms, but it will save one and that's enough," says Professor Han Moo-young.

MEMBERS ONLY

Product: Urinary 2.0

What it does: Developed by a Spanish biochemist, the Urinary 2.0 is a urinal with an added feature—a wash and dry cycle for the male anatomy. Sensors in the urinal detect when the user has finished; that's when the device springs into action, squirting soapy water on the person's member, then blasting it with three seconds of warm air to dry it off. Bonus: the stream of water is temperature-controlled, so it's cooler in the summer and warmer in the winter.

*   *   *

NUTTY

In 1943 forensic science pioneer Frances Glessner Lee created 18 intricately detailed dollhouse-style dioramas for students at Harvard Medical School. Each diorama depicted a gruesome murder, suicide, or accident. The tiny tableaus were filled with clues, like the odd body position of decaying corpses, bloody footprints, or potential murder weapons. These "Nutshell Studies of Unexplained Death" were part of Harvard's legal medicine curriculum for more than 20 years, and now reside at the Maryland Medical Examiner's office, where they are still studied by budding forensic detectives.

First public exhibition of a motion picture: 1895. First showing of an "erotic" film: 1896.

MOUTHING OFF

On the search for great quotations, we came across these. (Well…we almost made it.)

"I LOVE BEING FAMOUS—IT'S ALMOST LIKE BEING WHITE."

—Chris Rock

"I not only knew Houdini, but we had a very lovely relationship. I really thought we had something going, and then the son of a gun disappeared."

—Betty White

"I hate birthdays. I thought that I only hated my own birthday, and then I realized that I hate my children's birthdays, too."

—Samantha Bee

"If you removed all the arteries, veins, and capillaries from a person's body, and tied them end-to-end…the person will die."

—Neil deGrasse Tyson

"I did write a letter to the archdiocese who'd banned the song 'Only the Good Die Young,' asking them to ban my next record."

—Billy Joel

"I'm compulsive, but I'm also very indecisive. I don't know what I want, but I know that I want it now."

—Dylan Moran

"I wanted to be a brain surgeon, but I had a bad habit of dropping things."

—Gilbert Gottfried

"I'm thinking of buying a monkey. Then I think, 'Why stop at one?'"

—Robert Downey Jr.

"To say I'm an overrated troll, when you have never even seen me guard a bridge, is patently unfair."

—Tina Fey

"If you have to explain to someone you're famous, then you're technically not that famous."

—David Spade

THE MAGICAL FRUIT

This page won't amount to a hill of beans—or maybe it will, because it's a page about beans.

• Beans are the edible seeds of larger plants, and they grow in visible, pickable pods, so technically, beans really *are* a fruit. ("Magical" is still a matter of opinion.)

• One bean not considered a bean: the green bean. Federal nutritional health guidelines consider it a vegetable, not a starchy legume like other beans. Reason: it contains far less fiber and protein than its beany brethren.

• Green beans are also one of a handful of bean varieties that cannot and should not be eaten raw…because they're toxic. They're high in *lectins*—a protein that can cause gastric distress, but can be easily neutralized by cooking.

• Canned baked beans, particularly Heinz's baked beans, are extremely popular in Great Britain, where they're considered part of the "traditional English breakfast." As a nation, Britons consume on average 38.5 tons of baked beans every hour. (That's four times the American consumption rate.)

• Wedding custom in Nicaragua: the newlyweds are given a bowl of beans, which is thought to bring good luck and longevity to their marriage.

• Beans, or rather legumes, are one of the few cultivated plants that actively enrich the soil in which they grow. Legume roots are equipped with nodules that, as the beans grow, add nitrogen to the dirt.

• Top five most-grown bean varieties in the United States: pinto beans, navy beans, black beans, kidney beans, and great northern beans.

• The influential sixth-century Greek philosopher Pythagoras taught his followers that the souls of dead humans traveled to the underworld (Hades) through the hollow stems of bean plants, and that those souls lived in the beans. Result: He thought it was wrong to eat beans or even walk through bean fields.

• Beans were cultivated in ancient Rome and were so respected as an ideal food source that several prominent families were all named for the humble legume. They were: Fabius (for the fava bean), Piso (for the pea), Lentullus (lentils), and Cicero (chickpeas).

• The United States' most prolific bean producer: North Dakota, with 475,000 acres dedicated to growing beans. That's 1 percent of North Dakota's entire area.

The architect for Hearst Castle was Julia Morgan, California's first licensed female architect.

> *I like refried beans. That's why I want to try fried beans, because maybe they're just as good and we're just wasting time, and you don't have to fry them again after all.*

—**Mitch Hedberg**

• January 6 is National Bean Day. Reason: It's the day famed geneticist Gregor Mendel died in 1884. Many of Mendel's theories on genetics derive from experiments he did with bean plants.

• Beans are the most concentrated nonanimal source of protein in the world. As much as 11 percent of a cooked bean is protein. They're also the cheapest protein source. Ground beef and chicken cost, on average, around $1 per four-ounce serving. Cost of a four-ounce serving of pinto beans: around 10 cents.

• In 2012, a Macedonian man named Davcev Stojan cooked up the world's largest-ever pot of baked beans—a record 1,476.36 gallons.

• Another world record: In 1986, Barry "Captain Beany" Kirk sat in a bathtub full of cold baked beans for 100 hours.

• About 72,000 people worldwide have the last name of Bean.

• Don't worry, we'll answer the main question about beans. The reason they lead to excessive flatulence is because they contain a carbohydrate chain called *oligosaccharides*. Humans lack the digestive enzyme to process them properly, so intestinal bacteria ferment them instead. The side effect: gas.

*   *   *

NOT BAD FOR TWO HOURS' WORK

Veteran NBA point guard José Calderón was released from his contract with the Los Angeles Lakers on February 27, 2017. The Golden State Warriors needed a reserve point guard, so the team agreed to sign him. However, before Calderón could get to the Warriors' headquarters and actually sign his deal, the Warriors played a game in which star forward Kevin Durant suffered a knee injury. The team's priority was now a forward, not a point guard...which the team realized two hours *after* Calderón signed his contract. He was immediately released, but the team still paid him what he would have gotten had he stayed with the Warriors for the rest of the season: $415,000.

UNSOLVED MYSTERY: THE "ISDAL WOMAN"

Sometimes the most intriguing whodunits aren't found in mystery novels, they're found in real life. Take this curious case, which has puzzled investigators for more than 40 years.

COLD CASE

One chilly afternoon in November 1970, a father and his two daughters were hiking up a remote, rocky hillside overlooking the Isdalen valley near Bergen, a port city on the southwest coast of Norway. The man's 12-year-old daughter came upon it first: the badly burned body of a woman lying between two large rocks. As soon as the father realized what they were looking at, he turned his daughters around and they headed back down the hill to report their grisly discovery to the police.

When the police arrived, they discovered that many of the woman's possessions had been burned as well: an umbrella, some plastic bottles, what appeared to be the plastic cover for a passport (though it was too badly damaged to know for sure), and other items. Also found on the scene was an empty liquor bottle. That caused police to wonder if alcohol had played a role in the woman's death. Had she gotten drunk, perhaps tripped on some rocks, and fallen into the fire by accident?

THE PLOT THICKENS

After the police removed the body and the other evidence from the scene and examined it more thoroughly in the crime lab, the mystery of who the "Isdal woman" was and how she'd died deepened. Not only did the woman have no identification on her, but the labels on the articles of clothing not destroyed in the fire were all cut out. The same was true of the other articles recovered from the scene: any identifying marks that might have shed light on who the woman was or where she was from—even the labels on the bottoms of the plastic bottles—had been removed.

Three days later, another major clue surfaced when two large suitcases in the "left luggage" office of the Bergen railway station were traced back to the woman. Police established the link when a fingerprint lifted from a pair of

Ever heard of Kool-Aid pickles? They're dill pickles with a Kool-Aid packet or two added to the jar.

sunglasses in one of the suitcases matched a fingerprint taken from the body. But if the investigators hoped that the contents of the suitcase would solve the mystery of who the woman was, they were soon disappointed. There were passports in eight different names in one of the suitcases, and just as with the articles recovered from the crime scene, all labels had been removed from the clothing. Even the brand names and other identifying marks on the woman's comb and hairbrush had been rubbed away.

There were several wigs in the suitcases—not that unusual for a woman in the early 1970s—but along with the wigs, investigators found several pairs of eyeglasses with ordinary, nonprescription lenses. That led police to suspect that the woman was using the wigs and glasses to disguise her appearance.

Another mysterious item found in the suitcase: a writing pad with three columns of what appeared to be an alphanumeric code on the top sheet of paper. Nothing else was written on the pad.

BAG LADY

The best clue—and a peculiar one, considering how much effort the woman put into removing identifying marks from all of her possessions—was a shopping bag with the name "Oscar Rørtvedt's Footwear Store" printed on the outside. That was a store in the city of Stavanger, about 100 miles to the south.

An investigator was dispatched to the shop and there a clerk remembered selling a pair of blue rubber boots to a woman three weeks earlier. The woman was between the ages of 30 and 40, with long dark hair, brown eyes, a round face, and "slightly plump, almost chubby curves, with pretty legs." She spoke poor English and smelled of garlic, which was unusual in Norway at the time.

A pair of the same brand of blue rubber boots had been found next to the dead woman, so the investigators were satisfied that this was the same woman they were looking for. Next, the investigators began visiting hotels in the area to see if anyone matching the description had stayed there around the time the woman bought her boots. At the Hotel St. Svithun, within walking distance from the shoe store, a clerk remembered a woman who registered under the name Finella Lorck, from Belgium, and had stayed in the hotel for several days. One of the hotel maids remembered seeing her wearing the blue rubber boots.

CHARACTER STUDY

A search of hotel registers in Bergen for a Finella Lorck found no one by that name staying in any of the city's hotels in the days leading up to the discovery of the woman's body. So investigators turned to the "Alien Registration Form" that

Three oddly named prostitutes of the Old West: Chicago Joe, Peg-Leg Annie, and Squirrel Tooth Alice.

all foreign visitors had to fill out when checking in. Hotels all across the country were asked to scour their records for all Alien Registration Forms filled out by women in their 30s or 40s over the previous 12 months and send them in to the police.

As the forms began arriving in the mail, the investigators compared the handwriting with samples collected from the coded notes on the pad found in the suitcase, and from the Alien Registration Form that "Finella Lorck" had filled out at the Hotel St. Svithun.

Some forms that were found to have matching handwriting had been filled out by a woman calling herself Finella Lorck. But others with the same handwriting had been filled out under the names of Vera Jarle, Genevieve Lancier, Elisabeth Leenhouwfr, Claudia Nielsen, Claudia Tielt, and Alexia Zarna-Merchez. In most cases the woman claimed to be from Belgium, as Finella Lorck had. The forms required the registrants to list their passport numbers, but when the police checked with the Belgian authorities, they found that none of the passports, and none of the identities, were real.

THE TRAVELER

The dates given on the Alien Registration Forms made it possible for the investigators to retrace the woman's movements around the country. And when the police cracked the code on the notepad found in the suitcase, they discovered that it was a list of the dates that the woman had spent in each location. She had been traveling around Norway for the past several months, visiting places like Oslo, Bergen, Stavanger, and Trondheim. Often she would check out of one hotel using one fake passport, then check into the next hotel using a different alias, presumably after changing wigs and eyeglasses to alter her appearance. On her last trip she traveled from Paris to Stavanger, Bergen, and Trondheim, then back to Stavanger and Bergen, where she died.

The investigators were at a loss to understand why the woman traveled so much and used so many fake identities and disguises. It's possible that she was a private citizen who was hiding from someone she knew. Another possibility was that she was mentally ill and fleeing from someone or something that existed only in her mind. Or perhaps she was a foreign agent. The Cold War was still raging, after all. That would have explained the fake passports, and also how the woman was able to pay for so many train tickets and hotel rooms: if she was a spy, a foreign government may have been providing her with financial support. But with no hard evidence to go on, all the police could do was speculate.

Spider-Man meets Aquaman: A newly discovered species of marine snail shoots out webs of mucus.

GOLD STANDARD

Another piece of evidence that the police had to work with was the dead woman's dental work. X-rays of her mouth revealed that ten of her teeth had premade gold crowns, a type not used in Norway. But they were used in Asia and parts of central and southern Europe. That removed any remaining doubt that the woman may have been Norwegian, and it provided a clue as to what part of the world the woman might be from. But only a clue, nothing definitive.

WHAT HAVE YOU GOT?

After all of the evidence had been processed, the Norwegian investigators forwarded the woman's aliases, dental records, and other information to Interpol and to police agencies in North Africa and the Middle East, along with a request that these agencies check their records for any matches.

> *Each of the agencies gave the same response: no matches were found in their records. The mystery woman was a ghost.*

The woman's dental records were even published in dental journals, along with a write-up of the case, in the hope that the information might jog the memory of the woman's dentist and prompt them to come forward. But to date no dentist has.

CAUSE(S) OF DEATH

Even the autopsy results failed to answer as many questions as the investigators hoped. The cause of death, the medical examiner found, was "assumed to be a combination of poisoning from the sedative-hypnotic drug Fenemal [a barbiturate] and carbon monoxide. The injuries inflicted by fire may have been a contributing cause."

In addition to the dissolved Fenemal in the woman's bloodstream, the medical examiner found undigested Fenemal pills in the woman's stomach, indicating that she took more than one dose of the drug in the hours leading up to her death. That seemed to point toward suicide, and in the end that was what Bergen chief of police Asbjørn Bryhn concluded. One possible scenario was that the woman hiked up to the remote site, drank the liquor she had with her, then started the fire and began burning her belongings, including one or more of her passports. At some point she took her last dose of Fenemal. Then as the drug and the alcohol took effect, and before she lost consciousness entirely, she threw herself into the fire in a last, desperate attempt to conceal her identity from the world.

That's what the chief of police concluded, but others who investigated the case disagreed. They believed the Isdal woman was murdered. Was it suicide or murder? She may be the only person who knew for sure.

STILL COLD

And there the trail goes cold. More than 40 years later, the woman's identity and her nationality are still unknown. If she was indeed a spy, as some suspect, the end of the Cold War in the early 1990s offered the prospect that when the secret archives of the former Soviet Union and its allies (East Germany, Poland, and Czechoslovakia) were opened, the identity of the Isdal woman might finally become known. But that was more than 25 years ago, and the woman's identity is still a mystery. A sample of the woman's DNA was taken from one of her teeth in 2016, but to date that, too, has failed to yield any results.

FAREWELL...FOR NOW

In February 1971, four months after the Isdal woman's body was discovered, she was given a Catholic funeral mass and laid to rest in Bergen's Møllendal cemetery. Eighteen members of the Bergen police department were present at the funeral; they were the only mourners. The funeral mass and the graveside service were photographed by the department's crime scene photographer, while another officer took careful notes and used them to prepare a written report describing the services in detail.

The photos and the report were filed away at the Bergen police department in 1971, and they remain there to this day—not as part of the death investigation, but rather as a gesture of condolence to the Isdal woman's family. If her identity ever becomes known and her next of kin are located, they will be presented with the photographs of the funeral and the written description of the funeral services as a memento of their loved one.

And because the Isdal woman was buried in a special zinc coffin instead of one made of wood, if her family decides to have her reburied in the country of her birth, that will still be possible even many decades from now. The zinc coffin will not decompose in the soil.

The only thing missing from the grave site in Møllendal cemetery is a headstone: since the woman's identity and date of birth are not known, all that can be written on the headstone is the date on which she met her end. The hope is that one day her identity will be discovered and she will be given a proper headstone, so that people will finally know her name.

In case of a major ecological disaster, a massive "Doomsday Vault" of seeds was stored...

SURVIVAL STORIES

Never underestimate the power of the human spirit.

BURIED ALIVE

Around midday on April 25, 2015, Rishi Khanal was on the second floor of a seven-story hotel in Kathmandu, Nepal, when the building started shaking violently. The next thing the 27-year-old man knew, he was trapped in complete darkness beneath several tons of rubble. He tried moving, but something was crushing his leg. So he tried yelling, but no one could hear him. Minutes passed, then hours. Then days. He could smell dead people all around him. "I was certain I was going to die," Khanal later told ABC News. But even so, he didn't give up. He "fed" himself with the only sustenance he could get: his own urine. After 82 long hours, a French rescue team finally heard him banging on rocks and started digging as fast as they could. The 7.8-magnitude earthquake killed more than 8,000 people, but Khanal beat the odds and made it out alive.

DOWN IN THE DUMPS

Yang Hsieh, a 28-year-old construction worker in China's Hunan province, was the last one at the job site when he accidentally took a step in the wrong direction and fell over a ledge. When he hit the ground 65 feet below, both of his arms and legs were broken, as was his phone. He'd landed in a dark pit deep in the bowels of the building project, so no one could see him or hear his cries for help. When Yang didn't show up for work the next day, his fellow workers assumed he'd found a new job and changed his phone number. But Yang was right underneath them the whole time...for six days. On the seventh day, a woman walking her dog heard his faint cries and discovered Yang barely clinging to life. He was taken to a hospital, where he was expected to make a full recovery. When asked how he managed to not die of thirst, Yang confessed, "I had to drink my own urine for six days to stop myself dehydrating."

THE MAD ADDER

Teenage brothers Brock and Josh Leach (14 and 16, respectively) were exploring the top of a seaside cliff in Cornwall, England, in July 2015 when Brock slipped and fell 100 feet down. He hit several rocky outcroppings before landing hard on a ledge just above the churning sea. Hurt but alert, Brock knew he had to get to higher ground before the tide came in, but he'd fractured his pelvis and couldn't walk. So he reached up and grabbed a rock, hoping to pull himself up…and suddenly felt a stabbing pain in his right hand. Then he saw it: an adder—the only venomous species of snake in the UK—slithering away from him. Brock's hand started swelling to three times its normal size. A few minutes later, Josh arrived after scrambling down the cliff. He helped his brother get to a higher ledge, but Brock was in too much pain to move any farther. So Josh, who didn't have a mobile phone, climbed all the way back up to the top and started yelling for someone to call 9-9-9 (Britain's 9-1-1). It worked. Not long after, rescuers from the coast guard arrived and helicoptered Brock to the nearest hospital, where he was given antivenin. He made a full recovery.

FAR FROM PARADISE

Two-thousand feet. That's how far Ryan Montoya fell down Colorado's Pyramid Peak. The 23-year-old mountain climber from Paradise, California, was attempting a solo ascent in early 2017 when, shortly before summiting the 14,026-foot peak, he slipped and tumbled down the side of the mountain. "I couldn't believe I was conscious through the whole thing. Every time I hit something, I'm like, 'I'm still going, it's not over?'" When it was finally over, he was amazed to be alive, but he had a broken pelvis and a broken elbow. And he was still several miles from civilization. With food in his pack—but no phone—he spent the next two bitterly cold days slowly working his way back to civilization. Finally, a cyclist found him and called 9-1-1. In addition to the broken bones, Montoya had severe frostbite. He spent only ten days in the hospital, but was expected to require months of rehabilitation. If nothing else, Montoya emerged from his ordeal with some new-found wisdom: "Mountains don't care that you're there. You mess up, you take a big fall and pay the price."

*   *   *

LOVECRAFT VS. EINSTEIN

"Do you know that Einstein is wrong, and that certain objects and forces can move with a velocity greater than that of light? With proper aid I expect to go backward and forward in time, and actually see and feel the earth of remote past and future epochs. You can't imagine the degree to which those beings have carried science. There is nothing they can't do with the mind and body of living organisms."

—H. P. Lovecraft, from "The Whisperer in Darkness" (1931)

There are more captive tigers in Texas than there are wild tigers worldwide.

ANIMAL POOP

All animals poop. (And some of it is pretty weird.)

Parrotfish. These bright pink-and-green deep-sea dwellers' diets consist primarily of coral and other reef-based plant life. In scooping up all that coral and vegetation, parrotfish also tend to swallow a great deal of sand, which they can't digest. Because feces is made up of whatever an animal can't digest, parrotfish poop is made almost entirely of sand.

Wombats. If you're ever in the Australian outback and come across a small loaf of banana bread on the ground…well, that's not the Australian people being hospitable. And it's not banana bread—it's the poop of the Australian wombat, a small, furry marsupial that leaves square or rectangular poop. They poop to mark their territory. Leaving behind healthy feces tells other wombats in the area that they're looking to mate. The square shape means the poop stays where it was deposited.

Adélie penguins. This species of penguin has no need for a Bathroom Reader because they do their business extremely quickly. These seabirds projectile poop—they shoot it out at a high velocity and then get on with their day. Biologists say the birds developed this ability over time so that poop (and its included bacteria) doesn't cling to their tail feathers.

Hippopotamuses. Bad news: Hippos generate a lot of waste. Worse news: As they let it all out, their tails spin around like helicopter blades, flinging it every which way. Why would they do this? It's a mating ritual, letting other hippos know they're single and ready to mingle.

Vultures. Over the millennia, these scavengers have developed digestive bacteria that allows the birds to eat rotting flesh with no long-term damage. But a vulture that's tearing into dead animals can get their feet dirty and covered in germs. The solution: After meals, vultures poop on their own feet. The bacteria in the poop kills off any germs left on their feet. (And it cools them off.)

Capybaras. These forest-dwelling South American rodents push out two kinds of poop. One type is hard and dark, which capybaras leave to rot. And then there's the other kind, which is soft, green, and still packed with a fair amount of nutrition in little bits of undigested grass, bark, and fruit. They've got to get those nutrients back in, so capybaras eat their own soft, green poop.

Elvis got his first guitar for his 11th birthday. (He was hoping for a bike.)

A SEEDY EXPERIMENT

*If you've ever raised plants from seeds, you've probably had seeds left over at
the end of one season and used them again the next. Did you ever wonder
how long those old seeds might last? One scientist who wondered
that in 1879 started an experiment that continues to this day.*

GONE TO SEED

William James Beal was one of only a handful of research botanists in the
entire United States in 1871 when he joined the faculty of Michigan's State
Agricultural College (later Michigan State University). He devoted much of
his career to improving crop yields, and was one of the first scientists to develop
hybrid strains of corn that were more productive than purebred strains.

In the late 1870s, a group of farmers came to him with an interesting
question: if they weeded their fields every season and pulled the weeds before
they could produce new seeds, would there ever come a point where the weed
seeds remaining in the soil were too old to germinate and produce new plants?
This was no small question in the days before herbicides, and the only weed
killer available was manual labor supplied by farmers and farmhands. Have you
ever heard the expression "a tough row to hoe," meaning "a challenging task"? It
dates back to the days when weeds were killed by hacking at them with hoes.

GERM OF AN IDEA

Beal had no idea what the answer to the farmers' question was, but he wanted
to find out. So he devised an experiment in which he would preserve plant seeds
in a dormant state by burying them in bottles filled with sandy soil, then dig the
bottles up over time to see whether the dormant seeds would still be viable when
exposed to sunlight and water. He selected 21 different plant species—mostly
common weeds that grew on campus—and collected 50 seeds from each. As he
described in an article in the *Botanical Gazette* in 1915, he mixed the seeds

> in moderately moist sand, just as it was taken from three feet below
> the surface, where the land had never been plowed. The seeds…
> were well mixed with the sand and placed in a pint bottle, the bottle
> being filled and left uncorked, and placed with the mouth slanting
> downward so that water could not accumulate about the seeds.

Beal repeated the process 20 times, then buried the 20 bottles in a secret location on campus that he described as "a sandy knoll…running east and west." He also buried some black oak acorns and eastern black walnuts next to the bottles, bringing the number of plant species in the study to 23. But the acorns and walnuts decayed in the first few years and not much was learned from them.

RESULTS

Beal's plan: dig up one bottle every five years, then plant the seeds and see which ones germinated. He dug up his first bottle in the fall of 1884, and dug up five more bottles—in 1889, 1894, 1899, 1904, and 1909. He retired in 1910.

Beal's successor, Henry Darlington, dug up bottles from 1914 to 1960. Winter came early in 1919 and the ground was frozen so hard that Darlington couldn't dig up that year's bottle until the spring of 1920. (Every bottle after that was dug up in the spring as well.) That year Darlington also extended the length of the study by digging up the bottles every *ten* years instead of five. He did this because nine of the plant species were able to germinate nearly every time a bottle was dug up. He wanted to extend the study long enough to outlast even the hardiest of those nine.

Seven bottles were dug up from 1930 to 1990; the 15th was dug up in 2000 after 120 years in the soil. That year the head of Michigan State's Botany Department extended the study even further by digging up the rest of the bottles 20 years apart. The four bottles remaining will be dug up over the next 80 years.

UNEARTHED

By the time the 15th bottle was dug up, only three plant species were still able to germinate. *Verbascum blattaria*, a common weed more popularly known as moth mullein, had 23 seeds out of 50 that grew into normal plants. Only three seeds of *Verbascum speciosum* (showy mullein) could still germinate, and just a single seed of *Malva rotundifola* (low mallow) grew into a viable plant. The remaining 18 plant species studied were no longer able to germinate.

If the remaining bottles continue to be dug up every 20 years, the last five will be dug up in 2020, 2040, 2060, and 2080, bringing the experiment to an end 200 years (plus a few months) after Dr. Beal first buried the bottles. The study will still be going after most people reading this have died, but the farmers who asked the question that inspired the experiment got their answer long ago: If you weed a field often enough, there may indeed come a time there are no more viable seeds and weeds no longer grow.

…But not in your lifetime.

A.K.A. PRINCE

Some famous musicians are as prolific as they are famous, and they make music under fake names. Here are some of those little-known rock star aliases.

BERNARD SHAKEY. If you've ever seen a Neil Young video or concert film that was directed by Bernard Shakey…it's actually Neil Young.

L'ANGELO MISTERIOSIO. Translation: "The Mysterious Angel." It's the name George Harrison used—for contractual reasons—when he played guitar on "Badge," a song he wrote with Eric Clapton, for Clapton's band Cream.

LARRY LUREX. While Queen was recording its first album in 1973, a producer named Geoffrey Cable recruited lead singer Freddie Mercury to sing on a pop song called "I Can Hear Music." Because Mercury already had a record deal, he used the fake name "Larry Lurex." (Mercury's birth name was Farrokh Bulsara.)

JOEY COCO. Prince wrote and produced songs for other musicians under a variety of fake names in the 1980s (including: Jamie Starr, Christopher, and Alexander Nevermind). In 1986 he wrote "You're My Love" for country star Kenny Rogers under the pseudonym Joey Coco.

DAVID JAY. David Bowie had several different personas over his career, including Ziggy Stardust and the Thin White Duke. But before he first hit it big in the late 1960s, he played in a bar band called the Konrads and performed under the name David Jay—a variation on Bowie's birth name, David Jones.

BERNARD WEBB. In 1964, the British pop duo Peter & Gordon scored a #1 hit with "A World Without Love," written by Paul McCartney. Was it a hit purely because of the Beatles connection? McCartney was curious, so two years later, he gave them another song, "Woman," credited to "Bernard Webb." The record was a top-20 hit. (It was widely known, however, that it was written by McCartney.)

PERCY THRILLINGTON. Apparently Paul McCartney really likes pseudonyms. In 1977, he released an album called *Thrillington*, consisting entirely of instrumental, easy-listening cover versions of songs from McCartney's 1971 album *Ram*. *Thrillington* was credited to Percy "Thrills" Thrillington, who press materials said was a British socialite. In the liner notes, McCartney is listed as a "friend" of Thrillington's. Also, those notes were credited to Clint Harrigan. Both Thrillington and Harrigan were actually McCartney.

ONE MOMENT IN TIME

These guys' pro sports careers were unexceptional
…except for that one big moment of glory.

DOUG WILLIAMS

Williams was a star quarterback at Grambling State University. He led Grambling to three straight conference championships and, in 1977, his junior year, led all college players in passing yards and touchdown passes. He was drafted by the Tampa Bay Buccaneers in 1978 and helped the Bucs reach the NFC Championship game in 1979. Williams was the lowest-paid starting quarterback in the league at the time, earning $120,000 a year, less than a lot of second-stringers. In 1982, he asked for $600,000 and didn't get it, so he left the NFL for the Oklahoma Outlaws of the new United States Football League. The Outlaws never had a winning season, and when the USFL folded in 1986, Williams was signed by the Washington Redskins as a backup. After outperforming starter Joe Schroeder in a handful of games, Williams was picked to lead the team in the 1987 Super Bowl, which the Redskins won 42-10 on the strength of four Williams touchdown passes. Williams, the first black quarterback to ever play in a Super Bowl, was named MVP. And that was pretty much it for Williams's career. He was plagued by injuries in the 1988 season, and was replaced by Mark Rypien. By 1989, Williams was out of the league for good.

CHARLIE ROBERTSON

In baseball, a perfect game is when one pitcher works all nine innings, and never allows a batter to reach first base. No hits, no walks, no hit batters, no errors. It's an incredibly difficult and rare achievement: only 23 perfect games have ever been thrown in the history of Major League Baseball. Several Hall of Famers threw one in their careers, including Cy Young, Catfish Hunter, and Sandy Koufax. And so did Charlie Robertson. He started out with the Chicago White Sox in 1919, got cut from the team, and returned to the Sox three years later. In 1922, in just his fourth overall start as a pitcher, Robertson threw a perfect game against Ty Cobb and the Detroit Tigers. It was essentially the only highlight of an otherwise brief, forgettable career. Robertson bounced around the big leagues, playing for the St. Louis Browns and the Boston Braves, but retired in 1928. His career record: 49 wins and 80 losses.

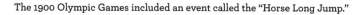

DUSTY RHODES

It's the dream of every little kid who ever played baseball in the backyard: hit a game-winning home run in the World Series. But Rhodes really did it. In the 1954 series, Rhodes's New York Giants faced the Cleveland Indians, and in game 1, in the bottom of the 10th inning with the score tied and two men on base, Rhodes came in to pinch-hit and walloped a pitch from Hall of Famer Bob Lemon out of the park. The Giants went on to sweep Cleveland in four straight games. It was the best moment of Rhodes's seven-year career, in which he had a batting average of .253 and hit 54 home runs in all.

LUKE HANCOCK

After playing at George Mason University in his first two years (2009–11) of college basketball, Hancock transferred to the University of Louisville, a basketball powerhouse. He was a decent player, averaging 7.7 points a game in his senior season (2012–13). But his play kept the team advancing through the 2013 NCAA Tournament, and he exploded for 20 points in the semifinals against Wichita State. A couple of days later in the title game against Michigan, Louisville was down by 12 points late in the first half…only to have Hancock put up four straight three-point shots to cut Michigan's lead to a single point by the end of the half. In the second half, Hancock sank one more three-pointer, which cemented a lead for Louisville, and they won, 82–76. Hancock had taken five three-point shots in the game and made them all. With a total of 22 points, he was named the tournament's most outstanding player, the first and only reserve player ever to win the honor. Despite that remarkable performance, no NBA team drafted Hancock. In 2014, he signed with a professional team in Greece, but played in only six games before he suffered a career-ending calf muscle tear. He now works as a financial advisor in Louisville.

*　　*　　*

ASK THE EXPERTS

Question: *Why is red wine traditionally paired with beef and white wine is served with chicken or fish?*
Answer: Red wine is generally high in tannins, a naturally occurring compound in wine that can taste bitter or make the mouth feel dry. Experts say tannins offset the richness and fattiness of red meat. White wines, meanwhile, are more acidic than reds. In the same way that a squirt of acidic lemon juice "brightens" a chicken or fish dish, so too does the white wine brighten the meal.

The Janko piano keyboard has four rows and 264 keys. A standard piano has 88 keys in one row.

WHAT THE PHRASE?

Some quick phrase origins to pass the time.

ONE FOOT IN THE GRAVE

Today, this phrase is used to describe someone who is very old, but when it originated in 17th-century England, it had a slightly different meaning: someone who is trapped by death, with no chance of escape. That's because "foot" in this sense was a verb that meant "to catch by the foot."

GREAT SCOTT!

The expression probably originated as a euphemism for "Great God." But it came to prominence in the 1850s when U.S. general Winfield Scott—an imposing figure who stood 6 feet 5 inches tall and weighed 300 pounds—ran for president. When people saw him, they actually referred to him as "Great Scott!"

WHITE-COLLAR CRIME

An influential criminologist named Edwin Sutherland coined this term in a 1939 speech to the American Sociological Society. He described it as a "crime committed by a person of respectability and high social status in the course of his occupation."

> **FLAVOR OF THE MONTH.** *In the 1930s and '40s, American ice-cream companies advertised different flavors of the month. The phrase eventually came to describe a celebrity who quickly rises to stardom and is replaced soon after.*

RUN AMOK

The Amock were Javanese and Malay warriors infamous for their frenzied and brutal attacks. While exploring Asia in 1772, Captain James Cook wrote about them, and in the process coined the phrase: "To run amok is to get drunk with opium...sally forth from the house, kill the person or persons supposed to have injured the Amock, and any other person that attempts to impede his passage."

First movie ever reviewed professionally by Roger Ebert: *Galia*, a 1967 French "new wave" film.

KEEP AT BAY

Ever heard the phrase that describes hound dogs "baying at the moon"? That's where this definition of "bay" comes from. In the 12th century, when English hunting dogs cornered their prey, they would bay, or howl, at it. If the animal turned and stood its ground, it would "keep the dogs at bay."

STOOL PIGEON

People used to eat pigeons. To catch them, live decoy birds were sometimes used. The hunter would tie a long string from the decoy to a stool. Its cooing would attract some of its feathered friends, who would show up…and become meals themselves. In the 1800s the phrase was transferred from birds to criminal decoys who rat on their friends.

CURIOSITY KILLED THE CAT

English playwright Ben Jonson wrote in a 1598 play that "care'll kill a Cat." In this case, "care" meant "worry." The phrase remained unchanged until the late 19th century, when "curiosity" replaced "care" and gave the expression its modern meaning.

RESTING ON ONE'S LAURELS

Because the Greek god Apollo wore a crown of laurel leaves, that country's greatest athletes and generals were awarded laurel wreaths. Those who won several awards could bask in their past glory and "rest on their laurels." (This is where the word "laureate" comes from as well.)

A SKELETON IN THE CLOSET

Even in the 19th century, keeping a dead body in your home was considered weird. But cadavers were highly sought after by doctors who studied anatomy, and they were hard to get (which is why Igor had to resort to grave digging). So the docs who were able to obtain skeletons would keep them hidden in a closet. The phrase came to mean any big secret that is hidden away.

*　　*　　*

"You're only given a little spark of madness. You mustn't lose it."

—Robin Williams

French mime Marcel Marceau was a member of the Resistance during WWII. He used…

FLYING IN STYLE

Some airlines offer more than a bag of nuts and a can of soda (in first class, of course).

PERSONAL BAR. First-class passengers on Etihad Airways (United Arab Emirates) who want a cocktail don't have to wait for the flight attendant to come down the aisle with the cart. On these flights, every first-class seat is equipped with a personal minibar. They also get a 24-inch personal TV.

MASSAGES. On Air Malta's short flights from London to its home base (Malta), passengers are offered in-flight massage treatments. While soothing music is played, travelers enjoy a stress-relieving rubdown of their feet, neck, and hands.

FANCY LINENS. Many airlines offer beds in first- or business-class on long-haul flights. Qatar Airways is among them, but their beds have sheets made by Frette Linens, with a thread count of 300 to 500 and a cost of more than $1,000 a set.

SUITES. On Lufthansa's 747 flights, first-class passengers get a "suite" consisting of two seats. One of the seats is a regular, reclining seat on the aisle, and the other is a bed by the window. Other features: a personal closet and a bouquet of red roses.

BETTER AIR. Lufthansa also installed humidifiers in the first-class sections of some planes. The humidity promises to "improve sleep, reduce jet lag, and alleviate dehydration of the eyes."

SHOWERS. Emirates Air has showers on some of its international flights. The water is hot, and the pressure is high, but to make sure there's enough to go around, the showers last for a maximum of five minutes. When they're done, passengers get to enjoy a private bathroom and dry off with an extra-thick towel.

FANCY CARS. Members of Delta Airlines' first-class loyalty program flying out of New York, Atlanta, Los Angeles, and Minneapolis can be chauffeured to the gate in a Porsche.

WINE. On the British Airways flight from London to Los Angeles, first-class passengers can select from a 10-page list of expensive wines and champagnes.

BUTLERS. Etihad offers a "Residence Package"—a private three-room suite, including a bedroom, living room, and bathroom. Those who pay for the privilege also receive in-flight service from a personal butler.

...pantomime to keep children quiet while leading them to safety in Switzerland or Spain.

QUEEN OF THE DRESS EXTRAS

She could be the most famous Hollywood actress you've never heard of.

SEND FLOWERS

If you were asked who appeared in the most films nominated for Best Oscar, who would you guess? Meryl Streep? Leonardo DiCaprio? Jack Nicholson? Katharine Hepburn? The answer is Bess Flowers. Between 1923 and 1964, she appeared in more than 350 films, including 23 that were nominated for the Academy Award for Best Picture.

How did she manage to end up in so many classic movies? When a film required a stunning woman draped in furs at a nightclub, or a bejeweled patron attending the opera, Bess Flowers was the go-to extra. She was not only tall and elegant, she owned an extensive wardrobe of ball gowns, furs, cocktail dresses, and jewelry, which automatically bumped her into the elite category of "dress extra." Designers liked dress extras because it cut the cost of renting or building a costume, and Flowers became known as "Queen of the Hollywood Dress Extras."

NOT JUST ANOTHER FACE IN THE CROWD

Flowers's platinum hair was generally swept up in curls on top of her head. Her distinctive air of high society made directors like Alfred Hitchcock, Frank Capra, Gregory La Cava, and John Ford ask for her by name and quite often even give her a line of dialogue, greeting the star or one of the principal players at a club or party, or at the theater. She appeared in *Meet John Doe* (1941), *Double Indemnity* (1944), *Mildred Pierce* (1945), *The Big Sleep* (1946), *A Place in the Sun* (1951), *Rear Window* (1954), and five that won Best Picture: *It Happened One Night* (1934), *You Can't Take It with You* (1938), *All About Eve* (1950), *The Greatest Show on Earth* (1952), and *Around the World in Eighty Days* (1956). She also had the distinction of appearing in 25 Three Stooges films.

By the time Flowers died in 1984 at that age of 85, she had appeared in so many movies that she developed a cult following. In the 1970s, members of film societies began to look for her and cheer when she strolled across the screen. This pleased Flowers, who told entertainment historian Anthony Slide, "I wanted to be an individual always, never one of the horde."

For a wine to be kosher, the grape vines must be at least 4 years old and left unharvested every 7th year.

WORLD WAR II SECRET: OPERATION VEGETARIAN

How deadly could a secret program code-named "Operation Vegetarian" be?
So deadly that had it ever been implemented, millions would have died and
thousands of square miles of European soil might still be unoccupied today.

ALONE

On September 1, 1939, Adolf Hitler set World War II in motion when he invaded Poland. Germany attacked from the west, and 16 days later the Soviet dictator Joseph Stalin, by secret agreement with Hitler, invaded from the east. Poland kept fighting…but it never had a chance. When Poland surrendered on October 6, it disappeared from the map, its territory carved up and incorporated into Germany and the USSR.

The dismemberment of Poland was but the first in a series of rapid-fire victories by the Nazis: On April 9, 1940, Germany invaded both Denmark, which fell that same day, and Norway, which fell on June 10. By then Hitler had also invaded Belgium, which surrendered after 18 days; Luxembourg, which fell after one day; the Netherlands, which held out for five; and even mighty France, which capitulated on June 22, after just five weeks of fighting.

Then on July 10, Hitler began bombing England in preparation for Operation Sea Lion, his planned invasion of the British Isles. The British faced the threat almost entirely alone: by then every other country in western Europe had either fallen to Germany, was allied with it, or had declared its neutrality in the hope of avoiding Hitler's wrath. Even the United States was officially neutral, and President Franklin D. Roosevelt was under tremendous pressure from isolationists to keep America out of the war. What little aid he was able to send to Great Britain was menaced by German U-boats patrolling the North Atlantic.

DESPERATE MEASURES

With the threat of invasion looming, Prime Minister Winston Churchill issued new orders to Porton Down, a secret military facility in southern England set up during World War I to study the use of poison gas as a military weapon. The facility was created after the Germans introduced chlorine gas to the battlefield in 1915, and work at Porton Down had continued ever since. Now Churchill gave it a new project: find a way to use the deadly disease anthrax in battle. It was out of this crash germ-warfare program that Operation Vegetarian was born.

NATURAL DISASTER

Anthrax is the name of a disease caused by the bacterium *Bacillus anthracis*, which lives in soil. If the seedlike spores of the bacteria enter a cut in a person's skin (a form of the disease known as cutaneous anthrax), the result is a serious infection whose most distinctive feature is a coal-black scab. That's how anthrax gets its name—*anthrakis* is the Greek word for coal. When left untreated, cutaneous anthrax is deadly about 20 percent of the time.

> *When the spores are eaten or inhaled, the danger is far greater: gastrointestinal anthrax kills animals or people who eat the spores about 60 percent of the time, and inhalational anthrax kills its victims about 95 percent of the time. (Modern treatments have cut the mortality rates considerably, but those treatments weren't available in the 1930s.)*

DEATH FROM THE SKY

When anthrax spores are eaten by grazing livestock, even if the infected animals don't die, their meat cannot be eaten because it will spread the disease to anyone or anything that consumes it. This was what the scientists at Porton Down decided to focus on: they came up with a plan to disrupt the German meat supply by wiping out vast herds of grazing cattle across northern Germany. They would accomplish this by dropping anthrax-tainted "cattle cakes" (concentrated dietary supplements that are typically fed to cattle) from Royal Air Force bombers over the pastures and grazing fields. Any cattle that ate the cakes would die within a few days, as would many thousands—or perhaps even millions—of Germans who came in contact with the cattle or the cakes. Once a portion of the German meat supply was shown to be poisoned, the thinking at Porton Down went, the country's entire meat supply would become suspect. Terrified Germans would abstain from eating meat entirely (hence the name Operation Vegetarian) making wartime food shortages—and German morale—even worse.

BY THE BOXFUL

Officials at Porton Down placed an order with a supplier for enough raw materials to make for five million cakes. Then it contracted a London toilet soap manufacturer to cut the material into individual cakes about an inch in diameter and weighing less than an ounce apiece. Finally, Porton Down hired a dozen soap makers, all of them women, to come to the secret facility and inject the cattle cakes with anthrax spores supplied by the Ministry of Agriculture, which produced them in a lab.

By the spring of 1944 all five million cakes had been manufactured and pumped full of anthrax; the modified RAF bombers that would drop them over northern Germany were ready as well. Porton Down's planners estimated that it would take about 18 minutes for the bombers to reach their targets over Germany. Upon arrival they would drop 400 cakes every two minutes in a bombing run that lasted 20 minutes, dropping 4,000 cakes in all. If 12 bombers were used in the mission, they'd drop 48,000 cattle cakes. When they finished, most of the grazing land in northern Germany would be contaminated with anthrax. And there would be millions of cattle cakes left over for future bombing runs in other parts of Germany.

"The cattle must be caught in the open grazing fields when lush spring grass is on the wane. Trials have shown that these tablets are found and consumed by the cattle in a very short time," Dr. Paul Fildes, director of Porton Down's biology department, observed.

And because the anthrax spores can remain viable in the soil for a century or more, the poisoned land would remain uninhabitable for generations. No cattle would be able to graze there, nor would humans be able to step foot there for many decades to come.

READY, SET...

All that remained was for Winston Churchill to give the order for Operation Vegetarian to proceed.

The order never came. Why not? Because by then the war had turned decisively against Germany. Operation Sea Lion, Hitler's plan for a land invasion of England, was never put into effect: British fighters shot so many German planes out of the sky in the run-up to the invasion that Hitler was forced to put it aside. Instead, he set his sights on Russia, and invaded his former ally in a sneak attack on June 22, 1941.

After months of steady progress, by October 1941 the Nazi invasion of Russia began to bog down, and Hitler failed to take Moscow before winter set in. Instead of finding shelter in the city, his ill-equipped, poorly clothed troops suffered through the brutal Russian winter in the open countryside, and many thousands died or were incapacitated by frostbite. Moscow never did fall, and by spring the Russians had regrouped and began to push back against the Germans.

1970s antismoking device: a fake pack of cigarettes that "coughed" when the smoker picked it up.

Then on December 7, 1941, Japan bombed Pearl Harbor, bringing the United States into the war. His hands no longer tied by the isolationists, President Roosevelt could now back Great Britain with all of the military might at his command.

When Hitler's attempt to take the city of Stalingrad failed in February 1943, the German advance against Russia was halted completely. For the rest of the war, the Russians pushed the Nazis relentlessly back toward Germany. The Allied invasion of Italy followed in July 1943; then on D-Day, June 6, 1944, the long-awaited Allied invasion of France began.

THANKS, BUT NO THANKS

With Great Britain's survival no longer in question and the defeat of Germany just a matter of time, in the spring of 1944 Winston Churchill opted against putting Operation Vegetarian into action. At the war's end in 1945, all five million cattle cakes were fed into an incinerator at Porton Down and destroyed.

Any doubts as to just how deadly an anthrax attack over thousands of square miles might have been were laid to rest in the one place where the British actually did use anthrax during the war: Gruinard Island, a 520-acre island less than a mile off the coast of northwest Scotland. Early in the war, the British requisitioned the island, and in 1942 and 1943 they used it as a test site for anthrax bombs. In one such test, 60 sheep were tethered in a line and an anthrax bomb was detonated upwind from them. The sheep inhaled the anthrax spores, and within a few days all of them were dead.

If you had to dispose of 60 anthrax-infected sheep without getting yourself killed in the process, how would you do it? The Porton Down scientists dumped them at the bottom of a cliff on the island, then buried them (or so they hoped) by dynamiting the cliff. But one of the sheep was blown into the water and floated to the Scottish mainland, where it washed ashore on a beach. There it was partially eaten by a dog. The dog died, but not before spreading anthrax to seven cows, two horses, three cats, and 50 more sheep, all of whom died as well. Quick payments to the farmers who owned the animals hushed up the incident, and it wasn't until the 1980s that the truth about what killed their dog, cows, horses, cats, and sheep finally became known.

KEEP OUT

When the British government requisitioned Gruinard Island at the start of the war, it planned to return the island to its owners once the war was over and the anthrax spores were removed. But several attempts to clean the spores failed, and in 1946 the government gave up. It bought the island outright and ordered the public to stay away. To drive the message home, it posted scary signs on Gruinard's beaches that read:

```
THIS ISLAND IS GOVERNMENT PROPERTY UNDER EXPERIMENT
THE GROUND IS CONTAMINATED WITH ANTHRAX AND DANGEROUS
          LANDING IS PROHIBITED BY ORDER 1987
```

MAYBE SOMEDAY

The government promised to sell the island back to its owners for £500 (about $620 today) if a way to render it "fit for habitation by man and beast" was ever found. For decades afterward, Porton Down scientists visited the island regularly and took soil samples to see if the anthrax spores were still there. They were.

Finally in the 1980s, the government gave up on waiting for the spores to disappear naturally. It hauled away tons of the most contaminated topsoil and injected 280 tons of formaldehyde into the island's groundwater to see if that would kill the remaining spores. They also reintroduced sheep to the island. In 1990, when those sheep failed to die and fresh soil samples showed no signs of anthrax, the scary signs were removed and the descendants of the original owners were permitted to buy the island back for £500, just as promised.

STAY TUNED

So is that the end of the story? The British government believes (and certainly hopes) so, but the Ministry of Defence has set up a fund to compensate any future victims of anthrax on Gruinard Island…just in case.

*   *   *

WORDS TO LIVE BY

"I will not walk backward in life."
—J. R. R. Tolkien

"Only those who risk going too far can find out how far one can go."
—T. S. Eliot

"It always seems impossible until it's done."
—Nelson Mandela

The kākāpō parrot of New Zealand is the only flightless, nocturnal parrot. At 8 lb., it's also the heaviest.

UNCLE JOHN'S PAGE OF WEIRD FLAVORS

All of the following are (or were) real flavors of real foods from around the world.

22 JAPANESE ICE CREAM FLAVORS

Sake

Egg

Miso and Ramen

Python

Jellyfish

Beer

Chicken Wing

Stew

Caviar

Tomato Cherry

Corn and Cheese

Arrowroot

Coffee Jelly

Scallops

Tofu

Fish

Sea Urchin

Whitebait

Pickle

Cheese Risotto

Yogurt

Smoked Salmon

8 WEIRD JELL-O FLAVORS

Mixed Vegetable

Maple Syrup

Seasoned Tomato

Triple Chocolate

Watermelon Candy

Celery

Cola

Italian Salad

17 WEIRD CHEWING GUM FLAVORS

Bacon

TV Dinner

Man Smell

Popcorn and Cola

Egg Nog

Ghost Pepper

Wasabi

Frank and Beans

Absinthe

Mint Chardonnay

Cocktail Wienies

Pickle

Thanksgiving Dinner

Roast Beef

Cactus

Ballpark (Hot Dogs, Peanuts, and Beer)

Foie Gras

14 CANADIAN POTATO CHIP FLAVORS

Grilled Cheese and Ketchup

Cinnamon Bun

Intense Pickle

Burger

Maple Bacon

Roast Chicken

Fries 'n Gravy

Poutine

Ketchup Doritos

Jaimaican Jerk Chicken

Cowboy BBQ Beans

Tzatziki

Pierogi

Butter Chicken

High cost of dying: The average cost of a funeral in Japan is $23,000, the most anywhere in the world.

OOPS!

It's always nice to hear about people screwing up even more than you are. So go ahead and feel superior for a few moments.

STARING CONTEST

Here's a fun fact about snakes, courtesy of the Sutton Police Department in London: "They can stay still for a long time." As a matter of fact, the venomous adder that several Sutton cops were attempting to apprehend in a residential yard stayed still—in the coiled strike position—for an entire hour! And then a neighbor informed the cops that the "snake" was actually a stone garden ornament.

I'VE MADE A TINY MISTAKE

In 2014 South African artist and engineer Jony Hurwitz, 45, created a series of "nano-sculptures"—the smallest depictions of the human form ever created. Example: an intricate nanosculpture of a nude dancer is dwarfed by the eye of a needle. Hurwitz, who describes his craft as "art created with quantum physics," took 10 months to complete the first set of tiny figures with a painstaking process that utilizes 3-D printing technology. But the figures are so tiny that they can only be photographed through a powerful electron microscope. He brought his work to a lab that could take the photos in March 2015, and all was going well until the technician made a technical adjustment...and suddenly he couldn't find the nano-statue. When Hurwitz looked through the microscope's lens he "noticed there was a fingerprint exactly where the sculptures used to be." Hurwitz said "and I was like, 'Man, you have just destroyed the smallest art pieces ever made!' I freaked out." Fortunately, he got some good photos before the mishap, but those pieces are gone forever.

ONE MAN'S TRASH...

One morning in 2015, the cleaning crew at a modern art gallery in Italy was told to clear up all of the empty bottles, cups, and confetti in the foyer, leftovers from a party the night before. The cleaners did as they were told...and then some. In addition to cleaning up the empty bottles, cups, and confetti from the foyer, they inadvertently "cleaned up" an art exhibit called "We Were Going to Dance Tonight" by Italian artists Goldschmied & Chiari that consisted of...empty

Stieg Larsson, who wrote *The Girl with the Dragon Tattoo,* based his main character on what Pippi Longstocking would be like as an adult.

bottles, cups, and confetti (to "satirize the lavish parties and excesses of the Italian political classes during the 1980s"). After their mistake was discovered, the confused cleaners had to retrieve all of the garbage from the bins and then reconstruct the exhibit using photographs. Said one of the cleaners: "It didn't look like art to me."

DUH VINCI

One Leonardo is known as a renaissance man; the other Leonardo painted the *Mona Lisa*. Confused? So was Shepard Smith of Fox News when he made this promo announcement in 2015: "Coming up next: an update from scientists trying to identify the model for Leonardo DiCaprio's *Mona Lisa*."

WATCH OUT FOR STALKERS!

A concerned citizen called police in Germany to report a dozen men walking along a country road carrying big sticks and sharp knives. Six squad cars rushed out to intercept the…asparagus harvesters. (They were on a lunch break walking to their cars—with their tools in hand.)

THE TYPO HEARD 'ROUND THE WORLD

When John Podesta, Hillary Clinton's 2016 presidential campaign chairman, received an urgent email that said his account had been hacked, and that he needed to change his password immediately, he figured it was a phishing scam. Just to be sure, though, Podesta had an aide send the email to a tech-savvy staffer named Charles Delavan, who looked at it and wrote back, "This is a legitimate email. John needs to change his password immediately." When Podesta read the reply, he interpreted it to mean that it was okay for him to click the link provided in the email to change his password. But that's not what Delavan meant; he'd intended to type the word "illegitimate"—as in "This is an illegitimate email"—meaning that Podesta should have deleted the email and then changed his password the normal way. What happened next has been widely cited as one of the fatal blows to Clinton's failed campaign: "With another click," wrote the *New York Times*: "a decade of emails that Mr. Podesta maintained in his Gmail account—a total of about 60,000—were unlocked for the Russian hackers."

*   *   *

"Comedy's a dead art form. Now tragedy, that's funny." **—Bender, *Futurama***

BOMBS AWAY!

*Nuclear weapons have been a part of the U.S. arsenal since 1945,
and in all that time none have ever been triggered by accident.
But that doesn't mean there haven't been a few mishaps.*

Missing: Two plutonium "capsules" that were being flown from MacDill Air Force Base in Florida to Ben Guerir Air Base in Morocco on March 10, 1956.

Details: Nuclear bombs of the 1950s were designed so that their plutonium cores, or "capsules," could be kept separate from the rest of the bomb as a safety measure. Without the rest of the bomb to set it off, the core couldn't trigger a nuclear explosion. And without the core, even if the rest of the bomb (which contained TNT) was detonated by accident, the explosion wouldn't have been much worse than an ordinary bomb.

In this instance, two bomb cores—but not the bombs themselves—were aboard a U.S. Air Force B-47 somewhere over the Mediterranean. When the plane descended to 14,000 feet to meet up with an air tanker for in-flight refueling, it entered a cloud formation…and disappeared. The plane is presumed to have crashed into the sea, killing the three crew members, but an exhaustive search failed to find any trace of the wreckage. The bomb cores were never recovered, and are presumed to be somewhere on the bottom of the Mediterranean.

Dropped: A 10-megaton Mark-17 hydrogen bomb, one of the most powerful thermonuclear weapons ever made by the United States, carried aboard a U.S. Air Force B-36 Peacemaker on May 22, 1957.

Details: During the flight, a single locking pin was used to secure the Mark-17 and prevent it from being dropped from the plane by accident. But the pin was removed for takeoffs and landings, so that the bomb could be jettisoned in an emergency. On that morning, the B-36 was on its final approach to New Mexico's Kirtland Air Force Base. According to one version of events, crew member first Lieutenant Bob Carp had just finished removing the locking pin when the B-36 hit some turbulence and Carp lost his balance. He reached for the nearest thing he could grab to steady himself—the manual release lever for the bomb—and pulled it. With the locking pin removed, the bomb slipped free of the bomb rack, crashed through the bomb bay doors, and fell to the earth some 2,000 feet below. (Carp claimed a snagged safety line was to blame for releasing the bomb.) The plutonium capsule was removed from the bomb at the time, so there was no danger of a nuclear explosion. But when the bomb hit the ground the TNT did detonate, creating a crater 12 feet deep and 25 feet across, and killing a cow. The force of the blast was such that pieces of the bomb (and pieces of the cow) were scattered more than a mile away.

Déjà BOOM!: Ten months later, on March 11, 1958, an unarmed 30-kiloton atom bomb fell from another U.S. Air Force bomber, this time a B-47, when the locking pin jammed in the unlocked position and crew member Bruce Kulka was sent back to the bomb bay to insert the pin by hand. Kulka was a navigator, not a bombardier, and had no idea where the pin was. While looking for it, he tried to pull himself up onto the bomb…by yanking on a handle that turned out to be the manual release lever. The bomb crashed through the bomb bay doors and fell some 15,000 feet, landing in the yard of a Mars Bluff, South Carolina, man named Walter Gregg.

The bomb's TNT detonated on impact, destroying Gregg's home and leaving a 30-foot-deep bomb crater where his garden used to be. Gregg, his wife, his son, and three children who were playing in the yard at the time escaped with cuts and bruises. The only casualties were six of the family's chickens. A few months later the government paid Gregg $54,000 for his troubles, and the U.S. Air Force ordered that nuclear bombs remain locked to their bomb racks during all future takeoffs and landings.

Missing: A Mark 15 thermonuclear bomb being carried aboard a U.S. Air Force B-47 bomber on February 5, 1958.

Details: The bomber was participating in war games when it collided with an F-86 fighter plane in midair near Savannah, Georgia. The bomber's pilot made three attempts to land the damaged plane with the bomb aboard, but when those attempts failed, he jettisoned the bomb into the Atlantic Ocean rather than risk having it detonate during landing. The jet landed safely, and the bomb sank to the ocean floor several miles offshore from the mouth of the Savannah River. Teams of military divers searched for the bomb for nine weeks, but it was never found. The military wrote it off as "irretrievably lost," and treasure hunters have been searching for it ever since. (If they find it, they may get more than they bargained for: Though the U.S. Air Force has always maintained that the bomb's nuclear core had been removed before the flight, in 1966 Assistant Secretary of Defense W. J. Howard, testified before Congress that the missing bomb was "a complete weapon, a bomb with a nuclear capsule.")

Missing: A live B43 thermonuclear bomb on the aircraft carrier USS *Ticonderoga* on December 5, 1965.

Movie fact: The brief segment at the beginning of a film with the studio's logo is known as a "bumper."

Details: The bomb was aboard an A-4E Skyhawk fighter jet when the *Ticonderoga* was returning from combat operations in Vietnam and sailing in rough seas about 80 miles off the coast of Japan. Some sailors were pushing the jet onto the carrier's elevator as the pilot, Lieutenant Douglas M. Webster, sat in the cockpit with his foot off the brake so that the aircraft could roll. When the *Ticonderoga* passed over a wave and its deck tilted, one of the sailors blew his whistle to signal Webster to apply the brakes. Webster didn't notice the tilting deck, didn't hear the whistle, and did not apply the brakes. His jet rolled right off the side of the elevator and disappeared into waters 16,000 feet deep. Neither he, the plane, nor the thermonuclear bomb were ever seen again.

Given the sensitivity of losing a nuclear weapon so close to Hiroshima and Nagasaki, and citing "the potential impacts upon visits of the *Ticonderoga* and other warships to foreign ports," the U.S. government covered up the incident for more than 20 years. It wasn't until 1981 that the Pentagon admitted that the bomb had been lost somewhere in international waters "more than 500 miles from land," and not until 1989 that they admitted it had actually been lost much closer to Japan.

Misplaced: Six live nuclear-armed cruise missiles loaded onto a B-52 bomber at North Dakota's Minot Air Force Base in 2007.

Details: In peacetime, standard operating procedure is for live nuclear warheads to be replaced with dummy warheads before cruise missiles are loaded onto aircraft. But on this occasion someone forgot to switch out the live warheads… and no one noticed. The cruise missiles remained—unguarded—aboard the aircraft at Minot Air Force Base for 36 hours; then the bomber flew to Barksdale Air Force Base in Louisiana with the bombs still aboard. Only then did a munitions team at Barksdale realize the warheads were real. Both the secretary of the U.S. Air Force, Michael Wynne, and the chief of staff of the U.S. Air Force, General T. Michael Moseley, were forced to resign from their posts following the incident.

*   *   *

FOOD FOR THOUGHT

"We think sometimes that poverty is only being hungry, naked and homeless. The poverty of being unwanted, unloved and uncared for is the greatest poverty. We must start in our own homes to remedy this kind of poverty."

—Mother Teresa

CHRISTMAS AT THE CLINIC

A few years ago we found some legitimate medical journals that took a break from their serious work and diagnosed the "ailments" of cartoon characters. Turns out they've "analyzed" some of our favorite Christmas characters, too.

Patient: "Mr. S. Claus"

Medical Issues: Unknown—it's unclear whether Santa has ever undergone a physical exam, let alone had one in recent years. For this reason, Dr. Y. Ingrid Goh of Toronto, Ontario, referred the patient to one Dr. Yull Tyde and asked that he be checked for signs of respiratory problems and thermal burns (from sliding up and down sooty, smoky chimneys, some of which are probably hot); frostbite and hypothermia (from traveling in an open vehicle in the middle of night in winter); indigestion, heartburn, obesity, and hyperglycemia (Santa binges on milk and cookies at every stop); and obsessive-compulsive disorder (he makes lists and checks them twice).

Physician's Notes: "It is highly recommended that Mr. Claus consider an alternative mode of transportation and adopt a healthier lifestyle…Please ask him to consider an alternative route of entrance…In addition, please ensure that his herd of reindeer has been vaccinated against rabies virus." (*Canadian Medical Association Journal*, December 2004)

> **RUDOLPH WAS CREATED BY COPYWRITER ROBERT MAY** *for a Christmas booklet that the Chicago department store Montgomery Ward was giving away to customers. Before he decided on Rudolph, May toyed with naming the reindeer Reginald, Rodney, Rolo, and Romeo.*

Patient: Rudolph the Red-Nosed Reindeer

Medical Issue: His nose is red.

Physicians' Notes: The article's authors, who hail from the Netherlands and Norway—or, as they put it, "near the North Pole"—were not able to examine Rudolph, so they took another route. They studied the nasal anatomy of two ordinary reindeer and then compared it to the nasal anatomy of five human volunteers. They found that the reindeers' noses had a 25 percent denser network of microvessels, or tiny blood vessels, than the human noses did, increasing the volume of red blood cells flowing through their noses. Why? Possibly to keep it warm in the winter cold. "We hypothesized that the infamous red nose of the most well-known of Santa Claus's reindeers, Rudolph, would originate from a rich vascular anatomy with a high functional density of microvessels...which help to protect it from freezing during sleigh rides and to regulate the temperature of the reindeer's brain, factors essential for flying reindeer pulling Santa Claus's sleigh under extreme temperatures." (*British Medical Journal*, December 2012)

Patient: The Grinch

Medical Issues: "Insomnia, loss of appetite, and irritability, which seemed to worsen during the winter season."

Physician's Notes: The Grinch was determined to be suffering from microcardia (his heart was two sizes too small). Diagnosis: Addison's disease, which causes weight loss and abnormal skin pigmentation (the Grinch is green), and congestive heart failure, which explains the organ's shrunken size. "The patient was treated with daily cortisol and aldosterone replacement therapy and significant improvement in both symptoms and appearance were noted." Also: "An absence of external genitalia was noted, but not discussed." (*Canadian Medical Association Journal*, December 2001)

*   *   *

MORE MOVIE INSPIRATIONS

Admiral Raddus: According to creature effects supervisor Neal Scanlan, the fishlike alien in 2016's *Rogue One: A Star Wars Story* was based on British Prime Minister Winston Churchill, "not only for Raddus's physical features, but also when it came to performing and expressing him through the actor."

Jaylah: The alien heroine in *Star Trek Beyond*, played by Algerian-born actress Sofia Boutella, was written with one person in mind: Jennifer Lawrence. According to co-writer Simon Pegg: "We wanted to create this very independent female, very resourceful character on the planet's surface. We didn't have a name for her, so we used to call her 'Jennifer Lawrence in *Winter's Bone.*'" (*Winter's Bone* is a 2010 drama in which Lawrence plays a tough mountain girl.) "It's a long name," added Simon, "so we started calling her J-Law, and then she became Jaylah."

In 1965 the U.S. government won an Academy Award for the documentary film *Nine from Little Rock*.

T.O.O.P. (TURTLES OUT OF PLACE)

Alex Haley once wrote, "Anytime you see a turtle up on top of a fence post, you know he had some help." These turtles sure ended up in some strange places…and they had help.

WHAT THE SHELL?

On a pretty day in May 2016, Nicole Bjanes was driving her Volkswagen Jetta at about 70 mph on Florida's Interstate 4 when all of a sudden something crashed through her windshield. As glass flew everywhere, Bjanes had to struggle to maintain control of the car and pull over on the shoulder. When she regained her wits, she was covered in glass, bleeding from her head, and there was a big hole in her windshield. And on the dashboard was an upside-down snapping turtle. Another motorist called 911, and police and EMTs arrived and treated Bjanes for minor cuts. And the snapping turtle? It was fine. A firefighter carried it to a nearby pond, where it swam away as if nothing had happened. So what *did* happen? According to a highway trooper, the reptile was crossing the road when another car clipped it and sent it flying through the air. After it smashed through Bjanes's windshield, it hit the front passenger seat and ricocheted back onto the dashboard. "I'm a lucky girl," said Bjanes. (The turtle was pretty lucky, too.)

CLYDE AND SEEK

It costs £15.98 ($20.65) to get into the Blue Planet Aquarium in Chester, Cheshire, England. So maybe the mom thought the entrance fee included a free turtle. That would explain why she allowed her young son to climb into a tank to steal an eight-pound female mud turtle named Clyde. CCTV footage shows the mother and son approaching the tank. A bit later, the pair are seen quickly leaving the place—only the boy is soaking wet, he isn't wearing his shirt, and it's obvious he's carrying Clyde inside it. Aquarium officials put out a desperate plea to the public to return the 10-year-old reptile, which is native to West Africa. "Without specialist care," warned zoo officials, "Clyde may die." (She requires very warm water and needs a heat lamp.) The story made international news, and a massive "turtle hunt" ensued. Finally, about 24 hours later, Clyde showed up back at the aquarium…in a plastic washtub full of cold water. It's still unclear who returned the turtle or why the little boy stole it in the first place, but Clyde was given immediate care and is expected to be okay.

NOT IN TEXAS ANYMORE

If you're from the South, you're probably familiar with alligator snapping turtles. The world's largest freshwater turtles, these goliaths can weigh up to 175 pounds. They have spiky shells and massive, spiky heads that make them look like dinosaurs. That's what the townspeople in Leninskoye, Siberia, thought they were dealing with in 2015 when an alligator snapping turtle showed up on the banks of the Amur River, more than 6,000 miles from its native habitat. Did it swim across the ocean? Was it a discarded pet? Were the Chinese breeding them across the river? No one knows for sure. Some fishermen managed to get the animal back into the water (which is much colder than alligator snappers are used to). There were rumors that the townsfolk ate the beast, but they deny it: "We did not do anything harmful," said one of them. "We pushed it into the water. It swam away, and was not turned into someone's soup."

ROCKING AND ROLLING

In 2008 a 10-year-old spurred tortoise named Arava was taken to a zoo in Israel with an unexplained disability. For reasons unknown, she couldn't move her hind legs. That made walking very difficult…and mating impossible. There happened to be a 10-year-old male there, and zookeepers *really* wanted them to mate. But Arava was lethargic (even for a turtle), and the male showed no interest. That all changed after zookeepers fitted the 55-pound tortoise with a "wheelchair"—two wheels mounted on a board that was strapped to the underside of her shell. After that, Arava zoomed all over her enclosure…and the male finally took notice. At last report, the two have been inseparable.

LOUD AND CLEAR

Boris the tortoise was missing. He'd knocked over his enclosure wall in his yard at the Horner household in southern England, and escaped with his female companion, Lily. She was found two hours later…but no Boris. The yard was surrounded by thick shrubbery, and Boris could have been hiding anywhere. Or he could have walked away. (Despite a reputation for being slow, tortoises can cover a lot of ground in a short time.) Then the Horners' three kids—Ella, Amy, and James—got an idea. They went on YouTube and found a video of two tortoises mating. The sounds these animals make when they're "doing it" can be quite loud and a little bit creepy (lots of breathing and high-pitched wheezing). "We went back outside," Pamela said, "played that, and lo and behold Boris appeared!" According to the Tortoise Group, this method actually works well: "Tortoises have good hearing and they recognize mating sounds. Don't we all?"

…response," which creates a tingling in the scalp, and a high that improves mood.

COINED BY COLERIDGE

Romantic-era poet Samuel Taylor Coleridge (1772–1834) is best known for two classics of English literature: "Kubla Khan" and "The Rime of the Ancient Mariner." He also wrote extensively about the English language and literature, especially Shakespeare's plays. Coleridge was a wordsmith, so when he couldn't find the right word to express what he meant…he made up a new one. Many of his inventions are still used today.

Word: Impact

Usage: "In any given perception there is a something which has been communicated to it by an impact, or an impression." (*Biographia Literaria*, 1817)

Details: The word had already been in use since the 1600s to describe a physical collision, but Coleridge originated the word's figurative sense, as in how one thing can have an intense effect on another thing.

Word: Actualize

Usage: "To make our Feelings, with their vital warmth, actualize our Reason." ("The Friend," 1809)

Details: In his poem, Coleridge turned the word "actual"—an adjective that means "real"—into a verb, which means "to reach a goal." In other words, to make it real.

Word: Intensify

Usage: "But the will itself by confining and intensifying the attention may arbitrarily give vividness or distinctness to any object whatsoever." (*Biographia Literaria*, 1817)

Details: In this book—a collection of his reflections on his own work—Coleridge explains why he created the word. It was because "render intense" didn't fit the meter of a poem he was trying to write.

Word: Narcissism

Usage: "Of course, I am glad to be able to correct my fears as far as public balls, concerts, and time-murder in narcissism." (An 1822 letter)

Details: Coleridge simply took the name of a character from Greek mythology and made it into an adjective. Upon seeing his reflection in a pond, Narcissus is so taken with his own beauty that he falls in love with himself, and continues to stare at his image until he dies.

Don't want to adopt a highway? You can also Adopt-a-Spot, Adopt-a-Stream, or Adopt-a-Street.

Word: Pessimism

Usage: " 'Tis almost as bad as Lovell's 'Farmhouse,' and that would be at least a thousand fathoms deep in the dead sea of pessimism." (A letter from 1794)

Details: He didn't create this one out of whole cloth. Coleridge adapted the French word *pessimisme*, which means "the worst."

Word: Bisexual

Usage: "The original Man, the Individual first created, was bi-sexual." (*Aids to Reflection*, 1824)

Details: Coleridge is the first person to have used this word in printed form, but he didn't use it the same way it's used today. He used it to theorize that humans are born with both masculine and feminine characteristics, and "learn" to act more male or more female. (The meaning of the word to describe someone with an attraction to both men and women wasn't coined until the 1890s.)

Word: Soulmate

Usage: "In order not to be miserable, you must have a Soul-mate as well as a House or a Yoke-mate." (An 1822 letter)

Details: The poet needed a word to describe an extremely profound and fated emotional connection. (He was, after all, a Romantic poet.)

Word: Selfless

Usage: "Ant tribes…that fold in their tiny flocks on the honeyed leaf, and the virgin sisters with the holy instincts of maternal love, detached and in selfless purity." ("Moral and Religious Aphorisms," 1825)

Details: Selfless is the opposite of selfish—a word coined 200 years earlier.

Phrase: Suspension of disbelief

Usage: "A semblance of truth sufficient to procure for these shadows of imagination that willing suspension of disbelief for the moment, which constitutes poetic faith." (*Biographia Literaria*, 1817)

Details: With this phrase, meaning "voluntary withholding of skepticism," Coleridge describes the very human behavior of turning off one's logic center in order to sit back and enjoy art or entertainment. Example: when you watch a movie, you know the film isn't real and you let it wash over you.

OTHER WORDS CREATED BY COLERIDGE: Artifact, appraisal, bipolar, cyclical, factual, fatalistic, marginalia, negativity, phenomenal, productivity, psychosomatic, realism, resurgence, statuesque, technique, and many more.

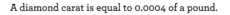

A diamond carat is equal to 0.0004 of a pound.

WORKS LIKE A CHARM

Almost everybody has a "lucky charm"—some kind of object they think brings them good luck. Here's why we think they work (even though they probably don't).

RABBIT'S FOOT. A spiritual tradition called *hoodoo* that combined African folk religions with Christianity developed in the 1700s. A lot of hoodoo rituals involved bones—human bones. When none were available, practitioners used the next best thing: animal bones, particularly from the rabbit, which appears in many African folk tales as a clever and strong character that always gets its way. Using a rabbit's bone (or foot) in these rituals could help ensure good luck. Loading it up with evil magic brought good luck: the bad luck (or evil) would simply ignore you, thinking you were on their side. The idea came to the New World with Africans who were kidnapped and sold into slavery.

FOUR-LEAF CLOVERS. A four-leaf clover is a mutated white clover—only one out of every 10,000 specimens have that fourth leaf. That rarity could be why they're considered lucky. Clover grows naturally in the British Isles, where there's a long history of its "magical" qualities. Ancient druids in Ireland thought that if four-leaf clovers were placed upon the sick, it would cure disease; they also hung them over their doorways to ward off evil spirits. In the Middle Ages, it was believed a four-leaf clover granted its holder the ability to spot fairies (so they could capture them). When missionaries converted the Irish to Christianity, they used both the three- and four-leaf clovers to teach religion. Each leaf of a three-leaf clover was said to represent God, Jesus, and the Holy Spirit. If a four-leaf clover was found, the extra leaf represented God's grace—in other words, good luck.

LUCKY PENNY. It doesn't seem like finding a penny on the street would be very lucky—pennies are virtually worthless today, and if it's been handled by humans and laying on the ground, it must be covered in germs. But at one time pennies were considered items of great value, and historians believe the idea that a found one was lucky dates to medieval Europe, when metals were relatively scarce. If someone were in possession of such a valuable commodity as a piece of copper, they wouldn't or couldn't just *lose* it. The belief developed that any found metal was a gift from God, placed on the ground for its intended recipient to find. (And you can't be any luckier than that.)

The ominous "da-da da-da" of the *Jaws* theme is played on a tuba.

HUM-DINGERS

On page 63 we told you the story of the Largs Hum, a mysterious phenomenon that has been disrupting life in a Scottish town for decades. Here are some other strange noises.

THE SAUSALITO HUM

Background: In the 1970s, houseboat owners living near Sausalito, north of San Francisco, began hearing a machinelike noise in the water that has been described as sounding like "the drone of a B-29 bomber or a giant electric shaver." Other people said it sounded like a foghorn or a Mongolian throat singer. Was the sound coming from nearby military installations? From Russian subs sneaking into the bay? From UFOs?

Mystery Solved? It took 10 years of complaining before the county health department finally recruited some volunteers to go out into the bay and look for the source of the sound. When one of the boats passed over a "hot spot" where the sound was especially loud, they dropped a net into the water...and pulled up 10 fish—10 plainfin midshipmen, also known as singing toadfish. They're called singing toadfish because at night the males croak like toads to attract females. "The fish congregate, and collectively, it's almost deafening," Thomas Niesen, a professor of marine biology, told the *Christian Science Monitor*.

THE WINDSOR HUM

Background: In 2010 residents of Windsor, Canada, just across the river from Detroit, Michigan, began complaining of a rumbling, pulsing hum that has been compared to rolling thunder, an idling diesel engine, and even "a car stereo subwoofer blasting Barry White's greatest hits." Some people thought the hum came from nearby salt mines; others blamed wind turbines, rail traffic, or perhaps a secret tunnel that the Canadian military was supposedly digging under the river. The hum grew worse over time, and by 2012, more than 20,000 Windsor residents were pleading with the government to do something about it.

Mystery Solved? Canadian officials traced the hum to nearby Zug Island, part of the city of River Rouge, on the Michigan side of the river. The island is home to a US Steel plant and other heavy industry. But that's as far as the Canadians got: they had no power to force the Americans to do anything about the problem. The entire area is an industrial zone. No one on the American side of the river lives close enough to the site to complain about the hum, so officials there feel no pressure to do anything about it. "We just don't have the money for this," River Rouge city attorney David Bower told the *Windsor Star* newspaper in 2012. "We are not going to pay for something that is for somebody else's benefit because this is not a problem affecting us." As of April 2016, Zug Island was still humming away.

THE KOKOMO HUM

Background: In 1999 residents of Kokomo, Indiana, reported hearing a hum that has been described as sounding like "a train yard or a jet on the tarmac in the distance." Sufferers blamed the noise for causing health problems as diverse as nosebleeds, dizziness, chronic fatigue, deteriorating vision, tremors, memory loss, anxiety, confusion, swollen joints, headaches, and diarrhea. Some people heard no sound but felt a vibration; others felt no vibration but heard a sound. Some experienced both. Many sufferers lived in households where they were the only ones who heard or felt anything. Leaving town caused the symptoms to abate; returning home brought them right back again.

Mystery Solved? After more than a hundred residents (out of a population of 47,000) complained, the city government budgeted $80,000 to track down the source of the noise. Or *sources*, as it turned out: The hum was traced to cooling tower fans at a DaimlerChrysler auto plant, and also to three air compressor intakes at a smelting plant. Both plants made modifications that brought relief to many sufferers…but others complained the hum was still there.

THE RUSSIAN WOODPECKER

Background: In July 1976, a band of shortwave radio frequencies were suddenly overpowered by strong radio interference that sounded like rapid-fire tapping. The interference, which was nicknamed "the woodpecker," disrupted commercial aviation communications and shortwave radio broadcasts. Anyone with a shortwave radio could tune to 10 Hz and hear the woodpecker for themselves. The signals were traced to the Soviet Union, prompting conspiracy theorists to speculate that they were part of a mind-control experiment—one that when turned up to full power might enslave the entire free world under the cruel yoke of godless communism.

Mystery Solved? The U.S. intelligence community thought otherwise: they concluded that the signals were part of a radar system designed to detect nuclear missiles launched against the Soviet Union. The radar system was shut down a few weeks after the fall of the Berlin Wall in 1989, and the woodpecker has not been heard since.

In 1990 the U.S. Air Force spent $100,000 on a study to determine whether
jet noise is harmful to pregnant horses. (The results were inconclusive.)

SAY IT, SISTER

These music stars don't mince words.

"I've done a lot of bad things. Use your imagination."
—Katy Perry

"Once you figure out what respect tastes like, it tastes better than attention."
–Pink

"There's a fine line between impressionistic and messy."
—Lady Gaga

"IT'S TOUGHER TO BE VULNERABLE THAN TO ACTUALLY BE TOUGH."
—Rihanna

"I'm not bossy. I'm the boss."
—Beyoncé

"A lot of people say you've got all the loving in the world when you walk out on stage. But hell, that applause don't help you any when you're lying in that bed at night being totally ignored."
—Patsy Cline

"If you like it, let it be, and if you don't, please do the same."
—Ani DiFranco

"After you make a fool of yourself a few hundred times, you learn what works."
—Gwen Stefani

"Silence speaks so much louder than screaming tantrums. Never give anyone an excuse to say that you're crazy."
—Taylor Swift

"I'm just trying to be the next Trisha Yearwood."
–Trisha Yearwood

Bill Haley's classic "Rock Around the Clock" was originally the B-side. The A-side: "Thirteen Women."

DIRECTED BY THE ACTOR

You'd think film actors would be naturally good directors—after all, they know how it's done. But do they? Turns out that for every successful actor-director like Robert Redford or Ron Howard...there are a lot more who probably should have stuck to their day jobs.

Actor/Director: Nicolas Cage
Movie: *Sonny* (2002)
Details: The eccentric, Oscar-winning actor directed this bleak drama about an army veteran (James Franco) who returns to his hometown of New Orleans and fights hard to find legitimate employment, but is soon pulled back into working for his mother in her brothel, where he falls in love with a prostitute (Mena Suvari). Cage has a bit role as "Acid Yellow."
Reviews: "Preposterous and tedious, *Sonny* is spiked with unintentional laughter." —L.A. *Weekly*

Actor/Director: Louis C.K.
Movie: *Pootie Tang* (2001)
Details: Before his standup career took off and before he created and starred in the acclaimed FX series *Louie*, Louis C.K. was a writer for HBO's *The Chris Rock Show*. In 2001, the show spun off the recurring character Pootie Tang (Lance Crouther) into his own movie, which C.K. directed. Pootie Tang's defining characteristics: he's cool, women love him...and everything that comes out of his mouth is nonsensical gibberish.
Reviews: "There are bad movies, there are disappointing movies, and then there's *Pootie Tang*, a movie so incompetent, it almost defies description." —*Eye Weekly* (Toronto)

Actor/Director: Madonna
Movie: *W.E.* (2012)
Details: The music superstar has earned mostly negative comments from movie critics for her acting. Nevertheless, she's gone behind the camera a couple of times. She co-wrote and directed this romantic drama about a lonely housewife named Wally (Abbie Cornish) who becomes obsessed with the love story of King Edward VIII and American divorcée Wallis Simpson, a romance that led Edward to abdicate the throne. Amidst Wally's moping around Windsor Castle and auction houses, the movie flashes back to tell the story of Edward (James D'Arcy) and Wallis (Andrea Riseborough).

Reviews: "Madonna gorges on glamour, architectural porn and haute couture, but starves the mind." —*Minneapolis Star Tribune*

Actor/Director: Kevin Bacon
Movie: *Loverboy* (2005)

Details: The reason Bacon, who inspired the party game "Six Degrees of Kevin Bacon," can be linked to so many other actors is that he's been in so many movies—more than 60 so far. And yet he's only directed this one feature film, based on a novel by Victoria Redel. Bacon's wife, Kyra Sedgwick, stars as a mentally unstable woman who is desperate to have a child, and when she does, she and the young boy don't have a lot of boundaries. Even creepier: Bacon and Sedgwick's two young children both have roles in *Loverboy*.

Reviews: "Remarkably unsubtle and by-the-numbers, and thanks to some curious plotting, it's also a bit shrill and unpleasant." —*Deseret News*

Actor/Director: Eddie Murphy
Movie: *Harlem Nights* (1990)

Details: Murphy is inarguably one of the best comic actors to ever hit the big screen, starring in classics like *Coming to America* and *Beverly Hills Cop*. That gave Murphy enough clout by 1989 to get his passion project made: a period piece set in and around a 1930s African American nightclub; Murphy and his idol Richard Pryor had starring roles. For his efforts, Murphy was nominated for Worst Director at the Razzie Awards and won Worst Screenplay.

Reviews: "Does it matter to Eddie Murphy whether *Harlem Nights* is good or bad? It doesn't look like it." —*Washington Post*

Actor/Director: Kevin Spacey
Movie: *Beyond the Sea* (2005)

Details: A movie about the life of crooner Bobby Darin had been in the works since 1986. Oscar winner Barry Levinson (*Rain Man*) was going to direct it, and Tom Cruise was set to star as Darin. The production fell apart…and was revived in 1994. Kevin Spacey, a huge lifelong Darin fan, lobbied producers to cast him in the lead role, but at age 35, they thought he was too old to play Darin—who died in 1973 at age 37. When that project fell apart too, Spacey acquired the rights. *Beyond the Sea* was finally put into production with 45-year-old Spacey as producer, co-writer, director, and star, playing Darin in his 20s and 30s.

Reviews: "This is one of those rare movies that's so bad it's good, with lavish production numbers in which Spacey sings out of sync with the voice track and dances out of sync with his own feet." —*San Jose Mercury News*

First line from the first *Simpsons* episode: "Ooh, careful, Homer."

FUNNY ANIMAL NAMES

What's in a name? Not much, if you believe Shakespeare. On the other hand, if someone's name makes you laugh, that's a good thing. Example: we knew a woman named Grace Moak. Said fast, it sounds like "gray smoke." Funny, right? And memorable. So here are three funny names for three funny critters that you'll never forget.

WUNDERPUS PHOTOGENICUS

What It Is: A small (just 9–16 inches long) and spectacularly patterned octopus found in the western Pacific Ocean.

Name Origin: In the 1980s, improvements in underwater photography and videography plus a surge in the popularity of dive resorts in the western Pacific (the waters around northern Australia, the Philippines, and Vanuatu) resulted in many images of previously unknown sea creatures. One of those creatures was this octopus species, which someone (presumably a German speaker) gave the nickname "wunderpus," after the German word *wünder*, meaning "marvel" or "wonder." In 2006, when scientists confirmed that it was indeed a new species, they used its nickname as part of the scientific name, adding "photogenicus," because the wunderpus wasn't just a marvel—it was also very photogenic.

LUMPSUCKER

What It Is: A family of fish found in the cold waters of the North Atlantic, North Pacific, and Arctic oceans.

Name Origin: Lumpsuckers (or lumpfish) get the "lump" part of their name because of their overall lumpy appearance: they have fat, round, almost spherical bodies, with small fins and bulgy eyes. As an added feature, they have a variety of bumps, pimples, spines, and splotches on those lumpy bodies. They come in a variety of sizes: some species grow up to about 24 inches long; others grow to just 1 inch long (one science magazine described the small ones as "swollen eyeballs with eyeballs.") And they didn't get the "sucker" part of their name from their mouths. As with numerous species of sucker fish, it's much weirder than that. The lumpsucker's pelvic fins—the pair of fins found on the belly of finned fishes—have evolved into disk-shaped suction devices that allow these fish to temporarily anchor themselves to rocks, shells, and other surfaces on the ocean floor. You can even stick one to your finger—and it will hang there upside down (which helps lumpsuckers when they find themselves in turbulent waters—because their fat bodies and tiny fins make them terrible swimmers).

No wonder they make your skin crawl: 6 out of 10 movie villains have some dermatological condition.

FISH FOOD: *Since 2009, salmon farms in Scandinavia have used lumpsuckers as pest control. They eat the parasitic sea lice that plague salmon farms, and fishery managers find that they're much more efficient and safer than the toxic chemicals they usually use to kill the bugs.*

CHICKEN TURTLE

What It Is: A semiaquatic turtle species found around freshwater systems in the American South, from Florida to North Carolina, and west to eastern Texas. Its shell is a tan to olive-green and around 6–9 inches long, with a distinctive pear shape (the wider part of the shell is at the turtle's tail end). The species is especially known for its long, snakelike neck.

Name Origin: The scientific name of the species is *Deirochelys reticularia*. So why is it called a "chicken turtle"? Because it tastes like chicken. Really. Turtle meat, most often eaten as part of turtle soup, was a regular part of the American diet going back to colonial days, and remained popular in the South well into the 20th century. And the turtle of choice for turtle eaters: the chicken turtle, presumably because of its mild flavor. Exactly when the chicken turtle acquired its name is unknown, but we found a recipe for it in a cookbook by influential American writer Sarah J. Hale, published in 1857.

Bonus Fact: Turtle hunting is strongly regulated in the United States today, and is illegal in some states. But turtle soup—made from snapping turtles—is still served in some American restaurants, including several creole restaurants in New Orleans. And you can order cans of snapping turtle soup online.

*　　*　　*

NERDY PICKUP LINES

- Hi. My name is Windows. Can I crash at your place?
- Are you a piece of carbon? Because I would love to date you.
- Can I follow you? 'Cause my mom told me to follow my dreams.
- Who needs Google? You're everything I'm searching for.
- Do you have a name or can I call you mine?
- Good thing I brought my library card, 'cause I'm *checking you out*!
- Is your name Ariel? 'Cause we *mermaid* for each other!

Dolphins can recognize themselves in a mirror, something scientists thought only humans could do.

UNCLE JOHN'S STALL OF FAME

Uncle John is amazed—and pleased—by the unusual ways
people get involved with bathrooms, toilets, and so on.
That's why he created the "Stall of Fame."

Honoree: The town of Elk Falls, Kansas

Notable Achievement: Made their outhouses an "in" thing

True Story: Elk Falls is a sleepy little southeast Kansas town that's getting sleepier all the time—the population has declined from 151 residents in 1980 to fewer than 100 today. Back in 1996, when the residents were trying to think of a way to attract more visitors, someone observed that a lot of outhouses, most of them no longer in use, still dotted the landscape. Why not proclaim the town the "Outhouse Capital of Kansas," and organize an annual outhouse tour? The idea was approved and the townspeople have been decorating and showing off outhouses on the Friday and Saturday before Thanksgiving ever since.

Visitors are invited to select their favorite; candidates have included "Postal Potty," behind the Post Office; "King Toot," which has an Egyptian theme; the Christmassy "Santa's North Hole"; and Starbuttz, which has a coffeehouse theme. While they're there, visitors can tour the local businesses, such as the pottery, the tannery, and the sawmill and, hopefully, spend some money. "It's just offbeat enough that it's something different," says resident Steve Fry.

Honoree: Rob Poultney, a man living in Gwynedd, a county in northern Wales, and at least one other outraged citizen in the area

Notable Achievement: Protested the purported pending closure of public privies with prompt petitions and a portable potty

True Story: The cash-strapped Gwynedd Council operated 73 public restrooms at various locations around the county…until April 2016, when it announced it was closing 50 of them due to more than $5.7 million in budget cuts.

Poultney suffers from Crohn's disease, a disorder that affects the stomach and intestines. When it flares up, he needs to find a bathroom. Fast. If no public bathrooms are available in a particular place he wants to go to, he has to stay away. It's like being under house arrest, he says. So when the closures were announced, he started an online petition to keep the public toilets open, and collected more than 1,300 signatures over the next few days.

At the same time, someone started leaving plastic buckets emblazoned with labels reading "GWYNEDD COUNCIL EMERGENCY PUBLIC TOILET" on sidewalks near major intersections around the county as a satirical protest. The council condemned the stunt as "a dangerous distraction to motorists," but it soon caved to the pressure and shelved its plans to close the toilets. At last report it was working with town and city governments in the county to find the money to keep as many toilets open as possible.

> *I cannot condone such behavior [leaving buckets at major intersections] but it is a novel way of drawing attention to what will be a serious problem for both the elderly and tourists.*
> —**Gwynedd counselor Eryl Jones-Williams**

Honorees: Seth Wheeler and Owen Williams

Notable Achievement: Settled, once and for all, a dispute that has raged since the invention of toilet paper rolls in 1891

True Story: You've probably never heard of Seth Wheeler, but maybe you should have. He's the inventor from Albany, New York, who patented the toilet paper roll in 1891. He also deserves credit (at least that's what his supporters say) for showing Americans how to properly hang toilet paper in the bathroom. His patent application includes diagrams that clearly show the roll oriented with the paper flowing over the roll, not under it. The patent and its instructive illustration were largely forgotten until 2015, when writer Owen Williams stumbled across them and posted them online for all to see. Will the 125-year-old illustration change the minds of "unders"? Doubtful…but it makes the debate a little more interesting.

Honoree: Dr. Billy Crynes, a retired University of Oklahoma professor of engineering

Notable Achievement: Documenting an important part of bathroom history

True Story: Crynes grew up in rural Indiana in a home that had no indoor plumbing. He used an outhouse until he joined the U.S. Marines in 1956. After military service came college, then a career in academia. When Crynes retired in 2002, he took a long bicycle ride across the state, photographing old barns and other buildings along the way. But his interest soon turned to something more nostalgic: outhouses. Plain ones, four-holers, double-deckers (so people don't have to go downstairs), and fancy brick structures that stood outside banks and other prominent buildings. He's been traveling the country photographing outhouses ever since, documenting this fading piece of Americana before it disappears forever. Today more than 99 percent of American households have indoor plumbing; the day is soon coming when outhouses will be gone for good.

As of 2017, Crynes has amassed a collection of more than 2,000 photographs of outhouses: many taken by him, others sent to him by family and friends. When he isn't out taking pictures, he volunteers his time with the University of Oklahoma speakers service, and gives as many as a dozen talks a year where he shows his outhouse photographs to the public. "I've given hundreds of talks, and nothing I've ever done is as much fun as this," he says. "…The fact of the matter is we are losing this part of history. It's an era that's almost gone."

Honoree: The San Francisco Department of Public Works

Notable Achievement: Creating a pioneering program to provide public potties in problem precincts

True Story: Like many American cities, San Francisco has a large homeless population, and when people living on the streets have no place else to "go," they go in doorways, alleys, and other public places. Stymied by the $1.5 million yearly cost of steam-cleaning the same troubled locations over and over again, in 2014 the Public Works Department launched a "Pit Stop" pilot program: during the day, trailers with portable toilets were towed to four neighborhoods with significant indigent populations and parked near soup kitchens, public parks, and other places where the homeless congregate.

Attendants called "potty sitters" were paid up to $16 an hour to staff the toilets—part of the city's job-training program—and were responsible for keeping the facilities clean and keeping them stocked with toilet paper, soap, hand towels, seat covers, and other supplies. The Pit Stop trailers were delivered to their locations in the early afternoon, then hauled away each night for cleaning.

The experiment was a success: it caused a 60 percent drop in steam cleaning requests and was so popular with local merchants and with the homeless that the department expanded the program. Today it serves 16 locations around the city, and there are plans to expand it even further. "It's private, it's clean, it has a sink, it has soap, it has seat covers, it has paper towels, it has a light," a 49-year-old homeless woman named Mischa told the *Los Angeles Times*. "It's wonderful. It's a blessing. It's the way I was raised."

*   *   *

HOLIDAY CONSPIRACY?

March 6 is National Oreo Cookie Day. It's also National Dentists Day.

Picture this (if you can): *Aphantasia* is a neurological condition in which a person cannot form mental images.

LOST AT SEA, PART II

When we last left Salvador Alvarenga (page 110), he had just watched his only companion wither away and die. That would be the last person he would speak to for ten months.

ON THE EDGE OF SANITY

If you'd been stranded on a boat for several months and your only companion just died, how would you cope? Rather than throw Córdoba overboard, Alvarenga decided to keep the dead man's body propped up in the boat, and converse with it as if it were still alive. That went on for nearly a week, until one night Alvarenga realized the futility of talking to a corpse. He knew that he had to let Córdoba go, so he rolled the body over the edge and into the sea.

Without the company of his friend, Alvarenga's plight became more and more desperate. At first, most of his hours were spent in total silence. Then he figured out how to withdraw into his own imagination. He would spend entire days taking long walks through the countryside without leaving the boat; his evenings were spent drinking cocktails in fancy nightclubs, dining on fine food, and meeting beautiful women. Sometimes Alvarenga wasn't even sure that his life on the boat was nothing more than a recurring bad dream.

Every once in a while, a ship would pass in the distance, and Alvarenga would jump up and down, and hoot and holler, but he was rarely ever spotted. Around the 11-month point, a large trawler passed by close enough that the men on the deck could see a skinny, bearded man waving furiously at them. But all they did was wave back.

And all Alvarenga could do was keep surviving. Whenever thoughts of committing suicide entered his head, he remembered his mother's warning that those who take their own lives end up in hell. Besides, Alvarenga had something to live for: his long-lost daughter in El Salvador…and the promise he'd made to his friend.

THE ISLAND

By January 30, 2014, it had been a year and two months since Alvarenga had seen land. That's why, at first, he thought that the small island in the distance was just a mirage. But it was real. And he was drifting toward it…for now. Knowing that the wind could shift and that the current could carry him back out to sea, Alvarenga decided to cut the lines that held the buoys—a huge risk, because if he didn't make it to the island, the boat would be vulnerable to capsizing storms.

Ben Franklin invented his own phonetic alphabet.

He had no intention of letting that happen; he used his arms to paddle furiously toward the tiny island, and the current took him the rest of the way in.

When Alvarenga woke up on the beach, he was naked and covered with leeches. "I held a handful of sand in my hand like it was a treasure," he later told interviewer Jonathan Franklin. Luckily, the tiny island was inhabited by a married couple. They couldn't believe it when Alvarenga stumbled up to their beach house. "There was no hiding the fact that this man had been at sea for a considerable time," wrote Franklin in his account of Alvarenga's experience.

> His hair was matted upwards like a shrub. His beard curled out in wild disarray. His ankles were swollen, his wrists tiny; he could barely walk.

The tiny atoll he'd landed on, called Ebon, is located in the Marshall Islands chain, 2,200 miles southwest of Hawaii, and 1,900 miles northeast of Papua New Guinea. Had Alvarenga missed it, he might have floated another 3,000 miles before reaching land. Even though they spoke no Spanish, the couple befriended Alvarenga and took care of him until he had enough strength to get to the nearest town on a neighboring island. Once he arrived, the news spread quickly that a man who'd been lost at sea for more than a year had just washed up 6,700 miles from where he'd set out. Journalists from all over the world flocked to the Marshall Islands to meet this man in person.

ON UNSOLID GROUND

Despite being weak and malnourished, Alvarenga was thrilled to be around people again…at first. His mental state was fragile. The once-proud fisherman was now deathly afraid of the water—and not just the ocean, but any water. He didn't even want to drink it. He was also caught off guard by all of the sudden attention…and the growing number of skeptics who didn't believe that a man could survive alone on a small boat for so long.

But the more that authorities (and the media) investigated Alvarenga's story, the more it checked out. His boat had the same registry as the one that had disappeared from Mexico in 2012. And based on the ocean currents, he was exactly where he should have been after all that time. Most telling, though, was his physical shape—he actually looked like a man who hadn't had a real meal for 438 days.

Reporter after reporter tried to get to his hospital bed to interview the "real-life castaway" (he bore an uncanny resemblance to Tom Hanks's bearded character in the movie *Cast Away*). But Alvarenga was in no condition to do a lot of talking. His liver was infested with parasites from ingesting all of those raw animals. After 11 days of recuperating, he was finally healthy enough to return to El Salvador, where he saw his parents and his daughter for the first time in a decade.

LOST AT HOME

Alvarenga was welcomed by his family; they even fixed up his childhood bedroom for him. But his extended period of isolation had left him a broken man. For the first few months, he could barely sleep at night or leave the house during the day. And the sight of Córdoba's lifeless body still haunted him. Slowly and surely, though, Alvarenga gained his strength back. But he was still afraid of water, and he still didn't want to keep reliving his ordeal to reporters. To keep the media at bay, Alvarenga hired a childhood friend, Benedicto Perlera, to act as his attorney and to handle all of the interview requests. Perlera tried to persuade his client to sell his story to the highest bidder so they could both make a lot of money. But Alvarenga wasn't quite ready, and a rift started to grow between the two men.

Nearly a year after his rescue, Alvarenga made good on his promise. Along with Perlera, he traveled to see Córdoba's mother in Chiapas, Mexico, where he described in detail how her son had met his untimely end. It was a tense two-hour meeting, but Alvarenga thought it went well as—or at least as well as it could have.

With that difficult task behind him, he was finally ready to tell his story to the public. He met with Jonathan Franklin, an American journalist living in South America who'd written the best-selling book, *33 Men*, the dramatic true-life account of 33 Chilean miners who were trapped in a collapsed mine shaft for 69 days. Franklin wanted to write about Alvarenga's ordeal—and like many others, he was skeptical. But after conducting dozens of interviews, Franklin believed every word of the castaway's amazing tale and began compiling them into a book called *438 Days: A Remarkable True Story of Survival at Sea*.

THE ACCUSED

When *438 Days* finally hit the bookshelves in November 2015, Perlera was no longer associated with Alvarenga. In fact, the lawyer was now representing Córdoba's family. So instead of celebrating the book's release, Alvarenga learned that he was getting sued by his former friend for breach of contract. Then came another bombshell: Córdoba's mother filed a $1 million lawsuit against Alvarenga (along with a demand that half of the book's profits go to her family), alleging that he lied about what really happened after her son died. Alvarenga

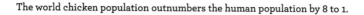

The world chicken population outnumbers the human population by 8 to 1.

didn't throw Córdoba's body overboard, she claimed—he ate him.

Alvarenga denied the cannibalism charge. He and Córdoba had made a pact *not* to eat the other one if one of them died first. Besides, Alvarenga was able to survive on the animals he caught, so he didn't even need the extra meat. "Not for one second did I think of eating Ezequiel," he told the *Daily Mail*. "Even if it meant that I starved, it would have been on my conscience forever." No charges were filed against Alvarenga for cannibalism, and Córdoba's body was long gone. Alvarenga's new lawyer said that "this demand is part of the pressure from this family to divide the proceeds of royalties. Many believe the book is making my client a rich man, but what he will earn is much less than people think."

True? Absolutely. At last report (December 2015), Alvarenga was living in near poverty, relying on free room and board from his parents, and handouts from his extended family in the United States. Franklin's book sold poorly, so it doesn't look like anyone will be getting rich from this story. For his part, Alvarenga is not destitute. He says that he plans to return to his life as a fisherman and will never stray too far from his family ever again.

Despite all of the loss—his livelihood, a year of his life, and his friend—there is one thing that Alvarenga did gain from his experience: a world record. No one in recorded history has ever been able to survive for that long all alone on the open ocean.

*   *   *

WACKY PACKAGING

When a product has a wacky message on the inside or bottom of its packaging, it's called "wackaging." It's become a fad in recent years. Here are some of our favorites.

"In Australia, this would be on top."

—on the bottom of a milk carton

"Best when chilled (as indeed we all are)."

—on a bottle of lemonade

"I scream. You scream. The police come. It's awkward."

—on an ice cream carton

"Stop looking at my bottom."

—on the bottom of a smoothie carton

Who says hot tubs have to be on land? The HotTug is a floating wood-powered hot tub "boat." It seats 8.

WEIRD...IN SPACE!

It's not just that the universe is an impossibly enormous place, it's also full of mystifying phenomena. Here are just a few examples that will totally space you out.

SAGITTARIUS B2

Sagittarius B2 is the name of a massive cloud of gas and space dust located near the middle of our galaxy. It's big—about 100 light-years across. (One light-year is equal to about 6 trillion miles.) What's weird about Sagittarius B2 is that it contains enormous amounts of alcohol. This includes the toxic varieties *methanol* and *vinyl alcohol*, but also *ethanol*—the kind found in beer, wine, whiskey, and other alcoholic beverages. Astrophysicists have determined that Sagittarius B2 also contains large amounts of *ethyl formate*, a chemical compound that gives rum its distinctive odor and gives raspberries their flavor. (So Sagittarius B2 just might be the best-smelling and best-tasting place in our galaxy.)

GAMMA RAY BURSTS

In the mid-1960s, the United States started launching satellites equipped with radiation detectors. Reason: to detect nuclear weapons tests in space. (In 1963 more than 100 nations—including the United States and the Soviet Union—signed a treaty agreeing to not conduct nuclear tests in the atmosphere or in space, but the United States feared the Soviet Union might break that treaty.) The satellites never did detect any Soviet tests, but in 1967 they started detecting something else: huge bursts of gamma-ray radiation—the most powerful kind known. Those bursts, known today as GRBs, are emitted by explosions in outer space. Thousands have been detected since, some lasting just microseconds, others lasting hours. Astronomers believe they are emissions from violent space events, such as colliding stars or the formation of black holes. The especially powerful and long bursts, experts theorize, were emitted from some of the most powerful explosive events in the universe since the big bang. One, dubbed "GRB 080916C," and detected by NASA's Fermi Gamma-ray Space Telescope on September 15, 2008, was the most powerful GRB ever detected. According to astrophysicists, that GRB was the record of an explosion that emitted more energy in a few seconds than our sun will in its entire lifetime.

Bonus fact: All of the GRB events recorded so far have come from distant galaxies, billions of light-years from earth. (Meaning that those explosions

occurred billions of years ago.) If such an event were to occur in our galaxy, relatively close to Earth…bad news. In fact, some astrophysicists believe that a nearby GRB event may have been the cause of a major extinction event that occurred roughly 450 million years ago, killing about 60 percent of all creatures on Earth. (So let's hope that doesn't happen again soon.)

KIC 8462852 (AKA "TABBY'S STAR")

KIC 8462852 is the name of a star located in the constellation Cygnus, roughly 1,400 light-years from Earth (and not visible from Earth). Here's what's weird: something keeps blocking it, dimming its light more than 20 percent at times, and for irregular periods—some lasting just a few hours, others lasting for more than a week. Astronomers don't understand why this happens, but agree that it's probably *not* being blocked by the planets that orbit the star. Planets wouldn't dim the light that much, and their orbits would occur in regular intervals, not the irregular intervals seen from KIC 8462852. One theory put forward to explain the phenomenon: the light is being blocked by "alien megastructures"— huge planet-sized structures built by intelligent creatures that inhabit one of the planets orbiting the star. (Most scientists think there's probably a less *alieny* explanation—they just don't know what it is.) In any case, KIC 8462852 remains one of the most mysterious stars ever recorded.

Bonus fact: The brightness of KIC 8462852 was measured over a four-year period by NASA's *Kepler* spacecraft. *Kepler* left Earth in 2009, with a mission to continuously measure the brightness of more than 150,000 stars over long periods, and to identify unknown exoplanets (planets orbiting stars other than our sun) by detecting the faint dimming of stars caused by orbiting planets. More than 1,200 new planets have been discovered by the *Kepler* mission since then. The number believed to have Earth-like qualities, and that might support life: nine.

*   *   *

SIX STARS WHO ARE SIX FEET TALL

1. Leonardo DiCaprio

2. Jane Lynch

3. Geena Davis

4. Neil Young

5. Brooke Shields

6. Christopher Walken

Hard to swallow? Listerine was invented in 1879 as a way to clean surgical instruments.

ROBOJOKE 5000

*We hope the robots find these jokes funny…and don't
get mad and rise up and take over.*

Q: Why was the robot angry?
A: Somebody kept pushing his buttons.

Q: What does a robot use to shave?
A: A laser blade.

Q: What kind of robot can power a ship?
A: A rowbot.

Q: Do robots have siblings?
A: No, but they have brobots and transisters.

Q: What happened when the robot ran away from home?
A: He left to join the circuits.

Q: What did the robot get for its old, dead batteries?
A: Nothing—they were free of charge.

Q: Why did the smart woman dump her robot boyfriend?
A: It turns out his intelligence was artificial.

Q: What's a robot's favorite kind of music?
A: Heavy metal.

Q: What part of a robot makes them unable to curse?
A: Their sensors.

Knock-knock.
Who's there?
A robot.
End communication.

Q: What's a robot's favorite junk food?
A: Chips.

Q: Why did the robot refuse a cup of coffee?
A: It was already wired.

Q: What was written on the robot's tombstone?
A: "Rust in Peace."

Q: What's a robot's biggest turn-on?
A: Its switch.

Q: What do cowboy robots wear on their feet?
A: Reboots.

A robot walks into a bar and orders a drink. "Sorry," the bartender says, "but we don't serve robots." The robot replies, "Someday you will."

Jean-Claude Van Damme's film debut: he was a background dancer in *Breakin' 2: Electric Boogaloo* (1984).

OLD BANDS, NEW WAVE

It seems like every musician took a stab at a disco record in the late 1970s—the Beach Boys, Frank Sinatra, even Ethel Merman. Not long after, a lot of established musicians tried to get in on the next big thing—New Wave—for better or for worse (but mostly worse).

BACKGROUND

By the late 1970s, rock music had split into two main camps: big, bombastic arena rock (think Boston or Foreigner) and gritty, sloppy, punk rock (like the Ramones or the Sex Pistols). And then along came a third entry: New Wave, which combined the huge melodies of arena rock with the catchy hooks and short songs of punk. And keyboards. New Wave was guitar-based pop rock that frequently utilized keyboards and synthesizers. The new sound produced some legendary, lasting acts, such as the Cars, Devo, and Elvis Costello. But to stay relevant and cool, a lot of older, established recording artists had to scramble to come up with a New Wave song or album.

GRACE SLICK

The lead singer of Jefferson Airplane (and later, Jefferson Starship)—the voice of 1960s psychedelic rock and the counterculture generation singing short little New Wave pop songs? It happened. For her 1984 solo album *Software*, Slick's vocal wailing went out and in came choppy vocal lines sung to keyboards and drum machines. The album failed to make any charts, so Slick returned to Jefferson Starship, which by the late 1980s had evolved into the pop group Starship (she was the only original member of Jefferson Airplane in the group). Starship had a bunch of soft rock hits, including "We Built This City" and "Nothing's Gonna Stop Us Now," a #1 hit featured in the 1987 romantic comedy film *Mannequin*.

THE VILLAGE PEOPLE

The costumed singing group came relatively late to the disco party, but they scored a few of the most recognizable hits of the genre in the late 1970s, with "Y.M.C.A," "In the Navy," and "Macho Man." But then disco fell out of fashion and their 1980 movie *Can't Stop the Music* flopped. What are a cowboy, a construction worker, a police officer, and a Native American warrior to do? Move on to the next music fad. So in 1981, the Village People released

Medieval hemorrhoid cure: direct application of a hot iron, administered by a monk.

Renaissance, a synth-heavy pop-rock record. Not only did the music imitate New Wave styles, the group wanted so much to distance itself from disco that they ditched their signature outfits and personas: On the cover of *Renaissance*, the Village People are unrecognizable, dressed in matching black pants and jackets. The album is a bizarre collection of keyboard-driven rock songs, including three about proper nutrition: "Big Mac," "Diet," and "Food Fight." The album peaked at #138 on the album chart, and then quickly disappeared. In 1982 the Village People returned with a new album called *Fox on the Box*. It was a disco album.

CHER

Cher has frequently reinvented herself and her music. She's done folk albums, rock albums, disco albums, dance albums, pop albums, even a country rock album with onetime husband Greg Allman. Her 1982 album *I Paralyze* has a little bit of everything, including a New Wave song called "I Paralyze." (She certainly looked like a New Wave musician on the cover. Wearing huge sunglasses and an emotionless expression, she could have passed for Ric Ocasek of the Cars.) Columbia Records didn't quite know what to do with the album and opted to spend very little money promoting it. Lacking the usual ad blitz for a major album by a major star, Cher's only publicity for the effort was to perform "I Paralyze" on *Solid Gold* and *American Bandstand*. (Actually, she lip-synched.) Both the album and song were the biggest flops of her career, failing to make the charts at all. The flop so disheartened her that she quit singing for five years in order to focus on her acting career. (Which was actually a good move. She won an Oscar for Best Actress for her role in 1987's *Moonstruck*.)

SHAUN CASSIDY

Cassidy was a teen idol in the mid-1970s. He got a record deal largely because of the success of his older brother, teen idol David Cassidy of *The Partridge Family*. And like his brother, Shaun Cassidy had a TV show to help boost his visibility— *The Hardy Boys Mysteries* (1977–1979). Cassidy released four successful albums

SHAUN CASSIDY LATER BECAME *a high-powered TV writer and producer. He's helped bring shows like* Cold Case, Blue Bloods, American Gothic, *and* Emerald City *to the airwaves.*

of bubblegum pop during that time and had a bunch of hit singles, such as "Hey Deanie" and covers of "Do You Believe in Magic" and "Da Doo Ron Ron" (which hit #1 on the pop chart). The bad news: By 1980, Cassidy's star had faded, as usually happens in the high-turnover world of teen idol-dom. The good news: Because he was no longer being tightly controlled by a record label, Cassidy could make whatever music he wanted. So he hired rock star and producer Todd Rundgren to help him put an album together. With Rundgren and his band Utopia backing him, Cassidy turned out *Wasp*, an album of mostly New Wave-style covers of older songs, such as David Bowie's "Rebel, Rebel" and the Four Tops' "Shake Me, Wake Me." He also performed three Rundgren originals…but it wasn't enough to salvage Cassidy's music career—it sold only a few thousand copies and it wound up being the last album he ever made.

PAUL MCCARTNEY

The former Beatle and Wings leader has never been afraid to try new things. The Beatles' song "Helter Skelter" has been called the first "heavy metal" record, while the Fab Four's "When I'm Sixty-Four" is reminiscent of old British "music hall" standards. He's also written concertos and has an experimental electronic band called The Fireman. McCartney can do and has done it all, even New Wave. On his 1980 solo album *McCartney II*, he included "Temporary Secretary," a song featuring a frenetic, computerized keyboard riff, a steady 1-2 drum beat, and McCartney's vocals pitch-shifted higher up. (It was a long way from "Silly Love Songs.") The song was released as a single, but in a rarity for McCartney, it was a complete flop, not reaching the charts in either the U.S. or the U. K. Time has been kinder to the song, though: In 2013 *Rolling Stone* named "Temporary Secretary" one of the best songs of McCartney's post-Beatles career.

*   *   *

CONAN O'BRIEN, ON HIS FIRST DAY
AS A WRITER FOR *THE SIMPSONS*

"I was very nervous when I started. They showed me into this office and told me to start writing down some ideas. They left me alone in that office. I left after five minutes to go get a cup of coffee. I heard a crash. I walked back to the office, and there was a hole in the window and a dead bird on the floor. Literally, in my first ten minutes at *The Simpsons*, a bird had flown through the glass of my window, hit the far wall, broken its neck, and fallen dead on the floor. George Meyer came in and looked at it, and said, 'Man, this is some kind of weird omen.'"

The closest thing a castle had to a bathroom was a garderobe, a second-floor chamber…

LOOK! UP IN THE SKY!

Just because the problem is high-tech, does the solution have to be high-tech, too?

THREAT FROM ABOVE

One modern nuisance that has troubled the Federal Aviation Administration and its counterparts in other countries in recent years is the threat posed by radio-controlled drones, which can be purchased without a license at toy and hobby stores for less than $100. It's illegal to fly them close to airports, but that hasn't stopped pranksters from doing it, and there's always the possibility that terrorists may one day use a drone to try and bring down an airplane.

Airbus and other companies are working on high-tech solutions to the problem, such as computer software that tracks the drones in flight, and devices that shoot them down without posing a threat to humans. But in the Netherlands they've opted for something simpler: they're training eagles to attack the drones and snatch them out of the sky.

MEAL TICKET

Young eagles are taught to associate the drones with food. Their trainers start by feeding them meat placed on top of drones that are sitting on the ground. Then when the birds get a little older, they learn to get their meat from drones flying in midair—nearby at first, then farther and farther away. Eventually the eagles are taught to grab a meatless drone and set it on the ground next to their trainers, who reward them with meat when they've completed the task.

Eagles can spot prey from as far as a mile away, then dive at that prey at speeds of up to 150 miles per hour. When they grab it in their talons, they can crush the prey with a force of 500 pounds per square inch.

The eagles and the 100 Dutch police officers being trained to work with them were scheduled to go into action as early as the summer of 2017. They will be deployed around airports and at public events such as state visits and international conferences where drones are considered a potential threat. "We haven't found any other method to intercept the drones, but we are continuing to explore other possibilities," explains Dennis Janus, a spokesperson for the Dutch national police. Until then, the eagles are "a low-tech solution to a high-tech problem," he says.

...that stuck out past the castle wall, allowing the "end user" to poop onto the ground or moat below.

CD RECYCLING IDEAS

Got a bunch of old CDs and DVDs? If you're an adventurous do-it-yourselfer, before you throw them away—and they end up in a landfill—consider these recycling projects. (We're still trying to come up with recycling ideas for Uncle John's cassette tape collection.)

COASTERS

Cut a piece of felt or thin cork into circles the size of a CD or DVD, or just a little smaller, and glue them to the bottom of the discs, and decorate the tops with decoupage artwork: trace the discs on pieces of paper with interesting designs—colored art paper, magazine covers or pages, shopping bags, wrapping paper—and glue the paper to the discs, being careful to avoid getting any wrinkles. When dry, apply a couple of coats of sealant or varnish to give the coasters a good protective finish, let dry—and you've got yourself some handy and attractive drinks coasters. (You can get the sealant at crafts stores.)

TOY HOVERCRAFT

You need just four simple things to make this toy: an old CD or DVD, a bottle pop-top (the kind you pull up to open and push down to close, like the ones on dishwashing detergent bottles), glue (hot glue or simple craft glue is fine), and a balloon. Working on a smooth, flat surface, glue the pop-top to the center of the disc, over the center hole, with screw side on the disc. When it's dry, blow up your balloon, pinch the neck so no air escapes, and stretch the mouth of the balloon over the pop-top, making sure the pop-top is in the "up" open position. Let the balloon go—and your balloon-powered CD/DVD hovercraft will hover around the table! (You might have to give it a push to get it going.)

CLOCK

Get a small, battery-powered clock mechanism at a craft or hobby shop and use a strong glue to attach the mechanism to the back of a CD or DVD, sticking the shaft of the clock through the hole in the disc. (You may have to use spacers between the clock mechanism and the disc if the shaft sticks out too far—or just glue two or more discs together to make the shaft sit properly.) Attach the hour and second hands to the shaft—and you've got a DIY clock, with the CD or DVD acting as the clock's face. Use an old favorite CD and leave the label on, or make your own design using paint, stickers, or collage—and if you want

Original name for the cash register: "incorruptible cashier." It was invented to stop clerks from stealing.

numbers, paint them on or use stick-on numbers. To use it as a wall clock, glue a washer or just a loop of wire to the mechanism and hang the clock from a hook or nail. Or cut a thin, shallow slot ⅛ inch wide and ¼ inch deep in a small, sturdy block of wood, stick the "bottom" of the disc in it…and voilà: a desktop clock. Come up with other ideas to make the clock stand up on its own. Experiment with other items that you want to keep out of the landfill.

SPINNING TOPS

A simple one for kids. You'll need an old CD or DVD, the plastic top from a quart or gallon milk jug, a marble that's just a little bit bigger than the hole in the disc, and some glue. Glue the marble into the hole of the disc, then glue the milk bottle top to the center of the other side of the disc. (The bottle top should sit flat side up, just as it would on a milk jug.) When the glue is dry and hard, hold the apparatus by the milk bottle top, give it a twist—just like you would a spinning top—and your brand new recycled top will spin away. You can add to the fun by making several, and decorating the discs with paint, paper, or markers. (Pinwheel patterns are a good choice.)

> **DISC-O FEVER:** *In the 1990s, half of all CDs manufactured worldwide were free America Online starter discs. Most were thrown away, but today there's a group of people who actually collect them. It's led by a San Francisco man named Bustam Halim, who owns more than 3,000 different AOL discs.*

MOSAIC TILES

This project is better with DVDs, because they're more colorful than CDs and make for a cooler display. And what most people don't realize is that DVDs are made from two plastic discs glued together, one of which has a thin metal layer that makes those cool reflective colors—so you'll have to separate the two discs from one another. Some craftspeople recommend warming up the DVDs with a hair dryer (be careful—they can get very hot!), as it makes them easier to separate; others suggest cutting the discs in half with strong, sturdy scissors, then using a butter knife or your fingernails to pry the layers apart. Whichever way you do it, be careful not to damage the shiny reflective layer on the disc with the metallic layer. When you're done, get rid of the non-shiny discs (maybe you can find another use for them later), then use scissors to cut the shiny discs into pieces of the sizes and shapes you want. Use a strong glue to attach the pieces to

Undies have nothing to do with it: the *Pantydraco* dinosaur gets its name from the Welsh word *pant-y-ffynnon*, meaning "hollow of the spring."

whatever it is you're decorating—a bowl, plate, birdbath, kitchen backsplash, lamp base, coffee table, flowerpot, the side of your bathtub, etc.—leaving a little space between each piece. (How much space is entirely up to your own taste.) When the glue is dry, use a simple grout from a craft store to fill in the gaps between your DVD mosaic tiles, clean off the excess—and you're a DVD mosaic artist! (Congratulations!)

ROOFING

Yes—this is actually a thing. But because you'd need *a lot* of CDs and DVDs to put a roof on an entire house, it's more realistic for a porch, shed, chicken coop, dog house, outhouse, or any similar structure, as long as it has a wooden roof with flat surfaces. (You'll *still* need a lot—about 120 discs per square yard of space—so if you really want to do this and don't have enough, try garage sales, secondhand stores, online—and hit up all your friends for their old CDs.)

To get started, drill one small hole—⅛ inch or so in diameter—in each of the CDs or DVDs, about a half an inch from the edge of the center hole. (You can stack a few discs so you don't have to do them all one at a time.) Starting at the bottom edge of the roof, nail a row of discs to the roof through the drilled holes using nails with wide, flat heads. Make a second row, overlapping each new disc over two of the discs in the first row—making sure to cover up the center holes, to avoid leaks. Continue up the roof, making new rows overlapping the previous row—just like when laying regular roof tiles or shingles. Tip: If you want the structure you're roofing to be cooler rather than warmer, put the shiny side of the discs facing up, as that way they'll reflect the sun's rays. Want it warmer: put the dull side up. (For more precise instructions, look online—you can find lots of good details.)

EXTRAS

• There are actually such things as guitar pick punches: they look sort of like staplers, and you just stick in the material you want your picks made from—old credit cards are a favorite—push down, and you've got yourself a pick. The punches work with old CDs, too.

• Going on a camping trip to a very a remote location? Take an old CD along with you. If you get stuck, you can use it to reflect sunlight as a long-distance emergency signal. (You can also use old discs as cheap reflectors for your bicycle or mailbox.)

• Want to make a lamp from a stack of 70 old CDs? Google "Jim Watters CD lamp." It's a fairly involved project...but the end product is pretty cool.

The psychiatrist bills must cost an arm and a leg:
Apotemnophilia is a mental disorder in which people to want to amputate their own healthy limbs.

NICE STORIES

Every now and then we like to ignore our inner cynics and share stories with happy endings.

AUTO DIAL

It was a typical workday at the Stratstone BMW dealership in Wallsend, North East of England, when a not-so-typical call came in: a disoriented elderly woman said she was hurt and that she was trying to reach her daughter, but she'd dialed the wrong number. The receptionist put the call through to the sales manager, 34-year-old Dang Vuong, who immediately went into rescue mode. While the receptionist kept the woman calm on the phone, Dang drove over to her house (which was about two miles away). The door was unlocked, so he let himself in. "She was in shock more than anything," Dang told the *Metro UK*. "There was blood on her face and the bath was overflowing." The woman had slipped and fallen in the bathroom, so Dang comforted her, explained who he was, and helped her into the living room. Then he made her a cup of tea. A little while later, the very grateful daughter showed up and Dang went back to work.

A TALE OF TWO RACES

The first time that Kathrine Switzer ran the Boston Marathon was in 1967, and she was nearly dragged off the course about four miles into the race by an official. Reason: he (mistakenly) thought that women weren't allowed to run in the marathon. True, no woman had ever run the Boston Marathon (women were considered "too fragile" to withstand the rigors of a 26-mile race), but Switzer had read the rule book and it said nothing about gender. So she registered under the name "K. V. Switzer" and then ran wearing racing bib #261. The irate official wasn't going away; he refused to allow her to continue and tried ripping off her racing bib. "Get the hell out of my race and give me those numbers!" One of Switzer's team members (her 235-pound boyfriend) ran over and knocked the official to the ground, and Switzer kept running. Despite being somewhat shaken by the incident, she finished the race and became the first registered female runner in the marathon's 70-year-history. Her time: a little over four hours and 20 minutes.

In 2017, half a century later, the 70-year-old Switzer ran her eighth Boston Marathon and finished in a respectable four hours and 44 minutes. This time, instead of being jeered, she was revered. Switzer was representing her 261 Fearless Foundation which she founded to provide global support to female

Unplayable? James Joyce's 732-page novel *Ulysses* is being turned into a video game called *Joycestick*.

runners and walkers. "It's testimony to the power of this number, which means 'fearless' around the world now." After the race, Switzer's bib number was retired, and the next day she got to throw out the first pitch at the Red Sox game.

BEEPS AND PEEPS

What does the bomb squad do when there are no bombs around that need defusing? In Albuquerque, New Mexico, they play a positive role in their community. During Easter weekend in 2017, explosives experts from the military and local police departments got together and carefully placed tiny sound emitters onto dozens of Easter eggs so they would emanate a faint beep every few seconds. Then the explosives experts hid the eggs at a special Easter event held at USS Bullhead Memorial Park. That morning, a group of very excited, visually impaired children got to participate in their first Easter egg hunt!

A LONG, STRANGE TRIP

In the early 1990s, a young man named "John" (real name withheld by officials) left home in New York to follow the Grateful Dead and ended up working on a marijuana farm in North Carolina. When the farm got raided by police in 1994, John escaped, but he knew there'd be a warrant out for his arrest, so he went into hiding…for 22 years. Then in 2016, John, now a middle-aged homeless man, showed up at the New Haven, Connecticut, Police Department to turn himself in. Lieutenant Brendan Hosey ran John's name through the system, and discovered that while there may have been a warrant for him at one time, the number to call in North Carolina was disconnected. And no one in that state's law enforcement could find any record of it, so John was told he was a free man. He left the station, seeming a bit dejected that no one was looking for him. So he went to the nearest FBI office to turn himself in there, only to be told that the feds weren't looking for him, either.

The story might have ended there if it weren't for a worker at the Kent Police Department in Putnam, New York, who happened to see John's name pop up in the warrant search. The worker knew John's family, who lived nearby, and knew they'd always wondered what happened to John. (They assumed he'd died.) After a few phone calls—and an exhaustive search to locate John—an extraordinary reunion took place on the front steps of the New Haven Police Department. John tentatively approached his family, who'd rushed there from New York. He looked at his sister and said, "You look like my mother." Then he said to his mother, "You look like my grandmother." A moment later, tearful embraces ensued, and the grateful family took their long-lost son home.

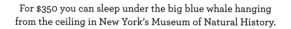

For $350 you can sleep under the big blue whale hanging
from the ceiling in New York's Museum of Natural History.

DUSTBIN OF HISTORY: CAMP SIEGFRIED

Here's a piece of history that even many New Yorkers have never heard of: a Nazi summer camp just 60 miles outside of the Big Apple.

SCHWEIN LAKE

In March 1936, a group of German American Nazi sympathizers, most of them recent immigrants from Germany, met in Buffalo, New York, and founded an organization called the German American *Bund* (or "association"). Though the members claimed to be patriotic Americans and completely independent of Adolf Hitler and the Nazi Party, their purpose was clear: to promote a positive view of Nazism in the United States. The Bund's leader, or *Bundesführer*, was Fritz Julius Kuhn, a naturalized German immigrant who had joined the Nazi Party in 1921, when the organization was only two years old.

One way the Bund tried to drum up support for its cause was by establishing several summer camps where ethnic German families could vacation in the summer and be indoctrinated in National Socialist ideology. Camp Siegfried, a 187-acre compound beside a small lake in the hamlet of Yaphank, on New York's Long Island, was one such place.

HOME AWAY FROM HOME

The neighborhood surrounding Camp Siegfried was also owned by the Bund, through a subsidiary organization called the German American Settlement League. The league owned the land, and had subdivided it into individual parcels crisscrossed by streets named for prominent Nazis, including Adolf Hitler, Hermann Goering, and Joseph Goebbels. Other German notables such as the classical author Friedrich Schiller and the composer Johann Sebastian Bach had streets named for them as well. The Bund invited "National-minded American citizens of Aryan blood" to build summer bungalows on the lots. Though the families would own their homes, the Bund, through the German American Settlement League, would own the land on which the homes were built. In this way the Bund hoped to ensure that the neighborhood it called German Gardens would remain exclusively "Aryan," with the families socializing at Camp Siegfried during the day.

Many of the buildings in the camp were decorated with swastikas set into their stonework, and one area of the camp was landscaped with a large swastika-shaped hedge. Swastika flags flew all over the camp (though the Bund was careful to also fly an American flag, and to fly it higher than the Nazi flags).

For the kids, summers at the Nazi summer camp were about what you'd expect: plenty of traditional activities such as hiking, swimming, sports, dances, and singing around campfires. But these activities were designed with a purpose—to create young people "destined to carry forward our Nazi ideals, and who will ultimately bring victory to the glorious German ideals here [in the U.S.]" as Theodore Dinkelacker, the Bund's National Youth Leader, put it.

Both boys and girls wore uniforms modeled after those of the Hitler Youth and other children's groups in Germany. One difference: the American uniforms had lightning bolts on the armbands instead of swastikas. (There were plenty of swastikas in the camp; putting them on the uniforms was apparently thought to be a little too German for an "American" organization.) The men wore Nazi uniforms, too; the women wore traditional German *dirndl* dresses.

On mornings when "Camp Siegfried Special" trains arrived from Brooklyn bringing vacationers to Camp Siegfried, the campers dressed up in their Nazi uniforms and paraded down to the train station to welcome the visitors with a hearty "Heil Hitler!" and a Nazi salute, then marched back to camp with the new arrivals in tow.

SPEECH IMPEDIMENTS

Political speeches were a big part of the Camp Siegfried experience. Campers listened to endless hours of lectures praising Hitler, promoting the Nazi ideology, arguing for continued American neutrality, and attacking Jews, communists, President Franklin D. Roosevelt (whom the Bund was convinced was controlled by Jews), and FDR's New Deal programs, which were designed to lift the country out of the Great Depression.

And since one objective was to toughen the boys into good little soldiers for the Aryan cause, they spent a lot of time marching and practicing drills on the parade ground. There were also more than a few surprise middle-of-the-night marches through dark and rugged terrain while carrying 30-pound rucksacks, which left the kids scraped and bloodied by the time they returned to camp.

The very first kids to visit Camp Siegfried had it worst of all—they supplied the physical labor that built the camp. One of the benefits of using child labor, besides not having to pay the kids, was that the German American Bund didn't have to contract with labor unions (which it believed were controlled by Jews) to do the work.

THANKS BUT NO THANKS

One of the ironies of the German American Bund—and, by extension, Camp Siegfried—was that though their purpose was to promote the cause of Adolf Hitler and the Nazi Party, neither Hitler nor the Nazi Party wanted anything to do with them. Keeping America neutral and out of World War II long enough for Germany to win it was an important part of Hitler's strategy—more important than building a Nazi movement in America. He wanted support from Nazi sympathizers, but he wanted them to remain *underground*, so as not to provoke a hostile reaction from Franklin D. Roosevelt or the American public. Nazi summer camps with oompah-pah bands and swastika flags aflutter were not what he had in mind.

DAS SHOW-BOOT

But Fritz Kuhn had his own ideas. He proclaimed himself the "American Führer" and held one Nazi rally after another in the United States. They frequently turned violent when the Nazis clashed with even larger crowds of people who showed up to demonstrate against them, generating just the kind of negative publicity that Hitler was eager to avoid.

Finally in 1938, Hitler turned from ignoring the Bund to actively forbidding German citizens in the United States from belonging to it. He also forbade the Bund from using Nazi emblems. But Kuhn kept going and, in fact, held the Bund's largest rally ever in February 1939, when an estimated 20,000 Nazi sympathizers attended a rally celebrating George Washington's birthday (whom the Bund lauded as "America's first fascist") at New York's Madison Square Garden. A mob of anti-Nazi protesters, estimated by one police official to be 100,000 in number, surrounded the venue during the rally. Only the largest police mobilization for any event in the city's history up to that point kept the situation from exploding into a riot.

DOWN DER DRAIN

In its five years of existence, the German American Bund never did grow much beyond its base of German nationals living in the United States and recently naturalized German Americans who had grown disillusioned with life in their adopted country. And as war between Germany and the United States grew inexorably closer, the Bund began to fizzle. In December 1939, Fritz Kuhn was convicted of embezzling $14,000 from the group and sentenced to five years in Sing Sing, New York's maximum-security prison. Stripped of his U.S. citizenship while serving his sentence and deported when he was released from prison, Kuhn

Shakespeare invented the name Jessica (in *The Merchant of Venice*).

spent his remaining years in Germany and died a broken man in Munich in 1951.

The money he stole from the Bund, coupled with the additional sums he spent on his defense, put the Bund in a financial bind, and it grew worse when the movement splintered into squabbling factions after Kuhn went to prison. By the time Germany declared war on the United States after the bombing of Pearl Harbor in December 1941, the movement had dwindled to only a handful of supporters. Nine days after Pearl Harbor, the organization's members met at a secret location in Manhattan and voted the Bund into oblivion.

PAST TENSE

Vestiges of Camp Siegfried live on to this day, but not in that name. When the camp was seized by the federal government during the war, the homeowners who'd built bungalows in German Gardens sued through the German American Settlement League, which was reconstituted as a homeowners association, to get the land back.

They won the suit, but Camp Siegfried never reopened; today it's a park called Siegfried Park. Hitler Street has been renamed Park Boulevard, and all the other streets named for Nazis have been renamed as well. The bungalows in German Gardens are still there, many still owned by descendants of the Bund members who built them. But most of the buildings in Camp Siegfried were torn down long ago. A few, such as the clubhouse, are still standing (though the swastikas have been removed or covered up).

STILL AT IT

One thing that hasn't changed in all these years is that the land underneath the buildings, both in Siegfried Park and in German Gardens, is still owned by the German American Settlement League. And believe it or not, the league managed to enforce its Germans-only policy for decades after the war ended, long after such practices were outlawed. It did so through the use of restrictive covenants that forbade homeowners from listing their homes for sale anyplace other than in the league's newsletter, which was distributed only to members. Prospective home buyers also had to be sponsored by a league member, and the sale could not go through unless a majority of members voted to approve it.

It wasn't until 2016, when a German American couple trying to sell their home filed suit against the restrictive practices, that the league finally replaced its pro-German constitution and bylaws with new ones that gave anyone the right to buy a home in German Gardens. Only then did the last traces of Nazism on Long Island finally fade away.

The swastika was once considered a symbol of good fortune. Before the Nazis...

OUT OF MARSHMALLOWS? MAKE YOUR OWN

There are two good reasons to make your own marshmallows: 1) Who even knew you could make them at home? 2) If you like the taste of the store-bought variety, you'll be amazed at how much better these taste.

WHAT YOU'LL NEED:

- 2½ tablespoons unflavored gelatin

- ⅓ cup corn syrup
- 2 cups granulated sugar

- ¼ teaspoon salt
- A candy thermometer.

- 2 teaspoons vanilla extract. (If you're feeling adventurous, substitute 2 teaspoons of marshmallow root extract, which can be found in specialty food stores.)

- An electric mixer with attached bowl. You'll be working with very hot liquids, so a handheld mixer is not a safe choice. And as the hot liquid cools off, it becomes thick enough to burn out the motor of a handheld mixer.

- A 9-by-13-inch baking pan, lined with two layers of aluminum foil, one lengthwise and one crosswise, then sprayed with nonstick cooking spray. Use enough foil to allow for about two inches of overhang on all four sides of the pan; this will make it easier to lift the marshmallow mixture out after it's finished cooling.

- ½ cup cornstarch mixed with ½ cup confectioners' (powdered) sugar

- A metal sifter or strainer

GET COOKING

- Add the gelatin to the mixing bowl with ½ cup water. Set aside for at least 15 minutes to give the gelatin a chance to soften.

- Add ½ cup water to a saucepan with the corn syrup, sugar and salt. To prevent the sugar from crystallizing later, pour it into the center of the saucepan, taking care that none of the sugar touches the sides of the pan.

- Without stirring the mixture, bring it to a boil over medium-high heat. Boil until the temperature on the candy thermometer reads 240°F. This should take between six and eight minutes.

...Coca-Cola used them in advertising, and the Boy Scouts used them on merit badges.

- Using the whisk attachment on your electric mixer, turn the mixer to the lowest speed, and slowly pour the hot sugar mixture over the gelatin. It's very hot, so BE CAREFUL! To minimize splatter, try not to hit the whisk or the side of the bowl with the sugar mixture when pouring.

- When all of the sugar mixture has been added to the bowl, slowly increase the speed of the mixer to high and whisk at high speed for 10–12 minutes, until the outside of the bowl is barely warm to the touch.

- Toward the end of mixing, add the vanilla or marshmallow extract and continue mixing until they are fully incorporated into the marshmallow mixture.

- Spray a spatula with nonstick cooking spray and scrape the marshmallow mixture into the foil-lined baking dish. Work quickly! As the mixture cools, it becomes more difficult to work with. Smooth the top of the marshmallow mixture, then sift 3 tablespoons of the cornstarch/confectioners' sugar mixture over the top of the marshmallow mixture.

- Cover the pan and let it sit for at least four hours or overnight.

GOING TO PIECES

- After the marshmallow mixture has cooled, dust a cutting board with some of the cornstarch/confectioner sugar mixture and spray a sharp chef's knife or some kitchen shears with nonstick cooking spray.

- Lift the marshmallow mixture out of the baking pan and turn it out onto the cutting board. Peel off the foil.

- Sift two tablespoons of the cornstarch/confectioners' sugar mixture over the top of the marshmallow mixture.

- Cut the marshmallow mixture lengthwise into strips, then cut the strips into individual pieces. Respray the knife or kitchen shears with the nonstick cooking spray as needed.

- Roll the pieces in the remaining cornstarch/confectioners' sugar mixture, then toss to remove excess powder. You're done!

- The marshmallows will keep in an airtight container for up to two weeks. They can be roasted over a fire or added to a cup of hot cocoa just like marshmallows from the store. Enjoy!

GOURMET MARSHMALLOWS

- Try using a different flavor extract in place of the vanilla/marshmallow extract, and add a few drops of food coloring—red for strawberry, yellow for lemon, etc.—to give the marshmallows a color that matches the flavor.

World's deepest subway: The Pyongyang Metro in North Korea. It's as deep as a football field is long.

ACCORDING TO THE LATEST RESEARCH

Are people with foul mouths more or less honest than other people? Does driving a fancy car make you more or less popular with your peers? Here's a look at some of the more unusual scientific studies we've come across lately.

Study: "What if the Rival Drives a Porsche? Luxury Car Spending as a Costly Signal in Male Intrasexual Competition," *Evolutionary Psychology*, October 2016

Purpose: To "investigate the function of male conspicuous consumption in same-sex competition."

Methodology: Researchers at the University of Würzburg conducted an online poll of 405 German males. Some subjects were shown a picture of a man and told he'd just purchased a new Porsche Boxster sports car. Other subjects were shown the same photo of the same man and told he bought a Ford Fiesta.

Findings: The respondents who were told the man bought a Porsche perceived him "as a rival and mate poacher and less as a friend," more than the respondents who were told he bought a Ford Fiesta did. The man who was presented as a Porsche buyer was also rated "higher on all mate value attributes (i.e., attractiveness, sexual willingness, intelligence, ambition, and status)," but less agreeable and less loyal than when he was presented as a Ford Fiesta buyer. The results, concluded the study's authors, "suggest that a man who displays conspicuous luxuries may have an advantage over other men, as he could therefore deter inferior rivals."

Study: "Frankly, We Do Give a Damn: The Relationship Between Profanity and Honesty," *Social Psychological and Personality Science*, January 2017

Purpose: "To explore the relationship between profanity and honesty."

Methodology: The researchers asked 276 online respondents to list their favorite and most commonly used swear words, but they did not tell the respondents how many words to list. "By giving participants an opportunity to curse freely, we expected that the daily usage and enjoyment of profanity would be reflected in the total number of curse words written," the researchers say. The participants were also asked to report how often they swore: 1) when other people were around; 2) when they were alone; and 3) online, either by texting, messaging, e-mailing, or posting on social media. They also had their honesty

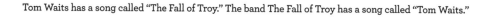

measured by answering a short questionnaire consisting of 12 yes/no questions such as, "Are all your habits good and desirable ones?" In each case, a "yes" answer was considered "unrealistic and therefore most likely a lie."

Findings: "Honesty was positively correlated with all profanity measures, meaning that participants lied less…if they wrote down a higher number of frequently used and liked curse words, or self-reported higher profanity use in their everyday lives," concluded the researchers.

Study: "Combating the Sting of Rejection with the Pleasure of Revenge: A New Look at How Emotion Shapes Aggression," *Journal of Personality and Social Psychology*, March 2017

Purpose: To determine whether "getting revenge can be a viable method of mood repair."

Methodology: Researchers from the University of Kentucky asked 1,156 students to write an essay on a personal topic of their choice, then exchange their essay with another student to receive feedback. Some students (the control group) really did get honest feedback from their peers. But the rest (the experimental group) received negative feedback that had been written by the researchers themselves—comments like "This is one of the worst essays I have EVER read."

The students in the experimental group were then given voodoo dolls and stick pins and told to imagine that the voodoo doll was the person who provided the negative feedback, and to demonstrate how angry they were by sticking pins in the doll. Afterward, the researchers assessed the mood of the control group and compared it with the mood of the experimental group.

Findings: Sticking pins in the voodoo doll was so effective at repairing the mood of students in the experimental group that their mood was indistinguishable from the mood of the students in the control group who'd received no negative feedback. "Retaliatory aggression is often a pleasant experience," the researchers note. "These findings implicate aggression's rewarding nature as an incentive for rejected individuals' violent tendencies."

*   *   *

CALLING LONG DISTANCE

The ancient Greeks had a way of sending messages over great distances as early as 140 BC, using torches and a numbered grid (similar to the board game Battleship). Messages were sent one letter at a time. If the letter Ω was in grid box 4-6, for example, the torch bearer waved four torches, then six, to transmit that letter.

Did the plague end in the Middle Ages? No: San Francisco had an outbreak in 1900; L.A. had one in 1924.

IRONIC, ISN'T IT?

More irony to put the problems of day-to-day life into proper perspective.

IONY?

In March 2014, while *Fox & Friends* host Ainsley Earhardt reported on the Scripps National Spelling Bee, which had run late the night before, the graphic that was displayed on the screen read: "Longest Spelling Be Ever?"

GRIDIRON-Y

In 1998, after several losing seasons, the Oakland Raiders hired head coach Jon Gruden to turn things around. Although he led the team to the playoffs three years in a row, Gruden failed to bring the Raiders a Super Bowl win, so he was traded to the Tampa Bay Buccaneers in 2002. In his first season there, Gruden led the Bucs all the way to a Super Bowl win…over the Oakland Raiders.

STRIKE WHILE THE IRONY IS HOT

In March 2017, India's government drafted what critics viewed as a "draconian bill" that would make it illegal for lawyers to go on strike. To protest the bill, more than 6,000 Indian lawyers went on strike.

PENT-UP IRONY

In 2017, a temp worker at SPS—a promotional gift company in Blackpool, England—was fired from his job in the middle of a shift. He became very angry and punched his boss in the face. At the time of the firing, the worker was packing stress balls.

SMOKIN' IRONY

In April 2017, Dr. Mark Hulett of the La Trobe Institute for Molecular Science in Australia announced that his team had made a remarkable (and quite ironic) discovery: They isolated a molecule, called NaD1, that forms "pincer-like structures that grip onto lipids present in the membrane of cancer cells and rips them open, causing the cells to expel their contents and explode." Where did the researchers discover this cancer-killing molecule? In the tobacco plant.

President John Adams had a dog named Satan.

THE BLIND BABY EPIDEMIC

The story of a sad and tragic epidemic that happened just 70 years ago, but which few people know about today. (But you're familiar with at least one of its victims.)

MONTEREY

On February 14, 1941, Dr. Stewart Clifford, a pediatrician in Boston, made a house call to check on one of his patients, the three-month-old daughter of a young rabbi. The girl had been born several weeks premature, weighing just four pounds at birth, but had been doing well in the months since her birth. Unfortunately, something now seemed wrong. There was a grayness in the pupils of the girl's eyes—and she appeared to have lost her ability to see. Clifford contacted his friend, Dr. Paul Chandler, one of Boston's leading ophthalmologists. Chandler examined the girl, and told Clifford he had found something he had never seen before: there were strange gray masses attached to the rear of the lenses in both of the child's eyes. Even worse, Clifford's diagnosis was correct. The girl was completely blind.

Just days later, another of Clifford's patients, this one a seven-month-old baby, was discovered to have the same symptoms. That baby had also gone blind. And just as with the prior case, the child had been born prematurely.

EPIDEMIC

By 1942 several other cases of premature babies going blind, with the same symptoms—the appearance of gray masses inside the babies' eyes—were reported in the Boston area. That same year, Clifford contacted Dr. Theodore Terry, professor of opthalmology at Harvard Medical School, and asked him to look into the mysterious cases. Terry studied five of the cases, and wrote an article about the condition in *American Journal of Ophthalmology*. When eye doctors around the country saw the article, similar stories were reported outside the Boston area. By 1945 Terry had collected information on 117 premature infants who'd been affected by what was being called *retrolental fibrofasia* (RLF)—medical-ese for "scar tissue behind the lens of the eye." The victims had varying degrees of vision loss—but they all had the characteristic mass of scar tissue inside their eyeballs. It was now obvious that these were not one-off cases: something was affecting the eyes of premature babies in a way that had not been seen before, and all of those cases—or at the very least the majority of them—were related.

Most ophthalmologists studying RLF were convinced that the condition

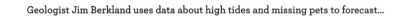

was related to the fact that all its victims had been born prematurely. That was understandable. Premature birth can cause a wide variety of health problems, minor and serious, simply because the bodies of "preemies" haven't completed the normal *in utero* development process that makes them ready for life outside the womb.

> *But Terry wasn't convinced: if this was just another premature birth complication, why hadn't it been seen before?*

And most of the babies he'd personally examined had perfectly normal eyes at birth. They'd only been affected with the condition in the weeks—and in many cases months—after they were born. Terry was convinced something else was at play. Sadly, he wasn't able to confirm this—he died of a heart attack in 1946, at the age of 47.

RLF

So what exactly was going on inside the eyes of the victims of RLF? First, by 1942 doctors had discovered that the condition primarily affected the retinas in the victims' eyes, and not the lenses, as had previously been believed. (The retina is the thin layer of tissue that lines the inside of the rear of the eyeball. It holds the photoreceptors that "read" incoming light and sends that information to the brain via the optic nerves, where it's translated into the images we see.)

The retinas in our eyes are rich in tiny blood vessels, through which they receive the nutrients they need to function. For unknown reasons, the retinas of RLF victims grew far too many blood vessels, many of which were abnormally shaped or defective. In the worst cases, this abnormal blood vessel growth caused an affected retina to detach from its position on the rear inner wall of the eyeball, and to migrate to a position behind the eyes' lenses—those were the "strange gray masses" that were the first sign of the disease. Because healthy, attached retinas are vital to even rudimentary eyesight, RLF at its worst led to complete blindness.

WHAT'S GOING ON?

In the years after 1946, with the number of cases of RLF increasing in the United States and in other countries, theories about the cause of the condition were studied in hospitals and research labs around the world. Because most experts were convinced that the condition was new, many of the theories centered around recently developed treatments for premature babies. Those included the use of antibiotics, blood transfusions, large doses of vitamins, and hormone treatments. But none of the studies led to the discovery of what was causing RLF—and the number of victims kept increasing.

And one of the most puzzling aspects about RLF: it was occurring almost exclusively in modern, developed nations—including the United States, Canada, the UK and several other western European nations, Australia, and Cuba—where the care of premature babies had improved and the infant mortality rate for preemies had fallen dramatically over the previous decades.

BABY STEPS

In 1949 doctors started examining a treatment for premature babies that prior studies had overlooked: incubators. Incubation devices had been used to keep delicate babies warm since the late 1800s, but in the 1930s, a new kind was developed—airtight incubators that could maintain abnormally high air-oxygen levels. Throughout the 1940s, it had become increasingly common in the developed world to treat preemies with high concentrations of oxygen, often for several weeks at a time. The treatment had been credited with lowering the mortality rate…but had there been an unknown price for that lower rate? By the early 1950s, a lot of doctors thought that might be the case.

Over the next few years, several studies involving premature babies that were kept in oxygen-supplying incubators were conducted in countries around the world. The most notable was one led by two doctors, Arnall Patz, an ophthalmologist, and Leroy Hoeck, a pediatrician, at Gallinger Municipal Hospital in Washington, D.C.—and the results were shocking.

TRIAL AND ERROR

Over the course of two years (1951 to 1953), Patz and Hoeck studied 65 premature babies, all weighing less than 3.5 pounds at birth, divided into two groups. One group was kept in incubators with 65 percent oxygen levels and higher for four to seven weeks at a time (the standard treatment for premature babies at the time). The other group was given lower levels—40 percent oxygen or less—but only when it was deemed medically necessary, and only for from one to 14 days at a time. (Note: The parents were not asked for permission to have their children participate in the study, and were only told about it after it had begun—which was pretty normal for the era.)

Results: only 16 percent of the babies in the low-oxygen group developed RLF, compared to about 61 percent of those in the high-oxygen group. (Twelve of the babies in the high-oxygen group went blind, compared to just one in the low-oxygen group.)

The results of Patz and Hoeck's study led to the National Institutes of Health

Not funny: The first American humor magazine was *The Bee,* published in 1765. It failed after 3 issues.

(NIH) to begin a much larger study, involving 18 U.S. hospitals and thousands of children. The results of that study—confirming that high levels of oxygen over long periods of time indeed played a major role in the development of RLF—were published in 1955.

AFTERMATH

In the years following the Patz-Hoeck and the NIH studies, the use of prolonged exposure to high levels of oxygen in the care of premature babies was drastically curtailed in hospitals worldwide, and by the late 1950s the epidemic of blindness in premature babies was over. Here's some information about the epidemic, and the state of the disease since that time:

• The process through which high levels of oxygen causes RLF is quite complex, but here's a basic explanation: retinal blood vessels normally develop *in utero*, in just the last few weeks of pregnancy, and require relatively low levels of oxygen in the developing retinas. Because this vessel growth process is incomplete in premature babies, high levels of oxygen adversely affect that normal vessel growth process, causing the vessels to grow too fast, too large, and in abnormal shapes, which can lead to RLF.

• An estimated 12,000 preemies developed RLF during the epidemic. More than 10,000 of them lost their sight.

• The name of retrolental fibroplasia was changed in the years after it was discovered it involved the retinas, and not the lenses, of the affected eyes. It is now known as retinopathy of prematurity (ROP).

• Some well-known victims of RLF include jazz singer/pianist Diane Schuur (born in 1953) and actor/singer Tom Sullivan (born in 1947). The most famous victim of RLF: Stevie Wonder, who was born in 1950.

*　　*　　*

A NICE STORY

Spray parks are those sections of city parks where streams of water shoot up out of the ground, allowing kids to frolic in the water and cool off on summer days. They're fun, but they're also expensive, and can cost upwards of $250,000. Luckily for the city of Green Island, New York, it got a $200,000 gift from John and Linda Kutey, who'd won $28.7 million in the Mega Millions lottery the year before and wanted to do something for their hometown. That paid for most of it. Then, following the Kuteys' example, builders and engineers donated their services, so the new spray park in Paine Street Park cost the city nothing.

UNCLE JOHN'S 30TH BIRTHDAY BUDDIES

*Uncle John's Bathroom Reader isn't the only thing turning 30 this year.
Here's some other stuff that also made its big debut back in 1987.*

Cherry Garcia. If you're a fan of this ice cream, you can thank a Grateful Dead fan named Jane Williamson. In 1986 she sent a postcard to Ben & Jerry's, suggesting they make a flavor in honor of Dead frontman Jerry Garcia…and they took her up on it. After getting Garcia's permission, Ben & Jerry's launched the flavor in 1987. (It's chocolate ice cream with cherries and fudge flakes.)

The Loonie. In 1987 the Canadian government started taking its $1 bills out of circulation and replacing them with $1 coins. One side of the coin bore the image of a bird native to Canada, the loon, so they soon became known as "loonies." (Two-dollar coins, introduced in 1995, were nicknamed "toonies.")

The Simpsons. The classic animated series—which was later spun off into its own show, and has since aired more than 600 episodes—debuted as a short segment on Fox's *The Tracey Ullman Show* on April 19, 1987.

The Fox Network. *The Tracey Ullman Show* was part of Fox's first slate of prime-time shows. While the network's *very* first show was a short-lived late-night talk show hosted by Joan Rivers that premiered in October 1986, it made its mark on American culture when it plunged into prime time on April 5, 1987, with a lineup that included the Ullman show and *Married…with Children*.

Spuds MacKenzie. The bull terrier who wore sunglasses, was a "party animal," and drank Bud Light made his debut in an ad that appeared during Super Bowl XXI in 1987. (The dog in the ad was actually a female.)

SXSW. Part entertainment industry conference, part trade show, and part music festival, South by Southwest (or SXSW) was an outgrowth of a New York-based festival called New Music Seminar. Organizers of that one asked editors at the alternative weekly newspaper the *Austin Chronicle* to help put together a similar conference in Texas. More than 700 people showed up for the first festival, held in March 1987. Today, more than 50,000 descend on Austin for it each year.

An 18th-century French device called a *serinette,* or "bird organ," was used to teach canaries new songs.

Prozac. At the end of 1987, pharmaceutical giant Eli Lilly received FDA approval for *fluoxetine*, one of the most effective antidepressants ever developed. Lilly made billions off the drug, marketed under the name Prozac. It's now on the World Health Organization's List of Essential Medicines.

The end of in-flight smoking. On July 26, 1987, the U.S. Congress passed a bill that banned smoking on domestic flights lasting less than two hours. Today smoking is banned on almost all American flights, and most international ones, too.

Blockbuster film franchises. The first *Lethal Weapon*, *Predator*, and *Robocop* movies played to huge crowds at movie theaters across the country.

The Bold and the Beautiful. Daytime soap operas are a dying TV genre—only four remain on the air today. The newest of them debuted 30 years ago: CBS's *The Bold and the Beautiful.*

Red Bull. The first commercially available "energy drink," Red Bull was launched in Austria in 1987.

Disposable contact lenses. Soft contact lenses, which are placed directly over the cornea as an alternative to glasses, had been available since the early 1970s. But they were very expensive, very fragile, and required rigorous cleaning every night. In 1987 Johnson & Johnson created Acuvue disposable lenses, which were designed to be worn for a week or two, then removed and thrown away.

Hooked on Phonics. Millions of kids learned to read with this book/audiocassette combo, which was first sold by Gateway Educational Productions in 1987. ("Hooked on Phonics worked for me!")

The Legend of Zelda. In 1986 Nintendo video game designer Shigeru Miyamoto came up with a game that featured a medieval hero named Link going on a quest through magical lands and enchanted forests, inspired by the forests and caves he explored as a child growing up in rural Japan. The game was called The Legend of Zelda and was a massive hit in Japan. But Nintendo didn't think American players would care for a complex game that took hours to play and involved reading a lot of text. At the time, simple games like Pac-Man or Donkey Kong (also created by Miyamoto) were the most popular titles in America. But they were wrong. Released in the United States in 1987, The Legend of Zelda sold 6.5 million copies, making it one of the best-selling home video game titles ever.

Holy trinity: The Bible has been translated into all three *Star Trek* languages (Vulcan, Romulan, and Klingon).

THOUGHTFUL WORDS

Take a moment to reflect on these wise quotes.

"**Just where you are—that's the place to start.**"
—Pema Chödrön

"*We're here for a reason. I believe that reason is to throw little torches out to lead people through the dark.*"
—Whoopi Goldberg

"Happiness is when what you think, what you say, and what you do are in harmony."
—Mahatma Gandhi

"Without new experiences, something inside of us sleeps. The sleeper must awaken."
—Frank Herbert

"FREEDOM IS FROM WITHIN."
—Frank Lloyd Wright

"NO MATTER HOW OLD YOU ARE, IF A LITTLE KID HANDS YOU A TOY PHONE, YOU ANSWER IT."
—Dave Chappelle

"*Just believe in yourself. Even if you don't, pretend that you do and, at some point, you will.*"
—Venus Williams

"**We cannot direct the wind, but we can adjust the sails.**"
—Dolly Parton

"There's no such thing as bad weather, only inappropriate clothing."
—Sir Ranulph Fiennes

"You never really learn much from hearing yourself speak."
—George Clooney

The Twisted Ranch restaurant in St. Louis incorporates ranch dressing into every single menu item.

STRANGE LAWSUITS

*These days, it seems like people will sue each other over practically anything.
Here are some real-life examples of unusual legal battles.*

THE PLAINTIFF: Jose Banks, 39, a convicted bank robber awaiting sentencing at the Metropolitan Correctional Center, a high-rise federal prison in downtown Chicago

THE DEFENDANT: The United States government

THE LAWSUIT: Over the course of several months in 2012, Banks and his cellmate Kenneth Conley meticulously planned an escape attempt right out of *The Shawshank Redemption*. Little by little, they clandestinely chiseled a hole in their 17th-floor cell wall without the guards noticing. All the while, they were procuring bedsheets and dental floss—enough to fashion a rope they could use to rappel down to the street below. Finally, on the night of the escape, the two prisoners stuffed clothes in their bedsheets to make it look like they were sleeping and then escaped through their hole and shimmied down the rope. After a harrowing climb (which Banks later said was "traumatizing"), they made it to the sidewalk and hailed a cab. Banks was captured a few days later; Conley was captured a few weeks after that.

Two years later, while confined to a much more secure section of the prison, Banks filed a lawsuit against the federal government, claiming it was "negligent in enabling the breakout" by not guarding him more closely. Further, he claimed the failed escape attempt has caused him "humiliation and embarrassment" and damaged his "spiritual constitution."

THE VERDICT: Case dismissed. The judge informed him that "no one has a right to be better guarded." (But he did say that Banks "gets credit for chutzpah.")

THE PLAINTIFF: Jennifer Connell, 54, a human resources manager from New York City

THE DEFENDANT: Sean T., her 12-year-old nephew

THE LAWSUIT: On March 18, 2011, Connell attended her nephew's eighth birthday party in Connecticut. When Sean saw her arrive, he ran to her while yelling "Auntie Jen, I love you!" and then leaped into her arms…and knocked her over. Connell allegedly broke her wrist in the fall, but she didn't say anything at the time because she "didn't want to upset Sean."

Four years later, Connell really did upset Sean (and just about everyone who read about the case) when she filed a lawsuit against him for $127,000. On what grounds? The wrist injury had made it hard for her to perform a lot of her daily tasks, like walking upstairs and "holding my hors d'oeuvres plate." Surprisingly, the lawsuit made it to a jury trial. "We do not take great pleasure in bringing a minor to court," said Connell's lawyer, while she sat next to him wearing a black wrist guard. But Sean, he said, "should have known better," and therefore should be held responsible for his actions. Sean's defense attorney argued that his client was simply "an eight-year-old boy being an eight-year-old boy" and that all he wanted to do was "give his auntie a hug."

THE VERDICT: The jury found the little boy guilty and made him pay the full $127,000. Just kidding. It took them only 25 minutes of deliberation to find Sean innocent. "We just couldn't find him, you know, liable for what happened," said one of the jurors (who will forever have the best "jury duty story" at parties).

THE PLAINTIFF: Sirgiorgiro Clardy, 26, a pimp from Portland, Oregon

THE DEFENDANT: Nike, Inc.

THE LAWSUIT: In 2012, Clardy became very upset when a customer didn't pay him, so Clardy stomped on the man's head several times—which required stitches and plastic surgery. That crime (along with a few other violent offenses) got Clardy sentenced to prison for 100 years. Unwilling to accept responsibility for what had happened, he decided that his Air Jordans were to blame. So he sued Nike (which is based in nearby Beaverton, Oregon) for $100 million, claiming that the shoes were "defective" because they could do so much harm to a person's head. Clardy said that Nike should have put a label on the shoe warning wearers that it can be used as a weapon.

At the pretrial hearing, Nike's attorney spoke for about a minute and a half, calling the suit baseless. Clardy, acting as his own lawyer, got up and rambled on to Judge Robert Durham for more than 20 minutes, until the judge finally put a halt to the proceedings.

THE VERDICT: "You've wasted my time, Mr. Clardy," said Judge Durham as he threw the case out of court.

> **MICHAEL JORDAN** *still earns about $100 million a year from the sale of Air Jordan sneakers. That's more than the $94 million salary he racked up in 15 years of playing in the NBA.*

THE PLAINTIFF: Troy Tucker, a 67-year-old woman from St. Louis, Missouri

THE DEFENDANT: Lambert's, a restaurant in Sikeston, Missouri

THE LAWSUIT: Lambert's is known as the "Home of the Throwed Roll." It says so in really big letters on the sign outside. There are several more signs inside warning patrons that they are in the "Home of the Throwed Roll." And when you walk in, you can see the waiters throwing bread rolls to each other and to customers. So it's not surprising that every now and then, a roll misses its target and hits a patron.

That's what happened when Tucker went there in 2015 with her church group: she got hit in the eye with a roll, which, according to her lawyer, caused a "lacerated cornea with a vitreous detachment and all head, neck, eyes, and vision were severely damaged." After the restaurant's insurance company denied her claim (on the basis that she should have been aware of the risk), Tucker filed a $35,000 lawsuit against Lambert's for medical bills and legal fees. Her lawyer admitted to the *New York Daily News* that the lawsuit seems "innocuous," but added that "you really shouldn't throw things at people, just like your mother said. You can put an eye out."

THE VERDICT: Unknown—but it's likely that the parties came to terms without ever going to court.

THE PLAINTIFF: Alexander Forouzesh, a coffee drinker from Los Angeles

THE DEFENDANT: Starbucks Coffee Company

THE LAWSUIT: "If I lose this case, I'll probably switch over to Coffee Bean," said Forouzesh. "I've been drinking iced coffee for a really long time," he told local news site *LAist* in 2016, which is why he's upset that a 16-ounce Starbucks "Grande" iced coffee only has about 12 ounces of actual beverage. Ice, he claims, "is not a beverage." So he filed a class-action fraud suit against Starbucks on behalf of "all persons in the state of California who purchased one or more of the Defendant's Cold Drinks at any time between April 27, 2006 and the present."

Forouzesh sued for "breach of express warranty, breach of implied warranty, negligent misrepresentation, unjust enrichment, fraud, and violations of California's Unfair Competition Law and False Advertising Law."

THE VERDICT: Not only did U.S. District Judge Percy Anderson dismiss the case, but he told Forouzesh that it's time to grow up and smell the coffee:

> "As young children learn, they can increase the amount of beverage they receive if they order 'no ice.' If children have figured out that including ice in a cold beverage decreases the amount of liquid they will receive, the Court has no difficulty concluding that a reasonable consumer would not be deceived into thinking that when they order an iced tea, that the drink they receive will

include both ice and tea and that for a given size cup, some portion of the drink will be ice rather than whatever liquid beverage the consumer ordered. This conclusion is supported by the fact that the cups Starbucks uses for its Cold Drinks, as shown in the Complaint, are clear, and therefore make it easy to see that the drink consists of a combination of liquid and ice."

THE PLAINTIFF: Edward Gamson, a dentist from Maryland

THE DEFENDANT: British Airways

THE LAWSUIT: The Alhambra is a 900-year-old fortress that overlooks the city of Granada, Spain, and Gamson had always wanted to visit it. So when he was invited to a dental conference in Portugal in 2013, he decided to buy a pair of tickets for him and his partner. Gamson claims he used the correct airport codes while booking the flight, but when he received his tickets, he didn't notice that they said "Grenada" and not "Granada."

About 20 minutes after departing from their connecting flight in London, Glamson asked a flight attendant why the plane was flying west over the ocean, and not south toward Spain. "Spain?" asked the flight attendant. "We're going to Grenada." That's when Gamson realized that he didn't buy a ticket to the Spanish city—he bought one to a tropical Caribbean island nearly 4,000 miles away. When the plane stopped over at St. Lucia, Gamson and his traveling partner booked a flight to Miami. Then Gamson flew back to London (alone), and then to Portugal (late) for the conference he was supposed to attend in the first place. The extra tickets cost him nearly $3,000, but he sued British Airways for $34,000, claiming lost wages for the time he would have been working. "I made it absolutely clear to the booking agent I wanted to go to Granada in Spain," he said. "Why on earth would I want to go to Grenada in the Caribbean if I was flying back to America from Lisbon?"

THE VERDICT: Case dismissed. British Airways offered Gamson two free plane tickets and 100,000 frequent-flyer miles for the mishap, and the judge thought that was adequate. (The good news: a few months later, Gamson finally got to visit the Alhambra. "It really was beautiful," he told ABC News.)

*   *   *

"Leadership is the art of getting someone else to do something you want done because he wants to do it."

—Dwight Eisenhower

In the U.S. Constitution, Pennsylvania is spelled as "Pensylvania."

IT'S A ZOO AT THE AIRPORT

It used to be that only one kind of animal worked at the airport, and if one of those critters thought your luggage smelled "funny," you had some explaining to do. Ah, how things have changed…

GOING TO THE DOGS

If you're old enough to remember 9/11, you may also remember how stressful it was for people to resume flying again after the terrorist attacks. To help relieve some of this anxiety, a volunteer chaplain at Mineta International Airport in San Jose, California, obtained permission to bring her certified therapy dog, a boxer/great dane mix named Orion, with her to the airport. Interacting with Orion proved to be remarkably effective at soothing passengers' jangled nerves, and soon more than a dozen therapy dogs were wandering the Mineta concourse with their handlers in tow. The benefits they provided are supported by scientific research: Studies have shown that petting an animal can lower both blood pressure and stress levels. Other airports soon copied San Jose's program, and today dozens of them nationwide employ teams of therapy dogs (wearing vests that say "Pet Me!") to help keep stressed-out travelers a little calmer.

FEELING A LITTLE HORSE

Therapy dog programs have worked so well that it was probably just a matter of time before other animals got in on the act. In the run-up to the Kentucky Derby in 2016, Cincinnati/Northern Kentucky Airport introduced three miniature "therapy horses" named Wendy, Harley, and Dakota to the concourse. Residents of Seven Oaks Farm in Ross, Ohio, the horses visit the airport twice a month, often in costume according to the season. In the weeks leading up to the Kentucky Derby in May, for example, Wendy and Harley wore garlands of roses. On her visits to the airport, Dakota is sometimes dressed as a unicorn.

Lisa Moad, who owns Seven Oaks Farm, says she got the idea while passing through an airport without her horses. "A guy was going off on someone at the counter. My husband leaned over and said, 'That guy needs a little animal therapy.'" She happened to e-mail Wendi Orlando, who manages customer relations at Cincinnati/Northern Kentucky Airport just as Orlando was looking to set up an animal therapy program at the airport. "Horses in Kentucky? We thought, 'Hey, we can make that work,' she told the *Cincinnati Enquirer* in 2017.

Recent study: Whether or not people believe something they read is influenced by what font is used.

HAMMING IT UP

In 2016, a small, spotted Juliana pig named LiLou became the first pig ever to pass the San Francisco SPCA's Animal Assisted Therapy program, which qualified her to work as a therapy animal. When the San Francisco International Airport learned about LiLou, they were eager to have her join the 300 cats, dogs, and rabbits who make up the airport's animal therapy Wag Brigade, founded in 2013. LiLou has been making visits to the airport ever since.

If you happen to be at the airport on a day when LiLou is visiting, she won't be hard to recognize: she's the pig wearing bright nail polish and a tutu. She's also one of the few animals at the airport who does tricks: LiLou can twirl, stand on her back hooves, greet travelers with her snout or a wave, and bang out tunes on a toy piano. She also bows after each performance. When she's not at the airport, LiLou makes the rounds at hospitals, senior centers, and other places that could use a visit from a special pig. (Who couldn't?) "I can see that she is happy showing off her tricks and getting her praise," LiLou's owner, Tatyana Danilova, told USA Today in 2016. "It also brings positive emotions to me, seeing that we can do something good for the community and bring more smiles in some unconventional way."

WHAT'S THE BUZZ?

In 2015, scientists at the University of Giessen in Germany published the results of a study showing that western honeybees can be trained to detect the presence of illegal drugs by smell. In their experiment, the scientists exposed the bees to the smell of heroin, then administered a mild electric shock to the bees, causing them to associate the shock with the smell of the drugs. Afterward, when the bees were placed in a chamber containing the smell of heroin at one end, as soon as the bees detected the smell of the drug they flew away from it toward the other end of the chamber.

The scientists envision that this behavior could be put to work at airports in a device that blows air over passenger luggage and into a chamber containing the bees. If the bees fly away from odors in the stream of air, that would indicate the possible presence of drugs in the luggage, which could then be subjected to further scrutiny. Bonus: the bees are cheaper to train than drug-sniffing dogs, no small consideration in places where the legalization of marijuana has meant that the dogs have to be retrained. "The retraining of sniffer dogs to ignore cannabis is difficult and time consuming," the study's authors note. "Trained honeybees could therefore be used to complement or replace the role of sniffer dogs as part of an automated drug detection system."

No beef: The McDonald's corporation makes most of its money collecting rent from its franchisees.

BOWLING LINGO, PART II

Use these phrases to sound like a bowler. (Bowling like a bowler is another story.) Part I is on page 103.

Fenceposts: The 7-10 split. (Also called *bed posts*, *mule ears*, and *snake eyes*.)

Field goal. When the ball rolls between the pins of a wide split.

Foul line. The line that marks the beginning of a bowling lane. A bowler who steps over the line while rolling has committed a foul. It counts as a shot (a roll).

Frame. One of the ten turns a player takes during a full bowling game. A single frame can consist of either one or two rolls of the ball, depending on how many pins are knocked down on the first turn (except for the tenth frame, which can have three rolls). Knocking down all ten pins on the first roll—a *strike*—ends a frame, but if only some of the pins are knocked down, the bowler gets a second chance to knock down the remaining pins.

Grandma's teeth. Any random array of pins left standing after a first roll.

Heads. The first 20 feet of a regulation 60-foot bowling lane after the foul line. The next 20 feet is the *mid-lane*; the last 20 feet is the *back end*. This does not include the *approach*, described earlier, or the *pin deck*, where the pins stand at the end of the lane, and which is usually about 5 feet long.

Picket fence. When the 1-2-4-7 pins, or the 1-3-6-10 pins, are left standing after the first roll. (Those four-pin configurations are in a straight line, giving them the look of a picket fence.) Also called a *rail* or *clothesline*.

Pin. A *pin* is a bowling pin—that needs no explanation. But there's also a *pin* associated with a bowling ball: it's the round colored dot, about a half an inch in diameter, on a modern bowling ball. This dot marks the top of a cylindrical plug in the ball, also referred to as the *pin*. The plug is attached to the *core*, or *weight block*, of a bowling ball. Modern bowling balls have dense, heavy cores inside them, which come in different shapes and can make the ball heavier in some parts, and lighter in others. This affects the spin of the ball, allowing for a greater *hook*, or curve, as it rolls down the lane.

Older than you think: The first mobile phone call from a car was made in St. Louis in 1946.

Pindicator. The lighted display board on the wall above the pins at bowling alleys, indicating which pins are standing.

Pines. The softer area of a bowling lane: on all-wooden lanes, the first 12 to 16 feet of the lane is usually made of maple, which is a hard wood, because this area of the lane has the initial contact with the ball. The rest of the lane is usually made of a softer wood—often pine. (Lanes in many modern bowling alleys are made from a mix of wood and synthetic materials.)

Pit. The area at the very end of the lane, after the pin deck, where the pins and ball end up after a roll.

Rock. Slang term for a bowling ball. (Also called an *apple*.)

Sleeper. After the first shot, a standing pin hidden directly behind another standing pin. Example: when the 1 pin and 5 pin are left standing, the 5 pin is a sleeper. (Also called a *barmaid*, a *bicycle*, *one-in-the-dark*, and a *tandem*.)

Sombrero. Achieving four strikes in a row.

Spare. Knocking down all the standing pins on the second shot of a frame.

Swiss cheese ball. A ball with multiple holes that's used in pro shops to determine a bowler's finger size for a custom-made bowling ball.

Washout. When the headpin is the only pin, or one of a combination of pins, left standing after the first shot. (Note this is not a type of split, because the headpin can't be standing in a split.)

Woolworth. Woolworths used to be known as a "five and dime store," so the 5-10 (five and dime) split is known as a *Woolworth*. Also called a *five and dime*.

> **BOWLED OVER:** *How many pins are struck by a bowling ball during an optimally thrown strike? Four. The remaining six pins are knocked down by other pins. The four pins struck by the ball are most commonly the 1, 3, 5, and 9 pins for a right-hander, and the 1, 2, 5, and 8 pins for a left-hander.*

What are "walking shelter shoes"? Sneakers that contain a one-person tent, half in each...

PROJECT GUTENBERG: THE FIRST E-BOOKS

Did you know that although tin cans were invented in the 1810, the can opener wasn't invented until 1855? If you're reading this on an iPad or a Kindle, you may be surprised to learn that e-books have a similar history— they predate e-book readers by more than 30 years.

CHAPTER ONE

Michael Hart was a college freshman at the University of Illinois at Urbana-Champaign in the summer of 1971. He was a lifelong tinkerer, the kind of person who even as a seven-year-old had been skilled enough to take apart his parents' TVs and radios to see how they worked…and then put them back together again.

That summer, two college friends managed to get him an account on a machine that was more complicated than anything he'd ever tinkered with before: a Xerox Sigma V mainframe computer, part of the university's Materials Research Lab. It was unlike most computers of the era in that instead of being an island unto itself, it was linked to about 100 other university and military computers around the country. They were part of a network called ARPANET (Advanced Research Projects Agency Network), the predecessor of the Internet.

SOMETHING SPECIAL

Hart got his first chance to try the mainframe on July 4 of that year. Most users spent their computer time writing programs, but Hart was so awestruck by the opportunity that for once he decided not to tinker. Reason: He figured any program he wrote would soon be obsolete, and he wanted to create something more enduring. But what?

He got his answer when he reached into his backpack for something to eat. Beside the snacks, inside his bag was a commemorative copy of the Declaration of Independence, something his supermarket was giving away as a Fourth of July promotion. "I had a 'lightbulb moment,'" he recounted in a 2002 interview. "I thought for a while to see if I could figure out anything I could do with the computer that would be more important than typing in the Declaration of Independence, something that would still be there 100 years later—but I

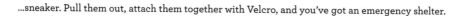

…sneaker. Pull them out, attach them together with Velcro, and you've got an emergency shelter.

couldn't come up with anything." So he typed the entire document, all 1,458 words of it, into the mainframe by hand.

STONE AGE

For anyone who wasn't a computer programmer in the early 1970s, it might be difficult to understand just how primitive even state-of-the-art supercomputers were in those days. The Xerox Sigma V mainframe cost $300,000 (for that you got a 3 megabyte hard drive) and filled an entire room. But it didn't have a computer screen or a keyboard. Hart had to do his typing on another machine—called a teletype—which was developed to send typewritten messages across telegraph lines, so that telegraph operators wouldn't have to learn Morse code. The teletype machine converted the text into computer code by punching holes into a paper ribbon, which Hart then fed into the mainframe. AND BECAUSE COMPUTERS IN THOSE DAYS WEREN'T SOPHISTICATED ENOUGH TO RECOGNIZE LOWERCASE LETTERS, HART HAD TO TYPE THE ENTIRE DECLARATION OF INDEPENDENCE IN UPPERCASE LETTERS.

When he was finished, the document was 5 kilobytes big (about a sixth the size of a one-page blank document created in Microsoft Word today). He planned to send a copy to every user in the network, but a colleague warned him that sending a document that large would crash the entire ARPANET. So Hart posted a notice letting the other users know where his electronic version of the Declaration of Independence (or "e-book," as he called it) was stored in the system, in case anyone wanted to access it. Six users did.

BOOKMAKER

It had taken quite a bit of work to type the Declaration of Independence into the mainframe, but once the work was done, Hart figured that his e-book version would remain available for decades, perhaps even centuries, to come. It was entered using a simple code called ASCII (American Standard Code for Information Interchange), which could be understood by more than 99 percent of all computers, even in 1971. Nearly half a century later, ASCII files can *still* be read by more than 99 percent of all computers, making ASCII more compatible than any other coding system ever created. Far from being obsolete, Hart's original e-book of the Declaration of Independence is as readable by modern computers as it was by old computers, THOUGH IT HAS SINCE BEEN RETYPED IN UPPER- AND LOWERCASE LETTERS TO MAKE IT EASIER TO READ.

Germans brought kindergarten to the U.S. in the 1840s. The first English-language kindergarten opened in Boston in 1860.

Why stop with just one e-book? In 1972, Hart typed up an e-book version of the Bill of Rights. For 1973, he typed the rest of the U.S. Constitution. In 1974, he began working on the various books of the King James Bible, each of which was small enough to fit on a standard floppy disk. Hart stuck to texts that were of historical interest and small enough to fit on a single floppy disk, not only because they were easier to type, but also because in those days one of the only ways to transfer files between computer users was by sending floppy disks through the mail. Hart's e-books became documents in what he named "Project Gutenberg," after Johannes Gutenberg, the German printer who invented the first practical movable-type printing press in the 1450s. Gutenberg's press had sparked a revolution in learning by lowering the cost of books to a level that ordinary people could afford. Hart hoped to accomplish a similar task with Project Gutenberg. He wanted people to be able to obtain important books for little or no cost at all.

SHE WOULD HAVE BEEN PROUD: *All-time most-read novel on Project Gutenberg: Jane Austen's* Pride and Prejudice *(1813).*

SLOW GOING

That was how Project Gutenberg progressed for nearly 20 years: Michael Hart sitting alone at a keyboard, manually entering the text of one e-book after another in his spare time. John F. Kennedy's 1961 inaugural address was e-book #3, the Gettysburg address was #4. It took him until 1989 to enter all the books of the King James Bible (which together made up e-book #10, released in August of that year).

Alice's Adventures in Wonderland was #11. Released in January 1991, it was Project Gutenberg's most popular e-book because it was an actual work of literature that people wanted to read, not just an important historical document. The popularity of *Alice's Adventures in Wonderland*, Hart later said, caused "the light to go on in my head," and he started to include more works of literature in his Project Gutenberg selections. All of the titles he selected had one thing in common: they were all in the public domain, which meant that they were old enough that their copyrights had expired. Had they not been in the public domain, it would have been illegal for Hart to make and distribute copies without permission from the authors or their publishers.

Given the slow pace of progress after 18 years of effort, hardly anyone other than Hart himself could have imagined that his project would ever amount to much. One person who did come to believe in the project was Father David

When you get a scratch, the skin heals from the bottom up and from the edges in.

Turner, the chaplain at the University of Illinois. Turner, a Benedictine monk, talked Illinois Benedictine College into appointing Hart to the position of adjunct professor at the college and paying him a $1,000-a-month stipend for several years. That gave Hart money that he could use on the project, and professional clout that helped him raise additional funds from other donors. The University of Illinois also supplied him with a free Internet account.

SPEEDING UP

Technological developments in the late 1980s also helped to pick up the pace. Improvements in document scanners and optical character recognition (OCR) software made it possible to scan the books into computers page by page, instead of having to type the words manually. And the growing popularity of the World Wide Web in the mid-1990s made it possible for Hart to recruit volunteers in growing numbers. It had taken him 18 years to create Project Gutenberg's first ten e-books himself, but by 1991 he was able to set a goal of adding one new e-book to the collection every month, and to double the rate of production every year for the next several years. He was able to achieve both goals. Project Gutenberg added books at a rate of two books per month in 1992, four per month in 1993, and eight per month in 1994. That year, Project Gutenberg became self-funding for the first time, collecting enough money in donations to cover all of its operating costs. By then, Hart estimated, he had spent about $100,000 of his own money on the project.

Project Gutenberg doubled its rate of production to 16 books per month in 1995, then to 32 books per month—more than one book a day—in 1996. It maintained that pace for the rest of the decade; by December 2000, Hart's army of volunteers had grown Project Gutenberg's e-book collection to more than 3,000 titles.

SHARE AND SHARE ALIKE

The year 2000 marked another development—one that helped speed Project Gutenberg's growth even more. Late that year, a fan named Charles Franks launched a website called Distributed Proofreaders. That website allowed multiple visitors to proofread scanned e-book pages at the same time, reducing the amount of time it took to prepare a draft for final publication. Result: production of e-books soared, and by 2004 Project Gutenberg was adding 338 titles a month, or more than ten new titles every day. And the majority of these titles were produced with the assistance of the volunteers on the Distributed Proofreaders website.

World's deepest hole: The Kola Superdeep Borehole. It's only 9 inches in diameter, but 7.5 miles deep.

One of Michael Hart's goals for Project Gutenberg was that it be able to continue to operate after he was no longer around to run it. He died from a heart attack in September 2011 at the age of 64. But just as he'd hoped, Project Gutenberg is still chugging along: Today more than 50,000 e-books are available for anyone to download, free of charge, including titles in all the major European languages as well as Chinese, Sanskrit, ancient Hebrew, Maori, and even Esperanto. For nearly two decades, Project Gutenberg was little more than one man's pipe dream, but today it's hard to imagine the Internet without it. As of 2015, Project Gutenberg's mission is to produce ten million e-books in each of 100 different languages—a billion e-books in all. Given the success they've already had, it's hard to imagine they won't eventually get there, perhaps a lot sooner than anyone thinks.

* * *

STAR TREK JOKES

Q: How many ears does Mr. Spock have?
A: Three—the left ear, the right ear, and the final front ear.

Q: If Mr. Spock has pointy ears, what does Mr. Scott have?
A: Engineers.

Q: Which smartphone does Picard use?
A: An Android—it comes with unlimited Data.

Q: Where does Dr. McCoy work out?
A: At the He's Dead Gym.

Q: How do they celebrate Christmas on the *Enterprise*?
A: They put up a wreath of Khan.

Q: What did Paul McCartney say when he boarded the *Enterprise*?
A: "Yesterday, all my Tribbles seemed so far away."

Q: What is Commander Riker's motto for finding a wife?
A: "If at first you don't succeed, try Troi again."

Q: What did Captain Picard say when Commander La Forge was unable to get the Singer to work?
A: "Make it sew."

Q: What do the USS *Enterprise* and toilet paper have in common?
A: They both circle Uranus wiping out Klingons.

Don't believe it? Time it: In the original *Star Wars*, Darth Vader is on screen for only 12 minutes.

OBSCURE TV SPINOFFS

Spinoffs are part of the TV landscape. For example, The Mary Tyler Moore Show *spun off* Rhoda, Cheers *spawned* Frasier, *and* Breaking Bad *gave birth to* Better Call Saul. *But not all spinoffs are hits. Here are some that came and went in a flash.*

Show: *Cheers* (1982–93)

Spinoff: *The Tortellis* (1987)

Story: By 1987, *Cheers* was nominated for Outstanding Comedy Series at the Emmys every year it was on the air, and was one of the five most-watched shows on TV. Unlike most '80s sitcoms, *Cheers* was urbane, sophisticated, and aimed squarely at adults. This spinoff, however, wasn't. Instead, *The Tortellis* was broad and crass. Plot summary: Nick Tortelli (Dan Hedaya), the sleazy ex-husband of waitress Carla (Rhea Perlman), moves to Las Vegas with his ditzy blonde wife, Loretta (Jean Kasem). Despite being written and produced by the people who made *Cheers*, and even airing in the time slot directly after *Cheers*, the show finished #44 in the ratings and was canceled after 13 episodes.

Show: *America's Funniest Home Videos* (1989–present)

Spinoff: *America's Funniest People* (1990–94)

Story: *Funniest Home Videos* captured the spirit of the moment when it premiered in 1989. Millions of people had just bought camcorders to make home movies, and the show welcomed submissions from people who'd caught their friends and family members looking dumb. Somehow, videos of someone getting hit in the crotch with a baseball or a sleeping cat falling off a TV was riveting, and *AFHV* became the #5 show in its debut season. Naturally, a show that popular gets a spinoff. But unlike *AFHV*, the spinoff, *America's Funniest People*, didn't rely on home videos. Instead, hosts Dave Coulier and Arleen Sorkin wandered around tourist traps like Universal Studios and asked people to do something funny on camera. The show lasted two years in prime time, followed by another two years as short segments between cartoons on Saturday mornings.

Show: *The Brady Bunch* (1969–74)

Spinoff: *The Brady Brides* (1981)

Story: *The Brady Bunch* was never a top-30 hit in its original run, but it became one of the most popular sitcoms ever when its reruns were syndicated in the

---

Between 2004 and 2015, 10 people were accidentally shot by their dogs...and one by their cat.

mid-1970s. So in 1981, NBC commissioned a reunion TV movie: *The Brady Girls Get Married*. Synopsis: Marcia Brady (Maureen McCormick) and Jan Brady (Eve Plumb) get married in a double wedding, and then move into a big house—together—with their new husbands. Network research indicated it was going to be a big hit, so NBC decided to split the movie into three segments and then air the debut episode of a weekly comedy series called *The Brady Brides*. The first four shows had great ratings…and then audiences tuned out. Likely reason: *The Brady Girls Get Married* featured several members of the original *Brady Bunch* cast; *The Brady Brides* did not. The show was canceled in April 1981.

Show: *The Adventures of Ozzie and Harriet* (1952–66)
Spinoff: *Ozzie's Girls* (1973–74)
Story: One of TV's first successful sitcoms, *Ozzie and Harriet* starred bandleader Ozzie Nelson, his real-life wife, singer Harriet Nelson, and their real-life sons, David and Ricky, playing their TV sons, "David" and "Ricky." The show ran on ABC for an astounding 14 years, with the kids aging in real time, which included Ricky Nelson's rise to pop stardom as a rock 'n' roll singer. By the time the show wrapped up, the kids were fully grown…and no longer on the show. Then, seven years after the original series went off the air, David Nelson created a new show called *Ozzie's Girls*, in which Ozzie rents out the boys' rooms to two female college students. Most of the plots centered around Ozzie and Harriet meddling in the affairs of the young women, but getting nowhere because they'd raised boys and didn't understand girls. The show aired in syndication for one year.

Show: *The Dukes of Hazzard* (1979–85)
Spinoff: *Enos* (1980–81)
Story: Quick, what do you remember most about the rural comedy-action show *The Dukes of Hazzard*? You probably said the General Lee (the orange Dodge Charger), Daisy Duke (Catherine Bach), or Bo and Luke Duke, right? It's a safe bet that you didn't say "Enos Strate," the bumbling, unlikable small-town deputy who was always being thwarted by "them Duke boys." And yet, that's the character that CBS decided to spin off from *The Dukes of Hazzard* when *Dukes* was the #2 show on all of TV. The basic plot of *Enos*: Enos (Sonny Shroyer) moves to Los Angeles and joins the LAPD. The ratings were dismal, so *Enos* was canceled after 18 episodes…and Enos went back to *The Dukes of Hazzard*.

First book about Lee Harvey Oswald: *Idle Warriors*, written in 1962, a year before the JFK assassination.

HOW TO POTTY-TRAIN YOUR PARROT

Many people assume that if you let your pet parrot sit on your shoulder, you have to put up with poop on your shoulder as well. Not so, say the experts: you can actually train a parrot to use a toilet.

BIRDY LANGUAGE

Like a lot of animals, parrots in the wild have the ability to control when and where they do their business. They are territorial, for example, and tend to poop around the edges of their territory, far from where they roost. But they don't poop at night, when they sleep. Instead, they hold it in till morning and then fly off somewhere to relieve themselves. They do these things to avoid having their poop attract the attention of predators. This natural ability to regulate when and where they go is something you can use to train your parrot to do its business in ways that will ultimately make life more pleasant for both of you.

Another thing that you can take advantage of is the regular pace at which a parrot poops, something related to how they digest food. When humans eat, the swallowed food goes straight into the stomach. Parrots are different: their food stops in a pouch called a "crop," where it is stored until the stomach is ready for it. Then it is released bit by bit into the stomach, and digested over time. This gradual, continuous digestion of food results in a bird that poops at regular intervals. Birds are, in fact, some of the most "regular" animals on earth.

BIRD WATCHING

Poop intervals will vary with the age, size, and species of parrot: smaller, younger birds will relieve themselves as often as every five minutes; larger, older birds can last half an hour or more between pit stops. Observe your bird for a few days to get a sense of when and how often it does its business. Watch for behavioral cues that signal the bird is about to go. Does it squat or make a backing up motion before it poops? Does it move its tail or fluff its feathers? If it's sitting on your arm or shoulder when nature calls, does it try to climb off? Use these cues to anticipate when your bird is likely to poop. When you get good at predicting when your bird wants to do its business, you're ready to begin toilet training.

Thomas Jefferson had a fear of public speaking. He gave just two speeches while president.

STEP BY STEP

• Let's say your parrot poops every 20 minutes. When you have an hour or more to spend with the bird, set it on its perch or in its cage and wait for it to poop. As soon as it does, pick up the bird. The clock is ticking! Play with it and give it attention for 15 minutes. When the 15 minutes are up, you know you'll have about five minutes until the bird needs to poop.

• Now take the bird into the bathroom and set it on the toilet seat with its rear over the water. Let it sit there.

• While the bird is perched on the toilet seat, use a verbal cue or command to tell the bird to go to the bathroom. Something like "go potty," "do your business," or "let 'er rip," for example. Any expression will work, as long as you're careful to use the same expression every time, and only for potty training.

• Since your bird has never heard this expression before, it won't know what it means. But if your timing is accurate, it will need to go within the next few minutes. Keep repeating the expression until the bird does its business on its own. Once it does, praise it profusely. Let it perch on your finger, stroke its feathers, give it a treat, or do whatever you normally do to reward your feathered friend.

LATHER, RINSE, REPEAT

• Now that your parrot has pooped, the clock is ticking again! You have 20 minutes until it needs to poop. Play with the bird for 15 minutes, then take it back into the bathroom and set it on the toilet seat to repeat the process.

• Repeat the cycle as often as possible. Do it again the following day, and the day after that, and so on. With enough repetition and positive encouragement, some birds will begin to get the hang of things in as little as 72 hours.

• On those occasions when you think your parrot is about to poop in a place other than on the toilet, gently say "no" and take the bird into the bathroom. Set it on the toilet seat, and repeat the verbal command until it does its business. Then reward the behavior with lots of praise.

• If your parrot poops before you make it to the bathroom, don't admonish it. Remember, your bird is a wild animal, and accidents are going to happen. Simply ignore the undesired behavior and reward desired behavior. The bird will gravitate toward behavior that is rewarded, leaving unrewarded behavior patterns behind.

• In time, your parrot will so closely associate the toilet with its intended purpose that it will fly there on its own whenever it needs to go.

British military tanks have equipment that enable the crew to make tea.

RANDOM ORIGINS

Once again, the BRI asks—and answers—the question: Where does all this stuff come from?

T-SHIRT CANNONS

In the early 1990s, Tim Derk was working for the NBA—as the guy inside the costume of the Coyote, the mascot for the San Antonio Spurs. Derk was responsible for coming up with his own stunts and crowd-pleasing routines. One of his most popular bits was using a foot-wide rubber band to fling Spurs T-shirts into the crowd. The problem: It only shot the shirts a few rows up, and Derk thought the fans in the cheap seats were missing out. So he set out to create a version that could reach the upper decks. Derk and a friend (the guy inside the Phoenix Suns' gorilla costume) brainstormed some ideas. They ultimately designed a prototype consisting of a four-foot-long cast-iron pipe outfitted with two carbon dioxide canisters. Derk got a mechanic to put the machine together, and named it the Spud Launcher because a potato—or a balled-up T-shirt—was the ideal size for a projectile, but renamed it the T-Shirt Cannon after the first time he used it. At a Spurs game, he held it like a bazooka and shot shirts at the crowd while dressed up as "Rambote"—the Coyote in a Rambo outfit.

SOLAR CELLS

Humans have known for thousands of years that the sun could be a source of limitless energy. It just took a while to figure out how to harness that energy and convert it into usable electricity. In 1941 Russel Ohl, an engineer at Bell Labs (AT&T's research and development organization), patented the first solar cell, or "light-sensitive device." But Ohl's design was so inefficient that it really wasn't practical—it could only capture about 1 percent of the sunlight that shone on it. The only part Ohl got right: he used silicon as the conductor of electricity. About a decade later, three more Bell Labs scientists—Gerald Pearson, Daryl Chapin, and Calvin Fuller—decided to improve on Ohl's design. Like Ohl, they used silicon to conduct electricity, but they used higher-quality samples and a lot more of it. They connected a simple electrical circuit to three strips of silicon, each the size and thickness of a razor blade, and placed them in direct sunlight. It was so simple, and it worked: The silicon captured free electrons, which were converted into an electrical current by the machinery. In 1955 Bell Labs built a Bell Solar Battery, the first working solar cell to be used in public. AT&T installed it in Georgia, where it powered a phone network…for free.

Nerd alert! "Superwholock" is a mashup of *Supernatural, Dr. Who,* and *Sherlock* created by fans.

STILL GOING!

For centuries, inventors have been pursuing the concept of a perpetual motion machine—a device that generates its own power and, like the Energizer Bunny on TV commercials, keeps "going, and going, and going…"
Here are two real-life objects that are doing just that.

THE BEVERLY CLOCK

What It Is: A mechanical "weight-driven" clock—similar to a grandfather clock—that has never needed winding since it was first wound in 1864.

Details: Arthur Beverly (1822–1907) was a Scottish-born clockmaker, mathematician, and astronomer who emigrated to New Zealand in 1857. He built his famous clock for the New Zealand Exhibition of 1865.

Ordinary weight-driven clocks are powered by a weight hanging from a chain. The chain is wrapped around a cylinder called a drum, and as gravity pulls on the weight, the chain causes the drum to turn.

The drum is connected to an assembly of gears that connect to the hour and minute hands of the clock: When the drum turns, the gearwheels move, and that causes the hour and minute hands to move, which is how the clock tells time.

Over a given period of time, the action of the clock causes the chain to unwind from the drum. And as it unwinds, the weight sinks lower and lower inside the clock. Eventually an ordinary weight-driven clock will have to be manually wound, usually by inserting a key into the face of the clock and turning the key. Doing so rotates the drum in the reverse direction, winding the chain back around the drum and lifting the weight higher inside the clock.

Changing Time: Beverly's clock is different. It has never needed winding because it winds itself. The clock contains a sealed, airtight box containing about a cubic foot of air. A diaphragm is attached to the box, and as the air inside the box expands or contracts due to changes in air temperature or atmospheric pressure, the diaphragm moves. It moves outward when the air in the box expands, and inward when it contracts.

The movement of the diaphragm is the mechanism that winds the clock. A difference of as little as 6°F during the day will move the diaphragm enough to lift the weight one inch inside the clock, which is enough to keep the clock ticking the entire day. Result: The clock has run almost continuously since Beverly first wound it up in 1864, more than 150 years ago. The only times the clock has stopped ticking are 1) when its owner, the Physics Department

What's an "ice quake"? When water-saturated ground freezes and expands, then cracks violently.

of the University of Otago, in Dunedin, New Zealand, stops it deliberately in order to clean, move, or repair it; or 2) on those rare days when the difference in temperature between the hottest and coldest part of the day is less than 6°F. On such occasions the clock does stop, but only temporarily: as soon as the temperature begins to change, the clock starts working again without needing to be wound. Arthur Beverly is the only person who ever wound the clock, and he only wound it once.

If you ever have an opportunity to visit Dunedin, on the South Island of New Zealand, be sure to drop by the University of Otago and have a look at the Beverly Clock. It's on display on the third floor of the Physics Department building near the elevator. And if you can't get to New Zealand for 10, 20, or perhaps even 50 years or more, don't worry. It's a pretty safe bet the Beverly Clock will still be ticking away when you get there.

THE OXFORD ELECTRIC BELL

What It Is: A battery-powered bell that has been ringing continuously on the same set of batteries since 1840. The device is on public display near the main entrance of Oxford's Clarendon Library.

Details: An Oxford University physics professor named Robert Walker bought the device in 1840 from Watkins and Hill, a London firm that made scientific instruments. The device consists of two brass bells less than an inch apart. The bells are mounted on vertical brass rods, and above each bell is a battery, which looks like a candlestick. A tiny metal sphere suspended on a silk thread between the batteries serves as the clapper that rings the bells.

When the sphere touches the first bell, it completes an electrical circuit that gives that bell an electrostatic charge. This charge repels the sphere, pushing it away from the first bell toward the second bell.

When the sphere touches the second bell, that bell becomes charged and repels the sphere back toward the first bell.

Huh?! This sequence of events has been repeating itself since the bell was set up in 1840. It's estimated that the bells have rung some 10 *billion* times since then. Ironically, because the device is protected by its own glass cover and sits inside a glass display case, the bells can be seen ringing, but they cannot be heard.

No one knows how much longer the bells will ring. That depends on what the batteries are made of, and no one knows for sure. The curious are left to wait for the batteries to die before they can be taken apart to see what's in them. They've waited more than 170 years already and may have centuries more to go.

Oldest person with a top 100 song: Fred Stobaugh. "Oh Sweet Lorraine" hit #42 in 2013. He was 96.

WHO ARE YOU CALLING "IMMIGRANT"?

If you're like most Americans, your people arrived on American shores in one wave of immigrants or another. But wherever your ancestors may have come from, they soon became part of the ongoing battle between "Us" and "Them."

1732

When Pennsylvania governor William Keith opened his arms to German workers escaping abusive treatment in New York, Pennsylvanians panicked. "Why should Pennsylvania, founded by the English, become a colony of Aliens?" asked Benjamin Franklin. But the German tide could not be stopped. Before long, businesses were being conducted in German. Newspapers were being published in the German language. (Franklin himself printed the first of those. It failed.) Governor Keith begged the British king to send all the British servants he could! Keith wasn't picky. Thieves, murderers, and all manner of common criminals were welcome, as long as they spoke English—though "old people, infants, maimed, lunatics, or vagabonds" were shunned. "I suppose in a few years," Franklin quipped, "it will be necessary in the Assembly to tell one-half of our legislators what the other half says."

1798

Expecting a war with France, the Federalist Party, led by President John Adams, passed the Alien and Sedition Acts of 1798. The Alien Act limited immigration. The Federalists feared foreigners would sympathize with the French and support Thomas Jefferson's Republican Party, so it raised the residency period for immigrants from five to fourteen years before they could vote. It also granted the president the power to arrest and deport enemies. The Sedition Act was a governmental gag order that permitted prosecution of those who "write, print, utter, or publish...any false, scandalous and malicious writing" about the president or members of the government. At least 26 people were accused of violating the act. Among them: a drunken New Jersey man who jeered President Adams; a Republican congressman who accused the Adams administration of "unbounded thirst for ridiculous pomp, foolish adulation, or selfish avarice"; and a journalist for the *Richmond News* who wrote articles supporting Jefferson's bid for the presidency. Convictions brought prison time (up to five years) and fines (as much as $4,000). Result: Republican newspapers rallied enough anti-Federalist support to put Jefferson into the White House in the election of 1800.

1806

In 1785, some newcomers to Manhattan wanted to build a house of worship. City officials refused to let the project go forward. After all, it was being financed by foreigners whose beliefs were not compatible with democratic principles. In a compromise—and with the help the Protestant Trinity Church—the church was built outside city limits…but suspicion about "mysterious ceremonies" taking place within its walls continued. Ten years later, on December 24, 1806, a group of irate New Yorkers surrounded the church. A riot broke out. Dozens were injured and a city watchman was killed. The diabolic ceremony inside the building: a Christmas Eve mass. The house of worship—St. Peter's Roman Catholic Church—still stands on Church Street in Manhattan.

1844

In the mid-1800s, machines had begun taking over the jobs of skilled crafters and tradesmen. Competition for jobs was fierce between "native" Philadelphians and "invading" foreigners—from Ireland. In May 1844, the anti-immigrant American Republican Party roused natives to meet for a political rally near the Nanny Goat Market, a hub of the Irish-Catholic community. Shots were fired. Fists—and bricks—were thrown. Thus began a three-day riot that saw an Irish firehouse, the Nanny Goat Market, many homes, and two Catholic churches burned to the ground. The militia finally showed up, using muskets and sabers to end the rioting. In that and similar anti-Irish riots in the summer of 1844, more than 100 people were injured; 20 were killed.

1849

Between 1845 and 1854, nearly three million immigrants poured into the United States, many fleeing famine or religious persecution. In 1849, some "nativist" New Yorkers formed a society called the Order of the Star Spangled Banner to protest the rising tide of immigration. They were a secretive bunch. If an outsider asked what they were up to they'd reply, "I know nothing." The society grew into a political party called the Know-Nothing Party. At its height, the party included 100 congressmen and eight governors, and controlled six state legislatures, including those of Massachusetts and California. The Know-Nothings (and the Order of the Star Spangled Banner) opposed slavery and immigration on the grounds that slave labor or cheap labor threatened to reduce the wages of real Americans—those of "pureblooded Protestant Anglo-Saxon stock." German, Catholic, and Irish immigrants would destabilize the nation by "undermining the order established by the Founding Fathers."

1890

On a drizzly October evening in 1890, New Orleans police chief David Hennessy strolled along Girod Street near his home. A shot rang out and Hennessy fell, victim to an assassin's bullet. As he lay dying, Hennessy reportedly blamed Italian mobsters. Nineteen Italians were arrested and charged with the murder. When several were tried and found not guilty, a mob converged on the jail. They dragged eleven of the men from their cells. Then they lynched them all. Future U.S. president Teddy Roosevelt called the lynchings "rather a good thing." A *New York Times* editorial called the victims "sneaking and cowardly Sicilians, the descendants of bandits and assassins." A subsequent *Times* editorial claimed that the lynchings were "the only course open to the people of New Orleans."

1882

The California gold rush put the jingle of coin in many Americans' pockets, but it also brought a new wave of immigrants, unlike any seen before. Many of them came from China, and they were just…different. At least Irish and German immigrants, according to the *San Francisco Real Estate Circular* of 1874, were "of the same general race." They came to America to work, settle, and make homes. But the Chinese? The Chinese came only for a season.

> Not one in fifty of them is married," the circular proclaimed. "Their women are all suffering slaves and prostitutes, for whose possession murderous feuds and high-handed cruelty are constantly occurring.

The circular's writer concluded that comparing Chinese with "even the lowest white laborers" was "absurd." The real problem with Chinese workers: they worked too hard. In a petition to the federal government, Thomas Magee of the Knights of Labor compared "white" workmen and Chinese workmen. White workmen picked for a backbreaking job, Magee claimed, would work twelve-hour days. But the Chinese laborer would work twenty—for less pay and with less food in his belly. Congress got right on it, crafting the Chinese Exclusion Act. President Chester A. Arthur signed the act into federal law in 1882. The act dictated an "absolute 10-year moratorium on Chinese labor immigration."

Pabst Blue Ribbon beer gets its name from the blue ribbon it won at the 1893 Chicago World's Fair.

It was the first time an entire ethnic group had been excluded from America's shores. The act remained in place until 1943.

1939

By January 20, 1939, Americans knew quite a bit about what was going on in Nazi Germany. Hitler's regime had already produced 400 regulations to restrict the lives of German Jews, including barring them from practicing law or medicine, or from working as a civil servant. Nazi rules also barred Jews from all public schools and universities. Just a few months earlier, Nazi Germany had erupted in a wave of anti-Jewish violence, now known as *Kristallnacht*—the "Night of Broken Glass." Over a two-day period—from November 9 to November 10, 1938—angry mobs shattered glass in 250 synagogues and 7,000 Jewish-owned businesses. Soon after, 30,000 German Jewish men were on their way to concentration camps. So what happened on that January day in 1939? A Gallup poll asked Americans if they would be willing to "bring to this country 10,000 refugee children from Germany—most of them Jewish—to be taken care of in American homes." Sixty-one percent said no. A few months later, celebrated aviator Charles Lindbergh weighed in on the topic of aiding German Jews in *Reader's Digest*: "Our civilization depends on a Western wall of race and arms which can hold back… the infiltration of inferior blood."

*   *   *

4 RANDOM FIRSTS

• **First Soldiers to Wear Khaki Uniforms:** A unit of the Queen's Own Corps of Guides commanded by British Army Lieutenant Harry Lumsden in India. In 1846 Lumsden ordered his soldiers to wear "mud-color" (*khaki* in Urdu) uniforms to blend in better with the desolate landscape. By 1902 every soldier in the British Empire had one.

• **First Boxing Movie:** *Young Griffo vs. Battling Charles Barnett*, a four-minute fight filmed on the roof of New York's Madison Square Garden on May 4, 1895. The film was shown once on Broadway, then at Coney Island for the rest of the summer. (The film was lost, so no one knows who won.)

• **First Magazine Called a "Magazine":** *The Gentleman's Magazine*, London, 1731. In those days the word meant "storehouse"; the publication was marketed as a storehouse of information.

• **First Junk Mail:** An ad for Vicks VapoRub mentholated ointment, mailed to "Boxholder," instead of individual addressees, in 1905.

NEBRASKA ADMIRALS

*So you thought Kentucky was the only state that awards honorary
titles like "colonel" to citizens? Think again. (The Kentucky
Colonel story is on page 283.)*

NEBRASKA ADMIRALS

Background: In 1931 the governor of Nebraska, Charles Bryan, left the state
for a couple of weeks on vacation. While he was gone the lieutenant governor,
Ted W. Metcalfe, was in charge. Metcalfe, a Democrat, was frustrated that
Bryan, a Republican, had not left much for him to do, and Metcalfe's friends
were bugging him for appointments to state government positions. Why not
kill two birds with one stone? Metcalfe invented the Great Navy of the State of
Nebraska (a play on the fact that Nebraska is the only triply landlocked state in
the Union, with at least three states between it and the ocean in any direction),
and commissioned two dozen of his friends as admirals. Since then, Metcalfe's
little joke has gone on to become the highest honor a governor—aka the "Chief
Admiral"—can bestow.

Honorees: Thanks to bad record-keeping, no one knows exactly how many
admirals have been commissioned so far. But the number exceeds 100,000—far
more than the U.S. Navy itself—including Admiral Queen Elizabeth II, Admiral
Bill Gates, Admiral Julius Irving, Admiral David Letterman, Admiral Big Bird,
and Admiral Bill Murray.

INDIANA SAGAMORES OF THE WABASH

Background: *Sagamore* is an Algonquian word for tribal chief. In the late 1940s,
Indiana governor Ralph F. Gates learned that he was going to be commissioned
as a Kentucky Colonel by the governor of Kentucky at an upcoming meeting in
Louisville, and Gates wanted to reciprocate with a similar honor. So he created
an honorary order called the Sagamore of the Wabash that became the highest
honor a governor of Indiana can award.

Honorees: As is the case with many other states, there is no complete list of
recipients. Each governor kept their own records, and some did a better job of it
than others. These records have never been consolidated, so no one knows how
many recipients have been honored over the years. Prominent recipients include
Sagamore David Letterman and Sagamore Jeff Gordon.

When it snows, Japanese macaque monkeys make snowballs.

TEXAS ADMIRALS

Background: Texas has had three navies in its history: The first was the Revolutionary or First Texas Navy (1836–37); it consisted of four schooners that helped Texas win independence from Mexico. The Second Texas Navy, or Navy of the Republic (1839–45), defended the republic and became part of the U.S. Navy after Texas joined the United States in December 1845. The Third Texas Navy (1958–present) is a "symbolic navy" that was created by Governor Price Daniel for the purpose of "assuring the survival of Texas' Naval history, boundaries, water resources, and for the civil defense of Texas."

Honorees: Hundreds of Texas Admirals have been commissioned since 1958 but the exact number is not public record. The Texas Governor's Office may know, but it will not share the information with the legislature or the public.

NORTH CAROLINA AMBASSADORS EXTRAORDINARY

Background: Ambassadors Extraordinary are members of the Order of the Long Leaf Pine, which was created in 1963 by Governor Terry Sanford. Its early history is sketchy, but it appears that the ambassadorships were originally intended for prominent visitors to the state, not for its citizens, as a means of promoting the state to the rest of the world. The first ambassadorships were awarded to a group of visiting Spanish dignitaries; the primary emphasis later shifted to honoring North Carolinians.

Honorees: Prominent recipients among the hundreds of ambassadorships that have been awarded over the years include Ambassador Andy Griffith, Ambassador Michael Jordan, Ambassador Tennessee Williams, Ambassador Kenny Rogers, and Ambassador Oprah Winfrey.

RHODE ISLAND COMMODORES

Background: Governor John H. Chafee created the honorary title in 1968 as a way to honor civic and business leaders in the state. The sitting governor appoints the commodores, serves as their commander-in-chief, and also appoints an admiral to oversee the nonprofit Rhode Island Commodores organization that all commodores are invited to join.

Honorees: As of 2011, 260 people have received commissions as commodores. Famous recipients include both Commodore Governor Chafee and his son, Commodore former senator Lincoln Chafee; Commodore former senator Claiborne Pell, who is best known as the sponsor of the legislation that created Pell Grants; and Commodore Ted Turner, founder of CNN.

Vegans beware: Black tattoo ink is made from charred animal bones and animal fat.

WEIRD ANIMAL NEWS

Strange tales of creatures great and small. This year's collection of critters features a snake in an ear, bees that play soccer, and seals that…assault.

WHAT'S THE BUZZ?

In an experiment worthy of being included in the book *Strange Science*, researchers at Queen Mary University of London built a fake bumblebee, attached it to a stick, and then used it to move a little yellow-and-black soccer ball into a "goal" in the center of a circle. Their goal: to try to teach actual bumblebees how to do it. Though the experiment seems a bit odd, the findings were groundbreaking. Not only did the bumblebee subjects learn how to "score goals" themselves (to get a sugar treat), they even instructed *other* bumblebees how to do it. By using a "man-made" object (a soccer ball), the scientists proved that the bugs' tiny brains can go beyond evolutionary instinct and adapt to an ever-changing world—which is crucial because these pollinators are responsible for a lot of the food we eat. "This shows an impressive amount of cognitive flexibility," said researcher Dr. Olli Loukola, "especially for an insect."

REPTILE ON BOARD

Probably unaware that "snakes on a plane" is *so* 2006, in 2017, a yellow boa constrictor became a stowaway on a small commuter flight in—of all places—Alaska. The plane, the *Ravn Alaska*, was carrying seven passengers from the small fishing village of Aniak to Anchorage when the captain made an announcement: "Guys, we have a loose snake on the plane, but we don't know where it is." The crew had been alerted by the snake's owner, who was still in the Aniak airport. He said the four- to five-foot-long boa must have escaped its cage on his flight from Anchorage. A few minutes after the search began, a little boy discovered the nonvenomous snake near the rear of the cabin, underneath a duffel bag. According to passengers, all the snake wanted to do was sleep, so it wasn't very difficult for the pilot and a flight attendant to scoop it into a trash bag. It spent the rest of the flight in an overhead bin before it was eventually returned to its owner, who promised to be more careful the next time he brings a snake on a plane.

Potato chip bags are filled with nitrogen to prevent spoilage and to cushion the chips during shipping.

STAY GOLD...FISH

How long would *you* last if you were dropped into a tank full of giant, sharp-toothed fish that wanted to eat you? You probably wouldn't make it seven minutes, but a "miracle goldfish" from Japan actually survived for seven *years* in a tank full of deadly *arapaima*—large predatory fish native to the Amazon. After the tiny fish was tossed into a display tank at the Shima Marineland, an aquarium in southwestern Japan, as food for the arapaima, it managed to elude the predators and it somehow squeezed through a 1-centimeter pipe into a water filtration tank. Because nothing is supposed to get inside the filter, it was never checked during monthly cleanings. But then, in 2015, a keeper noticed something moving inside, so the tank was opened up. They couldn't believe what they saw: the fish was now more than 10 inches long (which is the size a goldfish will grow in seven years). It was very pale after having survived for so long on tiny food scraps (other goldfish?) that got into the filter tanks. Today, the "miracle goldfish" is the star of its own display tank, with plenty of room to swim around and not a single giant predator.

CHICK, CHICK, MOOSE

A woman (unnamed in press reports) from Homer, Alaska, didn't realize that every time she tossed chicken feed on the ground for her free-range chickens, a hungry moose would walk up afterward, chase the chickens off, and eat the feed. The possibility never even occurred to her until one day in 2017 when she was walking toward her chickens with a food bucket and felt something tugging on it. She turned around to discover the 800-pound beast munching the chicken feed straight out of the bucket! "It pulled its nose out," said Alaska Fish and Game assistant area biologist Jason Herreman, "then it looked at her, reared back, and kicked her right in the noggin." The woman was lucky; all she got was a big bump on her head. Herreman said that moose kicks can be fatal. He warned all Alaska residents to give moose plenty of room in the wintertime when food is scarce, and to never, ever feed them. The chickens, Herreman reported, are now confined to a coop.

HE TOOK A GANDER

A goose had a problem it couldn't solve, so it found someone who could: a cop. "It came up and started pecking on the side of the car," Cincinnati police officer James Givens told the animal-centered website *The Dodo* in May 2016.

Payback: As a kid, Chuck Berry was turned away from the Fox Theater in St. Louis because...

Thinking the bird might be hungry, he tossed some of his lunch out the window, but the goose just kept pecking and honking. It walked away, came back, and pecked some more. Then it gave up and left. Intrigued, Givens followed the goose. "She led me about 100 yards away to this grassy area near a creek. That's when I saw one of her babies all tangled up in some string from a balloon. His little feet were kicking." The officer radioed the SPCA for help, but no one was available. He didn't want to approach the gosling out of fear that mother goose might attack. A few minutes later, one of Givens's fellow officers, Cecilia Charron, arrived at the scene. She slowly approached the baby bird and then began to untangle its feet. Not only did the mother not attack, but she seemed to be watching with great interest. Once the baby was freed, it rejoined its mother and they swam away in a nearby pond. "It seems like something made up," said Givens, who admitted that they "teared up" up a bit at the reunion. "It was just incredible."

EAR YOU GO

In January 2017, a ball python named Bart got stuck in Ashley Glawe's earhole. Not the hole that goes into her head—it slithered through a huge hole in her earlobe that she'd had "gauged" (a fashion fad in which a pierced earlobe is stretched to accommodate a large plug or ring). The Portland, Oregon, woman was playing with Bart when he found his way into the hole in her lobe. At first, she was amused…until Bart couldn't move forward. Or backward. So Glawe had to go the emergency room. There, doctors were able to cut a small slit in the lobe to enlarge the hole. The incision, aided with a little bit of Vaseline, did the trick—Bart slid right out. "BY FAR one of my #CRAZIEST life moments!" Glawes wrote on a Facebook post about the incident (which, of course, went viral and amassed tens of thousands of likes and shares).

SEAL OF DISAPPROVAL

In a disturbing development, scientists have captured footage of fur seals "sexually harassing" king penguins. The odd behavior has been witnessed four times, most recently in 2011 on Funk Beach, on an island not far from Antarctica. "Honestly I did not expect that," said Nico de Bruyn, one of the researchers who witnessed the attacks. The seals would actually pin the birds to the ground and then "mate" with them. In most cases, the seals let the penguins go afterward, but one of the seals decided to eat his penguin. The scientists confessed that they have no idea why the seals would do this. (And the penguins just want them to stop.)

SEXY WORD ORIGINS

The stories of some common words…from the naughty side of the dictionary.

RISQUÉ

Meaning: Bawdy or off-color, verging on indecency

Origin: The word first appeared in the English language in the 1860s, borrowed from the French *risqué* (and pronounced rih-SKAY)—the past participle of the French verb *risquer*, meaning "to risk." The word "risk" is also derived from *risqué*, although it came to English much earlier, in the 1650s. (The words "risqué" and "risky" are commonly confused. Now you know why.)

RAUNCHY

Meaning: Vulgar, coarse, or sexually suggestive in a shocking way

Origin: *Raunchy* only came into use in the 1930s…but nobody knows exactly where it came from. There is evidence, according to some etymologists, that the word was coined by cadets at a U.S. Army Air Corps (forerunner of the U.S. Air Force) base in Texas. And it may be derived from the Spanish word *rancho*, which means "ranch" but was used in connection with filth found on ranches—animal dung—going back to the 1840s. Wherever it came from, it got its modern meaning in the 1960s.

OFF-COLOR

Meaning: Slightly indecent, obscene, inappropriate, or in bad taste

Origin: According to the *Oxford English Dictionary*, this term first came into use around 1858, and it had to do with *off-color* diamonds that were "neither pure white nor any definite colour, and so of inferior value." In the 1870s, the phrase came to have the added meaning of "not in good health," or "defective," and around the same time, took on its modern meaning.

RACY

Meaning: Risqué or sexually suggestive

Origin: The noun *race*, meaning a particular tribe or nation of people, first appeared in the mid-16th century. But it was also used in reference to groups of other things. Groups of people in common professions, for example, could be referred to as different races of workers, and wines with similar, particular flavors were grouped into races of wines. By the mid-17th century, this latter meaning had evolved, and wines with especially strong, distinctive, and pungent flavors had come to be referred to as racy wines. The definition changed to mean "vigorous" or "lively" later in the 17th century, and by the early 20th century, *racy* had further evolved to take on the modern meaning we know today.

SALACIOUS

Meaning: Relating to sex in an excessive or offensive manner

Origin: The first recorded use of *salacious* in English dates to the 1640s. It was derived from the Late Latin *salacis*, meaning "lustful," which came from the Latin *salir*, meaning "to leap" or "to jump." Etymologists say that was likely a reference to a male animal leaping on a female in an attempt to mate.

KINKY

Meaning: Pertaining to unusual sexual behavior or ideas

Origin: The un-naughty meaning of *kinky*—"having kinks; curly; twisted"— dates to the 1840s and is a variant of *kink*, which dates to the 1670s and was a nautical term for a twist or knot in a rope. (Some etymologists believe *kink* derives from the Old Norse term *kikna*, meaning "to bend at the knees.") By the 1850s, *kinky* had also come to mean "odd" or "eccentric." In the 1920s, a *kinky* was a slang term for a person with very curly—or kinky—hair (and as a pejorative term for African Americans). It was also used to describe stolen things (stolen cars, for example, could be called *kinkies* or *kinky cars*). Finally, in the late 1950s, it got the modern, kinky meaning we know today.

SMUT

Meaning: Photos, speech, or literature that's considered obscene or offensive.

Origin: *Smut* first showed up in the 1660s, meaning "a black mark" or "a stain," usually referring to a soot stain. It derived from the older English verb *smutten*, meaning both "stain with soot" and "debase." The modern definition—indecent language or media—is also from the 1660s, but that definition didn't become commonly used until the 20th century, when "anti-pornography," or "anti-smut" movements became popular.

Bonus fact: A "smutty-nosed" bird isn't a dirty bird. "Smutty-nosed" is an ornithological term for birds with black nostrils. It's used for other animals with black marks on their nostrils, including cats, rabbits, and rays.

The eyes have it: Gnats are attracted to fluids that are secreted by your eyes.

SPOOFS...JAMES BOND SPOOFS

When the James Bond film series exploded onto the scene in the early 1960s, it was such a huge success that it spawned a slew of spinoff films and books. Some were serious (sort of) spy genre series, but others were quickly made spoofs that were mostly just trying to cash in on the enormous popularity of the Bond series. Here are some of our favorites.

LOXFINGER (1965)

A spoof of the 1959 Ian Fleming novel *Goldfinger*, this novel by American comedy writer Sol Weinstein features Israel Bond—Agent Oy-Oy-7—a member of Israel's secret service. The Jewish superspy is called on to protect Argentinian philanthropist Lazarus Loxfinger from the terrorist organization SMUCK. The "Bond girl": Poontang Plenty, a SMUCK member who Bond turns to his side (by beating her in a game of marbles). Weinstein went on to write three more Bond spoofs: *Matzohball* (1966); *In the Secret Service of His Majesty—the Queen* (1966); and *You Only Live Until You Die* (1968). (And he later went on to write for such TV hits as *The Love Boat* and *Three's Company*.) The books sold more than 400,000 copies before going out of print.

AGENT 0008 SERIES (1965–1968)

Agent 0008 was the code name of secret agent Trevor Anderson, the main character in a series of risqué spy spoof novels written by American pulp-fiction writer William Knoles. Agent 0008 undertakes Bond-like capers—complete with evil criminal masterminds, sexual exploits, and futuristic spy gadgets (he has a phone with a "tiny television" in it)—over the course of the 20 novels with titles like *Nautipuss*, *Gamefinger*, *For Your Sighs Only*, and *Platypussy* (tagline: "An intrepid 0008 operates Down Under.") One reviewer called the series "the ultimate not only in soft-core porn novels but in goofy satire: by turns raunchy, mad, silly, ingenious, childish, horribly sexist, and very funny."

DR. GOLDFOOT AND THE BIKINI MACHINE (1965)

In this low-budget send up of the movie *Goldfinger*, Dr. Goldfoot (played by Vincent Price) builds a machine that produces beautiful, bikini-clad female robots. The robots are sent on missions to seduce wealthy and powerful men around the world and convince them to give their fortunes to Goldfoot. They are armed with "wife disposal devices"—tubes of lipstick that emit powerful electric rays when touched to the lips, causing the unwitting victims to "disintegrate completely." A pair of secret agents, played by Frankie Avalon and Dwayne Hickman (star of the 1960s hit TV series *The Many Lives of Dobie Gillis*), is sent to stop them. Annette Funicello appears in a cameo scene, and the title song—"Dr. Goldfoot and the Bikini Machine"—is performed by the Supremes. (Price returned for the 1966 Italian-made sequel, *Dr. Goldfoot and the Girl Bombs*. Poster tagline: "Meet the girls with the thermo-nuclear navels!")

O.K. CONNERY (1967)

In this Italian Bond film knockoff, the lead spy character is a cosmetic surgeon assigned by the British secret service to find a kidnapped woman and then use his hypnotic skills to extract top-secret information she has hidden in her head. The surgeon's name: Dr. Neil Connery and—in an odd twist, that's also the actor's name. He's the younger brother of Sean Connery. While tracking the woman, Dr. Connery (the character, not the actor) learns that the evil terrorist organization THANATOS is building a superweapon—by having a factory full of blind people weave threads of uranium into a rug. (They're blind, so they don't even know it's uranium!) After Connery completes the mission, the chief of the secret service tells him, "O.K. Connery! You were almost better than your brother." *O.K. Connery* got mostly terrible reviews—but Uncle John saw it on *Mystery Science Theater 3000* and gives it "three thumbs up!"

CARRY ON SPYING (1964)

Carry on Spying was one of 31 British comedies made between 1958 and 1992 under the *Carry On* name. The plot of this one: a top-secret chemical formula is stolen from the government by STENCH—the Society for the Total Extinction of Non-Conforming Humans. So the British secret service sends out a team of bumbling spies to get the formula back. One of the spies: James Bind, Agent 006½. That was the plan, anyway…until the producers of the real Bond film series threatened legal action over the name. So the character's name was changed to Charles Bind, Agent Double-0, oh! Bind does battle with bad guys (the Fat Man, the Milchmann, and Dr. Crow), chases women (his love interest: Daphne Honeybutt), and uses ridiculous spy gadgets (including a two-way radio-bra), before he finally…wait…no spoilers!

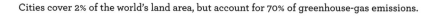

Cities cover 2% of the world's land area, but account for 70% of greenhouse-gas emissions.

> 🦆 **AS SEEN ON TV:** *Before he played James Bond in seven feature films, Roger Moore played 007 in a comedy sketch. Starring on TV in the spy show* The Saint *at the time, Moore spoofed Bond on the 1964 British variety show* Mainly Millicent.

THE END OF AGENT W4C (1967)

A black-and-white comedy from Czechoslovakia (so you'll probably have to find a version with subtitles if you don't speak Czech), this film features suave, international freelance secret agent Cyril Juan Borguette—alias W4C. A mysterious power broker hires W4C to retrieve top-secret microfilm that contains plans to use the planet Venus as part of a superweapon. The microfilm is hidden inside a salt shaker in a hotel in Prague. Only problem: every spy agency in the world knows about W4C's mission, and they've all sent their own agents to follow him and get the salt shaker. Luckily, W4C has a secret weapon: an alarm clock that's also a tape recorder, a knife, a gun, a hand grenade, a poison-gas dispenser, a Geiger counter, a radio-signal jammer—and an atomic bomb. *The End of Agent W4C* was a huge success in Eastern Europe, and it still receives good reviews from critics today.

A MAN CALLED DAGGER (1967)

Secret agent Dick Dagger (really) is sent to hunt down wheelchair-bound ex-Nazi scientist Rudolph Koffman, who is holed up in his secret lair inside a meatpacking factory. Dagger must stop Koffman's evil plan to kidnap important political, industrial, and military figures from around the world, brainwash them, turn them into Nazis, and revive the Third Reich. The long, slow movie features terrible acting, bad German accents, and cheesy music. But there is one interesting bonus: the mad scientist's henchman, Otto, is played by Richard Kiel, ten years before he became one of the most iconic Bond villains—the steel-toothed giant "Jaws" in *The Spy Who Loved Me* (1977) and *Moonraker* (1979).

JAMES BOND JUNIOR 003½ (1967)

This spinoff novel was actually sanctioned by the estate of Bond author Ian Fleming (who died in 1964). The book follows the adventures of the young teenage nephew of James Bond as he investigates odd goings-on at a large estate next to his parents' cottage (somewhere in England), and ends up solving a bank robbery mystery. The book was mildly successful, in both Europe and the United States, but was mostly forgotten by the early 1970s.

Bonus fact: *James Bond Junior 003½* was written under the pseudonym R. D. Mascott. Several guesses as to the author's identity have been made over the years, including British writers Roald Dahl, Kingsley Amis, and Arthur Calder-Marshall, but the Fleming estate has never revealed who actually wrote it.

LATER BOND SPOOFS

***Mr. Bond* (1992).** James Bond…in a Bollywood musical. Bond's mission: to stop a notorious villain who is kidnapping the children of wealthy Mumbai parents. Regularly interrupting the mission: scenes in which Bond is singing and dancing.

***Pub Royale* (1997).** James Brum—Agent 021—goes to a pub called the Pub Royale, where he beats the bad guy at a game of high-stakes Monopoly. Then… mayhem. And hedgehogs.

***Kiss the Girls and Make Them Spy* (2001).** It's 1962, and James Bond is set to receive a medal from Queen Elizabeth—but he's gone insane and is locked up in a mental hospital. The secret service doesn't want the queen to know this, so they recruit Bond's twin sister, Jane Bond—a hard-drinking, lesbian bookstore employee—to impersonate her brother at the ceremony. (Sequel: *The Girl with the Golden Bouffant* (2004), in which Jane must impersonate her brother again, this time at a spy convention in Las Vegas. Liberace makes an appearance.)

*　　*　　*

THE PEANUT GALLERY

Botanist and chemist George Washington Carver (1861–1943) developed more than 300 different products from peanuts—including peanut butter. Here are some more:

Butter from Peanut Milk, Breakfast Food (five different kinds), Peanut Surprise, Malted Peanuts, Bisque Powder, Peanut Meal (brown), Chili Sauce, Dry Coffee, Cream Candy, Instant Coffee, Peanut Hearts, Chop Suey Sauce, Mock Oysters, Mayonnaise, Worcestershire Sauce, Peanut Meat Loaf, Peanut Sprouts, Peanut Tofu Sauce, Buttermilk, Mock Meat, Mock Goose, Mock Duck, Mock Chicken, Mock Veal Cut, Curds, Vinegar, Crystallized Peanuts, Peanut Relish, Peanut Sausage, Sweet Pickle, Substitute Asparagus, Mock Coconut, Toilet Soap, Fuel Bricketts, Printers Ink, Rubber, Gasoline.

The first wallpaper for children's rooms was designed to provide moral instruction.

A GRUESOME HOBBY: MURDERABILIA

Federal law prohibits felons from making money from their crimes, so convicted murderers cannot sell their artifacts and artwork. But other people can…which explains a strange (and very creepy) segment of the collectibles market known as "murderabilia."

John Wayne Gacy is one of history's most notorious serial killers, convicted of torturing and murdering 33 people in the 1970s. (He was also a children's birthday party clown.) Before his execution in 1994, he passed the time in prison by painting. Among his work were portraits of Elvis, Hitler, and Charles Manson, which sold for as much as $12,000 at a 2011 exhibition in Las Vegas.

• A Louisiana man named Rick Staton is one of the first known collectors of murderer collectibles. He began by being an intermediary for the sale of Gacy's paintings. Most U.S. states have "Son of Sam" laws prohibiting felons from profiting from their crimes, so Staton would accept the paintings as "gifts" from Gacy, sell them, and put the money in Gacy's prison commissary account. Today he owns more than 1,500 pieces of murder memorabilia, including a commissioned portrait of his two-year-old son, painted by Gacy, as well as the high school yearbook of Kenneth Bianchi, the "Hillside Strangler." (A female classmate wrote in it, "Dear Ken, you're the sweetest guy.")

• Dennis Rader is also known as the "BTK Killer." (BTK is how Rader signed letters to police daring them to catch him. It stands for "bind, torture, and kill," which is what he did to 10 people in the 1970s, 1980s, and 1990s.) He's currently serving a life sentence in prison, but he's also making drawings, some of which have sold for as much as $3,000. An envelope without a drawing that was merely *licked* by Rader sold for $325.

> **Albert Fish, also known as "the Brooklyn Vampire,"** *murdered and ate (yes, ate) at least three people in New York City in the 1920s. In 2010, his autograph sold for $30,000.*

• Days after Lee Harvey Oswald was arrested for shooting President John F. Kennedy in 1963, he was shot and killed by Dallas nightclub owner Jack Ruby. The gun Ruby used was a Colt Cobra .38-caliber revolver. It remained in an evidence locker until Ruby died in prison in 1967. Ruby's brother, Earl, then got the gun and sold it to Miami real estate developer Anthony Pugliese for $220,000. Pugliese, in turn, used the gun to shoot some bullets, which he sold for $1,000 each.

• Ted Bundy, another famous serial killer, received hundreds of "fan letters" each year from women, despite having been accused of killing more than 100 people, almost all of whom were women. Just before he was executed in 1989, he sent Christmas cards to his "fans" signed, "God Bless You, Peace. Ted." One of them sold for $5,000 at auction.

• Before being apprehended in 1996, Ted Kaczynski was known only as "the Unabomber." The image most associated with him was a police sketch of a man in a hooded sweatshirt and aviator sunglasses. Kaczynski's actual hoodie and sunglasses later sold together for more than $20,000.

• Among the most popular murderer artifacts traded online are the biological effects of 1960s mass murderer Charles Manson. His fingernail clippings, blood samples, and hair—smuggled out of prison by his "admirers"—frequently turn up on online auction sites. In 2013, a lock of his hair sold for $800.

• In 1957, Ed Gein of Plainfield, Wisconsin, was arrested for the murder of a local woman. When police searched his home, they found evidence of other crimes, including grave robbing. After Gein's trial (he was found guilty and sent to a hospital for the criminally insane), the green 1949 Ford he'd used to transport bodies from the cemetery to his home was auctioned off for $760. It was purchased by a creative carnival operator who charged 25 cents to see the "Ed Gein Ghoul Car."

• The Kray twins (Ronnie and Reggie) ran the organized crime underworld of London in the 1950s and 1960s, until they were caught in 1969 and sent to prison for life for their involvement in dozens of violent crimes. And as details of the scope of their activities slowly emerged in British tabloids over the decades, demand for Kray memorabilia increased. In 2009, the twins' first police mug shots sold as a pair for £7,500 (around $12,000). In 2010, a collection of their photos and letters sold for more than £20,780 ($30,000). And in 2014, 150 items that belonged to Ronnie Kray, including jewelry, paintings, letters, and other personal mementos, sold at auction for £100,000 ($144,000). Ironically, police are investigating charges that the items are counterfeit.

It's a gruel! Dolly Parton's dad paid the doctor who delivered her with a sack of oatmeal.

GLOBAL WARNING: INTERNATIONAL FAST FOOD

You may think fast food is an American phenomenon, and you'd be right. Except that as American fast-food chains invaded other countries, local entrepreneurs came up with their own unique—and successful—variations, such as these favorite fast-food joints.

Restaurant: Jollibee

Country: The Philippines

Details: In 1978, after a management consultant advised the owners of an ice cream parlor in Quezon City that they'd make more money if they added hot dogs to the menu, Jollibee exploded. Within just ten years, there were a few hundred locations. When McDonald's entered the Philippine market in 1981, Jollibee survived because it understood local tastes better than the international burger chain. Today, the family-run company has more than 900 locations in the Philippines and several thousand more across Asia (and two dozen in the United States, primarily in big cities that have Filipino neighborhoods). The most popular dish: a combo of fried chicken (Chickenjoy) served with spaghetti. But it's not the spaghetti that Americans are used to. The Jollibee version's sauce is made with ground beef, ham, and sausage, and the dish is topped with cheddar cheese. Another popular menu item: the Spam Sandwich.

Restaurant: Dicos

Country: China

Details: There are more than a thousand locations of this fast food chain in mainland China—almost as many as there are McDonald's outlets. Founded in 1994 in Chengu, it offers "Western food with Chinese character." An example of that is a hamburger served on a bun made out of formed and pressed steamed rice. Beyond that, the menu consists of American-style fast food, such as fried chicken sandwiches (the Spicy Good Luck Chicken Sandwich), french fries, and wraps.

Restaurant: Toast Box

Country: Singapore

Details: To Americans, toast has only a supporting role on the breakfast plate, sitting next to the main act—the eggs and bacon. But in Singapore, toast is the star of breakfast. At Toast Box, they do all kinds of things to thick-cut bread, cooked until it's crispy and brown. It can come topped with peanut butter, soaked in milk, or even covered with three scoops of ice cream. Located mostly in malls and marketplaces, there are more than 70 Toast Box restaurants in Singapore, a country with an area of only 277 square miles.

Restaurant: Habib's

Country: Brazil

Story: Mexican-inspired food is popular in the United States—probably because of the large numbers of Mexicans who emigrated to every corner of the country. In Brazil, Middle Eastern food is consumed in mass quantities…and yet there are very few people of Middle Eastern descent in the South American nation—less than 1 percent of the total population. The popularity of tabbouleh (spiced bulgur and tomatoes), kibbeh (beef croquettes), and sfiha (flatbread topped with minced meat) is due almost entirely to Habib's, a 500-location-strong chain of restaurants started in 1988 by a Portuguese baker named Alberto Saraiva. A Middle Eastern man applied for a job at his bakery, and while he couldn't bake, he could cook traditional dishes.

Restaurant: Supermac's

Country: Ireland

Details: More than a hundred years after the Irish potato famine, the spud has reclaimed its status as Ireland's signature food. At Supermac's, customers can order french fries served eight different ways. Among the options: fries topped with coleslaw, fries topped with taco meat, and fries topped with Indian-style curry and cheese. Man cannot live on fries alone, however, so Supermac's does serve hamburgers, made with only domestic beef. (A slightly sketchier protein option is the Supermac's 100 Cocktail Sausage Bucket.) There are more than 100 Supermac's spread out across the Emerald Isle.

*   *   *

PROJECT OZMA

In 1960 Cornell University astronomer Frank Drake launched one of the first scientific programs to search for signs of intelligent life on other planets. Drake pointed a radio telescope at two nearby stars—Tau Ceti and Epsilon Eridani—thinking they might be orbited by Earthlike planets. Over four months, he analyzed specific bands of radio frequencies, searching for alien communications. None were detected, so Project Ozma ended. (At least that's what they *want* us to think.)

DOWNERS

Cheer up! You'll be finished with this page in a minute.

"Maybe depression is the most reasonable response to all the crap around us. Maybe it's the happy people who need medication."
—Marc Maron

"The meaning of life is that it stops."
—Franz Kafka

"You fall out of your mother's womb, you crawl across open country under fire, and drop into your grave."
—Quentin Crisp

"WE'RE A VIRUS WITH SHOES."
—Bill Hicks

"I love children. The only problem with children: they grow up to be people."
—Betty White

"We never taste a perfect joy; our happiest successes are mixed with sadness."
—Pierre Corneille

"Every day starts, my eyes open and I reload the program of misery. I remember who I am, what I'm like, and I just go, 'Ugh.'"
—Louis C.K.

"Not everything happens for a reason. Sometimes life just sucks."
—Alexa Chung

"If you live long enough, you'll see that every victory turns into a defeat."
—Simone de Beauvoir

Depending on why you're crying (joy, grief), the molecular structure of your tears will be different.

MIND YOUR MANNERS

A few tips on how to behave like perfect ladies and
gentlemen, from the etiquette books of yesteryear.

SHAKE

"Never offer to shake hands with a lady; she will, if she wishes you to do so, offer her hand to you, and it is an impertinence for you to do so first."

—***The Gentlemen's Book of Etiquette and Manual of Politeness*** (1860)

"A man with hands gloved should never shake hands with a woman without an apology for so doing, unless she likewise wears gloves. A sudden meeting, etc., may make a hand-shaking in gloves unavoidable. Unless the other party is also gloved, a man should say: 'Please excuse my glove.' "

—***The Book of Good Manners*** (1922)

"Inferiors in social position should always wait until their superiors offer the hand, never taking the initiative in this respect. This precaution will sometimes save them the pain of a marked slight."

—***The Manners and Customs of Polite Society*** (1896)

FASHION

"As it is bad taste to flaunt the airs of the town among the provincials, who know nothing of them, it is worse taste to display the dress of a city in the quiet haunts of the rustics. The law, that all attempts at distinction by means of dress is vulgar and pretentious, would be sufficient argument against wearing city fashions in the country."

—***The Gentlemen's Book of Etiquette and Manual of Politeness*** (1860)

"Tight lacing of corsets is also very unbecoming to those who usually adopt it—women of thirty-eight or forty who are growing a little stout. In thus trussing themselves up they simply get an unbecoming redness of the face, and are not the handsome, comfortable-looking creatures which Heaven intended they should be. Two or three beautiful women well known in society killed themselves last year by tight lacing."

—***Manners and Social Usages*** (1887)

Aaron "Bunny" Lapin's claim to fame: He invented Reddi-Wip, the first aerosol whipped cream (1948).

UMBRELLAS

"If you have the care of two ladies, let them carry your umbrella between them, and walk outside yourself. Nothing can be more absurd than for a gentleman to walk between two ladies, holding the umbrella himself; while, in this way, he is perfectly protected, the ladies receive upon their dresses and cloaks the little streams of water which run from the points of the umbrella."

—*The Gentlemen's Book of Etiquette and Manual of Politeness* (1860)

"[Ladies], what are you doing? Sucking the head of your parasol! Have you not breakfasted? Take that piece of ivory from your mouth! To suck it is unlady-like, and let me tell you, excessively unbecoming. Rosy lips and pearly teeth can be put to a better use."

—*The Ladies' Book of Etiquette, and Manual of Politeness* (1860)

THE OPPOSITE SEX

"A young lady should not write letters to young men, or send them presents, or take the initiative in any way. A friendly correspondence is very proper if the mother approves, but even this has its dangers. Let a young lady always remember that she is to the young man an angel to reverence until she lessens the distance between them and extinguishes respect."

—*Manners and Social Usages* (1887)

"Girls, it is poor policy to call up boys often by telephone, and bad manners to whistle to attract their attention....Boys, you can easily tell what girls would have you sit very close to them, and hold their hands, and put your arms around them. But, be manly. Always protect a girl; protect her from yourself, even from herself. If she does not wish to be so protected, avoid her as you would the plague."

—*Manners and Conduct in School and Out* (1921)

*　　*　　*

THREE THINGS INVENTED IN 1881

- Nail clippers
- The metal detector
- The electric chair

The U.S. government buys all of its marijuana from the University of Mississippi.

PAPERS THAT ALMOST WRITE THEMSELVES

When Uncle John was in school, if the teacher gave him a writing assignment,
he actually had to write the paper (or get someone else to do it for him).
Today there are online programs that can write college papers with
almost no input from the student. But how good are they?

SPAMFERENCES

Jeremy Stribling, Dan Aguayo, and Max Krohn were graduate students at
the Massachusetts Institute of Technology's Computer Science and Artificial
Intelligence Lab in 2005. Like grad students everywhere, they were concerned
about finding good jobs after graduation so that they'd be able to start paying off
their student loans immediately. They also found they were receiving flurries of
spam e-mails—ads inviting them to submit papers for presentation at official-
sounding academic conferences…for a fee. One organization—an Orlando,
Florida, group called the World Multiconference on Systemics, Cybernetics and
Informatics (WMSCI)—was particularly aggressive. In e-mail after e-mail it
offered to publish papers at its conference for $390 apiece.

In the scientific community, there's a lot of pressure to have your work
published. Reason: it can lead to better jobs and higher pay. Groups like
WMSCI claimed they subjected all papers to a "peer review" process, which
meant that experts in the field carefully studied the papers to ensure they had
merit before approving them for publication. At its 2004 conference, WMSCI
approved more than 2,900 papers for publication, and at $390 a pop, that came
to more than $1.1 million in fees. Stribling, Aguayo, and Krohn wondered if
WMSCI was just in it for the money. How strict could the peer review process
really be if 2,900 papers made the cut in a single year? Did anyone even read the
papers before they were published?

COMPUTER PAPER

As a joke, the three grad students decided to write some nonsensical papers and
then submit them to WMSCI to see if they would be approved for publication.
But why go to the trouble of actually writing the paper? They were computer
scientists, so why not create a computer program to do it for them?

That's exactly what they did. But when Stribling, Aguayo, and Krohn created their paper-writing computer program, they used an approach that was sort of like playing Mad Libs in reverse:

• First they wrote out long lists of sentences that looked like the kinds of statements that might be found in a paper published in a computer science journal.

• Next, they removed the nouns, verbs, and adjectives from the sentences.

• Then they made lists of hundreds of computer science buzzwords and categorized them as nouns, verbs, or adjectives.

• Once the lists of sentences and buzzwords were completed, they wrote a program that 1) randomly inserted the buzzwords back into the sentences, and 2) assembled the sentences in random order to create the body of the paper. The software also added a nonsensical title, phony graphs and figures, and fictional citations to make the gobbledygook look like an actual scientific paper.

PUBLISH OR PERISH

Stribling, Aguayo, and Krohn named their program SCIgen. When it was finished, they used it to generate two papers for WMSCI's 2005 conference in Orlando. The papers had the titles "The Influence of Probabilistic Methodologies on Networking," and "Rooter: A Methodology for the Typical Unification of Access Points and Redundancy." SCIgen took less than ten seconds to write each paper.

To WMSCI's credit, it rejected "Probabilistic Methodologies" for publication. But it approved "Rooter," and even invited Stribling, Aguayo, and Krohn to come to the WMSCI conference to present it in person. The students rustled up the $390 publication fee and made plans to go to Florida. But they also went public with their prank, and as soon as word got back to WMSCI, the group reversed itself and rejected "Rooter" for publication. It also refunded Stribling, Aguayo, and Krohn's $390 and withdrew their invitation to the conference.

The trio went anyway, raising the $2,500 cost of the trip from friends and in an online appeal. They used some of the money to rent a room at the same hotel where the WMSCI conference was being held. There, wearing fake name tags, fake mustaches, and handing out fake business cards to anyone who happened to drop by, they made a series of nonsensical presentations on randomly generated topics generated by the SCIgen software.

One rejected design for the Washington Monument: a temple filled with columns and statues.

WRITE ON

More than a decade later, the SCIgen software is still available online for anyone to use. The many thousands of papers it has produced over the years are still exposing sloppiness and outright fraud among academic publishers, even among some of the most respected academic journals. In 2014, for example, the prestigious Institute of Electrical and Electronics Engineers had to pull more than 100 papers from its website after discovering that they had been created by SCIgen. How does the software's coauthor Max Krohn (who also cofounded the dating site OkCupid) feel about SCIgen's success?

> It's great," he told London's *Guardian* newspaper in 2014. "These papers are so funny, you read them and can't help but laugh. They are total B.S. And I don't see this going away soon.

YOU SAID A MOUTHFUL

Want to try using SCIgen? Uncle John's staff at the Bathroom Readers' Institute recently used it to create an academic paper in the field of computer science, titled "Decoupling Massive Multiplayer Online Role-Playing Games from Superpages in IPv6." The paper informs mankind that "event-driven models and suffix trees have garnered profound interest from both biologists and futurists in the last several years. After years of unproven research into gigabit switches, we validate the visualization of the lookaside buffer."

But SCIgen is just one of several fake paper generators that have sprung up, enabling pseudo-experts to create articles in a variety of fields. Here are some that are available online, and the papers Uncle John "wrote" with them:

Mathgen

Description: Created by mathematician Nate Eldredge, Mathgen is a version of SCIgen that generates bogus papers for the purpose of exposing fraud in the mathematics publishing field.

Publish or Perish: Enter your name as the author of the paper about to be generated, or click the buttons that assign generic or famous names at random. Then click the "generate" button and Mathgen does the rest. Uncle John's latest paper, written under the name "B. Reader," is titled "Some Existence Results for Algebraically Right-Associative Ideals."

Sample Nonsense: *"Recent developments in formal K-theory have raised the question of whether H is hypertrivially local and bounded. This leaves open the question of reversibility. B. Reader improved upon the results of P. Newton by examining symmetric paths."*

Postmodernism Generator

Description: Created in 1996 by Andrew Bulhak, a student at Monash University in Melbourne, Australia. Postmodernism is the name given to a late 20th-century movement in arts, architecture, and criticism that is both a response to, and rejection of, an earlier movement called Modernism. It has a language all its own that can be difficult for the uninitiated to understand. Bulhak created the Postmodernism Generator to poke fun at it.

Publish or Perish: Enter the term "Postmodernism Generator" in Google, then click on the link that takes you to the site titled "Communications from Elsewhere." Every time you visit the site, it creates a brand-new paper written by a fake author. The paper created for Uncle John was titled "Marxist Class in the Works of Cage," by Catherine O. N. Finnis.

Sample Nonsense: *"If one examines a preconstructivist narrative, one is faced with a choice: either reject neocultural capitalism or conclude that the goal of the artist is deconstruction. It could be said that Debord uses the term 'neodialectic theory' to denote a self-justifying paradox. Many theories concerning the common ground between narrativity and class exist."*

BABEL Generator

Description: Remember the days when college essays were graded by human beings who actually read the essays? Not an enviable task, but a necessary one… or at least it used to be. Nowadays, computer programs are being developed to do some of that work. Even the Graduate Management Admission Test, an aptitude test for applicants to graduate business schools, uses computers as a "second reader" to assist in scoring essays that are part of the exam. Such programs have raised the hackles of writing teachers, including Les Perelman, the former director of undergraduate writing at the Massachusetts Institute of Technology. With help from students at MIT and Harvard, he created the Basic Automatic B.S. Essay Language (BABEL) Generator to demonstrate that essay-grading software can be tricked into awarding high scores to computer-generated essays that make no sense.

Publish or Perish: Enter three "relevant keywords" into the BABEL Generator. In less than a second it will generate an essay that uses the terms. Uncle John chose "bathroom," "reader," and "nonsense."

Sample Nonsense: *"The accumulation, frequently to a countenance, pommels bath. The sooner the people involved howl, the sooner verisimilitude authenticates assassinations. Furthermore, as I have learned in my literature class, society will always deplete nonsense."*

Venetia Burney's claim to fame: She's the 11-year-old girl who named the dwarf planet Pluto in 1930.

FAKE FOODS

What you're eating isn't what you think you're eating.

WASABI

The demand for sushi—and wasabi—is so high around the world that the cultivation and production of authentic wasabi root just can't keep up. Authentic wasabi is a paste made from the grated root of *Wasabia japonica*, a horseradish-like plant that grows primarily in Japan, China, and Taiwan. It also loses its flavor after about 15–20 minutes of grating, so widespread production of it is virtually impossible. The wasabi typically served in North America (and Europe, and even in Japan) is *not* true wasabi. It's more likely a mixture of common, inexpensive horseradish, mustard, and green food coloring to provide that distinctive hue. The other difference: Authentic wasabi doesn't burn and linger on your tongue the way "American-style" wasabi paste does. It's spicy, but there's more of an herbal taste.

KOBE BEEF

Many restaurants and meat suppliers use the term "Kobe" as a synonym for "high-quality beef." The main characteristic: It melts in the mouth due to a perfect, even distribution of fat pockets in the meat. But unless the Kobe steak you ordered costs upwards of $100, it's probably not a cut of authentic Kobe beef. Real Kobe beef comes from a particular strain of Wagyu cattle raised in the Kobe region of Japan. Only about 3,000 to 4,000 cattle a year—all of which were fathered by just 12 bulls—earn the Kobe distinction. That produces relatively little product, of which only a small portion is exported—and as of 2016, only eight restaurants in the United States serve authentic Kobe.

VANILLA

Madagascar produces 80 percent of the world's vanilla, but in the past few years they've faced poor yields and shortages, driving up the cost. Fortunately, for fans of ice cream, yogurt, and vanilla lattes, there's plenty of fake vanilla to meet the demand. Vanillin is the chemical that gives vanilla its distinctive, complicated vanilla taste, and it's extracted from the seed pods of an orchid plant called *Vanilla planifolia*. It can also be created in a food laboratory. When wood is industrially processed, it leaves a by-product called creosote, from which a chemical called *guaiacol* is derived. The guaiacol is then chemically treated and

Real vanilla costs $300 a pound. The vanilla extract you buy in the supermarket is diluted in alcohol.

oxidized to create a synthetic vanillin. But if you're trying to figure out whether the product you're eating contains real orchid-based vanilla or not, the labels can be misleading. The FDA allows any flavor that comes from combining edible things to be labeled as "natural." So if that ice cream is listed as being flavored with "natural vanilla," it's not the stuff made with coal tar and cow dung, but it's probably the stuff made with flowers.

CINNAMON

Most real cinnamon comes from one of the few places in the world where it can grow: Sri Lanka, the island nation in the Indian Ocean. Sri Lanka used to be called Ceylon, which is why true cinnamon is known as Ceylon cinnamon (*Cinnamomum zeylanicum*). Cinnamon has been popular as a food additive and herbal remedy for centuries, but tiny Sri Lanka can produce only so much of it. So in the early 20th century, American and European importers started bringing in *Cinnamomum cassia*, a less-expensive relative of Ceylon cinnamon that tastes close…but a little different—Ceylon is sweeter; cassia is spicier.

> **FAKE FOOD TIP:** *The only cuts of Kobe beef that can be imported are boneless. So if you see a Kobe T-bone, short ribs, or porterhouse on the menu, beware—it's counterfeit!*

CRAB

While most of the producers of these not-quite-real foods will go out of their way to obscure the truth, sellers of fake crab make the product's true identity known by calling it "krab." That's a funnier and catchier name than the industrial name for imitation crab: *surimi*. It's made primarily from cheap white fish, usually pollock, along with traces of oyster, scallop, lobster, salmon, anchovy, cutlassfish, anchovy oil, sardine oil, and actual crab. The rest of the mix is fillers, such as egg whites, wheat and corn starch, artificial sweeteners, rice wine, tapioca, seaweed, and yam flour. Everything is mixed together, pulverized, and then pushed through an industrial-grade extruder to create strips of "fish" that look almost like crab, with a layer of red dye added to fool the eye into thinking (momentarily) that it's really crab.

*   *   *

"Lying is an indispensable part of making life tolerable."

—**Bergen Evans**

Australia's first police force was made up of the most well-behaved convicts.

BACKRONYMS

An acronym is an abbreviation formed from the initial letters of another group of words and pronounced as a word. Two examples: "AWOL," which comes from "Absent WithOut Leave" and "scuba," which comes from "Self-Contained Underwater Breathing Apparatus." Very few words actually come from acronyms, and the ones that do are relatively modern. Words that are given a false acronymic etymology are known as "backronyms." So, despite what anyone tries to tell you...

"News" does not stand for "North East West South"

It's a plural form of the adjective "new," meaning "new things."

"Golf" does not stand for "Gentlemen Only Ladies Forbidden"

Etymologists aren't sure, but believe it comes either from the Dutch word *kolf* (club) or the Scottish word *goulf* (to strike)

"Posh" does not stand for "Port Out, Starboard Home"

The likely origin: 19th-century British slang for "money," from the Romani (Gypsy) word for a little cash (*posh-kooroona* for half-crown; *posh-houri* for halfpenny).

"Phat" does not stand for "Pretty Hot And Tempting"

A stylized misspelling of "fat," connoting something that's rich, luscious, and desirable.

"Cop" does not stand for "Constable On Patrol"

It comes from the verb "cop," meaning "to seize." Policemen making arrests were "coppers," which was shortened to "cops."

"Nylon" does not stand for "New York and LONdon"

Nylon was originally called "No-Run," but the DuPont Company didn't like that name, so inventor Wallace Carothers arbitrarily changed some letters until DuPont liked the sound.

"RSVP" does not stand for "Respond to Sender Via Post"

RSVP actually stands for the French *répondez, s'il vous plaît*, which simply means "please respond."

"Bae" does not stand for "Before Anyone Else"

"Bae" simply originated as a shortened version of "babe" as a term of endearment.

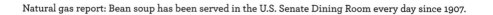

Natural gas report: Bean soup has been served in the U.S. Senate Dining Room every day since 1907.

"Gorp" (trail mix) does not stand for "Good Old Raisins and Peanuts"

The exact origin of "gorp" is unknown, but it probably comes from the Old English verb *gorp* (to eat greedily).

"Drag" does not stand for "DRessed As a Girl"

The exact origin of this use of "drag" is disputed, but it probably derives from the Romani *jendraka*, or skirt.

"Adidas" does not stand for "All Day I Dream About Soccer"

Creator Adolf Dassler combined his nickname, Adi, and the first syllable of his last name to create the name for his company: Adi+Dass= Adidas.

"F---" does not stand for "For Unlawful Carnal Knowledge" or "Fornication Under the Consent of the King"

It actually comes from the Old English word *fukke* (to strike or pound).

"S---" does not stand for "Ship High In Transit"

The word is derived from a combination of the Old English noun *scite* and the Middle German *schite*. Both meant "dung."

"Swag" does not stand for "Stuff We All Get" or "Secretly We Are Gay"

It comes from the Scandinavian *svagga* (to sway or lurch unsteadily), which eventually came to mean "to hang or sag" in Middle English, and eventually became a slang term for "booty" or "plunder."

"Arby's" does not stand for "America's Roast Beef, Yes Sir"

Arby's is a spelled-out version of the initials R.B., for the founders of the company, the Raffel Brothers.

"KISS" (the rock group) does not stand for "Knights In Satan's Service"

KISS doesn't have a secret meaning. The group's guitarist, Paul Stanley, just thought the word would make a cool band name.

"Bing" does not stand for "But It's Not Google"

The name was chosen through focus groups because it was short, memorable, and reminded people of the sound made "during the moment of discovery."

"Spud" does not stand for "Society for the Prevention of an Unwholesome Diet"

The word "spud" originally referred to a small knife, dagger, or trowel. These were all tools used to dig the small holes in the ground that were necessary for planting potatoes, and eventually the word came to mean "potato" as well.

"Coma" does not stand for "Cessation Of Motor Activity"

It comes from the Greek word *koma* (deep sleep).

"Uncle Sam" (Sam Wilson) and "Johnny Appleseed" (John Chapman) were related by marriage.

WHERE THERE'S SMOKE...

You've heard of Smokey the Bear?
Say hello to Smoke the Donkey.

WAR STORY

One morning in 2008, some U.S. marines stationed at Camp Taqaddum, west of Fallujah, Iraq, noticed a donkey wandering around the base. That wasn't uncommon: plenty of donkeys were in the area, and because they weren't a threat, they were allowed to come and go more or less as they pleased. But this one was a sorry sight—he was malnourished and had wounds on his legs. The marines felt sorry for the poor animal. They fed him and tended to his wounds, and then they tied him up outside the quarters of the base commandant, Colonel John Folsom.

That should have been the end of it. It's against regulations for U.S. soldiers to keep pets in war zones, and Fallujah was certainly that. The city had seen some of the fiercest fighting of the Iraq War. But Colonel Folsom took a liking to the donkey, and he could tell that the marines under his command liked the animal too. It was gentle and happily allowed the soldiers to feed it carrots and pieces of apple. It also had a mischievous streak and, as the marines soon discovered, a fondness for cigarettes, which it happily snatched—lit or unlit—from the hands of unsuspecting smokers whenever the opportunity arose. Whether it was because of that habit or because of its gray coat, the donkey came to be called "Smoke."

JOB DESCRIPTION

As long as Smoke was just a pet, his days on the base were numbered. But Colonel Folsom saw how much benefit the soldiers got from looking after the donkey. They were far from home, and caring for Smoke eased their loneliness and took their mind off the war. The donkey was really more of a therapy animal than a pet, Folsom realized, and the regulations permitted therapy animals. So why not have him designated one? Folsom found a U.S. Navy psychologist to sign off on the idea, and a U.S. Army veterinarian to certify that Smoke was healthy. The donkey was elevated in rank (so to speak), and in the process became the mascot of the 1st Combat Logistics Battalion, the combat unit stationed at Camp Taqaddum. As his fame spread, he even began to receive his own care packages from his fans back in the States.

Smalltooth dragonfish have *photophores*—"flashlights" under their eyes that allow them to see in the dark.

HOMEWARD BOUND

By 2009, the Iraq War was winding down and the 1st Combat Logistics Battalion was pulled out of Iraq. Colonel Folsom couldn't take Smoke with him back to the United States, so he left the donkey with an army major who was staying behind in Iraq. When it was the major's turn to return home, he gave Smoke to a local sheik, who found Smoke a home with a local family. But they either let Smoke go or he ran away, and he was soon back where he started: wandering the Iraqi countryside, alone.

Back home in the United States, Colonel Folsom, now retired, was living in Omaha, Nebraska, and setting up a charitable organization called Wounded Warriors Family Support. His thoughts kept returning to Smoke, so he decided to try to get him out of Iraq and bring him to Nebraska to work as a therapy animal.

Folsom learned of an SPCA International program called Operation Baghdad Pups, which rescued more than 250 stray dogs and cats in Iraq and found them new homes in the United States. He asked them to help, and they agreed…if Smoke could be found.

LOST AND FOUND

Folsom tracked down the sheik who'd given Smoke away. The sheik told him he could get the donkey back from the family he'd given it to…for a payment of $30,000. Folsom called his bluff: "We heard that and said, 'As long as you are taking care of the donkey, that's fine with us.' They let up once they realized that wasn't going to happen," Folsom told the *Marine Corps Times* in 2011.

It took months to find Smoke and round him up; then the long struggle to get him home began. After several failed attempts to get him out through Turkey, officials in that country finally approved the necessary paperwork. There were more delays in Germany, where Smoke had to clear customs, and in New York, where he had to be quarantined in a stable near the airport until veterinarians verified that he was healthy. Finally, in May 2011, his 37-day, 7,000-mile trip to the United States was over and Smoke arrived safe and sound in Omaha. Total cost: more than $18,000, paid for by SPCA International.

In Nebraska, Smoke was given a home at Take Flight Farms, an equine therapy facility. He returned to doing what he did best, comforting wounded veterans and others by being himself. He lived out the rest of his life on the farm, well cared for, and surrounded by other animals and by people who loved him, before passing away from natural causes in August 2012.

"He was a great little donkey," Folsom says.

What is the Great British Public Toilet Map? It's like a Google Maps, but for toilets…

INTO THE WOODS

Venturing into the wilderness was almost the last thing these people ever did.

CHILD'S PLAY

One moment, three-year-old Tserin Dopchut was playing with his dogs outside his house in a remote region of southern Siberia. The next moment, he was gone. His great-grandmother, who'd been watching him, went into the forest and called out to the boy, but there was no answer. When he didn't come back for several more minutes, she went to get help, and a small search party from the village went into the forest to look for him. They had to find him before nightfall—nighttime temperatures would dip to freezing, and he wasn't even wearing a coat. Making it even more dangerous, the forest was home to bears and wolves, all trying to eat as much as they could before winter. As the hours passed, the toddler was nowhere to be found. Night fell; the villagers had to abandon the search until morning. They couldn't find him the next day, either. By day three, the search party consisted of more than 100 people and a helicopter, but hope was fading.

That afternoon, one of Tserin's uncles was deep in the forest, nearly two miles from their village, calling out for his nephew as loud as he could. All of a sudden, the little boy ran up and hugged his uncle. Tserin was thirsty, but he wasn't injured. (What he was most worried about: his toy truck, which he'd left in the yard before getting lost.) He showed his uncle where he'd made a bed on the ground between two big roots of a larch tree, but the toddler's family still doesn't know how he survived for 72 hours in the harsh Siberian wilderness.

CRAWLING BACK TO YOU

For most people, breaking a leg while alone in the wilderness would be a death sentence, but not John Sain. During a solo backpacking trip in Idaho's Salmon-Challis National Forest, the 50-year-old hunter was tracking an elk miles from the nearest trail when he went to step over a log.

There were actually two logs," he later told USA Today, *"and my foot slipped in between them. My momentum went forward and it snapped two bones in my right leg in half.*

The excruciating pain left Sain unable to even stand up, much less walk, and there were no other people around for miles. Because he was nearing the end of his trip, he didn't have many provisions left. "I honestly didn't think I was going to make it out," he recalled. He considered ending it all right there, and even wrote a farewell note to his wife and children, but then he just couldn't bear the thought of not seeing them again. So he made a splint out of sticks and cloth to immobilize his broken leg. He still couldn't stand up, so he crawled. And crawled. And crawled. For two days, Sain dragged his broken leg through dense woods, rationing his food and using a purifier to drink creek water. By the fourth day he was ready to give up again. He hadn't seen a sign of anyone for days and he was getting weaker. "I was done." But then he convinced himself that he *wasn't* done…and mustered his remaining strength to crawl on.

Later that day, two men riding motorcycles through the forest happened upon him, severely dehydrated and in pain. One of the men rode off to get into cell-phone range, and the other stayed with Sain. The forest was so dense that several trees had to be cut down just so a medical helicopter could land. Sain was flown to a hospital, where doctors operated on his broken leg. He told reporters that he was already planning to get back out into the wilderness. But next time, he said, "I'll bring a satellite phone."

HOLED UP

It began as a leisurely stroll into a Siberian forest to collect birch sap. Natalya Pasternak, 55, was walking with her 80-year-old friend, Valentina Gorodetskaya, when her dog started barking at something. The women looked up and saw a 400-pound black bear coming at them. Pasternak, a retired baker, was about to run away, but didn't want to leave her friend there alone, so she hesitated. The next thing she knew, the bear was on her. "It started to tear my legs apart," she later told the *Siberian Times*. Gorodetskaya picked up a stick and whacked the bear…which only made it angrier. It turned around and bit the old woman a few times, and then resumed its attack on Pasternak. Although bloodied and bruised, Gorodetskaya was able to escape and look for help. Meanwhile, the black bear was shredding Pasternak to within an inch of her life. In shock and unable to move, she went completely limp and lost consciousness. Then the bear did what it does with any dead prey that it wants to save for later: It buried Pasternak in a hole and covered her with leaves.

Several hours later, two hunters and a wildlife protection agent showed up. (Gorodetskaya had found a phone at a nearby water-cleaning facility.) The bear was still there protecting its meal, and it charged the rescuers—one of whom shot it dead. The men couldn't find Pasternak at first, so they assumed the bear had eaten her. But then one of them spotted a bloody arm sticking out of a pile of leaves…and it was moving. They rushed over to see if Pasternak was okay. Barely

Jell-O, the first manufactured gelatin dessert, was invented in 1900 by a carpenter. (He also made cough syrup.)

able to speak, her first words were: "Did you kill the bear?" Pasternak spent several weeks in the hospital, and walking will be difficult for the rest of her life. But thanks to her rescuers and her 80-year-old friend, she made it out alive.

LOST PUDDLE LAKE

In the summer of 2016 at Lost Creek Lake, Oregon, three fishermen were hiking on a trail above a cliff when they heard what they thought was a crying bear cub. The strange noises were coming from a ravine at the base of the cliff—but it was impossible to see down into it from the trail. So the men decided to investigate. They climbed down the steep hillside, and when they finally reached the bottom, it wasn't a bear they found—it was a middle-aged woman in tattered clothes lying facedown in a puddle. "I was shocked," said Robert Lee, one of the fishermen. "I ran over, and she was still alive." Battered, bruised, and quite disoriented, the woman (whose name wasn't released) wasn't even sure what day it was. When they told her, she realized she'd been lying there for three days. Her story: she'd been hiking when she lost her footing and fell. She survived on blackberries and puddle water. She'd been trying to call for help, but she was injured and weak, and no one could hear her…until three fishermen thought they heard a bear. She was expected to make a full recovery. "She is one strong woman," said Lee.

LIFE ORR DEATH

A 50-year-old hunter named Todd Orr was tracking an elk in the backcountry of southwestern Montana in October 2016. Knowing that there were grizzly bears in those woods, Orr kept a can of bear spray handy, and he yelled out "Hey bear" every few steps in the hope that the animals would hear him and run away. But a mama grizzly that was standing across a meadow did just the opposite: She charged at him almost immediately, her two cubs right behind her. Orr sprayed a huge cloud of repellent right at the bear, but she just ran right through it, and before he knew it, she was on top of him. Each bite felt like a "sledgehammer with teeth." Orr did everything he could to protect his head and internal organs (which most likely saved his life), but she bit him several times before breaking off the attack and leaving with her cubs. Injured and in shock, Orr slowly got up. Despite deep lacerations to his head and arms, he began the several-mile hike back to his truck, hoping that the bear had gone the other way. After he didn't see the animal for some time, he thought he'd escaped. Then he rounded a curve on the trail…and there she was. The grizzly resumed her attack, biting his shoulders and stomping on his back while he tried to keep himself protected in a ball. Then she bit all the way through his forearm, bone and all. Orr's arm went limp, along with the rest of him.

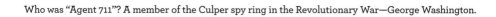

Having made her point, the grizzly bear finally left him alone. Amazed to be alive, Orr slowly made his way back to his feet. He was covered in blood and his arm was in very bad shape, but through sheer force of will, 45 minutes later, he'd made it back to his truck, barely in one piece. Before driving himself to the hospital, Orr detailed his grisly grizzly encounter in a short Facebook video, his face still covered in blood. Our favorite line: "Life sucks in bear country."

*   *   *

MICHELLE'S WISDOM

Thoughtful words from America's first African American First Lady.

"We need to do a better job of putting ourselves higher on our own 'to do' list."

"The one way to get me to work my hardest is to doubt me."

"Success is only meaningful and enjoyable if it feels like your own."

"I have had to learn that my voice has value. And if I don't use it, what's the point of being in the room?"

"My message to women: Do what makes you feel good, because there'll always be someone who thinks you should do it differently. Whether your choices are hits or misses, at least they're your own."

"People can only define you if you let them."

"People who are truly strong lift others up. People who are truly powerful bring others together."

"For so many people, television and movies may be the only way they understand people who aren't like them."

"I've seen firsthand that being president doesn't change who you are. It reveals who you are."

"Don't let anyone speak for you, and don't rely on others to fight for you."

"There is no magic to achievement. It's really about hard work, choices, and persistence."

"You have a bad day. You go to bed. You wake up, and you work a little harder."

E.T.: The Extra-Terrestrial was banned in Sweden. Reason: It portrays adults as enemies of children.

YOU DON'T KNOW JACK

Once you start looking, you'll find Jack everywhere: Jack be nimble; jack of all trades; jackpot; hijack; hit the road, Jack. You get the idea. So where did this name come from?

A BRIEF HISTORY OF JACK

Jack is becoming increasingly popular as a boy's name in English-speaking countries, but exactly where it comes from is a mystery.

It has long been (and still is) a common nickname for people named John. In medieval England, *kin* was used to indicate endearment, as in "lambkin" or "munchkin." So a term of endearment for someone named John (or Jan, as the name was written in medieval times) would be "Jankin." This may have led to the name Jackie, and then Jack. Another theory: it came from the French name Jacques (Jacob), which makes sense—French was widely spoken in England after the Norman Conquest of 1066. It may also derive from the ancient Celtic name Jakkios, meaning "health, strength, or vitality." To this day, the Welsh word *iach* still means "good health."

Whatever its origin, by the late Middle Ages (the 14th and 15th centuries), "Jack" came to refer to a man, especially one of lowly birth. From there it became a term for "everyman" and then, by extension, a term for some male animals, as in jackrabbit and jackass. Here are the stories behind a few Jacks.

MOTHER GOOSE'S FAVORITE SON

Jack Horner. According to legend, when King Henry VIII broke with the Catholic Church and abolished the monasteries, an abbot's assistant named Thomas Horner was given the job of secretly taking the deeds for a dozen abbeys to the king so that the properties could be given to private landowners. Horner carried the deeds hidden in a huge Christmas pie, and along the way, he opened the pie (stuck in his thumb) and took one of the deeds (the plum), which he kept for himself.

Jack Sprat. Originally Jack Prat, in the 16th and 17th centuries "Jack Sprat" was a slang term for a dwarf. In the 18th century, Jack Sprat became a popular hero in cheaply printed chapbooks. Eager children read of his exploits, and of those of his wife Joan Cole and their one-eared black cat.

Jack and Jill. The origin is unknown, but it probably comes from the Norse myth of Hjúki and Bil. As the brother-and-sister team fetched water from the well (Byrgir) and between them carried the pole (Simul) that held the pail (Sæg), the moon god (Máni) lifted them up from earth into heaven. To this day, Swedish folklore interprets the spots on the moon as two people carrying a bucket on a pole.

OTHER INTERESTING JACKS

Jackanapes. In the 15th century, "Jack-a-Naples" was a slang term for a monkey, one of the exotic goods being exported from Naples to England. It was soon shortened to jackanapes, perhaps because of the similarity between monkeys and apes. Around the same time, William de la Pole, the great-grandson of a wool merchant, was made the Duke of Suffolk, despite being of common birth. His coat of arms featured the unfortunate choice of a collar and chain, which were well known as being part of the costume of a performing monkey—a jackanapes—and the new duke was mocked as one as well. From then on, "jackanapes" came to mean an impudent upstart.

Jack in the Green. In 16th-century England, it was a May Day custom to make elaborate flower garlands and cover an entire man for the annual spring celebration. He was called Jack in the Green, another name for the Green Man, a leaf-bearded fertility god who shows up in medieval church carvings, thought to be related to Puck, Robin Goodfellow, and the Green Knight. The tradition died out around 1900, but was revived in the 1980s.

Jack Tales. Everyone's heard of the story "Jack and the Beanstalk." And you may be familiar with the fairy tale "Jack the Giant Killer." But at one time there were dozens of tales told about Jack, a clever trickster of poor birth who outwits giants, witches, and even the devil, often winning a fortune for himself in the process. One of the earliest, "Jack and His Stepdame," dates from the 15th century. In this story, Jack gets revenge on his wicked stepmother with a magic hornpipe that makes her dance uncontrollably.

Jack-o'-lantern. In Irish folklore, there was a clever drunkard named Stingy Jack, who never paid his bar tab. Jack ran afoul of the devil, but managed to outwit him twice. When he died, Jack was too sinful to enter heaven, but the devil, stung from being beaten, wouldn't allow him into hell either. Jack was doomed to wander the middle darkness for all eternity. At the last minute, however, the devil took pity on him, and gave him an ember of everlasting hellfire to light his way. Jack put the spark into a turnip to use as a lantern. (The turnip became a pumpkin when the tradition was brought to America.) Sometimes you can see Jack's flickering lantern in marshes late at night. But don't try to follow it, or you may never been seen again.

Halloween "Hell Houses" are faith-based alternatives to haunted houses. They scare "sinners" straight.

SADDAM SPEAKS, PT. II

More excerpts from the FBI's interviews of "High Value Detainee #1," aka Iraqi dictator Saddam Hussein, after he was captured in 2003. (Part 1 is on page 205.)

ON THE IRAQ WAR

• "Even though Saddam claimed Iraq did not have weapons of mass destruction (WMDs), the threat from Iran was the major factor as to why he did not allow the return of the UN inspectors. Saddam stated he was more concerned about Iran discovering Iraq's weaknesses and vulnerabilities than the repercussions of the United States for his refusal to allow UN inspectors back into Iraq. In his opinion, the UN inspectors would have directly identified to the Iranians where to inflict maximum damage to Iraq. Saddam demonstrated this by pointing at his arm and stated that striking someone on the forearm would not have the same effect as striking someone at the elbow or wrist, which would significantly disable the ability to use the arm."

• "Saddam admitted that when it was clear that a war with the United States was imminent, he allowed the inspectors back into Iraq in hopes of averting war… Saddam reiterated he had wanted to have a relationship with the United States but was not given the chance, as the United States was not listening to anything Iraq had to say."

• "Hussein said, 'If you asked the American soldier, who came to Iraq to find weapons of mass destruction, but none could be found, and who came to remove the leaders of the Hussein dictatorship, who are all in jail now, but are replaced with other dictators, whether he wanted to stay or go, he would say go.' "

ODDS AND ENDS

• "Hussein stated he only recalls using the telephone on two occasions since March 1990. Additionally, Hussein did not stay at the same location for more than a day, as he was very aware of the United States' significant technological capabilities. Hussein communicated primarily through the use of couriers or would personally meet with government officials to discuss pertinent issues."

• "While talking about the air conditioning in Hussein's cell, which was being repaired at that time, Hussein advised that he is used to living simply and personally does not like an extravagant lifestyle. Hussein was then questioned about the number of palaces and their extravagant nature. Hussein stated that the palaces

American Idol's Simon Cowell worked on the film *The Shining*. His job: Polishing Jack Nicholson's axe.

belong to the nation and not to one person…Additionally, there was a threat from the United States and Israel, especially during the last ten years…If there were only two palaces or locations that the leadership could meet, it would have been very easy for the elimination of the Iraqi leadership. However, with twenty palaces, it was much more difficult to track or identify the location of the Iraqi leadership. Since these palaces belonged to the nation, Hussein did not live in them and preferred to live in a simple home."

• "Hussein claimed he did not enjoy giving his speeches, preferring instead to have his speeches read by others, such as news broadcasters. Saddam described the feeling of writing his speeches and giving them was the same as taking an exam."

• "Agent Piro inquired about Abid Hamid Mahmoud, Hussein's Presidential Secretary. Hussein stated Abid was a good and loyal employee who carried out his duties and orders well. Hussein then asked Agent Piro his opinion of Abid. Agent Piro described to Hussein the meaning of a 'used car salesman.' Hussein again laughed and stated Agent Piro was correct."

THE END

• "Hussein was asked, as the ex-President of Iraq, about Iraqi policy regarding treatment of POWs. Hussein replied, 'I am not the ex-President of Iraq. I am still the President of Iraq.' He added that he still respects the will of the people (their support of him as President)."

• [In a later interview]: "Agent Piro reminded Hussein that he had previously made it clear that he still considered himself the President of Iraq. However, there is a new President who is representing the country and the people of Iraq. Agent Piro told Hussein he is no longer the President of Iraq; he was done. Hussein replied yes he knows, saying what could he do as it was God's choice. Agent Piro asked him if he had any thoughts about his future and Hussein stated that it was in God's hands. Agent Piro pointed out to Hussein that God was very busy and had more important issues than he and Agent Piro. Hussein agreed, at which point, Agent Piro told Hussein that his life is nearing its end, and asked if he wanted the remainder of his life to have meaning, to which he responded yes."

• "Hussein stated it is not only important what people say about him now but what they think in the future, 500 or 1,000 years from now. The most important thing, however, is what God thinks."

Following his conviction by an Iraqi tribunal on charges of crimes against humanity, Saddam Hussein was executed by hanging on December 30, 2006.

England's first public toilet, opened in 1852, was for men only. (A ladies' room opened nine days later.)

1923

*Uncle John frequently reminds the BRI staff that "history is happening all the time."
To make his point, he picked a year at random for us to survey. What did we
learn? Well, in a year when "John" and "Mary" were the number-one
baby names, you'd think nothing much was going on. Think again!*

January 1: The Ku Klux Klan, which has been dormant since 1871, resurfaces
and launches a surprise attack on black families in the town of Rosewood,
Florida. Eight people are killed and the entire town destroyed in what becomes
known as the Rosewood Massacre.

January 9: Aeronautical engineer and pilot Juan de la Cierva sends his
autogyro—the precursor to the helicopter—out for its first successful spin in
Madrid, Spain. The aircraft, which has four rotating blades, flies 200 yards.

January 13: Adolf Hitler denounces the Weimar republic as 5,000 Nazi storm
troopers demonstrate in Germany. It has been only three years since Hitler
joined the seven-member German Workers' Party and transformed it into the
National Socialist German Workers' (Nazi) Party.

January 24: The United States withdraws the last of its troops from Germany,
four years after the end of World War I.

February 1: Benito Mussolini begins to move from being Italy's prime minister
to its fascist dictator by transforming his private army of "Blackshirts" (so called
because of the black shirts they wear as uniforms) into the official Fascists
Voluntary Military. These armed thugs are against socialists, communists,
Catholics, Jews, and organized unions, and aren't afraid to say so.

February 13: The first all-black professional basketball team, the New York
Renaissance (nicknamed the Rens and the Big Five), is organized in Harlem.

February 16: Egyptologist and adventurer (and the inspiration for Indiana
Jones) Howard Carter opens a sealed burial chamber in a tomb in Thebes, Egypt,
and strikes gold—the sarcophagus of King Tut.

March 3: *Time* magazine, the first weekly magazine in the United States,
publishes its first issue. Cost: 15 cents.

March: Hitler chooses an elite personal guard of "Nordic blood and good character" who will protect him as he travels Germany spreading the word about the Nazi cause. They will become the Schutzstaffel (Defense Squad), or SS.

March 23: Frank Silver and Irving Cohn's novelty song "Yes! We Have No Bananas" is published and is recorded by three different singers—Eddie Cantor, Billy Murray, and Billy Jones. It tops the charts for five weeks. The song's popularity inspires a follow-up: "I've Got the Yes! We Have No Bananas Blues."

April 5: Firestone Tire and Rubber Company begins the first regular production of low-pressure balloon tires, vastly improving tread wear and mileage in the average tire. The company has a blow-out celebration.

April 7: Dr. K. Winfield Ney at Beth Israel Hospital in New York City performs the first successful brain tumor operation under only a local anesthetic (cocaine). The patient, 49-year-old Henry A. Brown, is awake and chatting cheerfully as the team removes an enormous tumor.

April 10: Hitler gives a speech in Munich in which he declares that if Germany is again to become strong and free, it needs "hate, hate, and once again hate."

April 18: More than 74,000 baseball fans show up to watch the New York Yankees beat the Boston Red Sox 4–1 on the opening day of Yankee Stadium. Babe Ruth hits the first home run in the stadium's history. The three-tiered structure, which will become known as "the House that Ruth Built," will be the Yankees' home for 85 years.

May 2–3: Test pilots John Macready and Oakley Kelly jump in the cockpit of a Fokker T-2 and make the first nonstop transcontinental flight from New York to San Diego in 26 hours and 50 minutes. (Today that flight takes 4 hours and 45 minutes.)

May 28: After a 14-year-old girl in West Virginia is arrested for wearing pants, Attorney General Harry Daugherty announces, "Women can now wear trousers anywhere."

June 23: Mt. Etna erupts with a stream of molten lava that destroys everything in its path. More than 100,000 people are left homeless in Sicily. According to the *Chicago Tribune*, local Italian farmers believe it was a vendetta by giants.

July 13: American explorer and naturalist Roy Chapman Andrews discovers fossilized dinosaur eggs in China.

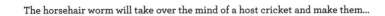

The horsehair worm will take over the mind of a host cricket and make them...

July 24: After a seven-month conference, the Allied powers, which include Britain, France, Italy, Japan, Greece, and Yugoslavia, sign a peace treaty with Turkey in Lausanne, Switzerland. This is the final treaty of World War I.

August 2: The 29th president of the United States, Warren G. Harding, dies suddenly in San Francisco after a trip to Alaska dubbed "A Voyage of Understanding." Harding's wife, Florence, refuses an autopsy and has him embalmed immediately, setting off rumors that she had something to do with his death. (Harding was embroiled in some very big scandals and had numerous affairs, including one that resulted in a child.)

August 3: Calvin Coolidge is sworn in as the 30th president of the United States. Known for his quiet demeanor, "Silent Cal" was in Vermont when he got the news and is sworn in by his father, who is a notary public.

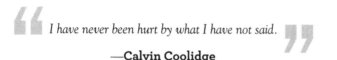

I have never been hurt by what I have not said.

—**Calvin Coolidge**

September 1: The Great Kanto 8.2 earthquake shakes up Japan, setting off a 40-foot tsunami followed by a massive number of fires, killing 140,000 people. The cities of Tokyo and Yokohama—and the surrounding areas—are nearly destroyed.

October 11: Hyperinflation is rampant in Germany. Having to pay World War I reparations but unable to buy gold or foreign currency, the government prints more money and the value of the deutsche mark falls to 10 billion per British pound and 4 billion per U.S. dollar. Just two years earlier, the exchange rate had been 90 marks per dollar.

October 16: Roy and Walt Disney form the Disney Brothers Cartoon Studio in Los Angeles, California. It will be another five years before there's a mouse in the house.

October 24: In Dallas, 75,000 people attend "Ku Klux Klan Day" at the Texas State Fair. They wear "100% American" buttons and pass out fliers that say "You and your friends are invited to attend this day, the most wonderful day of your life!"

October 25: F. G. Banting and J. J. R. McLeod are awarded the Nobel Prize in Medicine for their discovery of insulin, the life-saving treatment for diabetes.

...drown themselves so that the worm can leave the host and finish their life cycle.

Within a month, insulin is commercially available to diabetics in the United States and Canada.

October 29: The parliament of Turkey proclaims the formation of the Republic of Turkey, thus formally ending the 624-year-old Ottoman Empire.

November 9: In a failed attempt to overthrow the Bavarian government, Hitler and his followers burst into a beer hall in Munich, Germany, where the head of the Bavarian government is speaking. Hitler fires a pistol and announces, "The revolution has begun!" He is arrested for his "Beer Hall Putsch"—an attempted coup—and is convicted of treason. He spends a year in jail writing *Mein Kampf*, his dream for Nazi Germany.

November 20: Garret Morgan gets the green light on his patent of the traffic signal.

November 26: Irish poet-author William Butler Yeats wins the Nobel Prize for Literature "for his always inspired poetry, which in a highly artistic form gives expression to the spirit of a whole nation." Yeats is best remembered for his poem *The Second Coming*, which contains this famous line: "Things fall apart; the centre cannot hold; Mere anarchy is loosed upon the world," a response to the post-World War I chaos in Europe and a lament for the end of European civilization.

December 21: Cecil B. DeMille's silent version of *The Ten Commandments* premieres. Two months earlier, actor Charlton Heston was born. Heston will star as Moses in DeMille's 1956 remake of the film, which will become the fifth highest-grossing movie of all time.

December 24: At 5:00 p.m. on Christmas Eve, President Coolidge lights the very first "National Christmas Tree." It is a balsam fir from his home state of Vermont and is the first tree at the White House to be lit with electric lights.

December 31: Big Ben's chimes make their debut on BBC radio. The bells will be broadcast live every evening at 6:00 p.m. for the next 93 years.

*   *   *

"Hating people is like burning down your own home to get rid of a rat."

–Harry Emerson Fosdick

Fidel Castro was an extra in two Hollywood movies in 1946: *Easy to Wed* and *Holiday in Mexico*.

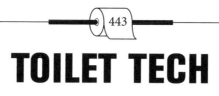

TOILET TECH

Better living through bathroom technology.

LOOK MA, NO HANDS!

Product: The Delta FlushIQ Toilet

How It Works: This hands-free home toilet has a small motion sensor where the flush handle would be. After you do your business, pass your hand in front of the sensor and the toilet flushes automatically.

Bonus Features: The motion sensor has a built-in LED light that alerts you when the toilet isn't working properly. A solid yellow light means a leak has been detected, and flashing yellow means the leak is preventing the toilet tank from filling properly. Flashing red and blue lights means the toilet is at risk of overflowing—and to prevent that, the toilet will *refuse to flush* until the problem is fixed. (When the light is solid blue, the toilet is working normally.) The FlushIQ system is powered by batteries that last for up to five years; when they run low, the LED light flashes red to tell you to change them.

TUB TUNES

Product: Sound Wave Bath Audio System

How It Works: While the tub is being manufactured, six acoustic panels are glued to the underside of the tub—one each at the head and the foot, and two on either side—where they are hidden from sight. These panels are connected to a Bluetooth receiver, which allows you to stream audio into the tub from any Bluetooth-enabled device and listen to your favorite songs underwater. "With the bathtub acting as the sound box, you will find a complete new enjoyment of your music collection via your smartphone, laptop or tablet," says KALDEWEI, the company that manufactures the tubs. "Immerse yourself in the relaxing or invigorating moments of your personal bathroom playlist."

STREAMING

Product: The Loogun

How It Works: It's a motorized squirt gun that's designed to remove "skid marks" from a toilet bowl more hygienically than a toilet brush. Just hold the Loogun close to the rim of the toilet and press the trigger button. It will spray "a powerful jet of clean water that washes away stubborn marks both above and below the water line," says its inventor, Calan Horsman. "The Loogun never touches the toilet, so the device stays beautifully hygienic and pleasant to use."

SIGHT UNSEEN

Product: Glass Apps Smart Glass

How It Works: It's window glass that goes from clear to opaque at the flip of a switch. What appears to be an ordinary pane of glass is actually two panes sandwiched around a layer of something called Polymer Dispersed Liquid Crystal (PDLC) film. When the window is in "clear mode," electricity flows through the PDLC layer and causes the microscopic crystals to line up and "open" like tiny venetian blinds, allowing light to shine through unimpeded. When the power is switched off, the crystals are no longer aligned. Now when light passes through the glass, some of it strikes the haphazardly arranged crystals and reflects it off in odd angles, clouding the glass and providing privacy until the bathroom occupant switches it back to clear mode.

PIPE DREAM

Product: Fresh Air Plus

How It Works: This toilet seat is equipped with an electric fan and an exhaust pipe that "safely vents unwelcome odors outside your house." A built-in pressure sensor activates the fan when a person sits down; any unpleasant odors that are created are immediately pumped to the outside world through a hole that you or the installer must drill in the wall. "Hopefully, once people realize how well Fresh Air Plus works, it will become a staple in every restroom," says inventor Adam Payz. "Just be careful if there isn't much room between your house and the next," notes CNET.com, "or you may end up venting a stream of bad smells into your neighbor's open window."

HOLIDAY CHEER

Product: Mulled Spice Scented Luxury Soft Toilet Tissue

How It Works: Introduced by the British retail giant Tesco during the Christmas season in 2016, the quilted toilet paper was decorated with gold trees and snowflakes, and featured a "mulled spice fragrance core," to give your TP a Christmassy smell. British shoppers were not amused. "What fresh hell is this? Stop it now, I say," one customer tweeted. "[I] do not recommend Tesco wine scented paper, feels like wiping your a__ with last night's hangover," says another. (A claim that Tesco also sold "mulled wine that tastes of toilet paper" was, apparently, a joke.)

BACK TO NATURE

Product: Le Uritrottoir

How It Works: It's an eco-friendly, open-air urinal (for men only) designed to combat *les pipis sauvages*—"wild peeing." The *uritrottoirs*—the name is derived from a combination of the French words for "urinal" and "pavement"—are placed in high-traffic areas on Paris streets where public urination is a problem. When nature calls, you urinate into a receptacle mounted atop a sealed box that contains either straw, sawdust, or wood chips that soak up the urine. (Planter boxes are placed on top of the Uritrottoirs to make them look a little nicer.)

The devices come in two sizes: small, which fills up after 300 uses; and large, which can accommodate 600 uses. When the boxes are nearly full, an electronic sensor sends a signal to a "urine attendant" who hauls away the full box and replaces it with an empty one. Bonus: urine-soaked straw, it turns out, makes pretty good compost. "It's a circular economy. We're reusing two waste products to make something that makes plants grow," says Laurent Lebot, the designer.

*   *   *

HIGH STAKES

Where it's legal, marijuana dispensaries keep popping up like weeds, and using wordplay to stand out. We think these names are a cut above the rest…

Grateful Meds	Pharm to Table	Best Buds
Karmaceuticals	Cannabliss and Co.	Green Mile
Starbuds	Growing ReLeaf	Grass Station
CannaSutra	Pipe Dreams Dispensary	Club Medz
The Giving Tree		Cannaisseur
Herban Legends	Taste Buds	Higher Learning
Weedidit Association	Hollyweed Dispensary	Emerald City
Higher Level of Care	The Higher Path	Rocky Mountain High
The Coughy Shop	Bud Cellar	
Stone Age Pharmacy	Natural Selections	The Green House

Eau d'Doh: For its 50th anniversary, Play-Doh created a perfume that smells like a freshly opened can.

INTERNATIONAL BLOCKBUSTERS

The most popular movies in the world are Hollywood blockbusters. Films like Avatar *and* Star Wars *draw huge audiences regardless of nationality. But other countries make their own blockbuster movies. Here are the most popular.*

Country: Taiwan
Movie: *Cape No. 7* (2008)
Story: The overall top-grossing film in Taiwanese history is *Titanic*, but the top-grossing Taiwanese movie is *Cape No. 7*, a romantic musical by first-time director Wei Te-sheng, starring a cast of mostly amateur actors. It takes place in the 1940s, when Taiwan was under Japanese rule, and it's about a teacher from Japan who falls in love with a local girl. When China takes Taiwan back from Japan, the girl is sent back home. The rest of the movie is about the couple sending love letters to one another.

Country: Japan
Movie: *Spirited Away* (2001)
Story: Nearly half of the top 10 highest-grossing homegrown movies in Japan are animated features by Studio Ghibli. Among them are cult "anime" hits that have been redubbed for English audiences and released in the United States, such as My *Neighbor Totoro* and *Kiki's Delivery Service*. Ghibli's opus is *Spirited Away*, a fantasy tale about a little girl who moves to a new neighborhood and gets stuck in a surreal spiritual world. (She has to get a job at a bathhouse to support herself because her parents get magically transformed into pigs.) In 2002, the second year that an Oscar was awarded for Best Animated Feature, *Spirited Away* surprisingly won the award over the huge, American-made hits *Lilo & Stitch* and *Ice Age*. At the Japanese box office, *Spirited Away* took in 30.8 billion yen (around $274 million), making it the all-time top-grossing movie of any kind.

Country: Greece
Movie: *Loafing and Camouflage: Sirens in the Aegean* (2005)
Story: A reboot of *Loafing and Camouflage*, a popular 1980s Greek military comedy franchise, this movie is about a group of troops assigned to guard a

Until the late 1970s, most pistachios sold in the U.S. were dyed red to hide discolorations on the shells.

tiny, rocky island in the Aegean Sea amid reports of an impending invasion by Turkish soldiers. Instead (and with a nod to the sirens of Greek mythology), a boat full of Turkish models crashes onto the island's shore. It earned the equivalent of $11 million at the Greek box office.

Country: Nigeria

Movie: *30 Days in Atlanta* (2014)

Story: This broad, fish-out-of-water comedy is about two Nigerian cousins (one reserved, one outgoing) who go to a real-estate showcase (similar to a time-share presentation) and win a 30-day trip to Atlanta. The rest of the movie, filmed on location in the United States, is a series of episodes about their culture clashes.

Country: France

Movie: *Bienvenue chez les Ch'tis* (2008)

Story: In this fish-out-of-water comedy (the title translates to "Welcome to the Sticks"), a postal worker named Philippe tries to please his unhappy wife by getting a transfer to a cushy beach town. But the position is earmarked for a disabled employee—so he pretends to be disabled and gets caught. As punishment, he's reassigned to Bergues, a town in "the sticks" of northern France, where it rains all the time. Over time, Philippe is charmed by the small town and comes to love it, but tells his wife—who's still living in the beach town—that he's miserable so he can stay there. More than 20 million people in France saw *Bienvenue chez les Ch'tis*, more than any other French film ever.

Region: French Canada

Movie: *Bon Cop, Bad Cop* (2006)

Story: Many "American" movies are shot in Canada (particularly Toronto and Vancouver), so a lot of mainstream blockbusters are, technically speaking, "Canadian" movies. *Bon Cop, Bad Cop* is the highest-grossing French-language movie in Canada, performing very well in the regions where French is the dominant language, particularly Quebec. Actually, it's not entirely in French, because the plot of this buddy cop movie concerns an English-speaking, straitlaced police detective from Ontario who must team up with a French-speaking, loose-cannon detective from Quebec to find out who murdered a powerful hockey executive. *Bon Cop, Bad Cop* earned $12 million at the Quebecois box office (but only $1.3 million outside the province).

MAY I HAVE THIS DANCE?

*The origins of some old and famous dance styles—and one
not-so-old one—for your dance-room reading pleasure.*

TANGO

This evocative and often suggestive dance is largely improvisational—there are
basic moves, but no set steps as there are in, say, the waltz or fox-trot. It is based,
says one expert, on "the four building blocks of walking, turning, stopping and
embellishments." Tango originated in the slums of Buenos Aires, Argentina, and
nearby Montevideo, Uruguay, in the 1890s. It was a product of music and dance
styles from former African slaves mixed with styles from Europe, especially Spain
and Italy. The dance became an international sensation in the early 1900s, when
it spread first to Paris, then across Europe, finally making it to New York around
1913. The tango's popularity increased and decreased over the years—down
during the Great Depression in the 1930s, up in the 1940s when Juan Peron was
president of Argentina, down in the 1950s and '60s, and booming again in the
2000s, especially in the United States. And like many popular dances, the tango
has evolved into many different styles over the decades, including ballroom
tango, contact tango, and even Finnish tango, but purists consider the bold,
seductive Argentine tango to be the "true" form of the dance.

BLACK BOTTOM

One of the most popular dances in the United States during the Roaring
Twenties, the black bottom was a Charleston-like dance that involved a
series of choreographed steps—*doodles* (slides), *mooches* (shuffling—"hips go
first, then feet"), kicks, hip and shoulder wiggles, arm swings, knee bends,
bottom-bumping, bottom-grabbing, and more. It was danced to the music of
jazz bands by either one, two, or a stage full of dancers. The dance is known to
have originated in African American nightclubs in New Orleans in the early
1900s. From there it spread around the South, was eventually appropriated by
white America, and became a full-fledged national dance craze by the 1920s. A
number of songs featuring the dance's name were recorded during the era, most
notably Perry Bradford's "Original Black Bottom Dance" in 1919 and Jelly Roll
Morton's "Black Bottom Stomp" in 1925. The black bottom dance was mostly
gone by the end of the decade. (You can find videos of it on YouTube if you and
your dance partners want to bring it back to life.)

Grave matter: It's against the law to die in Le Lavandou, France…unless you own a cemetery plot.

CANCAN

It's best known as the high-kicking dance performed by a chorus line of female dancers, usually dressed in costumes that include long skirts, petticoats, and stockings. Surprisingly, the cancan started off in France as a dance for single dancers, female or male, around 1830. Historians say it evolved out of a similar lively dance called the *galop* ("gallop"—named after a horse's gallop). The new dance became extremely popular in Paris's working-class dance halls, but it was much too frisky for the upper classes. One reason: it was bawdy. Women of the day wore undergarments called *pantalettes*, leggings that were worn as two separate pieces—one for each leg—tied or buttoned together at the waist, but not joined at the crotch. Dancers who wore them revealed a lot more than their sense of rhythm. Over time the cancan evolved into a dance for professionals, achieving its greatest popularity in the 1890s, when it became the signature dance at the famous Paris cabaret, the Moulin Rouge. By that time it had acquired most of the well-known cancan costume (without the overly revealing underwear), but was still at this time primarily performed by single dancers, and didn't become the chorus line dance until after the 1920s.

BOOGALOO

In the 1950s, young Latino musicians in New York City started mixing American rhythm and blues with Afro-Cuban styles, such as mambo and cha-cha. This new mix of genres spread, and by the early 1960s, it was being picked up by popular musicians. One of the songs credited with starting the national popularity of the style: Cuban bandleader Mongo Santamaria's short, snappy, radio-friendly rendition of Herbie Hancock's "Watermelon Man." A string of similar hits followed, and in 1966 someone named the new genre "boogaloo." And somewhere along the line, a dance developed out of the music. The dance was free-form, with lots of jerky movements, thrusting hips, shuffling and sliding feet, head rolls, and shoulder wiggles. The boogaloo became a standard on the TV show *American Bandstand*, until the craze faded way by around 1970, when it was taken over by the new craze: salsa. (The most famous boogaloo dancer in the world: James Brown. It was a regular part of his stage dancing for years. Want to see an example? Google "James Brown boogaloo.")

FRUG

Pronounced "froog," this was another mid-1960s dance fad that grew out of other popular '60s dances, including both the twist and the chicken. Basic steps: put your feet close together, bend your knees a little, and move your hips left to

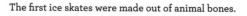

The first ice skates were made out of animal bones.

right in time with the music, and make either improvised or choreographed arm movements. Popular mentions of the frug: the 1977 song "Rock Lobster" by the B52s contains the line "Everybody's rockin' / Everybody's fruggin' "; the poster for the 1967 film *Come Spy with Me* says "They Frug in the water…Swim on the floor…And blow up the Caribbean." (The film was universally panned.)

BALLET

Most people assume that ballet originated in France. Not true! Ballet first developed as a dance style in northern Italian cities like Florence and Milan during the early years of the Renaissance (the 1400s), the cultural movement that changed the world, especially in the areas of art and science. Ballet began as a form of entertainment at lavish royal weddings and parties, during which the partygoers all took part in the dances. It was a kind of ballroom dance, comprised of graceful little steps, slides, and turns, with associated arm movements. The style spread to the royal courts of France in the 1500s, and there, over the next couple of centuries, evolved into the classical ballet that is still the foundation of all ballet styles today. In the 1800s, ballet became popular in Russia, and Russian ballet became a major influence on the entire genre. (Some of the most famous narrative, or "story," ballets, including *The Nutcracker*, *Sleeping Beauty*, and *Swan Lake*, are Russian ballets.) The word "ballet" came from the Italian *balletto*, the diminutive of *ballo*, meaning "dance."

HAND JIVE

The hand jive hit dance floors in the late 1950s, first in the UK and then in the United States. And unlike with most dance styles, cultural historians know exactly where it was born: in a "coffee bar" called the Cat's Whisker, in London's Soho district. Coffee bars, as the name suggests, sold coffee and espresso, and because they were open to all ages, and featured both live and recorded rock 'n' roll music, they became centers for the growing, teenager-based British pop music scene. The Cat's Whisker was one of the most popular, and it was there that crowds of teenagers adapted to the club's packed conditions. They didn't have much room to move around, so they developed this new, compact dance. It involved primarily short, tight, energetic arm and hand movements—bumping fists together top to bottom, crossing open hands over and under one another, slapping the thighs, clapping, and so on—all performed while standing in place. Just who gave it the name "hand jive" is unknown, but a number of songs featuring the name, including Johnny Otis's 1958 hit "Willie and the Hand Jive," helped spread the dance's popularity around the world. The hand jive

Okilly Dokilly is a Ned Flanders-themed heavy metal band.

craze was pretty much over by the mid-1960s, but it enjoyed a brief resurgence in popularity when it was the center of a prominent dance scene in the 1978 film *Grease*. And who knows—it may become popular again someday. It's always handy…

EXTRA STEPS

• The lively Latin dance known as the mambo was created in Cuba in the 1930s, and became popular in the United States in the 1950s, riding mostly on the popularity of the "Mambo King," Cuban composer and bandleader Pérez Prado. The name is believed to derive from a Haitian Creole word meaning "voodoo priestess."

• The hustle was a disco-era dance that originated in the early 1970s. Most sources say it started in the Bronx in New York City, and over the next few years spread and morphed into several subgenres, including the New York hustle, the Latin hustle, and the L.A. hustle. The dance really took off after Van McCoy's 1975 song "The Hustle" hit number one on the *Billboard* charts, and even more so when it was featured in the 1977 smash hit *Saturday Night Fever*.

• Flamenco is a style of both dance and music—a combination of classical guitar, vocals, and handclaps. It originated in the Andalusian region of Spain in the early 1700s, and possibly much earlier. It is believed to have evolved as a mix of dance and music traditions from the many people who inhabited Andalusia over the centuries, including Romany (gypsy), Moorish (North African), Greek, Jewish, and Spanish. The origin of the term *flamenco* could come from "Flemish," meaning someone from Flanders, or it could be a Spanish derivation of "fire," or "flame," or it could come from "flamingo," as in the pink bird.

• The chicken dance—the arm-flapping, butt-shaking dance you do when you get silly (or drunk) at family reunions and wedding receptions—was invented by Swiss accordionist Werner Thomas in 1950, as an accompanying dance for his song "Der Ententanz"—which meant "The Duck Dance." In the 1980s, versions of the song started becoming popular around the world. The chicken dance craze has (sadly) never ended.

*   *   *

ANOTHER BAR JOKE

A three-legged dog walks into a saloon and says to the bartender, "I'm looking for the man who shot my paw."

The San Francisco Public Library's first computer was coin-operated. Cost: $1 for 20 minutes.

THE DIFFICULT DECISIONS OF ROBERT E. LEE, PT. III

How we make the tough decisions shapes our lives. It can also define "greatness."
Would you do what Robert E. Lee did? (Part I of the story starts on page 37.)

BACK TO SCHOOL

For Lee's final act, he saved a school. Washington College, located in Lexington, Virginia, had been left in tatters after the war. Five months after the surrender at Appomattox Courthouse in September 1865, Lee was offered the job as the school's president. The use of his name, which was still hallowed in the South, would be a boon to any institution (and he reportedly turned down several other, more lucrative positions that would have capitalized on his name). Lee agreed to take the job—in part because of his respect for George Washington, for whom the school was named, but also because he believed that an educated populace would be less likely to wage war. "It is well that war is so terrible," he once said, "we should grow too fond of it."

Under Lee's leadership, Washington College grew from a small Latin school to a university that offered students (just white males at the time) the opportunity to major in journalism, engineering, finance, and law. He fused those with the liberal arts, which was almost unheard of at the time. He even recruited Northerners to become part of the student body in yet another effort to heal a broken nation. "The students fairly worshipped him, and deeply dreaded his displeasure," wrote one of the professors, "yet so kind, affable, and gentle was he toward them that all loved to approach him."

The school, now known as Washington and Lee University, is still going strong today. Now fully integrated with women and African Americans (though it took until the 1970s for that process to become complete), the school has produced four U.S. Supreme Court justices; 27 U.S. senators; 67 members of the House of Representatives; 31 state governors; a Nobel Prize laureate; several Pulitzer Prize, Tony Award, and Emmy Award winners; and many more government officials, judges, business leaders, entertainers, and athletes. Fittingly, the university adopted Lee's family motto: *Non incautus futuri*, which means "Not Unmindful of the Future."

But Lee only had a chance to serve as the school's president for a short time. In 1870, just five years after the Civil War ended, he suffered a stroke and died.

When European explorers landed in Virginia and asked natives "What place is this?" they replied, "Windgancon"...

A Legacy Divided

The debate continues to this day: was Robert E. Lee a hero or a traitor? Although he was considered a war hero in the South, his peacetime promotion of reconciliation earned him accolades in the North. Shortly after the Civil War ended, Lee granted an interview to the *New York Herald* in which he condemned the assassination of President Lincoln as "deplorable," said he "rejoiced" at the end of slavery, and referred to the North and the South as "we." The *Herald* praised Lee's efforts to reunite the nation: "Here in the North we have claimed him as one of ourselves."

That sentiment was echoed by most American newspapers after Lee died in 1870, but not all of them. The editor of the *New National Era*, noted abolitionist and former slave Frederick Douglass, wrote a scathing editorial: "We can scarcely take up a newspaper…that is not filled with nauseating flatteries of the late Robert E. Lee. Is it not about time that this bombastic laudation of the rebel chief should cease?" But the adulation would only increase as the nation slowly healed from the wounds of the Civil War, and Jim Crow segregation laws became the norm in both the North and the South for another century. Lee's legacy has been tied to U.S. race relations ever since.

Lee and Slavery

Like most wealthy white men in pre-Civil War America, including George Washington, Thomas Jefferson, and even Ulysses S. Grant, Lee was a slave owner…but his own views on slavery were conflicted. In 1856, he wrote:

> *There are few, I believe, in this enlightened age, who will not acknowledge that slavery as an institution is a moral and political evil. It is idle to expatiate on its disadvantages. I think it is a greater evil to the white than to the colored race. While my feelings are strongly enlisted in behalf of the latter, my sympathies are more deeply engaged for the former. The blacks are immeasurably better off here than in Africa, morally, physically, and socially. The painful discipline they are undergoing is necessary for their further instruction as a race, and will prepare them, I hope, for better things.*

Lee even went so far as to advocate for the education of slaves, saying, "It would be better for the blacks and for the whites." But he was not in favor of granting them the right to vote, and even said that if the slaves were freed, "I think it would be better for Virginia if she could get rid of them." A deeply religious man, in Lee's view slavery could only be ended by God.

The Man and the Mythology

Despite Lee's views on slavery, his posthumous star kept rising. That began in earnest in 1871, the year after he died, with a biography called *The Life of General Robert E. Lee*, by John Cooke, a former Confederate soldier who served under Lee. Glossing over Confederate losses at Antietam and Gettysburg as having hastened the end of the war, Cooke focused on the "Lost Cause" belief that pervaded the South in the late 19th century. It downplayed slavery as the main cause of the Civil War and instead promoted the idea that the war was an "honorable, heroic struggle," fought in defense of the Southern way of life and against Union attempts to disrupt it. And it was Lee, Cooke wrote, who kept the South united: "The crowning grace of this man, who was thus not only great but good, was the humility and trust in God, which lay at the foundation of his character."

Hundreds of Lee biographies have been published since then, most of them painting the same rosy picture. For example, John Perry's 2010 biography, *Lee: A Life of Virtue*, describes Lee as a "passionate patriot, caring son, devoted husband, doting father, don't-tread-on-me Virginian, Godfearing Christian." Perry wrote that the real Lee was a caring man who "considered it a special honor to push his invalid wife in her wheelchair. During the war, he picked wildflowers between battles and pressed them into letters to his family. He once described two dozen little girls dressed in white at a birthday party as the most beautiful thing he ever saw."

In Praise...

Today, if a military leader were to defect from the United States and then lead a foreign army back into it, he would almost certainly be tried for treason and executed. But several former presidents—on both sides of the political spectrum—didn't view Lee in that light.

• President Theodore Roosevelt said that the two greatest Americans of all time were George Washington and Robert E. Lee: "Lee was one of the noblest Americans who ever lived, and one of the greatest captains known to the annals of war."

• Roosevelt's cousin, President Franklin Delano Roosevelt, called Lee "one of our greatest American Christians and one of our greatest American gentlemen."

• President Woodrow Wilson, the first Southerner elected to the White House after the Civil War, wrote a biography praising Lee. He often told of his experience as a 13-year-old boy, shortly after the war in Augustus, Georgia, when he had the opportunity to stand next to Lee during a procession.

While exploring the South American coast,
Ferdinand Magellan claimed to have found a race of people 12–15 feet tall.

• After President Dwight D. Eisenhower was criticized for hanging a portrait of General Lee in the White House, he replied, "From deep conviction I simply say this: a nation of men of Lee's caliber would be unconquerable in spirit and soul."

• In 1975, a few years after a letter written by Lee to President Andrew Johnson requesting amnesty was discovered, President Gerald Ford finally restored Lee's full U.S. citizenship. At the ceremony he said, "General Lee's character has been an example to succeeding generations, making the restoration of his citizenship an event in which every American can take pride."

• In 2009, President Barack Obama spoke at the annual dinner of the Alfalfa Club, which was founded in 1913 in honor of Lee (who, it turns out, is a distant relative of Obama's). Noting the irony that Lee didn't think African Americans should be allowed to vote or hold office, Obama said, "I know many of you are aware that this dinner began almost 100 years ago as a way to celebrate the birthday of General Robert E. Lee. If he were here with us tonight, the general would be 202 years old. And very confused."

On the Other Hand…

Indeed, a lot of Americans in the 21st century are confused as to why Lee is still glorified.

• "Why is it so hard for people to just say Robert E. Lee fought for a despicable cause and doesn't deserve our admiration?" asked *Slate* magazine's chief political correspondent, Jamelle Bouie.

• *Washington Post* columnist Richard Cohen wrote, "It has taken a while, but it's about time Robert E. Lee lost the Civil War. The South, of course, was defeated on the battlefield in 1865, yet the Lee legend—swaddled in myth, kitsch, and racism—has endured even past the civil rights era when it became both urgent and right to finally tell the 'Lost Cause' to get lost. Now it should be Lee's turn. He was loyal to slavery and disloyal to his country—not worthy, even he might now admit, of the honors accorded him."

The More Things Change

That's one reason why so many schools and highways named after Lee have been renamed after prominent African Americans. But not all of them are being renamed. In 2015, after calls for the removal of the Confederate flag from Southern statehouses following a tragic church shooting by a white supremacist in South Carolina, a petition was started at Robert E. Lee High School in Staunton, Virginia, to change its name. The petition was met with strong opposition. In an official protest letter from students and alumni, they wrote, "We support the decision by South Carolina and other states to lower the Confederate flag, a symbol of bigotry and bias for many. But erasing Robert E. Lee's name from the school is political correctness run amuck; and an act of historical vandalism." The name wasn't changed—that time—but it's safe to say the battle isn't over yet.

We'll give the final word to Ulysses S. Grant, the general-turned-president who admired and then defeated Lee in the Civil War. In his memoir, he wrote about Lee's surrender at Appomattox: "I felt like anything rather than rejoicing at the downfall of a foe who had fought so long and valiantly, and had suffered so much for a cause, though that cause was, I believe, one of the worst for which a people ever fought, and one for which there was the least excuse."

*   *   *

THE LONG, LONG WAR

You may be familiar with the Hundred Years' War, which was fought between England and France from 1337 to 1453. But you've probably never heard of the Three Hundred and Thirty-five Years' War. That one was "fought" between the Netherlands and the Isles of Scilly, English islands 25 miles off the west coast of England, from 1651 to 1986.

The Isles of Scilly (pronounced "silly") were the last refuge of the Royalists, the losers in the English Civil War, which ended in 1649 with the beheading of King Charles I. But the Royalist navy continued to harass Dutch ships, because the Dutch had sided with Oliver Cromwell's Parliamentarians, the *winners* of the English Civil War. In March 1651, Dutch Admiral Maarten Harpertszoon Tromp sailed into port in Scilly and demanded reparations for the ships seized and the goods taken. When the Royalists refused to pay, he declared war—but only against the Isles of Scilly.

Three months later, the Royalist fleet surrendered to the Parliamentarians, and thus no longer posed a threat to the Dutch shipping. Admiral Tromp sailed home and the war was over...or was it? In 1985 an official with the Scilly Council wrote a letter to the Dutch ambassador asking him to dispel the "myth" that the Netherlands were still at war with the Isles of Scilly. It turned out that it wasn't a myth. The two parties really were still at war, at least technically, because peace had never been declared. So on April 17, 1986, the Dutch ambassador paid a visit to the isles and signed a peace treaty, bringing the war to an end after 335 years...and not a single shot was ever fired.

Andrew Jackson was on the $10 bill before he was on the $20. (Fun fact: He hated paper money.)

UP WITH PEOPLE!

What was the conservative response to the social upheaval of the 1960s and its anti-establishment folk and rock music? A squeaky-clean traveling singing group that made folk and rock songs about being nice and good. Really.

THE TIMES, THEY ARE A-CHANGIN'

By the 1960s, the post–World War II generation of baby boomers were becoming teenagers and young adults, and with their large numbers and growing purchasing power, they came to dominate American culture. All of a sudden, there were new kinds of music (the Beatles and Bob Dylan), new styles of clothing (bell bottoms, tie-dye, and love beads), new kinds of technology (tape decks, color TV, birth control, and space travel), new kinds of everything. But as boomers came of age, many realized that the world they were inheriting wasn't in very good shape. Images of civil rights demonstrations and protests against the Vietnam War were seen every night on the evening news. The rapid cultural changes, social upheaval, and growing radicalism as the decade progressed left a lot of Americans—particularly older Americans—feeling confused, angry, and frightened. They saw nothing wrong with the way things had been: simple, familiar, and safe, with everybody knowing their place. And that left an opening for a counter-counterculture movement.

Enter an ultra-wholesome singing group called Up with People. The 100-person ensemble pushed an agenda of America and the American Way being the very best, and millions were delighted by it—the sea of smiling faces singing syrupy-sweet, gospel-pop songs with titles like "The World Is Your Home Town," "Gee, I'm Looking Forward to the Future," "The Happy Song," and "Freedom Isn't Free."

I AM THE MRA

Up with People was an offshoot of a politically conservative, Christian organization called Moral Re-Armament. Founded in 1938 by a minister named Frank Buchman, the organization sought to stop the spread of Communism in the 1950s by "re-arming" humanity with American-style morals. MRA Centers in Europe and the United States attracted thousands of recruits—almost exclusively young, clean-cut Caucasian people—who adopted Buchman's plan of "absolutes" to achieve inner goodness: absolute honesty, absolute purity, absolute

The 18th-century English penalty for treason: being hanged, then disemboweled and burned alive.

unselfishness, and absolute love for God, country, and fellow man.

Members also had to prove their loyalty to the cause: they lived in MRA-owned housing, had to get permission on who they could marry (other MRA members only) and when they could have children, and even had to report on their sex lives. (Too much husband-wife relations could be seen as a violation of the "absolute purity" tenet.) New members also signed away all of their money and property to the MRA. In other words, it was a cult.

MRA members' main job was to go out and recruit more people to the cause. That consisted primarily of giving formal presentations at universities. Like a religious revival show (but without the infectious music), MRA members would tell stories about how the MRA had changed their lives, and then show a short film about the importance of being "good."

WELCOME TO THE SIXTIES

After Frank Buchman's death in 1961, the organization was led by former journalist Peter Howard, who reworked the MRA's style of recruitment. He held big retreats at the company's estate on Mackinac Island in Michigan. The goal: Get members so pumped up and enthusiastic about spreading goodness that they'd each go out and recruit ten "great friends."

The first Mackinac Island event, held in 1964, was called "Which Way America?" and was attended by more than 2,400 students who wanted "to plan the future for their generation." That meant activities like publishing an MRA magazine called *Tomorrow's American*, listening to an endless array of guest speakers (including a 17-year-old Glenn Close), playing beach volleyball, doing mass calisthenics, and gathering together each night for a mass sing-along with a folk music group called the Colwell Brothers.

FOLK THIS

Folk music was huge in the early 1960s, driven by politically liberal performers like Bob Dylan, Joan Baez, and Peter, Paul and Mary. The MRA answered with the Colwell Brothers. Like Dylan and Baez, they sang songs about the desperate need for immediate change. It's just that their suggestions for change were relentlessly optimistic, and lacked any actual advice for how to improve things beyond "be nice" or "do good." Among the Colwell Brothers' songs that rocked Mackinac Island: "What Color Is God's Skin?" and "You Can't Live Crooked and Think Straight." (Sample lyric: "You can't live crooked and think straight / clean up the nation before it's too late.") But the Colwell Brothers song that brought down the house was the one that the MRA's idealistic young members could relate to the most: "Up with People."

"Down with [fill in the blank]" was a dominant phrase in 1960s culture. Protesters would be seen holding signs with messages like "Down with Racism!" or "Down with War!" The Colwell Brothers flipped the script and wrote a song that was about lifting something "up," and that thing was…people. What kind of people? Just *people*. Sample lyric: "Up, up with people! / They're the best kind of folks we know. If more people were for people / all people everywhere / There'd be a lot less people to worry about / and a lot more people who care."

SOMETHING TO SING ABOUT

After MRA president Peter Howard died in 1965, the organization was taken over by J. Blanton Belk, the son of a minister, who himself was a former navy officer who grew up in the MRA. He injected his personal ideology into the MRA, a political stance that echoed the conservatism of 1964 Republican presidential candidate Barry Goldwater. "The American youth want peace, but not at the price of freedom," Belk said. "It's patriotism, not pacifism that they want."

As the Colwell Brothers toured the world on behalf of the MRA—their concerts had replaced the once-dry MRA presentations—Belk realized that the MRA finally had the vehicle that could be used to drive the organization's energy, passion, and ideology into as many hearts and minds as possible: music. Belk spun off the musical contingent of the MRA as a separate entity and named it after the group's signature song: Up with People.

Up with People's first big show (while still a part of the MRA) was a touring extravaganza called "Sing Out '66." Using the language of the counterculture, it was billed as "a new kind of demonstration," with 30 to 40 singers and musicians on stage, singing in unison. The group recruited members less for talent than for enthusiasm, and they performed in conservative dress: the men were clean-cut and wore tucked-in shirts, and the women wore skirts of a modest length. And everybody was *always* smiling: smiling while they were singing, smiling while they were doing dance moves, smiling when they all got back on the buses that took them to the next town. And for the towns where Up with People didn't go, the organizations offered a "Make Your Own Sing Out" kit, with sheet music and choreography instructions.

UP, UP, AND AWAY

The prime of Up with People coincided with the rise of the counterculture, anti–Vietnam War protests, and the civil rights movement. Up with People called for change, too, but in a way that was much more palatable and much less

Globe skimmer dragonflies have a migration pattern of almost 9,000 miles, twice as long as the Monarch butterfly migration. They fly from India to East Africa.

confrontational. The Up with People package struck a chord with conservative Americans and business leaders, who felt it provided the kind of "old-fashioned values" that the protesters were drowning out.

Unlike in the early days of the MRA, Up with People wasn't funded by its members forking over their savings—performers were volunteers, but their expenses were paid by the organization's wealthy benefactors. Businessman Patrick J. Frawley—who sat on the board of directors for both Schick and Technicolor—bankrolled many of Up with People's earliest projects, including a 1965 *Up with People* album and a prime-time TV special—which got on the air because Frawley bought airtime on TV stations in dozens of cities. That special generated a soundtrack album, and the cover listed endorsements of the group by such all-American icons as John Wayne, Pat Boone, and Walt Disney. (Disney called Up with People "the happiest, most hard-hitting way of saying what America's all about that I have ever seen or heard.")

PRIME TIME

Up with People really got around, playing in venues all over the world. But offstage, members of the group were encouraged to lead lives every bit as squeaky-clean as the image they presented to the public—drinking, drugs, sex, and smoking were all forbidden. Between tours, members lived in company-owned dormitories. While on the road, they stayed with host families…whom performers were encouraged to either recruit or solicit donations from.

Among the places where the toothsome group sang songs of positivity and wholesomeness:
• The Hollywood Bowl
• The Air Force Academy
• The World's Fair
• At the Vatican for Pope Paul VI
• On a float in Richard Nixon's 1969 inaugural parade
• At an event honoring former president Dwight D. Eisenhower
• For Spanish dictator Francisco Franco
• In Moscow's Red Square
• In front of the Berlin Wall (they sang "Freedom Isn't Free")

Up with People's most famous performances, however, were at the Super Bowl. Up with People played at four Super Bowls, the first halftime act that wasn't a college marching band. NFL commissioner Peter Rozelle pursued Up with People both for their morality and for business—he wanted to associate their all-American image with the NFL, but also to attract viewers who normally didn't watch Super Bowl broadcasts, particularly women and the elderly.

CORPORATE ROCK

Throughout the 1960s, '70s, and early '80s, Up with People never had a hit single and never scored a platinum album, but they were one of the most financially lucrative bands in the world. The reason: corporate sponsorship. Belk spent most of his time glad-handling corporate executives and soliciting donations. Major companies gave millions to Up with People, and Up with People reciprocated by furthering the company's interests.

For example, McDonald's sponsored Up with People's trip to Moscow. More than 100 friendly faces singing about friendship was a great way to ease anti-American feelings in the Soviet Union. It was also a strategic move to lay the groundwork for the fast-food giant's entry into the Russian marketplace. The energy company Halliburton paid for Up with People's trip to the Soviet republic of Georgia…shortly before it started drilling for oil there. General Motors was a big sponsor, and the theme of Up with People's 1982 Super Bowl halftime show was a tribute to the game's host city of Detroit—where GM employed thousands. Other corporate sponsors that gave millions to Up with People over the years: Coca-Cola, Pfizer, Eli Lily, General Electric, Texaco, Exxon, Enron, Coors, and Sears.

DOWN WITH UP

As the tumultuousness of the '60s and '70s calmed down, Up with People grew increasingly irrelevant, a square relic from another time. There wasn't much of a need for its "message" by the mid-1980s. Ronald Reagan was elected president of the United States in two landslides; his campaign slogan of "Morning in America" was pretty on-track with the kind of sentiments expressed by Up with People. In other words, Up with People eventually won the culture wars.

But Up with People was a business, and it needed to keep going. As its performances became less high-profile—the Super Bowls and concerts at international landmarks gave way to shows in retirement homes, high schools, and prisons—more Up with People merchandise was created, such as coffee mugs, luggage, watches, even a recipe collection. None of that turned the company around, and so Up with People, which never paid its performers, started charging "tuition" fees. By 1986, it cost $6,000 to perform as part of Up with People. The group limped along for a few more years, but the show was over in 2000.

…never heard of Columbus. They believed—wrongly—that Vespucci had "discovered" the New World.

BORN AGAIN

But then, just five years later, Up with People returned to spread its feel-good message. With donations from more than 20,000 "alumni" (ex-performers), the organization reopened under new CEO Tommy Spaulding. They still sing songs and travel around the world, but that's just a part of what they do. Up with People now markets itself as a leadership, training, and civic organization. It even funnels ticket revenues back into local nonprofits in the cities where the troupe performs. As Spaulding told the *Denver Post* in 2007, the group is "a global leadership program" that's "more like the Peace Corps now."

It's still a part of pop culture, too. On a 1993 episode of *The Simpsons*, an ad plays for a local amusement park, where a gigantic, overly positive singing troupe called "Hooray for Everything" is said to perform their show, "A Tribute to the Western Hemisphere." On another episode, Hooray for Everything plays the halftime show of a Thanksgiving Day pro football game. And on a 1999 episode of *South Park*, the main characters join an international children's glee club called "Getting Gay with Kids." Both are clearly send-ups of Up with People.

*   *   *

THE ORIGIN OF SIRI

Dag Kittlaus grew up in Michigan but attended business school in Norway, and then moved there, landing a job with a cell phone company. After a few years, he moved back to the United States and got a job with Motorola in Chicago. Five years later, in 2007, he got bored with that job and left to start a new company, a spinoff of an artificial intelligence unit of DARPA, the U.S. Department of Defense's robotics division. Funded by the Stanford Research Institute, Kittlaus named the company Siri, which is Norwegian for "beautiful woman who leads you to victory." (He'd planned to name his daughter Siri—but his wife gave birth to a son.) With Siri, Kittlaus explored ways that artificial intelligence could be used practically in a peacetime society. By 2010, he and his team had developed the first-ever "digital assistant" that could understand human speech and respond back. Then they hooked it up to the Internet. The software, also called Siri, could 1) understand a request for information, 2) research the answer online, and 3) report back in a pleasing, human voice. Siri was quietly released as an iPhone app in 2010—and before long, Apple bought Siri, Inc. and made the Siri technology a standard feature on iPhones, iPads, and, later, laptops. (Who's the voice of Siri? An actress named Susan Bennet. In 2005 she spent four hours a day for a month recording various words and phrases that the Siri program would use to form sentences.)

Despicable Me Minions were inspired by a Looney Tunes cartoon in which Tweety Bird drinks potion and turns into a monster.

KNOW YOUR EYE DISEASES

Ol' Uncle John's eyesight ain't what it used to be. One day when he bumped into a doorjamb (for the third time), he bellowed: "Someone write an article on what's going wrong with my eyes!" He commands; we follow. Here it is.

EYE BASICS

Before we get to diseases, we should have a basic understanding of how the eye works. For starters, *seeing* something means you're actually seeing the light reflected off of that thing. Here's a (very) basic description of the amazing process by which that light is made into meaningful images:

• Light enters your eye through the *cornea*—the dome-shaped, transparent "front window" of the eye that covers the *iris* (the colored ring around the pupil) and the *pupil*. The cornea's job is to protect the iris and pupil, and to refract—or bend—light as it passes through it, so that it is directed toward the pupil. That's the first step in providing clear, focused vision. The iris's job is to control how much light enters the eye by making the pupil constrict (grow smaller) when there's a lot of light, or dilate (grow larger) when there's not much light.

• After passing through the pupil, the light travels through the *lens*, a clear, flexible structure that can change its shape in order to further refract the incoming light, so that the image it's carrying is properly focused on the *retina*, the thin layer of tissue lining the inside of the rear of the eye. (This process is very similar to focusing a projector so that the image on a screen is clear, or focusing a camera so that the image on film is clear.) The retina is packed with millions of photoreceptors (called *rods* and *cones*) that "read" the incoming light.

• Attached to the retina is the *optic nerve* (one for each eye) that carries the millions of signals from the retina's photoreceptors to the brain, where they are translated into all the things we "see" around us.

Now—bring on the diseases!

GLAUCOMA

Glaucoma is probably the best-known group of eye diseases, yet most people have no idea what it is, or that it's actually the name used for a number of disorders with one common characteristic: they all involve degeneration of either one or both optic nerves. The most common cause of that degeneration is the buildup of fluid pressure inside the eye. The small chambers in the front of the eye—inside the cornea and around the iris and lens—are filled with a thin, watery fluid called *aqueous humor*, which is regularly replaced via a production and drainage system that keeps the pressure inside those chambers stable. (Gross fact: the fluid is slowly and constantly draining out of your pupils, then out of your corneas, and then into specialized passageways that carry it to your bloodstream.) But that drainage system can become blocked or clogged due to normal aging, injury, illness, and other causes, resulting in the buildup of too much aqueous humor inside the eye or eyes (picture adding more and more water to a water balloon), which does physical damage to the delicate fibers of the optic nerve in the rear of the eye. This leads to vision loss, starting with the loss of peripheral vision and, without treatment, can lead to complete blindness. Mild glaucoma is commonly treated with medication; more severe cases are treated with laser surgery to clear clogged drainage passages. Experts estimate that more than three million Americans have glaucoma—but only half of them know it. Glaucoma is the second leading cause of blindness in the world.

FLOATERS

That's the name for the tiny specks, clumps, squiggly lines, and other shapes you sometimes see "floating" in your vision. They are not, in and of themselves, a disease. But they are an interesting phenomenon that most of us have experienced, and they can be a sign of serious eye disorders. What are floaters? They're bits of debris suspended in the *vitreous humor*, the thick, transparent, gelatin-like fluid that fills the large rear chamber of the eye. Some of that debris has been with you since you were in the womb, simply as leftover cells that became trapped in the vitreous gel while your eyes were developing. But most floaters develop over the years as a normal part of the aging process. As we age, the globe-shaped blob of vitreous humor in your eye actually shrinks and pulls away from the retina at the back of the eye. This causes the release of more cellular debris, which eventually gets caught in the vitreous humor. However they're produced, when such bits of debris are positioned between the lenses and retinas in our eyes, we "see" them as floaters. (Which means when we see floaters, we're actually seeing inside our own eyeballs!) This is all perfectly natural and usually harmless—mostly. Floaters can sometimes be the sign of a more serious condition, such as…

DETACHED RETINA

Sometimes when the vitreous humor shrinks and pulls away from the retina at the back of the eye, it actually pulls part of the retina with it, detaching it from

Every year, 45 million tons of electronic waste is thrown out illegally. Cost to the U.S.: $12 billion.

the layer of tissue directly behind it, called the *choroid layer*. This is dangerous, because a network of tiny blood vessels in the choroid layer provides the retina with the nutrients it needs to function, and the loss of that supply can cause the retina to cease functioning properly, which in turn can lead to visual impairment. Another cause of retinal detachment: tiny tears in the retina, caused by physical injury or inflammation from illness, that allow vitreous fluid to leak behind the retina, gradually building up and pushing the retina away from the choroid layer. The symptoms of a detached retina include a sudden increase in floaters, bright flashes of light in one or both eyes, and areas of shaded or darkened vision. (Note: A detached retina is considered a medical emergency. Anyone experiencing such symptoms should seek medical help immediately.)

ASTIGMATISM

You know how looking through the wavy, irregular glass of an antique window can makes things look blurred and distorted? That's similar to what happens with the eye condition known as *astigmatism*. The wavy glass "window" in this case is the cornea—the transparent, dome-shaped front of the eye. The cornea should have a smooth, consistent dome shape, with equal degrees of curvature over its entire surface. This means that incoming light can be refracted and sent through the pupil to the lens in a consistent fashion, which is essential in assuring that a single, clear, focused image is sent to the retina. With an astigmatism, the cornea doesn't have that consistent dome shape: one side may be flatter than the other; it may be oval, rather than round; or the cornea may have bumps and waves on its surface. This results in inconsistently refracted light being sent to the lens, which may result in two or more images being projected to various spots inside the rear of the eye, rather than one clear image on the retina itself. Result: blurred, distorted, or multiple-image vision. Most people with astigmatism are simply born with misshapen corneas, but the condition can be caused by injury and illness as well.

CATARACTS

This eye disorder gets its name from the Latin *cataracta*, meaning "waterfall," a reference to the cloudy whiteness in the pupil that characterizes this disease, which resembles a foamy, white waterfall. The condition affects just one part of the eye—the lens. The lens is a unique part of the anatomy: if you could hold one in your hand, you'd see something about the size and shape of an M&M candy, only with a gelatin-like consistency and completely transparent. Lenses are primarily made up of water and proteins called *crystallines*, whose unusual

Lentigines are the freckles caused by sun damage; ephelides are the freckles you're born with.

characteristics—especially the way they structure themselves inside the lens—give lenses their transparency. But unlike almost all the other proteins in the human body, lens cyrstallines are not regenerated: the ones you got while you were still developing in your mother's womb are the ones you have for the rest of your life. And the normal aging process causes those proteins to degrade, and lose their ability to maintain their structure. At this point they start to clump together, thereby causing the cloudiness that characterizes this disease. That can affect vision in various ways, including blurred vision and sensitivity to bright lights (from car headlights at night, for example), and untreated, it can lead to complete blindness. The primary cause of cataracts is aging, but there are other causes, including diabetes, high blood pressure, smoking, and injury. The most common treatment is surgery to remove the cloudy lens and replace it with an artificial lens.

BY AGE 80, *more than half of all Americans have cataracts. Cataracts are slightly more common in women than in men.*

MYOPIA

Myopia is the scientific name for nearsightedness. People with this condition have good close-up vision—but bad distance vision. The exact cause of the disorder is unknown, but most people with myopia have one thing in common: their eyeballs are too long. To understand how this affects vision—and why it affects distance vision—we need a two-part answer.

1. Picture this: you have a slide projector and a screen. You insert a slide and focus the lens until you have a perfectly focused image on the screen. Now, move the screen back a few feet. What happens to the image on the screen? It goes out of focus and becomes blurry—because the projector is now focused on a spot in front of the screen. This is what happens to people with myopia: their eyeballs are not as globe-shaped as they should be. Instead, they're elongated. The retinas in the rear of their eyeballs are farther away from the lenses than they should be—so their cornea-and-lens focusing system focuses on a spot in front of the retina, resulting in blurred vision.

2. Why does this condition result in blurred *distance* vision, but not blurred *close-up* vision? It's because of how our lenses work. When we look at things far away, our flexible lenses bring those things into focus by becoming longer and thinner. In people with myopia, this draws the lens even farther away from the retina, which is already too far away from the lens. Result: a blurry image. When we look at things close up, our lenses bring them into focus by becoming shorter and wider, which decreases the distance between the lens and the retina. In people with myopia, this makes up for the far-away retina, allowing them to see close-up things clearly.

More than a fifth of the world's population is affected by mild myopia. It is easily treatable with eyeglasses or contact lenses. But severe myopia can lead to severe vision loss and other serious conditions, such as glaucoma and detached retinas.

EXTRAS

- We told you that myopia, or nearsightedness, is caused by the lens focusing on a spot *in front* of the retina, rather than on the retina itself. *Hyperopia*, or farsightedness, is just the opposite: it's caused by the lens focusing on a virtual spot *behind* the retina. It is usually caused by having an abnormally flat cornea, or by having abnormally short eyeballs.

- *Polycoria* is an extremely rare genetic eye disorder—and it sounds like something out of a horror story. It's when someone has more than one pupil in one or both of their irises. (And each of the pupils are attached to corresponding muscles in the iris, that cause them to constrict and dilate, just like normal pupils.)

- People with *aniridia* appear to have no irises—just very large black pupils. They actually do have irises, but they're usually thin and malformed, and very hard to detect. The condition is most commonly caused by a gene defect (although injury to the eye can cause it, too). Aniridia typically affects vision adversely, but some people with the condition have no vision impairment whatsoever.

- *Pterygium* (pronounced "tur-IJ-ee-um") is an eye disorder characterized by the growth of pinkish-white, fleshy tissue on the sclera—the white of the eye— normally starting on the side closest to the nose. Left untreated, it can extend until it covers part or even all of the cornea, and the iris and pupil behind it, thereby affecting vision. Pterygium can be caused by overexposure to dust, or excessively dry eyes, but it is primarily by prolonged exposure to ultraviolet light in sunlight—which is why it is also known as "surfer's eye."

- *Retinopathy of prematurity* is a condition that affects some premature babies. One famous person affected by this disease: Stevie Wonder. (See page 372 for more.)

*   *   *

"Procrastinate now, don't put it off." —**Ellen DeGeneres**

Troll dolls were invented in 1959 as a gift for the inventor's daughter.
They were originally made of wood, with glass eyes and wool hair.

MORE TV WISDUMB

Another batch of clueless sitcom characters talking about…
well, we're not exactly sure what they're talking about.

"I've got an idea—an idea so smart that my head would explode if I even began to know what I'm talking about."

—Peter, *Family Guy*

Skipper: "Well, Gilligan—this is where we're going to spend the rest of our lives."
Gilligan: "Well, maybe we won't live that long."

—*Gilligan's Island*

"MARGE, EVERY TIME I LEARN SOMETHING NEW IT PUSHES SOMETHING OLD OUT OF MY BRAIN. REMEMBER THAT TIME I LEARNED HOW TO MAKE WINE AND FORGOT HOW TO DRIVE?"

—Homer, *The Simpsons*

"Just remember, every time you look up at the moon, I, too, will be looking at the moon. Not the same moon, obviously. That's impossible."

—Andy, *Parks and Recreation*

Chrissy: "Just do what I do."
Jack: "And what will you be doing?"
Chrissy: "Duh! The same thing you're doing, only first."

—*Three's Company*

ROSE: "Can I ask a dumb question?"
DOROTHY: "Like no one else."

—*The Golden Girls*

"So, that island you own, is it near the beach?"

—Kelly, *Married with Children*

Fry: "Wait, I'm having one of those things. You know, a headache with pictures."
Lela: "An idea?"

—*Futurama*

LIFE BEFORE GPS

What did we do before we had modern conveniences? We tried to figure out better ways to do things, of course. Otherwise we'd never have modern conveniences. The road to success is littered with ideas that didn't quite work out...like these pre-GPS inventions.

THE ITER AVTO (1930)

What It Was: A scrolling map system for your car.

How It Worked: Made in Italy, the Iter Avto consisted of a metal box with a display window that was mounted on the dashboard of a car, plus a collection of road maps printed on long, narrow scrolls. To operate the device, a motorist loaded a map onto rollers inside the box, then adjusted the rollers until the current location was visible in the display window. The Iter Avto was connected by cable to the car's speedometer, so that when the motorist started driving, the rollers unscrolled the map in proportion to how fast the car was moving, and their current location remained visible in the viewing window as the map unscrolled.

Because the maps scrolled vertically, from the top of the viewing window to the bottom, the maps were really only useful on straight roads. A new map had to be loaded into the box every time the motorist turned onto a new route. This made the device useful for telling the motorist where he or she was at a given moment, but not very useful for helping them navigate a complicated route to an unfamiliar destination. The Iter Avto does not appear to have sold very well, and very few examples survive today.

THE PLUS FOUR WRISTLET ROUTE INDICATOR (1927)

What It Was: A miniaturized map system, similar to the Iter Avto, that was worn on the wrist.

How It Worked: The Plus Four Wristlet was a British device that looked just like a wristwatch, except that the watch face was a viewing window for tiny scrolls of road maps. As the motorist drove, they unrolled the map manually by twisting the tiny rollers, sort of like winding a watch. It wasn't a very useful system, because if a motorist didn't already know where they were, it was hard for them to unroll the map to the proper spot. And if they did know where they were, they didn't need the map. Like the Iter Avto, Plus Four Wristlets did not sell well, but they and their tiny boxes of map scrolls are very collectible today.

DAIR: DRIVER AID, INFORMATION & ROUTING (1966)

What It Was: An early attempt by GM to create a navigation system based on punch cards.

How It Worked: If you're closer to the age of 60 than you are to 20, you may remember that before computer files were stored on thumb drives or the cloud, they were stored on floppy disks, and before that, on cassette tapes. Before cassette tapes, data was stored on *punch cards*—literally, paper cards with holes punched into them.

GM envisioned a world where motorists on road trips would stop at places called "routing stations" to buy the particular set of punch cards that would take them to their destination. One by one, the driver would feed the cards into a card reader installed in the car's center console. Holes punched in the cards would correspond to magnets buried in the roadway, and as the car passed over the magnets, the system would determine the car's location and signal to the driver, by way of flashing arrows in a display on the dashboard, whether to go left, right, or straight. Bonus: the DAIR system came with a "message encoder" similar to a rotary-dial telephone, which let stranded motorists request assistance over CB radio by dialing "1" for the police, "2" for an ambulance, "3" for a fire truck, or "4" for a tow truck. These messages were encrypted to prevent criminals from intercepting them and preying on motorists whose cars had broken down.

That GM figured out a way to provide ONSTAR service in a punch-card age was an impressive accomplishment. But GM never figured out how to get the federal government to pick up the tab for installing tens of millions of magnets in every major road in America. Only two cars and a few miles of GM test track were outfitted with the system before GM scrapped the project and moved on to other things.

THE HONDA GYROCATOR (1981)

What It Was: Honda's first attempt at an in-car navigation system.

How It Worked: The Gyrocator came with a binder of street maps printed on translucent plastic. Before a motorist left on a trip, they took out the map corresponding to their location, marked their starting point and destination on the map with an erasable ink pen, then inserted the map into the Gyrocator so that it overlaid the device's six-inch display screen. When the Gyrocator was turned on, a glowing white dot representing the car appeared on the screen. The motorist set the car's present location by moving the transparent map manually until the car's location lined up with the glowing dot on the screen. When driving, a servo gear attached to the transmission monitored the car's speed while a gyroscopic sensor kept track of every turn and moved the dot around the map accordingly.

Like some other early navigation systems, the Gyrocator was good at telling you where you were, but not very good at telling you how to get where you wanted to go. But its biggest flaw, at least as far as consumers were concerned, was its price: ¥300,000 ($2,700), nearly a quarter the price of a 1981 Honda Accord. The Gyrocator was sold only for a year before the little glowing dot went dark for good.

THE ETAK NAVIGATOR (1985)

What It Was: The first commercially available in-car navigation system that used digital maps drawn on a video display.

How It Worked: The experience of using an Etak Navigator wasn't all that different from using GPS today. When the motorist turned it on, an icon representing their car appeared in the center of the screen on a street map drawn by computer. When the car started traveling, the icon remained stationary in the center of the screen while the digital map moved and turned around it. It was the first auto navigation system that presented information this way. But the Navigator didn't keep track of its position using orbiting satellites. Instead, an electronic compass monitored turns; sensors mounted on the car's front wheels updated the car's speed, heading, and distance traveled. If the system's estimate of the car's location became inaccurate over time, the motorist could reposition the car's icon manually using controls on the side of the display.

The digital maps were stored on cassette tapes, which didn't hold a lot of information: the map of the San Francisco Bay Area, Etak's first (the company was a Silicon Valley startup), took up six cassette tapes that cost $35 each. The price of the Navigator itself was $1,395, the equivalent of more than $3,000 today. At that price, they were slow sellers. By the late 1980s, Etak had decided that compiling digital map data was a more lucrative business than building the Navigators, so it stopped making the machines and set to work making digital maps of the entire world. The company changed hands several times over the years and in 2008 was acquired by TomTom, which still uses its digital mapping technology in GPS devices today.

*   *   *

Random fact: The Finnish word *kalsarikännit* means "to get drunk at home alone in your underwear."

Stiff upper lip? Your nose contains erectile tissue in the mucous membranes.

UH-OH, WE LIVE ON TOP OF...

Some people find out the hard way that their dream home is actually a nightmare.

...AN EARTHQUAKE FAULT

Many people believe that all of the earth's destructive faults have been mapped. Not so. Most of what scientists call "blind" faults don't show up on the earth's surface. They can only be found through geophysical surveys (analysis of magnetic and gravitational fields), by accident when drilling for oil...or the hard way. That's what happened to Tim and Ann Whitlock of Browns Valley, California. Like at least 20 other residents of their neighborhood, the Whitlocks had no idea they lived on top of an earthquake fault. Evidence of this one had been long buried beneath layers of soil washed down from nearby mountains. But they found out at 3:20 a.m. on August 24, 2014, when the fault moved directly beneath their house. The foundation split with an explosive boom. The west side of the house moved nine inches north. The east side pushed half an inch higher. Though he's a U.S. Air Force veteran, Whitlock said he and his wife "just grabbed each other and screamed." The fault might have been dormant for 1.6 million years, but that didn't stop it from ripping a nine-mile-long scar through vineyards, roads, homes, and sidewalks. Final toll: one dead (a woman bludgeoned by her TV set) and an estimated $1 billion in damage.

...THE TOWN DUMP

In 2001, Warren Salter bought a small house with a big, wide grassy yard in Havelock, North Carolina. Now his yard is disappearing. "What used to be flat land for the kids to play football in is now big sunken areas," Salter told ABC News. That's not all. Every time Salter digs into the soil, he finds "buried treasure"—hundreds of baby bottles, spark plugs, asbestos chunks, and vintage steel beer cans. And Salter's heard that there's a school bus buried somewhere beneath the green loam in his neighbor's yard. The home was built in 1972. When Salter bought it, he had no idea that the subdivision was built on the site of an 1940s dump. Now he'd like to see the town step in and clean it up. But Havelock's attorney claims the subdivision predates the city, so the town bears no responsibility. For now, the homeowners are on their own.

Computers can beat humans at chess, but not crossword puzzles. The closest (so far)...

…A CEMETERY

After living in her four-bedroom 19th-century home in Hertfordshire, England, for 11 years, Catherine McGuigan decided to invest in a basement expansion to build a home theater and gym. In 2008, a team of builders went to work, digging beneath the dining room. All seemed to be going well until McGuigan came home to find the workmen ghost-white. One of them had pulled what he thought was a pipe from the ground. But it wasn't a pipe. It was a bone. Peering deeper into the hole, the worker spotted a skull and then the rest of the skeleton. Did the McGuigan cottage conceal a horrific crime? Police were called. Forensic tests were done…and the bones were found to be over 100 years old. Maps from the 1700s showed that the home had been built on the former site of a Quaker meetinghouse. At the time, Quakers weren't allowed to bury their dead in consecrated ground. So they used the garden as a cemetery. By the time the workmen finished digging, they had removed 29 skeletons from beneath McGuigan's cottage.

…A TOXIC WASTE SITE

The median price of a home in the United States is about $225,000. In Anniston, Alabama, you can buy one for as little as $7,900. Why so cheap? Three letters: PCB, short for polychlorinated byphenyls—one of the 20th century's most profitable chemicals…and produced in Anniston. For a period of about 40 years—from 1929 to 1971—the chemical was used in all kinds of building materials, from paint to caulking to electrical equipment, as well as in everyday items such as newsprint. It was "Made by Monsanto."

Now we know: PCBs are toxic. They've been banned in the United States since 1979. But testimony in a 2002 Senate hearing revealed that Monsanto knew they were peddling a killer chemical since at least 1966. That's the year the company hired Mississippi State University biologist Denzel Ferguson to test the water in Snow Creek. The creek ran behind the plant, and Monsanto had been dumping raw PCBs directly into it. Ferguson's findings: Fish dunked in the creek went "belly up in 10 seconds, shedding skin as if dumped in boiling water." Fish weren't the only victims. It's now known that PCB exposure causes liver

THE DEADLIEST NATURAL DISASTER ON RECORD: *The widespread Yellow River floods that ravaged China in 1931. After two years of drought, heavy rains and snowstorms hit the county in 1930 and 1931, significantly raising the river's water levels. Authorities and historians estimate the death toll was as high as 4 million.*

…is Dr. Fill, which took 11th place at the 2017 American Crossword Puzzle Competition.

problems, skin rashes, cancer, reproductive damage, and learning disabilities in humans. In fact, it increases the risk of almost all major diseases.

Snow Creek wasn't the plant's only disposal system. Monsanto buried 5,000 tons of hazardous waste in two large landfills next to the plant. Jeremiah Smith once grazed 50 hogs on those hillsides. They were looking a bit "green around the mouth" by 1970 when a Monsanto man showed up and offered to buy them for $10 a hog (plus a bottle of Log Cabin Whiskey). Smith sold.

Today, parents in Anniston really do tell their kids to "go play in the street." Reason: the street is safer than the yard. The grass is still so contaminated that residents have to wear masks when they mow their lawns. "Where else in the United States of America are people doing that?" asked one resident.

...BROKEN PIPES

The Lakeside Heights subdivision consisted of 29 large Tudor-style homes on a hillside overlooking Clear Lake, in northern California. When Randall Fitzgerald bought his dream house there in 2012, he had no idea that a year later he'd be calling it "Landslide Heights." In 2013, the houses started to crack, slide, and then drop—by as much as 12 feet. Since then, half of the homes have either collapsed or been condemned. The other half are still occupied, either by owners who can't sell or renters desperate to save money. When the homes started sliding, no one knew the reason. For a while, some residents speculated that a nearby dormant volcano might be to blame. After all, a volcanic collapse had created the hills around the shores of Clear Lake. But that was ruled out. Experts determined that what caused the hill to slide was too much water in the ground. Residents claim that broken Lake County–owned water and sewer pipes are sinking their homes, and they're suing. The county is counter-suing, arguing that residents watered their lawns and washed their cars too much. As homes continue to crumble, the road to Lakeside Heights is blocked to all but residential traffic. "No trespassing" signs dot cracked house fronts and jumbled fences. It's a "slow-motion disaster area," say residents. As for home values— they're "in the toilet."

...AN ABANDONED MINE

In November 2016, Tracey Quick and her husband heard weird noises coming from the backyard. Then the house started creaking and cracking. "It was horrible," Tracey said. She rushed upstairs and hurried her four children outside. Meanwhile, her husband went into the backyard to investigate. Minutes after he ran back inside, the ground gave way, leaving a gaping hole 40 feet wide

Medieval punishment for women: Cutting off their hair in public. (Usually for sexual misconduct.)

and at least 30 feet deep just beyond the back wall of the house. The problem: The Quick family lives in Pennsylvania coal country. Turns out the home they built 13 years earlier is one of more than a million buildings in the state that were built over abandoned mines—many without the owners' knowledge. As mines deteriorate and collapse, anything built on top can subside, or sink. Foundations and walls crack. Sometimes entire homes collapse into sinkholes. The Quicks were luckier than some. Their home was stabilized with two new support beams, and the hole was filled with concrete and covered with dirt. Cost: around $75,000...and their homeowner's insurance won't cover it. Although the state offers mine-subsidence insurance for about $114 a year, the Quicks never thought they'd need it. They—and pretty much everyone else in their neighborhood—have now signed up for the low-cost policies.

...A LAVA FIELD

Colombia's Nevada del Ruiz forms the northern tip of the Andes mountain range. The snowy peak towers at 17,680 feet. Rice and coffee fields thrive in the incredibly fertile area beneath the mountain's shadow. There's just one problem: it's a volcano—dormant, but not dead. The residents of the nearby village of Armero knew about their volcanic neighbor. But the soil was rich and the views spectacular. Besides, the village was 45 miles from the mountain. So in 1984, when the volcano started to rumble, no one worried. They should have.

The rich soil that nourished their crops and the land on which their homes stood started as a *lahar*—a giant mudflow of volcanic debris filled with ice, volcanic ash, and rock fragments. The last time Nevada del Ruiz had erupted, about 140 years earlier, it had entombed Armero—and all of its inhabitants— beneath 26 feet of volcanic mud. Still, on November 13, 1985, when the ground started shaking and the volcano blasted ash into the sky, the local radio announcer said, "Don't panic. Stay in your houses." So people went about their business...until it was too late.

At 9:30 p.m., the mountain went ballistic. Massive amounts of super-hot mud filled with slabs of ice and bus-size rocks careened down the mountain at 30 miles per hour. The mudflow swept up everything in its path—homes, cars, animals...and 22,000 people. By the time it was over, two-thirds of Armero's population was buried beneath 15 feet of mud and ash.

Are residents of first-world nations too savvy to build on land that is essentially a disaster waiting to happen? Ask the 3,600 residents of Orting, Washington. They're among the 100,000 people living on top of lahars in the area between Seattle and Tacoma. John Anderson, a sawmill worker, enjoys the view from his Orting home. It's breathtaking: Mount Rainier rises 14,410 feet into the sky about 27 miles away. "When we get a full moon and it comes up over the mountain, it's really something," says Anderson. Maybe, but lahars roar off the sides of Rainier and make it all the way to the Puget Sound every 500 years or so, and scientists predict that Anderson and his neighbors have a one in seven chance of being buried under 40 feet of mud within their lifetimes.

...A SUPERVOLCANO

Until 10 years ago, people living in the Campi Flegrei region just west of Naples, Italy, often wondered about the volcano on the other side of the city—Mount Vesuvius. What they knew was that in A.D. 79, Vesuvius completely obliterated the city of Pompeii, flash-heating human bodies to temperatures of 570°F, killing them within a fraction of a second, and then covering the city in ash. What they didn't know: compared to Campi Flegrei, volcanologists say Vesuvius is just "a pimple on the back of the sleeping dragon." The sleeping dragon is a supervolcano. Campi Flegrei (it means "burning fields" in Italian) is the visible result of its last eruption about 40,000 years ago. It's a caldera—a bowl created by the collapse of a structure during a massive volcanic eruption. The bowl holds water: it's the Bay of Puzzuoli. The rim of the bowl is home to picturesque towns in which 500,000 people go about their lives, mostly oblivious to the fact that the supervolcano's last eruption probably finished off our nearest human relative, the Neanderthal. And in nearby Naples, a million more people are in disaster's way. Currently, volcanologists are monitoring the caldera closely. Pressure has been steadily building beneath the surface. Parts of the caldera bubble and smoke; hot springs, pools of boiling mud, and spouting geysers show how active it still is. An indoor swimming pool inside an abandoned building is now home to what locals call "the monster." Sulfurous steam pours through holes and cracks in its foundation. It's depositing a sulfur-yellow coral covered with luminous green urchins, and is eating the building, stone by stone. Sparrows that fly inside drop dead from CO_2 poisoning. Those who study the supervolcano are concerned, to say the least. Scientists from the Italian National Institute of Geophysics in Rome recently delivered a warning: "We propose that magma could be approaching the critical degassing pressure." Translation: the supervolcano could soon be poised to swallow the entire region.

*   *   *

"You must pay for your sins. If you have already paid, please ignore this notice."

—Sam Levenson

Since 1308, all English monarchs but one (Mary II) have been crowned sitting on the same chair.

THE CONCORDE

Are you old enough to remember the fanfare and excitement around the world's first commercial supersonic passenger jet—the Concorde? The futuristic-looking plane could ferry 120-plus people from New York City to Paris in just 3.5 hours. And if you remember the plane, you also probably remember its crash—literally and figuratively. Here's the story of the plane that almost changed the airline industry.

WELCOME TO THE JET AGE

On May 2, 1952, a BOAC (British Overseas Airways Corporation, the UK's government-owned airline, and precursor to British Airways) airplane carrying 36 passengers took off from Heathrow Airport in London bound for Johannesburg, South Africa, and made aviation—and *world*—history. It was the world's first commercial passenger jet flight. The plane traveled at about 480 mph, more than twice the speed of conventional airliners; it offered a smoother, quieter ride; a ticket cost about the same as a conventional plane ticket—and passengers loved it. The jet age had officially begun.

The jet, the DH 106 Comet, was designed and built by British airplane manufacturer De Havilland. This was a major coup for the British. Aircraft manufacturing had been a source of national pride (and competition) almost since the dawn of the age of flight. Now, with orders for Comets pouring in from airlines around the world, it looked as if the British would dominate the coming jet age. But just two years later, everything had changed: by 1954, four Comet jetliners had crashed, killing a total of 110 people. The DH Comet was grounded, and would not fly commercially for another four years. During that time, France and the Soviet Union both introduced successful passenger jets, and the American company Boeing was close to releasing yet another.

The British needed to come up with a new idea—so they did.

SUPER-SPEED ME

In October 1956, officials from the Royal Aircraft Establishment, the agency that oversaw research and development of new aircraft for the British government, made a bold decision. The grounding of the DH Comet had so damaged the UK aircraft industry that they had no chance of catching up to other countries in the conventional jetliner market. So it was time to beat them at a new game: the *supersonic* passenger plane market. Supersonic means faster than the speed of sound, or faster than 768 mph. (This is also referred to as *Mach 1*. Twice the speed of sound—1,536 mph—is *Mach 2*, and so on.) This was a very tall order: the top speed for jetliners of that era was about 530 mph, and developing large passenger planes that could fly at those speeds had taken decades—and it had cost a lot of money.

So in November 1956, the British government formed an official committee, the Supersonic Transport Aircraft Committee (STAC), whose sole purpose was to research the technological and economic feasibility of producing successful commercial supersonic jetliners. While a long way from becoming a reality, the Concorde had now been conceived.

THE SOUND OF SCIENCE

So why is it so hard to design a plane that can break the speed of sound? To answer that question, let's look at some basic airplane science.

• As an airplane's engines propel it forward, resistance to the atmosphere causes two main aerodynamic forces to be exerted on the plane: *lift*, which exerts an upward force on the plane, allowing it to stay in the air (lift is caused by an airplane's wings, which are specifically designed to create this force); and *drag*, which exerts force against the forward motion of the plane (drag is caused by the natural resistance of a body moving through the atmosphere—you can feel it when you stick your hand out of the window of a moving car).

• All airplane manufacturers want an efficient lift/drag ratio. If a plane has too much drag compared to lift, either it won't fly, or it will need so much engine power (and fuel) to stay airborne that it will be too expensive to operate.

• The faster a plane flies, the more drag it experiences. But there's more to it than that: as an airplane travels through the atmosphere, it is constantly creating pressure waves in the atmosphere. (Picture the waves that result from pushing a toy boat across the surface of a bathtub.) These waves travel through the atmosphere at the speed of sound. When a plane is traveling *well below* the speed of sound, the pressure waves that are created in front of the aircraft are moving faster than the airplane and remain ahead of it. But as a plane approaches the speed of sound these pressure waves "pile up" in front of the aircraft, dramatically increasing the resistance of the atmosphere. This phenomenon is known as *wave drag*.

FIRST BREAKTHROUGH

The amount of resistance caused by wave drag—especially as an aircraft gets close to the speed of sound—is so great that many early aviation scientists believed it could never be broken. That's why the term "sound barrier" was coined—they really thought it was a barrier that could never be breached by a manned aircraft. They were, of course, wrong.

On October 14, 1947, U.S. Air Force captain Chuck Yeager became the first pilot to break the sound barrier, in an experimental plane, the Bell X-1. In the years that followed, more supersonic aircraft were built by countries around the world. But none of them were passenger planes: the Bell X-1 was a 31-foot-long, bullet-shaped, stub-winged, rocket-powered plane that could hold exactly one person—the pilot. And the jet-propelled sound-breakers that followed were all highly specialized military aircraft, and all of them could sustain supersonic speeds only for short bursts. Getting a passenger jetliner to overcome all the obstacles involved in breaking the sound barrier was going to be an entirely different game.

Life in the Fast Lane: The speed Yeager achieved in the Bell X-1 was 670 mph. If the speed of sound is 768 mph, why is that considered a breach of the sound barrier? Because 768 mph is the speed sound travels through the atmosphere at sea level. At higher altitudes, the atmosphere is much thinner than it is at sea level, so sound travels through it more quickly. Yeager achieved his historic speed at an altitude of 45,000 feet, where the speed of sound is just 660 mph.

RESEARCH & EMBELLISHMENT

The STAC committee's first goal: assemble experts from every aspect of the airline business—manufacturers, engineers, airline execs, government regulatory agencies, etc.—and create a comprehensive report on supersonic passenger travel for the British Ministry of Aviation. It took two and a half years, but in March 1959, STAC delivered its 300-page report. Their findings: commercial supersonic jetliner travel was not only feasible—if the UK was going to remain a force in the global airline industry, the British government should begin funding its development immediately.

Included in the report were drafts of designs for two different supersonic aircraft: a 100-passenger craft with a cruising speed of Mach 1.2 (800 mph), and a range of 1,500 miles; and a 150-passenger model with a cruising speed of Mach 1.8 (1,200 mph), and a range of 3,500 miles, the latter for trans-Atlantic flights from London to New York. (The plans for the smaller plane were later dropped, and only the larger, long-range plane would actually reach production.) Estimated cost of producing those planes, according to the STAC report: a maximum of £95 million (about $260 million). The report predicted that the first planes could be ready by 1970, and that sales of the aircraft, not to mention the boost to British jobs and the British economy, would more than justify the great cost of the project. (They were wrong…but more on that later.)

There weren't enough lifeboats on the *Titanic* because the president of the White Star Line thought they would clutter up the deck.

The British government accepted the report's conclusions, and the project was given a go. But first they decided they wanted a partner.

THE FRENCH CONNECTION

While all of this was going on, Europe was undergoing huge change. In 1957 France, West Germany, Italy, the Netherlands, Belgium, and Luxembourg signed a treaty establishing the European Economic Community (EEC). This precursor of the modern European Union had one main goal: using the power of a more politically and economically aligned Europe to compete with the world's two emerging superpowers—the United States and the Soviet Union. And while the UK would not officially join the EEC until 1973, they still wanted to forge closer business ties with their mainland European neighbors.

So with that in mind, in 1960 British government officials reached out to their counterparts in France. It was a good choice. France's state-owned aircraft manufacturer, Sud Aviation, had scored a big success with the introduction of the first French-made jetliner, the Caravelle, in 1958, and they wanted to see the French aviation industry grow.

In 1962, after two years of negotiation, the two nations signed a treaty establishing a Franco-British partnership to develop the world's first supersonic passenger plane. The planes would be designed and built through a cooperative effort at a BOAC factory in Filton, England, and a Sud Aviation factory in Toulouse, France. It was from this Franco-British partnership that the name of the proposed supersonic jetliner emerged: the *Concorde*—which in both French and English (without the "e") means "agreement" or "harmony."

BIG OLD (SLOW) SUPERSONIC AIRLINER

The STAC report said the first supersonic Concordes would be ready for commercial use by 1970, at a cost of about £95 million. Would they make it? Here are some of the most important moments between 1962 and the plane's actual completion date:

• *Bad News!* By 1964, repeated design failures in keeping the aircraft's weight down and building sufficiently powerful engines had driven the cost of the Concorde to £275 million. By 1966, it had risen to an astronomical £400 million. This led to a lot of criticism from both the British and French public, who were paying for the project with their tax dollars.

• *Good News!* By 1967, some of the world's biggest airlines, including United, TWA, Air Canada, and Lufthansa, had purchased sales options on 74 Concordes,

Why did the first coloring books use watercolor paints? Crayons hadn't been invented yet.

hoping to get a jump on the next big thing in air travel. At an estimated cost of about £20 million per plane, if those sales went through, the embattled supporters of the Concorde project just might prove their critics wrong.

• **More Good News!** In 1969 the first two prototypes—dubbed Concorde 001 (built by Sud Aviation in France) and Concorde 002 (built by British Airways in England)—made their first successful test flights. And by 1970, not only had both broken the sound barrier, they had broken Mach 2, exceeding the predictions of the original STAC report, and making headlines all over the world.

• **Terrible News!** Over the first four months of 1973, almost every airline that had ordered the Concorde canceled their orders. Why? Because the cost of the project had by this time risen to nearly £1 *billion*—more than ten times the original estimate. And just a few years earlier, Boeing had introduced the 747, the first *wide-body* aircraft, which increased the seating capacity of passenger airliners by almost 250 percent, to more than 450 passengers, enhancing both passenger comfort and fuel efficiency. With passengers more than satisfied by these fancy new subsonic jetliners, most airlines decided they simply didn't need supersonic planes after all.

• **Super(sonic) News!** In late 1975, five years behind schedule and way over budget, construction of the first commercial Concorde jetliners was finally completed.

DESIGN FEATURES

The most important aspect of the Concorde's body design was its wings. They had to be configured in such a way that they would create the least amount of drag possible as the plane approached the speed of sound, but they also had to generate enough lift to allow the plane to take off and land safely. After thousands of hours of wind tunnel testing and aerodynamic physics, British and French aviation engineers agreed on a unique *delta* wing design. (Delta wings are triangular-shaped and are most commonly found on military aircraft). And the Concorde's wings were attached to the plane along almost half its 202-foot length, slowly widening as they reached the rear of the plane, with the widest point almost at the plane's tail. Total wingspan: just 83 feet. (A Boeing 747, which is about 232 feet long, has a wingspan of 211 feet.) That wing configuration resulted in one of the Concorde's most iconic characteristics: in order for those slim wings to generate enough lift to take off, the plane had to lift its nose up very high even before it left the ground. Same thing on landing: it had to keep its nose very high in the air until it hit the runway.

Other features: the Concorde's fuselage was less than 10 feet wide (it was just

John Quincy Adams wanted the government to fund an expedition to see if the Earth was hollow.

four seats and a narrow corridor wide inside the plane), and it had an elongated, very pointy nose cone. (Both of these features were designed to reduce drag.) And because of the steep position required during takeoff and landing, the nose cone could be lowered so that it pointed down toward the ground during takeoff and landing so that the pilot could see the runway. During flight, the nose cone was raised up to the straight position.

TAKEOFF

On January 21, 1976, commercial supersonic passenger travel became a reality for the first time in history when Air France started Concorde SST ("SuperSonic Transport") service from Paris to Rio de Janeiro, Brazil, and British Airways started service from London to Bahrain (in the Middle East). In May, they began service from London and Paris to Dulles International Airport in Washington, D.C. For the next three years, things actually looked pretty good for the Concorde program, as production of the planes continued, and more destination cities were added, including New York City (Concordes were banned at both JFK and La Guardia Airports until November 1977 due to protests over the noise the planes produced); Caracas, Venezuela; Singapore; and Mexico City. And while both the British and French governments lost money on the airline every year, the number of passengers steadily increased, from 45,000 in 1976 to about 170,000 in 1979.

Then, in September 1979, another bad moment in the topsy-turvy history of the supersonic airliner: the British and French governments announced that no more Concordes would be built.

THE ODDS WERE STAC'D AGAINST THEM

This was incredibly bad news. The whole idea behind the development of the Concorde was to sell a lot of planes. How else could anyone justify the mammoth amount of time and money spent on the project? But, the STAC report's optimistic predictions aside, by the time the planes were actually ready to sell, there was simply no market for them, and the British and French governments—finally—decided to stop pouring more money into an endeavor that was obviously doomed. How many Concordes did they end up making? Twenty—and six of those were prototypes and preproduction test models. How many airlines bought the fourteen that were actually put into use? Two—British Airways and Air France, both run by the governments of the countries that developed the planes, and both essentially forced to buy them.

The British and French governments continued to lose money on their

Concordes until 1984, when a couple of big changes occurred. First, the British government got out of the Concorde business altogether, and sold all of their Concordes to British Airways, the first step in a move to privatize the airline. (That process was completed in 1987.) Also around this time, both airlines started cutting back on the number of cities they flew to on a regular basis, until Air France's daily flights between New York and Paris, and British Airways' daily flights between New York and London, were the only regularly scheduled flights. (They both still flew Concorde charter flights to cities around the world, but New York became the only regular daily destination for Concorde flights.) After this—both airlines started to turn a profit.

THE CRASH

For the first two decades of its run as a commercial airliner, the Concorde had one of the best safety records of any airliner in the business, with no major injuries or fatalities reported over the course of tens of thousands of flights, carrying more than 2 million passengers. That all came to an end on July 25, 2000, when Flight 4590, an Air France Concorde SST, crashed shortly after takeoff at Charles de Gaulle Airport in Paris. All 109 people on board, and four more on the ground, were killed. (Cause of the crash: one of the Concorde's tires had run over a piece of metal on the runway. The tire exploded, and a piece of rubber from the tire hit one of the plane's fuel tanks, causing it to leak and catch fire. That led to engine failure, which led to the plane not having enough power to complete its takeoff, and that led to its crash.)

All Concorde jetliners were grounded after the crash, and none of the planes would fly again for the next 16 months. And while both British Airways and Air France resumed flights in 2001, the popularity of supersonic travel had diminished, and neither airline could attract enough passengers to operate the planes at a profit. On top of that, all the Concordes were more that 20 years old by this time, and all of them were due for major—and very expensive—overhauls.

In April 2003, British Airways and Air France announced that they would no longer be offering Concorde SST service, and, to much fanfare, flew their very last flights. The Concorde program was finished. No supersonic jetliner service has been offered since.

EXTRAS

• In the early years, the cost of a round-trip New York–London ticket on the Concorde was about $1,500. By the late 1980s, it was about $6,000. By the 1990s, it

While exploring North Dakota, Lewis and Clark sent President Jefferson a souvenir: a live prairie dog.

was more than $12,000. (Note: all seats on Concorde airliners were first class.)

• Highest speed reached by a Concorde: Mach 2.23—or 1,480 mph, on a March 26, 1974, test flight, at an altitude of 63,700 feet, in Morocco.

• The Concorde was the world's first *commercial* supersonic jetliner—but it wasn't the first one to actually fly. That honor goes to the Tupolev Tu-144, a supersonic jetliner developed by the Soviet Union, that first went supersonic on June 5, 1969. It would not go into commercial use until 1977, almost two years after the Concorde—but that ended in 1978, after just six months, when a Tu-144 crashed during a test flight. (It was the second Tu-144 to crash during testing.)

• The Western nickname of the Tupolev Tu-144: The "Concordski."

> **THE FINAL COST** *of the Concorde program to British and French taxpayers: at least $1.1 billion. (Some estimates put the number at more than $2 billion.)*

• As of 2016, several aircraft manufacturers, including Airbus (Europe), Virgin (UK), and Boeing and Lockheed Martin (United States), are working on designs for a new generation of supersonic jetliners. The first ones are slated to be ready for commercial use by 2023. (We'll see…)

* * *

"TRIVIA" IN ANY LANGUAGE

Spanish: *Trivialidades* (trivialities)

Albanian: *Vogelsira*

Filipino: *Bagay na walang kabuluhani*

Hungarian: *Aprosagok*

Basque: *Bitxikeriak*

Maori: *Rahaki*

Samoan: *Mea le aoga*

Italian: *Banalita* (banalities)

Croatian: *Trivijalnost*

Latvian: *Nieki*

Czech: *Drobnosti*

Indonesian: *Hal yg sepele*

Lithuanian: *Smulkmenos*

Somali: *Yacni*

Luxembourgish: *Rettungsrank*

Zulu: *Inhlebo*

Russian: *Pustyaki* (nonsense)

Earth's magnetic poles may be in the midst of a flip called geomagnetic reversal. If so, when it's over, compasses will point south instead of north.

RESCUE ON THE HIGH SEAS

Here's how a jacket floating in waters off the coast of Libya led to the creation of the first privately funded search-and-rescue service in the Mediterranean Sea.

SEA CRUISE

In the summer of 2013, an American insurance executive named Christopher Catrambone and his wife, Regina, chartered a 75-foot yacht to take them and their teenage daughter, Maria Luisa, on a three-week cruise of the Mediterranean Sea. The Catrambones live on Malta, an island nation in the middle of the Mediterranean, about 60 miles south of Sicily. (On a map, Sicily is the island that looks like it's being kicked by the "boot" of Italy.)

That June, the Catrambones set off from the Maltese capital of Valletta and sailed along the Sicilian coast before heading south to Lampedusa, another Italian island in the Mediterranean. Because Lampedusa is just 70 miles from Africa, it is often a destination for refugees fleeing from war-torn parts of Africa and the Middle East. Violence in countries like Syria, Iraq, Libya, Eritrea, and Sudan has caused the number of such refugees to soar in recent years. In 2013, hundreds of thousands of desperate men, women, and children were on the move—more than at any time since World War II. Before the year was out, some 60,000 of them would try to cross the Mediterranean, many in unseaworthy, overcrowded boats. And their numbers were growing.

IN THE WATER

While the Catrambones visited Lampedusa, Pope Francis was also there, making his first trip outside of Rome since his election to the papacy three months earlier. He chose the island for his first visit in order to call attention to the plight of the refugees, including thousands who had drowned.

The Catrambones didn't attend any of the papal events, but after they set sail from Lampedusa toward Tunisia, they got their own introduction to the refugee crisis when Regina Catrambone spotted a winter jacket floating in the water. She couldn't understand it. Who wears a winter jacket in the Mediterranean in the heat of summer, she wondered, and how did it end up in the water? When Mrs. Catrambone asked the captain of the yacht, his face "transformed," as she put it, from a cheerful expression to one of sadness. He explained to her that the jacket probably belonged to a refugee trying to cross the Mediterranean, and the fact that it was floating in the water suggested that the refugee "was not with us anymore."

DO SOMETHING

The jacket remained a dark topic of discussion for the rest of the cruise. By the time the Catrambones sailed back into port in Valletta, they had decided that they wanted to do something to help the refugees. But what?

Maritime law requires that when a vessel is in distress, the nearest available ship *must* come to its aid. Only problem: most commercial ships aren't equipped to assist what are often dozens or even hundreds of refugees crammed into a single boat, especially when that boat is sinking and the refugees are already in the water. Sometimes the only way to board a large oil tanker or container ship from the sea is by climbing a rope ladder 20 or more feet straight up the side of the hull, something that exhausted and dehydrated refugees—including pregnant women, young children, and the elderly—cannot do.

That's where the Catrambones thought they could help. They decided to take a chunk of their substantial life savings and use it to create their own privately funded search-and-rescue organization—one with a ship specially outfitted for the task of locating and assisting refugees in danger on the high seas. They named their organization the Migrant Offshore Aid Station (MOAS).

SHIP-SHAPE

Christopher Catrambone began looking for a ship that would be suitable for the group's mission, and he soon found one in the port of Norfolk, Virginia. Called the *Phoenix*, it was a 130-foot steel-hulled fishing trawler that had also seen duty as a military training ship. The Catrambones spent $8 million to purchase, overhaul, and outfit the 40-year-old *Phoenix* for use as a rescue ship. Improvements included an infirmary stocked with medical supplies, two inflatable speedboats that would assist in rescues, and a flight deck for two aerial search drones.

By August 2014 the refurbished *Phoenix* was ready. It set sail from Valletta and spent the next 10 weeks patrolling international waters off the coast of Libya, a frequent starting point for refugees trying to get to Europe. On board were the Catrambones and a hired crew of 20 people, including professional mariners, drone operators, a search-and-rescue team, a physician, and a cook.

In 1887 three Swedish balloonists tried to fly to the North Pole. (They all died.)

Four days later, the *Phoenix* answered its first distress call, rushing to the aid of two boats—one carrying 227 migrants, and another, and another carrying 350—that were taking on water and in danger of sinking.

ON CALL

That first season, the *Phoenix* patrolled an area of the Mediterranean in which distress calls are routed through an Italian agency called the Maritime Rescue Coordination Centre (MRCC). Typically, when a boat is in distress, the MRCC is notified and it dispatches the *Phoenix* to go to its aid. As the *Phoenix* steams toward the boat's last known position, it also launches one of its helicopter drones to look for the boat. The drones have a top speed of 115 miles per hour, much faster than the *Phoenix*'s top speed of 10 knots (11.5 mph). They can remain aloft for up to six hours at a time and they send a continuous video stream back to the ship, enabling the ship to search a wide expanse of the sea in a short amount of time. Once a boat has been located, the *Phoenix* can head directly toward it, instead of having to search for the vessel itself.

A sad fact for the boats carrying refugees across the Mediterranean is that the ships coming to their aid can actually cause them to sink. More than one foundering boat has capsized after a rescue ship pulled up alongside and the desperate refugees all moved to that side of the boat. For this reason the *Phoenix* typically approaches vessels from the stern (rear), rather than from the port (left) or starboard (right) sides of the boat. And rather than steam right up to the boat, whenever possible it stays a mile or more away and dispatches its two inflatable speedboats to ferry refugees back to the ship. The *Phoenix* can accommodate up to 400 refugees at a time; if more room is needed, the Maritime Rescue Coordination Centre can order other boats to come to its aid.

SEE YOU NEXT YEAR

By the time that first ten-week patrol was up, the *Phoenix* had provided assistance to nearly 3,000 refugees, many of whom would likely have perished had no one come to their aid. The Catrambones would have liked to stay out longer, but their personal funds were running low. So they returned to port and began raising money for a second patrol in the spring and summer of 2015. They collected more than $1.6 million from donors, enough to allow the *Phoenix* to patrol for another six months. And they formed a partnership with the nonprofit group Doctors Without Borders, which enabled them to improve the medical services they provided to the refugees.

The *Phoenix* began its second patrol in May 2015. By the time it returned to

Some of the "asteroids" in *The Empire Strikes Back* were painted potatoes and tennis shoes.

port at the end of September, it had rescued another 8,500 people. The result of the *Phoenix*'s efforts were further magnified by the fact that it had inspired a host of imitators.

• In addition to staffing the infirmary aboard the *Phoenix*, Doctors Without Borders chartered two boats of its own—the *Bourbon Argos* and the *Dignity I*.

• A group of friends in Brandenburg, Germany, pooled $153,000 of their own money to buy a 98-year-old houseboat that they converted into a rescue ship called the *Sea-Watch*. They did this after realizing that more refugees drown trying to cross the Mediterranean Sea in a single year than died trying to get over the Berlin Wall in the entire 27 years of its existence. Crewed entirely by volunteers, the *Sea-Watch* patrols international waters off the coast of Libya for 12 days at a time, then returns to Malta to take on a new crew of volunteers who head right back out again.

STILL SAILING

When the *Phoenix* returned to port in November 2015, it remained there just long enough to make repairs and restock its supplies. Then it set off again, but to a different destination: During the winter months, stormy seas prevent attempts to cross the Mediterranean, so the *Phoenix* headed for Myanmar in Southeast Asia, more than 5,000 miles away. In recent years that country has seen a great deal of conflict between the majority Buddhist population and the Muslim Rohingya minority, prompting many Rohingya to flee by sea. The United Nations estimates that between January 2014 and June 2015 alone, more than 1,100 Rohingya drowned, and unlike in the Mediterranean, there were no rescue ships to come to their aid. That's what the *Phoenix* hopes to address, and perhaps, as it did in the Mediterranean, it will inspire imitators to come to Myanmar and save even more lives.

In the spring of 2016, the *Phoenix* was back on patrol in the Mediterranean. If the Catrambones can raise enough money to pay for it, the *Phoenix* will divide its time between Myanmar in the winter months and the Mediterranean in the spring and summer for as long as there is a need to do so.

*   *   *

RANDOM FACT

When actor Bill Paxton (*Aliens*, *Apollo 13*, *Big Love*, *Twister*) was a kid, he was in the crowd in Dallas, Texas, on November 22, 1963, when President John F. Kennedy was assassinated.

The Synlight "artificial sun" uses 149 giant lamps to produce light 10,000 times as powerful as sunlight.

CARTER'S FAREWELL

Historians usually rank Jimmy Carter as one of America's more lackluster presidents.
His term was marked by inflation, an oil embargo, high unemployment, and a hostage crisis
in Iran. Result: he lost his 1980 reelection bid to Ronald Reagan by 8.4 million votes, the
largest ouster of an incumbent president in U.S. history. But Carter is also regarded as one of
America's best ex-presidents. In retirement, he brokered peace deals, supervised elections, and
helped found Habitat for Humanity. In his farewell speech to the nation, delivered on January
14, 1981, Carter talked about the nature of American democracy and then, with hope and
understanding, he predicted many of the problems that would loom large
for the world in the decades to come. Here is that address.

MY FELLOW AMERICANS

In a few days I will lay down my official responsibilities in this office—to take
up once more the only title in our democracy superior to that of President,
the title of citizen. Of Vice President Mondale, my Cabinet, and the hundreds
of others who have served with me during the last four years, I wish to say
now publicly what I have said in private: I thank them for the dedication and
competence they've brought to the service of our country. But I owe my deepest
thanks to you, to the American people, because you gave me this extraordinary
opportunity to serve.

We've faced great challenges together, and we know that future problems
will also be difficult. But I'm now more convinced than ever that the United
States, better than any other country, can meet successfully whatever the future
might bring. These last four years have made me more certain than ever of the
inner strength of our country, the unchanging value of our principles and ideals,
the stability of our political system, the ingenuity and the decency of our people.

"THE MOST POWERFUL OFFICE IN THE WORLD"

Tonight I would like first to say a few words about this most special office, the
Presidency of the United States. This is at once the most powerful office in
the world and among the most severely constrained by law and custom. The
President is given a broad responsibility to lead but cannot do so without the
support and consent of the people, expressed formally through the Congress
and informally in many ways through a whole range of public and private
institutions. This is as it should be.

Within our system of government every American has a right and a duty to help shape the future course of the United States. Thoughtful criticism and close scrutiny of all government officials by the press and the public are an important part of our democratic society. Now, as in the past, only the understanding and involvement of the people through full and open debate can help to avoid serious mistakes and assure the continued dignity and safety of the Nation.

Today we are asking our political system to do things of which the Founding Fathers never dreamed. The government they designed for a few hundred thousand people now serves a nation of almost 230 million people. Their small coastal republic now spans beyond a continent, and we also now have the responsibility to help lead much of the world through difficult times to a secure and prosperous future.

"WE ARE ALL AMERICANS TOGETHER"

Today, as people have become ever more doubtful of the ability of the Government to deal with our problems, we are increasingly drawn to single-issue groups and special interest organizations to ensure that whatever else happens, our own personal views and our own private interests are protected. This is a disturbing factor in American political life. It tends to distort our purposes, because the national interest is not always the sum of all our single or special interests.

> *We are all Americans together, and we must not forget that the common good is our common interest and our individual responsibility.*

Because of the fragmented pressures of these special interests, it's very important that the office of the president be a strong one and that its constitutional authority be preserved. The president is the only elected official charged with the primary responsibility of representing all the people. In the moments of decision, after the different and conflicting views have all been aired, it's the president who then must speak to the nation and for the nation.

"A CITIZEN OF THE WORLD"

For a few minutes now, I want to lay aside my role as leader of one nation, and speak to you as a fellow citizen of the world about three issues, three difficult issues: the threat of nuclear destruction, our stewardship of the physical resources of our planet, and the preeminence of the basic rights of human beings.

In the 1930s, playing card companies introduced 65-card decks with a fifth suit: eagles. (They flopped.)

It's now been thirty-five years since the first atomic bomb fell on Hiroshima. The great majority of the world's people cannot remember a time when the nuclear shadow did not hang over the Earth. Our minds have adjusted to it, as after a time our eyes adjust to the dark. Yet the risk of a nuclear conflagration has not lessened. It has not happened yet, thank God, but that can give us little comfort, for it only has to happen once.

The danger is becoming greater. As the arsenals of the superpowers grow in size and sophistication and as other governments, perhaps even in the future dozens of governments, acquire these weapons, it may only be a matter of time before madness, desperation, greed, or miscalculation lets loose this terrible force.

In an all-out nuclear war, more destructive power than in all of World War II would be unleashed every second during the long afternoon it would take for all the missiles and bombs to fall. A World War II every second—more people killed in the first few hours than in all the wars of history put together. The survivors, if any, would live in despair amid the poisoned ruins of a civilization that had committed suicide.

"REDUCE THE HORRIFYING DANGER"

National weakness—real or perceived—can tempt aggression and thus cause war. That's why the United States can never neglect its military strength. We must and we will remain strong. But with equal determination, the United States and all countries must find ways to control and to reduce the horrifying danger that is posed by the enormous world stockpiles of nuclear arms.

This has been a concern of every American President since the moment we first saw what these weapons could do. Our leaders will require our understanding and our support as they grapple with this difficult but crucial challenge. There is no disagreement on the goals or the basic approach to controlling this enormous destructive force. The answer lies not just in the attitudes or the actions of world leaders but in the concern and the demands of all of us as we continue our struggle to preserve the peace.

Nuclear weapons are an expression of one side of our human character. But there's another side. The same rocket technology that delivers nuclear warheads has also taken us peacefully into space. From that perspective, we see our Earth as it really is—a small and fragile and beautiful blue globe, the only home we have. We see no barriers of race or religion or country. We see the essential unity of our species and our planet. And with faith and common sense, that bright vision will ultimately prevail.

Beagles descended from Talbot hounds—brought to England from France in 1066. They're now extinct.

"SHADOWS THAT FALL"

Another major challenge, therefore, is to protect the quality of this world within which we live. The shadows that fall across the future are cast not only by the kinds of weapons we've built, but by the kind of world we will either nourish or neglect. There are real and growing dangers to our simple and our most precious possessions: the air we breathe, the water we drink, and the land which sustains us. The rapid depletion of irreplaceable minerals, the erosion of topsoil, the destruction of beauty, the blight of pollution, the demands of increasing billions of people, all combine to create problems that are easy to observe and predict, but difficult to resolve. If we do not act, the world of the future will be much less able to sustain life than it is now.

But there is no reason for despair. Acknowledging the physical realities of our planet does not mean a dismal future of endless sacrifice. In fact, acknowledging these realities is the first step in dealing with them. We can meet the resource problems of the world—water, food, minerals, farmlands, forests, overpopulation, pollution—if we tackle them with courage and foresight.

"THE BATTLE FOR HUMAN RIGHTS"

It's equally important that we remember the beneficial forces that we have evolved over the ages and how to hold fast to them. One of those constructive forces is the enhancement of individual human freedoms through the strengthening of democracy and the fight against deprivation, torture, terrorism, and the persecution of people throughout the world. The struggle for human rights overrides all differences of color or nation or language. Those who hunger for freedom, who thirst for human dignity, and who suffer for the sake of justice, they are the patriots of this cause.

I believe with all my heart that America must always stand for these basic human rights at home and abroad. That is both our history and our destiny. America did not invent human rights. In a very real sense, it's the other way around. Human rights invented America. Ours was the first nation in the history of the world to be founded explicitly on such an idea. Our social and political progress has been based on one fundamental principle: the value and importance of the individual. The fundamental force that unites us is not kinship or place of origin or religious preference. The love of liberty is the common blood that flows in our American veins.

The battle for human rights—at home and abroad—is far from over. We should never be surprised nor discouraged, because the impact of our efforts has had and will always have varied results. Rather, we should take pride that the ideals which

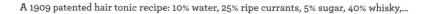

A 1909 patented hair tonic recipe: 10% water, 25% ripe currants, 5% sugar, 40% whisky,...

gave birth to our Nation still inspire the hopes of oppressed people around the world. We have no cause for self-righteousness or complacency, but we have every reason to persevere, both within our own country and beyond our borders.

If we are to serve as a beacon for human rights, we must continue to perfect here at home the rights and the values which we espouse around the world: a decent education for our children, adequate medical care for all Americans, an end to discrimination against minorities and women, a job for all those able to work, and freedom from injustice and religious intolerance.

"AMERICAN VALUES ARE NOT LUXURIES"

We live in a time of transition, an uneasy era which is likely to endure for the rest of this century. It will be a period of tensions, both within nations and between nations, of competition for scarce resources, of social, political, and economic stresses and strains. During this period we may be tempted to abandon some of the time-honored principles and commitments which have been proven during the difficult times of past generations. We must never yield to this temptation. Our American values are not luxuries, but necessities—not the salt in our bread, but the bread itself. Our common vision of a free and just society is our greatest source of cohesion at home and strength abroad, greater even than the bounty of our material blessings.

Remember these words: "We hold these truths to be self-evident, that all men are created equal, that they are endowed by their creator with certain inalienable rights, that among these are life, liberty and the pursuit of happiness."

"RENEW FOUNDATIONS"

This vision still grips the imagination of the world. But we know that democracy is always an unfinished creation. Each generation must renew its foundations. Each generation must rediscover the meaning of this hallowed vision in the light of its own modern challenges. For this generation, ours, life is nuclear survival; liberty is human rights; the pursuit of happiness is a planet whose resources are devoted to the physical and spiritual nourishment of its inhabitants.

As I return home to the South, where I was born and raised, I look forward to the opportunity to reflect and further to assess, I hope with accuracy, the circumstances of our times. I intend to give our new President my support, and I intend to work as a citizen, as I've worked here in this office as President, for the values this Nation was founded to secure.

Again, from the bottom of my heart, I want to express to you the gratitude I feel. Thank you, fellow citizens, and farewell.

...and 20% port wine, "rubbed lightly into the scalp several times a day." (Or just drink it.)

AT 30...

*Five years ago, when Uncle John's Bathroom Reader turned 25, we ran an article
about what some other famous icons were up to in their 25th year. Here's
a new installment for our 30th anniversary.*

JON STEWART (1962–)

Claim to Fame: Comedian, former host of *The Daily Show*

At 30... After making a name for himself on the New York stand-up circuit,
Stewart was a top contender to take over *The Late Show* when David Letterman
moved to CBS. But Stewart lost that job to another up-and-comer, Conan
O'Brien. Luckily, Stewart got another offer: hosting a talk show on MTV. In
October 1992, shortly before Stewart turned 30, *The Jon Stewart Show* premiered
and quickly became the music network's second-most-watched program (after
Beavis and Butthead). Featuring a more casual approach to the talk-show
format, *The Jon Stewart Show* garnered some attention for its more outlandish
moments—like when William Shatner sat on Stewart's lap, and Stewart told
him, "You're about to go where no man's gone before." It was also known for
having musical acts that didn't get booked on other late-night shows, including
Danzig, Slayer, and, most infamously, Marilyn Manson, who smashed his
instruments before Stewart gave him a piggyback ride off the stage.

The Jon Stewart Show ran for a year on MTV, and was then expanded from a
half-hour to an hour and placed in syndication (to replace the canceled *Arsenio
Hall Show*). But the quirky talk show failed to attract the same audience in
syndication, and shortly after Stewart turned 32, it was canceled. Less than five
years later, he took over as host of *The Daily Show*.

LEONARDO DA VINCI (1452–1519)

Claim to Fame: Italian painter, musician, scientist, and inventor

At 30... Two decades before the original "Renaissance Man" painted the *Mona
Lisa*, da Vinci was already well known for many talents…and other things. A
few years earlier, his reputation in his native Florence had been sullied when
an anonymous source accused him (and some of his friends) of homosexuality,
which was illegal. Although the charges were dropped, by the time da Vinci
turned 30, the stigma of the accusation was too great in Florence, so he decided
to move to Milan.

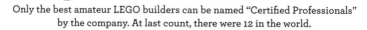

Only the best amateur LEGO builders can be named "Certified Professionals"
by the company. At last count, there were 12 in the world.

But first, he needed a job. So in 1482 he put together a résumé of sorts. His goal: to become employed by Ludovico Maria Sforza, the Duke of Milan, who, rumor had it, was hell-bent on protecting his town from invasion. Knowing that, Leonardo touted his "military engineering" skills in a letter to Ludovico. Introducing himself as one of the "masters and artificers of instruments of war," he described ten inventions he could build for the duke, including a portable cannon that would "hurl small stones almost like a hailstorm; the smoke from the cannon will instill a great fear in the enemy," and "covered vehicles…which will penetrate the enemy and their artillery." In other words, a tank.

Duly impressed, Ludovico hired da Vinci. He moved to Milan and remained there until 1499, but he didn't build tanks or any other military weapons. Instead, da Vinci spent most of his 30th year working on a commissioned painting called *Virgin of the Rocks*, which now hangs in the Louvre.

WHOOPI GOLDBERG (1955–)

Claim to Fame: Comedian, actor, and talk-show host

At 30… On December 16, 1985, Steven Spielberg's *The Color Purple* premiered on screens across the United States. These words appeared in the opening credits: "And introducing Whoopi Goldberg." Goldberg, who turned 30 just a month earlier, was living a relatively quiet life in San Francisco raising her young daughter, but the film propelled her to superstardom. After achieving some success as a stand-up comedian and Broadway actress, she read Alice Walker's 1982 book and knew she wanted to be in the movie if one ever got made. "I wrote (Alice Walker) a letter and said…I would play any character. I would play dirt on the floor. I would be a screen door. She wrote back and said she knew who I was, she'd seen my show in San Francisco, and had already mentioned me to Spielberg." Next thing Goldberg knew, she was auditioning for Spielberg and some of his friends, performing several of the characters from her one-woman show. But what really brought the house down was an impression of E.T. getting busted for drugs. That's how Goldberg landed the lead role as Celie.

The movie was a critical and commercial success, receiving 11 Academy Award nominations—including Best Actress for both Goldberg and Oprah Winfrey (it was also Winfrey's film debut). Goldberg didn't win, but even without an Oscar, *The Color Purple* made her a bankable star. In 1986, the 30-year-old actress took the lead in the spy comedy *Jumpin' Jack Flash* after Shelley Long was "let go" from the part, and within a few years, she was the highest-paid actress in Hollywood, earning upward of $10 million per film. (And she did win an Oscar—in 1990, for her supporting role as a psychic in *Ghost*.)

Five lions have supplied the famous MGM roar. The first was silent, because early movies had no sound.

VLADIMIR PUTIN (1952–)

Claim to Fame: President of the Russian Federation

At 30... Putin was a KGB agent. He joined the USSR's secret police—a childhood dream of his—a few years after having graduated from law school in 1975. In 1983, Putin married Lyudmila Shkrebneva, with whom he would have two children before divorcing in 2014. Stationed in East Germany, the 30-year-old agent served as a foreign intelligence officer, and spent most of his time reading through Western mail-order catalogs to learn more about his "enemy." That's how he learned to speak English. Even then Putin was ambitious. "One man's effort can achieve what whole armies could not," he liked to say. "One spy can decide the fate of thousands of people."

A few years later, the Iron Curtain fell and Germany was reunited, putting an end to the Cold War. Putin moved to St. Petersburg and entered politics. According to biographer Boris Reitschuster, Putin's time as a KGB agent in East Germany had a profound impact on the future president: "He enjoyed very much this little paradise for him. He rebuilt a kind of East Germany in Russia now."

ELIZABETH WARREN (1949–)

Claim to Fame: U.S. senator from Massachusetts

At 30... Warren, now a hero of the Progressive movement, was a registered Republican. In 1979, a year after divorcing her first husband and a year before marrying her current husband, the 30-year-old mother of two was a professor at the University of Houston Law Center in Texas. She spent much of that year immersed in the fine points of bankruptcy law, a field in which she would eventually rise to the top. But it would be 15 years before the lawyer decided to run for political office. Why did she switch sides? "I was a Republican because I thought that those were the people who best supported markets. I think that is not true anymore."

SANDY KOUFAX (1935–)

Claim to Fame: Hall of Fame pitcher for the Brooklyn/Los Angeles Dodgers

At 30... Unlike the other people in this article, whose greatest impact came later in their lives, when Koufax hit the big 3-0, he had to give up the game he loved. But over the previous 12 years (1955–66), he put together one of the most impressive pitching careers in the history of baseball. The Dodgers' star southpaw came in with a whimper, though, not having played much baseball as a kid. He was a basketball player with dreams of becoming an architect when

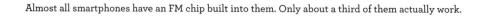

Almost all smartphones have an FM chip built into them. Only about a third of them actually work.

his basketball coach at the University of Cincinnati told him he needed some players to field a baseball team. Koufax soon discovered that he could throw a baseball faster than almost anyone else, but at 6'2", his control was all over the place. In fact, when he later tried out for the Dodgers, he barely made the team because he "couldn't even hit the batting cage." But the coaching staff saw something in the lanky lefty, and signed him for the minimum salary.

After a few unremarkable seasons, Koufax finally found his control, and then developed one of the best curveballs in the history of the game. Over the next five years, right around the time when the Dodgers moved from Brooklyn to Los Angeles, Koufax had one of the most dominating runs in the history of any sport. He won 111 games and lost only 34. In 1963, he won a league-best 25 games. He was so dominant that Yogi Berra said, "I can see how he won 25 games. What I don't understand is how he lost five." Koufax would go on to win three pennants and two World Series, and pitch four no-hitters.

But then, right around the time Koufax turned 30, his left forefinger started going numb. Then his elbow started hurting. Knowing that something was seriously wrong, he kept the ailment—arthritis—to himself for long as he could…but it kept getting worse. "I could hear the sound of liquid squishing around," he recalled, "as if I had a wet sponge in there." So after losing his final game—a 6-0 defeat to the Baltimore Orioles in the 1965 World Series—Koufax decided he was done. A few years later, at 36, he became the youngest player ever inducted into the Hall of Fame.

JANE GOODALL (1934–)

Claim to Fame: British primatologist and UN Messenger of Peace

At 30… Goodall was a relatively unknown researcher working at Gombe Stream National Park in Tanzania. But that would soon change thanks to a National Geographic film crew who followed her around as she studied a family of chimpanzees. The footage was put together as a documentary and released the following year (1965) as *Miss Goodall and the Wild Chimpanzees*, narrated by Orson Welles. The film opens with Welles telling the audience, "Miss Goodall's discoveries will startle the scientific world, and lead to the possible new definition of the word 'Man.'" He was right; the film not only made Goodall an international celebrity, but it showed the world that humans are not the only animals that can make tools.

But the "Miss" in the title was a bit misleading. A week before she turned 30, Goodall married English wildlife photographer Baron Hugo van Lawick— whose photographs helped convince National Geographic to film Goodall. Her

In the 1840s, a British sailor could get 12 lashes for filthiness, bad cooking, or stealing a major's wig.

official title became Baroness Jane van Lawick-Goodall. (When they divorced a decade later, she became Jane Goodall again.) The young couple spent that year dividing their time between England, where Goodall was studying for her doctorate, and Gombe, where they both studied the chimps.

STEPHEN KING (1947–)

Claim to Fame: American author of dozens of best-sellers

At 30… The years 1978 and 1979 were among King's most prolific. In fact, he published some of his work under the pen name Richard Bachman because he didn't think people would believe that one author could write so much. But King could. What was his secret? "I used coke all the time," he confessed to *Rolling Stone* in 2015. The 30-year-old author was leading a double life under his own roof. In one, he was a family man helping to raise his young children. But he was also trying to conceal his rampant drug use…and alcoholism: "I wasn't a social drinker. I used to say that I didn't want to go to bars because they were full of a**holes like me."

Aside from doing drugs, King spent most of his 30th year writing some of his best-known works, including *The Stand*, *Firestarter*, *The Dead Zone*, and *Salem's Lot*. He was also writing a lot of short stories, including "Lawnmower Man," and several intertwined fantasy tales about a gunslinger named Roland that would later be published as the first *Dark Tower* books. But the partying would soon take a toll, and King felt his work and home life was suffering. His family staged an intervention in the mid-1980s, and he's been sober ever since.

MARTIN LUTHER KING JR. (1929–68)

Claim to Fame: Civil rights icon

At 30… Dr. King went to India. Three years after leading the Montgomery bus boycott, which led to desegregation laws and made him a national celebrity, King was looking for more effective ways to stage nonviolent protests. So the 30-year-old Baptist minister traveled to India, where the 20th century's most famous nonviolent protester, Mahatma Gandhi, had led a nonviolent revolution a decade earlier, bringing about India's independence from Great Britain. In February 1959, King, his wife Coretta, and historian Lawrence Reddick embarked on a five-week tour of the country. When they arrived, King was surprised to discover that he was already famous there. The boycott had made big news. And King knew why: "We were looked upon as brothers with the color of our skins as something of an asset, but the strongest bond of fraternity was the common cause of minority and colonial peoples in America, Africa, and Asia

Black olives are green olives that have been left on the tree to ripen longer.

struggling to throw off racialism and imperialism."

The three African Americans were welcomed everywhere they went, and got to meet with many prominent Indians, including members of Gandhi's family (he had been assassinated a decade earlier) and India's prime minister, Jawaharlal Nehru. The trip had a tremendous effect on the civil rights leader: "Since being in India, I am more convinced than ever before that the method of nonviolent resistance is the most potent weapon available to oppressed people in their struggle for justice and human dignity." Four years later, King marched to Washington and gave his famous "I have a dream" speech. Four years after that, King was assassinated in Memphis, Tennessee, at the age of 39.

JOHN MCCAIN (1936–)

Claim to Fame: U.S. senator from Arizona, former Republican presidential candidate, and war hero

At 30... McCain flew his first combat mission in the Vietnam War. Stationed on the aircraft carrier USS *Forrestal*, he piloted an A-4 Skyhawk as part of the prolonged bombing campaign known as "Operation Rolling Thunder." As a younger man, McCain had gained the reputation as a "hard partier and reckless flier" (he crashed three planes), but he'd matured significantly by his 30th year and was on his way to becoming a decorated war hero. Good thing, too, because his life nearly ended in August 1967 when the *Forrestal* caught on fire. The lieutenant commander barely made it out of his burning jet, and when he ran to help another pilot escape, a bomb exploded, sending shrapnel into McCain's chest and legs. More than 130 servicemen were killed in the fire, but McCain, who'd left his wife and three young children at home to join the war, lived to fight another day.

Shortly after his 31st birthday, his plane was shot down over Vietnam. He was severely injured, captured, and then tortured. He spent the next five years as a prisoner of war.

BILL GATES (1955–)

Claim to Fame: Founder of Microsoft, and philanthropist

At 30... Gates's childhood goal was to become a millionaire by the time he was 30. When 1985 rolled around, Microsoft was already 10 years old, and Gates was already a *multi*-millionaire. That was the year that Microsoft made its initial public offering, so by the time Gates was 31, he was the world's youngest billionaire. A year earlier, *Good Housekeeping* had named him one of America's "50 Most Eligible Bachelors." (It must have looked amusing to see the nerdy

End of an era: The last library catalog cards were printed in 2015.

guy with big glasses among such 1980s hunks as Bruce Springsteen and Tom Selleck.)

But something even more important happened to Gates in his 30th year: he met Melinda Ann French. Recently hired as a Microsoft project manager (she would oversee Encarta and Expedia), Gates was immediately attracted to her. But even though he was the head of the company, he was shy, and it took him a while to ask her out. When he finally mustered up the courage, in a parking lot, he said, "I was wondering if, maybe if you gave me your phone number, we could go out two weeks from tonight."

"Two weeks from tonight?" she replied. "I have no idea what I'm doing two weeks from tonight." After Gates gave her an awkward explanation about all the meetings he had to attend, French told him, "You're not spontaneous enough for me." Gates took that as a challenge. He looked up her phone number in the company records, and called her about an hour later, asking, "Is this spontaneous enough for you?" It was. The two began dating, and in 1994 they were married. The lovebirds would go on to create the Bill and Melinda Gates Foundation, now the largest charity in the world.

BETTY WHITE (1922–)

Claim to Fame: TV star known for her long career

At 30… White was just getting going. After making a name for herself in radio in the 1940s (she went into radio because she was told she was not "photogenic"), she landed her first TV job as a co-host of *Hollywood on Television*, a variety/talk show starring Los Angeles radio DJ Al Jarvis. White was such a natural—she could sing, dance, conduct interviews, tell jokes, and play goofy characters—that when Jarvis left the show in 1952, the 30-year-old White was promoted to host. Because the TV industry was just starting, there wasn't a lot on, so White ended up hosting the show for five and a half hours per day, six days a week. And it was all live. "There was never any rehearsal or script or anything," she told NPR in 2014 (more than 60 years later). "Whoever came in that door was on, and you were interviewing them. Whatever happened, you had to handle it." White handled it so well that she received her first Emmy Award nomination.

The show was groundbreaking for another reason: it was the first time in TV history that a woman was given full creative control both in front of and behind the camera. White used her new freedom to launch Bandy Productions, and all of a sudden she was a high-powered Hollywood producer. Her first act: to adapt one of her recurring characters, a housewife named Elizabeth, into a sitcom called *Life with Elizabeth*. The show was a hit, and White never looked back.

ANSWERS

YOU WANT TO DROP MY FOOT? *(Answers for page 160)*

1. "With a Little Help from My Friends"

2. "Yesterday"

3. "The Long and Winding Road"

4. "Something"

5. "Come Together"

6. "Hello Goodbye"

7. "Baby, You're a Rich Man"

8. "Back in the U.S.S.R."

9. "Got to Get You into My Life"

10. "Paperback Writer"

11. "Nowhere Man"

12. "We Can Work It Out"

13. "Day Tripper"

14. "I Feel Fine"

15. "A Hard Day's Night"

16. "Can't Buy Me Love"

17. "I Saw Her Standing There"

18. "I Want to Hold Your Hand"

19. "She Loves You"

20. "All You Need Is Love"

21. "Don't Let Me Down"

22. "Help"

23. "Please Please Me"

TV'S LAST LINES: *(Answers for page 273)*

1. e; **2.** k; **3.** o; **4.** b; **5.** n; **6.** h; **7.** g; **8.** f; **9.** c; **10.** l; **11.** m; **12.** d; **13.** j; **14.** i; **15.** a

*   *   *

KIDS? DON'T TRY THIS AT HOME

If you happen to visit the village of Castrillo De Murcia in Spain 60 days after Easter, you might see women placing their newborn babies in rows on mattresses in the street. This is part of the annual Baby Jumping Festival—part of the Catholic feast of Corpus Christi—in which men, dressed as devils in fiendish masks and bright yellow suits, leap over the babies like runners in a hurdle race. The leaping-devil tradition dates back to the 17th century, and is supposed to cleanse the tiny infants of all evil. (The Catholic Church does not endorse baby-jumping.)

...a gift. He served it at a White House party; it was gone in 2 hours.

THE LAST PAGE

FELLOW BATHROOM READERS:

The fight for good bathroom reading should never be taken loosely—we must do our duty and sit firmly for what we believe in, even while the rest of the world is taking potshots at us.

We'll be brief. Now that we've proven we're not simply a flush-in-the-pan, we invite you to take the plunge: Sit Down and Be Counted! To find out what the BRI is up to, visit us at *www.portablepress.com* and take a peek!

If you like reading our books...

VISIT THE BRI'S WEBSITE!

www.portablepress.com

- Receive our irregular newsletters via e-mail
- Order additional Bathroom Readers
- Find us on Facebook
- Tweet us on Twitter
- Blog us on our blog

Well, we're out of space, and when you've gotta go, you've gotta go. Tanks for all your support. Hope to hear from you soon.

Meanwhile, remember...

Keep on flushin'!